# APPLIED SPORT MANAGEMENT SKILLS

## THIRD EDITION

**Robert N. Lussier, PhD**
Springfield College

**David C. Kimball, PhD**
Elms College

HUMAN KINETICS

**Library of Congress Cataloging-in-Publication Data**

Names: Lussier, Robert N., author. | Kimball, David Charles, 1959- author.
Title: Applied sport management skills / Robert N. Lussier, PhD, Springfield
    College, David C. Kimball, PhD, Elms College.
Description: Third edition. | Champaign, Illinois : Human Kinetics, [2020] |
    Includes bibliographical references and index.
Identifiers: LCCN 2018051077 (print) | LCCN 2018055173 (ebook) | ISBN
    9781492589747 (epub) | ISBN 9781492570165 (PDF) | ISBN 9781492570158
    (print)
Subjects: LCSH: Sports administration.
Classification: LCC GV713 (ebook) | LCC GV713 .L87 2020 (print) | DDC
    796.06/9--dc23
LC record available at https://lccn.loc.gov/2018051077

ISBN: 978-1-4925-7015-8 (print)

The web addresses cited in this text were current as of November 2018, unless otherwise noted.

**Acquisitions Editor:** Andrew L. Tyler; **Managing Editor:** Derek Campbell; **Copyeditor:** Kevin Campbell; **Proofreader:** Pamela Johnson; **Indexer:** Rebecca McCorkle; **Permissions Manager:** Dalene Reeder; **Graphic Designer:** Julie L. Denzer; **Cover Designer:** Keri Evans; **Cover Design Associate:** Susan Rothermel Allen; **Photograph (cover):** Josh Barber/Angels Baseball LP/Getty Images; **Photographs (interior):** © Human Kinetics, unless otherwise noted; © Paul Yates/fotolia.com (p. 25); © Aurelien Meunier/Getty Images (p. 55); © Ben Smawfield/fotolia.com (p. 79); © Getty Images/Hero Images (p. 173); © Dominique LUZY/fotolia.com (p. 211); © Brand X Pictures (p. 257); © PhotoAlto/Sandro Di Carlo Darsa/Brand X/Getty Images (p. 287); © Bettmann/Getty Images (p. 319); © Photodisc/Getty Images (p. 347); courtesy of Robert Lussier (p. 377); **Photo Asset Manager:** Laura Fitch; **Photo Production Manager:** Jason Allen; **Senior Art Manager:** Kelly Hendren; **Illustrations:** © Human Kinetics, unless otherwise noted; **Printer:** Walsworth

Printed in the United States of America     10 9 8 7 6 5 4 3

The paper in this book was manufactured using responsible forestry methods.

**Human Kinetics**
1607 N. Market Street
Champaign, IL 61820
USA

*United States and International*
Website: **US.HumanKinetics.com**
Email: info@hkusa.com
Phone: 1-800-747-4457

*Canada*
Website: **Canada.HumanKinetics.com**
Email: info@hkcanada.com

E7365

**Tell us what you think!**
Human Kinetics would love to hear what we
can do to improve the customer experience.
Use this QR code to take our brief survey.

To my wife, Marie, and our six children:
Jesse, Justin, Danielle, Nicole, Brian, and Renee

—RNL


To my wife, Amy, and our two children:
Carly and Jacob

—DCK

# CONTENTS

# PART IV  Leading

# PART V  Controlling

Unlike most college textbooks, this book takes a how-to approach to management. Research has shown that we are more likely to implement our knowledge when we learn by doing something rather than simply by reading, listening, or thinking. Leaders and researchers in both business and sport management are calling for textbooks that can be applied by sport managers on the job. They want students to be able to develop their management skills by putting principles into action. To that end, we have written a textbook that focuses on applying sport management principles and fostering practical skills you can use in your personal life and in your profession.

## Objectives of the Book

This book uses a three-pronged approach, with these objectives:

- To teach you the important principles, concepts, research, and theories of management
- To develop your ability to apply the management principles to sport organizations
- To develop your management skills in your personal life and in your profession

The book offers some unique features to further each of these three objectives, as summarized in the following table.

### Features of This Book's Three-Pronged Approach

| | |
|---|---|
| **Principles (learning about management)** | • Text discussion of concepts and theories, based on business and sport research<br>• Figures<br>• Learning Outcomes<br>• Key Terms<br>• Chapter Summary<br>• Review and Discussion Questions |
| **Application (applying the concepts)** | • Opening cases with applications throughout the chapter<br>• Sport examples<br>• Time-Outs—applications of concepts to your sport or work experience<br>• Applying the Concept<br>• Cases<br>• Sports and Social Media Exercises—on companion web study guide<br>• Game Plan for Starting a Sport Business—on companion web study guide<br>• Internet exercises—on companion web study guide |
| **Skill development (job and personal)** | • Developing Your Skills<br>• Pop-up questions related to practicing managers<br>• Self-Assessments<br>• Step-by-step behavior models for handling management functions<br>• Skill-Builder Exercises—on companion web study guide |

- *Management principles*—Throughout this book, you will learn management principles and concepts used in sport organizations, and you will read about the difficulties and challenges managers face. Your knowledge of management concepts is vital to your success as a manager.

- *Application of management principles*—It is essential to understand theory and concepts before moving to the next level: applying the concepts. If you don't understand the concepts, how can you develop the critical thinking skills you need to apply them? As shown in the table, this book offers eight features to help you develop the critical thinking skills you will need to apply the concepts.

- *Development of management skills*—The third and highest-level objective is to develop management skills that you can use in your personal life and in your profession, as both a leader and a follower. You can develop your management skills, and this book offers five features to help you do so.

## Web Study Guide

A web-based study guide has been created specifically to supplement the text. It is available at www.HumanKinetics.com/AppliedSportManagementSkills. This study guide includes interactive versions of most of the activities in the chapters.

In the study guide, an online flash card activity helps you learn the key terms for each chapter. You can take the self-assessments for each chapter online; your responses will be recorded automatically and you'll instantly see your final score for each assessment. All of the Applying the Concept practice quizzes in the web study guide are auto-scored, and you get feedback on your response to each quiz question. And there are links to numerous websites and apps in the study guide that you'll use to hone your research skills.

This is the full list of activities available in the web study guide:

- Key Terms Flash Cards
- Auto-Scoring Self-Assessments
- Applying the Concepts Practice Quizzes
- Time-Outs
- Internet Resources
- Internet Skills
- Review and Discussion Questions
- Case Study and Questions
- Skill-Builder Exercises
- Sports and Social Media Exercises
- Game Plan for Starting a Sport Business

The Time-Out, Internet Resources, Internet Skills, Review and Discussion Questions, Case Questions, Skill-Builders, Sports and Social Media Exercises, and Game Plan for Starting a Sport Business all include downloadable Word files that you can save, complete online, and submit to your instructor or upload to a learning management system.

## Practice and Flexibility

As with sport and just about everything in life, you cannot become skilled by simply reading about or trying something once. You need discipline, you have to practice, and you have to keep repeating it. The great football coach Vince Lombardi said that leaders are made by effort and hard work. If you want to develop your management skills, you must not only learn the concepts in this book but also practice with the applications and Skill-Builder exercises. But most important, to be successful, you need to practice using your skills in your personal life and in your profession. We hope the variety of sport industries covered in the textbook motivates you to find internships, part-time jobs, full-time jobs, and long and successful careers in sport.

This book has so many features that it is unlikely that all of them can be covered in the course during a semester. Your instructor will select the features that best meet the course objectives and the amount of time available, but you may want to cover some or all of the other features on your own or with the assistance of others outside class.

Sport management is a growing field, and this growth has created the need for a how-to book on becoming a sport manager. Most people using this book will not be professional athletes; they will be managers in sport industries. Thus, our purpose is to provide a fully integrated textbook with a companion web study guide (www.HumanKinetics.com/Applied SportManagementSkills) that constructively applies the principles of business management to the sport industry.

We provide a meticulous and comprehensive overview of management topics with an in-depth focus on how to manage sport organizations. We provide thorough coverage of the principles of management concepts combined with robust sport applications and exercises to develop sport management skills that students can use in both their personal lives and professional lives. Adopters of *Applied Sport Management Skills* and reviewers clearly agree that the book is the best on the market for developing sport management skills.

## Commission on Sport Management Accreditation (COSMA)

Here is how our book covers the 2016 Common Professional Component (CPC):

- The major focus of our book is on the Foundations of Sport Management—Management Concepts (CPC topic B1). Also, Foundations of Sport Management—International Sport (topic B3) is discussed in chapter 2, with some discussion and examples throughout the book.

- We cover the Functions of Sport Management—Sport Operations (topic C1) in chapter 14, Functions of Sport Management—Sport Communications (topic C3) in chapter 10, and Functions of Sport Management—Sport Finance and Economics (topic C4) in chapter 13.

- The Sport Management Environment—Legal Aspects of Sport Management (topic D1) and Sport Management Environment—Ethical Aspects of Sport Management (topic D2) are briefly covered in chapter 2. Coverage of Sport Management Environment—Diversity Issues in Sport Management (topic D3) is in chapter 2 and chapter 6.

Our book is a perfect fit for any sport management program that offers a course teaching the principles of management concepts. We cover essentially all the topics in traditional business principles of management textbooks with a functional approach (planning, organizing, leading, and controlling). But unlike texts offering a general business focus, we focus on sport examples and cases with an applied skill-building focus, including coverage of sport facilities and event management.

## North American Society for Sport Management (NASSM)

Our book addresses NASSM concerns about the theoretical and applied aspects of management theory and practice specifically related to sport. Topics of interest to NASSM members that we cover include a major focus on management competencies. We also have entire chapters or major sections that discuss leadership (chapter 12), personnel management (chapter 7), facility management (chapter 14), organizational structures (chapter 5), and conflict resolution (chapter 8). In addition, the topic of sport and the law is briefly discussed in chapters 2 and 7.

# Three-Pronged Approach

As indicated in the title of the book, *Applied Sport Management Skills*, the book presents the principles of management, sport applications of the principles, and skill development. Following is a list of features for each.

## Principles of Management Concepts

The text uses several features to present the principles of management concepts:

• *Research*—The references at the end of the book are primarily from two types of sources, academic research journals to support the theory and popular publications to provide sport management examples and cases.

• *Learning Outcomes*—Each chapter begins with a list of Learning Outcomes stating what students will be able to do after studying the chapter.

• *Key Terms*—Important terms are listed in the opening of the chapter and are defined within the chapter (terms appear in boldface where defined). Students can also complete an interactive Key Terms matching exercise at the book's companion web study guide.

• *Chapter Summary*—Each chapter ends with a summary, which lists the Learning Outcomes with their answers.

• *Review and Discussion Questions*—Approximately 15 questions appear after each Chapter Summary. Students can also complete these questions online at the book's companion web study guide.

## Applications to Sport

Each chapter includes six types of applications that provide students an opportunity to apply the management principle to actual sports and sport organizations to develop critical thinking skills through the following features:

• *Reviewing Their Game Plan*—Each chapter begins with an opening case featuring real-world sport organizations and their managers. Throughout the chapter, examples illustrate how the organization uses the text concepts.

• *Sport examples*—As the concepts are presented, we provide many examples of how real-world sport organizations use the principles of management. We discuss a variety of organizations, including professional, college, and high school teams, and we provide examples from sport businesses, such as Nike, and nonprofit organizations, such as the YMCA and Jewish Community Center.

• *Time-Outs*—Open-ended questions require students to explain how the text concepts apply to their own sport and work experiences. Students can draw from sport experience at any level as well as present, past, summer, full-time, or part-time employment. The questions help students bridge the gap between theory and the real world. The Time-Outs can be completed online at the book's companion web study guide.

• *Applying the Concept*—Each chapter contains a series of two to five Applying the Concept boxes that require the student to determine the management concept being illustrated in a specific sport example. The Applying the Concept boxes offer an interactive experience for the student at the book's companion web study guide.

**Self-Assessments** help students gain knowledge about themselves.

**Applying the Concept** activities require students to determine the management concept being illustrated in an example.

**Situation-based questions** ask what sport managers should do under a given set of circumstances.

**Learning Outcomes,** which are also listed at the start of the chapter, describe what students should be able to do after reading the material.

**Key Terms** are listed at the start of the chapter and appear in boldface in the text.

---

## SELF-ASSESSMENT 12.1

### Are You a Theory X or Theory Y Leader?

Note the frequency with which you do (or would do, if you have not yet held a position of leadership) each action. Be honest. There are no right or wrong answers. This Self-Assessment is easiest to complete online.

U = usually
F = frequently
O = occasionally
S = seldom

_____ 1. I set objectives for my department alone; I don't include staff input.

_____ 2. I allow staff members to develop their own plans rather than developing them myself.

_____ 3. I delegate to staff several of the tasks that I enjoy doing rather than doing them myself.

_____ 4. I allow staff members to solve problems they encounter rather than solving them myself.

_____ 5. I recruit and select new employees alone; I don't solicit input from staff.

_____ 6. I orient and train new employees myself rather than having members of my team do it.

_____ 7. I tell staff members only what they need to know rather than giving them access to anything they want to know.

_____ 8. I praise and recognize staff efforts; I don't just criticize.

_____ 9. I set controls for the team to ensure that objectives are met rather than allowing the team to set its own controls.

_____ 10. I often observe my group to ensure that it is working and meeting deadlines.

For items 1, 5, 6, 7, 9, and 10, give each U answer 1 point; F, 2 points; O, 3 points; and S, 4 points. For items 2, 3, 4, and 8, give each S answer 1 point; O, 2 points; F, 3 points; and U, 4 points. Total your score, which should be between 10 and 40.

You have just measured your theory X, theory Y behavior. This theory was developed by Douglas McGregor (1906-1964), who contrasted the two theories based on the assumptions managers make about workers. Theory X managers assume that people dislike work and need managers to plan, organize, and closely direct and control their work in order for them to perform at high levels. Theory Y managers assume people like to work and do not need close supervision. Place a check on the continuum that represents your score.

**Theory Y Behavior**

---

## APPLYING THE CONCEPT 10.2

### Barriers to Communication

Identify the barriers in the following messages or responses as

a. perceptual filter
b. information overload
c. wrong transmission channel
d. emotions
e. trust and credibility
f. distortion
g. failure to listen

_____ 6. Relax. You shouldn't be so upset that our young team didn't win the championship.

_____ 7. I don't have any questions. (Really thinking, "I was lost back on step one and don't know what to ask.")

_____ 8. We are right on schedule in building our new athletic facility. (Really thinking, "We are actually behind, but we'll catch up.")

_____ 9. I said I'd do it in a little while. It's only been 15 minutes. Why do you expect it to be done by now?

_____ 10. You don't know what you're talking about when you give your opinions on how to play defense. I think we will do it my way.

### Distortion

Distortion, or filtering, occurs when we alter information that we send and receive; it's a nice word for lying. We don't want to use the word "lying" because we may offend someone. We may do this for innumerable reasons. We don't like the truth, so we twist a message to fit our version of the incident and the "facts"—we believe what we want to believe. Tell the truth. Many people have said that things are going well only to get burned at the last minute when they can't deliver.

This results in lost trust and credibility; it's better to let people know of problems early because they may be able to help you. Likewise, when receiving messages, we hear what we want to hear. In these situations, you may have to repeat your message. You may have to reframe it. Asking for feedback helps you discern what the receivers are hearing. Listen carefully. Avoid having "yes" employees who filter out bad news—problems get solved only when they are faced honestly. Some executives build truth-telling cultures.

 What other decoding barriers can you think of?

## Using the Channels

Sometimes the difference between failed communications and those that hit their mark is your choice of channel. When you are encoding a message, select the best channel.[27] The channels through which we transmit our messages are nonverbal, oral, written, and visual (see table 10.1).[28]

**LEARNING OUTCOME 3** ▶ Use transmission channels well.

### Nonverbal Channels

Every time we talk to someone, we use words, but we also communicate nonverbally.[29] **Nonverbal communication** consists of the messages we send without words. It includes

**Developing Your Skills** gives an overview of the skills that are emphasized in a chapter.

**Reviewing Their Game Plan** features real-world sport organizations and managers.

## DEVELOPING YOUR SKILLS

You can't win in business or sport without motivated players. In this chapter, you will learn about the motivation process, one reinforcement-based motivation theory, and four content-based and three process-based theories, and you will find tips on motivating with each theory. Giving praise is motivational and is not used nearly enough. You can develop this skill using a four-step model for giving praise.

## REVIEWING THEIR GAME PLAN

### Famous Motivational and Leadership Quotes

Sport coaches and athletes are known for their many memorable quotes about motivation and leadership. Vince Lombardi is well known for his amazing words of wisdom. We use a few of his quotes here to focus your attention on how exciting motivation can be.

**Vince Lombardi**

"It is essential to understand that battles are primarily won in the hearts of men."

"In great attempts, it is glorious even to fail."

"Leaders are made, they are not born. They are made by hard effort, which is the price which all of us must pay to achieve any goal that is worthwhile."

"The harder you work, the harder it is to surrender."

"It's not whether you get knocked down, it's whether you get up."

"The quality of a person's life is in direct proportion to their commitment to excellence, regardless of their chosen field of endeavor."

"There's only one way to succeed in anything, and that is to give it everything. I do, and I demand that my players do."

"If you aren't fired with enthusiasm, you'll be fired with enthusiasm."

"Once you learn to quit, it becomes a habit."

"Winning isn't everything—but wanting to win is."[1]

**Special Olympics Motto**

"Let me win, but if I cannot win, let me be brave in the attempt."[2]

**Coach Darrell Royal**

"Luck is what happens wh[...][3]

[...]bility to think under pressure."[4]

[...]ance

[...]are used to influence employ-[...]ed players and employees to[...]d motivators.[6] Great leaders[...]t great motivators, but they[...] to succeed." Do you need to[...]ter?

[...] others, and you will learn[...]ion of the motivation pro-[...] overview of the motivation

---

3. *Problem identification.* Change agents use interviews or feedback surveys to help the team to identify its strengths and its weaknesses (areas it would like to improve). The team next lists several areas where it can improve and then prioritizes these areas in terms of how improving each area will help the team to improve performance.

4. *Problem solving.* The team takes the top priority and develops a solution. It then moves down the priorities in order of importance. Force-field analysis may be used here for problem solving.

5. *Training.* Team building often includes some form of training that addresses the problems facing the group.

6. *Closure.* The program ends with a summary of what has been accomplished. Team members commit to specific improvements in performance. Follow-up responsibilities are assigned, and a meeting is scheduled to evaluate results.

### Process Consultation

Process consultation is often used in the second stage of team building, but it is also commonly used as a separate, more narrowly focused intervention. **Process consultation** improves team dynamics. Whereas team building often focuses on how to get the job done, process consultation focuses on how people interact as they get the job done. Team dynamics (or processes) are about how the team communicates, allocates work, resolves conflict, and handles leadership and how leadership solves problems and makes decisions. Change agents observe team members as they work to give them feedback on the operative team processes. Under the change agent's guidance, the team discusses its processes and how to improve them. Training to improve group processes may also be conducted at this point. The ultimate objective is to train the group so that process consultation becomes an ongoing team activity. (We examine team dynamics in more detail in chapter 9.)

 **TIME-OUT 8** Give an example of an OD intervention used recently in your firm or team. Was it effective? Why or why not?

**Time-Outs** are open-ended questions that relate the text concepts to students' experiences.

### Direct Feedback

Situations can occur, particularly with rapidly changing technologies, that require a solution outside the company's core expertise. In these situations, outside consultants are often brought in to act as change agents and to recommend action directly. For example, some teams have hired Amazon and IBM to set up their cloud computer systems.

## LEARNING AIDS

**Learning Aids** at the end of each chapter include a summary, review questions, and case studies.

### CHAPTER SUMMARY

1. **Identify the driving forces behind change.**
   The forces for change come from the external and internal environment. Changes in economic, social, demographic, and technological forces require organizations to adapt to their environments.

2. **List the four variables of change.**
   Change occurs in strategies, structures, technologies, and people.

3. **Differentiate between fact, belief, and values.**
   Facts are provable statements that identify reality. Beliefs cannot be proven because they are subjective, not objective. Values address what is important to people.

167

- *Sport Management Professionals @ Work*—Following the Review and Discussion Questions is a sport manager profile highlighting that person's career progression, ending with questions to apply the managerial topics from the chapter and to get students thinking about their own career paths.

- *Cases*—Next, an actual coach or manager and sport organization are described. The student learns how the manager or organization applies the concepts from the chapter. Each case is followed by multiple-choice questions and some open-ended questions to help students to apply the concepts to the sport organization. The Case Questions can be answered online at the book's companion web study guide.

## Skill Development

The difference between learning about management and learning to be a sport manager is the acquisition of skills. Each chapter includes four features that provide students with the opportunity to apply management principles to develop sport management skills they can use both in their personal lives and in their professions.

- *Developing Your Skills*—In the chapter opener, students are given an overview of the skills they can develop through the chapter.

- *Situation-based questions*—Usually related to the opening case, these questions build managerial competencies by asking what the sport manager should do in a given situation.

- *Self-Assessment exercises*—Each chapter includes at least one Self-Assessment. Students complete the Self-Assessments to gain personal knowledge. Many of the assessments are tied to exercises within the book, thus enhancing the impact of the activities. All information for completing and scoring the assessments is contained within the text, but the book's companion web study guide also offers students an interactive format for completing these exercises.

- *Behavior models*—Some of the tables and figures are behavior models that include step-by-step guidelines for handling situations. Models include how to set objectives and set priorities, how to prepare for and conduct a job interview and train employees, how to negotiate and handle a conflict, how to give motivational praise and delegate, and how to coach an employee to increase performance and to discipline when needed. Almost all of the behavior models are used in exercises to develop the skill.

## Ancillary Support

To ensure fully integrated support for every faculty member, the following ancillaries are available to adopters of *Applied Sport Management Skills, Third Edition*, at www.Human Kinetics.com/AppliedSportManagementSkills.

- *Instructor guide*—Each chapter includes a chapter outline, a lecture outline for class lecture enhancement, definitions of key terms, Learning Outcome answers, Time-Out sample answers, answers to Review and Discussion Questions, Applying the Concept answers, answers to Case Questions, and suggestions for using the Skill-Builders, Sports and Social Media Exercises, and Game Plan for Starting a Sport Business exercises, as well as tips for grading students' answers to these exercises.

- *Test package*—Each chapter includes between 50 and 100 test questions in true-or-false, multiple-choice, and essay formats. Many of these questions were written specifically for the test package, but they may also include items taken verbatim from the text: Applying the Concept questions, Review and Discussion Questions, Learning Outcomes, and Time-Outs.

- *Presentation package*—More than 350 PowerPoint slides are provided to enhance class lectures. They include text, figures, and tables.

- *Web study guide*—Created specifically to supplement the text, this includes Internet resources and exercises and matching activities for the Key Terms. Many features of the textbook are also available online in the web study guide and may be completed and sent to the professor if he or she wishes. An online flash card activity helps students learn the key terms for each chapter. They can take the self-assessments for each chapter online; students' responses will be recorded automatically and they will instantly see their final score for each assessment. All of the Applying the Concept practice quizzes in the web study guide are auto-scored, and students get feedback on their response to each quiz question. And there are links to numerous websites and apps in the study guide that they can use to hone their research skills. The other activities (Time-Out, Internet Resources, Internet Skills, Review and Discussion Questions, Case Questions, Skill-Builders, Sports and Social Media Exercises, and Game Plan for Starting a Sport Business) are available as downloadable documents that students can save, complete online, and submit to your instructor or upload to a learning management system. These resources are especially helpful for teaching the course online.

## Major Changes in This New Edition

- The text content has been heavily revised with an increased focus on how to be a sport manager with expanded and new content. During the revision, it was thoroughly updated with more than 1,300 new references, and 97 percent of the references are new to this edition.
- A new Sport Management Professionals @ Work profile has been added to each chapter.
- The opening cases and end-of-chapter cases have been either updated or replaced with new cases.
- Current sport examples of how the principles in the text are used in the real world of sports have been added to each chapter.
- There are two new Self-Assessment exercises.
- There are two new Skill-Builder exercises in the web study guide.

For a detailed list of the changes made in each chapter, see the instructor guide. Knowing the changes from the previous edition will help you transition to this new edition of *Applied Sport Management Skills*.

## Contact Us With Feedback

We wrote this book for you. Let us know what you think of it. Specifically, how can it be improved? We will respond to your feedback. If we use your suggestion for improvement, your name and college or university will be listed in the acknowledgments section of the next edition.

Dr. David Kimball
Director of Sport Management
Elms College
291 Springfield Street
Chicopee, MA 01013
413-265-2572
kimballd@elms.edu

# PART I

# Introduction to Sport Management

# Managing Sports

## LEARNING OUTCOMES

After studying this chapter, you should be able to

1. describe career opportunities in sport management;

2. describe a sport manager's responsibilities;

3. define the five management skills;

4. define the four management functions;

5. explain the interpersonal, informational, and decisional roles of management;

6. diagram the hierarchy of management levels;

7. describe general, functional, and project managers; and

8. explain how skills and functions differ by management level.

## KEY TERMS

| | | |
|---|---|---|
| sport management | people skills | organizing |
| sport manager | communication skills | leading |
| manager's resources | conceptual skills | controlling |
| performance | decision-making skills | management roles |
| management skills | management functions | levels of management |
| technical skills | planning | types of managers |

## DEVELOPING YOUR SKILLS

The first step in developing your **sport management** skills is to understand what managers are responsible for, what it takes to be a successful leader, what sport managers do, and how managers differ. To develop your skills, observe effective leaders and copy their behavior, and complete the Skill-Builder exercises in the web study guide. You can also apply the principles of management by taking on leadership roles in your classes, in your job, and on your team—practice does make perfect.

## REVIEWING THEIR GAME PLAN

### Dick's Sporting Goods Knows Sports

Dick's Sporting Goods is headquartered in Pittsburgh, Pennsylvania. Dick's Sporting Goods (DSG) also owns and operates Golf Galaxy, Field & Stream, True Runner, and Chelsea Collective specialty stores. DSG was started in 1948 by an entrepreneur, Dick Stack, whose grandmother funded his new store with $300. DSG sells a full line of sport and fitness equipment, bikes, athletic shoes and apparel, and hunting and fishing goods and apparel. DSG focuses on quality products with competitive prices. DSG knows that its customers are passionate about sports.

Instead of resting on its history of opening over 650 stores, DSG has to be well aware of the threat of other sporting goods stores such as Foot Locker, Big 5 Sporting Goods, and Cabela's. But even more threatening is the rise of Internet retailers led by Amazon. Nike and Amazon recently announced a partnership whereby Amazon would sell Nike apparel directly to consumers through its well-trafficked website.[1]

Still, DSG is going to defend its market position by offering aggressive promotional offers to buy products in its stores online. DSG also has a growth strategy to build new stores in growth markets such as Florida. Like all the sport-related businesses you will read about in this textbook, DSG has learned to adapt its products and services in a rapidly changing marketplace.

Successful retail operations depend on merchandising and marketing skills. DSG successfully uses a marketing strategy of inserting weekly fliers into local Sunday newspapers around the country.

Based on Dick's Sporting Goods. https://www.dickssportinggoods.com/s/about-us

# The Sport Industry

Sports are a big and growing part of the U.S. and world economies. Sports have strong links to other economic sectors, and the number of sport jobs and managers has increased over the years.[2] Think about teams that made you love going to work out and jobs that didn't make you want to go to work. Did the coach or manager figure in your answer? Very likely it did, because managers set the tone, create the culture, and have the power to make or break the team. As management guru Henry Mintzberg said, "No job is more vital to our society than that of a manager."[3] As we focus on sport management, let's include coaches as managers, and because business jobs include teams, we will refer to teams in both sport and business settings.

Are you thinking about answers to these questions: "What can I get from this book?" and "What's in it for me?"[4] A simple answer is that the better you can work with people as a team player—a key objective of this book—the more successful you will be in your personal and professional lives.[5] You are probably taking this course because you are interested in a career in sport management. This means you already have energy, ambition, a desire to make a difference, and some people and leadership skills. Now it's time to put your energy and ambition to work.

Being involved in sport, you probably realize the importance of working well with people as a team. Team and management skills can be developed,[6] and this book will help you hone the skills you have and develop new ones. The skills that you develop in this course will serve you well in both personal and professional realms. So let's get going.

# What Is Sport Management?

We begin this section by talking about jobs in sport management. We then present an interview with a sport manager and end with a discussion of the sport manager's responsibilities and resources.

Sport management is relatively young as an academic discipline, but the number of sport management programs continues to grow.[7] A major reason for the growth in academic programs is that the value of sport depends on how it is managed. In sport, as in other businesses, managers determine organizational performance both on and off the playing field. Sport management programs train people for management positions in such areas as community and youth sport, high school and college athletics, professional teams, fitness centers, recreational centers, coaching, officiating, marketing, sport tourism, and sporting goods manufacturing and retailing. There are many different careers in the sport industry. The following are some examples:

Athletic directors (ADs) and their assistants hold excellent administrative jobs in high schools and colleges. Most colleges need an athletic director for intercollegiate and interscholastic athletics. Colleges also have sport information directors, professionals who are responsible for managing and distributing information about their college teams. This textbook often refers to athletic directors to illustrate points about sport management.

Stadiums and arenas need general managers, business managers, operations managers, box office managers, and event managers to run their organizations. These jobs are exciting if you like to help produce live sporting events.

Sport marketing agencies manage corporate-sponsored events. Sports like golfing and NASCAR rely heavily on sport sponsorships, and they need managers to make sure their products gain attention at sponsored events.

Sport marketing agencies and independent agents represent athletes, handling the business side of affairs for the athlete.

Sport broadcasting includes careers in daily sport news programs, all-sports radio, and live game broadcasts. All-sports radio stations have become very popular, and they are excellent places to find internships. The Internet has opened up positions managing websites and providing statistical data for sport teams.

Recreation management is a broad term for careers such as athletic directors at YMCAs and Jewish Community Centers, directors of public parks and recreation, workers in leisure fields such as in fitness centers, and directors of activities at resorts.

Sporting goods manufacturers such as Nike, New Balance, and Wilson need employees in sales, operations, human resources, and finance. Sporting goods stores such as Dick's Sporting Goods need purchasing agents and accountants and employees to staff the human resources (HR) departments at their headquarters. Managers are also needed to operate each store and its departments.

The most obvious career path is working in professional leagues. Major League Baseball (MLB), the National Football League (NFL), the National Basketball Association (NBA), and the National Hockey League (NHL) are professional leagues in the United States that sport management students often dream about when planning their careers. An internship with professional teams in these leagues is a good way to get started. However, in almost all situations you will have to start at the bottom of the organization and work your way up the ladder. Newer professional leagues such as MLS (Major League Soccer), MLL (Major League Lacrosse), and AFL (American Football League) offer additional opportunities to work for professional teams.

◀ LEARNING OUTCOME 1

Describe career opportunities in sport management.

The study of sport management includes aspects of management science and business administration with application to both theory and practice. Sport management is a multidisciplinary field that integrates sport and management, and the same management skills have application to both business and sport.

## Interview With a Sport Manager

Cheryl Condon, athletic director for Elms College (Chicopee, Massachusetts), started as an admissions counselor at Elms. She has always loved and lived sports, and she pursued her passion by coaching Elms' women's softball team. Her coaching successes and her management skills did not go unnoticed, and she was eventually promoted to athletic director.

**Question:** Although opportunities to play sports have never been greater for women, opportunities in management are still few and far between. How did you prepare for the job of athletic director (AD) of a small college?

**Answer:** With my background in coaching and being around sports for so many years, I have the experience to do my job professionally and properly. I've been around sports all my life.

**Question:** Before you were an AD, you were an admissions counselor. How did your career path evolve?

**Answer:** The previous AD left for a similar position at another college. I interviewed for the position and was fortunate enough to be selected by the search committee. I was very fortunate to be able to move from a career in recruiting student-athletes into an administrative sport position. I believe that the key reason I was able to get the position was the extra effort I put into coaching the women's softball team. Coaching was not one of my required job responsibilities, and the college realized my commitment to sports by my extra efforts to make the team a success.

**Question:** What responsibilities do you have as an AD?

**Answer:** Many, many responsibilities. Hiring coaches, scheduling gymnasiums and fields for teams to practice and play regular-season games, arranging for van and bus transportation to away games, printing tickets and game programs, acquiring advertisers for the game programs, fund-raising, and watching many games. When I watch the games, I appreciate all the work that my staff and the students have put into making the event a success.

**Question:** Now you are about to take on different responsibilities as director of intramural sports. Why make the change?

**Answer:** The number of teams at my college is increasing, and the new AD will be responsible for managing even more budgets, teams, coaches, and game logistics. However, my college has never had any intramural sports. I want to get the whole student body more involved in sports on a daily basis, and I think an intramural program is the way to bring this about.

**Question:** What do you think is the most important issue for sport managers?

**Answer:** Ethics. Sport managers need to live by a high moral code. They need to make sure the physical environment is safe for all athletes and fans. They need to conduct themselves in a professional managerial role whether they are on or off the athletic field.

**LEARNING OUTCOME 2 ▶**

Describe a sport manager's responsibilities.

## Sport Manager's Responsibilities

Without resources, you don't have an organization, and the resource-based view says that the better the resources, the more successful the organization. A **sport manager** is responsible for achieving the sport organization's objectives through efficient and effective use of resources. To begin with a good perspective on what sport managers are all about, let's take a closer look at a couple of these terms. *Efficient* means getting the most out of your available resources. *Effective* means doing the right thing (following the proper strategy) to attain your objective; it also describes how well you achieve the objectives. The **manager's resources** include human, financial, physical, and informational resources.

## Human Resources

People are a manager's most valuable resource.[8] As a manager, you will try to recruit and hire the best people available. These people must then be trained to use the organization's other resources to maximize productivity. Whether you are managing a team of players or a team of employees, they will not be productive if they cannot work well together. Throughout this book we focus on how you can work with others to achieve your organization's objectives. It is people who come up with the creative ideas and technologies to improve the use of the other three resources.

## Financial Resources

Most managers have budgets. Their budgets state how much it should cost to operate their department, store, or team for a set period of time. In other words, a budget tells you what financial resources you have available to achieve your objectives. As a manager, you will be responsible for seeing that your department does not waste resources. Cheryl Condon spends her budget creatively to make sure that each sport at Elms has a chance to have a successful season.

## Physical Resources

Getting the job done requires effective and efficient use of physical resources. For a retailer like Dick's Sporting Goods, physical resources include store buildings (more than 850 of them), the merchandise it sells, the fixtures that display the merchandise, and the computers used to record sales and inventory. The Dick's Sporting Goods physical resources also include supplies such as price tags, hangers, and charge slips.

Managers are responsible for keeping equipment in working condition and for making sure that materials and supplies are readily available. Current sales and future business can be lost if Dick's Sporting Goods physical resources are not available when needed or are not used and maintained properly.

## Informational Resources

Information gives you power[9] in our information age.[10] Managers need all kinds of information. Dick's managers need to know how sales in Fairfax, Virginia, compare to those in Nashua, New Hampshire. These managers need to know which suppliers will get them golf balls fastest and most cheaply. Computers store and retrieve information like this for all of the Dick's stores and for the home office in Pittsburgh, Pennsylvania. When managers at Dick's check their texts, voice mails, and email; give employees directions on setting up displays; and attend the district meeting, they are using informational resources.

Sport teams at all levels keep lots of statistical information and use it to win more games. If you watched the movie *Moneyball*, you saw a good example of how sport teams such as the Oakland A's use algorithm-based statistical information to improve team performance. Billy Beane brought algorithms to MLB to use big data to go from intuition-based decision making to improved decisions based on data. Billy said, "You don't get partial credit for losing. I never doubted the Moneyball approach."[11]

 What kinds of resources would a Little League baseball team be able to tap into? What kinds of resources would Cheryl Condon have at her disposal?

 Name some informational resources that your team or organization uses.

 **TIME-OUT 1** Categorize the resources used by one of your present or past coaches or managers.

# What Does It Take to Be a Successful Manager?

Let's start by stating that success is based on the level of performance, and **performance** is a measure of how well managers achieve organizational objectives. Managers are responsible for meeting these objectives and are evaluated on how well they meet them using their resources effectively, efficiently, and creatively. Coaches who don't win enough games can be fired, such as Earl Watson of the NBA Phoenix Suns or Tom Rowe of the NHL Florida Panthers. Next, we discuss qualities of good and poor managers, the five skills that all managers need, a list of topics of interest to North American Society for Sport Management (NASSM) members, and the findings of the Ghiselli study.

## Traits of Good Managers

In a Gallup survey conducted for the *Wall Street Journal*, top executives were asked, "What are the most important traits for success as a supervisor?"[12] Before you read their answers, complete Self-Assessment 1.1 to find out whether you have what they think it takes. To improve, we need self-awareness[13] and self-assessment.[14] We present self-assessments for you to complete in every chapter of this book.

**TIME-OUT 2**

Think about a coach and a manager you know and explain what makes them good managers or poor ones. In what ways are they alike? In what ways do they differ? Give examples to support your conclusions.

The executives in the Gallup poll listed integrity, industriousness, and the ability to get along with people as the three most important traits of successful managers.

## Management Skills

LEARNING OUTCOME 3 ▶
Define the five management skills.

Skills are used to perform an activity or task well. We define **management skills** to include (1) technical skills, (2) people skills, (3) communication skills, (4) conceptual skills, and (5) decision-making skills (see figure 1.1). Technical skills are primarily concerned with things; people and communication skills are concerned with people; and conceptual and decision-making skills are primarily concerned with ideas. Technical skills are often called hard skills; people, communication, conceptual, and decision-making skills are called soft skills. Organizations seek employees with soft skills who can communicate clearly, take initiative, problem-solve, and work well with coworkers.[16] Soft management skills are critical, so they are the focus of this book. Management skills can be developed if you work at them through this course.

**Technical skills** are those that enable you to use methods and techniques to perform a task. When managers work on budgets, they use spreadsheet software such as Microsoft Excel, so they need computer skills; they also need some knowledge of accounting (a great deal of accounting has to do with budgets and finances). Dick's managers need computer skills just to open the store, and of course they also need these skills when they record transfers and sales. Technological advances improve sport performance, but it is people working in teams who develop new and improved technology.[17]

Most people are promoted to their first management positions on the strength of their technical skills. Because technical skills vary widely from job

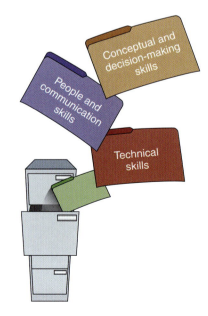

**FIGURE 1.1** Management skills.

## SELF-ASSESSMENT 1.1

# What Are Your Management Traits?

**Objective:**

To assess your own management traits

**Preparation:**

The following questions relate to key qualities that successful managers have.[15] Rate yourself on each item by writing the number (1-5) that best describes your behavior for that item.

1 = not very descriptive of me

2 = somewhat descriptive of me

3 = neutral

4 = descriptive of me

5 = very descriptive of me

_____ 1. I'd rather work with a team than work alone.

_____ 2. I can get others to try hard to win at sports or work.

_____ 3. People want to be on my team or work with me.

_____ 4. I'm a team player, not a ball hog seeking to be the star high scorer.

_____ 5. I enjoy influencing others to improve.

_____ 6. I always give it my best effort in sports and at work.

_____ 7. I can motivate myself.

_____ 8. I overcome obstacles that keep me from reaching my objectives.

_____ 9. I work on my own to continually improve my sport and work performance.

_____ 10. I push myself to the limit to succeed at sport and work.

_____ 11. Others know they can count on me to be on time and do what I say I'll do.

_____ 12. I don't trash talk my teammates and coaches or my boss and coworkers.

_____ 13. I seek to know my weaknesses and to change to improve.

_____ 14. I do not lie to, steal from, or cheat anyone (I compete within the rules).

_____ 15. I don't discriminate against or take advantage of others.

_____ (Add up your total score, between 15 and 75.)

The higher your score, the better your chances of succeeding in sport management. If you are or want to be a sport manager, review your subtotals for your ability to get along with people (items 1-5; average score 1-5), your industriousness (items 6-10; average score 1-5), and your integrity (items 11-15; average score 1-5), in this course and in your personal life, including sport and work. If your scores are not what you would like them to be, what will you do to improve?

to job, developing these skills is not a focus of this book. However, in our discussion of controlling skills (chapters 13 and 14), we give you a brief overview of the financial and budgetary tools you will use as a manager.

**People skills** enable you to work well with people. Today, people want partnership relationships with their managers rather than the outdated superior–subordinate relationship. Not only do employees want to participate in management; management encourages

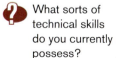 What sorts of technical skills do you currently possess?

group decision making (see chapter 3). Your people skills are what will make athletes, parents, employees, and other coaches want to work with you and for you. **Communication skills** are the skills that enable you to get your ideas across clearly and effectively. Without communication skills, you cannot be an effective team member or manager.[18] With the increased use of teams comes the need for good people skills. The combination of people skills and communication skills is called *interpersonal skills*, and they are becoming more important than technical skills.[19]

The resources you need to get the job done are made available through relationships.[20] So another key area of interpersonal skills is political savvy—"street smarts" help you manage teams, develop a power base and political skills to get the resources you need, manage conflict, and improve employee performance. Our interpersonal skills can be developed. Throughout this book and the web study guide, in the Skill-Builders and other exercises, you will learn to work with diverse people, hone your people skills, improve your communication skills, and motivate and lead others. As director of the athletic department at Elms, Cheryl Condon has many stakeholders (see chapter 2) to satisfy—she wouldn't last a minute if she didn't have great people skills and great communication skills. We focus on developing interpersonal and leadership skills in part III.

**Conceptual skills** refer to the ability to understand abstract ideas through critical thinking. Another term for conceptual skills is systems thinking, or the ability to understand an organization or department as a whole and the relationships between its parts. Sport managers regularly run projects and special events that require project management conceptual skills to pull everything together. **Decision-making skills** are those that enable you to select alternatives to solve problems. The decisions you make affect you today and in your future. Managerial decisions affect the success of organizations and teams,[21] especially decisions about the employees and players that they recruit and play; when they don't win, they sometimes get fired. Recruiters seek job candidates with conceptual skills who can make decisions that solve problems.[22] Also, firms train employees to improve their decision-making skills.[23] An important part of Cheryl's job is to decide what facilities to use, which marketing strategies will work, which coaches fit with Elms' objectives, and which student-athletes she should recruit. You will develop your creative problem solving and decision-making skills in chapter 3.

TIME-OUT
3

Think about a coach and a manager you know, and list the management skills they use on the job. Be specific, and try to identify each of the five skills discussed here.

## North American Society for Sport Management (NASSM) Topics

The North American Society for Sport Management (NASSM) is the major professional association for college and university sport management academics, and it offers student membership for career development. NASSM's website (www.nassm.org) lists sport management programs worldwide.

NASSM supports professionals in sport, leisure, and recreation. The purpose of NASSM is to promote, stimulate, and encourage study, research, scholarly writing, and professional development in sport management—both theoretical and applied aspects. Sport management scholarly research is published in NASSM's *Journal of Sport Management* and *Sport Management Education Journal* through Human Kinetics. The website also has a link with a list of other "Journals Serving Sport Management." Topics of interest to NASSM members include the following:[24]

- Sport marketing (we briefly discuss marketing in chapter 13)
- Future directions in management (current and future trends are discussed throughout the book)

## APPLYING THE CONCEPT 1.1

### Management Skills

Identify the skill used in each situation:

a. technical skills

b. people skills

c. communication skills

d. conceptual skills

e. decision-making skills

_____  1.  The ability to see the game as a whole and the effects of the players' performance on the score.

_____  2.  The ability to motivate athletes to do a good job

_____  3.  The ability to perform departmental jobs such as ticket taker

_____  4.  The ability to correct a problem

_____  5.  The ability to write effective memos and letters

- Employment perspectives (we have already listed jobs, and we discuss careers in sport management in the appendix)
- Management competencies (the focus of every chapter is on developing your management skills)
- Leadership (we discuss leading in five chapters, 8-12)
- Sport and the law (we discuss employment law in chapter 7)
- Personnel management (we discuss human resource management in chapter 7)
- Facility management (we discuss facility management in chapter 14)
- Organizational structures (we discuss organizing in chapters 5-7)
- Fund-raising (we briefly discuss fund-raising in chapter 13)
- Conflict resolution (you will learn how to resolve conflicts in chapter 8)

The focus of the book is on management, with a heavy dose of leadership. Reading the list of topics, you may realize that your school offers entire courses in some of these areas. You may be required to complete multiple courses to gain knowledge and skills in these areas. NASSM influences sport management curriculum, but it does not give accreditation.

### The Commission on Sport Management Accreditation (COSMA)

COSMA is an accrediting body whose purpose is to promote and recognize excellence in collegiate sport management education worldwide through specialized accreditation.[25] Some schools elect to go through accreditation, and others don't. Visit its website (www.cosmaweb. org) for a list of accredited programs and for more information regarding accreditation.

## Management Ability

In his classic 1971 study, Professor Edwin Ghiselli identified six traits that are important for managers, although not all are needed to succeed as a manager.[26] They are, in reverse order of importance, (6) initiative, (5) self-assurance, (4) decisiveness, (3) intelligence, (2) need for occupational achievement, and (1) supervisory ability. The number-one trait, supervisory ability, requires skills in planning, organizing, leading, and controlling. Ghiselli's four areas of supervisory ability are more commonly referred to today as the management functions; we discuss them in the next section and throughout the book.

# What Do Sport Managers Do?

LEARNING OUTCOME 4 ▶

Define the four management functions.

Sport managers do lots of things, as you can well imagine, but the things they do can be classified into the four functions of management and 10 management roles.

## Management Functions

Managers get the job done through others. They plan, organize, lead, and control to achieve organizational objectives—these are the four **management functions**.

This book is organized around the four management functions. Each function serves as a title for a part of the book, and two to five chapters are devoted to developing skills in each function. Here and in later chapters, we examine each function separately. However, the starting point of all functions should be to set objectives.[27] So you set an objective and then plan, organize, lead, and control to achieve the objective. But keep in mind that the four functions together compose a system; they are interrelated and are often performed simultaneously.

### Planning

The people who work for organizations, from the CEO to the summer intern, need goals and objectives as well as plans by which they will achieve them. **Planning** is the process of setting objectives and determining in advance exactly how the objectives will be met. Performance tends to be based on effective plans.[28] Start with an objective, and then develop a plan to achieve it.[29] Note that organizing, leading, and controlling are also based on achieving your objectives. You will learn how to write effective objectives in chapter 4 and how to plan in part II.

 What planning functions does your team or organization perform? Which managers are responsible for different aspects of planning?

Managers schedule the work that employees perform, and they also develop budgets. At Dick's, managers schedule employees' work rotations so that high-volume times in stores are well covered, and these managers also select the merchandise that Dick's will sell. Performing the planning function well requires strong conceptual and decision-making skills.

### Organizing

Successful managers also design and develop systems to implement plans. **Organizing** is the process of delegating and coordinating tasks and resources to achieve objectives. How you organize your resources affects your performance.[30] Organizing includes assigning people to various jobs, athletic positions, and tasks. At Elms, Cheryl Condon plans for regular-season games, holiday tournaments, and postseason games. To do this, she has to organize the athletic department employees (including coaches, assistants, equipment people, and ticket takers) so that they cover every game.

Staffing is also part of organizing. It's the process of selecting, training, and evaluating employees.[31] Cheryl is responsible for staffing her teams with coaches. Effective organizing requires both conceptual and decision-making skills as well as people skills and communication skills. You will learn how to organize in part III.

### Leading

Leadership affects organizational success, so leadership is an important skill for everyone.[32] Recruiters seek job applicants with leadership ability.[33] This is especially important for managers who work with employees and athletes daily.[34] **Leading** is the process of influencing employees to work to achieve objectives. An important part of Cheryl's job at Elms, as for all sport managers, is to communicate objectives and then motivate and lead individuals and teams. Effective leaders develop positive relationships based on strong people and communication skills.[35] You will develop your leadership skills in part IV.

### Controlling

We know we are achieving our objectives by monitoring our progress through controlling.[36] **Controlling** is the process of creating and implementing mechanisms to ensure that objectives are achieved. You need to measure your progress to know whether you are on target to meet the objective,[37] and when you are off target, you need to take corrective action.[38] The great thing about sports is that there is almost always a score, so you know if you are meeting your objective of winning. If you are ahead, you tend to keep things the same, but when you are losing, you make changes, such as new plays or athletes in different positions to score and win. Cheryl and the coaches monitor the progress of each team and make adjustments as needed. You will learn control systems and processes in part V.

**TIME-OUT 4** Using the coach and manager you've analyzed in previous Time-Outs, give examples of how they perform each of the four management functions.

## Nonmanagement Functions

All managers perform the four functions of management as they and their teams complete the job. But managers may perform nonmanagement employee work. If Cheryl makes a photocopy of the athletic department budget she is working on, she is performing a nonmanagement function. Working managers perform both management and employee functions. If you walk into a Dick's store during its busy hours, it is not uncommon to see managers waiting on customers and running the cash registers. They also may be filling in for employees who are out sick, at lunch, or on break.

Successful coaches display strong interpersonal and managerial skills.

## Transition to Sport Management

*Go suit* is the term used for getting promoted to management.[39] Going from being an employee or player to being a manager or coach is not an easy transition.[40] New managers often don't realize just how hard and different the job is. Managers use interpersonal skills[41] and manage people to get them to do the job[42]—coach versus athlete.

For most athletes, it's difficult to go from playing to coaching or to working to make the games possible as a sport manager. The athletic technical skills you needed to win games are very different from the management skills you need to succeed as a coach or sport manager. This book is designed to help you successfully make that transition. Some great athletes don't want to coach, and others make poor coaches: Wayne Gretzky's tenure as coach of the NHL Phoenix Coyotes was mediocre; Magic Johnson of the NBA Los Angeles Lakers coached for a total of 11 games before it became too frustrating; Isiah Thomas of the NBA New York Knicks traded the franchise's future away for players who never achieved their potential. On the other hand, some not-so-great athletes make great coaches and sport managers, such as Brad Stevens with the NBA Boston Celtics and A.J. Hinch of the MLB Houston Astros.

## Management Functions as a System

The management functions relate to each other as a system.[43] They do not always work sequentially. Managers don't simply plan, then organize, then lead, and end with control. The functions are both separate and interrelated, and this calls for conceptual skills. Sport managers often perform the four functions at the same time. Each function affects the others. For example, if you start with a poor plan, your objective may not be met, even though things are well organized, well led, and well controlled. Plans need controls to monitor progress and to take corrective action to ensure the objective is met. Figure 1.2 illustrates this process. So the management functions are based on setting (planning) and achieving (organizing, leading, and controlling) objectives.

## Management Roles

Henry Mintzberg identified 10 roles that managers assume to accomplish their planning, organizing, leading, and controlling functions. A role is a set of expectations for how one will behave in a given situation. How well managers implement the management roles affects their performance. Mintzberg categorized the 10 management roles as shown in figure 1.3.[44] **Management roles** characterize the behaviors managers engage in to accomplish the management functions.

**FIGURE 1.2**   Management skills and functions.

## APPLYING THE CONCEPT 1.2

### Management Functions

Identify which function fits the situation described.

a. planning
b. organizing
c. leading
d. controlling
e. nonmanagement

_____  6. Coach Sally shows Kelly how to kick a ball.

_____  7. Coach Tom determines how many players were hurt during the first half of the game.

_____  8. Ace forward Jason has missed practice several times. Coach Dave is discussing the situation with Jason to get him to understand that he cannot continue to miss practice.

_____  9. Coach Sheryl is interviewing applicants for the position of physical therapist.

_____ 10. Coach Terry is fixing a broken weight training machine.

**FIGURE 1.3**   Ten roles managers play. *Note that the starting point is with setting objectives. **Managers play the necessary role while performing management functions to achieve objectives.

### Interpersonal Roles

Interpersonal roles include figurehead, leader, and liaison. When you play interpersonal roles, you need people and communication skills. Managers are *figureheads* when they represent the organization or team in ceremonial and symbolic activities. Cheryl Condon played the figurehead role at Elms College when she granted an interview to one of the authors. Managers are *leaders* when they motivate, train, communicate with, and influence others. Throughout the day, Cheryl functions as a leader when she directs players to prepare for the upcoming game. Managers are *liaisons* when they interact with people outside their team for information and favors. Cheryl plays liaison when she solicits local businesses to place advertisements in game programs.

◀ LEARNING OUTCOME 5

Explain the interpersonal, informational, and decisional roles of management.

## Informational Roles

Informational roles include monitor, disseminator, and spokesperson. When you play informational roles, you need people and communication skills. Managers are *monitors* when they gather information—a controlling function. Cheryl continually monitors her situation by following the performance of other local colleges and other Division III teams in her league. Managers are *disseminators* when they send information. They are *spokespersons* when they provide information to people outside the organization. Cheryl is both disseminator and spokesperson when she gives interviews to the local newspaper.

## Decisional Roles

Decisional roles include entrepreneur, disturbance handler, resource allocator, and negotiator. When you play decisional roles, you need conceptual and decision-making skills. Managers are *entrepreneurs* when they innovate improvements in products and processes. Cheryl demonstrates an entrepreneurial spirit in her desire to start an intramural sport program. Managers are *disturbance handlers* when they take corrective action to defuse disputes or crises. Cheryl is a disturbance handler when she negotiates a settlement in a dispute between a coach and the coach's players. Managers are *resource allocators* when they use people, finances, physical, and information resources. Cheryl is a resource allocator when she authorizes departmental budgets and the purchases made against these budgets. Managers are *negotiators* when they bargain with others to gain and use resources to achieve objectives. Cheryl negotiates the athletic department budget with the VP of finance.

**TIME-OUT 5** Using the coach and manager you've analyzed in previous Time-Outs, give examples of how they perform their management roles.

---

## APPLYING THE CONCEPT 1.3

### Management Roles

Identify the role played by management in each situation.

a. interpersonal
b. informational
c. decisional

_____ 11. Baseball Commissioner Rob Manfred discusses the players' contract with union representatives.

_____ 12. An Adidas HR manager shows a new hire how to fill out a form.

_____ 13. The Cincinnati Reds' Walt Jocketty reads *Street & Smith's* with his cup of coffee first thing in the morning.

_____ 14. Cheryl Condon develops new total quality management techniques.

_____ 15. The Raiders' sales and ticket managers discuss a complaint with a customer.

# How Do Managers Differ?

Although all managers need the same skills and perform the same functions, at various levels of management, different management skills are needed more than others, different management functions are performed more often, and different roles are played. Managers who work for large organizations typically have more specialized jobs than those who work for small organizations, and there are also some differences between managing for-profit and nonprofit organizations. In this section, we explain these differences.

## Three Levels of Management

The three **levels of management** are top, middle, and first-line management (see figure 1.4).

◀ **LEARNING OUTCOME 6**
Diagram the hierarchy of management levels.

### *Top Managers*

These executives have titles to help identify the level of management,[45] such as chief executive officer (CEO), chief operations officer (COO), president, and vice president. They manage the entire organization or major units or departments of it. They develop the organization's mission, objectives, and strategies. Their supervisors are the board of directors or other executives, and they supervise the middle managers. The presidents of Elms and your college are top managers.

### *Middle Managers*

They have titles such as general manager, athletic director, sales manager, branch manager, and department head. Middle managers carry out top management's strategies. Their supervisors are executives, and they supervise first-line managers. Cheryl Condon is a middle manager at Elms College.

### *First-Line Managers*

Titles at this level include coach, ticket manager, event manager, supervisor, and office manager. First-line managers supervise day-to-day operations and report to middle managers. They supervise operative employees or athletes, not other managers.

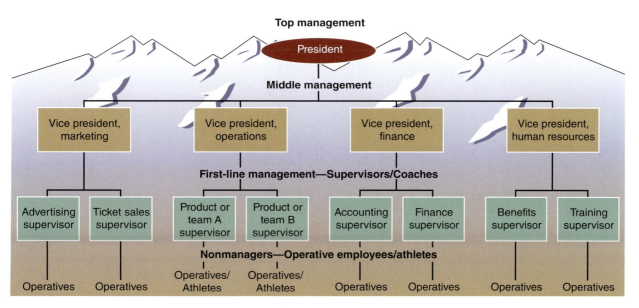

**FIGURE 1.4** Management levels and functional areas.

### Team Leaders and Captains

As you know, most sport teams have captains who help the coach. Duke University basketball coach Mike Krzyzewski said that a large part of his success was based on team leadership to motivate players to give it their all and win games. Sport businesses also have team leaders for various tasks, such as a committee to complete a project.

### Nonmanagement Operatives: Employees and Players

The workers and athletes who compose the teams that managers lead do not hold management positions. Operatives, as we use the term here, are the people who report to first-line managers and possibly team leaders. Operatives work in concessions, take tickets, make the products, wait on customers, and perform repairs.

TIME-OUT
6

Think about a sport organization you are familiar with, and identify the levels of management in the organization by level and title. Does this organization use all three levels? Why or why not?

## Types of Managers

**LEARNING OUTCOME 7** ▶
Describe general, functional, and project managers.

The three **types of managers** are general, functional, and project managers. Top-level and some middle managers are *general managers* because they manage several departments.

Middle and first-line managers are often *functional managers* who supervise related jobs and athletic positions. The major functions, often called departments, are marketing (sell tickets), operations (game day) and production (make sport goods), finance and accounting (budgets), and human resources (recruiting employees and players).

Project management positions are needed in organizations with team-based structures.[46] A *project manager* coordinates resources across functions to accomplish a goal or task.[47] One example would be a multiple-team athletic tournament like the yearly Hoop Classic held at Springfield College, the birthplace of basketball. You will learn more about managing events in chapter 14.

TIME-OUT
7

Which type of manager have you worked for? Write a job description for this person, and categorize the tasks he or she performs by function.

## Management Skills

**LEARNING OUTCOME 8** ▶
Explain how skills and functions differ by management level.

All managers need technical skills, people and communication skills, and conceptual and decision-making skills. However, the need for these skills differs by the level of management. Various studies have determined the skill needs at each level of management, and it is generally agreed that the need for people skills and communication skills is fairly constant across all three levels. Top-level managers have a greater need for conceptual and decision-making skills; first-line managers need better technical skills. This is logical—as managers move up the corporate ladder, they are less concerned with the daily details of conducting business and more concerned with the big picture, conceptualizing and strategizing. First-line managers focus on the detail—the day-to-day practice for games and creation of the product or service. Middle managers typically need a balance of all three skills, but this varies from organization to organization.

## Management Functions

As we have already noted, every manager plans, organizes, leads, and controls. However, the focus and time spent on each function differ based on the level of management. It is generally agreed that first-line managers spend more time leading and controlling as they focus on getting the day-to-day work done, middle-level managers spend equal time on all four functions, and top managers spend more time focusing on long-term planning and organizing. Table 1.1 summarizes the differences by management levels.

## APPLYING THE CONCEPT 1.4

### Differences Between Management Levels

Identify the level of management in each situation.

   a. top

   b. middle

   c. first line

_____ 16. Coaches the professional players

_____ 17. Owns the team

_____ 18. Spends time motivating and developing skills

_____ 19. Is the athletic director reporting to the president

_____ 20. Has a more balanced need for the management skills and functions

### TABLE 1.1   Skills and Functions Performed by Management Level

| Management level | Primary management skills needed | Primary management functions performed |
|---|---|---|
| Top | Conceptual and decision-making skills | Planning and organizing (long-term) |
| Middle | Balance of all skills | Balance of all four |
| First-line/coach | Technical and people and communication skills | Leading and controlling (short-term) |

## Managing Large Businesses and Small Businesses

Table 1.2 lists the major differences between managers in large and small businesses. These are general statements, and many large and small businesses share certain characteristics. Sport managers in all organizations need the same skills and perform the same managerial functions. However, jobs in large firms tend to be more specialized than those in small ones. It's not unusual to coach a couple of sports at the youth and small high school level but only one at the college level. Small business can be defined in many ways. This is the Small Business Administration (SBA) definition: "A small business is an independent business having fewer than 500 employees." But the SBA also provides different definitions based on type of industry that are used in government programs and contracting.[48] Elms College is a small business.

## Managing For-Profits and Not-For-Profits

Whether you work for your local Little League team (nonprofit) or for the Brazilian World Cup champions (for-profit), you need the same management skills, perform the same management functions, and play the same roles.

That said, the two types of organizations do exhibit key differences. These are mainly seen in how they measure performance, how they staff their organizations, and how they get funds. The primary measure of performance in for-profit organizations is, well, profit. In addition, organizations that are in business to make money must pay their workers. Nonprofit organizations measure performance differently—for example, by whether they can pay for the team's swimming pool rental fees, whether team membership is increasing, and whether they are reaching their stakeholders (such as inner-city kids). Typically, many of the staff members of nonprofits are unpaid *volunteers*.

Nonprofits also commonly conduct *fund-raisers* and get money from the government, whereas for-profits don't. When funds are cut back, many school and college athletic programs depend on fund-raising.

We can also separate not-for-profits into nongovernment organizations (NGOs) and government organizations. You could work for an NGO, such as the private University of Notre Dame, or a governmental organization, such as the public Ohio State University. Three primary areas of difference that distinguish for-profits, NGOs, and government organizations relate to ownership and profits, revenues, and staffing. See table 1.3 for a list of differences.

## TABLE 1.2   Functions and Roles in Large and Small Businesses

| Functions and roles | Large businesses | Small businesses |
|---|---|---|
| Planning | Formal long-term strategic plans with a global business focus | Usually have informal plans with a local focus |
| Organizing | Formal organization charts with clear policies and procedures and with specialized jobs | Commonly have informal structures with fewer than three levels of management and no clear job descriptions |
| Leading | Managers tend to use participative leadership, allowing employees to make decisions | Entrepreneurs tend to be autocratic leaders who make the important decisions |
| Controlling | Have more sophisticated computerized control systems | Often rely on direct observation of employees and finances |
| Important management role | Resource allocator | Entrepreneur |

## TABLE 1.3   Contrasting For-Profit, Not-For-Profit, and Government Organizations

| Function | For-profit | Not-for-profit (NGO) | Government |
|---|---|---|---|
| Ownership and profits | The primary universal measure of performance is bottom-line profit. Owners are entitled to take profits out of the firm. | Organizations are mission driven; as in all businesses, profits are the objective. However, any excess revenue remains in the organization. There are no individual owners. | Organizations are mission driven; profits are not the goal. Ownership resides with an entity of government. |
| Revenues | Money comes into the business primarily through sales. | Money often is raised through donations, grants, memberships, and investments, as well as sales or fees. | Money is raised through taxes, fees, and sales. |
| Staffing | Employees are primarily all paid employees. | Many NGOs rely on both volunteer workers and paid employees to accomplish their mission. | Employees are primarily all paid employees; however, some entities rely on volunteers. |

Reprinted by permission from Dr. Kathryn Carlson Heler.

## Objectives of the Book

Research indicates that knowledge is more likely to be used when it is acquired from active learning than when it is acquired from passive reading, listening, or thinking. This book uses an active, "how-to" three-pronged approach, with these objectives:

- To teach you the important concepts of sport management
- To develop your ability to apply the sport management concepts through critical thinking
- To develop your sport management skills in your personal and professional lives

The book offers some unique features to further each of these three objectives, as summarized in table 1.4.

### TABLE 1.4  Features of This Book's Three-Pronged Approach

| | |
|---|---|
| Features that present sport management concepts | • Chapter text<br>• Key Terms<br>• Learning Outcomes<br>• Chapter Summaries<br>• Review and Discussion Questions |
| Features that help you apply what you learn | • Reviewing Their Game Plan cases<br>• Sport organizational examples<br>• Time-Outs<br>• Applying the Concepts<br>• Cases |
| Features that foster skill development | • Self-Assessments<br>• Step-by-step models for handling sport management functions<br>• Sports and Social Media Exercises*<br>• Game Plan for Starting a Sport Business*<br>• Skill-Builder exercises* |

* Available in the web study guide.

## Practice

Like in sports, you can improve,[49] or you can develop your sport management skills.[50] That is the major goal of this book. When it comes to sport, we don't have to tell you about the need for practice. Vince Lombardi, the late great football coach of the Green Bay Packers, said that leaders are made by effort and hard work. If you want to develop your sport management skills, you must not only learn the concepts in this book but also practice with the applications and Skill-Builder exercises. But most important, to be successful, you need to practice using your sport management skills in your personal and professional lives just as you do in sports.

## LEARNING AIDS

### CHAPTER SUMMARY

1. **Describe career opportunities in sport management.**

   Sport management is a multidisciplinary field that integrates sport and management. Sport management programs train interested people for management positions in such areas as college athletics, professional teams, fitness centers, recreation centers, sport tourism, coaching, officiating, marketing, youth organizations, and sporting goods manufacturing and retailing.

2. **Describe a sport manager's responsibilities.**

Sport managers are responsible for achieving organizational objectives through efficient and effective use of resources. Sport managers use their organization's human, financial, physical, and informational resources to achieve the objectives.

3. **Define the five management skills.**

The five management skills are technical skills, people and communication skills, and conceptual and decision-making skills. Technical skills enable us to use methods and techniques to perform a task. People skills enable us to work well with people. Communication skills enable us to get our ideas across clearly and effectively. Conceptual skills enable us to understand abstract ideas, and decision-making skills enable us to select alternatives to solve problems.

4. **Define the four management functions.**

The four management functions are planning, organizing, leading, and controlling. Planning is the process of setting objectives and determining in advance exactly how the objectives will be met. Organizing is the process of delegating and coordinating tasks and resources to achieve objectives. Leading is about influencing employees to work toward achieving objectives. Controlling is the process of creating and implementing mechanisms to ensure that the organization achieves its objectives.

5. **Explain the interpersonal, informational, and decisional roles of management.**

Managers play the interpersonal role when they act as figureheads, leaders, and liaisons. Managers play the informational role when they act as monitors, disseminators, and spokespersons. Managers play the decisional role when they act as entrepreneurs, disturbance handlers, resource allocators, and negotiators.

6. **Diagram the hierarchy of management levels.**

The three levels are top, middle, and first-line management.

7. **Describe general, functional, and project managers.**

General managers supervise the activities of several departments or units. Functional managers supervise related activities such as marketing, operations, finance, and human resources management. Project managers coordinate employees and other resources across several functional departments to accomplish a specific task.

8. **Explain how skills and functions differ by management level.**

Top managers have a greater need for conceptual and decision-making skills. Middle managers need a balance of all skills. First-line managers need better technical skills.

## REVIEW AND DISCUSSION QUESTIONS

1. What is sport management? Name some possible career opportunities available to sport management majors.

2. What are the five management skills? Do all sport managers need these skills?

3. What are the four functions of management? Do all sport managers perform all four functions?

4. What are the three management roles? Do all sport managers perform all three roles?

5. What are the three types of managers? How do they differ?

6. Is it more important for a sport manager to be efficient or effective? Can you be both?

7. Should a sport management course focus on teaching students about sports or about management? Explain your answer.

8. Can college students develop their management skills through a college course? Why or why not?

9. Do you believe that sport management theory is or should be as precise as physics or chemistry? Explain your answer.

10. What are three career paths in sport management that you find interesting?

11. Why is it important to take this management course?

12. Are you interested in being a manager?

13. Some people say that hard skills (technical, finance, quantitative analysis) are more important for managers than soft skills (people and communication skills), and some say the opposite is true. What is your view?

14. Is your college professor a manager? Why or why not?

## CASES

### Sport Management Professionals @ Work: Joe Esile

Joe Esile attended Elms College from 2005 to 2009. He was a management major because, like many colleges at that time, Elms College did not yet offer a sport management major. Joe went to Marshall University for a master of science degree in sport administration. Like most master's programs, this took two years to complete. During those two years, Joe was involved in field maintenance and game operations.

After graduation, Joe became the game operations assistant at the University of Missouri. His duties included football game-day operations, which entailed overseeing customer service for all fans in the stadium. This included monitoring a student section of over 10,000 general admission student seats and a 10,500 reserved chair back section. He also collaborated with many outside entities, including keystone event staffing, Missouri University Police Department (MUPD), and facility operations, to preserve order and safety.

Joe then moved to the University of Pittsburgh to be the athletic facilities and game operations coordinator for three years. His responsibilities included coordinating all projects and routine inspections for five athletic facilities in the areas of carpentry, plumbing, painting, and cleaning. He was also responsible for many renovation projects such as technology upgrades, turf installation, carpet installation, furniture replacement, and varied field maintenance projects.

Joe is currently the athletic facilities and events director for the University of California, Berkeley.[51] Joe has traveled all over the country to follow his sport management dreams!

### Case Questions

1. Which of the five management skills—(1) technical skills, (2) people skills, (3) communication skills, (4) conceptual skills, and (5) decision-making skills—does Joe appear to use in furthering his career?

2. How has Joe used the four functions of management (planning, leading, organizing, and controlling) in his different positions?

3. What is your opinion on how Joe progressed from a small Division III private New England college to a very large public research university in California?

### Special Teams to Special Leader at Under Armour

Under Armour is one pretty dry company! Under Armour's mission is to provide technically advanced products engineered with superior fabric construction, exclusive moisture management, and proven innovation. Under Armour produces highly technical gear marketed to provide climate control for athletes.

Founded in 1996 by former University of Maryland football player Kevin Plank, Under Armour is the originator of performance apparel—gear engineered to keep athletes cool, dry, and light throughout the course of a game, practice, or workout. Amazingly, Under Armour (UA) pretty much created the entire high-end performance apparel market on its own.

While Plank was a special teams captain of the University of Maryland football team, he grew tired of his sweaty T-shirt. He wanted to create the ultimate T-shirt, one that wouldn't absorb moisture. Nearly 10 years later, Plank developed his unique synthetic fiber concept to create one of the most unusual lines of sporting goods products since the founding of Nike.

Where did Under Armour find the nerve to compete against a giant like Nike? Kevin Plank.

It seemed as if overnight, Under Armour was available in all the major sporting goods stores, such as Modell's and Dick's Sporting Goods. In addition, professional leagues and their players became avid users of the unique clothes.

Plank oversees all operations and strategic planning, including sales and marketing, production management, forecasting, and general management functions. Today, Under Armour has more than 14,000 teammates worldwide. The company has successfully added athletic cleats to diversify its product line. Under Armour sells footwear, sports and casual apparel, and sporting equipment to compete directly against long-standing giants such as Nike and Adidas.

Lisa Delpy Neirotti, director of George Washington University's sport management MBA program, thought it was a brilliant move. "It's like anything in business . . . being a little bit different . . . gets attention and people talk about it."[52]

Recently, Under Armour was involved in a rare bit of negative publicity. Some people felt that CEO Plank didn't quite express himself properly in regard to the travel ban on immigrants ordered by President Donald Trump. Plank responded in an open letter stating UA was united against the travel ban. He went on to express how UA had built a 30,000-square-foot community center where kids and families could learn, play, and have fun. UA has also built a Manufacturing Boot Camp to train people in skills that can help them live a good life. Plank wanted it to be known that UA creates jobs and believes immigration is a source of strength, diversity, and innovation for global companies based in America like Under Armour.[53] In today's world shaped by technology, social media, and social unrest, CEOs of sport organizations are increasingly responding to issues that previously were the domain of government officials.

Has Under Armour reached its peak? Sales of footwear and athletic apparel dropped 5 percent from 2016 to 2017. The United States market lost sales, which hurt since this was UA's largest market. Sales did grow in smaller UA markets in Europe, Latin America, and Asia. But UA has a much smaller market share in those areas of the world. UA has lowered its sales projections.

What caused the drop in sales? Superstar NBA player Steph Curry was signed to represent UA, but the style of his footwear has not been well received. Social media have portrayed the footwear as uncool. One area where UA has to grow is in women's footwear and athletic clothing.[54]

For current information on Under Armour, visit its website at www.ua.com.

Go to the web study guide to answer questions about this case study.

## @ TAKE IT TO THE NET

Please visit www.HumanKinetics.com/AppliedSportManagementSkills and go to this book's companion web study guide, where you will find the following:

A list of websites associated with the concepts in this chapter

Skill-Builder exercises, Sports and Social Media exercises, and a continuing Game Plan for Starting a Sport Business

Online versions of chapter exercises and end-of-chapter learning aids

An exercise that helps you define the Key Terms

# The Sport Industry Environment

## *Globalization, Ethics, and Social Responsibility*

### LEARNING OUTCOMES

After studying this chapter, you should be able to

1. describe the five components of the internal environment;

2. explain the two primary principles of total quality management;

3. explain how factors in the external environment affect the internal business environment;

4. state the differences between domestic, international, and multinational businesses;

5. list the lowest- and highest-risk ways to take a business global;

6. explain the stakeholders' approach to ethics; and

7. discuss the four levels of social responsibility in business.

### KEY TERMS

| | | |
|---|---|---|
| internal environment | customer value | joint venture |
| mission | total quality management (TQM) | direct investment |
| stakeholders | external environment | ethics |
| systems process | international business | stakeholders' approach to ethics |
| structure | multinational corporation (MNC) | social responsibility |
| quality | global sourcing | |

## DEVELOPING YOUR SKILLS

Top-level managers routinely analyze their company's environment and management practices and those of their competitors. Analyze the company you work for in terms of its internal environment (What is its mission? What resources does it use to make and deliver its products or services?) and external environment (How does it get and treat customers? Who are its competitors?). Are the employees ethical, and is the firm socially responsible?

## REVIEWING THEIR GAME PLAN

### Major League Baseball (MLB) Goes Global

New York is a very big city, and it can be hard to find success—especially if you are a pitcher from Japan. The New York Yankees signed Masahiro Tanaka from Japan in 2014. As Masahiro himself said at the press conference, "They gave me the highest evaluation and are a world-famous team."[1] Tanaka signed a seven-year contract for $155 million. The Yankees' decision to sign Tanaka is a result of their efforts to use their internal environment to find players in their external marketplace. The Yankees management team of Randy Levine, Brian Cashman, former manager Joe Girardi, assistant general managers Billy Eppler and Jean Afterman, pitching coach Larry Rothschild, special assistant Trey Hillman, and translator George Rose decided that Tanaka's ability to perform at a high level in Japan would translate to the large New York market. Along with the ability to pitch at a high level of excellence, Tanaka was a big catch for the Yankees to show the other MLB teams they could outbid them for the services of highly talented athletes. Attracting Tanaka to play in New York would help to recruit more free agents to the New York marketplace.

The Yankees' investment included paying a $20 million posting fee to Rakuten, Tanaka's Japanese team, under the terms of baseball's posting system with Nippon Professional Baseball. The large-market Yankees had the internal financial resources to secure the services of Tanaka for seven years with an opt-out clause for Tanaka to seek a new contract in the eighth year.

After having success in the 2017 season and playoffs—Tanaka was 2-1 with a 0.90 earned run average in three playoff starts—he decided not to use his opt-out clause, and he planned to remain with the Yankees for three more years.

In 2017, another Japanese baseball star announced his decision to leave Japan to pursue a career in Major League Baseball. Shohei Ohtani, a two-way player for the Hokkaido Nippon Ham Fighters, was known as the Japanese Babe Ruth due to his unique ability to excel as both a pitcher and a hitter. At age 23 and with five years of professional experience, Ohtani threw a 100-mile-per-hour fastball and had hit 48 home runs.[2] Major League Baseball owners voted unanimously to approve an agreement with Nippon Professional Baseball that resulted in Ohtani being put up for bid to all major league teams for the maximum $20 million posting fee. Major league front offices were then required to prepare presentations in both Japanese and English for the Ohtani family that included a detailed organizational plan, talent evaluation, player development philosophy, facility information, marketplace information, and resources for Shohei's cultural assimilation. Ultimately, Ohtani signed with the Los Angeles Angels.[3]

Will Masahiro Tanaka and Shohei Ohtani's fame help to spread MLB baseball in Japan? Will other foreign players be recruited in hopes of finding the next international superstar?

# Internal Environment and Quality in Sport

Organizations have people working together for a common purpose to provide goods or services.[4] The term *product* is commonly used to mean both goods and services because many products have an element of both, so when we use the term *product* throughout this book, we mean both goods and services The organization's **internal environment** includes the factors within its boundaries that affect its performance. Organizations have control over their internal resources, as opposed to external environmental factors they can't control. The five internal environment factors that you will learn about in this section are management, mission, resources, the systems process, and structure, and we also discuss quality in sport as part of the internal environment. We cover the external factors in the next major section.

## Management

Managers are responsible for their organization's performance as they develop the visionary mission, strategies, and plans to successfully compete.[5] They plan, organize, lead, and control using internal factors,[6] and how they manage is affected by the external environment they compete in.[7] Or they need to use their internal factors[8] and adjust them to stay competitive in their changing external environments.[9] Clearly, the NBA Dallas Mavericks would not be the team it is today if team owner Mark Cuban didn't continually scrutinize both environments. Managers are also responsible for developing the organizational culture that will identify the values and beliefs needed to achieve the mission. We will discuss organizational culture in chapter 6.

**◄ LEARNING OUTCOME 1**
Describe the five components of the internal environment.

Which environmental factors are important to a general manager of the Dallas Mavericks?

## Mission

The organization's **mission** is its purpose or reason for being. The mission provides identity by answering the question, Who are we as an organization?[10] Developing the mission is the responsibility of top management. Shorter mission statements are easier to understand and carry out. For an example, "The mission of Springfield College is to educate the whole person in spirit, mind, and body for leadership in service to others."[11] What is your college's or university's mission?

Missions should be relevant to stakeholders.[12] **Stakeholders** are people affected by the organization's activities. There are internal (within the organization, employees) and external (outside the organization, customers and fans) stakeholders. We list external stakeholders in the next section and also in figure 2.3. Managers must make trade-offs when stakeholder interests conflict. For example, professional athletes want more pay, and fans want lower prices to attend games. Salaries and prices (tickets, food and drinks, parking) affect image and attendance.

A mission and objectives can also be defined as the outcome that the organization strives to achieve. The other internal environmental factors—management, resources, systems process, and structure—are the means the organization uses to achieve its ends[13] (see figure 2.1). Managers develop the mission statement and set objectives, but they are also one of the four means to achieve the ends. As a sport manager, you may not write the mission statement and set organizational objectives, but you will definitely be responsible for helping to achieve them.

 **TIME-OUT 1** State the mission of a sport organization. Does it differ in any way from the missions of other types of organizations?

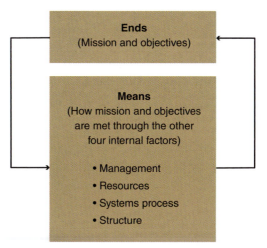

**FIGURE 2.1** Internal environmental means and ends.

## Mission

The value of a mission statement is often revealed in the process of discussing what it should address. For example, the hypothetical BAS University with 25,000 students might form a committee to discuss what should be included in its mission statement. The statement might be, "BASU initiates intellectual discussion, innovating curriculum and researching topics concerning the area of sport management." In comparison, the BASU Sport and Recreation Management department's mission might be, "Our program prepares students to face challenges in a number of capacities in the sport and recreation industries."

## Resources

Organizations need resources to accomplish their mission. As stated in chapter 1, organizational resources can be human, financial, physical, and informational. Human resources are critical[14] because people develop the mission and achieve it with the other resources.[15] Performance-based differences between firms can be seen in how they acquire and use their resources. For example, the team that gets and develops the best players wins more games, and teams like the MLB New York Yankees have the money to get top baseball players. As a sport manager, you will use these four resources to achieve your organization's mission.

## Systems Process

The **systems process** is the method used to transform inputs into outputs. The final outputs are organizations' products.[16] To be successful, firms strive to accelerate the systems process to increase performance through teamwork.

As shown in figure 2.2, the systems process has four components:

1. *Inputs.* Inputs are the resources (human, financial, physical, and informational) used to provide the organization's products. The athletes are the inputs for teams such as the NBA L.A. Lakers.

2. *Transformation processes.* Inputs are transformed into outputs. The L.A. Lakers play a game against the Boston Celtics.

3. *Outputs.* Outputs are the products offered to customers and fans. Either the Lakers or the Celtics win the game.

4. *Feedback.* Feedback is used to improve the systems process at all three stages—it's a controlling function. As the game is being played, Laker and Celtics coaches are giving feedback to their players on how to win the game. After the game is over, the teams review areas they can improve on and work on through practices.

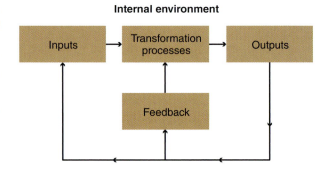

**FIGURE 2.2**   The systems process.

**TIME-OUT 2** Describe the systems process for an organization you have worked for or a team you have played on.

Putting it all together, what is the systems process for your college or university? It's not an easy one. You are an input to your college, your educational experience is the transformation, and when you graduate you are an output of your college. Most colleges ask students to assess faculty to gather feedback on their level of satisfaction and to make instructional improvements.

## Structure

Organizations structure their resources so that they can transform inputs into outstanding output—products.[17] An organization's **structure** is the departmentalization of its resources to accomplish its mission and objectives.[18] Organizations are commonly structured by functional departments—finance/accounting, marketing, production/operations, and human resources/personnel. As part of a system (chapter 1), each department (or player on a team) affects the organization (or team) as a whole, and each department (player) affects every other department (player during the competition—teamwork). As a sport manager you will be responsible for some part of the organization's structure—perhaps a department or a team within the department. We discuss the organizing management function in chapters 5 through 7.

## Quality in Sport

Quality is needed within the systems process to ensure successful outcomes. Proponents of total quality management (TQM) believe that customers (fans in the case of many sport organizations) assess the **quality** of the organization's outputs by comparing what they need (or want) from the product (goods and services) to their actual experience with the product. **Customer value** is the benefits that customers obtain if they buy a product or attend a sport event. Customers and fans are not simply buying a product or attending an event. They are also buying the benefit (value) they expect to derive from it. Value therefore motivates us either to buy or not to buy products or attend events. When fans buy tickets to a MLB New York Yankees versus Los Angeles Angels game, they expect to watch a high-quality game because star players such as Mike Trout and Giancarlo Stanton will be

◀ **LEARNING OUTCOME 2**
Explain the two primary principles of total quality management.

---

## APPLYING THE CONCEPT 2.1

### Internal Environment

Match each statement with the internal environmental factor it pertains to.

a. management
b. mission
c. resources
d. systems process
e. structure

_____ 1. We take these chemicals and make them into a liquid, which then goes into these molds. When it's hard, we've got golf balls.

_____ 2. We deliver pizza and buffalo wings to the basketball tournament.

_____ 3. The people here make this team what it is.

_____ 4. As we grew, we added a new department for human resources services.

_____ 5. Management does not trust us. All the major decisions around here are made by top-level managers.

playing for their teams. Sport organizations pay close attention to quality and value because these are what attract and retain fans and customers.

Total quality management isn't just about coaches and athletes striving for continuous improvement. **Total quality management (TQM)** is the process through which everyone in the organization focuses on the customer or fan in order to continually increase value. Enjoying a professional sport event is not simply about your team winning—it is entertainment. When you attend, you also want speedy ticket sales, helpful ushering, good food, and clean restrooms. The major principles of TQM are (1) to deliver customer and fan value and (2) to continually improve the systems processes. (We discuss quality and TQM in more detail in chapters 6 and 13.)

# External Environment

**LEARNING OUTCOME 3** ▶

Explain how factors in the external environment affect the internal business environment.

The organization's **external environment** includes factors outside its boundaries that affect its performance. Although managers can control the organization's internal environment, their influence over what

Sport organizations should continually seek new, innovative ways to enhance event value for customers.

happens outside the organization is limited, so they need to monitor the environment and change to continuously improve. The external environment includes nine factors.

1. *Fans and customers.* Without giving customers value, you don't have a successful business.[19] Pro teams would go out of business without enough loyal fans who buy tickets. The Dallas Cowboys had the most highly attended games in the NFL in 2016 with a total of 740,318 spectators, an average of 92,539 fans per game. The Los Angeles Dodgers remained the best-supported team for the third year in a row for MLB with a total of 3.7 million fans in 2016, an average of 45,719 spectators per game.[20]

2. *Competitors.* Organizations must compete for customers and fans. Scouts gather information to help their teams beat the other teams. Today in some areas, fans can choose from competing teams, like the MLB New York Yankees or New York Mets. Sport is entertainment, and people can select other things to do besides watch sports. This tends to happen when teams lose too many games.

 **TIME-OUT 3** Give an example of how one sport firm's competitors have affected the firm's performance.

3. *Suppliers.* Dick's buys equipment and apparel from suppliers to sell to its retail customers. Nike, Reebok, and Under Armour compete and pay big to be the official apparel company for each pro team and to sponsor athletes to help sell their apparel. Suppliers play an important part in an organization's success.[21]

4. *Athletes and workers.* Sport business success depends on having good employees throughout the organization. The best athletes are highly recruited by college coaches and are paid millions by the pros.

5. *Team owners and shareholders.* The owners of a corporation or pro sports team, known as *shareholders*, influence management.[22] Michael Jordan (MJ) is the first athlete to become a billionaire and major owner of a professional team. MJ acquired a 90 percent ownership stake in the NBA's Charlotte Hornets.[23] In 2017, Derek Jeter was part of a group of investors

## APPLYING THE CONCEPT 2.2

### External Environment

Identify each statement by its external environmental factor.

a. customers
b. competition
c. suppliers
d. workforce
e. shareholders
f. society
g. technology
h. governments
i. economy

_____ 6. Some critics blame the media for the escalating salaries of Major League Baseball players.

_____ 7. At one time, Nike was the coolest sneaker company, but then others came along and took some of its market share.

_____ 8. I applied for a loan to start my own dance company, but I might not get it because money is tight these days, and the bank may not provide a loan.

_____ 9. Team owners have threatened to fire the general manager if the team doesn't improve this year.

_____ 10. Management was going to sell our team to Disney, but the feds said that would be in violation of antitrust laws.

that gave him about a 4 percent stake in the group buying the MLB Miami Marlins. Also part of the group, Jordan now owns approximately half of 1 percent. Jeter and Jordan became part owners of the Marlins after a $1.2 billion purchase from Jeffrey Loria that included $800 million in cash.[24] Derek Jeter was ranked first on the Entrepreneur magazine list of "The Most Entrepreneurial Athletes of 2017."[25]

6. *Society and activists.* Our society, to a great extent, determines what are acceptable business and athletic practices.[26] Individuals and activist groups pressure organizations to make changes, such as renaming the NFL Washington Redskins.

7. *Technology.* In the sport industry, intuition is being replaced by science to improve athletes' performance with better diets, supplements, training, and sport apparel and equipment. Moneyball big data is technology driven.

 TIME-OUT 4 Give an example of how technology has affected several different sport organizations.

8. *The economy.* Organizations have no control over economic growth, inflation, or interest rates. Sports are an important part of the economy in many countries.[27] When economic activity, measured by GDP (gross domestic product), is slow or in recession, fewer fans attend games at the stadium. With inflation, prices of tickets and other sport products go up.

9. *Sport regulations and governments.* National, state, and local governments all set laws and regulations that organizations must obey, and these laws and regulations can change.[28] In America, Title IX of the Education Amendments of 1972 required athletic opportunities for females in high school and college. Title IX led to explosive growth in the number of female athletes, creating a large new market for sport equipment and apparel businesses

like Spalding and Nike. DraftKings was required by some state laws to change or stop fantasy sports games.[29] Although not government owned and operated, sport organizations such as the NCAA (National Collegiate Athletic Association) make rules that colleges are required to obey.

# Conducting Sport Business in a Global Environment

We now expand the external sport environment to competing in the more complex global environment. Do you realize that no matter where you are, you live and work in a global environment? You will likely interact with people from different cultures.[30] An employee works with diverse coworkers, suppliers, and customers. You may play on the same team and compete against foreign athletes, and you could coach them at home. As a customer, you may buy foreign products from diverse sales reps online or in a local store. As a student, you have most likely interacted with foreign exchange students in and outside of class. A global mind-set will help you advance in your career.[31]

In this section, we discuss globalization and how to classify businesses in the global economy, the importance of understanding cultural differences, ways to take a business global, and some of the risk in sport management. For a review of the organizational environment, including globalization, see figure 2.3.

## The Globalization of Sport and Classifying Business in a Global Environment

If you are thinking that sport businesses should just stay local, think again. They are going global in search of the best athletes, coaches, and sport managers and to increase revenues. Here we explain that sport has been global for many years, and we describe how businesses are classified in the global environment.

### The Globalization of Sport

The growing trend toward globalization will continue[32] as sport manufacturers and teams compete globally.[33] Internationalization is not new to sport; the Olympic Games were held centuries ago in Greece, and the Games are now run by the International Olympic Committee (IOC). The NHL has U.S. and Canadian teams, MLB has the Toronto Blue Jays, and the NFL plays regular-season games and exhibitions in Europe. Tennis and golf tournaments have been global for many years.

Although many of the same sports are played around the world, how they are regulated and managed varies greatly. Organizations that help coordinate global sport include the International Sport Management Alliance, which in turn includes the North American Society for Sport Management (NASSM) (discussed in chapter 1), the European Association for Sport Management, the Sport Management Association of Australia and New Zealand, the Fédération Internationale de Football Association (FIFA), and the IOC, to name a few.[34]

You may be thinking, Well, this doesn't affect an organization such as the YMCA! Think again. YMCAs are at work in more than 120 countries around the world, serving more than 45 million people. About 230 U.S. YMCAs maintain relationships with Ys in other countries. Think about the complexity of complying with the rules and regulations of multiple countries with different economic systems, workforces and labor laws, and cultures.

The globalization of sport allows sport management programs to have an international focus through teaching and directly working in other countries. Sport businesses are recruiting students with international experience.[35] American and other global athletes and sport management graduates are going abroad to play and work for professional teams.

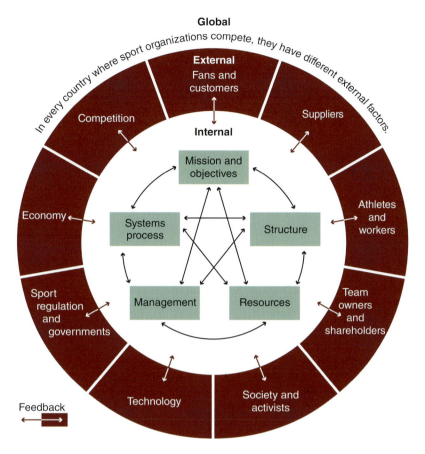

**FIGURE 2.3**  The business environment.

Based on idea from Abbas Nadim, University of New Haven, unpublished work.

### Classifying Business in a Global Environment

There are three classifications of businesses in a global environment. A domestic firm conducts business in only one country, although it may have to compete against global firms at home. The local Max's Gym competes for members with the global Gold's Gym[36] and YMCAs. An **international business** is primarily based in one country but transacts business in other countries. The common international business model is importing and exporting from the home country. Ferrari makes race cars and competes in Formula 1, and sport cars are made in Italy and imported for sale by car dealers in other countries. A **multinational corporation (MNC)** has significant operations in more than one country, including Gold's Gym, Nike, and YMCAs.

◀ **LEARNING OUTCOME 4**

State the differences between domestic, international, and multinational businesses.

## Understanding International Cultural Differences and GLOBE

If you wonder why some groups of people think and act differently, it's often largely based on their countries' national cultural differences.[37] To be successful in the global village, it is important to understand and be able to work with people from different cultures,[38] making this an important career skill.[39] Local and regional cultural patterns greatly affect the popularity of certain sports. Two of the most popular football or soccer leagues in the world are La Liga in Spain and the English Premier League in England. Meanwhile, the National Football League (NFL) is extremely popular in America. Organizational leaders

## TABLE 2.1  GLOBE Dimensions

| Dimension | Low | Moderate | High |
|---|---|---|---|
| **Assertiveness** (aggressive vs. passive) | New Zealand Switzerland | Ireland Philippines | Spain United States |
| **Future orientation** (longer term vs. shorter term) | Argentina Russia | India Slovenia | Canada Netherlands |
| **Gender differences** (similar vs. different roles based on gender) | Denmark Sweden | Brazil Italy | China Egypt |
| **Uncertainty avoidance** (acceptance vs. avoidance of uncertainty) | Bolivia Hungary | Mexico United States | Austria Germany |
| **Power distance** (acceptance vs. rejection of power differences) | Netherlands South Africa | England France | Spain Thailand |
| **Societal collectivism** (teamwork vs. individualism) | Greece Germany | Hong Kong United States | Japan Singapore |
| **In-group collectivism** (pride in team membership vs. lack of pride) | Denmark New Zealand | Israel Japan | China Morocco |
| **Performance orientation** (striving for high performance vs. lack of striving) | Russia Venezuela | England Sweden | Taiwan United States |
| **Humane orientation** (kindness to others vs. lack of kindness) | Singapore Spain | Hong Kong United States | Iceland Indonesia |

Adapted from M. Javidan and R.J. House, "Cultural Acumen for the Global Manager: Lessons from Project GLOBE," *Organizational Dynamics* 29, no. 4 (2001): 289-305.

must be aware of cultural issues to avoid expensive errors like the time Nike used a design on the soles of its shoes that meant Allah in Arabic, which caused an embarrassing and expensive recall.

**GLOBE** is the acronym for **Global Leadership and Organizational Behavior Effectiveness**. GLOBE is an ongoing cross-cultural project to compare leadership and national culture. The GLOBE research team used data from 62 countries and identified nine dimensions in which national cultures are either similar or different. (See table 2.1 for a list of the dimensions with examples of country ratings.) Based on GLOBE, there are major cultural differences,[40] especially between Eastern and Western country cultures.[41] Thus, sport organizations need to manage differently in various countries based on the culture.[42] Have you heard the expression, Think globally, act locally?

 **TIME-OUT 5** Select a sport-oriented business, and identify as many of its global practices as you can.

# Taking a Sport Business Global

**LEARNING OUTCOME 5** ▶

List the lowest- and highest-risk ways to take a business global.

To manage a global sport business successfully, you need to understand the differences in practices between internationals and MNCs and the six forms of global business, which we discuss in this section.

Sport businesses go global in six ways—by global sourcing, importing and exporting, licensing, contracting, engaging in joint ventures, and making direct investment. In figure 2.4, these six approaches are mapped by cost and risk and by whether they tend to be the strategy of international businesses or that of MNCs.

1. *Global sourcing.* **Global sourcing** is the use of worldwide resources for inputs and transformation. Other terms include *outsourcing* and *offshoring*, and global sourcing will continue to increase.[43] The difference between domestic managers and global managers lies in where they look for the best deal on inputs and where they think inputs can be

most advantageously transformed into outputs.[44] Some U.S. colleges and most professional teams don't just search for talent in the United States; they have scouts all over the world looking for the best athletes.

2. *Importing and exporting*. With importing, domestic firms buy products from other countries and sell them as is (they are not part of their products—that's outsourcing) at home.[45] U.S. retailers must thus import Adidas (based in Germany) sneakers in order to sell them. With exporting, domestic firms sell their products to buyers in other countries. Companies like Spalding export their products to almost every country in the world, and professional sport teams sell their team products globally as well.

3. *Licensing and franchising.* Under a **licensing** agreement, one

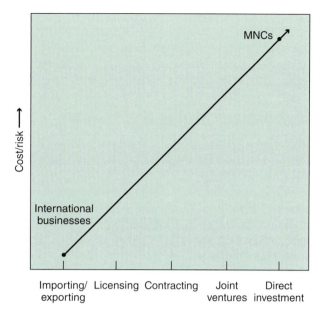

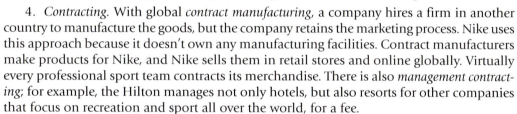

**FIGURE 2.4** Taking your business global. Note: Global sourcing can be used alone (at low cost and risk), but it is commonly used with the other approaches.

company allows another to use its intellectual assets, such as brand name, trademarks, technology, patents, or copyrights. For a fee, Disney allows companies around the world to make all kinds of products using the ESPN brand, and so do professional sport teams. In **franchising**, the franchisor licenses the entire business to the franchisee for a fee and a share of its ongoing revenues. The franchisor provides help, such as its trademark, equipment, materials, training, managerial and operational guidelines, and advertising to the franchisee.

4. *Contracting*. With global *contract manufacturing*, a company hires a firm in another country to manufacture the goods, but the company retains the marketing process. Nike uses this approach because it doesn't own any manufacturing facilities. Contract manufacturers make products for Nike, and Nike sells them in retail stores and online globally. Virtually every professional sport team contracts its merchandise. There is also *management contracting*; for example, the Hilton manages not only hotels, but also resorts for other companies that focus on recreation and sport all over the world, for a fee.

 What sorts of inputs and transformations do you think are good candidates for global sourcing?

5. *Joint ventures and strategic alliances.* A **joint venture** is created when firms share ownership (partnership) of a new enterprise. IMG and Mandalay Sports Media entered into a joint venture that will see the two companies work together to develop, finance, and produce sport-focused feature films. They plan to produce 10 sport-related films for distribution to streaming platforms and traditional movie theaters.[46] IMG will provide access to athletes, while Mandalay will add its skills in media services to produce the films. A **strategic alliance** is a partnership sharing resources that usually does not create a new company. The companies remain separate and share resources to sell products in other countries, to develop new or improved products, or to build and share production facilities and sport stadiums. Does your college have study abroad program strategic alliances?

6. *Foreign direct investment*. This approach is becoming increasingly popular.[47] It virtually eliminates foreign trade barriers.[48] **Direct investment** occurs when a company builds or purchases operating facilities (affiliates or subsidiaries) in another country. This is a common strategy for large MNCs. In 1991, to globalize American football, the NFL developed the NFL Europe subsidiary. However, on June 29, 2007, the NFL owners decided that it was not worthwhile to invest more money in NFL Europa (the last name the league was known by) just to keep the league afloat. A major factor in the failed venture was culture—

Europeans prefer soccer—which resulted in low ticket and merchandise sales. However, the NFL continued trying to invest in Europe with a 15-year agreement to hold regular-season games in England. Additional games will be in Mexico and Germany. The NFL expects to have a permanent franchise in England by 2022.[49] It is important for the NFL to understand global culture to find the right way to grow its business globally.

## Risk Management in Global Sport

Risk management refers to the potential for damage to property, equipment, athletes, spectators, and employees before, during, and after an event. Coaches are responsible for the safety of their athletes, and officiating crews need to control games and prevent athletes from injuring each other. Identifying and managing risk and controlling crowds are also very important responsibilities of sport facility managers, operations managers, and event coordinators. With the growth of terrorism, preventing and dealing with violence and fan control around and inside sport facilities have become increasingly important to sport management.

It is impossible to ensure a risk-free environment at sporting venues. Incidents will happen and emergencies will arise. What matters is how managers prepare for, respond to, and recover from emergencies at a sporting venue. Employees and volunteers need to be properly trained to help manage risk in order to prevent mistakes and accidents that can result in damage, injuries, and expensive lawsuits.

Sport management students should understand four global sport issues. First, large global corporations and teams are using developing countries' workforces to manufacture sportswear and sport equipment. Second, there is an increase in the number of athletes whose country of birth and origin are no longer a limitation on where the athletes play and compete. Third, extremely large global organizations such as FIFA, the IOC, and the NBA play a major role in organizing sports worldwide. And fourth, students of sport management should understand how globalization will affect their careers.

# Ethics in Sport Management

**Ethics** refers to the standards of right and wrong that influence behavior. Being ethical means being honest and not taking advantage of others—no lying, cheating, or stealing. Today, ethics is a major concern. Business and sport management programs are including more ethics throughout their curricula.[50] You may be required to take an entire course in sport ethics. Thus ethical understanding is an important competency.

An organization's ethics are the collective behaviors of its employees. If each athlete and employee acts ethically, the actions of the organization will be ethical, too. The starting place for ethics, therefore, is you. Are you an ethical person? It's an important question, and one that you should devote some thought to. To answer this question, complete Self-Assessment 2.1. In this section, we discuss ethics in sports, explain why ethical behavior pays, discuss why good people do unethical things, provide some simple guidelines for ethical behavior, and discuss how you can manage employee ethics.

Unfortunately, there is no shortage of unethical behavior in sports. Here are a few examples of recent troubling scandals:

1. FIFA, soccer's world governing body, has fired many top-level officials since Swiss investigators detained seven FIFA officials at their Zurich hotel. Racketeering, conspiracy, wire fraud, money laundering, and bribery were some of the charges brought against them.[51]

2. Female bicyclist Femke Van den Driessche, a former European youth cyclocross champion from Belgium, became the first person to be banned for using a hidden electric motor.[52]

3. The International Weightlifting Federation (IWF) banned nine nations from the World Championships and beyond for repeatedly testing positive for doping. Russia,

Kazakhstan, China, Ukraine, Armenia, Azerbaijan, Belarus, Moldova, and Turkey were banned for a year. The IWF has increased doping testing at their championships.[53]

4. Rick Pitino was ousted as the NCAA basketball coach at the University of Louisville. Federal prosecutors accused two Louisville Cardinals coaches of directing money provided by the university's apparel partner, Adidas, to two high school prospects. Pitino indicated he had no knowledge of providing money to high school students to attend Louisville.[54]

5. These charges came only three months after Pitino and his program were sanctioned by the NCAA for a scandal in which prostitutes were provided to players and teenaged recruits.[55] In an interview, Pitino blamed the graduate assistant responsible for athletes in their dorm life.[56]

6. Chris Correa, a former scouting director for the MLB St. Louis Cardinals, was sentenced to almost four years in prison for hacking into the Houston Astros' computer database to obtain valuable player information. This case is important because it broke federal laws. The judge valued the unique database and player information that was stolen at $1.7 million.[57]

## Yes, Ethical Behavior Does Pay

Not many days go by without the media reporting on some scandal involving unethical behavior. Laws and regulations exist to govern business behavior, but ethics go beyond legal requirements. Although unethical behavior may result in short-term gains, in the long run people often get caught and pay the price because they sabotage themselves.[58] Ethics scandals hurt the team's and organization's reputation. Many organizations seek integrity in job applicants, and they even test for ethics.[59]

Do you want to be happy and have job satisfaction and success? Happiness comes primarily from relationships.[60] Trust is the foundation of good relationships;[61] people need to trust you.[62] Lying is a common unethical behavior.[63] If you know a person lies to others, there is a good chance that they lie to you, too. Years of a trusting relationship can be hurt or lost by one lie. Do you consider people who are unethical with you to be your friends? Unethical behavior may result in some short-term gain, but truth does matter,[64] so being ethical does pay off in the long run.[65]

 Have you or any of your friends taken performance-enhancing drugs? Have you ever bought or sold a ticket for more than the event price?

## Why Good People Use Unethical Behavior

We aren't simply good or bad people. Around 98 percent of us will be a little unethical[66] if given "incentives" that we really want to have or avoid.[67] The incentive is usually for some personal gain[68] (cheat to win the game) or to avoid getting into trouble (lie and say you didn't cheat). Also, some people cheat because they don't believe in following the rules.[69] Four important factors contribute to a person's electing to use ethical or unethical behavior: personality, moral development, the situation, and justification.

### *Personality, Moral Development, and the Situation*

Here are three factors that affect our use of ethical or unethical behavior. Think about how your personality and moral development affect your decisions and about situations in which you are more or less likely to use unethical behavior.

**Personality**    We will discuss personality and attitudes in more detail in chapter 8. Integrity (chapter 1) is considered a personality trait, so some people are more ethical than others. Unfortunately, a culture of dishonesty has infected business, sport, and society as lying, stealing, and cheating have become more acceptable. Do you know any people who don't even realize they are dishonest, or don't see anything wrong with being dishonest?[70]

**Moral Development**    Moral development is the process of distinguishing right from wrong that influences behavior.[71] Moral development affects people's ethical decisions.[72] Recall

As you could be asked in court, do you tell the truth, the whole truth, and nothing but the truth?

## SELF-ASSESSMENT 2.1

### Sport Ethics

**Objective:**

To practice thinking ethically

**Preparation:**

Respond to the same set of statements twice. In your first responses, focus on your own behavior and the frequency with which you use it. In the first column, place the number (1-5) that represents how often you did, do, or would do the behavior if you had the chance. These numbers will allow you to determine your level of ethics. Be honest—students will not share their ethics scores.

In your second responses, focus on current or past coworkers. Place an *O* on the line after the number if you observed someone doing this behavior. Also place a *W* on the line if you blew the whistle on this behavior within the organization or externally.

| Column 1: | Frequently | | | | Never |
|---|---|---|---|---|---|
| | 1 | 2 | 3 | 4 | 5 |
| Column 2: | O (observed) | W (reported) | | | |

**College**

____ 1. ____ Cheating on homework assignments

____ 2. ____ Trying to pass off someone else's work as your own work

____ 3. ____ Cheating on exams

**Team (or replace with workplace terms)**

____ 4. ____ Coming to practice late

____ 5. ____ Leaving practice early

____ 6. ____ Taking longer breaks than allowed

____ 7. ____ Calling in sick to skip practice when not sick

____ 8. ____ Socializing or goofing off during practice rather than working diligently

____ 9. ____ Socializing or goofing off during games

____ 10. ____ Using the team phone to make personal calls

that 98 percent of us will be unethical at times, but just a little.[73] So we can be on different levels for different issues and situations. Three levels of personal moral development are presented in table 2.2. What level of moral development do you consider yourself to have reached? What can you do to further your moral development?

**The Situation**     It can be very tempting to be unethical for personal rewards, such as when you are paid on commission or negotiating with someone.[74] Unsupervised people in highly competitive situations who are under high pressure to achieve bottom-line results are more likely to use unethical behavior. Tom Brady of the New England Patriots was accused of deflating footballs to improve his performance. Joe Montana, Hall of Fame quarterback of the San Francisco 49ers, commented that his star wide receiver, Jerry Rice, used adhesive "stickum" to help him catch balls and that his offensive linemen used silicone on their

_____ 11. _____Using the team copier for a personal purpose

_____ 12. _____Mailing personal things through the team mail

_____ 13. _____Taking home team supplies and keeping them

_____ 14. _____Taking home team equipment without permission for personal use and returning it

_____ 15. _____Giving team merchandise to friends or allowing them to take merchandise without saying anything

_____ 16. _____Falsifying reimbursement paperwork for meals and travel or other expenses

_____ 17. _____Drinking alcohol the night or day before games

_____ 18. _____Taking spouse or friends out to eat and charging the expense to the team

_____ 19. _____Taking a spouse or friend on business trips and charging the expense to the team

_____ 20. _____Taking illegal drugs to enhance performance (or being high at work)

To determine your ethics score, add up your numbers. Your total will be between 20 and 100.

Place your score here _____ and circle it on the following continuum.

**Unethical**                                                              **Ethical**

   20     30     40     50     60     70     80     90     100

## Discussion Questions

1. For the college items 1 through 3, who is harmed and who benefits from these unethical behaviors?
2. For team items 4 through 20, select the three unethical behaviors (circle their numbers) you consider the most serious. Who is harmed and who benefits from these unethical behaviors?
3. If you observed unethical behavior but didn't report it, why did you not do so? If you did blow the whistle, why did you do so? What was the result?
4. As a manager, it is your responsibility to hold your team to high standards of behavior. If you know employees are behaving unethically, will you take action to enforce compliance with your organization's code of ethics?

shirts to make them more slippery.[75] People are also more likely to be unethical when their performance is low—when they are losing the game.

    People are more likely to be unethical when there is no formal ethics policy. We also consider the chances of getting caught and the penalty or reward for being unethical. People are more unethical when they believe they will not get caught or when the punishment is minimal, so even if they get caught the gain is greater than the punishment—the behavior results in net rewards.[76] Ever made an intentional foul to stop an easy basket or goal? Even worse, players and employees are more unethical when coaches and managers ask them to use and reward them for using unethical behavior.[77] You may know that some coaches have been caught giving their athletes illegal performance-enhancing drugs. Ever been asked by a coach or manager to be unethical?

**TABLE 2.2  Levels of Moral Development**

| Level | | Description of behavior | Examples |
|---|---|---|---|
| | **3. Postconventional level** | People do the right thing regardless of the norms of leaders or one's team. They don't behave unethically due to peer pressure. | "I don't lie because it's wrong." "I don't cheat and take performance-enhancing drugs because it is wrong and against the rules." |
| | **2. Conventional level** | People copy the behavior of leaders or of those on one's team. They do unethical things, even if they disagree with them, to be liked or to fit in. They give in to peer pressure. | "I lie because the others do." "I take performance-enhancing drugs because we all take them." |
| **1. Preconventional level** | | People do whatever it takes to gain rewards, and they only follow rules to avoid punishment. | "I lie for personal gain and when I'm in trouble." "I take performance-enhancing drugs to get an advantage over my competitors." |

## Justification and Escalation of Unethical Behavior

Do you know any people that use unethical behavior? If you question the behavior, will they admit straight out that they lie, steal, or cheat? Or will they give you excuses for using the behavior? Most people tend to justify their unethical behavior, and they tend to escalate it.

**How and Why We Justify Our Unethical Behavior**    Most of us see ourselves as ethical,[78] so we justify our behavior by determining whether the action was rationally or reasonably acceptable.[79] Therefore, when we are only a little dishonest,[80] we justify the behavior to protect our *self-concept* so that we don't feel bad about it.[81] People at the preconventional and conventional levels of moral development commonly use the following thinking processes to justify their unethical behavior.[82] Our memory tends to fade as we forget about unethical behavior, so we repeat it, and it can become a habit for some.[83]

**Justifications for Unethical Behavior**    Here are some common justifications for our unethical behavior:

- *Everyone does it (conventional rationalization)*—Everyone cheats in college, and athletes take performance-enhancing drugs; We all take things home (steal).
- *I did it for the good of others, the team, or the organization (moral justification and euphemistic labeling)*—I lied to prevent Joan from getting into trouble; I intentionally hurt the player so he'd be taken out of the game so my team could win; We are not terrorists, but we are freedom fighters who bomb to help our cause.
- *I was only following orders, so it's not my fault (displacement of responsibility and attribution of blame)*—My coach told me to do it; My teammates made me take the drugs.

- *I'm not as bad as the others (advantageous comparison)*—I only miss practice when I'm not sick once in a while, and others do it all the time.
- *Disregard for or distortion of consequences*—No one will be hurt if I cheat or take drugs, and I will not get caught; If I do get caught, I'll just be out of the game for a short time.

Have you or your family members, friends, or teammates said any of these things?

Unethical behavior that you justify might give you some type of short-term gain. But in the long run, you sabotage your own conscience, undermine your own pride, and open yourself up to the risk of harm. Such harm can include the loss of trust, reputation, and friends; receiving disciplinary action or being fired or kicked off the team; facing lawsuits; and going to jail.

**Relativism, Individualism, Hedonism, and Minimalism**    *Relativism* creates ethical confusion by saying there is no absolute truth or right or wrong (which itself is an absolute statement). Based on relativism, three other "-isms" are commonly claimed to bring us happiness and success—but they don't. *Individualism* is being selfish by just looking out for ourselves (for example, being a ball hog) and taking advantage of others for our own personal gain. We only act when there is something in it for us. *Hedonism* tells us not to do something if we don't feel like doing it; we should just do what makes us feel good. *Minimalism* tells us to do the least we can to get by. Do you know any relativists who are selfish, hedonistic, or minimalist people? Do you like them? Are they really happy and successful? Will they ever be?

**Caution Against Escalation of Unethical Behavior**    Our character and integrity are based on our repeated behavior.[84] You should realize how unethical behavior can gradually take hold of you. It's tempting to change the rules or the truth and to be unethical for personal gain, justifying the behavior to ourselves. We easily forget about our unethical behavior, so we repeat it, and it can become a habit.[85] Little white lies are not little, as one lie leads to another lie.[86] Our unethical behavior escalates because the more we are unethical, the easier it is to be unethical, especially if we don't get caught. We also tend to start with minor unethical behaviors that tend to lead to more major unethical behaviors. The truth tends to be revealed eventually, so it's better not to start.[87] The important lesson here is, don't take the first step that leads you to escalate unethical behavior. It's not always easy to do the right thing, but being ethical does pay off in the long run.[88]

Did the people at FIFA start out planning to lie, cheat, and steal? Most didn't. What tends to happen is that the organization accepts a small gift to hold an event at a certain time or location. The gift becomes larger with each successive agreement to hold an event. Eventually the "gift" is more like a bribe as it grows in size. The same types of exchange happen for years and reach the point that no one is able or willing to admit their unethical or illegal nature until they get caught.

# Simple Guidelines to Ethical Behavior

Improving team and organizational ethics begins with you;[89] it begins with your setting a leadership example for others to copy.[90] Being ethical isn't always easy,[91] and it is not always easy to distinguish between ethical and unethical behavior. A gift in one country is a bribe in another, and in some countries bribes are standard business practice. Self-Assessment 2.1 helped you measure how ethical your behavior is in different situations. We all can improve by adhering to the following guidelines when faced with ethical dilemmas.

## *Golden and Platinum Rules*

The Golden Rule is to treat others as you would have them treat you. Most religions have a variation of the biblical Golden Rule. Treating people the way you want to be treated can lead to ethical behavior. But in today's diverse global world, not everyone wants to be treated the way you do. So a new Platinum Rule was developed, which says to treat other people as they want to be treated. Legendary former NBA basketball coach Phil Jackson said, "Much of my outlook in life is from a spiritual direction."[92] These are simple rules to remember, but they are often broken. Do you follow these rules? Imagine what a great world this would be if everyone followed these rules.

## Four-Way Test

The Rotary International slogan is "Service Above Self." This organization developed the four-way test to frame our thinking and business actions in an ethical manner. When you are faced with an ethical dilemma, ask yourself the following about your choice: (1) Is it the truth? (2) Is it fair to all concerned? (3) Will it build goodwill and better friendship? (4) Will it be beneficial to all concerned? If you can answer yes to these questions, you are probably making an ethical choice.

For example, a former coach of the women's basketball team at Howard University was found to be in violation of rules governing recruitment inducements. The coach knowingly made an improper payment for an airline ticket for a prospective student-athlete to visit the university. The coach then approached the players on her team, requesting that they provide false information about the visit. The National Collegiate Athletic Association (NCAA) ruled that the coach cheated, and the coach was fired.[93] Would you ask others to lie for you? Would you lie for others?

## Stakeholders' Approach to Ethics

**LEARNING OUTCOME 6** ▶

Explain the stakeholders' approach to ethics.

With the **stakeholders' approach to ethics**, you try to create a win–win situation for all relevant stakeholders so that everyone benefits from the decision. Unfortunately, because multiple stakeholders often have conflicting interests in such cases as cutting or benching a player or laying off a worker, not everyone can benefit from every decision.[94] However, you need to try, and that requires talking to multiple stakeholders.[95] The higher up in management you go, the more stakeholders you have to deal with. So in muddy situations, ask yourself two simple questions: Am I proud to tell my stakeholders of my decision? Am I justifying my answer and trying to cover up my behavior?[96] If you are proud of a decision and not simply trying to justify it, then your decision is probably ethical.

## Going Beyond the Stakeholders' Approach to Ethics

We hope you can be among the few who go beyond the minimum ethical guidelines to the postconventional level of moral development. Some managers, called servant leaders, create win–win situations and make sacrifices for others' benefit. Most likely your parents, a coach or two, and others have made sacrifices to help you get to where you are today. How often do you look out for number one without concern for, or at the expense of, others? How often do you go out of your way to help others without expecting anything in return? Recall that happiness and success are based on relationships, and doing things for others clearly improves relationships, which leads to happiness and greater success.

## Discernment, Advice, and Using an Ethical Guideline

Thinking before you act applies to ethics. So use ethical guidelines to judge whether a behavior is ethical or not before you act. If you don't know if the behavior is ethical or not, ask your coach, boss, higher-level managers, and other ethical people. If you are not willing to ask others about your ethical dilemma, and worse, if you don't want them to know about it, your behavior may not be ethical.

Making a decision without using ethical guidelines leads to less ethical behavior. Using an ethical guideline helps keep you honest.[97] So if you want to be happy and successful and to have good relationships, make it a habit to use an ethical guideline and to behave ethically.

## APPLYING THE CONCEPT 2.3

### Stakeholders

Identify each statement by its stakeholder.

   a. employees
   b. customers
   c. society
   d. competitors
   e. suppliers
   f. government

_____ 11. We're going to fight this—we do not want a baseball stadium downtown!

_____ 12. I bought an ice-level seat for the hockey game. The glass shattered in my face when a player was checked into the boards, causing me injury.

_____ 13. The town board is very political, so you have to play games if you want to get a liquor license for home games.

_____ 14. I'm sorry to hear your retail sales are down at your sporting goods stores because that means we'll have to cut back production on team T-shirts.

_____ 15. I bid on the job, but another printer got the contract to print the programs for home games.

## Managing Ethics

A team and organization's ethics are based on the combined behavior of its athletes and employees. If each person is ethical, so is the team and organization. So as a sport manager, it's your job to enforce the use of ethical behavior. To this end, managers develop their team and organization's guidelines and train for ethical behavior, set the example, and enforce the rules they want to play by. But ultimately, individuals are responsible for their own behavior, and they must pay the consequences for violations, including being fired or going to jail. Trying to justify unethical and illegal behavior by saying everyone else does it, or the coach made me do it, are not getting you off.

### Codes of Ethics and Training

Codes of ethics (also called codes of conduct)[98] state what is and isn't ethical behavior.[99] Most large sport organizations have written codes of ethics, and many train employees to use the code. Knowing and following the code can help keep you honest and out of trouble. The code of ethics for the National Federation of State High School Officials (NFHS) provides guidelines for ethical standards of conduct for all interscholastic officials.[100]

### Support and Example of Top Management

It is the responsibility of sport management from the top down to develop codes of ethics to ensure that employees are taught what is and is not considered ethical behavior and to enforce compliance.[101] However, managers' primary responsibility is to lead by example. Managers, especially top managers, set the standard because employees tend to imitate managers' unethical behavior.[102] In the doping cases that led to the 2016 International Weightlifting Federation Championships scandal, it was revealed that some of the top IWF

## APPLYING THE CONCEPT 2.4

### Ethical Approach

Identify each statement by its approach to making ethical decisions.

   a. Golden and Platinum Rules
   b. four-way test
   c. stakeholders' approach
   d. discernment and advice
   e. code of ethics

_____ 16. I try to treat people the way I want them to treat me.

_____ 17. Cindy, what do you think of my decision for handling this situation?

_____ 18. I'm a member of Rotary International, so I use its approach when I make decisions.

_____ 19. I follow the guidelines the company gave all of us to use to make sure I'm doing the right thing.

_____ 20. I try to make sure that everyone affected by my decisions gets a fair deal.

members were corrupt, others followed their lead, and still others allowed this unethical behavior to continue by ignoring it. Eventually, measures were taken to stop the unethical behavior, and more drug-testing procedures were added to the 2017 IWF Championships.[103]

Coaches and physical education teachers hold a special responsibility when it comes to "talking the talk" of ethical behavior in sports. Paul "Bear" Bryant, former football coach at the University of Alabama, once stated, "We have the opportunity to teach intangible lessons to our players that will be priceless to them in future years. We are in a position to teach these young people intrinsic values that cannot be learned at home, school, or any place outside of the athletic field."[104]

### Enforcing Ethical Behavior

If employees are not punished for unethical behavior, they will continue to pursue questionable business practices.[105] To help keep people honest, many organizations create ethics committees to be fair in judging and punishing those accused of unethical behavior.[106] One of the corrective actions that is being taken when a university is in violation of an NCAA rule is to add an assistant director position in the compliance office to increase the understanding and enforcement of NCAA rules on campus.

To help prevent unethical behavior, employees should be encouraged to *blow the whistle* on questionable activities. Whistle-

TIME-OUT 6 — Examine a recent scandal in the sport industry, preferably a local one, and identify which decisions led to unethical behavior and why.

blowing occurs when employees report unethical behavior. Historically, this has been a dicey action to take. Whistle-blowers have ended up being harassed on the job by peers and managers and even losing their jobs. However, sport managers are coming around to the idea that listening to whistle-blowers is in their best interest because it is also illegal to retaliate against whistle-blowers, and lawsuits are common and very expensive.

How do you feel about reporting unethical behavior to your professor, coach, or managers? What if they are the ones engaging in the behavior—would you go outside the organization to report them? It's not an easy decision because we have a deeply embedded cultural reluctance to "tattle." It would behoove you to give this some thought, however, because you will most likely face this dilemma at work. As pointed out in Self-Assessment 2.1, you probably already have.

# Social Responsibility and Sustainability

Social responsibility (SR), often called *corporate social responsibility* or *CSR*,[107] is an extension of the stakeholders' approach to ethics.[108] SR focuses on the duty of sport and business to do good things that benefit society.[109] Equally important is the idea of doing no harm.[110] **Social responsibility** is the conscious effort to operate in a manner that creates a win–win situation for society. SR is important to sport because sports are significant social institutions in their communities. In this section, we discuss the need to be a good corporate citizen, why it pays to be socially responsible, the four levels of social responsibility, and sustainability.

## Corporate Citizenship

Let's discuss what it takes to be a good corporate citizen and why it does pay to be socially responsible, and describe a B Corp that strives to be socially responsible.

### Being a Good Corporate Citizen

Today, sport and business are expected to benefit society[111] by helping solve social problems[112] because stakeholders are increasingly pressuring them to be socially responsible.[113] There are many things that SR teams and companies can do to improve people's quality of life.

Corporate citizenship involves a commitment to improve community well-being through discretionary business practices and contributions of corporate resources. Organizations invest athlete and employee time and money in pro bono work, philanthropy, support for community education and health, and protection of the environment.

MLB Boston Red Sox top-level managers and baseball players work closely with the Dana-Farber Cancer Institute to help children, and NFL Indianapolis Colts football players work with kids. The Red Sox often have Dana-Farber patients attend home games and sometimes even throw out the first pitch. Dana-Farber and the Red Sox also sell a license plate with the Red Sox logo to raise funds for patient care and cancer research. As stated, SR teams and companies also try to avoid harm to society. Nike tries to provide safe products, and the NBA Hornets try to provide a safe environment for their players and fans at basketball games.

Do you shop at Walmart? If you don't think Walmart is ethical and socially responsible, should you shop there anyway?

### It Pays to Be Socially Responsible

The value of the goodwill won by being a good corporate citizen is difficult to quantify in financial statements, but company stakeholders benefit, and that is a win–win situation for the company. Although research is inconsistent on support for a clear link between SR and the bottom line, many teams and sport companies would answer with a resounding yes![114] Some companies are even using SR to increase profits.[115] In a recent study, companies considered to be high in SR had an average return of 13.6 percent compared to 9.9 percent for those having low SR ratings.[116] If being a good corporate citizen didn't benefit the team or organization in some way, why would virtually all pro teams and major corporations like Adidas and Nike have SR programs?

### The B Corp

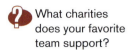

**What charities does your favorite team support?**

*B Corps* (*benefits corporations*) use their business resources to solve social and environmental problems; they clearly believe that it pays to be socially responsible. You can't just use the term B Corp; the title is given to companies that meet the certification requirements. "Individually, B Corps meet the highest standards of verified social and environmental performance, public transparency, and legal accountability, and aspire to use the power of markets to solve social and environmental problems."[117] There are more than 2,650 certified B Corps from over 60 countries, including ZogSports, Senda Athletics, LA 25 SPORT, Kusaga Athletic, Fit 4 Life NYC, and Newton Running.[118] For information on certification requirements, visit www.bcorporation.net.

## Levels of Corporate Social Responsibility

Businesses do vary greatly in their SR activities, based on the overall level of CSR at which they decide to operate.[119] Figure 2.5 illustrates the four levels of social responsibility in a continuum from the lowest level to the highest one.

### The Four Levels of CSR

**LEARNING OUTCOME 7 ▶**

Discuss the four levels of social responsibility in business.

1. *Social obstruction.* At this level, managers deliberately perform, or request employees to perform, unethical or illegal business practices. For example, Rick Pitino, head basketball coach at the of the University of Louisville, was fired in September 2017 for recruiting violations. So far Pitino has denied knowing about any payments made to high school recruits.[120]

2. *Social obligation.* At this level, managers meet only the minimum legal requirements. Compliance is an approach in which firms rely on easy solutions and resist voluntarily initiating socially responsible programs. Economists Adam Smith and Milton Friedman theorized that when a business makes a profit, it is being socially responsible because it is providing jobs for employees and goods and services for customers. Thus, a corporation has no responsibility to society beyond that of obeying the law and maximizing profits for shareholders. Although this level is ethical, most firms today operate at a higher level.

3. *Social reaction.* Here, managers respond to appropriate societal requests. The most common type of social reaction takes place when civic groups ask companies for donations for the arts, college scholarships, or antidrug programs; sponsorship of sport teams; or the use of company facilities for meetings or sport teams. These firms are *philanthropic*, giving gifts of money, or other resources—often called giving back.[121] For example, each year SportsStuff and other retailers give merchandise to the Holy Cross Athletic Association to raffle off to raise money for its sport teams.

4. *Social involvement.* At this level, managers voluntarily initiate socially responsible acts. CVS voluntarily stopped selling legal cigarettes at an estimated cost of $2 billion a year.[122] As discussed earlier, most pro teams and major international corporations have social involvement programs.

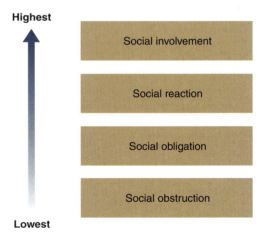

**Highest**

Social involvement

Social reaction

Social obligation

Social obstruction

**Lowest**

**FIGURE 2.5** Four levels of social responsibility.

**TIME-OUT 7** Select a sport organization and identify its level of social responsibility for a current issue.

### Social Audit

Although not a level of social responsibility, a social audit measures CSR. Businesses often set social objectives and then measure whether they have met their objectives. Most large corporations include a social audit in their annual reports. Although certain organizations maintain their social responsibilities at a given, consistent level, others score at different levels for different issues. In place of or in addition to the social audit, many organizations present information about their social responsibility activities on their websites. Where to find the social information varies. Some companies provide links from their home page, and others include the information in their "About Us" link.

### A Situational Approach to CSR

First, let's be realistic. A company can't operate at the socially reactive and socially involved levels of CSR if it is not making a profit to give away.[123] Although companies tend to operate at a fairly consistent level of CSR, the level can and does change based on the activity. According to the principle of *enlightened self-interest*, companies are motivated to engage in CSR activities when the benefits outweigh the costs.[124]

Resources allocated to CSR are limited. Therefore, each request by nonprofits for social reaction and suggestions for social involvement programs by employees requires analysis. Giving to one organization's cause versus another creates winners and losers. So how do the various stakeholder relations affect the overall well-being of the firm?[125] As you can see, selecting who gets your limited resources, and how much of them, is not an easy decision to make.

## APPLYING THE CONCEPT 2.5

### Social Responsibility

Identify each statement by its level of social responsibility.

a. social obstruction
b. social obligation
c. social reaction
d. social involvement

_____ 21. We agree—a Boys & Girls Club downtown would help develop new sport programs in our city. We'll give you $1,000 to get the ball rolling.

_____ 22. I'm disappointed with the reading levels of players coming from our local high school. Betty, I want you to contact the principal and see if you can work together to develop a program to improve reading skills.

_____ 23. Bill, the auditor will be here next week, so we'd better make sure that the hockey equipment we took from inventory does not show up as missing.

_____ 24. We reviewed factory workers' hourly labor rates in Vietnam because of the bad press we were receiving. Now we pay higher than the minimum wage in Vietnam, which is more expensive for our company.

_____ 25. As of June 1, the new regulations go into effect. We will have to cut the amount of waste we dump into the river by half. Get the lowest bidder to pick up the other half and dispose of it.

## Sustainability

Let's discuss what sustainability is, explain the triple bottom line, and give examples of some sustainability practices.

### What Is Sustainability?

*Sustainability* is meeting the needs of today without sacrificing future generations' ability to meet their needs.[126] Society expects and pressures managers to use resources to operate their businesses responsibly with minimal harm to society's stakeholders. Customers expect safe products and employees safe working conditions. People expect to live in a safe environment with minimal pollution in their communities.[127] Thus, focusing on sustainability is an important part of being socially responsible to stakeholders. Sustainability is important,[128] so managers must include the environment as an important external stakeholder.[129] Because of growing global environmental problems,[130] sustainability has become a buzzword.[131] Organizations are using more renewable energy[132] as sustainability standards are raised around the world.[133]

### The Triple Bottom Line

Today's managers need to go beyond profits and create benefits for the natural environment and social welfare.[134] SR accounting has moved from a single bottom line—profits—to using *triple bottom-line* accounting: making profits, benefiting society, and helping the environment. Southwest Airlines' triple bottom line motto is: profits, people, planet.[135] Managers are focusing on sustainability changes because it's the right thing, the benefits outweigh the costs, and it can be profitable.[136]

### Sustainability Practices and Green Companies

Sustainability includes reducing the organization's environmental impacts.[137] A *green company* engages in behavior that minimizes harm or improves the environment. Environmental problems have created opportunities for entrepreneurs who are creating green management companies to help solve environmental problems.[138]

Professional sport organizations are becoming more active in developing sustainable practices. NASCAR is focused on cutting costs by recycling, conserving, and generating its own energy. NASCAR has also implemented green initiatives such as collecting used fuel, planting trees to offset carbon emissions, and even using sheep to cut the infield grass at racetracks. Professional sport teams such as the MLB St. Louis Cardinals and the Seattle Mariners recycle and conserve energy. The NBA Portland Trail Blazers, the Miami Heat, and the Orlando Magic play in energy-efficient arenas certified by the United States Green Building Council. NASCAR suppliers, such as Coca-Cola, have significantly increased their efforts to recycle waste at sporting events.

## LEARNING AIDS

### CHAPTER SUMMARY

1. **Describe the five components of the internal environment.**

   *Management* refers to the people responsible for an organization's performance. *Mission* is the organization's purpose or reason for being. The organization uses human, physical, financial, and informational *resources* to accomplish its mission. The *systems process* is the organization's method of transforming inputs into outputs. *Structure* refers to the way in which the organization groups its resources to accomplish its mission.

2. **Explain the two primary principles of total quality management.**

   The two primary principles of total quality management are to (1) focus on delivering customer value and (2) continually improve the system and its processes. To be successful, businesses must continually offer value to attract and retain customers. Without customers, you don't have a business.

3. **Explain how factors in the external environment affect the internal business environment.**

   Customers should determine what products the business offers, for without customer value there are no customers and there is no business. Competitors' business practices, such as features and prices, often have to be duplicated to maintain customer value. Poor-quality inputs from suppliers result in poor-quality outputs without customer value. Without a qualified workforce, products and services will have little or no customer value. Shareholders, through an elected board of directors, hire top managers and provide directives for the organization. Society pressures the business to perform or not perform certain activities, such as pollution control. The business must develop new technologies, or at least keep up with them, to provide customer value. Economic activity affects the organization's ability to provide customer value. For example, inflated prices lead to lower customer value. Governments set the rules and regulations that businesses must adhere to.

4. **State the differences between domestic, international, and multinational businesses.**

   Domestic firms do business in only one country. International firms are primarily based in one country but transact business with other countries. Multinational corporations have significant operations in more than one country.

5. **List the lowest- and highest-risk ways to take a business global.**

   Importing-exporting is the lowest-risk strategy, and direct investment is the highest-risk strategy. Global sourcing can be part of either method.

6. **Explain the stakeholders' approach to ethics.**

   In this approach to ethics, organizations create a win–win situation for the parties affected by the decision. If as a manager you are proud to tell stakeholders of your decision, it is probably ethical. If you are not proud or you keep rationalizing your decision, it may not be ethical.

7. **Discuss the four levels of social responsibility in business.**

   Social responsibility can be divided into four levels, which range from low to high. At the low end, social obstruction, managers behave unethically and illegally. At the next level, social obligation, managers meet only the minimum legal requirements. With social reaction, managers respond to societal requests. At the highest level, social involvement, managers voluntarily initiate socially responsible acts.

## REVIEW AND DISCUSSION QUESTIONS

1. Do most sport organizations focus on creating customer value? Use specific examples to defend your position.

2. Do you think that all sport organizations should use TQM? Why or why not?

3. Describe the relationship between management and an organization's mission, resources, systems process, and structure. Which of these internal factors are ends and which are means?

4. What technological breakthrough in sports has had the greatest impact on the quality of your life, and why?

5. Should government regulation of sport and business be increased, be decreased, or remain the same? Defend your position.

6. Categorize a few sport companies you are familiar with as international or multi-national.

7. For the companies you listed in question 6, identify their methods of going global.

8. Do you believe that ethical behavior pays off in the long run? Why or why not?

9. What guides your behavior now? Will you use one of the ethical guides from the text? If yes, which one and why?

10. Can ethics be taught and learned? Defend your position.

11. How do companies benefit from being socially responsible? Give some examples.

12. If you were a CEO, what level of social responsibility would you aspire to? How might you go about attaining it?

13. Did Alex Rodriguez demonstrate that he was worth $30 million a year? Does his ethical behavior on and off the field have anything to do with this?

14. Research what socially responsible activities Alex Rodriguez is involved with off the playing field.

15. If you can't control the external environment, why be concerned about it?

16. Should people in the United States make an effort to buy products made in America? If yes, how should "made in America" be defined?

## CASES

### Sport Management Professionals @ Work: Noah Volain

Students often forget that people with interesting careers in sport started their careers as lower-level employees. Noah Volain started as a counselor at the local Jewish Community Center. He studied hard at the local inner-city high school and was accepted into the prestigious sport management major at the University of Massachusetts. At UMass he was involved in the UMass Association for Student Sport Managers, activities, and trips to the Pawtucket Red Sox; participated in Career Internship Fairs at Gillette Stadium; and mentored freshman sport management students.

Noah worked hard to find his first job in the world of sport management. He didn't just graduate and immediately move into a professional position. Noah worked on the box office staff at UMass using the Archtics program to sell tickets to customers. He also worked at the will-call booth prior to UMass athletic events.

His next stop was as a project statistics associate at ESPN. He received clock and score updates, scoring play-by-play and entering box scores of college football and basketball games for display on ESPN.com and ESPN BottomLine.

Noah was the sales representative for the Holyoke Blue Sox baseball team, networking throughout western Massachusetts with the goal of driving ticket sales for Holyoke Blue Sox games. That was the last time Noah worked fairly close to home!

The next stop was ticket sales manager for the Tampa Bay Rays in Florida. His job was to contact previous single-game ticket buyers and local businesses to generate season ticket and partial season ticket sales through both cold calls and face-to-face appointments.

The next stop was the Philadelphia area. Noah became the account executive at Penn State IMG Learfield Ticket Solutions. Noah contacted previous ticket buyers and local adult and youth organizations to generate ticket sales for groups and season tickets for football, men's basketball, women's basketball, men's hockey, women's volleyball, softball, and other Penn State athletics through cold calls and maximizing and upselling inbound calls.

Other stops along the way included working as a sales associate with the Philadelphia 76ers before being promoted to senior sales associate. He also worked for a time at Custom

Promotions as a sales associate. He was a multimedia account executive at Philadelphia Media Network. For the last few years he has been working as the outbound business sales representative for Comcast.Business.

There is a well-known expression that we will do many jobs in our lifetime. Noah has successfully moved from one organization to another quite gracefully, but almost every position he held was based on selling tickets to sporting events.

## Case Questions

1. How many different jobs did Noah have in his career? Comment on some of his stops along the way.

2. Would you take a job in ticket sales?

3. Would you consider moving across the country to attain the job you desire?

## Ethics and the Olympics 2002 to 2018

The scandals associated with the 2002 Salt Lake City Olympics (the bribery involved in the site selection process and the judging practices used to award the figure skating medals, among others) forced the IOC to reevaluate its practices. The IOC faced two problems that had been difficult to manage. First, there was the long-standing problem of illegal doping by athletes. Second, the committee looking to bring the Olympics to Beijing in 2008 had to address long-standing human rights violations attributed to China's leaders. Issues of further concern included a lack of media freedom and free speech and the mistreatment and torture of human rights activists. The 2008 Olympic torch relay was slightly delayed by protestors in major cities such as London and San Francisco. Protesters were concerned about human rights issues in China. Still, the IOC hoped that media attention would be on sports and not on human rights problems.[139]

The IOC president, Belgium's Jacques Rogge, said that the reforms implemented in the wake of the 1999 Salt Lake City bribes-for-votes scandal strengthened the IOC by widening its committee base (which originally included only national VIPs) to include heads of major international sport federations and athletes.

One of the challenges ahead was the fight against doping: Rogge commented, "You can win many battles, but the war is more difficult. You find ways to discover drugs, but there are new drugs coming." He hailed the collaboration between the World Anti-Doping Agency and governments, which "have means we don't have like customs and police investigations." However, he also noted, "The end of this fight is very far from now. The war is very difficult. But with the new World Anti-Doping Agency, there is a very good collaboration now between the world of sport and governments. For the last few years, governments have become very interested in this fight."[140]

The 2008 Beijing Olympics turned out to be a big success. The opening ceremonies were spectacular; the U.S. men's basketball team "redeemed" themselves by winning a gold medal; Chinese and U.S. women gymnasts both won hard-earned gold medals; and U.S. swimmer Michael Phelps broke many Olympic records by winning eight gold medals.

With regard to the management of the Games, only one unfortunate incident resulted in a death; a family member of the U.S. volleyball team. A solitary attacker assaulted the tourist for reasons still unknown.

In summary, concerns about environmental issues, freedom of speech, and the use of banned drugs did not lead to any controversies.

The 2012 Summer Olympic Games were held in London, England. Rogge has tried to help the Olympic movement be more transparent and open about its activities. However, the memories of the 2002 Salt Lake Games still linger. Potentially much worse, there were riots in the streets of London in August 2011 before the 2012 Summer Games in London were held. The riots were started by demonstrators who felt that police used too much force when they killed a local Englishman. Two important soccer games were postponed. Although the riots were a blemish on the London Games, it seemed that the streets of London were back to being an orderly tourist attraction.[141]

The 2016 Rio Olympics were troubled before they began. There was concern that the cost of building the infrastructure in Rio was too high considering the economic crisis the country was experiencing. There was also a major political shift as Brazil's president was impeached right before the games began. A potential pandemic caused by the Zika virus was also a major health concern.[142]

Once the Rio games began, most competitions lived up to their expectations. However, Ryan Lochte, a U.S. swimmer, lied in a story about being robbed.[143] The water was badly polluted at sailing events, causing delays in the events. An Irish Olympic leader was arrested in a ticket re-selling scheme.[144] An Egyptian judo competitor refused to shake hands with his Israeli counterpart for political and cultural reasons.[145] Unfortunately, Rio was also charged with not having enough trained staff on hand to implement anti-doping procedures. Many volunteers simply never showed up or walked away from their positions.[146] For details on the planning and implementation of the Olympics, visit the official website at www.olympic.org/.

Go to the web study guide to answer questions about this case study.

## @ TAKE IT TO THE NET

Please visit www.HumanKinetics.com/AppliedSportManagementSkills and go to this book's companion web study guide, where you will find the following:

A list of websites associated with the concepts in this chapter

Skill-Builder exercises, Sports and Social Media exercises, and a continuing Game Plan for Starting a Sport Business

Online versions of chapter exercises and end-of-chapter learning aids

An exercise that helps you define the Key Terms

# PART II

# Planning

# Creative Problem Solving and Decision Making

## LEARNING OUTCOMES

After studying this chapter, you should be able to

1. describe how meeting objectives, solving problems, and making decisions are connected;

2. explain how management functions, decision making, and problem solving relate;

3. list the six steps in decision making;

4. identify programmed and nonprogrammed decisions and recognize certain, risky, and uncertain business conditions;

5. know when to use the different decision models and when to make decisions as a group or as an individual;

6. state the difference between an objective and "must" and "want" criteria;

7. explain how creativity and innovation differ;

8. describe the three stages in the creative process; and

9. explain how quantitative and cost–benefit analyses facilitate selecting alternatives.

## KEY TERMS

| | | |
|---|---|---|
| problem | programmed decisions | creative process |
| problem solving | nonprogrammed decisions | devil's advocate |
| decision making | decision-making conditions | brainstorming |
| reflexive decision style | criteria | synectics |
| reflective decision style | creativity | nominal grouping |
| consistent decision style | innovation | consensus mapping |

Organizing Leading Controlling Planning Organizing Leading Controlling Planning Organizing
ontrolling Planning Organizing Leading Controlling Planning Organizing Leading Controlling Planni
Leading Controlling Planning Organizing Leading Controlling Planning Organizing Leading
anning Organizing Leading Controlling Planning Organizing Leading Controlling Planning
ading Controlling Planning Organizing Leading Controlling Planning Organizing Leading Controll
Organizing Leading Planning Organizing Leading

## DEVELOPING YOUR SKILLS

The decisions you make will affect your sport management career. Problem solving and decision making are crucial skills of effective managers. By following the six steps in the decision-making model presented in this chapter, you can improve your ability to solve problems and make decisions.

## REVIEWING THEIR GAME PLAN

### Implementing Adidas' Decision to Design Fashion Footwear

For the past 80 years, legendary soccer players trotted around playing fields all over the world, from Seoul to Manchester to Sao Paulo to Kabul, sporting the three-stripe Adidas logo on their footwear. Yet, caught in the downdraft that swept through the athletic footwear industry in the 2000s, Adidas—the original sport brand—somehow lost its firm footing on the bottom line. Even the purchase of Reebok in 2005 didn't help Adidas to decrease the market share lead, nor the style advantage, that Nike has held for decades.[1]

By 2016, new CEO Kasper Rørsted felt Adidas had focused too much attention on the functional marketing principles of the business and not enough on being customer-focused. His decision was to cut down on different models and focus on being able to change products based on consumers' desire.

Adidas has decided to use fewer celebrities, but to allow the few that represent their brands, such as rappers Pharrell and Kanye West, to have the freedom to be more creative and innovative.[2] The goal is to blend the introduction of new brands such as NMD's, NEO, and Y3 that consumers will wait in line to buy. Ultraboost footwear has such a comfortable sole that Adidas expects it to compete with Air from Nike. At the same time, traditional products such as casual sneakers Stan Smith footwear will continue to be profitable, so Adidas can support the development of new footwear.[3]

Under Kasper Rørsted's leadership, Adidas has decided to bet heavily on the fashion footwear markets in Germany and the United States.[4] It will be important for Kasper Rørsted to evaluate his decisions on a regular basis to make sure the new strategies he has put in place are successful.

For current information on Adidas, visit www.adidas.com.

# An Overview of Problem Solving and Decision Making

Problem solving and decision making are important skills.[5] In fact, decision making is one of the five important management skills (chapter 1), and conceptual skills help in decision making. Organizations recruit employees with problem-solving skills.[6] We all make decisions in our personal and professional lives. As coaches and sport managers we teach and encourage our players and employees to make good decisions because the success of the individual, team, and organization is based on the decisions we make. Clearly, team performance is based on the selection decisions of the coaches and athletes and the decisions they make on and off the field.

Top management decisions have a direct effect on the success of the entire organization.[7] When Michael Jordan (MJ) went to the NBA, he sought a sponsorship with Adidas. But Adidas executives made a poor decision in rejecting MJ, saying he wasn't tall enough and that no one could relate to him.[8] Nike made a good decision and signed MJ and also took the NBA sponsorship away from Adidas-owned Reebok.[9] But Nike has made poor decisions, too, like buying Umbro for $484 million and selling it at a 46 percent loss for only $225 million in 2012.

We do not always make the best decisions, but we can improve our decision-making skills;[10] that's what this chapter is all about. Let's continue this section and discuss the relationships between objective setting, problem solving, and decision making; the relationships among the management functions, decision making, and problem solving; and the six steps of the decision-making model that will help you make better decisions. You will also learn about your own decision-making style and understand the need to use the ethical guidelines from chapter 2 when making decisions.

## Objective Setting, Problem Solving, and Decision Making

You and your boss will sometimes set objectives together, and your boss will sometimes assign objectives for you and your team to achieve. Objectives are often not achieved.[11] When you don't meet your objectives, you have a problem. When you have problems, you must make decisions.

A **problem** exists when objectives are not being met. In other words, you have a problem when a difference exists between what is happening and what you and your team want to happen. **Problem solving** is the process of taking corrective action to meet objectives. **Decision making** is the process of selecting a course of action that will solve a problem. It may be hard to believe, but half of the managerial decisions made fail to solve their problems.[12]

When faced with a problem, your first decision is whether to take corrective action or not. Some problems result from outcomes that differ little from the original objectives, and they are not worth spending the time and effort it would take to solve them. Sometimes you will accept the problem or change the objective. However, it's your job to achieve objectives, so to be successful, you must figure out how—that's what sport managers get paid to do.

 **TIME-OUT 1** Give an example of an objective from your manager or coach that was not met. Identify the problem created and the decision that prevented the objective from being met.

## Management Functions, Decision Making, and Problem Solving

In chapter 1 you learned that all managers perform the same four management functions. To perform each of these functions, managers must make decisions. Keep in mind that every action is preceded by a decision. As *planners*, sport managers decide on the objectives they want to pursue and when, where, and how the objectives will be met. The better you can develop plans that prevent problems before they occur, the fewer problems you will encounter and the more time you will have to take advantage of opportunities and respond to competitive threats.[13] As an *organizer*, you decide what to delegate and how to coordinate the department's resources, including whom to select for each position and how to train and evaluate them (staffing). As a *leader*, you must decide how best to influence employees to meet objectives. As a *controller*, you assess whether—and how well—objectives are being met and how to take corrective action.

Also, recall that management has a systems effect because the decisions made in each functional area also affect other areas. Selecting the wrong plays (planning), putting athletes in the wrong positions (organizing), failing to motivate the athletes (leading), or unsuccessfully monitoring team performance (controlling) can cost you the game.

Adidas saw opportunity in new markets. Its objective? Provide a broader selection of sporting goods than its competitors. Its decision? Enter the skiing, golf, and cycling markets. However, Adidas' decision to diversify has not been without problems. Adidas thus faces important decisions—how best to share skills, abilities, and resources.

 **TIME-OUT 2** Give an example of a poor decision made by your manager or coach. Describe the management function he or she was performing at the time and the problem created as a result of the decision.

## Decision-Making Model

To make important decisions, managers are often taught to follow the steps of the classical decision-making model, which is based on years of research to determine how the most successful managers make decisions.[14] The model works, but you need to know when to use it, which you will learn in step 1 of the model.

The model consists of six steps (see figure 3.1). Each step is presented in detail in separate sections after this overview section. In the sports world, you will not always proceed in the conveniently sequenced manner implied in figure 3.1. At any step in the process you may find yourself returning to a prior step to make changes. Let's say you have gotten to implementation, but it isn't going well. Perhaps this time you simply need to tweak the implementation plan, but other times you will need to backtrack and select a new alternative or even change your original objective. A problematic implementation may reveal that you haven't defined the problem precisely enough, and you may have to return to square one.

The Dallas Cowboys believe they have a streamlined decision-making process. The club owner, Jerry Jones, does not hire a general manager. This means the Cowboys can eliminate the step in a normal decision-making process in which a general manager has to get permission to sign or drop a player. Fewer people in the decision-making process should mean that decisions are made swiftly. However, not having an experienced general manager can prove costly if the owner does not have the experience to draft or trade for the players the club needs in order to improve.

Following the steps laid out in figure 3.1 will not guarantee that you will make good decisions every time. However, using the model increases your chances of success.[15] Think of it like this: Using the model will not result in a goal or hit every time, but it will increase the number of goals or the batting average you achieve during the season. Consciously use these six steps for important decisions in your daily life, and you will improve your ability to make effective decisions.

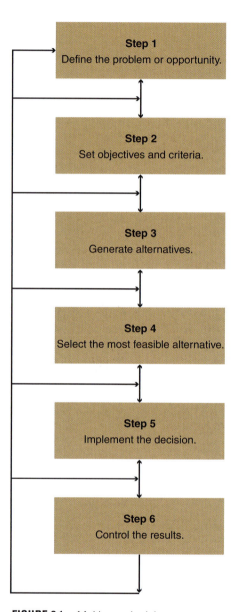

**FIGURE 3.1**  Making a decision.

## APPLYING THE CONCEPT 3.1

### Making Decisions

Identify which step in the decision process each statement represents.

  a. step 1
  b. step 2
  c. step 3
  d. step 4
  e. step 5
  f. step 6

_____   1.  We brainstorm to solve problems.

_____   2.  Betty, is the machine that makes baseball caps still jumping out of sequence, or has it stopped?

_____   3.  I don't understand what the new owners are trying to accomplish.

_____   4.  What symptoms have you observed that indicate the team has a problem?

_____   5.  Break-even analysis should help us in this situation.

## Decision-Making Styles

What approach do you use when you are faced with having to make a decision?[16] Let's start by finding out whether your decision-making style is more reflexive, reflective, or consistent by completing the following Self-Assessment.

### Reflexive Decision Style

Decision makers who use the **reflexive decision style** "shoot from the hip"—that is, they make snap decisions without taking the time to get all the information they need and without considering many alternatives. Reflexive decision makers are decisive—they do not procrastinate, and they sometimes score on short-lived opportunities. However, hasty decisions made without adequate information can be a dangerous form of "business roulette."

If you tend to make fast decisions, you may want to slow down and spend more time gathering information and analyzing more alternatives when you have to make important decisions. Resist your natural tendency to jump in too quickly; don't rely on emotional intuition—also called "winging it"—without using rational reasoning processes.[17] Bad intuition leads to bad decisions[18] because it proceeds from biases and false beliefs.[19]

### Reflective Decision Style

Decision makers who use the **reflective decision style** are slow to decide, gathering considerable information and analyzing many alternatives. They certainly don't make hasty decisions. In fact, they tend to procrastinate and waste valuable time and resources, and they often miss out on short-lived opportunities. Too much information can lead to paralysis, and being too slow to make decisions with athletes and employees can result in their viewing you as wishy-washy and indecisive.

If you are too reflective, think about what Andrew Jackson said: Take time to deliberate—absolutely—but when the time for action comes, stop thinking and get moving. Even a correct decision is wrong when it was made too late.[20]

## SELF-ASSESSMENT 3.1

### What Is Your Decision Style?

To determine whether your decision-making style is reflexive, reflective, or consistent, select a number from 1 to 5 on the following continuum that best describes your behavior in relation to each statement.

1 = a very common behavior

2 = a somewhat common behavior

3 = neutral

4 = a somewhat uncommon behavior

5 = a very uncommon behavior

**Overall**

_____ 1. I make decisions quickly.

**When Making Decisions**

_____ 2. I usually don't stop to define the problem clearly.

_____ 3. I usually don't set specific objectives for what the end result of my decision will be.

_____ 4. I go with my first thought or hunch.

_____ 5. I don't bother to recheck my work.

_____ 6. I gather little or no information.

_____ 7. I consider very few alternatives.

_____ 8. I usually make a decision well before the deadline.

_____ 9. I don't ask others for advice.

**After Making a Decision**

_____ 10. I don't look for other alternatives or wish I had waited longer.

_____ Total score

To determine your style, add up your answers. Your total score will be between 10 and 50. Place an X on the continuum that represents your score.

| Reflexive | Consistent | | Reflective |
|-----------|------------|------|------------|
| 20 | 30 | 40 | 50 |

### Consistent Decision Style

Decision makers who use the **consistent decision style** don't rush and don't waste time. They know when they need more information and when it's time to stop analyzing and get moving. Consistent decision makers also boast the best decision-making record. Today, making better decisions faster is important to success.[21] Thus, many companies and teams are analyzing big data as consistent decision makers.[22] Not surprisingly, when faced with important decisions, they typically follow the steps outlined in figure 3.1, so maybe you should, too.

Jerry Seeman, former referee and senior director of officiating for the NFL, personified consistent decision making. According to Seeman, being on the field is like being in a fishbowl: Everyone is waiting for your decision. Above all, you have to keep your cool. One of the biggest errors that officials fall into is making calls too quickly. When things happen in a split second, it can be tempting to throw a penalty flag before you know what happened. That's why officials need to work in cruise control and consult with each other to get information from different angles. Using the consistent style to make calls may upset some who want a split-second decision without consultation or watching the tape, but bad calls will make everyone angry and will result in poor performance reviews.

## Ethics and Social Responsibility in Decision Making

Don't forget to consider the ethics of your decisions.[23] Recall from chapter 2 that one of the touchiest ethical issues in sport involves the use of illegal drugs, including steroids, to enhance performance as well as just to get high. A major trap with drugs is that some athletes are looking to get an advantage over competitors, so they take drugs. Others find out and reason that they also have to take drugs in order to compete. Others take drugs under peer pressure. The final result is that no one has the advantage, but they are all on drugs and don't stop while competing unless they have to, usually because of suspension from the sport, injury, health problems, or death. Can the vicious cycle ever end?

As an old ad stated, no kid says, I'm going to grow up to be a drug addict. But those who take drugs all justify it by saying, I can handle it, there is nothing wrong with it, and nothing will happen to me. You can probably think of at least one person who took drugs and did suffer consequences, and that person's team, school, friends, and family suffered consequences as well. Many good coaches have helped prevent drug use and have helped people quit, but some coaches have ignored drug use, encouraged it, or even given players drugs.

The decisions we make can affect the rest of our lives, and those of others, and we need to consciously follow our ethical guidelines (chapter 2) during each step of the decision-making process. Now let's learn how to perform each step of the model so that we can use it in our personal and professional lives to make important decisions.

# Step 1: Define the Problem or Opportunity

In the first step in your decision process, you define the problem you want to solve or the opportunity you want to capitalize on. This step requires that you classify the problem so you know which decision model to use, select an appropriate level of employee participation, and distinguish the cause of the problem from its symptoms.

## Classify the Problem

Problems can be classified in terms of how the decision is structured, the conditions in which decisions are made, and the decision model to be used based on the structure and condition.

◀ **LEARNING OUTCOME 4**

Identify programmed and nonprogrammed decisions and recognize certain, risky, and uncertain business conditions.

### *How Problem Decisions Are Structured*

Decision structure can be categorized as programmed or nonprogrammed. **Programmed decisions** are recurring or routine situations in which the decision maker should use decision rules or organizational policies and procedures to make the decision. Here is a typical decision rule for Dick's: Order X number of Titleist golf balls every time stock reaches level Y. So, it is not necessary to follow all the steps of the decision model.

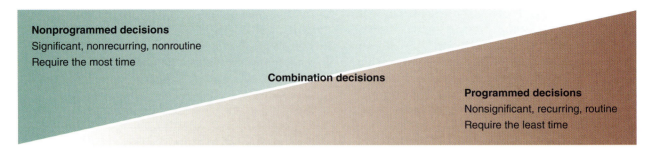

**FIGURE 3.2** The continuum of decision structure.

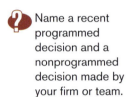

Name a recent programmed decision and a nonprogrammed decision made by your firm or team.

**Nonprogrammed decisions** are significant but nonrecurring and nonroutine situations in which the decision makers should use the decision-making model. To qualify as significant, a decision must be expensive (e.g., purchasing major assets) or have major consequences (e.g., launching a new product ). Adidas made a nonprogrammed decision when it purchased Reebok.

Nonprogrammed decisions should take longer to make than programmed decisions. Note also that decisions fall along a continuum from totally programmable to totally nonprogrammable, with many combinations of the two types in between (see figure 3.2).

You must be able to distinguish between the two types of decisions because they alert you to the time and effort you should be spending. Upper-level managers typically make more nonprogrammed decisions than do lower-level managers, who tend to make programmed decisions.

## Decision-Making Conditions

Decisions are made in an environment of certainty, risk, or uncertainty; these elements are called **decision-making conditions**. When you make decisions in a *certain* environment, you know the outcome of each alternative in advance so you can usually take quick action.[24] When you make decisions in a *risky* environment, you don't know each outcome in advance, but you can assign probabilities of occurrence to each one. In an *uncertain* environment, lack of information or knowledge makes the outcomes unknown,[25] or accurate probabilities can't be made.[26] Top-level managers tend to make more risky and uncertain decisions than lower-level managers do.[27]

Although risk and uncertainty can never be accurately predicted, they can be reduced with information (big data).[28] The key is for event decision makers working in an increasingly fast-paced environment to plan for the event (come game time) by having risk assessments and contingency plans.[29] In the sport world, conditions can't always be neatly categorized as certain, risky, or uncertain. As shown in figure 3.3, the conditions are on a continuum.

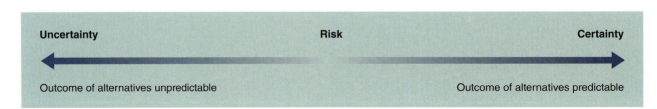

**FIGURE 3.3** The continuum of the decision-making environment.

### Decision Models

The two primary decision models are the classical rational model and the bounded rationality model. The *rational model* uses "*optimizing*"—that is, it endeavors to select the best possible alternative. The *bounded rationality model*, a subset of the rational model, uses "*satisficing*"—it selects the first alternative that meets certain specified minimal criteria. Figure 3.1 presents the rational model. With satisficing, only parts, or none, of the model would be used.

The more unstructured the decision and the higher the risk and uncertainty, the greater the need to conduct the research required in the rational model. Thus, you want to optimize when you make nonprogrammed decisions in uncertain or high-risk conditions (follow the rational six-step model), and you should satisfice when you make programmed decisions in low-risk or highly certain conditions (use the bounded rationality model without following all six steps of the model).

> **TIME-OUT 3**
> Analyze a recent decision of your organization, and decide which decision model your managers used. Identify the environmental conditions and the type of decision (programmed or nonprogrammed).

◄ **LEARNING OUTCOME 5**
Know when to use the different decision models and when to make decisions as a group or as an individual.

## Select an Appropriate Level of Employee Participation

When a problem or opportunity exists, you must decide who should participate in solving the problem or making decisions. Should you make the decisions yourself, or should a team be used?[30] Employees generally want to participate in making decisions,[31] especially when they are directly affected by them,[32] and groups tend to solve problems and make better decisions than individuals.[33] Decision making with team participation will continue to increase.[34] Therefore, you must know when and how employees should participate in the process. To begin, let's examine individual and group decision making.

---

**APPLYING THE CONCEPT 3.2**

### Classify the Problem

Classify the following problems according to the type of decision and the environmental conditions in which the decision is being made.

a. programmed, certain
b. programmed, uncertain
c. programmed, risky
d. nonprogrammed, certain
e. nonprogrammed, uncertain
f. nonprogrammed, risky

_____ 6. When I graduate from college, I will buy an existing fitness center rather than work for someone else.

_____ 7. Sondra, the owner of a health center, has experienced a turnaround in her small business; it's now profitable. She wants to be able to keep her excess cash accessible in case she needs it to cover shortfalls. How should she invest it?

_____ 8. Every six months, a purchasing agent selects new materials for the soccer balls his company makes.

_____ 9. In the early 1970s, investors decided to start the World Football League.

_____ 10. A manager in a department with high turnover hires a new employee.

Realize that even though the trend is toward team decision making, it does have disadvantages, and it is not always better than individual decision making.[35] The key to successful group decisions is to avoid the pitfalls and capitalize on the strengths of the group process.

## Upsides of Group Decision Making

When group members participate in the decision process, six advantages often accrue:

- *Better-quality decisions.* Groups tend to do a better job of solving complex problems than would the best individual in the group going solo. Thus, groups do well with nonprogrammed decisions in risky or uncertain conditions.

- *More information, more alternatives, and heightened creativity and innovation.* Groups typically bring more information to the table than individuals do. Group members bring different points of view to bear on the problem and can thus generate more alternatives. Creative, innovative ideas (and products) emerge from the synergy of members' building on each other's ideas.

- *Better understanding of the problem and the decision.* When people participate in the decision-making process, they gain a fuller understanding of the alternatives and why the final selection was made.

- *Greater commitment to the decision.* People involved in a decision are more committed to making the implementation succeed. This makes implementation easier.

- *Improved morale and motivation.* Teams help meet social needs. "Ownership" of the process, the decision, and the results improves morale and motivates people to meet objectives.

- *Good training.* Participation in decision making trains people to work in groups by developing group-process skills. Group participation helps employees better understand problems faced by the organization, and this results in greater productivity.

## Downsides of Group Decision Making

Effective leadership is required to avoid the following pitfalls of group decision making:

- *Wasted time and slower decision making.* It takes longer for groups to reach consensus, and during this time employees are not performing their jobs. Because group involvement costs the organization time and money, for programmed decisions in certain or low-risk business conditions, individual decision making is generally more cost-effective.

- *Satisficing.* Groups are more likely to satisfice than individuals. Satisficing tends to occur when meetings are not run effectively. Members may take the attitude, "Let's be done with this. I'm not responsible for the decision anyway, the group is."

- *Domination by subgroup or individual and goal displacement.* An individual or subgroup can control the process and make the decision. Goal displacement occurs when an individual or subgroup gets its decision accepted for personal gain rather than allowing the team to find the best solution.

- *Conformity and groupthink.* Members may feel pressured to agree with the group's decision without raising reasonable criticisms because they fear rejection or they don't want to cause conflict. Groupthink occurs when members withhold their divergent views to conform with the group. This offsets one of the strong points of effective groups—their diversity. Conformity is especially problematic in highly cohesive groups because members can put getting along ahead of finding the best solution.

- *Social loafing.* People may become free riders by not giving their best effort or not performing their share of the work. Have you ever been a social loafer or gotten stuck doing more than your share of the work at school or on the job?

### *When to Use Individual and Team Decision Making*

Group decision making generally works well with nonprogrammed decisions made in conditions of risk or uncertainty. Individual decision making works well with programmed decisions in low-risk or certain conditions. See figure 3.4 for an illustration of how to define the problem by structure, conditions, and choice of decision model and level of participation.

**TIME-OUT 4** Give an example of a group decision and an individual one from your organization or team. Describe the strengths and weaknesses encountered in each process.

## Distinguish Symptoms from the Cause of the Problem

This is a cause-and-effect relationship. The systems effect tells you a problem exists, but not the cause. If attendance at games is down, you know this symptom. You need to find out what is causing the ticket sales decline so you can act to increase attendance. Tony, your

**1. Categorize the decision structure.**

Nonprogrammed decision
Significant, nonrecurring, and nonroutine

Programmed decision
Nonsignificant, recurring, and routine

**2. Check the conditions in the environment.**

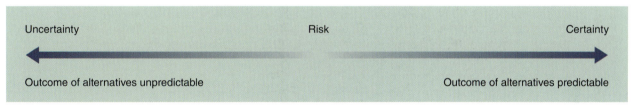

Uncertainty       Risk       Certainty

Outcome of alternatives unpredictable       Outcome of alternatives predictable

**3. Choose the decision model.**

Rational model       Bounded rationality model

Optimizing       Satisficing

**4. Choose the level of participation.**

Group decisions       Individual decisions

**FIGURE 3.4**   Four continuums in classifying the decision.

Name some other possible causes of lost net income. Do any of these causes fit the merger of Adidas and Reebok?

star first baseman, has been late for practice more times in the last month than in the past year. So, what is the problem? If your answer is that he is being late, you are confusing symptoms with the cause. Why is Tony late? If the causes of problems are not discovered and addressed, symptoms usually continue or reappear.

While Adidas was buying Reebok in 2015, there were symptoms of a problem since Reebok had a slightly lower net income. The causes (notice that there are several), as defined by Adidas, were the use of smaller low-end retailers, overcapacity to produce products from Indonesian factories, and the inability to reach the higher-end target markets. The price that Adidas paid for Reebok and the timing of that purchase were not optimal. Remember that defining the problem is the key to successful solutions and strategies. When making nonprogrammed decisions in high-risk or uncertain conditions, take your time, and clearly distinguish symptoms from causes.

**TIME-OUT 5**

Define a problem your organization or team is facing or an opportunity it would like to capitalize on. Clearly distinguish symptoms from causes.

## Step 2: Set Objectives and Criteria

**LEARNING OUTCOME 6** ▶

State the difference between an objective and "must" and "want" criteria.

Once you have defined the problem, your next step is to set an objective that states the end result to solve the problem or capitalize on the opportunity.[36] In chapter 4, you will learn how to set effective objectives. One goal of Adidas is to reduce purchasing costs. This will help the company reduce overall production costs.

When writing an objective, you should also specify the criteria for achieving the objective. **Criteria** are the standards that must be met to accomplish the objective. It is a good idea to distinguish between "must" and "want" criteria. *"Must" criteria* have to be met to achieve the objective, whereas *"want" criteria* are desirable but not absolutely necessary. Thus, every acceptable alternative (and there may be several that are acceptable in the initial stages of the decision process) has to meet the "must" criteria. Thereafter, you must decide which alternative meets the most "want" criteria. With satisficing, you select the first acceptable alternative; with optimizing, you try to choose the best possible option, one that meets as many "want" criteria as possible. It is also often important to *weigh criteria*, as some of the must and want criteria are more important than others.

Go to a recent Adidas annual report and find a company objective that addresses an opportunity in the marketplace. Can you write an objective for Adidas to achieve with regard to successfully merging Adidas and Reebok?

With simple programmed decisions, the objectives and the criteria have already been set. Therefore, you don't have to implement steps 2 through 4 of the decision-making model. However, with important nonprogrammed decisions, you should implement all six steps in the decision-making model (figure 3.1). Suppose your coach has quit and you must hire a new one. Your objective is to hire a coach by June 30, 20xx. Your "must" criteria include, among other things, three years' experience as a coach. Your "want" criterion is that the coach be from a minority group (can be a female, or white in an inner city). That is, you want to hire a minority employee but will not hire someone who is significantly less qualified than a majority applicant. In this situation, you would optimize the decision following the six steps of the model, rather than satisfice. We discuss criteria again later in this chapter.

**TIME-OUT 6**

List the qualifications for a job at an organization that you are familiar with and distinguish between "must" and "want" criteria.

## Step 3: Generate Alternatives

After you and your team have defined the problem and set objectives and criteria, it is time to generate alternatives. Often there is more than one way to solve a problem, so don't shortchange yourself—explore your alternatives.[37] Base your alternatives on facts, not just opinion.

With a programmed decision, step 3 can be skipped because the alternative has already been selected and stated as policies, procedures, and rules. However, with nonprogrammed decisions, the time and effort invested in generating alternatives pays off. In this section, we examine innovation and creativity, the use of information and technology to generate alternatives, and group methods for generating creative alternatives.

## Use Innovation and Creativity

**Creativity** is a way of thinking that generates new solutions to problems and new ways to approach opportunities.[38] It's about looking at and seeing things differently.[39] Ever been told to think outside the box? Creativity is about coming up with new ideas, but they are useless if they are not implemented through innovation.[40] An **innovation** alters what is established by introducing something new. Two classifications of innovation are *product innovation* (new things including products) and *process innovation* (new ways of doing things). Creativity is needed, but it is essentially useless if not implemented.[41]

◄ **LEARNING OUTCOME 7**
Explain how creativity and innovation differ.

Let's be fair to Adidas. The company took a risk in purchasing TaylorMade at a premium price to enter the growing golf business. It entered the equipment business even though its experience was in footwear and apparel. However, its managers were creative and tried an innovative approach. Unfortunately, Adidas bought TaylorMade in 2012 for $1.7 billion. Their risk was not rewarded, since they sold the business for only a little more than $500 million by 2017.[42] Still, it is important for management to be creative and innovative if a company expects to keep abreast of changes in the external environment—but you must make good decisions.

## Creative Process

We all have the ability to be creative, and it's possible to enhance your own creative juices. The three stages in the **creative process** are (1) preparation, (2) incubation and illumination, and (3) evaluation. Following these stages, which we discuss next, can get your creative juices flowing.

◄ **LEARNING OUTCOME 8**
Describe the three stages in the creative process.

1. *Prepare.* What is the problem, and how do you solve it? Get others' opinions, feelings, and ideas, but also get the facts. Dream big (you can always scale back). At this stage, don't limit your thinking—take the attitude that everything goes as you come up with lots of alternatives. Also, don't evaluate your own ideas or those of others; criticism comes later.

2. *Incubate and illuminate.* Take a break and let ideas incubate; sleep on your idea. Don't worry—you are working on the problem, just subconsciously. Allowing your idea to incubate gives you insight you might not gain otherwise,[43] including the solution—*illumination*.[44] Illumination is also referred to as the "Aha, now I get it" phenomenon.

3. *Evaluate . . . and then reevaluate.* Don't rush to implement your creative idea. You should evaluate it to be sure it addresses the problem and not just a symptom. In one useful evaluation approach, playing **devil's advocate**, some group members defend the idea while others try to come up with reasons why it won't work. The focus is on more creativity as the idea is improved upon before it is tried.

## Use Information and Technology

Successful managers use data (big data), information, knowledge, and facts to make creative and innovative decisions.[45] Technology leads to innovation. Unlike managers from an earlier generation, you have a new world of tools to use on problems and opportunities. You also have a new problem, however—too much information and too many tools.

 TIME-OUT
**7**
Think about some problem whose solution you were particularly proud of (or some other solution that really impressed you as outstanding). Break down the solution process into parts—do the three stages discussed here apply to this solution?

As you solve problems and take advantage of opportunities, you will often ask yourself, How much information do we need, and where should we get it? Unfortunately, there are no simple answers. The more important the decision, the more information you need (generally). However, too much information can paralyze the decision process. That is, the decision becomes too complex, and you never get to the best choice. So tech and data are your decision tools, not your boss.[46] Therefore, it helps to know what constitutes useful information.

Useful information has four characteristics: (1) timeliness, (2) quality, (3) completeness, and (4) relevance (see figure 3.5). Timely information is information that you get in time to make your decision. High-quality information is accurate, whereas false information misleads and results in bad decisions. Complete information is of course extensive—no holes, no gaps. Relevant information pertains to the group's objectives. Having a clear objective and good criteria helps you to chuck irrelevant information.

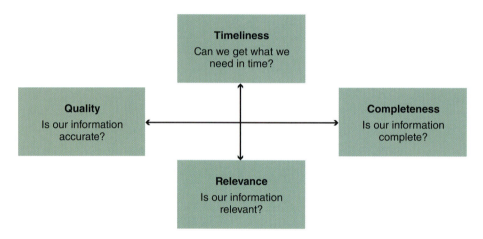

**FIGURE 3.5**   Characteristics of useful information.

## Get Groups to Use Creativity and Innovation

The trend today is to use groups to develop creative ideas and innovative decisions[47] because small groups generally outperform individuals[48] by combining and improving creative ideas.[49] As noted earlier, there are downsides to group decision making, but you can help your group to avoid these difficulties. Figure 3.6 lists five widely used methods for generating creative ideas.

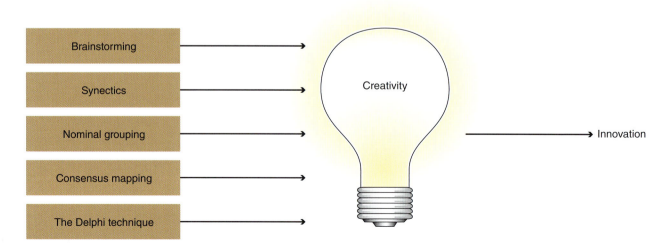

**FIGURE 3.6**   Methods that foster creativity and innovation in groups.

## Brainstorming

When selecting members for a brainstorming group, choose a diverse group.[50] In **brainstorming**, group members generate as many alternatives as they can in a short time. The group is presented with a problem and asked to develop as many solutions as possible. A short time period (10-20 minutes) is specified. Members are encouraged to make wild, off-the-wall suggestions and to build on suggestions made by others. Three rules include: (1) Everyone (presidents to janitors) should have an equal voice. (2) No criticizing ideas while brainstorming.[51] (3) Don't evaluate ideas until all possible alternatives have been presented to the group.[52]

With online technology, you can use *e-brainstorming*. Participants send ideas electronically from anywhere in the world and build on others' ideas like in traditional brainstorming.

## Synectics

In **synectics**, novel alternatives are generated through role-playing and fantasizing. Synectics groups are used to generate unique ideas. To avoid preconceptions and focus on novel ideas, the problem is not stated at first.

Nolan Bushnell wanted to develop a new family dining experience. He started with a group discussion on leisure activities having to do with eating out. The novel idea was a restaurant–electronic game complex where families could entertain themselves playing games before, during, and after eating pizza and other food and drinks. The business that emerged from this process is called Chuck E. Cheese.

## Nominal Grouping

In **nominal grouping**, a structured voting method is used to generate and evaluate alternatives. It helps to eliminate the downsides of group decision making. This process involves six steps:

1. *List ideas.* Participants generate ideas in writing.
2. *Record the ideas.* Participants suggest ideas while the leader writes them for all to read. This continues in a round-robin manner until all ideas are posted.
3. *Clarify the ideas.* Ideas are discussed and improved, and additional alternatives are listed.
4. *Rank the ideas.* Participants rank-order the top three ideas. The low-ranked alternatives are eliminated.
5. *Discuss the rankings.* Participants explain their choices and their reasons for making them.
6. *Vote.* A secret vote is taken to identify the top-ranked alternative.

Used properly, nominal grouping minimizes the downsides of group domination, goal displacement, conformity, and groupthink.

## Consensus Mapping

**Consensus mapping** is a process for developing group agreement on a problem's solution. The Japanese like consensus and use the term *ringi*. Consensus mapping can be used instead of voting to come to an agreement on the most feasible decision after brainstorming. Consensus is generally the best approach because it gives members a better understanding of the problem and its solution, and it secures their commitment to implement the decision. However, as a

 **TIME-OUT 8** Give examples of problems in your organization or team for which brainstorming, nominal grouping, or consensus mapping would be appropriate.

## APPLYING THE CONCEPT **3.3**

### Using Groups to Generate Alternatives

For each situation, identify the most appropriate technique.

   a.  brainstorming

   b.  synectics

   c.  nominal grouping

   d.  consensus mapping

   e.  Delphi technique

_____ 11. A consultant leads a group of company employees and young soccer players to come up with ideas for new cleats.

_____ 12. Our team is suffering from morale problems.

_____ 13. We need new matching desks for the 10 of us in this office.

_____ 14. We need to reduce waste in the production department to cut costs and increase productivity.

_____ 15. Top managers are projecting future trends in the retail sporting goods industry as part of their long-range planning.

sport manager, you can't always get a consensus, and there are times when you can't wait and have to make the decision yourself.

### *Delphi Technique*

In the Delphi technique, a series of confidential questionnaires are used with a panel of experts to reach agreement on an issue. It is commonly used to identify trends, such as technology, that will affect a team or organization. Delphi group members typically are recruited from the "best of the best"; they are widely acknowledged as experts in their field, and—this is important—they are outsiders, not from the organization that is hiring them. Responses from the first open-ended questionnaire are analyzed and resubmitted to participants in a second questionnaire. This process may continue for five or more rounds before a consensus emerges. Because of the nature of the process, they may never need to come together.

Upper-level managers may use the less commonly used synectics and the Delphi technique in their nonprogrammed decision making. Brainstorming, nominal grouping, and consensus mapping are often used at the department level by managers or human resource specialists. Whichever of these methods suits your decision situation, be sure to guard against responses that snuff out creativity. The sidebar contains a list of examples of "killer" statements. If a team member makes a killer statement, make sure everyone realizes that such negative attitudes are counterproductive.

## Use Decision Trees

So you've got some alternatives—now what do you do? You might make a decision tree, which is a diagram of alternatives. The tree gives you a visual tool to work with, which makes it easier for some people to analyze the alternatives.

To construct a decision tree, write down every alternative you can think of that could solve the problem you are grappling with. For each alternative, list potential outcomes. Next, list the choices (decisions) to be made with each alternative. Continue doing this,

---

## Great Ways to Kill Creativity

- It can't be done.
- We've never done it.
- Has anyone else tried it?
- It will not work in our department (or company or industry).
- It costs too much.
- It isn't in the budget.
- Let's form a committee.

---

breaking each alternative into subalternatives, until you are satisfied you have explored each alternative in enough detail. At Adidas, alternatives that would have been generated in the decision process included (among many others) doing nothing, developing a new advertising campaign, introducing new fashion-oriented footwear products, creating new unrelated products, and creating new related products.

# Step 4: Select the Most Feasible Alternative

Like brainstorming, steps 3 and 4 of the decision process are separate steps. There is a good reason for this: Generating and evaluating alternatives at the same time tends to kill creativity and often leads to satisficing. So after generating evidence-supported alternatives,[53] you analyze them using *analytical thinking*.[54]

◀ **LEARNING OUTCOME 9**
Explain how quantitative and cost–benefit analyses facilitate selecting alternatives.

You want to select the "best" alternative.[55] But notice that step 4 says "the most feasible"; the most feasible alternative may not always be the best alternative because we have limited resources. For example, NCAA Division III teams have limited budgets for coaches, so these teams generally can't attract and hire coaches with the same experience as those hired by Division I and pro teams. So they hire the most feasible coaches, who are often internal employees, including team graduates who know the college athletic program.

As you and your team evaluate alternatives, "think forward," and try to predict possible outcomes by synthesizing information.[56] Use an ethical guide to consider the ethics of each alternative.[57] Use the objectives and criteria you developed in step 2 of the decision process to critique each alternative. Then compare how each alternative measures up against your other alternatives. To assist you in this process, become familiar with (if not adept at) two types of techniques: quantitative analysis and cost–benefit analysis. To get you started, we present a brief overview here.

## Quantitative Analyses

Quantitative techniques use mathematical analysis to assess alternative solutions. Microsoft Excel spreadsheets and other software make this process easier. The field of sport management is increasingly using quantitative methods. Recall our MLB *Moneyball* example and the increasing use of statistics (big data) in baseball and other sports at all levels.[58]

### Break-Even Analysis

Break-even analysis involves forecasting the volume of sales and the cost of production. The break-even point (payback) occurs at the level where no profit or loss results. As a manager at a skating rink, you buy a pair of skates for $50. Each time you rent the skates you get $5. How many rentals does it take to break even? It takes 10 rentals to pay back the $50,

What other factors might have been critical in Adidas's break-even analysis?

and every rental after that is profitable. Break-even analysis is commonly used to determine the number of tickets that need to be sold to cover the cost of an event.

### Capital Budgeting

Capital budgeting is used to analyze investments in assets that will be used to generate revenues, such as machines to make sport products and equipment to provide a food service at games. It's used for *make-or-buy*, *fix-or-replace*, *upgrade-replacement*, and *rent/lease-or-buy* decisions. Building a new stadium is a major capital budgeting decision for any NFL or MLB team. The break-even approach calculates the number of years it will take to pay back the initial cash investment. Another technique that is useful when yearly returns of various alternatives differ is the average rate of return. Discounted cash flow takes into account the time value of money because the value of a dollar you get today is higher than that of a dollar you will get in the future through a capital expenditure.

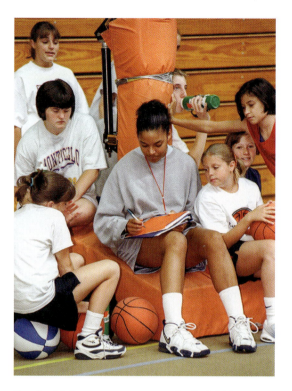

Small athletic programs may make their hiring decisions based on the most feasible option, such as hiring a less-experienced coach from a pool of former athletes or staff that they know and trust.

### Queuing Theory

This technique addresses waiting time. Using too many employees to wait on customers or fans is an inefficient use of resources and is costly. Too few employees providing service can also be costly if poor service drives customers away. Queuing theory helps organizations to balance these two costs. Event managers use queuing theory to determine the optimum number of ticket takers to reduce customers' waiting time when entering an event or game. Retail Dick's stores use queuing theory to determine the optimum number of checkout clerks, and Wilson Sporting Goods production departments use it to schedule equipment maintenance.

### Probability Theory

Analysts use probability theory to help managers make decisions in risky environmental conditions. A probability for the chance of success or failure is assigned to each alternative. Expected value, which is the payoff or profit from each combination of alternatives and outcomes, is then calculated. Usually done on a payoff matrix or decision tree, the assigned probability of

**TIME-OUT 9** Choose two or three decisions of various importance facing your team, and decide whether break-even analysis, capital budgeting, queuing theory, or probability theory is an appropriate technique to use in your decision process.

the outcome is multiplied by the assigned benefit or cost. It is commonly used to determine whether and how much to expand sport facilities to select the most profitable use of finances or to determine inventory levels. On a simple level, like some coaches and fans, have you ever assigned a probability to the outcome of an athletic competition?

## APPLYING THE CONCEPT 3.4

### Selecting a Quantitative Technique

Choose the appropriate technique to use in each situation:

a. break-even analysis

b. capital budgeting

c. queuing theory

d. probability theory

_____ 16. Claudia needs to repair the swimming pool's filtering system or replace it with a new one.

_____ 17. Ben is investing money for the team.

_____ 18. Employees at a sporting goods store sometimes hang around with nothing to do, and at other times they work for hours without stopping.

_____ 19. A bicycle shop owner wants to know how many times a bike must be rented out to make it worth purchasing.

_____ 20. Fans had to wait so long in the ticket line that they missed most of the first quarter of the game.

### Big Data

*Big data* is the analysis of large amounts of quantified facts to aid in maximizing decision making; data scientists are in demand.[59] Big data is commonly calculated through algorithms using software programs. The use of big data will continue to increase;[60] it reveals patterns and opportunities that 99 percent of managers would not capitalize on.[61] Big data is being used in all industries.[62] Organizations using big data can make faster decisions and more profits than companies that don't use big data.[63]

Sport managers must use big data,[64] for whoever has the data and uses it correctly wins today.[65] Organizations are adding math departments to provide the big data to coaches and managers and to the operations, marketing, accounting/finance, and other functional departments.[66] When you are online, do you receive ads for products you bought in the past or are likely to buy, or ads to reorder? That's big data.

## Cost–Benefit Analysis

Cost–benefit analysis and intuition are more subjective than quantitative analysis, but the two types of analysis are commonly used together. Quantitative methods objectively compare alternatives using mathematical techniques. But no technique is ever completely objective; each method has to start with underlying assumptions that are, by their very nature, subjective. Even with the use of mathematical techniques, managers tend to use at least some intuition when judging alternatives. So decision making is not a simple choice between data and gut analysis;[67] data and intuition are commonly used together.[68] Managers who understand big data and how to use it will make the best gut decisions.[69]

As effective as mathematical techniques are, circumstances don't always allow their use, but data use can enhance intuition.[70] Sometimes it is impossible to assign a probability to a benefit received for a cost. How much is a human life worth, and how do you place a number on getting an athlete off drugs? Cost–benefit analysis can combine subjective methods and mathematical techniques to compare alternative courses of action. Also called pros and cons analysis, cost–benefit analysis looks at the advantages (benefits) and the

**FIGURE 3.7** Continuum of analysis techniques.

disadvantages (costs) of each alternative. However, you need to be careful in judging the alternatives, and you must be sure to make evidence-based decisions.[71] Figure 3.7 shows the continuum from quantitative techniques to cost–benefit analysis.

Whichever method you use to analyze alternatives, keep your end goal in mind—that of selecting the optimal alternative that meets the criteria you and your team have established. If none of the alternatives meet the criteria, you have two options: (1) Return to step 2 and change the criteria, or (2) return to step 3 and generate more alternatives. Adidas has changed its criteria for selecting athletes to endorse its footwear. The company has chosen more entertainers such as Kanye West or Pharell. These multifaceted entertainers have helped Adidas to reach consumers outside of the athletic footwear market.

 How accurate do you think general managers can be in deciding which player will become the next marketing superstar?

Every year Adidas needs to generate new endorser alternatives based on new criteria. Traditionally, Adidas would only consider athletes. Adidas still uses athletes such as soccer stars Lionel Messi and Gareth Bale. But it also has "a number of strategic partnerships" with designers, including Yohji Yamamoto and Stella McCartney, and music stars Kanye West, Pharrell Williams, and Rita Ora.[72]

**TIME-OUT 10** Describe a recent decision in your organization in which cost–benefit analysis would have been particularly appropriate, and lay out a few of its pros and cons.

## Step 5: Implement the Decision

Decisions can be made but not implemented successfully.[73] Have you ever made a New Year's resolution, like to lose weight, but didn't succeed? Why? A key reason is not developing a detailed plan to achieve your objective. So once you make a decision, you need to commit to meeting the objective and developing a plan to achieve it.[74]

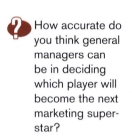 Judging from Adidas' results with its Taylor-Made clubs, do you think the implementation went smoothly?

Your plan of action should include a schedule for implementation. You also need to get the necessary resources[75] and coordinate them with your current resources to implement the plan that will achieve the objective.[76] We examine the details of planning in chapter 4. Communicating the plan to all employees is also critical. (We discuss effective communication in chapter 10.) Delegating (discussed in chapter 5) is also key to smooth implementation. You may need multiple implementation plans. Adidas, for example, developed a plan to sell TaylorMade golf clubs, a plan to advertise them, and a plan to distribute the clubs at the retail level.

## Step 6: Control the Results

Control methods should be developed as part of your plan.[77] Establish checkpoints to monitor progress to determine whether the chosen alternative is solving the problem. If not, consider corrective action.[78] You will learn how to control in chapters 13 and 14. More important, if the implementation continues to go poorly, don't remain with your decision—that is, change your tack. For example, if a team is losing, it often tries different plays and players in various positions to score and win.

If you are off track to achieve your objective, you don't want to give up too soon and miss it, but you also don't want to be a victim of the *escalation of commitment*[79]—not admitting to having made a bad decision and staying too long with a plan that is not working.[80] We all face *loss aversion*, the feeling that the pain of losing would be greater than the joy of winning. Do you have a tendency to stay with a plan, even when you get bad news, by wasting more resources and throwing good money after bad?[81] Why? Is it because you don't like to lose and don't want to admit that your plan is not effective at meeting the objective, even to yourself? Do you know anyone who will never admit to making a mistake?

When you make a poor decision, admit it, and quickly change plans to take corrective action. You may need to go back to prior steps in the decision-making model. You also need to learn from your mistakes so that you don't repeat them. The good news is that poor decisions and failure can often be rectified[82] and may even lead to greater success.[83] Sometimes taking the star player out of the game leads to the substitute contributing to victory.

The following is an example of corrective action in the NFL. The NFL has denied that the league had a problem with player health due to concussions. Sports media such as *ESPN Outside the Lines*, *Sports Illustrated*, and a *PBS Frontline* all reported the NFL was in denial about player concussions. After settling a lawsuit with 4,500 former players, the league has implemented comprehensive corrective actions. The first action is to make the current games safer. The second is to invest in research on brain injuries. The third action is to develop youth football education and training programs.[84]

It will be several years before Adidas managers can determine whether their decision to diversify into new fashion-oriented sneaker markets was a good strategic move. Although moving into TaylorMade golf equipment didn't go as well as planned, the fashion sneaker market appears to have a much stronger fit with Adidas' traditional lines of athletic footwear.

As we bring this chapter to a close, you should understand your decision-making style and how to use the decision-making model when making important nonprogrammed decisions—define the problem, set objectives and criteria, generate alternatives, select the most feasible alternative, implement the decision, and control the results.

## LEARNING AIDS

### CHAPTER SUMMARY

1. **Describe how meeting objectives, solving problems, and making decisions are connected.**

    Managers are responsible for setting and achieving organizational objectives. When managers do not meet objectives, problems result. When problems exist, decisions must be made about what, if any, action must be taken.

2. **Explain how management functions, decision making, and problem solving relate.**

    When managers plan, organize, lead, and control, they make decisions. When managers are not proficient in these functions, they are part of the problem, not part of the solution.

3. **List the six steps in decision making.**

    (1) Define the problem or opportunity, (2) set objectives and criteria, (3) generate alternatives, (4) select the most feasible alternative, (5) implement the decision, and (6) control the results.

4. **Identify programmed and nonprogrammed decisions, and recognize certain, risky, and uncertain business conditions.**

Programmed and nonprogrammed decisions differ in how often they recur, whether they are routine, and their level of significance. Nonprogrammed decisions are nonrecurring, nonroutine, highly significant decisions. Programmed decisions are recurring, routine, and less significant decisions.

Decisions are made in environmental conditions that are certain (you know the outcome of each alternative), risky (you can assign probabilities of success or failure to the outcomes), or highly uncertain (you cannot assign probabilities of success or failure to the outcomes).

5. **Know when to use the different decision models and when to make decisions as a group or as an individual.**

Use the rational model with group decision making when a nonprogrammed decision must be made in high-risk or uncertain conditions. Use the bounded rationality model when you work solo on programmed decisions made in low-risk and certain conditions. Note, however, that this is a general guide; there are always exceptions to the rule.

6. **State the difference between an objective and "must" and "want" criteria.**

An objective is the end result you want from your decision. "Must" criteria are the requirements that an alternative has to meet to be selected. "Want" criteria are desirable but are not absolutely necessary.

7. **Explain how creativity and innovation differ.**

Creativity is a way of thinking that generates new ideas. Innovation is the implementation of new ideas.

8. **Describe the three stages in the creative process.**

The three stages are (1) preparation, (2) incubation (take a break from the problem and let your subconscious work on it) and illumination (recognize when the light bulb goes on), and (3) evaluation (critique your idea to make sure it is a good one).

9. **Explain how quantitative and cost–benefit analyses facilitate selecting alternatives.**

Quantitative analysis uses math to objectively choose the alternative with the highest value. Cost–benefit analysis combines subjective analysis with some math, although alternatives don't necessarily have to be quantified to be compared (as in the pros and cons approach).

## REVIEW AND DISCUSSION QUESTIONS

1. Why are problem solving and decision making important in sports?

2. Why is it necessary to determine the decision structure and the conditions surrounding the decision?

3. Why do organizations use groups to solve problems and make decisions?

4. Which pitfall of group problem solving and decision making is most common?

5. Is a decrease in ticket sales or profits a symptom or a cause of a problem?

6. Would setting a specific maximum price to spend on a cycle exercise machine be an objective or a criterion?

7. Are creativity and innovation really important to a soccer team?

8. We have all made decisions using information that was not timely, high quality, complete, or relevant—we are human, after all. Reflect on a decision your team made with poor information. What was the result?

9. What is the major difference between nominal grouping and consensus mapping?

10. Why are generating alternatives and selecting alternatives separate steps in the decision process?

11. Have you ever used any of the techniques discussed in the text to analyze an alternative? If so, which one? If not, how might you have improved on a recent decision using one of these techniques?

12. Should managers be ethical in their decision making? If so, how should ethics be used in decision making?

13. Have you or anyone you know experienced escalation of commitment to a bad decision? If yes, explain.

## CASES

### Sport Management Professionals @ Work: Christopher Atwood

Christopher Atwood has made many important decisions to help him build his career as a sport information director. Chris started out as an undergraduate student at Springfield College with a bachelor of science degree in communications and sport journalism. He then completed a master of science in sports administration from Marshall University. He was a sports information graduate assistant at Marshall. He was the primary media relations contact for Marshall's volleyball and baseball programs.

Chris became the sport information director at Elms College in 2009. At that time, he really was the SID for all of the sports on campus. He spent five years developing his SID skills at Elms College. He made a tough decision to move to Amherst College as the assistant sport information director.

Chris recently made a life-changing job change by accepting a position as the assistant executive director of the Southern California Intercollegiate Athletic Conference. As Chris said, it was a chance to move from a single college to helping run an entire conference.

### Case Questions

1. Would you be able to take a position as the assistant SID after being the SID at a smaller college?

2. What decisions do you think are part of moving from the West Coast to the East Coast of the United States?

3. Would you rather work for a single college or university or for an entire conference?

4. What conference is your college or university affiliated with in regard to their athletic teams?

### Draft-Day Decision Making

How would you make the decision on what player to pick if you had the number-one NBA draft pick? The 2017 NBA draft posed quite a dilemma for Danny Ainge, the general manager for the Boston Celtics. The Celtics owned the first pick for the first time in 22 years. What decision should Ainge make with such a valuable pick?

*Option 1.* Was Markelle Fultz worth the top draft spot? Recent number-one picks hadn't exactly turned into Michael Jordan, who was picked in round one, number three in 1984 or Stephan Curry, who was round one, number seven in 2009. Markelle was from Washington University, not exactly the most well-known college basketball program. However, the top basketball experts in the country felt he was clearly the best player in the draft. He could play at three levels—shooting three-point shots, taking mid-level jumpers, or driving to the hoop.

*Option 2.* A range of other players also offered skills the Celtics needed to complement their Eastern Division Championship team from the 2016-2017 season. Lorenzo Ball appeared to be determined to go to the Los Angeles Lakers with the second pick since he didn't have any intention of playing on the East Coast. Josh Jackson from Kansas was a shooting forward the Celtics could use to open up the game on the offensive side of the court. Jason Tatum from Duke was also a shooting forward the Celtics were considering to move into their starting lineup. DeArron Fox was a small backcourt player with electric speed, but the Celtics had plenty of guards on their roster.

*Option 3.* The Celtics could decide to trade the top pick for a current star such as Jimmy Butler, who played some outstanding offense and defense against the Celtics in the last year.

*Option 4.* Trade the number-one pick for a lower pick in the draft and a draft pick or two in the future. The Philadelphia 76ers were rumored to be very interested in Fultz. The 76ers were picking number three in the first round. Philly had two number-one picks in the 2018 draft to also toss into the swap of draft positions.

*Option 5.* Focus on free agents. To make the decision more difficult, the Celtics wanted to acquire a top-name free agent or two. The money spent on the number-one pick would mean less money to spend on free agents such as Gordon Haywood, who played for Celtics coach Brad Stevens when they both were at Butler University.

So, what did the Boston Celtics decide? How did the decision turn out?

For current information on the Boston Celtics and to find out whether their draft-day strategy appears to be working, go to www.bostonceltics.com.

Go to the web study guide to answer questions about this case study.

## @ TAKE IT TO THE NET

Please visit www.HumanKinetics.com/AppliedSportManagementSkills and go to this book's companion web study guide, where you will find the following:

A list of websites associated with the concepts in this chapter

Skill-Builder exercises, Sports and Social Media exercises, and a continuing Game Plan for Starting a Sport Business

Online versions of chapter exercises and end-of-chapter learning aids

An exercise that helps you define the Key Terms

# Strategic and Operational Planning

Planning Organizing Leading Controlling Planning Organizing Leading Controlling Planning Organizing Leading Controlling Planning Organizing Leading Controlling Planning Organizing Leading C Controlling Planning Organizing Leading Controlling Planning Organizing Leading Controlling Planning O Leading Controlling Planning Organizing Leading Controlling Planning Organizing Leading Controlling Planning Organizing Leading Controlling Planning Organizing Leading Controlling Planning Organizing Leading Controlling Planning Organizing Leading Controlling Planning Organizing Leading Controlling Planning O Planning Organizing Leading Controlling Planning Organizing Leading Controlling Planning Organizing Leading Controlling Planning Organizing Leading Controlling Planning Organizing Leading Controlling Planning Organizing Leading Controlling Planning Organizing Leading Controlling Planning Organizing Leading Controlling Planning Organizing Leading Controlling Planning Organizing Leading Controlling Planning O

## LEARNING OUTCOMES

After studying this chapter, you should be able to

1. explain how strategic and operational plans differ;

2. describe the differences between corporate-, business-, and functional-level strategies;

3. explain why organizations analyze industries and competitive situations;

4. explain why organizations analyze the company situation;

5. discuss how goals and objectives are similar but not the same;

6. describe how to write objectives;

7. describe the four corporate-level grand strategies;

8. describe the three growth strategies;

9. discuss the three business-level adaptive strategies; and

10. list the four functional-level operational strategies.

## KEY TERMS

strategic planning

operational planning

strategic process

strategy

three levels of strategies

situation analysis

SWOT analysis

competitive advantage

goals

objectives

management by objectives
(MBO)

grand strategies

corporate growth strategies

merger

acquisition

business portfolio analysis

adaptive strategies

operational strategies

## DEVELOPING YOUR SKILLS

Effective managers develop sound strategic plans and set achievable objectives. Does the organization you work for or play for have a plan? What are the objectives it intends to achieve this year? in two years? in five years? In this chapter, by following the steps in the strategic process, you can improve your strategic planning skills. At the more personal level, follow the steps of the writing objectives model to develop effective objectives for your personal, sport, and professional lives.

## REVIEWING THEIR GAME PLAN

### Building the House of FIFA

Whole regions, peoples, and nations across the globe share neither mores, culture, language, nor religion, but they do share a passion—football. Not to be confused with American-style football, football (soccer to Americans) is not only the world's number-one game but is also a major player in international commerce and politics. With more than 200 million active players, the game also constitutes a substantial chunk of the global leisure industry. Whole nations (from Yemen to Germany to Brazil to South Korea and Japan) dream about winning the World Cup, and their citizens pay money (and lots of it!) to travel to see matches, to see them at home, to wear shoes like those of their favorite players (whose status makes that of movie stars pale in comparison), and to buy numerous football products.

FIFA (Fédération Internationale de Football Association) is one reason for the world's love affair with football. Founded in Paris in 1904, it has survived the turmoil of two world wars and today includes over 200 member organizations, making it the biggest and most popular sport federation in the world.

In 1998, at the 51st FIFA Ordinary Congress in Paris, Joseph Blatter (Switzerland) succeeded João Havelange (Brazil) as the eighth FIFA president. This victory elevated Blatter, who had served FIFA in various positions for 23 years, to the highest position on the international football stage. Blatter was viewed as a versatile and experienced proponent of international sport diplomacy (this is crucial with a global sport like soccer) who was totally committed to serving football, FIFA, and the world's youth.

With the new president came a fresh strategic approach to issues facing world football. Blatter lost no time in presenting his vision of FIFA's future priorities, and he worked tirelessly to win widespread approval in FIFA's Congress and Executive Committee. His vision was wide ranging and ambitious and included the following:

- FIFA's Goal Program, which seeks to educate and support national associations by providing aid for special projects to further develop football within countries.
- FIFA's Quality Concept initiative, whose goal is to improve the actual football (soccer ball).
- Development of coaching, refereeing, and administration courses to help national football associations. Special emphasis was placed on the need for football associations to have proper communication and good media relations—otherwise known as marketing and event planning.
- An aggressive stance against player doping. An ethical code against doping was developed. The last three World Cups have been dope free and a real success story after years of players with doping problems.

However, President Blatter was barely reelected as president of FIFA in June 2011. Preceding the elections, there were allegations of payoffs before the vote on host countries for the 2018 and the 2022 World Cup games. The payoffs were to influence the voting on site selections for those tournaments. Ultimately, the decision was to hold the 2018 World Cup games in Russia and the 2022 World Cup games in Qatar.[1]

Blatter was accused of making poorly worded remarks about some of the biggest issues that FIFA faces. He offended female players by saying they should dress in a more feminine way, as they do in volleyball, if they want to increase the popularity of the sport. He also offended LGBT (lesbian, gay, bisexual, and transgender) people by saying they should refrain from sexual activities during the 2022 World Cup games in Qatar, where homosexuality is illegal.[2]

By 2015, Blatter and Michel Platini were banned from FIFA for eight years for an illegal payment authorized by Blatter to Platini. FIFA has since reduced the punishment to six years for both former FIFA leaders. Platini's ban has since been further reduced to four years by the Court of Arbitration for Sport.[3]

The current FIFA president is Gianni Infantino. Unfortunately, he was recently investigated by the ethics committee, but he was cleared after an investigation into his expenses.[4] So the question remains, can FIFA develop a strategy to continue the growth of the game of football while developing leaders who exhibit ethical behavior?

For current information on FIFA, visit www.fifa.com.

# An Overview of Strategic and Operational Planning

Strategic leadership and planning are major determinants of organizational performance.[5] There is a relationship between formal plans and team performance.[6] Planning is one of the most important tasks managers do, and it is crucial today. Planning has three major benefits: speedier decision making, better management of resources, and clearer identification of the action steps needed to reach important goals. The North American Society for Sport Management (NASSM) expects sport management students to learn how to plan.[7]

◀ **LEARNING OUTCOME 1**

Explain how strategic and operational plans differ.

Top-level management and the board of directors have the primary responsibility for strategic planning. Sport governance is the responsibility for the overall direction of sport organizations. National organizations, such as the United States Olympic Committee (USOC), state high school athletic associations, and professional sport teams need to provide direction to their organizations. Strategic development is a key component of corporate governance. One key issue is that CEOs need to work closely with their boards of directors to make sure that important strategic goals are reached.

However, poor planning of the use of organizational resources can lead to failure. If you fail to plan, you plan to fail. A prime example is the now-defunct XFL, which was

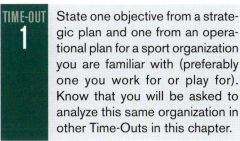

TIME-OUT
1
State one objective from a strategic plan and one from an operational plan for a sport organization you are familiar with (preferably one you work for or play for). Know that you will be asked to analyze this same organization in other Time-Outs in this chapter.

the World Wrestling Federation's attempt to develop a new professional football league. The XFL failed to assess the control that the NFL has over player talent. Although the XFL was able to secure some television coverage, the quality of the players and ultimately of the game itself was not high enough to make watching worthwhile. Better planning might have led to creating an alternative football league, such as the Arena Football League (AFL), instead of competing directly against the NFL. The AFL is played indoors on a much shorter field than regular football, and it uses nets on the goalposts to help keep the ball in play. However, after an absence of a few years, the XFL has announced the league will return to the playing field in 2020. The WWE founder and president of the XFL, Vince McMahon, has stated the new XFL will feature shorter, faster-paced games that are family oriented and easier to understand. Player safety will be a main consideration in all decisions.[8]

Although planning alone won't secure the success of new ventures, planning increases their likelihood of survival.[9] Good planning is based on conceptual and decision-making skills. Before we examine the planning process and the various levels of strategic planning, complete Self-Assessment 4.1 to determine how well you plan.

## SELF-ASSESSMENT 4.1

## Are You an Effective Planner?

Indicate how well each statement describes your behavior by placing a number from 1 to 5 on the line before the statement.

1 = not very descriptive of me

2 = somewhat descriptive of me

3 = neutral

4 = descriptive of me

5 = very descriptive of me

_____ 1. I have a specific end result to accomplish whenever I start a project of any kind.

_____ 2. When setting objectives, I state only the end result; I don't specify how the result will be accomplished.

_____ 3. I have specific and measurable objectives; for example, I know the specific grade I want to earn in this course.

_____ 4. I set objectives that are difficult but achievable.

_____ 5. I set deadlines when I have something I need to accomplish, and I meet the deadlines.

_____ 6. I have a long-term goal (what I will be doing in three to five years) and short-term objectives to get me there.

_____ 7. I have written objectives stating what I want to accomplish.

_____ 8. I know my strengths and weaknesses, am aware of threats, and seek opportunities.

_____ 9. I analyze a problem and alternative actions rather than immediately jumping right in with a solution.

_____ 10. I spend most of my day doing what I plan to do rather than dealing with emergencies and trying to get organized.

_____ 11. I use a calendar, appointment book, or some form of to-do list.

_____ 12. I ask others for advice.

_____ 13. I follow appropriate policies, procedures, and rules.

_____ 14. I develop contingency plans in case my plans do not work out as I expect.

_____ 15. I implement my plans and determine whether or not I have met my objectives.

Add up the numbers you assigned to the statements to see where you fall on the following continuum.

| Effective planner | | | | | Ineffective planner | |
|---|---|---|---|---|---|---|
| 75 | 65 | 55 | 45 | 35 | 25 | 15 |

Don't be too disappointed if your score isn't as high as you would like. All of these items are characteristics of effective planning. Review the items that did not characterize you. After studying this chapter and doing the exercises, you can improve your planning skills.

# Strategic Process

In **strategic planning**, management develops a mission and long-term objectives and determines in advance how they will be accomplished. Long-term generally means longer than a year. In **operational planning**, management sets short-term objectives and determines in advance how they will be accomplished. Short-term objectives are those that can be met in a year or less. Much of team management is evolving from a focus on winning as a means of realizing short-term profits to a focus on strategic management of the team brand as a means of realizing long-term appreciation in franchise value.

Strategic planning and operational planning differ primarily by time frame and by the management level involved. Strategic plans are typically developed for five years and are reviewed and revised every year so that the organization always has a five-year plan.[10] Ferrari developed a five-year strategy to increase sales.[11] Top-level managers develop strategic plans. Operational plans are developed for time frames of one year or less; middle managers or first-line managers develop operational plans.

The strategic process is about developing both the long-range and short-range plans that will enable the organization to accomplish its long-range objectives. If we use the means and ends analysis (chapter 2), top managers determine the ends, and middle- and lower-level managers find the means to accomplish the ends. Hosting major sport events requires long-term strategic plans that are well coordinated with short-term plans. The investments must fit into the city's long-term plan to make the event economically successful. The Olympic Games require extensive long- and short-term planning by the IOC and the cooperation of the host country and city.

In the **strategic process**, managers (1) develop the mission, (2) analyze the environment, (3) set objectives, (4) develop strategies, and (5) implement and control the strategies. Developing strategies takes place at three levels. As you can see from figure 4.1, the process is not a linear one. Managers continually return to previous steps and make changes—planning is an ongoing process. Also note that management performs the four management functions—planning, organizing, leading, and controlling—in the strategic process.

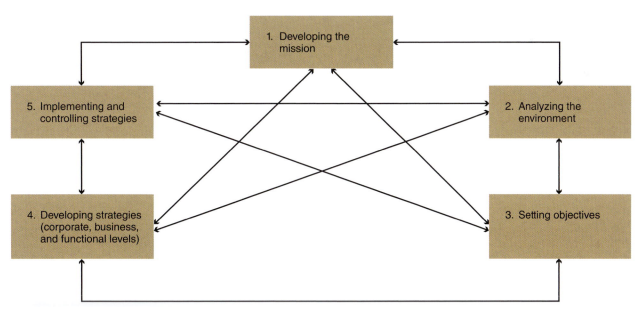

**FIGURE 4.1**   The strategic process.

## Levels of Strategies

An organization's **strategy** is its plan for pursuing its mission and achieving its objectives. The **three levels of strategies** are corporate, business, and functional. We examine these three levels in more detail later in this chapter. Here we simply define them to give you an overview.

Corporate-level strategy is the organization's plan for managing multiple lines of businesses. Many large companies are actually several businesses. Adidas, for example, sells footwear, golf equipment, and cycling products—the company treats each product line as a separate line of business.

Business-level strategy is the organization's plan for managing one line of business. Each of Adidas' businesses has its own strategy for competing in its market. In fitness, Reebok's aim is to be the leading performance fitness footwear in the world in terms of sales and profitability. Reebok has made significant gains in the fitness market by sponsoring CrossFit programs. For example, the best CrossFit athletes in the world come together to compete for the titles of Fittest Man and Fittest Woman on Earth at the Reebok CrossFit Games.[12]

Functional-level strategy is the organization's plan for managing one area of the business. Functional areas include marketing, finance and accounting, operations and production, human resources, and others, depending on the specific line of business. Managers in each of Adidas' business lines are involved with these functional areas. For example, Reebok has combined product marketing, brand communication, and retail marketing into one fully integrated global marketing team. Reebok has used Instagram, Twitter, and Facebook to make sure Reebok is well known in the CrossFit market. Reebok has been the main marketing sponsor for CrossFit for the last eight years. CrossFit exercises include tire flipping, box jumps, pull-ups, and weightlifting, among many other rugged exercises.[13] Figure 4.2 shows the relationships between corporate-, business-, and functional-level strategies.

> **TIME-OUT 2** List the lines of business your organization is involved in.

## Development of the Mission

Developing the organization's mission is the first step in the strategic process. The mission provides the foundation on which the plan, via the four remaining steps, will be constructed. The organization's mission, as noted in chapter 2, defines who the organization is and why it exists. The mission describes management's vision (which may be a separate statement) for the company—where the company is headed and why. FIFA's mission is stated as "Using a number of guiding principles but also concrete and measurable objectives, FIFA's new

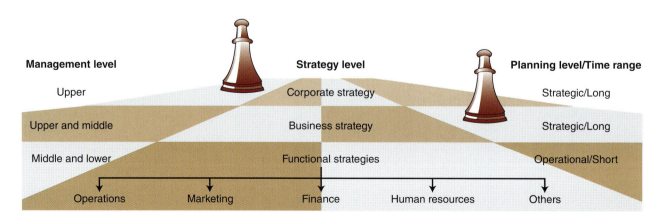

**FIGURE 4.2** Strategic planning.

vision as stated in FIFA 2.0 is to promote the game of football, protect its integrity and bring the game to all."[14]

 Name three ways FIFA is fulfilling its mission and three areas in which it could improve.

The field of sport management is monitored by NASSM. NASSM's mission is to be actively involved in supporting and assisting professionals working in the fields of sport, leisure, and recreation. The purpose of NASSM is to promote, stimulate, and encourage study, research, scholarly writing, and professional development in the area of sport management—both theoretical and applied aspects.[15] NASSM membership has increased significantly over the years, which is a sign that it is achieving its mission of helping members interested in sport management. NASSM has a strategic plan, which its members continue to discuss and update.

# Analysis of the Environment

To create value, a strategy must fit with the capabilities of the firm and its external environment.[16] The organization's internal and external environmental factors (chapter 2) are analyzed as step 2 in the strategic process, which determines the fit. Another term for analyzing the environment is situation analysis. A **situation analysis** draws out those features in a company's environment that most directly frame its strategic window of options and opportunities. The situation analysis has three parts: analysis of the company's industry and its competition, analysis of the company's particular situation, and analysis of the company's competitive advantage (or lack thereof). Companies with multiple lines of business conduct environmental analyses for each line of business.

## Industry Analysis and Five Competitive Forces

Industries vary widely in their business makeup, competitive situation, and growth potential. Different sport management strategies are needed in different areas. To determine whether an industry is worth entering requires answers to such questions as, How large is the market? What is the growth rate? How many competitors are there? Thus, competitive analysis is important to strategic planning. Callaway Golf Company, for example, faces strong competition from Acushnet (Titleist brand), Adams Golf (Tight Lies Fairway Woods), TaylorMade, and Orlimar (TriMetal Fairway Woods).

**◀ LEARNING OUTCOME 3**
Explain why organizations analyze industries and competitive situations.

Michael Porter uses the idea of five competitive forces to analyze the competitive environment.[17] Following is a list of the five forces; see figure 4.3 for Nike's five-force competitive analysis.

- Rivalry between competing firms
- Potential development of substitute products and services
- Potential entry of new competitors
- Bargaining power of suppliers
- Bargaining power of consumers

Companies use analyses of the industry and their competitors primarily at the corporate level when they are deciding which lines of business they should consider entering (or exiting) and how to allocate resources between their product lines. (We will return to this topic later in the chapter.) Nike bought Bauer, a hockey equipment manufacturer, because the company decided that this was an attractive industry.

 **TIME-OUT 3** Using figure 4.3 as a guide, do a simple five-forces competitive analysis for your organization.

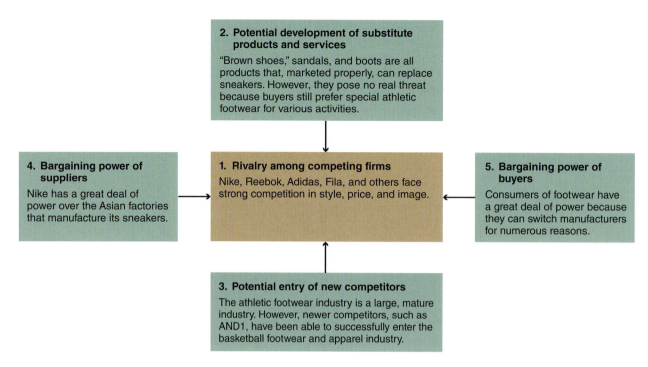

**2. Potential development of substitute products and services**

"Brown shoes," sandals, and boots are all products that, marketed properly, can replace sneakers. However, they pose no real threat because buyers still prefer special athletic footwear for various activities.

**4. Bargaining power of suppliers**

Nike has a great deal of power over the Asian factories that manufacture its sneakers.

**1. Rivalry among competing firms**

Nike, Reebok, Adidas, Fila, and others face strong competition in style, price, and image.

**5. Bargaining power of buyers**

Consumers of footwear have a great deal of power because they can switch manufacturers for numerous reasons.

**3. Potential entry of new competitors**

The athletic footwear industry is a large, mature industry. However, newer competitors, such as AND1, have been able to successfully enter the basketball footwear and apparel industry.

**FIGURE 4.3**   Nike's five-forces competitive analysis.

## Analysis of the Company Situation

**LEARNING OUTCOME 4** ▶

Explain why organizations analyze the company situation.

Managers use analyses of the company situation when they develop business strategies and when they determine which issues need to be addressed in the next three steps of the strategic process. A complete company situation analysis has five steps, as shown in figure 4.4.

- *Step 1: Assess present strategy.* This assessment can be a simple comparison or a complex analysis of performance measures (wins, championships, attendance, market share, sales, net profit, and so on) over the past five years.

❓ How would you expect Gianni Infantino would have assessed FIFA when he became the president of the association?

- *Step 2: Analyze SWOTs.* A highly recommended strategic tool,[18] **SWOT** (**S**trengths, **W**eaknesses, **O**pportunities, **T**hreats) **analysis** is used to assess strengths and weaknesses in an organization's internal environment and opportunities in its external environment. (See chapter 2 for a discussion of internal and external environments.) SWOT helps you know how the firm is doing.[19] The sidebar "Nike's Company Situation Analysis" includes a SWOT analysis.

- *Step 3: Assess competitive strength.* For a strategy to be effective, it must be based on a clear understanding of competitors. Management should always be wondering, What are we missing in the marketplace? Did Nike miss the emergence of fitness and CrossFit-type programs that Adidas and Reebok capitalized upon? Did Nike miss entering the performance

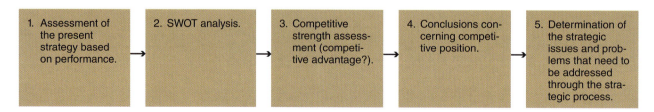

1. Assessment of the present strategy based on performance.

2. SWOT analysis.

3. Competitive strength assessment (competitive advantage?).

4. Conclusions concerning competitive position.

5. Determination of the strategic issues and problems that need to be addressed through the strategic process.

**FIGURE 4.4**   Steps in the analysis of the company situation.

wear market that Under Armour did so well in creating a whole new line of sporting apparel? Skechers went from a marginal fashion footwear company to having comfortable shoes with memory foam endorsed by Sugar Robinson, Rob Lowe, and Brooke Burke-Charvet. This has helped the Skechers stock price increase quite significantly.[20]

Looking at critical success factors can help improve a company's assessment of its competition. Critical success factors (CSFs) are pivotal activities that the business must perform well if it is to win its race. It is imperative that management compare its CSFs for each product line to those of each of its major competitors. This takes a great deal of business acumen and objectivity. Organizations typically use one of two approaches. The first (and simpler) approach rates each CSF from 1 (weak) to 10 (strong) and tallies the ratings to rank competitors. The second approach uses the same rating system but weights the CSFs by importance, with the weighted total equal to 1.00. The weight is multiplied by the rating to get a score for each firm on each factor. Scores are totaled to determine the final rankings. "Nike's Company Situation Analysis" shows weighted CSF rankings for Nike, Under Armour, and Adidas-Reebok.

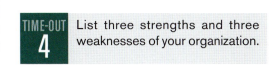
TIME-OUT 4 | List three strengths and three weaknesses of your organization.

- *Step 4: Make conclusions.* The questions here are simple to ask but not always so easy to answer. How is the business doing compared with its competition? Is our market share improving or slipping?

 What issues did Joseph Blatter and FIFA decide to improve on?

- *Step 5: Decide what issues to address.* Using information developed in steps 1 to 4, management now asks, What needs to be done to improve our competitive position?

## Competitive Advantage

Strategic planning helps organizations create a competitive advantage. **Competitive advantage** specifies how the organization offers unique customer value. It identifies, What makes us different from and better than the competition?[22] and Why should a person buy our product or service rather than the competition's?[23] A sustainable competitive advantage[24] (1) distinguishes the organization from its competitors, (2) provides positive economic benefits, and (3) cannot be readily duplicated. The key to producing sustainable competitive advantage is effective management of people.[25] In athletics, a team is only as good as its players and their teamwork. Many organizations focus on quality as a means to beat the competition.

If you ever consider starting your own business, be sure to answer these questions: "What will make my business different from the competition? Why should a person buy my product or service rather than the competition's?" If you don't have answers to these crucial questions, go back to the drawing board! Why? Because your business is very likely to join the ranks of failed businesses, those that don't have a competitive advantage and don't have a strategic plan for developing one.[26] The Self-Assessment later in the chapter will help you determine whether you have what it takes to be a successful entrepreneur, and in the exercise you will develop a strategic plan for a new business.

Finding core competencies and benchmarking go hand in hand with developing competitive advantage. A *core competency* is what a firm does well—in other words, its strengths. Management that focuses on core competencies can create new products and services that take advantage of the company's strengths. Through *benchmarking*, you compare your firm with its competitors, as was done in the situational analysis. You also copy others' successful strategies.

TIME-OUT 5 | Describe your organization's competitive advantage. If you don't think it has one, state how it resembles its competitors in its products or services.

## Nike's Company Situation Analysis

### Present Strategy Assessment

Nike's present strategy is working well. Nike is profitable and continues to be the leading company in the sport footwear and apparel industry. However, finding new ways to grow the footwear business is difficult because Nike already has such a large percentage of the footwear market. Increasing sales globally will be important—that is, trying to lessen the importance of the North American market. Nike's stock price has been steady, but not spectacular, in the $50 to $60 range.

So far, the company has been able to hold off strong competitors such as the merged Adidas–Reebok combination. But growth in areas such as golf could be harder to achieve since Tiger Woods, the centerpiece of Nike golf sales, is starting to use more TaylorMade woods to help revitalize his golf career. Tiger will still represent Nike golf apparel, but it appears he will become more closely affiliated with TaylorMade in the future.[21]

### SWOT Analysis

*Strengths:* Nike's strength is its reputation for high-quality and innovative footwear. Nike is also known for its innovative marketing. Nike ads are part of the pop culture—an impressive achievement. Famous campaigns feature Bo Jackson, Michael Jordan, and Tiger Woods. The Nike "Swoosh" is highly recognizable worldwide. Nike's recent comeback has been greatly helped by increased sales of Nike apparel. Nike+ works with Apple products to help runners calculate their distance and speed. NIKEiD allows customers to design their own footwear.

*Weaknesses:* Tiger Woods' personal troubles off the golf course and his lack of winning on the golf course threaten to slow down Nike's gain in market share in the golf industry. Improved research and development by Adidas-Reebok threatens the perception that Nike is the technology leader in the footwear industry. Another area of some concern is that global sales, for example in Europe and Asia, have increased at a much faster pace than domestic sales in the United States.

*Opportunities:* Nike has an opportunity to capitalize on its own Nike+ technology. This is a sensor placed in Nike footwear that interacts with Apple's iPod to record the distance a runner has completed and the calories that have been burned. Another opportunity will be to capitalize on an endorsement deal with LeBron James after his NBA Playoffs and Championship Series appearances. NIKEiD is a unique website that allows consumers to design their own footwear. It is a fun and creative site that could be further marketed.

*Threats:* The U.S. economy and relations with other countries is a bit rocky while President Donald Trump is in the White House. Competitors such as Under Armour and Adidas-Reebok have been able to secure contracts with colleges, the NBA, the NFL, and the NHL for their apparel businesses. Younger target segments often prefer video games, such as the Madden games, instead of watching or attending the real games. These consumers will prefer to use more technology-oriented products as advances are made to shrink technology that athletes can wear while playing their sport. Nike needs to be seen as a sport-related product that also includes high technology.

# Setting of Objectives

Setting objectives is the third step in the strategic process. Individuals, teams, and organizations need goals to be successful. For strategies to succeed, management must commit to a carefully thought-out set of objectives. The idea is to set objectives that are compatible with the mission and that address strategic issues identified in the situation analysis. Objectives are then prioritized so that the organization can focus on the more important ones. (In chapter 5 you will learn how to prioritize.)

Objectives are end results that you wish to attain—they do not tell others how to achieve them. Therefore, setting objectives is just the beginning of your task because you need to develop plans to achieve your objectives. That is also why you need to know the difference

## Competitive Strength Assessment

As illustrated in table 4.1, each factor is rated on a weighted scale (rating 1 [low] to 10 [high] for each firm—rating × weight). Quality is determined to be the most important criterion, with a weight of 0.50, followed by marketing and price at a weight of 0.25 each. In terms of quality, Nike, Under Armour, and Adidas all have a perfect score of 10: 10 multiplied by the weight of 0.50 equals a score of 5.0. Thus, all three companies have superior-quality products. Overall, Nike is the strongest company at 9.50, followed by Adidas at 9.25; Under Armour is a 9.00. Scores are determined by executives at the companies, students in a class, or (in this case) authors. Scoring is based on completing a SWOT and should foster debate. The authors lowered the score for Nike's marketing since it really hasn't been unique since Michael Jordan retired and Tiger Woods failed to win any major golf tournaments.

**TABLE 4.1   Nike's Company Situation Analysis**

| Critical success factors | Weight | Nike | Under Armour | Adidas-Reebok |
|---|---|---|---|---|
| Quality | 0.50 | 10 = 5.0 | 10 = 5.0 | 10 = 5.0 |
| Marketing | 0.25 | 9 = 2.25 | 8 = 2.0 | 8 = 2.0 |
| Price | 0.25 | 9 = 2.25 | 8 = 2.0 | 9 = 2.25 |
| | 1.00 | 9.50 | 9.00 | 9.25 |

## Conclusions About Competitive Advantage

Nike's advantage lies in name recognition and quality image in many different markets. The Nike name and Swoosh logo continue to be worldwide status symbols.

Nike is the leading (and hence strongest) competitor and will remain so through continual improvement of the technology used in its footwear, equipment, and apparel lines. Continued growth in these divisions will be supported by new and creative marketing campaigns. However, Nike needs to monitor the success of the recent merger of Adidas and Reebok, which created a competitor nearly as large as itself. Reebok has relaunched its brand to help capture the fitness and CrossFit markets. At the same time, Nike needs to shift market share in the high-performance athletic apparel market away from Under Armour. Nike is a latecomer to this market, so gaining an edge here might take longer than Nike expects.

## Determination of Strategic Issues

Nike needs to focus on (1) improving U.S. footwear sales, (2) continuing to increase international sales, (3) building U.S. sales in its high-performance athletic apparel, (4) continuing to monitor the product desires of each new generation, and (5) improving the sustainability of the environment as a source of innovation and growth for the company.

between goals and objectives, how to write objectives, criteria for effective objectives, and the concept of management by objectives (MBO), all of which we examine in the following discussion.

# Determining Goals and Objectives

Some people use the terms *goals* and *objectives* synonymously. This is not a good idea. Precise language makes for precision thinking, which of course enhances your ability to accomplish your organization's mission. **Goals** state general targets to hit. **Objectives** state what is to be done in specific and measurable terms by a certain target date. Goals are your target; objectives guide your development of operational plans and help you to know if you are

◀ **LEARNING OUTCOME 5**

Discuss how goals and objectives are similar but not the same.

hitting the target. Goals thus translate into objectives. Likely goals and objectives for Nike's apparel and footwear divisions give a few likely goals for Nike as a whole.

## Writing Objectives

**LEARNING OUTCOME 6** ▶

Describe how to write objectives.

Successful people set goals[27] that they then strive to attain, and they write explicit objectives to help them get there.[28] The writing of the objectives is itself a clarifying and focusing endeavor and is one reason why motivational gurus and career counselors swear by written objectives. If you don't have career objectives, your resolution should be to get some. The Skill-Builders in the web study guide will help get you started. To keep your focus on your end goals, post your objectives on your desk or wall.

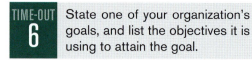

**TIME-OUT 6** State one of your organization's goals, and list the objectives it is using to attain the goal.

Here's a simple and effective way (which we adapted from Max E. Douglas' model) to set objectives.

1. Start with the word *to*:
   To—
2. Attach an action verb—typical ones are *increase, improve, enter, revive* (you get the picture):
   —obtain—
3. Now think of a single, specific result that you want to achieve and that can be measured:
   —a batting average of 300—
4. Choose a target date.
   —during the 2020 season.

This is too simple, you say? What do you think managers do when they write objectives? Table 4.2 shows one of Nike's objectives diagrammed. We'll show you some other examples when we discuss criteria.

### TABLE 4.2  Writing Objectives Model

| To write an objective | Nike's objective |
|---|---|
| 1. Start with *to*. | To |
| 2. Add an action verb. | increase |
| 3. Insert a single, specific, and measurable result. | the sales of eco-friendly footwear by 5% |
| 4. Choose a target date. | by November 2020. |

## Using Criteria to Write Objectives

You've seen one of Nike's objectives diagrammed. Now let's look a little more critically at what makes an objective useful. An objective must lead to a single result that is specific and measurable and must include a target date. These criteria are discussed next.

1. *Single result.* Write each objective so that it describes only one result. Later, you will have the luxury of stating that the objective was met or not met. If your objec-

**TIME-OUT 7** Using the guidelines given here, write one objective that your organization should pursue.

tive involves multiple possible results, you're going to sound wishy-washy and apologetic when you are reduced to saying that the objective was partially met, somewhat but not quite met, or almost met. Because there is nothing like an example to drive home a point, let's look at the objectives written by OB Iffy and OB Sharp, two young floating managers who work for various organizations.

**OB Iffy:** To increase sales by 25 percent and to achieve a 5.4 percent market share.

**(What if Iffy meets one goal but not the other—is this objective met or not met? Also, sales of what? Market share of what? And by when?)**

**OB Sharp:** To increase tennis racket sales by 25 percent by December 31, 2020.

To achieve a 5.4 percent market share of tennis rackets by December 31, 2020.

2. *Specific result.* State the exact level of performance expected. Years ago, research showed that people with specific goals perform better than those with general goals.

**OB Iffy:** To maximize profits in 2020.

**(How much is "maximize"? Is this gross profit or net profit?)**

**OB Sharp:** To earn a net profit of $15 million in 2020.

3. *Measurable result.* If you can't measure your progress, you're going to have trouble determining whether your objective has been met.

**OB Iffy:** Perfect service for every customer.

**(How do you measure perfect service?)**

**OB Sharp:** To attain 90 percent "excellent" in customer satisfaction ratings for year-end 2020.

4. *Target date.* Set a date for accomplishing the objective. Deadlines make all of us focus earlier and try harder.

**OB Iffy:** To achieve attendance of four million fans.

**(For every game? For all time?)**

**OB Sharp:** To achieve attendance of four million fans for the 2020 MLB season.

**OB Iffy but Getting Better:** To double international business to $5 billion annually within five years.

**(Will anyone remember the date five years from now?)**

**OB Sharp:** To double international business to $5 billion annually by year-end 2020.

**OB Sharp:** To keep rejected products to less than 1 percent. (Note: Some objectives are ongoing and therefore do not require a target date.)

In addition to the "must" criteria (a single result that is specific and measurable and has a target date), three "want" criteria will help you achieve objectives: The objective (1) is realistic, (2) is set by the team, and (3) has team commitment. With must criteria, you can read the objective and tell if it meets all the criteria. However, the want criterion of realistic is subjective, and you can't tell by a written objective if it was set by an individual or a team and if the team is committed to achieving it or not. Some people like to set *SMART goals*—Specific, Measurable, Attainable, Realistic, and Timely.

5. *Realistic objective.* People perform at higher levels when they work toward realistic objectives. That is, the objective should be difficult, but it must also be achievable. People do less well when the objective is too difficult (we often don't try or we give up when we believe something is impossible), when the objective is too easy (we just meet the objective and hold back performance), and when the objective is an open-ended, do-your-best

instruction (most people don't do their best but say they did). So set objectives that will challenge you to work hard,[29] but remember to use ethical behavior to achieve the objective to attain the reward for doing so.[30]

6. *Team-set objective.* Work groups that set their own objectives generally outperform groups that are assigned objectives (chapter 3), but we must use the appropriate level of participation for the group's capabilities.

7. *Team commitment to the objective.* A team that commits to an objective will work harder to achieve it. Participation in the decision-making and problem-solving process that usually precedes the setting of an objective is often key in attaining team commitment (see chapter 3).

For a review of these key seven criteria, see figure 4.5. You can tell if the objective must criteria are met (top row) when reading the objective, but you can't tell if the want criteria (bottom row) are met. When putting the criteria together, include team members in setting difficult, realistic objectives that meet the must criteria, and get them to believe they can achieve the objectives; they will then most likely be motivated to commit to and achieve objectives. Get them thinking and believing, "I/we can do it."[31]

## Using Management by Objectives

**Management by objectives (MBO)** is the process by which managers and their teams jointly set objectives, periodically evaluate performance, and reward according to the results. Other names for MBO include work planning and review, goals management, goals and controls, and management by results. There are three steps in the MBO process.

- *Step 1: Set individual objectives and plans.* With each team member, you jointly set objectives. These objectives should meet the seven criteria.

- *Step 2: Give feedback and evaluate performance.* Communication is critical to the success of MBO. Thus, you and team members must meet to review progress. The frequency of monitoring progress and evaluating results depends on the team member and the job performed. However, most managers probably do not conduct enough review sessions.

- *Step 3: Reward according to performance.* Team members' performance should be measured against their objectives. Those who meet their objectives should be rewarded through recognition, praise, pay raises, and promotions.

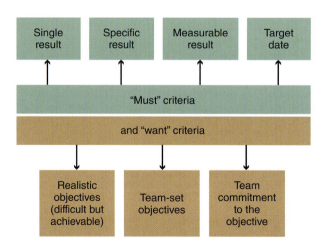

**FIGURE 4.5**   Key criteria for achieving objectives.

Former head football coach Lou Holtz (currently a motivational speaker, author, and ESPN commentator) is known for turning around Arkansas and Minnesota teams and leading the University of South Carolina and the University of Notre Dame to national championships. Holtz is a strong believer in setting objectives, stating that all good performance starts with clear goals. He used MBO to motivate players. Holtz had players set objectives, and then he approved them, reviewed them during the season, gave feedback, and rewarded (primarily with playing time) players who were accomplishing the objectives.[32] Do you have clear, well-written objectives? Skill-Builder 4.1 in the web study guide will help you write objectives using the model.

# Corporate-Level Strategy

After the mission is developed, the environmental analysis is completed, and objectives are set, the organization's strategy (step 4 in the planning process) is developed at the corporate, business, and functional levels. You need to develop a plan to achieve each objective.[33] With a corporate strategy, the parent corporation has subsidiaries or business units (companies within one company), and it allocates and coordinates resources between its different business units. Berkshire Hathaway is the parent of more than 60 companies, including Brooks Sports and Fruit of the Loom,[34] which is the parent company of Russell Athletic, which owns Spalding Sporting Goods and American Athletic.[35] In this section, you will learn about corporate-level strategy: grand strategies, corporate growth strategies, and portfolio analysis.

## Grand Strategies

An organization's **grand strategies** are its corporate strategies for growth, stability, turnaround and retrenchment, or a combination thereof. Each grand strategy has different objectives as described in its strategy.

◀ **LEARNING OUTCOME 7**

Describe the four corporate-level grand strategies.

- *Growth.* Companies with a growth strategy aggressively try to increase their size through increased sales, market share, and fans. We will return to growth strategies in a moment. The sport industry is growing, and many organizations have growth strategies.

- *Stability.* Companies with a stability strategy try to hold and maintain their present size or to grow slowly. Many companies are satisfied with the status quo. Some college and pro teams, such as the MLB Red Sox, virtually sell out every game. With no real growth in ticket sales, they seek to keep fans coming.

- *Turnaround and retrenchment.* A turnaround strategy is an attempt to reverse a declining business as quickly as possible to prior levels. A retrenchment strategy is a reduction in operating size by the divestiture or liquidation of assets and laying off employees. We list them together because most turnarounds involve retrenchment. Turnaround strategies try to improve cash flow by increasing revenues, decreasing costs, and selling assets. Converse, the longtime maker of athletic footwear, tried many turnaround strategies to save that company. In the end, Nike bought Converse in 2003 for $305 million. At the time, Converse had annual sales of just over $200 million. Nike has since returned Converse to profitability and is in the process of opening Converse stores in major U.S. cities. Converse had sales of nearly two billion dollars in 2016.[36]

- *Combination.* A corporation may simultaneously pursue growth, stability, and turnaround and retrenchment across its different lines of business. We discuss this idea in more detail in the business portfolio analysis section.

 **TIME-OUT 8** State your organization's grand strategy.

## Corporate Growth Strategies

**LEARNING OUTCOME 8 ▶**

Describe the three growth strategies.

Companies that want to grow have three major options. **Corporate growth strategies** include concentration, backward and forward integration, and related and unrelated diversification. Figure 4.6 summarizes an organization's choices when its grand strategy is growth.

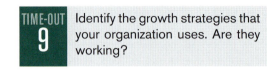

**TIME-OUT 9** Identify the growth strategies that your organization uses. Are they working?

- *Concentrate.* An organization with a concentration strategy grows its existing lines of business aggressively. Dick's Sporting Goods continues to open new stores.

- *Integrate.* An organization with an integration strategy enters *forward* or *backward* lines of business (see figure 4.7). In forward integration, the line of business is closer to the final customer. In backward integration, the line of business is farther away from the final customer. Some manufacturers, including Reebok, open factory stores and fitness centers to forward-integrate; that is, they bypass traditional retail stores and sell their products directly to the customer. Instead of buying rubber for its balls, Spalding could make a backwards integration and buy a rubber producing farm.

- *Diversify.* An organization with a diversification strategy goes into *related* or *unrelated* lines of products. Nike pursued related diversification when it decided to add beach-style sport clothing (Hurley) as a business line. Figure 4.6 summarizes the grand strategies used at the corporate level.

- *Growth strategies include mergers and acquisitions.* Organizations also grow through mergers and acquisitions (M&As). Competing companies sometimes use M&As to compete more effectively with larger companies; to realize economies of size; to cut expenses; and

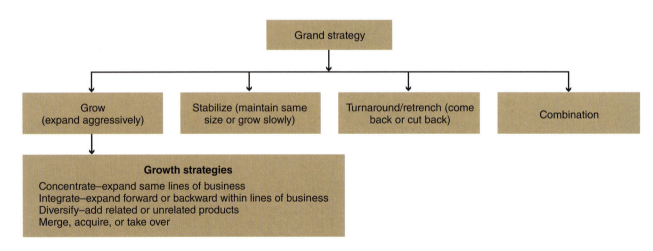

**FIGURE 4.6**  Corporate grand and growth strategies.

**FIGURE 4.7**  Forward and backward integration.

**APPLYING THE CONCEPT 4.1**

## Corporate Growth Strategies

Identify the growth strategy used by each company.

a.  concentration

b.  forward integration

c.  backward integration

d.  related diversification

e.  unrelated diversification

_____  1.  Spalding buys a rubber company to make the rubber it uses in its sneakers.

_____  2.  General Motors buys the Sea World theme park.

_____  3.  Dick's opens a new retail store in Worcester, Massachusetts.

_____  4.  Adidas opens its own retail stores.

_____  5.  Nike buys Bauer Hockey Equipment.

to achieve access to markets, products, technology, resources, and skilled managers. In a **merger**, two companies form one new company. The Canadian Amateur Hockey Association and Hockey Canada merged to form the Canadian Hockey Association. In an **acquisition**, one business buys all or part of another business. Companies also use acquisitions to enter new lines of businesses—it is less risky to buy an established, successful business than it is to start a new one. PepsiCo acquired Quaker Oats to get its sport drink, Gatorade, whereas Coca-Cola started its own POWERADE brand.

When a target company's management rejects an offer to be acquired by another company, the purchasing company can make a bid to the target company's shareholders to acquire it through a *takeover*—these are typically not friendly actions (hence the term *hostile takeover*).

## Business Portfolio Analysis

You are no doubt familiar with the idea of individual investment portfolios. Businesses use the term *portfolio analysis* somewhat differently than would an individual investor. In **business portfolio analysis**, corporations determine which lines of business they will be in and how they will allocate resources between the different lines. As noted, a business line—also called a strategic business unit (SBU)—is a distinct business with its own customers that operates rather independently from its parent corporation. What constitutes an SBU varies from company to company—SBUs are variously divisions, subsidiaries, or single product lines. Adidas has divisions for footwear, cycling equipment, and golf equipment. Corporations use the environmental analysis they perform on each business line (step 2 in the strategic planning process) to analyze their portfolios. Another method, the BCG matrix, places each line of business in one matrix.

### BCG Growth-Share Matrix

One commonly used method for analyzing corporate business portfolios is the Boston Consulting Group's (BCG) growth-share matrix. A BCG matrix for Nike is shown in figure 4.8. The four cells of the matrix are as follows:

1. Cash cows are good-selling products that generate a lot of revenue. They may exhibit low growth, but they have high market share (e.g., Air Jordan sneakers). Cash cows typically use stability strategies since there is no reason to change them. Air Jordans sell very well, even though Michael Jordan has been retired from the NBA for nearly 20 years. Footwear was an $18 billion dollar cash cow for Nike in 2016.

2. Stars are emerging businesses with a rapidly growing market share. The strategy is for a star to eventually gain enough market share to become a cash

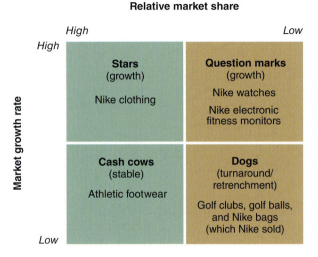

FIGURE 4.8  Nike's BCG matrix.

cow. Nike Apparel is a good example of a star that should become a cash cow. Consumers certainly like to purchase clothing with the Nike swoosh on the front. However, Under Armour taught Nike that new styles and technology can create whole new segments of the apparel industry. Apparel was an $8 billion star for Nike in 2016.

3. Question marks are new lines of business with a low market share in an expanding market that the corporation believes can be grown into stars. The commitment of resources to these lines is, of course, not without risk because question marks can become dogs. One of Nike's question mark product areas is the use of technology in its footwear and apparel—for example, the NIKEiD on-court customization initiative. Nike's endorsers Kobe Bryant, LeBron James, and Kevin Durant have all played using NIKEiD on-court customization. In effect, Nike customers can design their own footwear.[37] But it is yet to be proven that consumers would rather design their own footwear than just buy the latest styles directly from Nike or Foot Locker stores. Equipment was a $1.8 billion business in 2016.[38]

4. Dogs give low returns in low-growth markets, and they have low market share. Therefore, if a turnaround strategy doesn't work, firms often divest or liquidate their dogs. Nike has the largest market share for footwear, around 33 percent in 2016. So products that are dogs are not typical for Nike. However, the company's size can be a hindrance when it must pivot to address new fashion changes. Thus, Nike could consider developing a footwear line such as Tom's Shoes with a mission of giving a pair of shoes to charity for every pair sold. Or it could offer a line of more fashion-oriented footwear to protect its sales from fashion-oriented competitors such as Skechers.

Business portfolio analysis helps corporate-level managers to figure out strategies and the allocation of cash and other resources to its business lines. Managers use profits from cash cows to fund question marks and sometimes stars. Any cash from dogs is also given to question marks and stars, as are any resources from their sale.

## Entrepreneurial Strategy Matrix

The BCG matrix works well with large companies with multiple lines of business. Matthew Sonfield and Robert Lussier developed the entrepreneurial strategy matrix (ESM) for small businesses.[39] Before you read about the matrix, complete Self-Assessment 4.2.

The ESM identifies different combinations of innovation and risk for new ventures and then suggests ways to optimize performance. The matrix answers such questions as "What venture situation am I in?" and "What are the best strategic alternatives for a given venture?"

Innovation is the creation of something new and different. The newer and more different a product or service is, the higher its level of innovation. Risk is the probability of a major financial loss. Entrepreneurs need to determine the chances that their venture will fail and ascertain how serious the financial losses would be. Figure 4.9 shows how the ESM uses a four-cell matrix to assess innovation and risk.

The ESM suggests appropriate strategies for each cell (also shown in figure 4.9). Entrepreneurs use the first part of the matrix to identify which cell their firms are in. Then, based on their cell, they follow the suggested strategies.

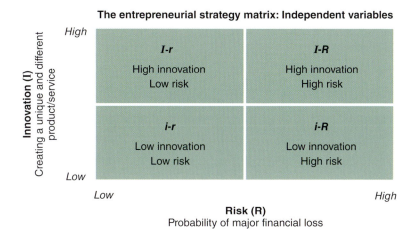

**The entrepreneurial strategy matrix: Independent variables**

Innovation (I): Creating a unique and different product/service

|  | **I-r** | **I-R** |
| High | High innovation / Low risk | High innovation / High risk |
| Low | **i-r** Low innovation / Low risk | **i-R** Low innovation / High risk |

**Risk (R)**
Probability of major financial loss

**The entrepreneurial strategy matrix: Appropriate strategies**

Innovation (I)

**I-r**
- Move quickly
- Protect innovation
- Lock in investment and operating costs via control systems, contracts, etc.

**I-R**
- Reduce risk by lowering investment and operating costs
- Maintain innovation
- Outsource high-investment operations
- Joint venture options

**i-r**
- Defend present position
- Accept limited payback
- Accept limited growth potential

**i-R**
- Increase innovation; develop a competitive advantage
- Reduce risk
- Use a business plan and objective analysis
- Minimize investment
- Reduce financing costs
- Franchise option
- Abandon venture?

**Risk (R)**

**FIGURE 4.9** The entrepreneurial strategy matrix.

Reprinted from *Business Horizon*, Vol. 40, No. 3, May-June, M.C. Sonfield and R.N. Lussier, "The Entrepreneurial Strategy Matrix Model for New and Ongoing Ventures," pgs. 73-77, Copyright 1997, with permission from Elsevier.

## SELF-ASSESSMENT 4.2

# Do You Have Entrepreneurial Traits?

**Objective:**
To assess your entrepreneurial qualities

**Preparation:**
Would you like to be your own boss? Ever thought about operating your own business? This Self-Assessment will help you decide whether you've got what it takes to be a successful entrepreneur.

**Entrepreneurial Qualities**
Select the number on the scale that best describes you.

1 = not very descriptive of me

2 = somewhat descriptive of me

3 = neutral

4 = descriptive of me

5 = very descriptive of me

_____ 1. I have a strong desire to be independent

_____ 2. I enjoy taking reasonable risks

_____ 3. I usually don't make the same mistake twice

_____ 4. I am a self-starter

_____ 5. I seek out competition

_____ 6. I enjoy working long, hard hours

_____ 7. I am confident of my abilities

_____ 8. I need to be the best or the most successful

_____ 9. I have a high energy level

_____ 10. I stand up for my rights

**Scoring**
Add your assessment numbers. Your total score will be between 10 and 50. Place your score on the following continuum.

**Entrepreneurial Qualities:**

| Strong | | | | Weak |
|---|---|---|---|---|
| 50 | 40 | 30 | 20 | 10 |

Generally, the higher your score on this assessment, the better your chances of becoming a successful entrepreneur. Keep in mind, however, that simple self-assessments aren't always good predictors. If you scored low on this scale but you really want to start a business, you can still succeed. You may not have all the qualities that typically mark entrepreneurs, but you can develop them.

# Business-Level Strategy

Each business unit must develop its own strategic plan following the five-step process shown in figure 4.1. Corporate- and business-level strategies for organizations with a single business are the same. So we are still at step 4 of the strategic planning process—developing strategies. Here we discuss adaptive strategies, competitive strategies, and the product life cycle.

## Adaptive Strategies

Because it can be confusing to use similar names for corporate- and business-level strategies, business-level strategies are commonly called adaptive strategies. These correspond to the grand strategies, but their emphasis is on adapting to changes in the external environment. Table 4.3 gives a brief overview of the criteria used to select the three **adaptive strategies**—prospecting, defending, and analyzing. The objectives are different for each adaptive strategy.[40]

◄ LEARNING OUTCOME 9

Discuss the three business-level adaptive strategies.

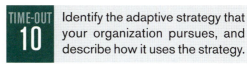

TIME-OUT **10** Identify the adaptive strategy that your organization pursues, and describe how it uses the strategy.

## TABLE 4.3   Choosing an Adaptive Strategy

| Rate of environmental change | Potential growth rate | Adaptive strategy | Corresponding grand strategy |
| --- | --- | --- | --- |
| Fast | High | Prospect | Growth |
| Moderate | Moderate | Analyze | Combination |
| Slow | Low | Defend | Stability |

### *Prospect*

The prospecting strategy calls for aggressively offering new products or entering new markets seeking growth opportunities.[41] Businesses that successfully implement a prospecting strategy tend to be the most successful.[42] Modell's sporting goods continues to open new stores to enter new markets to compete with Dick's.

### *Defend*

Businesses that implement a defensive strategy stay with their current product lines and markets and focus on maintaining or increasing market share. PepsiCo's Gatorade is defending its position as the leading sport drink against the rival Coca-Cola POWERADE brand.

### *Analyze*

The analyzing strategy is in the middle of the continuum between prospecting and defending. Business units that analyze move into new markets cautiously and deliberately, or they seek new opportunities to offer a core product group. Analyzers tend to let the prospectors come out with the new products, and if the products succeed, analyzers will come out with the same products. Coca-Cola and Pepsi were both well aware of Gatorade and analyzed its sales for years. With the growth of sport drinks, they both entered this market.

Although the adaptive strategies model has no turnaround and retrenchment, business units use this model when they cut back or stop sales of dog products. If the firm does not replace its dogs with improved or new question mark products that become stars, it risks going out of business.

## APPLYING THE CONCEPT 4.2

### Adaptive Strategies

Identify the appropriate adaptive strategy for each situation.

a. prospector
b. defender
c. analyzer

_____ 6. Industry leader Gatorade uses a primary strategy in the U.S. sport drink market.

_____ 7. Reebok comes out with a new zipper sneaker to compete with Nike's zipper sneaker.

_____ 8. Dick's Sporting Goods opens restaurants in the state of Washington.

_____ 9. Wilson pioneers a baseball glove that can be folded up and put in your pocket.

_____ 10. Champion develops a strategy when other companies copy its sweatshirts.

# Competitive Strategies

Michael Porter developed three typologies of effective business-level competitive strategies: product differentiation, cost leadership, and focus.[43]

## Product Differentiation

Companies that implement a differentiation strategy stress the advantages of their products over those of their competitors. Nike, Spalding, Reebok, Adidas, and others use their logos in prominent places on their products to differentiate them—indeed, the logos themselves become a selling feature.

## Cost Leadership

Companies that implement cost leadership strategies stress lower prices to attract customers. Walmart sells more brand-name sport and recreation goods than any other company in the world.

## Focus

Companies that implement a focus strategy target a specific regional market, product line, or buyer group. Focusing on a specific target segment or market niche, the business may use a differentiation or cost leadership strategy, but it shouldn't use both. It would be very difficult to compete head-on with *Sports Illustrated* or *Street & Smith's*, but lots of smaller magazines that focus on just one sport are making good profits, as are websites.

# Product Life Cycle

The product life cycle is the series of stages—introduction, growth, maturity, and decline—that a product goes through over its lifetime. The speed at which products go through their life cycle varies. Many products, like an MLB baseball or an NFL football, stay around for many years; however, the products and styles of the merchandise change. Fad products,

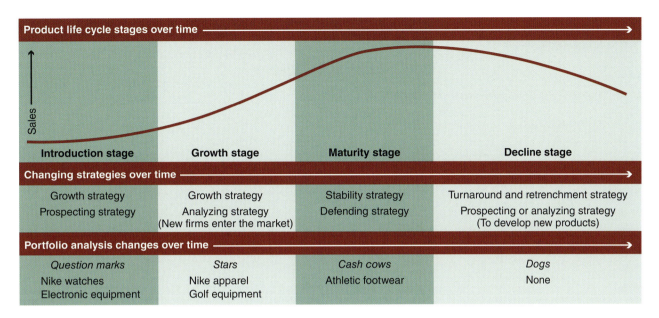

**FIGURE 4.10**  Nike's strategies for products at different life cycle stages.

like golfing products marketed to improve one's score, may last only a few months. Figure 4.10 gives appropriate portfolio analyses, grand strategies, and adaptive strategies for each life cycle stage for various Nike products.

Pricing strategies are important to growing and maintaining market share. They also change over the product's life cycle. Prices typically are higher at the product's introduction because there is little, if any, competition. Prices decline as sales volume increases because economies of scale allow for lower product unit costs, and prices also drop as new competing products appear.

## Introduction

When a new product (a question mark in the business portfolio) is introduced, a prospector company tries to clearly differentiate it while using a focus strategy. That is, the company will focus on getting customers to embrace the product. Resources will be used to promote (advertise) the product and to get production up and running.

## Growth

During the growth stage, sales expand rapidly. When analyzer companies see that a prospector company is doing well, they may try to bring out their own version of the product. Analyzer companies may use differentiation, focus, or cost leadership to gain market share during their product's growth stage. They focus on quality and systems process improvements to achieve economies of scale. They may lower prices, even though this reduces profit per unit, to gain market share.

## Maturity

When a product is mature, sales may grow slowly, level off, and even begin to decline. In a saturated market, the company's strategy changes to one of stability (a defensive strategy). Cost becomes an issue, and cost-cutting efforts are emphasized. Mature products are usually cash cows.

## APPLYING THE CONCEPT 4.3

### Product Life Cycle

Select the life cycle stage of each product.

a. introduction
b. growth
c. maturity
d. decline

_____ 11. Baseball gloves

_____ 12. Racquetball rackets

_____ 13. Baseball caps

_____ 14. Skiing helmets

_____ 15. Recumbent exercise bicycles

### Decline

As the product nears the end of its life cycle, sales decrease. A product can be in decline and remain profitable for many years. In the business' portfolio, aging products are considered dogs and may eventually be divested. The company's strategy must change from that of stabilizer-defender to turnaround and retrenchment and back to prospector and analyzer as the company needs replacement products to stay in business.

Grand strategies and adaptive strategies complement one another. Companies select their strategies based on their mission, the external environment, and their objectives.

 Determine at what stage in the product life cycle FIFA and soccer itself are located.

**TIME-OUT 11** Identify the life cycle stage for one of your organization's products. Is the strategy you identified in Time-Out 10 appropriate for this stage of the product's life cycle? Explain.

## Functional-Level Strategies

**LEARNING OUTCOME 10 ▶**
List the four functional-level operational strategies.

Thus far we have examined long-range strategic planning. We now turn our attention to short-term operational strategies, still within the fourth step of developing strategies. **Operational strategies** are used by every functional-level department—marketing, operations, human resources, and finance, among others—to achieve corporate- and business-level strategy objectives. The primary task of functional-level departments is to develop and implement strategies that achieve the corporate- and business-level missions, strategies, and objectives. These are the operational strategies that functional departments use as they do their work. They include the daily decisions and actions that make or break the team and organization.

In this section, we briefly describe the functional departments—marketing, operations, human resources, finance, and others—and how they are used based on the firm's strategy. You may have already taken (or probably will take) one or more courses devoted to each functional department.

## Marketing Functions

The marketing department's primary responsibility is defining the target market, finding out what the customer wants, and figuring out how to add customer value. This department therefore is responsible for the four Ps—product, promotion, place, and price. The marketing department decides which products to provide, how they will be packaged, how they will be advertised, where they will be sold, how they will get there, and how much they will be sold for.

The sport mass media (such as *Sports Illustrated* and ESPN) have been very influential in promoting sport, and so have TV commercials, athlete endorsements, and venue signage. Brand identity is an important topic in sport that has four categories, or dimensions, of assets: brand awareness, brand loyalty, perceived quality, and brand associations. Companies budget large amounts of money to develop brands that stir excitement and cement customer and fan loyalty. NASCAR hired a public relations agency to reconstruct its brand identity. To gain brand identity, many organizations develop trademark images and slogans like the Puma animal, "Wheaties, the Breakfast of Champions," the Nike swoosh, and "Just Do It!"

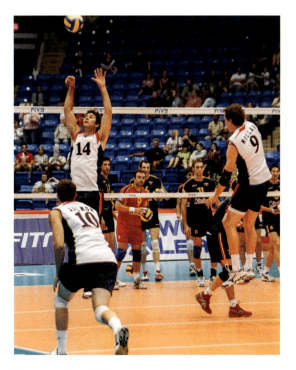

How would marketing, operations, human resources, and finance teams function together to fill this volleyball stadium or market sportswear to the players?

## Operations Functions

The operations (or production) department is responsible for systems processes that convert inputs into outputs (chapter 2). This department focuses on quality and efficiency as it produces the products that marketing determines will provide customer value. We return to the operations function in chapter 13.

## Human Resources Functions

Human resources (HR) departments work with all functional departments to recruit, select, train, evaluate, and compensate employees. HR commonly develops policies, procedures, and rules for the entire organization. We examine human resources more fully in chapter 7.

## Finance Functions

Finance departments perform at least two major functions. (1) They finance business activities by raising money through the sale of stock (equity) or bonds and loans (debt), they decide on the debt-to-equity ratio, and they pay off debt and pay out dividends (if any). (2) They record transactions, develop budgets, and report financial results (the income statement and balance sheet). A third function that finance departments perform in many organizations is optimizing the company's use of its cash reserves—that is, investing the company's cash as a means of making money. In the nonprofit sector, fund-raising is an important source of revenues. We discuss finance in chapter 13.

## APPLYING THE CONCEPT **4.4**

### Functional Strategies

Identify the function described in each statement.

- a. marketing
- b. operations
- c. finance
- d. human resources
- e. other

_____ 16. Cleans up and repairs the arena

_____ 17. Sends out the bills

_____ 18. Transforms inputs into outputs

_____ 19. Decides where the product will be sold

_____ 20. Manages labor relations

---

If the company is a prospector, finance raises money to cover the functional-area budgets, and dividends will be low, if any are paid. If the company is defending its market share, finance pays off debt and also generally pays a dividend. If the company is an analyzer, finance raises money and pays off debt. If the company finds itself in a turnaround situation, finance may try to raise money and sell assets to pay for the comeback. In a retrenchment, finance sells assets but does not typically pay dividends, or it pays very low ones.

 **TIME-OUT 12** Describe the operational strategy of a functional area in your organization.

## Other Functional Areas

Depending on the type of business, any number of other functional departments need strategies to achieve their objectives. One area that varies in importance depending on the nature of the company's business is research and development. Businesses that sell products usually allocate more resources (budgets) for research and development than do service businesses. Nike, Under Armour, and others continue to develop new and improved products to help athletes perform at their best. As another example, a team may have a ticket, food, or merchandise department.

## Implementing and Controlling the Strategies

The first four steps in the strategic process involve planning. The fifth and final step involves implementing and controlling the strategies to ensure that the organization's mission and objectives at all three levels are achieved. Top managers usually develop corporate and business-level strategies, whereas the lower-level functional managers and employees implement the strategies on a day-to-day basis. Successful implementation of strategies requires effective and efficient coordination and cooperation throughout the organization. You need to have the right people in the right positions doing the right things to achieve your objectives.[44]

Executives in the United States have been credited with doing a great job of developing strategies, but they have been criticized for doing a poor job of implementing the strategies.[45] Game plans and plays are use-

**TIME-OUT 13** Describe some of the controls used in your organization.

less without good execution during the game, and so are business strategies. The implementation of strategic plans is often a stumbling block because organizations have difficulty translating business strategies into cohesive competitive strategies (results). The need for greater integration of corporate-, business-, and functional-level strategies has long been recognized. Another thorny issue is achieving greater cooperation across functional departments. One suggestion is to develop functional-level strategies for each stage of a product's life cycle; then these strategies can be used to integrate the functional areas.

Those in the trenches would say that if implementation isn't going well, strategic planners probably didn't do their jobs. Things that look good on paper may not necessarily be doable or practical. Another reason strategic plans fail is that they often end up buried in bottom drawers, and no action is taken to implement them. In chapters 5 through 12, you will learn how to implement strategy.

Strategy implementation is successful when effective controls are used. Controlling features mechanisms to ensure that objectives are achieved in a timely and cost-efficient manner. This involves monitoring and measuring progress and taking corrective action when needed.[46] Controlling is about overcoming the barriers that hinder you from achieving your objectives.[47] Budget issues are an important part of controlling, as is being flexible about the budget when necessary to meet new challenges in the environment. You will develop your controlling skills in chapters 13 and 14.

Recall from chapter 2 that as a business expands and competes *globally* as a multinational corporation (MNC), its operations become more complex. MNCs like Nike and Adidas, which conduct business in more than 100 countries, have to develop strategic plans and manage differently for each country. With their wide global diversity, MNCs must develop different strategies to appeal to varied cultures and customs and to comply with local laws in order to sell their products and get fans to watch their games.

As we bring this chapter to a close, you should understand the strategic planning process; be able to complete an analysis of the environment; know how to set objectives using a model; understand corporate-, business-, and functional-level strategies; and understand the need to coordinate the three levels for successful implementation and control of the strategies.

## LEARNING AIDS

### CHAPTER SUMMARY

1. **Explain how strategic and operational plans differ.**

    They differ by time frame and management level involved. In strategic planning, a mission and long-range objectives and plans are developed. Operational plans state short-range objectives and plans. Upper-level managers develop strategic plans, and lower-level managers develop operational plans.

2. **Describe the differences between corporate-, business-, and functional-level strategies.**

    They primarily differ in focus, which narrows as strategy moves down the organization, and in the management level involved in developing the strategy. Corporate-level strategy focuses on managing multiple lines of business. Business-level strategy focuses on managing one line of business. Functional-level strategy focuses on managing an area of a business line. Upper-level managers develop corporate- and business-level strategy, and lower-level managers develop functional-level strategy.

3. **Explain why organizations analyze industries and competitive situations.**

The industry and competitive situation analysis is used to determine the attractiveness of an industry. It is primarily used at the corporate level to decide which lines of business to enter and exit and how to allocate resources between the organization's lines of business.

4. **Explain why organizations analyze the company situation.**

The company situation analysis is used at the business level to determine issues and problems that need to be addressed through the strategic process.

5. **Discuss how goals and objectives are similar but not the same.**

Goals and objectives are similar because they both state what is to be accomplished. However, goals can be translated into objectives. They also differ in detail. Goals state general targets, whereas objectives state what is to be accomplished in specific and measurable terms by a target date.

6. **Describe how to write objectives.**

(1) Start with the word *to*; (2) add an action verb; (3) insert a single, specific, and measurable result to achieve; and (4) set a target date.

7. **Describe the four corporate-level grand strategies.**

Firms with a growth strategy aggressively pursue expansion. Firms with a stabilizing strategy maintain the same size or grow slowly. Firms with a turnaround strategy attempt a comeback; those that are retrenching decrease their size to cut costs so that they can survive. Firms with a combination strategy use different strategies across different lines of business.

8. **Describe the three growth strategies.**

Firms that concentrate try to grow existing lines of business aggressively. Firms that integrate grow their lines forward or backward. Firms that diversify grow by adding related or unrelated products.

9. **Discuss the three business-level adaptive strategies.**

A prospector company aggressively offers new products or services or aggressively enters new markets. Prospecting is a growth strategy used in fast-changing environments with high growth potential. A defender company stays with its product line and markets. Defending is a stable strategy used in slow-changing environments with low growth potential. An analyzer company moves into new markets cautiously or offers a core product group and seeks new opportunities. Analyzing is a combination strategy used in moderately changing environments with moderate growth potential.

10. **List the four functional-level operational strategies.**

Companies develop operational strategies in four major functional areas: marketing, operations, human resources, and finance. Other functional-level strategies are developed as needed, depending on the organization's business and environment.

## REVIEW AND DISCUSSION QUESTIONS

1. Explain why strategic planning and operational planning are important.

2. How do plans and strategies differ?

3. Should all sport organizations have corporate-, business-, and functional-level strategies? Why or why not?

4. Should a mission statement for an athletic department be customer focused? Why or why not?

5. Why would a situation analysis be part of the strategic process of redesigning a sport organization?

6. Why is competitive advantage important to sport organizations?

7. Are both goals and objectives necessary for managing a health club? Why or why not?

8. Develop a SWOT for the North American Society for Sport Management (NASSM).

9. As a manager or a coach, would you use MBO? Why or why not?

10. Which growth strategy would you say is the most successful? Defend your answer.

11. What is the difference between a merger and an acquisition?

12. Develop a BCG matrix for Adidas.

13. Why would a sport organization use a focus strategy rather than try to appeal to all customers?

14. Give examples of "other" functional departments.

15. Is it ethical to copy other teams' or companies' ideas through benchmarking?

## CASES

### Sport Management Professionals @ Work: Michael Cometa

The reason Michael Cometa selected sport management as his major at Springfield College was due to his part-time job in high school. During the summer between his junior and senior years, he started working as an outside operations member at a golf course near his hometown. This involved getting the course ready for regular golfers and, for a couple of days during the week, large tournaments. In addition, there was a private course on campus that had a hundred members which he helped service as well. The combination of greeting golfers and members as they arrived, serving them and preparing their golf outing, and then welcoming them back after their round was done was something he cherished. Seeing the satisfaction on their faces after they spent the day on the course and knowing he was responsible for setting that up was what he enjoyed most in his job. Alongside the operational aspect of his job, building relationships with the members was something he also found rewarding. He always had a passion for sport. This led him to pursue a career in sport management on the event management and client service side.

While he was attending Springfield College, Michael took several internships. He believed internships, whether paid or unpaid, for credit or not for credit, were very important. Along with volunteer work, they could strengthen his résumé and create networks that would help him to get a job in the future. He took two internships that he believed paved the way to his first full-time job with the Boston Red Sox. The first was with the Baltimore Ravens between his junior and senior years of college. He applied on Teamworkonline, thinking there was no shot he would get an email or call. However, based on his volunteer work, internship with the local AHL hockey team, and involvement with the Sport Management Club and Springfield athletics, he received a call back. Instead of taking a Skype or phone interview, he drove down to Baltimore to interview in person and was called back with a job offer. At the Ravens, he worked hard every day, was a team player, and built great relationships with his coworkers, including managers and supervisors.

After college, he hoped to find a full-time job, but he quickly realized that the ideal job would not come easily and that another internship might be the best route. He applied for a corporate sponsorship seasonal role with the Atlanta Falcons. He asked around about the position. One person he asked was his supervisor with the Ravens. "She told me that the hiring manager for that role was one of her good friends and that she just had dinner with her the other day. A few weeks later after an interview, I received the job." Mike tells this story to every current student he talks to. Working hard, making connections, and networking can pay off big in the long run.

Mike finds working in professional sports very exciting. Not only are you doing what you love to do, he says, but you are also rooting for your team to succeed. Even if you had a favorite team growing up, that has changed now, and you root for the name on your paychecks. Mike has been very fortunate to experience a championship with the Red Sox in 2013. One of his managers at the time said at the start of the postseason, "Make sure you don't take this for granted as this is a once-in-a-lifetime opportunity. To be there with your family or friends or coworkers celebrating all of the hard work you put in throughout the season and seasons prior is what working in sports is really all about."

Another note about networking: Mike was fortunate to have good classmates and friends throughout his time at Springfield College. He is still close with most of them today, and they can comfortably discuss jobs, current Springfield sport management students, and other sport industry issues. Mike has also kept in touch with the sport management professors. He would tell current students to do the same. "Get to know your classmates and professors. Even though you are competing for jobs, you will ultimately need each other's help down the road. Some alumni send job openings to the professors, and then the professors can send them out to you. That is how I started my career at the Red Sox." A former alumnus working for the Sox sent the job opening to a professor; the professor knew Mike's current internship was ending and forwarded it to him.

## Case Questions

1. What would you write for Michael's personal mission statement?

2. How does the personal mission statement differ from the organizational mission statement where you work or go to college?

3. Explain whether you think college students understand the role of networking in being hired for a mid-level corporate job.

## Strategic Planning at the NHL: Entering the Esports Market

Leagues, teams, and companies of all sizes need to develop a corporate strategy. You can imagine how complex such strategies get when the organization is the National Hockey League (NHL). You probably haven't heard too much about esports, so you might be surprised to learn that professional sport leagues such as the NBA and NHL are making it part of their strategic planning to maximize revenue from the esports platform.

The NHL's strategic plan focuses on a growth strategy of developing the sport in the online sport marketplace. Its goal was a seamless distribution of esport online entertainment to as many markets across the United States as possible. An obvious focus was a concentrated strategy at gaming tournaments, such as the 2018 NHL Gaming World Championship. Players could match up one-on-one, but there were also plans for leagues and tournaments to offer two-versus-two or three-versus-three.

The NHL hopes diversifying into online sports will attract new fans and connect with current fans in a different way than attending a physical game or watching the game from home. NHL executive vice president and chief revenue officer Keith Wachtel said, "This is the most basic way for our fans to play."

The 2018 NHL Gaming World Championship is a venture with NHL global broadcast partners NBC Sports, Sportsnet, and Viasat. Each broadcast sponsor was to present one of the regional tournaments. The NHL's Twitch channel is the official tournament platform for the competition.[48]

The NHL has also fulfilled the strategic goal of being a global player in hockey. NHL players are from countries throughout Europe. Russia has the KHL, which is the Russian NHL. The 2018 Gaming World Championships were held in Canada and Europe using the PlayStation 4 and Xbox One. The championship was held at Esports Arena Las Vegas.[49]

To find current information about the NHL, visit www.nhl.com. Be sure to search for esports.

Go to the web study guide to answer questions about this case study.

## @ TAKE IT TO THE NET

Please visit www.HumanKinetics.com/AppliedSportManagementSkills and go to the book's companion web study guide, where you will find the following:

A complete list of websites associated with the concepts in this chapter

Skill-Builder exercises, Sports and Social Media exercises, and a continuing Game Plan for Starting a Sport Business

Online versions of chapter exercises and end-of-chapter learning aids

An exercise that helps you define the Key Terms

# PART III

# Organizing

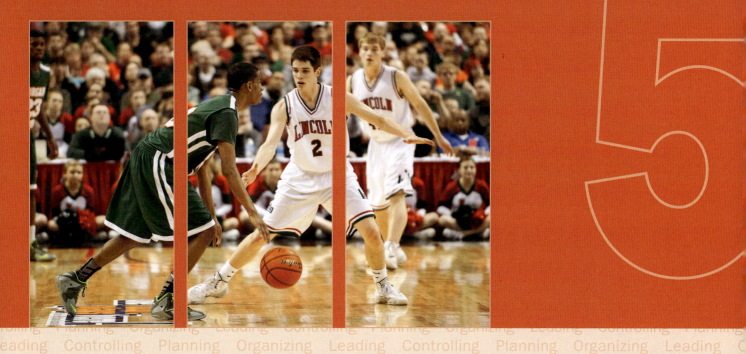

# Organizing and Delegating Work

## LEARNING OUTCOMES

After studying this chapter, you should be able to

1. explain how flat organizations and tall organizations differ;

2. describe liaisons, integrators, and boundary roles;

3. differentiate between formal and informal authority;

4. explain the four levels of authority;

5. describe the relationship between line and staff authority;

6. describe organization charts;

7. explain how internal departmentalization and external departmentalization differ;

8. state the similarities and differences between matrix and divisional departmentalization;

9. explain how job simplification and job expansion differ;

10. describe the job characteristics model and what it is used for;

11. set priorities; and

12. delegate.

## KEY TERMS

| | | |
|---|---|---|
| span of management | line authority | departmentalization |
| responsibility | staff authority | job design |
| authority | centralized authority | job enrichment |
| delegation | decentralized authority | job characteristics model |
| levels of authority | organization chart | delegation model |

## DEVELOPING YOUR SKILLS

It is important to understand how sport firms are organized—the basic principles of organization, authority, organization charts, and types of departmentalization used to achieve the sport firm's mission and objectives. On a more personal level, in this chapter you will learn to organize yourself and set priorities by answering three questions, which can be part of a to-do list. By following the steps in the delegation model, you can improve on this skill as well.

## REVIEWING THEIR GAME PLAN

### Learning to Organize the Springfield Sting

Zach Baru is a master of the four functions of management: A day doesn't go by that Baru doesn't plan, organize, lead, and control. Zach has been owner of the Springfield Sting of the American Basketball Association (ABA), Western Massachusetts, for the past two years.

Zach learned from internships that he completed for other smaller professional teams. He was an intern at the Springfield Armor that folded in 2011. The Armor played their home games at the Mass Mutual Center, which was much too large for the sparse crowds that attended. Zach knew that to keep the programs alive and well he would need a strategic plan. Part of the plan was to have home games played at the Naismith Memorial Basketball Hall of Fame, which is home to more than three hundred inductees and more than 40,000 square feet of basketball history.[1]

As owner, Zach organizes something every day. He has to hire key people, such as the coach for his team. Local college students are hired as interns to give them experience managing and organizing a sport facility. The interns help staff the ticket booth, merchandise table, and concessions. Zach uses family members to help with audio, time clocks, and other aspects of the event.

Zach's leadership skills were forged through many years of teaching high school. He is always around greeting, encouraging, mentoring, and coaching staff and players.

Control issues are just as important to Zach as they are to managers in other organizations. He carefully oversees the budgets that need to be prepared for the different operational areas of the team. Zach found the marquee aspect of being at the Hall of Fame did help with free publicity. But the building does not have key features such as locker rooms for the players. Thus, for the second year, Zach decided it was more cost effective to split the home games between a local community college and an area high school court.[2] So far, the Sting have been successful on the court (they score well over 100 points a game), and they are successful off the court in regard to positive community relationships. The key will be if Zach can stick with the strategic plan and keep growing the number of fans and followers as the team enters its third season.

For more information about the Springfield Sting, visit www.springfieldsting.com/www. sportsworld.cc.

# The Organizing Function

Organizing is the second function of management, and we defined it in chapter 1 as the process of delegating and coordinating tasks and resources to achieve objectives. Managers design formal structures to organize four types of resources[3]—human, physical, financial, and informational; and the structure influences innovation and success.[4] On a company-wide basis, organizing is about grouping activities and resources. Effective managers know that organizing their team's resources and putting the right person in each position is instrumental in achieving objectives.

The organization's mission and strategy (chapter 4) influence its structure because the organization must be structured to meet the mission and strategy.[5] The organizational structure must be aligned with the external environment to achieve objectives.[6] But how does management know the best organizational structure? Managers answer at least six key questions. The questions are listed in table 5.1, and the answers are discussed in more

**TABLE 5.1    Organizing Questions**

| Organizational questions | Chapter topic |
|---|---|
| Whom should each individual report to? | Chain of command (p. 115); span of management and control (p. 116) |
| How many individuals should report to each manager? | Span of management and control (p. 116) |
| How should the work be grouped? | Division of labor (p. 116); departmentalization (p. 123) |
| How do individuals and groups work together as a united team? | Coordination (p. 117) |
| At what level of management should decisions be made? | Centralized and decentralized authority (p. 121) |
| How should the entire firm be structured? | Departmentalization (p. 123) |

detail throughout the chapter under the topics indicated. In this section, we discuss eight organizational principles, listed under Principles of Organization, that are commonly followed in organizations and help to answer the organizing questions.

## Unity of Command and Direction

*Unity of command* means that each employee should report to only one boss. Having more than one boss can be confusing and frustrating when different bosses want different things done. When we are goal oriented,[7] *unity of direction* means that all activities focus on the same objectives—winning the game. When a team doesn't pull together, it often loses the game.

## Chain of Command

Chain of command, or the scalar principle, is the clear, hierarchical line of authority from the organization's top to its bottom.[8] Everyone in a company needs to know whom they report to and who, if anyone, reports to them. The chain of command also identifies the formal path for communications. It forms the hierarchy shown in organization charts,[9] which we examine later in this chapter.

TIME-OUT 1 — Follow the chain of command from your present position (or a past one) to the top of your organization. Identify anyone who reported to you and to whom you reported; list that person's title, that person's boss' title, and so on, all the way to the top manager.

## Principles of Organization

- Unity of command and direction
- Chain of command
- Span of management and control (flat and tall organizations)
- Division of labor (specialization)
- Coordination
- Clarification of responsibilities and scope of authority
- Delegation
- Flexibility

Team captains are the part of the chain of command that links coaches and players. Team captains in the NHL often have as much influence over their teammates as do the coaches. Choosing the captain of a team, therefore, is not a decision to be taken lightly. Duke University Coach Mike Krzyzewski (Coach K) has stated that a large part of his success is based on his team captains.

## Span of Management and Control

**LEARNING OUTCOME 1** ▶

Explain how flat organizations and tall organizations differ.

The **span of management**, or span of control, is the number of employees that report directly to the same manager. There is no optimal number of employees to manage. But the trend is to increase the span of management.[10] Typically, lower-level managers have a wider span of control than do higher-level managers. (Of course, *directly* is the operative word here—second-level managers are responsible for first levels in their departments and also for all the staff under the first-level managers, even though they do not supervise them directly.)

Examining how an organization sets up its spans of management tells you a great deal about whether it is a flat or a tall organization. Flat organizations have very few levels of management, and these levels have wide spans of control. Tall organizations have many levels of management with narrow spans of control. Figure 5.1 illustrates these two different approaches. Notice that the flat organization has only two levels of management and the tall one has four. In recent years, organizations have been flattening their hierarchies by cutting as many levels of management as they can to speed up decision making and processes while cutting costs.[11]

## Division of Labor

Division of labor occurs when jobs are organized by specialty—for example, sales reps work in the marketing department, and football players are on the offensive or defensive squad. The MLB American League has specialized batting and pitching roles

**TIME-OUT**
**2**
Think about a current boss or coach and describe his or her span of control. Describe your own span of control if you are a manager or coach. How many levels of management exist in your organization, and would you characterize it as flat or tall?

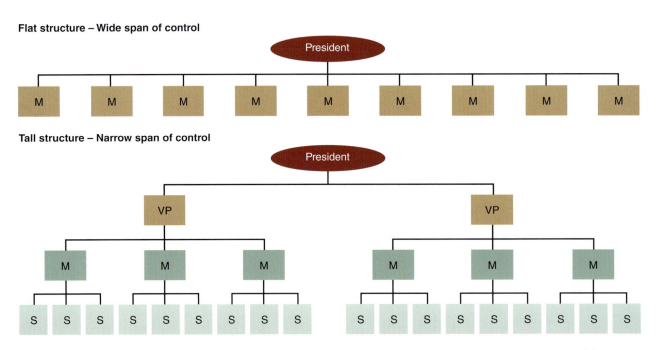

**Flat structure – Wide span of control**

**Tall structure – Narrow span of control**

**FIGURE 5.1**   The span of control in flat and tall organizations. Key: vice president (VP); manager (M); supervisor (S).

with its designated hitter. Managers usually perform less specialized functions as they move up the management ladder. Paul Lawrence and Jay Lorsch coined the terms *differentiation* and *integration*.[12] Differentiation is about organizing work groups into departments, and integration is about coordinating departmental activities.[13] You need to balance the two.[14]

## Coordination

Coordination is about departments and individuals in an organization working together to accomplish strategic and operational objectives for its environment. Coordinating across jobs and departments requires systems-based analysis and conceptual skills. Zach Baru needs to coordinate the event planning to hold a professional basketball game (i.e., the safety of the court, concessions, parking lot, and ticket sales), support the coaching staff, and keep the locker rooms clean. This coordination must be focused on meeting the needs of the teams and players.

◄ **LEARNING OUTCOME 2**
Describe liaisons, integrators, and boundary roles.

Every aspect of the organizing function involves coordination, and coordination also requires cooperation. Examples of coordinating activities include the following:

 What sorts of coordinating activities do you think would be involved in starting a new professional basketball team?

- Direct contact between people from the same department or from different departments
- Liaisons who work in one department and coordinate information and activities with other departments
- Committees formed to organize just about everything—for example, building a new fitness center
- Integrators, such as product or project managers, who don't work for a specific department but coordinate multiple-department activities; also called linking pins
- Boundary roles in which staff (from sales, customer service, purchasing, and public relations, for example) work with people in the external environment

## Clarification of Responsibilities and Scope of Authority

Management must ensure that each person's responsibilities in the organization are clearly defined, that employees are given the authority they need to meet these responsibilities (i.e., that their scope of authority should match their responsibilities), and that employees are held accountable for meeting their responsibilities. **Responsibility** is one's obligation to achieve objectives by performing required activities. Managers are responsible for the results of their organizations, divisions, or departments, and you have to trust others with responsibility to get the job done.[15]

**Authority** is the right to make decisions, issue orders, and use resources. As a manager, you will be given responsibility for achieving departmental objectives. You must also be given a certain level of authority if you are to get the job done. Accountability means you are evaluated on how well you meet your responsibilities.

Managers are accountable for everything that happens in their departments. As a manager, you will routinely delegate responsibility and authority for performing tasks, but your accountability stays with you. Coaches have authority to manage their teams. But they don't play the game; they delegate that responsibility to athletes. However, they are held accountable for winning, and some get fired for losing.

## Delegation

**Delegation** has to do with assigning responsibility and authority for accomplishing objectives. Responsibility and authority are delegated down the chain of command. To improve accountability, the IOC delegated the control function of decision making to a board and the management function to internal agents. Delegation is an important skill for managers,[16]

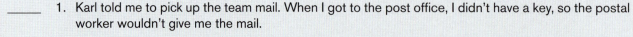

## APPLYING THE CONCEPT 5.1

### The Organizing Function

Note which aspect of the organizing function is operative in each situation.

    a.  unity of command and direction

    b.  chain of command

    c.  span of management

    d.  division of labor

    e.  coordination

    f.  clarification of responsibility and authority

    g.  delegation

    h.  flexibility

_____  1.  Karl told me to pick up the team mail. When I got to the post office, I didn't have a key, so the postal worker wouldn't give me the mail.

_____  2.  The players on the football team are on either the offensive squad or the defensive squad.

_____  3.  My job can be frustrating. Sometimes my department manager tells me to do one thing, but my project manager tells me to do something else at the same time.

_____  4.  Middle manager: I want Sam, who works for Sally, to deliver this package, but I can't ask him to do it directly. I have to ask Sally to ask him.

_____  5.  There has been an accident in the game, and the ambulance is on the way. Jim, call Dr. Rodriguez and have her get to emergency room C in 10 minutes. Pat, get the paperwork ready. Karen, prepare room C.

and we examine it later in this chapter. For now, you should realize that true delegation occurs when you assign something new to an employee. When you simply tell an employee to do a task, it is not really delegating.

## Flexibility

Many managers and employees focus on following company rules without exceptions.[17] Flexibility has to do with understanding that there can be exceptions to the rule. Going by the book does not always produce the best results. Progressive organizations want employees to be flexible and make exceptions to create customer satisfaction.[18] They want employees to be flexible and quickly resolve problems.[19] But when you take the authority and responsibility for breaking a rule, you will be held accountable for the end results.[20] You may be rewarded for your efforts, but you could be punished for breaking a rule. Does your organization want you to simply follow the standard procedures and rules or to be flexible? Are you willing to be flexible?[21]

 **TIME-OUT 3** Is your organization flexible? Explain why or why not.

## Authority

Authority comes in many different forms and in many different styles. Understanding formal and informal authority, scope of authority, levels of authority, line and staff authority, and centralized and decentralized authority—the topics of this section—will help you become a more effective sport manager.

How would an effective sport manager communicate and outline the authority of staff managing a large triathlon?

## Formal and Informal Authority

Formal authority is the approved way of getting work done through specified relationships between employees and between departments. When your boss tells you what to do, that's formal authority. The organization chart shows the lines of formal authority of reporting relationships. But most organization charts don't come close to describing organizational life, and it's not easy to understand how things really work through the informal organization.

    Informal authority comes from a constellation of collaborations, relationships, and networks.[22] If you note that someone is competent, is dependable, and continually comes up with strategies that get the job done, you (and others) are very likely to turn to that person for leadership—this is informal authority. It can be as powerful as formal authority—indeed, many times it is more powerful. Although it is not formally specified, it is very real. Duke University's Coach K says he relies on team leaders to motivate others to perform at their best on the basketball court to win. Have you ever known a player who had more influence on other athletes' performance than the coach? Informal authority can be used to overcome the burdens and limitations that formal authority imposes on employees. Informal authority often gets the job done and gets it done quicker.

**◀ LEARNING OUTCOME 3**

Differentiate between formal and informal authority.

## Scope of Authority

People's formal scope of authority narrows the farther down their job is in the organization chart.[23] A CEO has more authority than presidents and vice presidents, who have more authority than managers, and so on. The Ohio State University athletic director has more authority than the coaches, who have more authority than their assistant coaches and graduate assistants. Responsibility and authority flow down the organization, whereas accountability flows up the organization, as figure 5.2 illustrates. The right column illustrates a typical pro sports team.

## Levels of Authority

Every manager needs to know the scope of his formal authority. For example, what authority would the athletic director (AD) at Springfield High School (SHS) have to alter a medi-

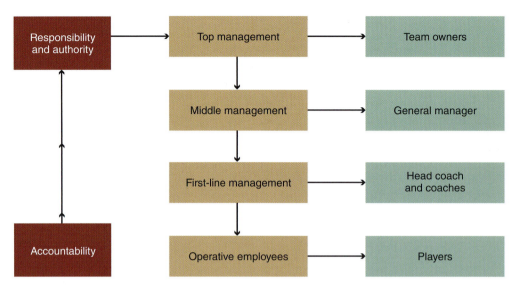

**FIGURE 5.2**   Scope of authority.

cal record that she believes is in error? The **levels of authority** are informing authority, recommending authority, reporting authority, and full authority. Levels of authority vary from task to task. Let's examine the SHS AD's authority to hire a new basketball coach, illustrated under each level.

LEARNING OUTCOME 4 ▶

Explain the four levels of authority.

• *Informing authority.* At this level, you inform the leader of possible alternatives. The leader then analyzes the alternatives and makes the decision. People in administrative assistant (adman) positions often have only informing authority because the job calls for gathering data for others.

At the informing level of authority, the SHS adman would simply organize, record, and give the applications for the coaching job to the AD.

• *Recommending authority.* At this level, you generate alternative actions, analyze them, and recommend action to the leader who may or may not implement the recommendation. Committees are often given recommending authority.

At the recommending level of authority, the SHS AD would give the top applications for the coaching job to the principal with a recommendation as to which candidate to hire. However, the principal may select a different candidate.

• *Reporting authority.* At this level, you have the authority to select a course of action and carry it out. However, you routinely report the courses of action to your leader.

At the reporting level of authority, the SHS AD would hire the coach and simply report doing so, maybe by introducing the coach to the principal.

• *Full authority.* At this level of authority, you can get the job done your own way without telling the leader. However, there may be times when you want to consult the leader for advice on your planned action. Also, full authority does not mean you can do whatever you want for your benefit. You must act with sound judgment within the confines of formal authority to benefit the team or organization.

At the full level of authority, the SHS AD would simply hire the coach without telling the principal.

 TIME-OUT 4   Think about a task you do routinely for your company or team and describe your level of authority for this task in detail.

## Line and Staff Authority

**Line authority** is the responsibility to make decisions and issue orders down the chain of command. Operations and marketing are usually line departments, but some organizations also organize financial activities as line departments. Line managers are primarily responsible for achieving the organization's objectives, and their staff or team follows the directives that the line manager develops to achieve those objectives. SHS coaches are line managers because they are responsible for leading their team to victory.

◀ **LEARNING OUTCOME 5**

Describe the relationship between line and staff authority.

**Staff authority** is the responsibility to advise and assist other personnel. Human resources (HR), public relations, and management information systems are almost always staff departments. The line departments are internal customers of the staff departments. Therefore, the two types of departments have a collaborative partnership. When the SHS AD hires a new coach, the AD gets help from the HR department, which places the coaching job in newspapers and online and collects the applications. But HR doesn't select the new coach; the principal line manager does.

**TIME-OUT 5** Identify several line and staff positions in your company or team. State whether they are general or specialist staff positions.

The staff's primary role is to advise and assist, but situations occur in which they can give orders to line personnel. Functional authority is the right of staff personnel to issue orders to line personnel in established areas of responsibility. The SHS financial manager can't tell the AD which coach to hire but she has authority to require the AD to stay within the budget and fill out the proper paperwork when hiring the new coach. The AD can tell the coaches how to coach, but the financial manager can't.

Staff managers may have dual staff and line authority. For example, public relations (staff) managers advise and assist all departments in their organization. However, they also have line authority within their own departments and issue orders (a line function) to their groups. The SHS financial manager can tell the bookkeepers what to do.

There are also two types of staff. General staff work for only one manager. Often called "assistant to," they help the manager in any way needed. Specialist staff help anyone in the organization who needs it within their scope of authority. The SHS principal has an assistant principal who primarily takes care of discipline; the AD has no assistant (though many colleges do have assistant ADs) but can get help from the school's administrative assistants who help all school staff as needed.

## Centralized and Decentralized Authority

These structures differ in where the authority to make the important decisions resides.[24] With **centralized authority**, important decisions are made by top managers. With **decentralized authority**, important decisions are made by middle- and first-level managers. *Micromanagement* is a term used to describe managers who closely watch their employees to make sure they follow standard procedures and rules, and they don't let employees make decisions without their approval.[25] The trend for top managers is to decentralize authority and accountability.[26] Employees are given authority to determine how they do their jobs and make decisions.

Authority is actually on a continuum, and most organizations function with a blend of centralized and decentralized authority. With the exception of very small companies, which tend to be centralized, most organizations lie somewhere between the two extremes. Finding the right balance

**TIME-OUT 6** What type of decision authority is most prevalent in your firm or team? Are there reasons that make this choice appropriate in this environment? Or is it not as effective as it could be? Explain.

APPLYING THE CONCEPT 5.2

## Authority

Identify the type of authority implied in each situation.

    a.  formal

    b.  informal

    c.  level

    d.  line

    e.  staff

    f.  centralized

    g.  decentralized

_____   6.  I like my job, but it's frustrating when I recommend potential employees to the production and marketing managers and they don't hire them.

_____   7.  It's great working for a team that encourages everyone to share information.

_____   8.  Coaches here run their teams the way they want to.

_____   9.  I'm not sure if I'm supposed to get a list of company cars for Wendy or recommend one to her.

_____  10.  That is a great idea, Jean. I'll talk to Pete, and if he likes it, I'm sure he'll want us to present your idea to his boss.

between the two, the one that serves the business' environmental contingencies and its business model best, leads to success. For example, production and sales are often decentralized, whereas finance and labor relations are centralized to provide uniformity and control.

# Organizational Design

It's time we address how entire firms are organized. Top-level managers develop the strategic plan,[27] and they design formal organizational structures for achieving the organization's mission and objectives.[28] Organizational design is the arrangement of positions into work units or departments and the relationships between them. Here we discuss organization charts and departmentalization.

## Organization Chart

**LEARNING OUTCOME 6** ▶

Describe organization charts.

The formal authority structures that define working relationships between the organization's members and their jobs are illustrated in organization charts.[29] An **organization chart** lays out the organization's management hierarchy and departments and their working relationships. As shown in figure 5.3, the boxes represent positions in the organization, and the lines indicate the reporting relationships and lines of formal communication. Figure 5.3, a hypothetical organization chart for a university, illustrates the following four major aspects of organizations.

    • *The level of management hierarchy.* The organization chart shows the top-down hierarchy structure[30] by the levels of management.[31] In figure 5.3, the board of regents and president are the top two levels of management; the vice presidents are middle-level management; and department managers, such as athletic facilities managers, are first-level management.

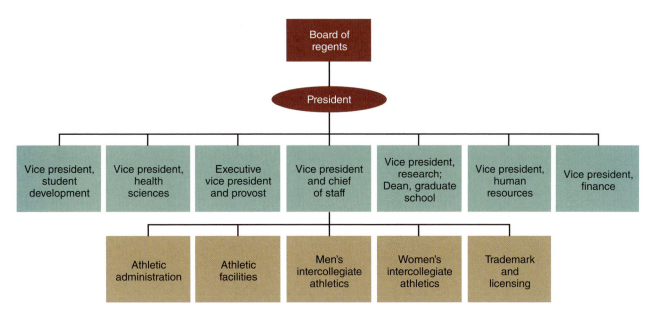

**FIGURE 5.3**    Organization chart for a university, highlighting athletic administration.

• *Chain of command.* The chart shows the supervisory reporting relationship. As you follow the lines in figure 5.3, you will see that the president reports to the board of regents. The vice presidents report to the president, and the department managers report to the vice presidents.

• *The division and type of work.* The chart divides the university by "product" by indicating different academic areas such as health sciences and graduate programs. The university is also organized by functional area (finance and HR).

• *Departmentalization.* The organization chart also shows how the business of the firm is divided into work units, commonly called departments. The university's athletic departments are under the control of two people, the vice president for administration (not shown) and the chief of staff. The departments are athletic administration, athletic facilities, men's intercollegiate athletics, women's intercollegiate athletics, and trademark and licensing.

Now that you know what an organization chart shows, let's discuss what an organization chart doesn't show. Virtually every large firm has at least two organization charts.[32] The first is the formal one on paper we just discussed. The second is the informal chart that is not included in the formal one, but it reveals how day-to-day activities are performed, whom to talk to get the job done, how politics work, and who really has the influence to help you achieve your objective. You will learn how to successfully navigate the informal organization in chapter 8.

## Departmentalization

**Departmentalization** is the grouping of related activities into work units. Departments have either an internal focus or an external one. Departmentalization around internal operations or functions and the resources needed to accomplish the unit's work is called functional departmentalization. External or output departmentalization is based on activities that focus on factors outside the organization; this is also called product or service, customer, and geographic or territory departmentalization.

◀ **LEARNING OUTCOME 7**

Explain how internal departmentalization and external departmentalization differ.

## Functional Departmentalization

Functional departmentalization organizes departments around essential input activities,[33] such as financing, making and selling the products, or event tickets. Virtually all sport companies use some form of functional departmentalization. An example is Spalding Sporting Goods. The first chart in figure 5.4 shows functional departmentalization listing the four common activities all organizations must perform.

## Product or Service Departmentalization

This approach organizes departments around sporting goods produced or services (like sport entertainment) provided. Companies with multiple products commonly use product departmentalization. Retail stores like Dick's Sporting Goods have product departments in each store. The second chart in figure 5.4 exemplifies product departmentalization.

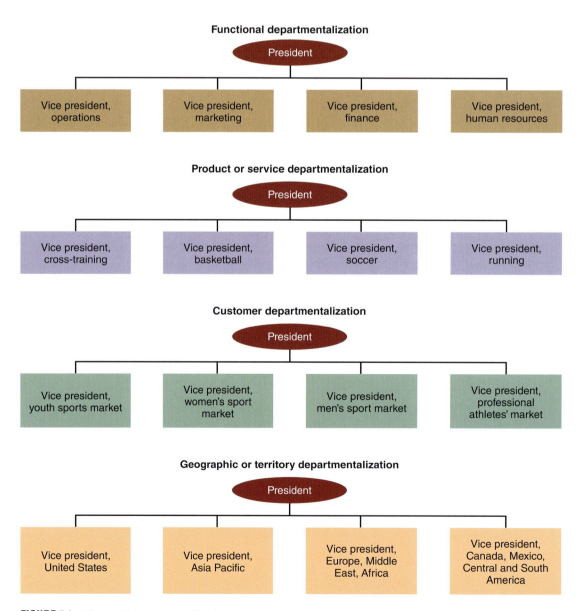

**FIGURE 5.4** Types of departmentalization.

### Customer Departmentalization

Customer departmentalization organizes departments around the needs of different types of customers. The product or service may be the same or slightly different, but the needs of the customers vary, so your four Ps of marketing change by customer (in the type of products, packaging and quantity, location, prices, sales staff, and so on). Nike has different customers, including individuals online and at retail stores, schools, and colleges and pro teams. So Nike has different employees making and selling the standard or customized products to meet the different customer needs. The third chart in figure 5.4 shows customer departmentalization.

### Geographic or Territory Departmentalization

This type of departmentalization organizes departments by each area in which the enterprise does business. Nike divides its financial reporting into four geographic regions. The EMEA division consists of Europe, the Middle East, and Africa. The Americas division includes Canada, Mexico, and Central and South America. The other two divisions are Asia Pacific and the United States. Each region reports numbers for sales and expenses.[34] The final chart in figure 5.4 organizes by geographic area.

## Multiple Departmentalization

Many large, complex businesses use multiple departmental structures to create hybrid organizations.[35] The mixture of structures varies based on the business. Most businesses have functional departments, but they also organize sales by territory with separate sales managers and salespeople in different territories.

### Matrix Departmentalization

Matrix departmentalization blends jobs between functional and product departmentalization. That is, staff are assigned to a functional department but work on one or more products or projects. With a matrix, the firm can temporarily and quickly reorganize for high-priority projects. When a project is done, they work on another one or just go back to doing their functional jobs. But the employees have two managers—a functional boss and a project boss—which can make coordination difficult and can cause conflicts to arise because of the different objectives of multiple managers. Figure 5.5 shows a matrix structure.

◀ **LEARNING OUTCOME 8**
State the similarities and differences between matrix and divisional departmentalization.

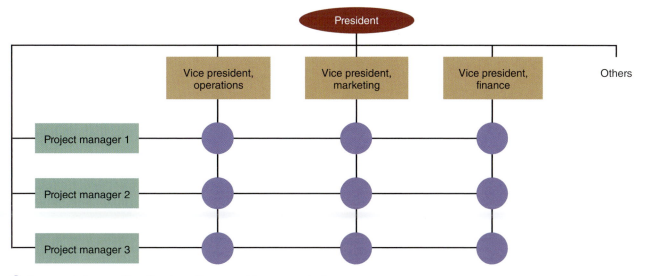

● Represents teams of functional employees working on a project

**FIGURE 5.5** Matrix departmentalization.

### *Divisional Departmentalization*

Divisional departmentalization is used for large companies that have corporate-level strategies managing semiautonomous strategic business units—companies within a company (chapter 4). This structure is also called multidivisional or M-form.[36] Recall that Berkshire Hathaway has more than 60 business units, including Brooks Sports,[37] Russell Athletic, Spalding Sporting Goods, and American Athletic.[38] You couldn't buy stock in Gatorade because it is a division of PepsiCo, as are Frito-Lay snacks and Tropicana juices.

**TIME-OUT 7** Draw a simple organization chart for your company or team. Identify the type of departmentalization and staff positions used.

## Athletic Director and Divisions and Conferences

An important decision facing high school and college ADs (and pros as well) is which division and conference to compete in. Let's focus on colleges that tend to be able to select the division level and then the conference. The conferences themselves, such as the Big Ten, ACC, Pac-12, Big East, SEC, and Big 12, do face an organizational issue when teams ask to enter the conference or when some leave for another conference. Another option is to be independent and try to play any team you want to; Notre Dame is an example.

## APPLYING THE CONCEPT 5.3

### Departmentalization

Identify the organizing approach used in the following five charts.

   a. function

   b. products and services

   c. customer

   d. territory

   e. matrix

   f. division

_____ 11. All-Sports Consulting Company

_____ 12. Fitness Publishing Company

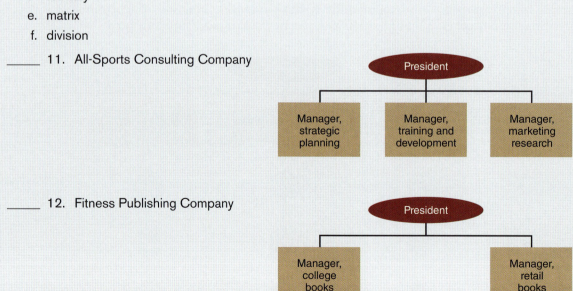

# Job Design

The work performed by organizations is grouped into functional departments, which are further grouped into jobs to accomplish objectives.[39] **Job design** is the process of combining the tasks that each employee is responsible for completing. How jobs are designed affects job satisfaction and productivity.[40] As you will learn in this section, jobs can be simple (and contain few tasks) or they can be expanded (and contain many tasks) to include teamwork. There is a job characteristics model that can be used to design jobs.

## Job Simplification

Job simplification makes jobs more specialized and efficient by working smarter, not harder. Thus, job designers break a job into workflow steps to improve performance.[41] Job designers take three approaches:

- *Eliminate.* Does the task have to be done at all? If not, don't do it. Some sport stores have stopped requiring a paper signature for small credit card sales or have gone all electronic to speed up checkout times.

TIME-OUT 8

Describe how you would simplify a job at your firm or company. Specify whether you are eliminating, combining, or changing the sequence of tasks.

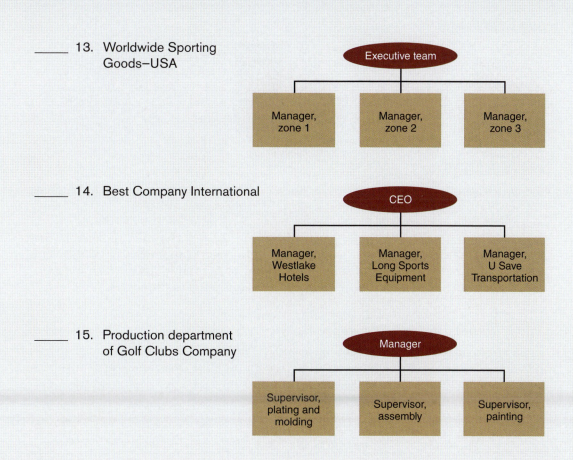

_____ 13. Worldwide Sporting Goods–USA

Executive team

Manager, zone 1 — Manager, zone 2 — Manager, zone 3

_____ 14. Best Company International

CEO

Manager, Westlake Hotels — Manager, Long Sports Equipment — Manager, U Save Transportation

_____ 15. Production department of Golf Clubs Company

Manager

Supervisor, plating and molding — Supervisor, assembly — Supervisor, painting

- *Combine.* Combining tasks often saves time. Make one trip to the mailroom at the end of the day instead of several throughout the day, if this makes sense.
- *Change sequence.* Changing the order of tasks can save time. Start your day getting important tasks done, and save the email until later when you are tired, if you can.

Jobs that are too simple bore people, and they may not be productive. However, used appropriately, job simplification can motivate people. Often, people don't hate the job, just some aspect of it. Rather than ignoring or simply putting up with aspects of their jobs that they don't like, sometimes employees can change their jobs.

## Job Expansion

LEARNING OUTCOME 9 ▶

Explain how job simplification and job expansion differ.

Job expansion makes jobs less specialized in order to empower workers and to make them more productive. The trend is to give employees more job autonomy.[42] Jobs can be expanded through job rotation, job enlargement, and job enrichment.

### Job Rotation

In this approach, people perform different jobs for a set period of time. For example, employees making sneakers on a New Balance assembly line could rotate so that they get to work on different parts. Many large firms have training programs that rotate management trainees through various departments.

Cross-training is related to job rotation. With cross-training, staff members learn to perform different jobs so they can fill in when someone is on break, out sick, or on vacation.[43] This also increases skills, which makes people more valuable to the organization.

### Job Enlargement

This approach to job design adds more tasks in order to provide variety. For example, the New Balance sneaker workers could perform four tasks instead of just two. However, only adding more simple tasks to an already simple job is not a great motivator.

 TIME-OUT 9 Describe how you would expand a job at your company or team. Specify whether you are using job rotation, job enlargement, or job enrichment.

### Job Enrichment

**Job enrichment** builds motivators into a job to make it more interesting and challenging. The goal is to engage employees on the job so that they are satisfied at work while also making them more productive.[44] To enrich jobs, many firms are offering flexible work arrangements, such as telecommuting (working from home), flextime (individualizing starting and finishing times), compressed workweeks (four 10-hour days per week), and job sharing (two employees splitting one job). A simple way to enrich jobs, which any sport manager can do, is to delegate more variety and responsibility to employees.

## Work Teams

Today, the trend is to design jobs for work teams, or, rather, to allow teams to redesign members' jobs. The trend is to empower teams to cross-train and to determine which members perform which roles. Teamwork is as vital for successful companies as it is for successful NFL teams. Moving to work teams is a form of job enrichment. The two common types are integrated teams and self-managed teams.

### Integrated Work Teams

With traditional work groups, the manager assigns tasks and supervises the work. With integrated work teams, the manager is usually also a team member sharing leadership. Teams are assigned a number of tasks by the manager, and the team itself then assigns specific tasks to members and oversees the work with the manager having the final say on decisions.[45]

### Self-Managed Work Teams

These teams are assigned an objective, and the team plans, organizes, leads, and controls the work in order to achieve that objective. Self-managed teams operate without a designated manager; everyone on the team functions as both manager and worker. Teams select their own members and evaluate each other's performance and have the authority to discipline and fire members of the team.

Have you ever been on a self-managed team project at your college and received a grade based on team performance? If so, you know the importance of teamwork. In chapter 9, we discuss how you can develop your skills as a team member and leader.

> **TIME-OUT 10** Describe how your firm uses—or could use—work teams. Indicate whether the teams are integrated or self-managed.

## Job Characteristics Model

Developed by Richard Hackman and Greg Oldham, the job characteristics model provides a complex conceptual framework for designing enriched jobs. The job characteristics model (JCM) is commonly implemented by people trained to use it effectively. Our goal is not to teach you to be a trained user of JCM, but rather to understand its components and know when to call in a pro. So we keep the description brief, focusing on the JCM in figure 5.6.

◄ **LEARNING OUTCOME 10**
Describe the job characteristics model and what it is used for.

---

## APPLYING THE CONCEPT 5.4

### Job Design

Identify the job design implied in each situation.

a.  job simplification
b.  job rotation
c.  job enlargement
d.  job enrichment
e.  work teams
f.  job characteristics model

_____ 16.  Jack, I think you need a challenge, so I want you to develop some new offensive plays.

_____ 17.  Sales reps who have business lunches with clients that cost less than $20 no longer need to provide sales receipts.

_____ 18.  We'd like to change your fitness center job so you can develop new skills, complete entire jobs by yourself so that the job is more meaningful, do the job the way you want to, and know how you are doing.

_____ 19.  To make your athletic assistant job less repetitive, we're adding three new responsibilities to your job description.

_____ 20.  I'd like you to learn how to run the stopwatch so that you can fill in for Ted while he's at lunch.

The **job characteristics model** addresses core job dimensions, critical psychological states, and employees' growth needs (their need to grow on the job) to improve the quality of working life for employees and productivity for the organization.

### Core Job Dimensions

As shown in figure 5.6, five core dimensions determine a job's personal outcomes (quality of working life for employees) and work outcomes (productivity for the organization). By enhancing each dimension (skill variety, task identity, task significance, autonomy, and feedback), you can increase both outcomes.

### Critical Psychological States and Personal and Work Outcomes

As the three critical psychological states (experienced meaningfulness of work, experienced responsibility for work, knowledge of the results of work)—which are developed through the five core job dimensions—improve, so do the job's personal and work outcomes (high internal work motivation, high-quality work performance, high satisfaction with the work, low absenteeism and turnover), as shown in figure 5.6.

### Employee Growth-Need Strength

A person's growth-need strength determines her interest in improving the five core dimensions. Note that if a person is not interested in enriching the job, the JCM will fail to increase personal and work outcomes. We examine needs and motivation in more detail in chapter 11. Figure 5.6 shows how this JCM process works.

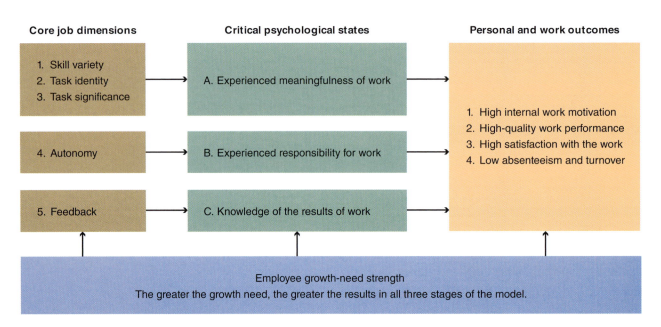

**FIGURE 5.6** The job characteristics model.

# Organizing Yourself and Delegating Work

Let's move from realizing how you must manage within an organization structure and job design[46] to learning how to organize yourself by setting priorities to achieve important things[47] and delegating to get work done through employees.[48] It's important to realize that productivity results aren't based on how busy you are[49] or how many hours you work;[50]

productivity comes from managers effectively setting priorities[51] and delegating work.[52] Complete Self-Assessment 5.1 to determine the priorities that are important to you.

## Setting Priorities

As we have already noted, setting priorities is an important aspect of organizing anything[53]— a department, a job, yourself. At any given time, you must perform several tasks. Prioritizing makes this easier and more successful,[54] and a to-do list is a good place to begin.[55] List the tasks you need to do and then rate each one by importance.[56] Then focus on accomplishing only one task at a time by its priority.

◀ LEARNING OUTCOME 11

Set priorities.

To begin, as a manager, ask yourself three yes-or-no questions:[57]

1. Do I need to be personally involved? When you are the only one who can do the task, you must be involved. But if your answer here is no, you don't need to answer the remaining questions for this task because you can delegate it to an employee.

2. Is the task my responsibility, or will it affect the performance or finances of my department? You are responsible for completing certain managerial tasks yourself, overseeing the performance of your department, and staying within your budget.

3. Is quick action needed (for a deadline)? Do you need to work on this activity right now, or can it wait? Time is relative, but you need to start soon enough to meet the deadline. This may sound obvious, but people often miss deadlines simply because they start too late, so it bears repeating: don't procrastinate.

## SELF-ASSESSMENT 5.1

### What Are Your Personal Priorities?

For the following 16 items, rate how important each one is to you on a scale of 1 (not important) to 10 (very important).

| Not important | | | | Somewhat important | | | | Very important | |
|---|---|---|---|---|---|---|---|---|---|
| 1 | 2 | 3 | 4 | 5 | 6 | 7 | 8 | 9 | 10 |

_____ 1. An enjoyable, satisfying job

_____ 2. A high-paying job

_____ 3. A good marriage

_____ 4. Meeting new people, attending social events

_____ 5. Involvement in community activities

_____ 6. Relationship with spirituality or religion

_____ 7. Exercising, playing sports

_____ 8. Intellectual development

_____ 9. A career with challenging opportunities

_____ 10. Nice cars, clothes, home

_____ 11. Spending time with family

_____ 12. Having several close friends

*(continued)*

_____ 13. Volunteer work for nonprofit organizations like the Cancer Society

_____ 14. Meditation, quiet time to think, pray

_____ 15. A healthy, balanced diet

_____ 16. Educational reading, TV, self-improvement programs

Transfer your rankings for each item to the appropriate column, and then add the two numbers in each column.

**Professional**

1. _____

9. _____

Totals _____

**Financial**

2. _____

10. _____

Totals _____

**Family**

3. _____

11. _____

Totals _____

**Social**

4. _____

12. _____

Totals _____

**Community**

5. _____

13. _____

Totals _____

**Spiritual**

6. _____

14. _____

Totals _____

**Physical**

7. _____

15. _____

Totals _____

**Intellectual**

8. _____

16. _____

Totals _____

The higher your total in any area, the more highly you value that area. The closer the numbers are in all eight areas, the more well-rounded you are.

Think about the time and effort you put into your top three priorities. Is your effort sufficient for you to achieve the level of success you want in each area? If not, what can you do to change your level of effort? Is there any area that you believe you should value more? If yes, what can you do to give more priority to that area?

Consider how you value physical activity. Do you value exercise, playing sports, and eating properly as much as you thought you would? Do you think your valuing of physical activity can be transferred to community, spiritual, and intellectual pursuits? Is it realistic to expect that the values we learn in sport will transfer to other activities? Is sport, as Plato thought, a most valuable tool in instilling the right attitudes and values in young people? Or are we expecting too much from our passion for sports?

### Assigning Priorities

Based on your answers to the three yes-or-no questions we presented under Setting Priorities, you can now assign each task a priority.[58]

- *Delegate priority (D)*. Delegate the task if your answer to question 1 is no (N). The task will go on your and another team member's to-do lists with a priority. You also need to plan the delegation and when it will take place. We discuss how to delegate in the next section.

- *High priority (H)*. Assign a high priority for the task if you answered yes to all three questions (YYY), but don't have too many *H*s because you can lose focus on determining which task is really most important.[59]

- *Medium priority (M)*. Assign a medium priority if you answered yes to question 1 but no to question 2 or question 3 (YNY or YYN).

- *Low priority (L)*. Assign a low priority if you answered yes to question 1 but no to both questions 2 and 3 (YNN).

### *Prioritizing Your To-Do List*

Figure 5.7 is a quick way to prioritize your to-do lists as a manager. Make copies of this figure (or make an electronic version) and use it on your job as follows:

1. List the tasks to be performed in enough detail so you know what you have to do later.

2. Answer the three prioritizing questions Y (yes) or N (no). Note the deadline and the time needed to complete the task. You may also want to note a deadline for starting the task as well as its completion date.

3. Assign a priority (D, H, M, or L) to the task. The top left part of figure 5.7 helps you to do this at a glance. If you wrote D, note when the task should be delegated.

4. Determine which task you should work on now. You may have more than one high-priority task, so select the most important one. When you have completed your high-priority tasks, start on the medium-priority ones, and finally work on your low-priority tasks.

You're not finished at this point—in fact, you've only just begun. You will need to continually update your list and add new tasks as they arise, but avoid the tendency to put off a high-priority task to work on a new lower-level task. Let the distractions (your phone) and so-called emergencies and urgent things that don't need to be done now wait until the more important things are done. Also, as time passes, priorities change. Writing a report or paper due in one month starts as an M or L priority, but the day before the due date it's an H priority.

**TIME-OUT 11** Make a copy of figure 5.7, and use it to list three to five tasks you must complete in the near future and prioritize them.

As we note in chapter 14, if you deal with a wide variety of changing tasks and you need to carve out time for long-range planning, we strongly suggest that you use the time management system. Your prioritized to-do list dovetails neatly with that system. If your job is more routine and you basically plan for the short term, the to-do list will probably suffice to keep you both organized and focused. Skill-Builder 5.1 in the web study guide uses the to-do list to help you develop your prioritizing skills.

## Delegating

When you delegate, you assign others the responsibility for accomplishing a task and give them the authority to meet the objective with the resources to complete the task. Remember that you can delegate responsibility and authority, but as a sport manager, you are held accountable for the actions of your employees. When delegating, you are coaching others to do the task. Directing others to do work that is part of their job description is *not* delegating; delegation is giving others tasks that are not part of their regular jobs. The delegated task may become a part of their job, or it may be a one-time task.

◀ **LEARNING OUTCOME 12**
Delegate.

### *Why Should You Delegate?*

As a coach and sport manager, in most cases you can't be a player. Your job is to get the work done by delegating it to athletes and employees.[60] When more tasks are accomplished, productivity rises.[61] Face it, there are tasks that others can do better than you can, anyway, so why not delegate those tasks to improve performance?[62] Also, delegating gives you time

# Prioritized To-Do List

| Assigning a priority | | Priority determination questions | | | | |
|---|---|---|---|---|---|---|
| **D** Delegate priority | **N** No to question 1 | 1. Do I need to be personally involved? | 2. Is it my responsibility, or will it affect performance or finances of my department? | 3. Is quick action needed? | Deadline/Time needed | Priority |
| **H** High priority | **YYY** Yes to all three questions | | | | | |
| **M** Medium priority | **YNY** or **YYN** Yes to question 1 and no to 2 or 3 | | | | | |
| **L** Low priority | **YNN** Yes to question 1 and no to questions 2 and 3 | | | | | |
| **Task** | | | | | | |
| | | | | | | |
| | | | | | | |
| | | | | | | |
| | | | | | | |
| | | | | | | |
| | | | | | | |
| | | | | | | |
| | | | | | | |
| | | | | | | |

**FIGURE 5.7** Prioritized to-do list.

to perform your high-priority tasks,[63] and when you are away from the job, the work still gets done.[64] Delegating challenges others and improves their self-esteem,[65] trains them for future opportunities, and eases the stress and burden on you. Wise delegation of work enriches jobs and improves personal and work outcomes. To help stop corruption, the IOC delegated separate tasks to different committees and internal agents to enable them to check on each other.

## What Stops Managers From Delegating?

Managers get used to doing things themselves—that's a habit and is relatively easy to fix. Many managers believe that they can perform a task more efficiently than others,[66] and they fear one of two things: (1) that the person will show them up, or (2) that the person will fail to accomplish the task, thereby making things worse, not better.[67] Recall that as a manager you can delegate responsibility and authority, but you cannot delegate accountability. Some managers don't realize that delegating work is an important part of their jobs. Others who know it is important are reluctant to delegate because they don't know what to delegate, or they don't know how to delegate (we'll teach you soon).[68] If you want to be an effective manager, make delegating part of your job. But first learn when and what to delegate, and to whom.

## How Can Managers Know That They Delegate Too Little?

Several flags indicate that managers are delegating too little: (1) They take work home; (2) they perform employee tasks; (3) they are continually behind in their work; (4) they continually feel pressured and stressed; (5) they are always rushing to meet deadlines; (6) they rarely meet deadlines; and (7) their employees always seek approval before acting. If you are a manager, does this sound like you?

 **TIME-OUT 12** Think about a situation at work where you believe the manager isn't delegating enough. Identify the obstacle preventing the manager from delegating, and list the flags that told you he or she isn't delegating enough.

# Getting to Delegating

An important part of delegating is knowing which tasks to delegate.[69] Effective delegators know which work to delegate, when to delegate it, and the right people to delegate it to.

## What and When to Delegate

The question of what to delegate and when will make you grateful that you have a prioritized to-do list because the answer is in the list. Here are the types of things you should consider delegating:

- *Paperwork.* Employees really can write reports, memos, and letters.
- *Routine tasks.* Employees really can check inventory, schedule, and order.
- *Technical matters.* Your top employees really can deal with technical questions and problems. (If they can't, it's time to train them!)
- *Tasks with developmental potential.* Employees like learning new things. Give them the opportunity to show the stuff they're made of.
- *Problem solving.* Train your people to solve their own problems. If they ask you what to do, ask them what they think they should do. More than likely they will have the answer, and they will catch on to the fact that they don't need to run to you to make all the decisions. Your team will be more effective, and you will be less stressed.

## What You Shouldn't Delegate

This is pretty clear-cut—do not delegate the following:

- Personnel matters—performance appraisals, counseling, disciplining, firing, and resolving conflicts.
- Confidential activities (unless you have permission to do so).
- Crises—these are why you are a manager, and you won't have time to delegate them, anyway.
- Activities assigned to you personally by your boss.

## Find the Right Person

This is where you earn your pay. You've got to know your people. If you choose wisely—that is, if the person has the skills, the growth-need strength, and the time to get the job done right by the deadline—you will have a happy employee and good results. If you choose unwisely, the person may fail, and the job will still need doing. So consider an employee's skills and the requirements of the job very carefully, and give him or her the coaching needed to succeed. Make sure the person has the temperament to work under pressure if a deadline is looming. When you hire employees, consider whether they can handle delegation to expand their skill set on the job.

## Now It's Time to Delegate

Delegating tasks quickly without a detailed plan often results in the employee not meeting your objective.[70] The following four-step model helps ensure that the job you need to get done gets done right. Note how these steps mesh with the job characteristics model, core job dimensions, and critical psychological states. The **delegation model** steps are to (1) explain the need for delegating and the reasons for selecting the team member; (2) set objectives that define responsibility, the level of authority, and the deadline; (3) develop a plan that will meet the objective; and (4) establish control checkpoints and coach as needed.

1. Explain why you are delegating this job and your reasons for selecting the team member. We all like to know why—indeed, one can make a strong case that we *need* to know why. Remember the "experienced meaningfulness of work"? Here is where you give work meaning. Telling people why they've been chosen is a very natural and genuine way to make them feel valued. Don't say things like, "it's a lousy job, but someone has to do it." Statements like this can make an employee feel negative and even resentful about the assignment. Be positive; make team members aware of how fans or customers, the team, department, or organization, and they themselves can benefit by completing the task. Employees should be motivated, or at least willing, to do the job.

2. Set an objective that defines the person's responsibility, the scope of her authority, and the deadline. State the objective, the end result, and the deadline using table 4.2, Writing Objectives Model, in chapter 4. Deadlines are important because they create pressure to get the job done on time.[71] Saying "Do it when you have time," "when you get a chance," or "as soon as possible (ASAP)" are not deadlines. Not having an established deadline leads to procrastination or to the task not getting done when you need it done. Define the employee's responsibility and level of authority (inform, recommend, report, or full).

Here is some career advice. If you can't meet a deadline, tell your manager (customer or other person) as soon as you know it—don't surprise them at the deadline. Be sure to set a new, realistic deadline, and meet it.[72] If you want excellent performance reviews that can lead to raises and promotions, exceed your boss' expectations, and follow Professor Lussier's motto: "I don't meet deadlines—I beat deadlines." When your name comes up, your boss should be thinking and saying what a great employee you are.

3. Develop a plan to meet the objective. What level of participation in developing the plan should you use: (1) you develop the plan alone, (2) you and the team member develop the plan together, or (3) the team member develops the plan alone? This will depend on team members' experience and ability to plan on their own. You (and the team member) may find it helpful to use a planning tool (see scheduling tools in chapter 14).

4. Establish control checkpoints, and coach as needed. Obviously for short, simple tasks, you don't need to set control checks to monitor progress toward the objective. But you should check progress on tasks that have multiple steps or that will take some time to complete. Consider the team member's capabilities and experience. The lower the capabilities or experience, the more often you should check on his work, and vice versa. The role-playing scenarios in Skill-Builder 5.2 in the web study guide will give you some practice in delegating.

For complex tasks and projects, more formalized control and accountability benefit everyone concerned. For one thing, this creates a healthy flow of information. Discussing and agreeing on the form of progress checks (phone calls, visits, memos, or detailed reports) and their time frame (daily, weekly, or after specific steps are completed) before work begins will prevent future misunderstandings. It is also helpful to formalize control checkpoints in writing (possibly on the planning sheet itself), distributing copies of it so that everyone involved has a record. In addition, all involved should record pertinent control checkpoints on their calendars. If someone doesn't report as scheduled, find out why. Evaluate performance at each checkpoint and also upon completion of the task to provide immediate feedback. (Sound familiar? This is the "knowledge of the results of work" that we discussed earlier.) Praising progress and successful completion of the task is always a good motivator. We will return to the subject of praise in chapter 11.

 **TIME-OUT 13** Think about a manager or coach for whom you have worked or played, and analyze how well he delegates. Which steps did your manager or coach do well, and which steps could he have done better?

Figure 5.8 summarizes the delegation process model.

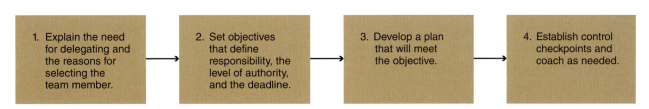

1. Explain the need for delegating and the reasons for selecting the team member. → 2. Set objectives that define responsibility, the level of authority, and the deadline. → 3. Develop a plan that will meet the objective. → 4. Establish control checkpoints and coach as needed.

**FIGURE 5.8** How to delegate.

LEARNING AIDS

## CHAPTER SUMMARY

1. **Explain how flat organizations and tall organizations differ.**

   Flat organizations have fewer layers of management with wide spans of control. Tall organizations have many layers of management with narrow spans of control.

2. **Describe liaisons, integrators, and boundary roles.**

   Liaisons, integrators, and people in boundary roles are all coordinators. Liaisons and integrators coordinate internally, whereas people in boundary roles coordinate efforts with customers, suppliers, and other people in the external environment. Liaisons work in one department and coordinate with other departments, whereas integrators coordinate department activities without working for a specific department.

3. **Differentiate between formal and informal authority.**

   Formal authority specifies relationships between employees. It is the sanctioned way of getting the job done. Informal authority comes from the strength of relationships that evolve as people interact—it works through trust and respect. With centralized authority, top managers make important decisions; with decentralized authority, middle-level and first-line managers make important decisions.

4. **Explain the four levels of authority.**

   (1) Informing authority—the person simply presents an alternative. (2) Recommending authority—the person presents alternatives and suggests one. (3) Reporting authority—the person can take action in his own area of expertise and regularly informs the boss. (4) Full authority—the person takes action in her area of expertise and usually does not have to inform the boss.

5. **Describe the relationship between line and staff authority.**

   Staff advise and assist line personnel, who are responsible for making decisions and directing others down the chain of command.

6. **Describe organization charts.**

   Organization charts show the organization's levels of management hierarchy, chain of command, the division and type of work, and the departmentalization of the entire organization.

7. **Explain how internal departmentalization and external departmentalization differ.**

   Internal departmentalization focuses on functions performed inside the organization, usually operations/production, marketing, accounting/finance, human resources, and others. External departmentalization focuses on the product, the customer, or the territory in which the organization does business.

8. **State the similarities and differences between matrix and divisional departmentalization.**

   Both are ways to set up departments. Matrix departments combine functional and product structures to focus on projects. Divisional departments are based on semiautonomous strategic business units and focus on portfolio management.

9. **Explain how job simplification and job expansion differ.**

   Job simplification makes jobs more specialized by eliminating tasks, combining tasks, or changing the sequence of work. Job expansion makes jobs less specialized by rotating employees, enlarging the job, or enriching the job to make it more interesting and challenging.

10. **Describe the job characteristics model and what it is used for.**

    This model is a conceptual framework for designing enriched jobs. It uses core job dimensions, critical psychological states, and employee growth-need strength to improve employees' personal and work outcomes and productivity for the organization.

11. **Set priorities.**

    Setting priorities involves asking three questions: (1) Do I need to be personally involved? (2) Is the task my responsibility or will it affect the performance or finances of my department? (3) Is quick action needed? Delegate when you don't need to be personally involved. Assign a high priority when your answers to all three questions are yes (YYY). Assign a medium priority when your answer is yes to question 1 but no to question 2 or 3 (YNY or YYN). Assign a low priority when your answer to question 1 is yes and your answers to questions 2 and 3 are no (YNN).

12. **Delegate.**

    To delegate effectively, (1) explain why you are delegating the task and the reasons you chose the team member to do the work; (2) clearly state objectives that define responsibility, the team member's scope of authority, and the deadline; (3) develop a plan for achieving the objective; and (4) establish control checkpoints and coach as needed.

## REVIEW AND DISCUSSION QUESTIONS

1. What is the difference between unity of command and unity of direction?

2. What is the relationship between the chain of command and the span of management (span of control)?

3. What do the terms *differentiation* and *integration* mean?

4. What is the difference between responsibility and authority?

5. Can a coach delegate accountability to a player?

6. How does the scope of authority change in an organization, and what is the flow of responsibility, authority, and accountability?

7. What is the difference between a general staff person and a specialist staff person?

8. What does an organization chart show? What doesn't it show?

9. What is the difference between product and customer departmentalization?

10. What is job design, and why is it necessary?

11. What is the difference between an integrated and a self-managed work team?

12. What is the importance of employee growth-need strength to the job characteristics model?

13. Why is it important to update priorities on a to-do list?

14. What is the first and most important question you ask to determine what and what not to delegate?

15. Explain why each of the four steps of delegating is necessary.

16. Why has there been a trend toward more team, network, virtual, and learning organizations? Is this a fad, or will it last?

17. Matrix structures violate the unity of command principle. Should companies not use the matrix structure?

18. Is centralized or decentralized authority better?

## CASES

### Sport Management Professionals @ Work: Nash Birch

From Springfield College to the major leagues! Well, maybe not in such an effortless path. Upon graduation, Springfield College alum Nash Birch had worked diligently during her 10-month internship to secure a full-time position working for Major League Baseball. Nash graduated magna cum laude from Springfield College, earning her bachelor's degree in sport management with a minor in business. Upon completing her in-credit internship with the New York Red Bulls, did Nash have any idea she would be working for Major League Baseball?

During the spring semester of her junior year, Nash completed a semester abroad in Barcelona, Spain. She completed a study abroad program at Universitat Autònoma de Barcelona, taking courses ranging from Doing Business in Emerging Markets to Nations Without State: A Case of Catalonia. During her four months abroad, Nash traveled to seven additional countries, exploring different cities, experiencing diverse cultures, tasting authentic food, and learning new languages.

Growing up with the financial support of her family, Nash has always felt the need to give back. Nash backpacked through Malawi, Africa, at the age of 16, which gave her a "bigger picture" perspective on life. Watching shoeless children running around a tiny grassy area strewn with broken bricks, which they called their soccer field, made a huge impact on Nash's life. Nash knew from this moment on that it was her duty to give back as much as possible. A few other organizations that have had an influential effect on Nash's life were Special Olympics, Feel Your Boobies Foundation, and the American Cancer Society. Nash continues to volunteer through events held by Major League Baseball, along with other organizations such as the ALS Association, New York Cares, and Save a Child's Heart.

During her academic career, Nash worked for the New York Red Bulls in varying capacities for three seasons. She worked game days as a member of the Premium Team staff. While a Premium Team member, she completed two internships, one in the Training Programs department and the other in the Marketing Partnerships department. Nash has cultivated remarkable relationships during her time working for the New York Red Bulls, which has helped her secure her internship with Major League Baseball.

All of her experiences have led her to accept an internship in Consumer Products at Major League Baseball. After 10 months of hard work and perseverance, her internship turned into a full-time position as the coordinator of the MLB authentication program. This position requires Nash to manage the authentication inventory and e-commerce duties; to consolidate club requests and provide scheduling to authenticators; to create, approve, and assign authentication sessions for proper authentic contacts; to create purchase orders that are expensed to clubs, licensees, and other third parties; to create a monthly newsletter to use as a communication conduit for the authenticators; to use data analysis to strategically plan for the growth of Star Wars authentic business; to create tools to improve the processes and functions of the program; and much more.

Along with all these sport experiences, Nash would like to encourage more young professionals to work diligently and follow their passion. No dream is too large, no obstacle cannot be overcome, and you never know where the road may lead if you shoot for the stars!

## Case Questions

1. Where have you volunteered? How can you apply your volunteering to sport management?

2. What did Nash achieve by studying abroad?

3. Why would the MLB like Nash's experience with the New York Red Bulls?

## Rebuilding Championship Teams in Boston

Boston is known for beans and the Red Sox. In the last decade, Boston has also been known as a city of well-organized championship teams. What is the organizing secret that led to all four professional teams' winning a championship? Even more interesting, how do championship teams rebuild to stay on top for a long period of time?

The Red Sox won the World Series in 2004 and 2007. Before then, the last time they had won a World Series was in 1918. Under the artful guidance of Terry Francona, known as a "player's manager," the team flourished with a "cowboy up" team philosophy.

Not to be outdone, the New England Patriots won three NFL Super Bowls in the decade of the 2000s. The Patriots won under the stern leadership of Bill Belichick. He is a no-nonsense coach who will release players who do not exhibit team spirit. He is also not afraid to release or trade valuable veterans before their contract expires, even if it appears they have some good playing years left. It should be noted that Belichick drafted Tom Brady, his Hall-of-Famer-to-be quarterback, with the 199th pick of the football draft—a wise choice and decision by Belichick.

Meanwhile, the Boston Celtics rekindled the magic of earlier decades by winning the NBA Championship in 2008. Led by General Manager Danny Ainge and Coach Doc Rivers, the team turned a decade of losing into a season of glory by reorganizing around three aging veterans. Kevin Garnett was acquired from the Minnesota Timberwolves and Ray Allen was acquired from Seattle, and they blended extremely well with longtime Celtic Paul Pierce. Coach Rivers took over and created a team atmosphere where a young guard (Rajon Rondo) was able to develop to help the experienced veterans. The new "Big Three" reminded fans of the original Big Three of Larry Bird, Kevin McHale, and Robert Parrish and their championship seasons.

Lastly, the city of Boston was able to enjoy the reorganization of the NHL Boston Bruins. The Big Bad Bruins were led by Coach Claude Julien, who had been expected to be fired for another lackluster playoff loss. However, the Bruins got the hot hand and worked hard in the corners to win the NHL Stanley Cup in 2011. Julien's style of play (with players working together as a scrappy, hard-nosed team) took a little time for people to learn. But with the hot goaltending of Tim Thomas and some balanced scoring, the result was a championship in a hard-fought series against the Vancouver Canucks.

Still, time goes by for all teams and organizations. Owners, coaches, and players all eventually need to change. Even the fans change from generation to generation, although families tend to stay loyal to their local teams.

In Boston, the new Big Three retired. However, Danny Ainge was able to use the draft picks he received by trading the older players, right before their skills eroded, to the Brooklyn Nets. Younger players picked in the draft, such as Jason Tatum from Duke, are ready to lead the Celtics to future NBA championships.[73]

The player-oriented baseball coach, Terry Francona, was replaced by the more stoic John Farrell, who won the 2013 World Series and two back-to-back Eastern Division titles in 2016 and 2017. Farrell was then replaced by the younger Alex Cora. The Red Sox have the highest payroll in MLB baseball, so ownership has used the free agency route to reorganize their team with talented players such as Hanley Ramirez, David Price, and J.D. Martinez. The Red Sox have also developed talented draft picks such as Mookie Betts and Jackie Bradley Junior.[74]

The Boston Bruins had to last through some hard times after winning their championship. The team fired Claude Julien after 10 years in 2017. However, under the guidance of General Manager Don Sweeney and new coach Bruce Cassidy, the team has rebuilt a core of new players acquired via the draft. Young players such as Charlie McAvoy and Jake DeBrusk are ready to lead the team for many years.[75]

The New England Patriots stand out as the team that hasn't changed its management, coach, or key player in over 15 years. Owner Robert Kraft, Coach Bill Belichick, and star quarterback Tom Brady are all still leading the team. Although rumors put them at odds on certain decisions that have been made, they insist their goals are aligned to add to their six Super Bowl victories. The ultimate goal is not only build, but rebuild and maintain excellence.[76]

For more information, visit redsox.com, bruins.nhl.com, celtics.com, and patriots.com. Go to the web study guide to answer questions about this case study.

## @ TAKE IT TO THE NET

Please visit www.HumanKinetics.com/AppliedSportManagementSkills and go to the book's companion web study guide, where you will find the following:

A list of websites associated with the concepts in this chapter

Skill-Builder exercises, Sports and Social Media exercises, and a continuing Game Plan for Starting a Sport Business

Online versions of chapter exercises and end-of-chapter learning aids

An exercise that helps you define the Key Terms

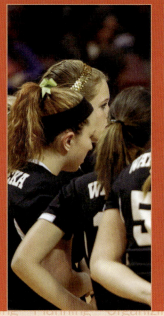

# Sport Culture, Innovation, and Diversity

## LEARNING OUTCOMES

After studying this chapter, you should be able to

1. identify the driving forces behind change;

2. list the four variables of change;

3. differentiate between fact, belief, and values;

4. describe the three components of organizational culture;

5. state the core values of TQM;

6. describe a learning organization;

7. explain how diversity can affect innovation and quality;

8. state how force-field analysis and survey feedback differ; and

9. explain the difference between team building and process consultation.

## KEY TERMS

variables of change

management information systems (MISs)

stages in the change process

organizational culture

components of culture

core values of TQM

learning organization

organizational development (OD)

OD interventions

force-field analysis

survey feedback

team building

process consultation

## DEVELOPING YOUR SKILLS

Change is a fact of life. Your ability (or inability) to change with the ever-shifting demands of the business environment may make (or break) your career. And if you are to succeed in management, one task you must learn to do—and do well—is to implement change. In this chapter, you will learn to identify and overcome resistance to change, which can mean the difference between a successful transition and a failed one. You will also need to work within the sport organization's culture; you will need to be able to work with a diversity of people; and you may be involved in an organizational development change intervention, such as team building.

## REVIEWING THEIR GAME PLAN

### Diversity Issues in Sport Management

The topic of diversity is certainly one of the most popular in the *Journal of Sport Management*. The titles of the articles should help you to appreciate the wide spectrum of issues about diversity in sport management.

- "Gendered Leadership Networks in the NCAA: Analyzing Affiliation Networks of Senior Woman Administrators and Athletic Directors," by Matthew Katz, Nefertiti A. Walker, and Lauren C. Hindman, *Journal of Sport Management* 32, no. 2 (2017): 135-149.[1] The purpose of this study was to examine and compare the informal networks of both senior woman administrators (SWAs) and athletic directors (ADs) within National Collegiate Athletic Association Division I institutions.

- "The Gendered Experiences of Women Staff and Volunteers in Sport for Development Organizations: The Case of Transmigrant Workers of Skateistan," by Holly Thorpe and Megan Chawansky, *Journal of Sport Management* 31, no. 6 (2017): 546-561. This study offers insights on female transmigrant workers from Africa who relocated to work for a skateboarding project in Afghanistan. The article focuses particularly on how formal and informal management strategies are experienced by international female staff and volunteers.[2]

Learning more about these articles from the *Journal of Sport Management* will help you to learn more about diversity in sport management.

# Managing Change

New York Yankees former player and coach Yogi Berra once said, "The future ain't what it used to be." It has been predicted that between now and 2020, virtually every facet of how we live and work will change.[3] Today, an organization's long-term success stands directly on the shoulders of its ability to manage change.[4] Things are changing fast,[5] and managers can't get stuck in the way they currently do business. Do you know that the early term for a smartphone was a BlackBerry because that device dominated sales? It failed to change, and it lost sales to Samsung and Apple; in 2016 it stopped making phones.[6] Change leadership is an important skill that recruiters seek in job candidates.[7] An important career question to ask yourself is, "Am I willing to constantly make changes?" If you answer no, don't expect to advance far in your career.

In this section, we discuss forces for change, management functions and change, variables of change, stages in the change process, resistance to change and how to overcome it, and a model for identifying and overcoming resistance.

## Forces for Change

We examine five different forces for change:

◄ LEARNING OUTCOME 1
Identify the driving forces behind change.

- *Environmental forces.* As we noted in chapter 2, the environment is becoming increasingly global and competitive,[8] and organizations need to align their internal and external environments.[9] Innovative organizations strive to make internal changes to stay ahead of the competition, but as they interact continually with their external environment, they often must make internal changes just to keep up.[10]

- *Economic forces.* When the economy and jobs are growing, there is more money to spend on sport programs from youth through the pros and more money to spend on sport apparel, equipment, and tickets. Today more sports, such as track and field, offer a path for amateur athletes to become pros. Even athletes with average skills make millions of dollars per year. MLB has become a sport where big-market teams like the New York Yankees and Boston Red Sox can generate more revenues than small-market teams like the Kansas City Royals and thus can afford to spend more money to acquire star players. More star players mean more fan and media interest.

- *Social forces.* The sociology of sport is an academic discipline that has evolved significantly in the past 40 years. Social forces cause the popularity of sports to increase and decrease. You may not know it, but bowling was once a popular professional sport. Social forces also lead to the maxim that everyone loves a winner—fan attendance at games does change during winning and losing streaks.

 Do you believe your college is a melting pot where people blend together? Or is it more like a kaleidoscope where people hold onto their unique differences?

- *Demographic forces.* Teams must take into consideration the diverse populations in their marketplaces. As the U.S. white population continues to decrease and Hispanic and other minorities increase, teams should recruit minorities who will attract fans. Some teams already offer media and marketing materials in other languages. We will discuss diversity later in this chapter.

**TIME-OUT 1** Think about a change that the organization you work for or play for has faced recently, and identify the force driving the change.

- *Technological forces.* Sport apparel and equipment companies like Nike and Under Armour continue to improve their products to improve athletic performance. Information technology is very different today than it was only a few years ago. Fewer sport fans are getting their sport news from print newspapers and traditional TV broadcasts. What devices do you use?

## Management Functions and Change

Leaders manage change every workday. Managing change requires conceptual skills to understand changes in the environment, and it requires decision-making skills to effectively implement the management functions (chapter 1) to make the changes.[11] When you set an *objective*, the *plans* that you develop to achieve it require changes. *Organizing* structures and job designs produces changes in working relationships and in the work performed. *Delegating* tasks can add new responsibilities to jobs. The process of hiring, orienting, and training employees and evaluating their performance may reveal that aspects of their jobs or the approach to their jobs must change. Managers need to apply their leadership influence with employees to continually make changes to improve performance. Controls are used to monitor progress toward meeting objectives, and changes are made to keep on track to achieve the objectives.

## Variables of Change

**LEARNING OUTCOME 2** ▶

List the four variables of change.

The four **variables of change**—strategy, structure, technology, and people—refer to what organizations must adapt to, adjust, shift, or re-create to stay current, to keep or grow market share, or to remain viable as they are bombarded with changes they must address in the marketplace (see table 6.1). You need to consider how a change in one variable will affect the other variables through the systems effect and plan accordingly.

### Strategy and Structure

As discussed in chapter 5, organizations adjust strategies in order to adapt to changes in their environments. Structure typically follows strategy. In other words, a change in strategy changes structure. Over time, organizational structures evolve to adapt to emerging needs. We examined organizational structure in chapter 5; figure 5.3 briefly summarizes key elements in organizational structure.

### Technology

Technology increases productivity and thus helps organizations gain competitive advantage and improve our quality of life. Technology advances two to three times faster than organizations can keep up with.[12] Technology, especially the Internet and smartphones, has changed the way we live and work.[13] Technology often drives changes in strategy, structure, and people. Here are a few examples of the innumerable ways technology affects changes:

- *Machines.* Athletes look to their equipment suppliers (Nike, Spalding, Wilson, and many others) to provide cutting-edge shoes, bats, skis, and bicycles and to their trainers and therapists to provide cutting-edge training techniques and rehabilitation methods to facilitate recovery from injuries. Do you have some type of a Fitbit or app?

- *Systems process.* In chapter 2 you learned that the *systems process* is the technology used to transform inputs into outputs. Every organization has some type of operations

**TABLE 6.1** **The Four Variables of Change**

| Strategy | Structure | Technology | People |
|---|---|---|---|
| Corporate (growth, stability, and turnaround and retrenchment) | Principles (unity of command and direction, chain of command, span of management, division of labor, coordination, balanced responsibility and authority, delegation, and flexibility) | Machines | Skills |
| Business level (prospecting, defending, and analyzing) | Authority (formal and informal, line and staff, and centralized and decentralized; levels of authority) | Systems process | Performance |
| Functional (marketing, operations, finance, and human resources) | Organizational design (departmentalization) | Information process | Attitudes |
|  | Job design (job simplification, rotation, enlargement, enrichment, and work teams) | Automation | Behavior |

department that has a systems process to create its goods or services, and technology is what makes the systems process work.

- *Information process.* With the advent of the computer, organizations have radically changed the way they do business using big data. **Management information systems (MISs)**, also called information systems, are formal systems for collecting, processing, and disseminating information that aids managers in decision making. MISs centralize and integrate the organization's key information, such as finance, production, inventory, and sales. Departments plugged into MISs can better coordinate their efforts, and this translates into a more focused organization and higher productivity. Just think about how much easier computers have made it to record and maintain all the statistics of each team and each player in all the sports at all levels,

What are some ways that technology may drive changes in strategy, structure, and staff for major sports teams?

© Steve Debenport/Getty Images

especially in professional leagues like the NFL that keep records on hundreds of players.

*Moneyball* is still as controversial today as it was in 2003. The concept that statistical analysis can outperform the wisdom of experts has spread to other sports and many other industries. Moneyball is so popular that decision makers in many fields rely on analytical data instead of trusting the experts in the field.[14] The concern about Moneyball is that teams have actually relied on analytics too much. Boston Red Sox owner John Henry stated that the team relied too much on analytics in making major decisions. He has added managers who rely often on their instincts.[15]

- *Automation.* Computers and other machines have enabled organizations to replace people with robots. Automation has increased the speed of making athletic equipment and its quality and helped keep prices down. Automation takes away some jobs and adds others. It also changes the types of work people do. Pressing needs for better training, retraining, and higher levels of skill will continue to help athletes to break records for the foreseeable future. *Artificial intelligence (AI)* is the use of any device that perceives its environment and takes actions to achieve its goals, such as a self-driving car continuing to adjust to road conditions to get you safely to your destination. AI will continue to automate how we work (with robots), and live (in home appliances).

- *Incremental and discontinuous change. Incremental change* is continual improvement of an existing product within the current technology cycle.[16] *Discontinuous change* (also called *creative destruction*) is a significant breakthrough in technology that leads to a new product, often a replacement product, creating a new technology cycle.[17] This requires competitors to make radical changes or go out of business.[18] The technology of recording music on vinyl records was incrementally improved for years but began to be overtaken by music recorded on tape. Cassette tapes were disrupted by CDs and MP3 players, which are being disrupted by streaming.

## People

Common types of people change occur when members join or leave your team and receive education and training to enhance their job skills, including receiving college degrees. People have always been, and always will be, the key variable of change.[19] Why? Because changes in the other three variables will not be effective without people.[20] It is people who develop and implement strategy, structure, and technology; they are the most valuable resource for

## APPLYING THE CONCEPT **6.1**

### Variables of Change

Identify the change variable involved in each situation.

a. strategy

b. structure

c. technology

d. people

_____ 1. We installed a new computer system to reduce the time it takes to bill ticket customers.

_____ 2. With the increasing number of pro basketball leagues, we're going to have to devote more time and effort to keeping our existing customers.

_____ 3. Jamie, I'd like you to consider getting a college degree if you're serious about a career in management with this team.

_____ 4. We're changing suppliers to get higher-quality components for our tennis rackets.

_____ 5. We are laying off some assistant coaches to increase the number of players reporting to one coach.

change.[21] When any other variables change, a change in people skills is needed. This may require adding new people or training current employees. To stay current and advance in your career, view learning as a life-long process, and continue to keep up with the latest trends and skills in your field.[22] A change in organizational *culture* is also considered a people change, and we will discuss it in the next major section.

**TIME-OUT 2** Describe a recent change in your organization or team, and identify the variables of change affecting it or affected by it.

## Stages in the Change Process

People in the midst of a change commonly go through four distinct **stages in the change process**—denial, resistance, exploration, and commitment.

1. *Denial.* When people first hear rumors that change is coming, they go into denial—"It won't happen here!" Prudent managers manage change proactively; they don't wait until change rudely knocks on the door. They start addressing the change and its ramifications early on to both lessen the impact of the change and smooth the transition.

2. *Resistance.* Once people get over their initial shock and realize that change will happen, they often doubt there is a need for the change and resist changing. We all tend to resist change, and we discuss the reasons in the next section.

3. *Exploration.* When implementation begins, people explore the change, often through training, and they begin to better understand how it will affect them. It is helpful to solicit input from those affected. Inviting and encouraging them to be part of the change process are important to successful implementation.

4. *Commitment.* Through exploration, people commit (or don't commit) to making the change a success. One's level of commitment can also change. Be alert for naysayers, and carefully and patiently address statements like "It's always been done this way."

Figure 6.1 illustrates the change process. We present the stages as occurring in a circular fashion because change is rarely linear. People go back and forth—they waver in their resistance and commitment, as the arrows show.

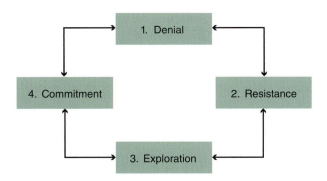

**FIGURE 6.1**   Stages in the change process.

## Resistance to Change and How to Overcome It

When change programs fail, it is usually because the people involved resist—even sabotage—the change efforts.[23] Do you really like to change your habits and routines?[24] It is important to understand that we all—in one way or another, and at one level or another—resist change. "Only a baby with a wet diaper likes change."[25]

Although U.S. law changed to give females equal rights to participate in sport (Title IX of the Education Amendments of 1972), people resisted, and some are still resisting. As a manager, your job is to enact changes. To do so, you need to understand why people resist and then find ways to counter resistance. See table 6.2 for an overview.

### Why Do We Resist Change?

Here are some of the major reasons.

- *We fear uncertainty and learning.* Fear of the unknown is a universal human trait, and people resist change in order to cope with their anxiety and fear of the unknown and failure. Even thinking about learning something new can create anxiety—*learning anxieties*.

- *We don't like to be inconvenienced and change successful habits.* We often don't want to disrupt our routines or the way things are because they are comfortable.[26] We become fixed in our habits of repetition.[27] Even if the change is easy and we don't have learning anxieties, it's easier to do things the same old way than to change.

    When you are successful at something, do you want to change at the risk of a decrease in performance? Have you, or anyone you know, been pretty good at playing a certain position but been asked by the coach to play another position requiring different skills for the good of the team? How did you feel? Did you resist changing positions?

- *We always move to protect our self-interest.* When people hear about change, they ask, "How will it affect me?" Of course people will resist change if it threatens their self-interest.[28]

 Describe how the AD at a Division III college would use the strategies in table 6.2 to overcome the players' resistance to change. Assume that the AD is adding more women's teams to comply with Title IX of the Education Amendments of 1972.

### TABLE 6.2   Overcoming Resistance to Change

| Why people resist change | How to overcome resistance |
| --- | --- |
| Uncertainty creates fear. | Create a trust climate. |
| Inconvenience is off-putting. | Develop a change plan. |
| Their self-interest is threatened. | State why change is needed and how it affects people. |
| They fear loss. | Create a win–win situation. |
| They don't want to lose control of their jobs. | Involve people and provide support. |
|  | Follow through. |

We are usually more concerned about our own best interest than that of the team or organization. Know any ball hogs who don't want to become team players?

• *We fear loss.* Change often brings loss of jobs, or it may require pay cuts—witness older players who can no longer demand high salaries as they did when they were rising stars. Ever feared the loss of a good friendship when you or a teammate changed teams? Aging athletes are often happy to prolong their careers for a year or two just to spend more time with their teammates.

• *We like to be in control, or at least feel as if we're in control.* Actual or perceived losses in power, status, security, and especially control often come with change programs. Aging athletes often want to prolong their careers to keep control of their status as pro athletes and because they fear the uncertainty of a new career.

**TIME-OUT 3** Describe an instance in which you resisted change. Specify which of the five reasons were behind your resistance. Now, be your own manager and prescribe some proactive ways you could have overcome your initial reluctance.

## How Can You Overcome Your Resistance to Change?

You cannot change anything without your mind accepting the change.[29] So you need to have a mind-set that embraces change.[30] Yes. It is easier said than done. But face it. If you know you have to make a change, resisting it doesn't help, does it? So accept it, and make the change willingly. Follow Nike's advice and Just Do It!

In addition to changing our thoughts, we need to make the changed behavior a habit to make it successful.[31] If you say you will exercise more, but you don't make a scheduled time to work out (routine habit), you may not work out. Developing a habit takes conscious planning and effort—schedule time to work out. A habit has three parts, and here is an example.[32]

1. *Cue.* Leave your running shoes near your bed at night so they remind you to run.
2. *Routine.* Run first thing in the morning.
3. *Reward.* Endorphin rush, feel good about yourself and healthier, better athletic performance, weight loss and more energy; eat a healthy breakfast.

Are there any good habits you should develop (like eating healthier)? Are there any bad, self-destructive habits you should drop or replace (such as hanging out with people who are a bad influence on your behavior, or taking drugs, or drinking too much)? Are you willing to be more positive about change and develop habits that can help you succeed as an athlete and sport manager? Skill-Builder Exercise 6.3, New Habits, in the web study guide can help.

## How Can You Overcome Others' Resistance to Change?

Now that you know why people resist change and how to overcome your resistance to change, let's focus on overcoming others' resistance to change. The good news is that there are ways to alleviate their fears and overcome their resistance as well as more ways to overcome your own resistance. Here are some key ones:

• *Create a trust climate.* You do this by carefully developing and maintaining good relations with your team so that they trust you.[33] Make sure your colleagues understand that you have their best interests in mind. Constantly look for better ways to do things. Encourage people to suggest changes and implement their ideas. They are valued members of your team—show it!

• *Develop a change plan.* Successful implementation of change is no accident. Behind every successful implementation stands a good plan. Develop one and then use it. Identify possible resistance to change, and plan ways to overcome it. View change from your team's position. Set clear objectives so that everyone knows exactly what to do during and after the change. And make sure your plan addresses the next five issues.

- *State why the change is necessary and how it will affect your team.* Communication is the key. People need to know all the whys and all the hows. "Why are we doing this? How will it affect us?" Give them the good news and the bad news. Be open, honest, and ethical in bringing about change. You've taken great care to build trust—don't squander it. Giving everyone the facts as early as you can not only prevents their fears but also helps them feel in control. (Now they can make plans.) If the grapevine starts spreading incorrect information, correct the information quickly and firmly.

- *Create a win–win situation.* Obviously, you can't always do this, but often you can meet employee needs and achieve the objectives you've been given. Think about how you can answer the question everyone is thinking but nobody is asking: "What's in it for me?" People who see how they will benefit from a change will be more open to it. So, how do you create this win–win scenario? Read on.

- *Involve people.* It's a fact—a group's commitment to change is critical to its success. Here's another fact—people who help develop change are more committed to the success of the change than are those who don't. It's about ownership and it's about control. It helps if you phrase your own ideas as if a team member said them so that they commit to your idea for change without realizing it. If we feel we "own" the change, we feel in control, and we'll work hard to make it succeed.

- *Provide support.* Training is very important to successful change; therefore, it behooves you and your organization to provide as much training as you can before, during, and often after a change is made. Thorough training reduces learning anxieties, alleviates frustration, and helps people realize they will "have a life" after the change. Get them to believe, "I can do that."[34]

- *Follow through.* Coaching in the office or on the field is all about persistent follow-through to maintain and improve performance. If a Little League or MLB coach sees a player drop his lead elbow as he swings the bat, do you think that simply telling the player once to change his technique is enough?

## Model for Identifying and Overcoming Resistance

Before initiating change of any sort, savvy managers anticipate how their team will react. Looking at three key components of the resistance itself—intensity, source, and focus—will help you understand why certain members of your group may be reluctant to change.[35]

### Intensity

We all view change differently. Some of us even thrive on it (with low intensity), and others are upset by having to change. Most of us resist change at first but gradually accept it (with medium intensity), yet some of us resist it forever (with strong intensity). And we view different changes differently. To implement change, it helps to know the intensity of your group's response. To lower the intensity, follow the seven methods for overcoming resistance to change. Let's discuss the other two variables.

### Source

Resistance to change arises from three sources:

- *Facts.* All of us at one time or another have used facts to prove our point. Using fact can help overcome others' fear of the unknown and uncertainty about the change.

- *Beliefs.* Factual statements can be proven. But beliefs cannot because they are subjective opinions—they are our perceptions. How we perceive a situation colors whether

◀ **LEARNING OUTCOME 3**

Differentiate between fact, belief, and values.

we believe that a change will be beneficial or detrimental. People sometimes resist change by refusing to believe facts, even though they are proven. It is often hard to prove how a change will affect your team, so the issue becomes a matter of their beliefs versus yours. Our beliefs are influenced by others, so it helps to get a person that your team members trust to encourage the team members to make the change.

- *Values.* We have beliefs about everything. But values go beyond beliefs because what we value is extremely important to us. Values pertain to right and wrong behavior (ethics and religion), and values help us prioritize what is important. Sometimes the facts collide with our values—in such situations, values often win.

### Focus

When we resist change, we do so from three viewpoints—that is, we choose a focus:

- *Ourselves.* All of us ask, What's in it for me? What will I gain or lose through the change? When we perceive (correctly or incorrectly) that a proposed change will affect us negatively, we will resist the change.

- *Others.* After considering what's in it for us, or when the change does not affect us, we consider how the change will affect other people who are of value to us. If we believe the change will affect important others negatively, we may also be reluctant to embrace the change.

- *Work environment.* The work environment includes where we work and the work itself. We like to be in control of our situation, and we resist changes that take away our feelings of control. Has a manager asked you to do a task you didn't want to do?

The resistance matrix in figure 6.2 gives examples for each component. Use the matrix to identify the intensity, source, and focus of your team. This will help you decide which strate-

Sources of resistance (fact →belief →values)

| **Focus of resistance (work → other → self)** | **1. Facts about self**<br><br>• I have never done the task before.<br>• I failed the last time I tried. | **4. Beliefs about self**<br><br>• I'm too busy to learn it.<br>• I'll do it, but don't blame me if it's wrong. | **7. Values pertaining to self**<br><br>• I like the way I do my job now. Why change?<br>• I like working in a group. |
|---|---|---|---|
| | **2. Facts about others**<br><br>• She has the best performance record in the department.<br>• Other employees told me it's hard to do. | **5. Beliefs about others**<br><br>• He just pretends to be busy to avoid extra work.<br>• She's better at it than I am; let her do it. | **8. Values pertaining to others**<br><br>• Let someone else do it; I do not want to work with her.<br>• I like working with him. Don't cut him from our department. |
| | **3. Facts about the work environment**<br><br>• We are paid only $8 an hour.<br>• It's over 100 degrees. | **6. Beliefs about the work environment**<br><br>• This is a lousy job.<br>• The pay here is too low. | **9. Values pertaining to the work environment**<br><br>• I don't care if we meet the goal or not.<br>• The new task will make me work inside. I'd rather be outside. |

Intensity (high, medium, or low for each box)

**FIGURE 6.2** Resistance matrix.

Based on Hultman (1979).

gies will lead people to buy into making the change work. Note that intensity is outside the matrix because it can be strong, moderate, or weak for the other nine components. In Skill-Builder 6.1 in the web study guide, you will use the resistance matrix to identify the source and focus of resistance to various changes.

**TIME-OUT 4** Think about the situation you identified in the preceding Time-Out, and then use the resistance matrix in figure 6.2 to determine your level of intensity, the focus of your resistance, and its source.

# Organizational Culture

**Organizational culture** is the set of values, beliefs, and standards for acceptable behavior that its members share. It should create an internal environment that enables the firm to achieve its mission by living its values and beliefs daily.[36] The culture should be one in which people care about each other, the team, and their work.[37] When you understand an organization's culture, you can understand how it functions and how you can fit in. Fit with the culture is one of the top criteria recruiters look for when hiring new employees. It's a shared understanding of the organization's identity. Think of culture as the organization's personality. Sport team culture adds a special dimension to the idea of organizational culture because bonds within teams are often very strong. With sport teams come special ways of behaving or goofing off, a special determination to win, ways of dealing with winning and losing—in short, all the bonding mechanisms are in full display.

Add to this mix the fans who closely identify with or idolize a particular team's culture, image, or personality, and you have many strong forces at play. NCAA Division I and III teams tend to have distinctive cultures determined in part by their focus on academics. Professional teams often have distinct personalities. Think of "good guy" teams like the Seattle Mariners and "bad guy" teams like the Oakland Raiders.

## Components of Culture

In this section, you will learn that the three **components of culture** are behavior, values and beliefs, and assumptions. We will also examine strong and weak cultures and how we learn about an organization's culture.

◄ **LEARNING OUTCOME 4**
Describe the three components of organizational culture.

### *Behavior*

Behavior is observable action—what we do and say. Artifacts are the results of our behavior, and we will discuss artifacts in more detail after we differentiate strong and weak cultures.

### *Values and Beliefs*

Values represent the way we think we ought to behave and identify what we think it takes to be successful. Beliefs can be expressed as if–then statements. (If I do X, then Y will happen.) Values and beliefs are the operating principles that guide decision making and behavior in an organization; they influence ethical or unethical behavior. We observe values and beliefs only indirectly, through the behaviors and decisions they drive. Values and beliefs are often described in an organization's mission statement, but take care here—sometimes an organization's talk (its stated values and beliefs) doesn't match its walk (values and beliefs put into action).

 What is the image of the Indianapolis Colts as a team? the Indianapolis Colts as an organization?

### *Assumptions*

Assumptions are deeply ingrained values and beliefs whose truth we never question. Because our assumptions are the very foundation of our belief system, they are patently obvious to us—and we assume to everyone else—so we rarely discuss them. They are the automatic pilots that guide our behavior. Naturally, when our assumptions are challenged, we feel threatened. Question a teammate on why things are done in certain ways; if the response is, "That's the way it has always been done," you have probably run into an assumption. Assumptions are often the most stable and enduring part of culture and the most difficult to change.

## Strong Cultures and Weak Cultures

Organizational cultures range from strong to weak. In organizations with strong cultures, people unconsciously share assumptions and consciously know the organization's values and beliefs. That is, they agree with the organization's assumptions, values, and beliefs and behave as expected. In organizations with weak cultures, many employees don't behave as expected—they don't share underlying assumptions. They question and challenge the beliefs. When people don't agree with the generally accepted values and beliefs, they may rebel and fight the culture. This can either strengthen or weaken an organization. Culture is both an entrenched phenomenon and a fluid one. Hence cultures resist change, but they also continually adapt to the times. In essence, with a strong culture everyone behaves the same (exhibited by such things as the use of common jargon, dress, and material objects), but they don't in a weak culture.

TIME-OUT 5

Give examples of behaviors that show your organization's culture working. What values, beliefs, and assumptions underlie these behaviors? Does the organization have a strong culture or a weak one?

There is good news and bad news about strong cultures. Strong cultures make communication and cooperation easier and better. Unity is common, and consensus is easier to reach. The downside is potential stagnation and a lack of diverse opinion (no one thinks about alternative ways of doing things). The continually changing business environment requires that assumptions, values, and beliefs be questioned occasionally and changed when they no longer adequately address the needs of the marketplace.

A change in culture is a people change. To be effective, changes in culture have to occur in all three components (people's behavior, values and beliefs, and assumptions). A culture of success allows for change, and businesses that fail to move with the times lose their competitive advantage.

## APPLYING THE CONCEPT 6.2

### Strong Cultures and Weak Cultures

Identify each statement as characteristic of an organization with (a) a strong culture or (b) a weak culture.

_____ 6. Walking around this athletic department during my job interview, I realized I'd have to wear a jacket and tie every day.

_____ 7. I'm a little tired of hearing about how our team founders conducted their business. We all know the stories, so why do people keep telling them?

_____ 8. I've never met with so many people who all act so differently. I guess I can just be me rather than trying really hard to fit in.

_____ 9. It's hard to say what is really important in our department. Management says quality is important, but the supervisors force us to work too fast, and they know we send out defective athletic equipment all the time just to meet orders.

_____ 10. I started to tell this ethnic joke and the other employees all gave me a dirty look.

Successful organizations realize that managing culture is not a program with a starting and ending date. It is an ongoing endeavor that is part of organizational development (OD). You will learn about OD later in this chapter.

## How Team Members Learn the Culture

So you graduate and get a sport management job. How do you learn the organizational culture, and how do you know how to behave at work? First, observe the behavior of your coworkers. You may want to dress like them and use the same jargon. Next, learn the values and beliefs of your team. Recall that artifacts are the results of behavior; they convey values and beliefs. Let's discuss six artifacts that organizations use to convey and live their cultures so that you can observe and learn about the culture.

1. *Heroes.* Managers, particularly founders, have a strong influence on their organization's culture. The late Tom Yawkey of the Boston Red Sox and George Halas of the Chicago Bears were legends in their own time and are legends still to fellow players, colleagues, and fans alike who relish the tales and anecdotes surrounding these enduring personalities.

2. *Stories.* The stories are often about founders or other heroes. Have you ever heard of or seen the movie about Notre Dame football coach Knute Rockne, heard the expression "win one for the Gipper," or seen the movie about Rudy? The *Knute Rockne* and *Rudy* football movies are old, but they are worth watching.

3. *Slogans.* Dick's Sporting Goods' slogan is "Best Price Guarantee," and Nike has "Just Do It!" Which men's college football teams are the Fighting Irish and the Buckeyes, and which women's basketball team is the Huskies?

4. *Symbols.* What is your college logo and team mascot? Do your teams get any jackets, pins, or plaques? Nike uses the swoosh on every product. Ever won a trophy?

5. *Rituals.* Ever seen NFL players giving chest bumps? Ever watched the Olympic gold medal winners stand in victory as their national anthem was played?

6. *Ceremonies.* Does your college have any sports banquets or award ceremonies for academic achievement?

## Innovation, Quality, and the Learning Organization

In chapter 3 we noted that creativity is a way of thinking that generates new ideas and that innovation is the implementation of a new idea, making innovation extremely important to organizational success.[38] Recall the importance of keeping up with the latest technology.[39] Fortune 500 company CEOs ranked the rapid pace of technology change as their single biggest challenge.[40]

Two important types of innovation are product innovation (new things) and process innovation (new ways of doing things).[41] You need to actively seek opportunities and to take action to create new products and processes. You have to be able to adapt your current practices and thinking and go for innovation.

Amer Sports' mission is "to provide everyone from first-time participants to professional athletes with the world's best sports and fitness equipment, footwear and apparel."[42] Amer Sports owns a variety of famous athletic brands such as Salomon, Louisville Slugger, Wilson, and Atomic. Amer Sports believes developing new products requires being innovative and always questioning the way things are done.

Process innovation occurs when coaches bring in new concepts for how games are played or how players should train for games. For example, computers are now used extensively during preparation for football games, eliminating much of the time-consuming gathering of video and organizing of notes. NFL coaches can call up any play on the computer that either their own team or a competitor has run in previous games. They can retrieve all plays called for a certain down and yardage combination (e.g., third down and 8 yards to gain) and what defense the other team played (e.g., a dime defense).

 What product innovations have occurred in baseball in the past 10 years? What product innovations have occurred in football in the past 10 years?

## Innovation

Organizations need formal structures to coordinate internal activities,[43] but rigid bureaucracy makes it difficult and slow to implement innovations.[44] So-called tall organizations have superfluous layers of management, which slows decision making and makes them less able to move quickly on opportunities. Organizations are developing innovative cultures by using flat organizational structures. As noted in chapter 5, flat organizations limit their bureaucracies, divide labor along generalist lines (not by specialties), and routinely use cross-functional teams to get the work done, solve problems, and identify opportunities. Flexibility is the name of their game. Systems are informal, and authority is decentralized. Jobs are designed to be richer in content and in responsibility, and work teams are used to make continuous improvements.[45]

TIME-OUT 6 Describe an innovation from an organization you have worked for or played for. Was it a product innovation or a process innovation?

Large companies commonly create within their divisions the small units and teams that are so essential to innovation. Innovative organizations commonly create separate systems for innovative groups, such as new venture units. They also recruit creative people and train their workforce to think creatively (yes, this can be done!). Their reward system encourages people to think about new ways to do things. Many organizations reward individuals and groups that come up with innovative ideas; cash, prizes (such as trips), praise, and (always) recognition encourage people to explore the less traveled path.

## Quality

**LEARNING OUTCOME 5** ▶

State the core values of TQM.

High-performing organizations believe that innovation and quality go hand in hand. In fact, the characteristics that make a corporate culture innovative are essentially the same characteristics found in organizations that pursue total quality management (TQM). Outdoor sport and mail-order catalog firm L.L. Bean established a total quality and human resources (TQHR) department that led the company's efforts to improve quality, efficiency, and customer service. The TQHR department has saved the company millions of dollars annually from process improvements.

---

## APPLYING THE CONCEPT 6.3

### Getting to Innovation

Check each statement that describes an innovative corporate culture by placing an (a) for an innovative culture and (b) for a noninnovative culture on the lines.

_____ 11. We have a very tall organization in our local soccer league.

_____ 12. I tried for months to develop a stronger skate blade for hockey, but it didn't work. However, my boss thanked me profusely for trying.

_____ 13. It drives me nuts when I'm given a task and my boss tells me exactly how to do the job, down to crossing the T's and dotting the I's. Why can't I meet the objective my way for a change?

_____ 14. This athletic footwear company has a policy, procedure, and rule for everything under the sun.

_____ 15. We strive mightily to make sure that our coaches' jobs are broad in scope and that coaches have a lot of autonomy to get the job done their way.

The **core values of TQM** involve a companywide focus on (1) delivering customer value and (2) continuously improving the system and its processes. TQM cultures emphasize trust, open communication, a willingness to confront and solve problems, openness to change, internal cooperation against external competition, and adaptability to the environment. In TQM organizations, people are the most important resource. Therefore, TQM organizations go to great lengths to make sure their workforce gets the best training available, and they stress teamwork. Employees use cutting-edge technology and innovations to improve customer value. TQM cultures are strong cultures in which values support and reinforce the organization's strategic purpose—that of aligning people, processes, and resources to create value for customers through continuous improvement.

 Do the Patriot teams led by Bill Belichick in the past several years fulfill the two core values of TQM?

The late W. Edwards Deming developed 14 points that are pivotal in creating a TQM culture. Deming's points improve people's job satisfaction as well as product quality, productivity, effectiveness, and competitiveness. For a list of the 14 points, visit the Deming Institute website link (https://deming.org/explore/fourteen-points).[46]

 **TIME-OUT 7** Identify whether TQM values are operative in your organization or team. Give specific examples to support your conclusions.

## The Learning Organization

As you know, people can learn. But do you appreciate the fact that everyone you meet in your personal and professional life knows more about something than you do? Make it a habit to get others to pass their knowledge on to you so you can continually learn and improve your performance,[47] and make it a mutual learning experience by sharing your knowledge.[48] Also, like individuals, organizations can learn—that is, they can operate as learning organizations. In addition, companies are now able to make products that learn, such as a Fitbit, and *learning products* are the current and future challenge for learning organizations because they will change the basis of a business.[49]

◀ **LEARNING OUTCOME 6**
Describe a learning organization.

Today's managers are knowledge workers, which is a change in the traditional realm of management. Knowledge is a dominant source of competitive advantage because it leads to creativity and innovation.[50] Success often comes from recognizing new opportunities through knowledge of a market, industry, or customers. The learning organization is based on knowledge.[51] In a learning organization, everyone understands that the world is changing rapidly and that they must not only be aware of these changes but also must adapt to the changes and, more important, be forces for change. The **learning organization** has a capacity to learn, adapt, and change as its environment changes to continuously increase customer value.

Organizations need to focus on building "corporate learning," which is a much broader idea than simply developing individual skills and knowledge. The learning organization appears to be an effective model for a fast-changing work environment. Learning organizations thus focus on developing good human resources (HR) policies that will ensure that they can recruit, retain, and develop the best and the brightest. Learning organizations see that knowledge flows horizontally—this increases corporate learning because everyone in the organization participates in the transfer, sharing, and leveraging of individual knowledge and expertise. Learning organizations also create alliances with other firms to share knowledge horizontally.[52]

Trust is a crucial part of the learning culture because only by trusting one another can workers fully exploit their own knowledge and expertise. Creating a learning organization demands strong leadership, team-based structures, a commitment to empower people, open information, strategies built through full employee participation, and a strong, adaptive culture.[53]

# Diversity

**LEARNING OUTCOME 7** ▶

Explain how diversity can affect innovation and quality.

When we talk about diversity, we mean characteristics of individuals that shape their identities and their experiences in the workplace. Diversity refers to the degree of differences between members of a team or an organization. People are diverse in many ways. As workers, we are commonly classified by our race or ethnicity, religion, gender, age, and "other." A few of the "other" categories are military status, sexual orientation, lifestyles, socioeconomic class, and work styles.

## Importance of Diversity

Effective organizational cultures value innovation, quality, and diversity. Quality and diversity have a special relationship. To improve the quality of their products and services, organizations must first understand and address the needs of their workforce, and this includes valuing diversity. Innovative organizations have long recognized the realities of the new workforce and how they affect efficiency and effectiveness. Thus, sport managers are promoting diversity for the benefits and value it brings to the organization. In this section, we discuss the importance of diversity, valuing diversity, and gender diversity.

### Discrimination

One of the many reasons diversity is important is that discrimination is illegal. If you think that prejudice and discrimination are no longer real problems, think again. Discrimination is one of the more pressing issues in organizations today, including those in sport and leisure. Discrimination is still evident from youth sports through college, including NCAA Division IA intercollegiate athletics. Women and minorities are underrepresented in coaching and upper-level management positions of sport organizations. There are also still negative attitudes about lesbians and gay men, confirming sexual prejudice and discrimination.

### U.S. Diversity

If you think that diversity doesn't really matter, or that it will not affect you, think again. Have you given any thought to the fact that there are people from all over the globe living in America? The United States was populated by a diversity of global immigrants. Have you been on teams that demonstrated diversity? Have you interacted with people at college and at work from other countries?[54]

The U.S. Census Bureau estimates that the U.S. population of more than 327 million people will continue to grow slowly and diversify.[55] The Caucasian population is decreasing because more of them are dying than are being born every day. Population growth in the United States occurs among minorities (Hispanics are now the largest minority group) and immigrants. One in 12 children born in the United States, about 8 percent of those born, have parents who immigrated illegally. Fewer than half of Americans will be Caucasian by the year 2040. By 2060, it is estimated that Caucasians will make up about 43 percent of the U.S. population, and one in three people (33 percent) will be Hispanic.

In the global village, the world population of 7.46 billion people will continue to grow.[56] But the decrease in the Caucasian percentage of the total global population will decline at an even faster rate than in the United States. This is especially true in the European Union, where the death-to-birth ratio is higher.

The diversification of America is clearly affecting individuals, sports, businesses, and government. This trend isn't going to change, and you will witness the shifting percentages as you continue to age. Can any professional team function without minority employees and players?

# From Equal Employment Opportunity to Inclusion

In this section, we present how the focus has shifted from focusing primarily on equal employment opportunity (EEO) to affirmative action, to diversity, to valuing diversity, to inclusion.

## *From Equal Employment Opportunity to Affirmative Action to Diversity*

Diversity programs have replaced most equal employment opportunity (EEO) and affirmative action programs. EEO laws required organizations to treat all employees equally, whereas affirmative action was created to correct the past exclusion of women and minorities from the workforce. Affirmative action programs established percentages and quotas. Although quotas are no longer commonly used, many organizations actively recruit women and minorities with specific quantitative objectives because it's the right thing to do.[57] The NFL developed the Rooney rule, which requires teams to interview minorities for head coaching and general manager jobs before they are filled. Art Rooney was the owner of the Pittsburgh Steelers for many years. Rooney wanted to give minorities an equal chance to be selected for head coach or general manager.[58]

Most large organizations today moved from complying with EEO laws and affirmative action quotas to actively recruiting a diverse workforce because research supports the idea that diversified teams and organizations are more innovative and profitable.[59] In other words, diversity is a good strategy for gaining competitive advantage. People with diverse backgrounds bring diverse experiences and viewpoints to bear on problems, and more creative solutions are often the result. Diversity helps the individual, the team, and the organization.

## *From Valuing Diversity to Inclusion*

When organizations value diversity, they focus on training everyone in their workforce—from all the different races and ethnicities, religions, ages, and abilities, as well as both men and women—to work together effectively so that everyone is treated fairly and justly.[60] The goal is a climate of dignity and trust, and in such a climate everyone wins. The organization wins because its workforce has a synergy that is fertile ground for creativity and innovation, and this can only help the organization in its ultimate goal of continuously improving customer value. The workforce wins because work becomes a place people can enjoy and value for its fairness and team spirit and on which they can build a good life. So don't view diversity training as a task to be merely tolerated—it is an opportunity to understand your world better and an opportunity for personal and professional growth. Most organizations have moved from EEO to affirmative action to accepting diversity to valuing diversity to inclusion.[61] The terms *diversity* and *inclusion* have different meanings. Inclusion has the goal of valuing all types of diversity and integrating everyone (not just specific groups like minorities and women) to work together while maintaining and valuing their differences.[62] *Inclusion* is the practice of ensuring that all employees feel they belong as valued members of the team or organization. An inclusion culture creates a feeling of supportive energy and commitment from others so that everyone can do their best work by incorporating personal diversity.[63] To help make the shift to inclusion, many organizations are now replacing the word *diversity* with the term *inclusion*. MLB now has an ambassador for inclusion.[64]

## *Inclusion in Sport*

For teams and sport managers, inclusion is more about recruiting people with the diversity of skills needed to be successful without discriminating against anyone. Not everyone can be the pitcher or quarterback. It takes the right combination of skills and everyone's being respected and valued for their contributions to maximize team performance. Reflect on a present or past sport team or job. Did you feel included as a valued member? Was the team or organization truly inclusive, or were there in-groups and out-groups and individuals? Should all teams and organizations strive for inclusion?

### Being Personally Inclusive

Answering these questions may help you to be more inclusive. Have you ever felt the pain of being excluded? Have you caused others pain by discriminating or excluding them? Are you sincerely open to letting others who are different from you and your group be who they are? Do you try to make them look and act like you or do things your way? Do you ever make remarks that put them down in some way, either to their faces or behind their backs? You can make a personal effort to look for the good in others and accept people for who they are and value their differences. You can reach out to others and include them. Next time you see someone off by herself, go over to be with her or bring her to be included in your group.

## Gender Diversity

Before we discuss gender issues, complete Self-Assessment 6.1 to determine your attitude toward women in the workplace. Female readers should complete this assessment also; you may be surprised at what you learn!

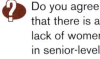 Do you agree that there is a lack of women in senior-level athletic administration positions?

### Sex, Gender, and Stereotypes

Do you know that *sex* and *gender* are different? *Sex* distinguishes biological males and females. Sex is part of gender, but gender also includes common behavioral characteristics, including clothes, hair style, the use of makeup, and other things. We learn our expected gender behavior through social interactions and through the stereotyped language used to describe it—that is, by labeling behavior as *masculine* or *feminine*. Ever heard that boys are tough and play competitive games, while girls are nurturing and play with dolls; boys are good at math, and girls are good at English? We are also pressured into conforming to gender stereotypes. Ever heard he's a sissy; she's a tomboy?

Stereotypes about leadership result in gender discrimination against women who try to advance in management. Men are stereotyped as having leadership qualities, such as assertiveness, confidence, and independence. Women are stereotyped to be helpful, nurturing, and kind. Women who use aggressive male leadership characteristics are often criticized as being "bossy" or a "bi--h."[65] Facebook COO Sheryl Sandberg said that America and the world are not comfortable with women in leadership roles,[66] so we have to address our culture's discomfort with female leadership to let women advance.[67] How did you score on Self-Assessment 6.1?

### Gender Discrimination

Let's start with some facts related to all females in the workforce, which includes women in sport industries. Women make up about half of the U.S. workforce,[68] but they are paid just 77 cents on the dollar compared to men,[69] and highly educated women face greater discrimination.[70] Women perform equally well when compared to men, but they are paid significantly less,[71] and it is more difficult for women to advance.[72] Women are underrepresented at entry levels and every management level. Men have an estimated 30 percent greater chance of being promoted into management positions.[73] Facing the glass ceiling, few women are promoted to high-level management positions, especially women with children.[74] The most significant factor keeping both women and minorities out of the top jobs is discrimination.[75] The United States has the Equal Employment Opportunity Commission (EEOC) to handle legal charges of sex-based discrimination, and a federal Glass Ceiling Commission to help eliminate the problem. However, as you just read the facts, even though discrimination is against the law, they haven't made much progress.[76] It has been estimated that if women globally were offered the same opportunities as men, $28 trillion would be added to global gross domestic product by 2025.[77]

Now let's discuss sport. Yes! Title IX opened the doors for equality of the sexes in the United States, but female athletes often don't truly have equal coaching support and resources, and women face constraints in sport organizations. Although women's sports are growing, it's hard to make social change to true equality between the sexes. The glass ceiling is still a fact of life as women struggle to access middle and upper managerial jobs in sport organizations. Part of the reason is that men have the power in all types of sports and so far have been keeping it.

Women have largely been limited to coaching other women, whereas men commonly coach both men and women. Men coach women's NCAA basketball and the pro WNBA, but women do not tend to coach men's NCAA basketball or the NBA. In youth sport in

## SELF-ASSESSMENT 6.1

### Attitudes About Women in the Workplace

For each statement, select the response that best describes your belief. (Be honest!)

1 = strongly agree

2 = agree

3 = not sure

4 = disagree

5 = strongly disagree

_____ 1. Women lack the education necessary to get ahead.

_____ 2. Women's entering the workforce has caused rising unemployment among men.

_____ 3. Women are not mentally strong enough to succeed in high-pressure management jobs.

_____ 4. Women are too emotional to be effective managers.

_____ 5. Women managers have difficulty in situations calling for quick and precise decisions.

_____ 6. Women work to earn extra money rather than to support a family.

_____ 7. Women are out of work more often than men.

_____ 8. Women quit work or take long maternity leaves when they have children.

_____ 9. Women have a lower commitment to work than men.

_____ 10. Women lack the motivation to get ahead.

_____ Total

To determine whether you have a positive or a negative attitude, total your score and place it on the following continuum.

| Negative attitude | | | | Positive attitude |
|---|---|---|---|---|
| 10 | 20 | 30 | 40 | 50 |

Each statement represents a commonly held attitude about women in the workforce. However, research has shown all of these statements to be false. Such statements stereotype women unfairly and create glass ceilings.

many areas, mothers are generally not role models because it is much more common for the fathers to coach their daughters. Females are also much more willing to watch males play sports than males are to watch females.

Getting back to inclusion, are you aware of gender stereotypes and discrimination against them? Do you judge and criticize others because they don't fit into your view of how males and females should look and act? Again, can you improve your inclusiveness, including gender?

## Sexual Harassment

Women are also more commonly sexually harassed than men at work, and same-sex harassment also takes place at work. In 2018, several women came forward bringing the widespread problem of sexual harassment to the national spotlight. In simple terms, sexual harassment is any unwelcome behavior of a sexual nature. Behavior is sexual harassment when it explicitly or implicitly affects one's employment, unreasonably interferes with one's work performance, or creates an intimidating, hostile, or offensive work environment.[78] Actions such as touching private body areas (defined for kids as the bathing suit area) are *hostile work environment sexual harassment;* and requiring sex for getting, keeping, or advancing on the job are considered *quid pro quo sexual harassment.* With other sexual behavior, however, things are not always so clear, as illustrated in Applying the Concept 6.4. When you are in doubt, tell the person not to repeat the behavior or you will report the offense as sexual harassment; if the behavior is repeated, report it internally; and if no satisfactory action is taken, consider legal action with the Equal Employment Opportunity Commission (EEOC). For more information on sexual harassment, visit the EEOC website at www.eeoc.gov.

## Mentoring

A word about mentoring is pertinent here. Mentors are highly skilled people who prepare promising employees for advancement; they function at every level of the organization. Mentoring enhances management skills, encourages diversity, and improves productivity. Mentoring programs help women and minorities break the glass ceiling.

Skilled mentors can help you develop expertise, poise, confidence, and business savvy. Ask about mentoring opportunities at work. If your organization doesn't have a mentoring program, seek out a person whose professional attributes you admire and would like to emulate and ask him or her to mentor you.

## APPLYING THE CONCEPT 6.4

### Sexual Harassment

Check each behavior that would be considered sexual harassment in the workplace by placing an (a) if it is sexual harassment or (b) if it is not sexual harassment.

_____ 16. Jose tells Claire she is sexy and he'd like to take her out on a date.

_____ 17. Sue tells Josh he'll have to go to a motel with her if he wants that promotion.

_____ 18. Joel and Kathy hang pictures of nude men and women in their office cubicles in view of people walking by.

_____ 19. For the third time after being politely told not to, Jamal tells Anita a sexually explicit joke.

_____ 20. Ray puts his hand on his secretary Lisa's shoulder as he talks to her.

# Organizational Development

**Organizational development (OD)** is the ongoing planned change process that organizations use to improve performance. HR departments (discussed in chapter 7) are usually responsible for OD and change agents.[79] Change agents are people selected by HR management to be responsible for the OD program.[80] Change agents may be members of the organization (commonly for ongoing issues) or hired consultants (often for new changes requiring their expertise through direct feedback).

## Change Models

Here are two change models that can be used when making organizational changes.

### Lewin's Change Model

In the early 1950s, Kurt Lewin developed a model that is still used today to change people's behavior and attitudes. Lewin's change model consists of three steps:

1. *Unfreezing.* This involves reducing the strength of the forces that maintain the status quo. Organizations often accomplish unfreezing by introducing information that reveals the need for the change by showing the discrepancies between desired performance and actual performance.
2. *Moving.* In this step, behavior begins to shift to the desired changed behavior. That is, people begin to learn the new desired behavior, and they also begin to embrace the values and attitudes that go with it. Shifts in strategy, structure, technology, and people or culture may be needed to attain the desired change.
3. *Refreezing.* The desired change becomes the new status quo. Reinforcement and support for the new behavior are often required for refreezing behavior to become a habit.

An allegory for this change process is taking an ice cube and melting it back to water and then refreezing it into a new shape.[81]

### Comprehensive Change Model

Today's rapidly evolving business environment has obliged us to expand Lewin's original model. Note that as shown in table 6.3, the comprehensive model extends the Lewin model from three steps to five more detailed steps. Research indicates that the Lewin model is effective at making minor incremental changes; however, the comprehensive model is more effective for making discontinuous changes.[82] The expanded model involves the following actions:

1. Recognize the need for change. Clearly state the change needed; set objectives. Consider the systems effect—that is, how will the proposed change affect other areas of the organization?

## TABLE 6.3  Two Change Models

| Lewin's change model | Comprehensive change model |
| --- | --- |
| Step 1: Unfreezing | Step 1: Recognize the need for change.<br>Step 2: Identify possible resistance to the change and plan how to overcome it. |
| Step 2: Moving | Step 3: Plan the change interventions.<br>Step 4: Implement the change interventions. |
| Step 3: Refreezing | Step 5: Control the change. |

2. Identify possible resistance to the change and plan how to overcome it. Use the resistance matrix in figure 6.2, and then follow the guidelines in table 6.3.

3. Plan the change interventions. A careful diagnosis of the problem (step 2) often indicates the appropriate interventions. (Interventions are discussed next.)

4. Implement the interventions. Change agents oversee the interventions (from start to finish) to bring about the desired change.

5. Control the change. Follow up to ensure that the change is being implemented and maintained. Make sure the objective is met. If not, take corrective action.

# Change Interventions

**OD interventions** are specific actions taken to implement specific changes. What follows is a brief survey of nine common interventions (see figure 6.3).

## *Training and Development*

Training is the process of developing skills, behaviors, and attitudes that will enhance performance. Does anyone ever get a job without any type of training to do their work? Most interventions include some form of training and development. MLB players, for example, spend the month of March in Florida and Arizona in spring training developing hitting, pitching, and fielding skills. (We examine training and development in more detail in chapter 7.)

Job design, discussed in chapter 5, is also an OD intervention. Job enrichment, which is part of job design, is commonly used. Training to perform the redesigned job is common.

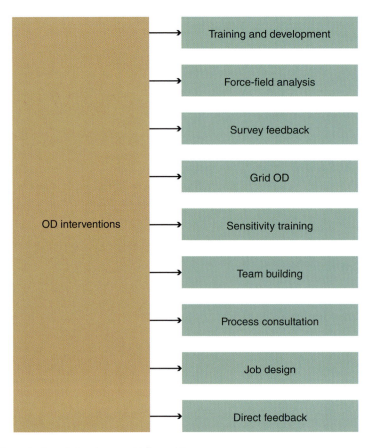

**FIGURE 6.3** Organizational development interventions.

## Force-Field Analysis

Particularly useful for small groups of 4 to 18 members in problem solving, **force-field analysis** involves assessing current performance and then identifying the forces hindering change and those driving it. The result is a diagram that gives an overview of the situation; see figure 6.4 for an example. The process begins with an appraisal of current performance—this assessment appears in the middle of the diagram. Forces that are holding back performance (hindering it) are listed at the left side of the diagram. The forces driving change are listed at the right side. Diagramming the situation clarifies thinking and helps change agents and the small group to develop strategies.

◀ **LEARNING OUTCOME 8**
State how force-field analysis and survey feedback differ.

The basic thrust is to find ways to strengthen the driving forces and simultaneously to diminish the hindering forces. The diagram often points the way to a promising strategy. As an example, we created a force-field diagram (figure 6.4) for a hypothetical footwear company that has been losing market share. Our analysis indicates that the footwear company should focus on production and sales forecasting.

## Survey Feedback

One of the oldest and most popular OD techniques, **survey feedback** uses a questionnaire to gather data that are used as the basis for change. Survey feedback is commonly used in step 1 of the change model. Different change agents use slightly different approaches; however, a typical survey feedback includes six steps:

1. Management and the change agent do preliminary planning to develop an appropriate survey questionnaire.
2. The questionnaire is administered to all members of the organization or unit.
3. The survey data are analyzed to uncover problem areas for improvement.
4. The change agent presents the results to management.
5. Managers evaluate the feedback and discuss the results with their teams.
6. Corrective intervention action plans are developed and implemented.

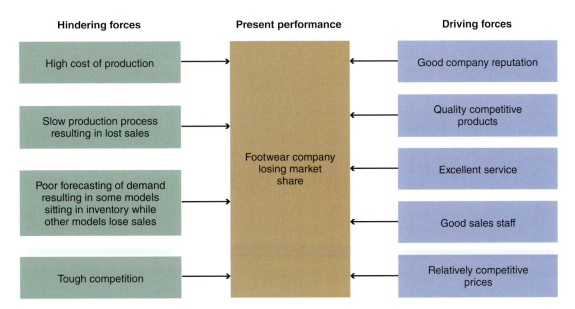

**FIGURE 6.4** Force-field diagram for a footwear company.

## Grid OD

Robert Blake and Jane Mouton developed the Grid OD, a six-phase program, with a standardized format, procedures, and fixed goals, designed to improve management and organizational effectiveness. The six phases are (1) training, (2) team development, (3) intergroup development, (4) organizational goal setting, (5) goal attainment, and (6) stabilization.

## Sensitivity Training

Sensitivity training includes a training group (a T-group) of 10 to 15 people. The training sessions have no agenda. People learn about how their behavior affects others and how others' behavior affects their own. Understanding each other's styles and qualities helps people get along better. The popularity of T-groups peaked in the early 1970s as organizations began to question the on-the-job value gained from the training. Although T-groups are still used, they have largely been replaced by team building and process consultation.

## Team Building

**LEARNING OUTCOME 9** ▶

Explain the difference between team building and process consultation.

Team building is probably the most widely used OD technique besides training; it includes training, and its popularity will continue to grow as more companies use teams.[83] **Team building** helps work groups to improve structural and team dynamics and thus performance. Team building is a powerful tool and a crucial one as well because effectiveness and ineffectiveness, both within teams and between teams, will affect the results of the entire organization. Team building can be used as a comprehensive program in which top executives first go through the program and then go through it with their middle managers, who then go through it with their groups, and so on throughout the organization. However, team building is more widely used by new or existing groups to pinpoint ways to improve effectiveness.

Team-building activities are quite diverse—indeed, they use many techniques developed in coaching sports. Teams may play in a golf tournament, play a single game of baseball or rugby, or participate in an "autocross" competition in which teams are timed as they drive cars through obstacle-course drills until a winning team is determined. The activities are tied to classroom instruction on the principles of effective team building.

**Team-Building Goals**   The goals of team-building programs also vary considerably, depending on the group's needs and the change agent's skills. Typical goals include the following:

- To clarify the objectives of the team and the responsibilities of each team member
- To identify problems preventing the team from accomplishing its objectives
- To develop team problem-solving, decision-making, objective-setting, and planning skills
- To develop open, honest working relationships based on trust and an understanding of group members

**The Team-Building Program**   Team-building agendas and the length of time vary with team needs and the change agent's skills. Typical programs go through six stages:

Discuss a part of the team-building program that Tony Dungy used successfully.

1. *Climate building and goals.* The program begins with change agents establishing a climate of trust, support, and openness. Change agents discuss the program's purpose and goals based on data gathered before the program. Team members learn more about each other and share what they would like to accomplish through team building.

2. *Structure and team dynamics evaluation.* Team building endeavors to improve both how the work is done (structure) and how team members work together as they do the work (team dynamics). The team evaluates its strengths and weaknesses in both areas.

3. *Problem identification.* Change agents use interviews or feedback surveys to help the team to identify its strengths and its weaknesses (areas it would like to improve). The team next lists several areas where it can improve and then prioritizes these areas in terms of how improving each area will help the team to improve performance.

4. *Problem solving.* The team takes the top priority and develops a solution. It then moves down the priorities in order of importance. Force-field analysis may be used here for problem solving.

5. *Training.* Team building often includes some form of training that addresses the problems facing the group.

6. *Closure.* The program ends with a summary of what has been accomplished. Team members commit to specific improvements in performance. Follow-up responsibilities are assigned, and a meeting is scheduled to evaluate results.

## Process Consultation

Process consultation is often used in the second stage of team building, but it is also commonly used as a separate, more narrowly focused intervention. **Process consultation** improves team dynamics. Whereas team building often focuses on how to get the job done, process consultation focuses on how people interact as they get the job done. Team dynamics (or processes) are about how the team communicates, allocates work, resolves conflict, and handles leadership and how leadership solves problems and makes decisions. Change agents observe team members as they work to give them feedback on the operative team processes. Under the change agent's guidance, the team discusses its processes and how to improve them. Training to improve group processes may also be conducted at this point. The ultimate objective is to train the group so that process consultation becomes an ongoing team activity. (We examine team dynamics in more detail in chapter 9.)

 **TIME-OUT 8** Give an example of an OD intervention used recently in your firm or team. Was it effective? Why or why not?

## Direct Feedback

Situations can occur, particularly with rapidly changing technologies, that require a solution outside the company's core expertise. In these situations, outside consultants are often brought in to act as change agents and to recommend action directly. For example, some teams have hired Amazon and IBM to set up their cloud computer systems.

## LEARNING AIDS

### CHAPTER SUMMARY

1. **Identify the driving forces behind change.**

   The forces for change come from the external and internal environment. Changes in economic, social, demographic, and technological forces require organizations to adapt to their environments.

2. **List the four variables of change.**

   Change occurs in strategies, structures, technologies, and people.

3. **Differentiate between fact, belief, and values.**

   Facts are provable statements that identify reality. Beliefs cannot be proven because they are subjective, not objective. Values address what is important to people.

# APPLYING THE CONCEPT 6.5

## OD Interventions

Identify the appropriate OD interventions for each situation.

a. training and development
b. force-field analysis
c. survey feedback
d. grid OD
e. sensitivity training
f. team building
g. process consultation
h. job design
i. direct feedback

_____ 21. We're not winning, our fans are leaving in droves, our costs are skyrocketing, the voters are unhappy about funding expensive stadiums that are often empty at games, and the players are about to go on strike.

_____ 22. Everyone can see that team morale is at an all-time low—but why?

_____ 23. We need a new scouting system; our present one isn't delivering the goods.

_____ 24. We've got a cutting-edge fitness machine and no one to run it.

_____ 25. We've got a lot of prima donna star athletes who are more interested in publicity than in winning.

4. **Describe the three components of organizational culture.**

   The three components are (1) behavior (the actions we take), (2) values (the way we think we ought to behave) and beliefs (if–then statements), and (3) assumptions (values and beliefs that are so deeply ingrained we never question their truth). The values, beliefs, and assumptions of an organization guide its decision making and behavior.

5. **State the core values of TQM.**

   The core values of TQM involve a companywide focus on (1) delivering customer value and (2) continuously improving the system and its processes.

6. **Describe a learning organization.**

   Learning organizations consciously create a culture in which people have the capacity to learn, adapt, and change with the environments to continuously increase customer value.

7. **Explain how diversity can affect innovation and quality.**

   A diverse workforce can be more innovative and also more effective at achieving quality.

8. **State how force-field analysis and survey feedback differ.**

   Force-field analysis is used by small groups to diagnose and solve specific problems. Survey feedback uses questionnaires with large groups to identify problems; the group does not work together to solve the problem. Force-field analysis is used to solve problems identified through survey feedback.

9. **Explain the difference between team building and process consultation.**

    Team building is broader in scope than process consultation. Team building improves both how the work is done and how team members work together as they do the work (team dynamics). Process consultation improves team dynamics.

## REVIEW AND DISCUSSION QUESTIONS

1. How do the management functions relate to change?

2. How does the systems effect relate to the four variables of change?

3. List the four stages in the change process.

4. Which of the five reasons for resisting change do you believe is most common?

5. Which of the six ways to overcome resistance to change do you believe is the most important?

6. Select two sport organizations and discuss the differences between their cultures.

7. Discuss how the two types of innovations could be used by a manufacturer of golf balls.

8. Discuss how you would use team building to improve the effectiveness of a team you are playing on or have played for.

9. Do you agree with the core values of TQM? If not, how would you change them?

10. Do you believe that online surveys are an effective method for analyzing the effectiveness of Title IX in the United States?

11. Do you consider yourself to be a creative, innovative person? Why or why not?

12. How has diversity affected you personally?

13. Should men break the glass ceiling and promote more women to top positions? Why or why not?

14. Should the government get involved in breaking the glass ceiling? Why or why not? If yes, what should the government do? State pros and cons of government involvement.

15. Do you believe that it is acceptable for people who work together to date each other?

16. Do you have a mentor? Will you get one? Why or why not?

17. As a manager, which, if any, OD interventions will you use?

## CASES

### Sport Management Professionals @ Work: Jacob Ray

Why sport management? As a college student who chose this major, Jacob Ray knows you will get this question all of the time because he did. However, the answer was easy for Jacob—Why not? He was a former athlete who wasn't quite talented enough for the collegiate level, but he still had a passion for sports, and he wanted to choose a career where sports were present. A sport management major was the perfect and obvious choice.

As a freshman at Ashland University, Jake initially followed the coach and athletic director career sequence. After taking a few classes, he saw that there were countless opportunities that a sport management degree could yield—recreational sports, brand activation, and many more. Knowing that there were all of these options was huge for Jake because it provided him with opportunities that he didn't even know existed. He took the same approach of exploring his options when he selected his internships. He wanted to get experience in different fields to find what exactly he wanted to do for a career, but more importantly, find what he also did not want to do.

Jacob currently works at the Pro Football Hall of Fame in Canton, Ohio, as the Youth and Education Coordinator. His main job responsibility is handling all of the educational programming that takes place within the museum.

Before being hired as a full-time employee, Jake was an intern in the Youth and Education department while still in college. After graduating, instead of going to graduate school, he took a part-time job opportunity at the Football Hall of Fame, which ultimately led to a full-time job at the hall.

The most important thing Jake took away from his experiences while earning a degree in sport management was to participate in all of the opportunities that appear. You never know who you are going to meet, who is watching, or what an opportunity might lead to!

## Case Questions

1. Look online for more information about brand activation.

2. Why is it more likely that Jacob would work full-time at the Football Hall of Fame than at the Basketball Hall of Fame?

3. Who would you consider to be Jake's teammates?

## Big-Time ADs

Until the late 1970s, the job of a college AD was easy. In the old days, colleges often gave the AD job to the football coach when he retired. Playing golf with alumni was a big part of the job then. The times, how they change!

To say that ADs have many more job responsibilities today is a bit of an understatement. ADs in the United States supervise coaching staff and teams, oversee million-dollar budgets and requisitions, work with coaches to schedule events and travel itineraries, help plan facilities, issue contracts for home contests, watchdog player eligibility, maintain records of players and insurance coverage for all athletes, manage crowd behavior at events (are you tired yet?), fund-raise, attend booster club meetings, supervise the sport information director, maintain marketing publications, attend professional meetings, develop staff, and conduct weekly meetings to monitor progress!

The AD job is just one of many positions in large U.S. collegiate organizations—college sports are big business today. The AD may have an associate director, a sport information director, academic advisors, ticket managers, and event managers. For instance, at Ohio State University, Gene Smith is in his thirteenth year as AD. He oversees a department of more than 36 varsity sports and over 1,000 athletes participating in Big Ten Conference and NCAA Championships.[84] Ohio State must comply with these rules or face sanctions.

AD jobs are also more complicated because external factors are changing so rapidly. ADs must keep up with legal issues such as Title IX in the United States, which requires equal access to education (including athletics) for women. Recruiting athletes is increasingly competitive because more colleges actively pursue athletes as they try to build winning teams. And unfortunately, athletes (like the wider population) face a wide variety of social problems, such as AIDS, drug addiction, and sexual harassment.

Fund-raising is a constant endeavor—athletic operations are extremely expensive. The athletic department at Ohio State is expected to operate like a business and at least break even. As AD, Gene Smith uses the sales and marketing strategies of professional sport: seat licenses, luxury boxes, corporate sponsorships, new arenas, and high ticket prices.

Urban Meyer, the football coach, was the highest paid public employee in Ohio in 2016, making $4.61 million in salary and bonus pay. In comparison, athletic director Gene Smith only made $1.98 million.[85] Total athletic revenue at Ohio State was $169.9 million. Football revenue was $88.65 million.

Gene Smith and Urban Meyer were suspended from their positions for parts of August and September of 2018, when Meyer stated he "mishandled domestic assault allegations made against former Buckeyes assistant coach Zach Smith and misrepresented what he knew about the situation in a public statement in July." Smith was suspended because he did not alert others to red flags about Zach Smith's conduct after he learned that police were investigating accusations of domestic abuse in 2015.[86] Both men have returned to their positions and are more aware then ever of following NCAA rules and regulations.

Would you like to be an AD? An assistant AD? A coach? A sport information director? Visit www.jobsatosu.com for information on jobs in Ohio State's athletic department.

Go to the web study guide to answer questions about this case study.

## @ TAKE IT TO THE NET

Please visit www.HumanKinetics.com/AppliedSportManagementSkills and go to this book's companion web study guide, where you will find the following:

A list of websites associated with the concepts in this chapter

Skill-Builder exercises, Sports and Social Media exercises, and a continuing Game Plan for Starting a Sport Business

Online versions of chapter exercises and end-of-chapter learning aids

An exercise that helps you define the Key Terms

# Human Resources Management

## LEARNING OUTCOMES

After studying this chapter, you should be able to

1. describe the four parts of HR management;

2. differentiate between a job description and a job specification, and explain why they are needed;

3. state the two parts of the process of attracting employees;

4. explain how hypothetical questions and probing questions differ;

5. state the purposes of orientation and training and development;

6. describe job instructional training;

7. define the two types of performance appraisals;

8. explain the concept "You get what you reward";

9. state the two major components of compensation; and

10. describe how job analyses and job evaluations are used.

## KEY TERMS

| | | |
|---|---|---|
| human resources management | assessment centers | compensation |
| bona fide occupational qualification (BFOQ) | orientation | job evaluation |
| strategic human resources planning | training | labor relations |
| job description | development | collective bargaining |
| job specifications | vestibule training | strike |
| recruiting | performance appraisal | lockout |
| selection | | |

## DEVELOPING YOUR SKILLS

The most important resource of any organization is its people, its human resources (HR). You need to understand the HR laws and regulations—the rules of the game—to be a successful sport manager. HR managers need to recruit and select talented employees and players to win games. They also need good managers and coaches to train and develop the human resources. In addition, they need to evaluate the HR performance, retain top talent, and possibly engage in union negotiations. On a more personal level, in this chapter, you can develop your skills by using the models to interview candidates, train HR, and assess their performance. You may also consider HR management as a sport management career.

## REVIEWING THEIR GAME PLAN

### Finding Job Openings in Sport Management

The goal of many sport management students is to work in the sport industry. How do you achieve this career goal? Learn to work with HR departments. The HR department of an organization is involved in the entire hiring process. This includes helping write the criteria for the job opening, posting the advertisement in various publications and on websites, selecting the initial set of candidates, interviewing the candidates, and negotiating a salary and benefit package for the chosen candidate.

The first step in job searching is to research the field of interest. Conduct a broad search of current job openings to gain some insight into the various types of positions that HR departments are trying to fill. As of this writing, the following were seven available positions advertised at www.teamworkonline.com. This site has been considered very valuable by the sport management alumni in our Sport Management Professionals @ Work cases at the end of each chapter.

- Director, Video Production, Los Angeles Galaxy (Carson, CA)
- Media-Social Media Community Relations Manager, Binghamton Devils (Binghamton, NY)
- Web Designer, Portland Trailblazers (Portland, OR)
- Ticket Representative, Inside Sales, Detroit Pistons (Auburn Hills, MI)
- Inside Sales Representative, AEG Sports (Los Angeles, CA)
- Vice President, Human Resources, IRONMAN (Tampa, FL)
- Guest Relations Team Member (Part-Time) Summer/Fall, Denver Broncos/Stadium Management Company (Denver, CO)

The vice president of human resources at IRONMAN listed was specifically in the field of human resources. The vice president for IRONMAN will be involved with talent acquisition, talent management, compensation and benefit administration, employee relations, employee recognition, performance management, policy and procedure development, and training. The vice president of human resources is also responsible for global strategic human resource planning to position the organization as an employer of choice.[1] HR careers often start at the assistant level and can lead to a position as the vice president of HR for an organization. Would you like to work in HR?

For current information on job openings in sport management, please visit www.teamworkonline.com. (For more information on careers in sport management, see the appendix.)

# Human Resources Management Process and Department

Every team and organization is only as good as its players and workers. People are the most valuable resource[2] because they give the team a competitive advantage to beat the competition.[3] Therefore, how you and the organization manage its people will determine its success or failure.[4] Thus, the key driver of business success is HR management practices of hiring and developing great people to continuously increase productivity,[5] which is challenging.[6] **Human resources management** (also known as staffing) consists of planning, attracting, developing, and retaining employees. Figure 7.1 gives an overview of this four-part process; the arrows indicate how the parts mesh to create a systems effect.

◀ LEARNING OUTCOME 1
Describe the four parts of HR management.

**TIME-OUT 1** Describe your experiences with the HR department in the organization you work for or play for.

One of the four major functional departments in organizations, the HR department is a staff department that advises all other departments and helps them to manage employees. Larger companies tend to have a separate HR department that plans HR practices for the entire organization. Many firms, especially small businesses, outsource most or parts of their HR management functions, such as payroll and benefits.[7] HR managers are responsible for developing HR practices and systems, which you will learn about throughout this chapter.

# Legal Environment

All organizations have to conduct business in accordance with the law. It is the job of the HR department to ensure that everyone in the organization complies with the law. The laws tell organizations what they must and must not do. Recall the importance of Title IX, which requires equality for females in sport in the United States.

You are not legally allowed to discriminate and hire, promote, or fire whomever you want. Title VII of the Civil Rights Act of 1964 *prohibits employment discrimination based on race, color, religion, sex, and national origin.* Just as all athletes should be treated fairly and justly, so should all employees. The legal environment affects HR practices in significant ways, so understanding HR law is important to sport management. As a manager, you will most likely be involved in hiring employees; if you break the law, you and your organization can get into legal trouble and end up in court, and you can even be sent to jail. This section teaches you the basics of equal employment opportunity law and what you can and can't ask candidates during employment recruiting.

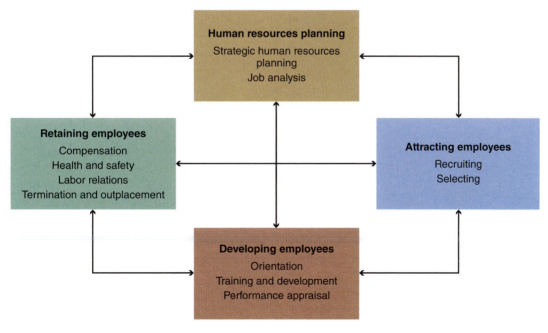

**FIGURE 7.1** Managing human resources.

## Equal Employment Opportunity

The Equal Employment Opportunity (EEO) Act, a 1972 amendment to the U.S. Civil Rights Act of 1964, prohibits discrimination in the workplace and applies to virtually all private and public organizations in the United States with 15 or more employees. Who is considered a minority by the EEO? Just about anyone who is not a white male, not of European heritage, or not adequately educated. Thus, in the United States, Hispanics, Asians, African Americans, American Indians, and Alaskan natives are minorities. Women are not a minority—in some occupations, such as nursing and teaching, they are a majority, but they also get protection. The EEO also protects disadvantaged young people, disabled workers (Americans with Disabilities Act), and people over age 40 (Age Discrimination in Employment Act).[8]

In addition to federal EEO laws that you must obey, all 50 U.S. states have additional laws. Some cities also have additional laws, such as minimum wage laws, that vary from place to place. There are far too many differences to discuss here, but if you are an HR management specialist, you need to know the laws because ignorance of the law is not a legal defense in court. We will discuss compensation (pay and benefits) in the last major section of this chapter.

The **Equal Employment Opportunity Commission (EEOC)**, which is responsible for enforcing EEO mandates, has field offices across the United States and operates a toll-free line (1-800-USA-EEOC) around the clock to provide information on employee rights. It also has a website (www.eeoc.gov). If you are not sure whether your HR policies are legal, contact the EEOC.

The U.S. General Counsel is responsible for conducting EEOC enforcement litigation under Title VII, the Equal Pay Act, the Age Discrimination in Employment Act, and the Americans with Disabilities Act. Violation of antidiscrimination laws can lead to investigation by the EEOC or to class action or individual lawsuits. Courts find discrimination when selection criteria are vague, elusive, unstructured, undefined, or poorly conceived. As a manager, you should be familiar with your organization's EEO compliance, and if you are truly inclusive, you most likely will not be in violation of the law. As discussed in chapter 6, discrimination in HR practices still exists in the United States.

## Preemployment Inquiries

No one in your organization—not recruiters, interviewers, other HR staff, or line managers—can legally ask discriminatory questions, either on the application or during interviews. Here are two rules to guide you:

1. Be sure that every question you ask is job related. When developing questions, make sure you have a purpose for using the information. Ask only for information that you plan to use in the selection process.

2. Ask all candidates the same general questions. Asking women and minorities different questions can lead to legal problems.

The list under Preemployment Inquiries summarizes U.S. laws concerning what you can ask for during the selection process (lawful information you can use to disqualify candidates) and what you cannot ask for (prohibited information you cannot use to disqualify candidates). Complete Applying the Concept 7.1 for a better understanding of what questions are and are not legal to ask.

An organization can discriminate legally for a **bona fide occupational qualification (BFOQ)** for the job. A BFOQ allows organizations to base their hiring decisions on otherwise discriminatory attributes that are reasonably necessary to the normal

TIME-OUT 2

Have you or anyone you know ever been asked for discriminatory information when you were screened for a job? If yes, explain the situation.

# Preemployment Inquiries

| Topic | Can ask | Cannot ask |
|---|---|---|
| Name | Current legal name and whether the candidate has ever worked under a different name | Maiden name or whether the person has changed his name |
| Address | Current residence and length of residence there | Whether the candidate owns or rents her home |
| Age | Whether the candidate's age is within a certain range (if required for a particular job; for example, an employee must be 21 to serve alcoholic beverages); if hired, can ask for proof of age | How old are you? What is your date of birth? Can you provide a birth certificate? How much longer do you plan to work before retiring? |
| Sex | Candidate to indicate sex on an application if sex is a BFOQ | Candidate's sexual preference |
| Marital and family status | Whether candidate can adhere to the work schedule; whether the candidate has any activities, responsibilities, or commitments that may affect attendance | Specific questions about marital status or any question regarding children or other family issues |
| National origin, citizenship, or race | Whether the candidate is legally eligible to work in the United States, and whether the candidate can provide proof of status if hired | Specific questions about national origin, citizenship, or race of candidate or parents and relatives |
| Language | What languages the candidate speaks, writes, or both; can ask candidate to identify specific language or languages if these are BFOQs | What language the candidate speaks when off the job or how the candidate learned the language |
| Criminal record | Whether the candidate has been convicted of a felony; if the answer is yes, can ask other information about the conviction if the conviction is job related | Whether the candidate has ever been arrested (an arrest does not prove guilt); for information regarding a conviction that is not job related |
| Height and weight | Whether the candidate meets BFOQ height or weight requirements and whether the candidate can provide proof if hired | Candidate's height or weight if these are not BFOQs |
| Religion | Whether candidate is of a specific religion if religious preference is a BFOQ; whether the candidate must be absent for religious reasons or holidays | Candidate's religious preference, affiliation, or denomination if not a BFOQ |
| Credit rating or garnishments | For information if a particular credit rating is a BFOQ | Unless it is a BFOQ |
| Education and work experience | For information that is job related | For information that is not job related |
| References | For names of people who are willing to provide references or who suggested the candidate apply for the job | For a reference from a religious leader |
| Military record | For information about candidate's military service that is job related | Dates and conditions of discharge from the military, National Guard, or reserve unit of candidate |
| Organizations | About membership in job-related organizations, such as unions or professional or trade associations | About membership in any non-job-related organization that would indicate candidate's race, religion, or the like |
| Disabilities | Whether candidate has any disabilities that would prevent him from performing the job being applied for | General questions about disabilities (focus on abilities, not disabilities) |
| Past salary/Pay | If the candidate was employed by a prior organization | How much the candidate was paid for her previous jobs |

## APPLYING THE CONCEPT 7.1

### Legal or Illegal Questions?

Use the Preemployment Inquiries list to identify the following 10 preemployment questions as

    a.  legal (can ask)

    b.  illegal (cannot ask)

_____    1.  What languages do you speak?

_____    2.  Are you married or single?

_____    3.  How many dependents do you have?

_____    4.  Are you a member of the racecar drivers' union?

_____    5.  How old are you?

_____    6.  Have you been arrested for stealing on the job?

_____    7.  Do you own your own car?

_____    8.  Do you have any form of disability?

_____    9.  What type of discharge did you get from the military?

_____  10.  Can you prove you are legally eligible to work?

operation of a particular organization. For instance, being a practicing Jew is not a BFOQ for a fitness instructor at a Jewish Community Center; however, being a practicing Jew is a BFOQ for a rabbi and teacher of Jewish religion classes. If challenged, the organization must provide evidence that the BFOQ is needed to do the job.

What BFOQ would an HR assistant for the Memphis Grizzlies have to be concerned with if she were trying to fill a senior equipment mechanic position?

# Human Resources Planning and Job Design

**LEARNING OUTCOME 2** ▶

Differentiate between a job description and a job specification, and explain why they are needed.

HR develops the HR plans to hire and manage good people for the entire organization.[9] HR practices strategically guide employees as they carry out the mission, strategy, and objectives of the firm.[10] **Strategic human resources planning** is the process of staffing the organization to meet its objectives. The job of the HR department is to provide people with the right skills at the right time to meet their goals.[11] Strategic human resources management is important because it matches the HR practices with the strategy.[12] If a company's strategy is growth, then employees will need to be hired. If its strategy is retrenchment, then there will be layoffs. Hiring strategies in professional sport are important to the competitive balance between teams and revenue sharing.

General managers (GMs) of professional sport teams need to be involved in strategic HR management. The director of player development for a professional team typically spends time finding replacements for injured players, working on problems with the coaching staff, and preparing for contract negotiations. The GMs help to decide when a team releases an aging player, when a player is no longer worth a long-term contract, and which free agents are worth large amounts of cap money.

General managers in football are involved in everything having to do with the football team. That includes the field, video, trainers, doctors, players, coaches, travel, and logistics.

Other people are involved in these activities, but the GM is often approached for answers.[13] If GMs don't answer the questions correctly, they will likely be fired.

Strategic HR planning determines the number of people and the skills needed, but it does not specify how each job is to be performed. So, before you rush off in search of a new employee, you need to conduct a job analysis[14] so that you and the job candidate know what the job really is and so that you have an accurate title for the position.[15] Job design (chapter 5) is the process of developing and combining the tasks and activities that make up a particular job. *Job analysis* is the process of determining what the position entails and the qualifications needed to staff the position. Thus, job analysis is the basis for the job description and the job specifications.

**TIME-OUT 3**

Perform a job analysis on your current job or one you recently held. Use your analysis to write a simple job description and job specifications. Were you given a realistic job preview when you were hired? Explain.

The **job description** identifies the tasks and responsibilities of a position. It should list the skills needed to perform the tasks.[16] In other words, it identifies what employees do all day to earn their pay. See the sample job description for the athletic director of Division III Elms College.[17]

The next step is to determine **job specifications**. Job specifications identify the qualifications needed to staff a position to ensure that the candidate matches the job requirements.[18] The job specifications thus identify the types of people needed. They answer the question, What competencies are important for performing the job?

The process of planning and job analysis is an important first HR activity because it is your basis for the other three HR processes: attracting, developing, and retaining employees. If you don't understand the job, how can you select employees to perform it? How can you train them to do the job? How can you evaluate their performance? How do you know how much to pay them? The job analysis should be updated as the tasks performed and qualifications for performing them change with the internal and external environment.[19]

An essential part of job analysis is developing a *realistic job preview (RJP)*. The RJP provides the candidate with an accurate, objective understanding of the job.[20] Some managers make the job sound better than it really is by describing the positive duties and not the negative ones.[21] But new hires are often disappointed and quit, creating turnover problems.[22] Research supports the idea that employees who believe they were given accurate descriptions are more satisfied and express less desire to change jobs than do those who believe they were not given an accurate job description. The RJP can lead to job satisfaction, which tends to improve performance.[23]

The Occupational Information Network (O*NET) is your tool for career exploration and job analysis! O*Net is sponsored by the federal government's Department of Labor (DOL). O*NET OnLine has detailed job descriptions, including specifications of hundreds of jobs for use by job seekers, workforce development and HR professionals, students, researchers, and more.[24] Visit www.onetonline.org to view the DOL website.

## Attracting Employees

Team and organizational success depend on the ability to attract and retain the best athletes and workers[25] because they directly affect organizational performance.[26] A lack of good team members in all positions can cause a variety of problems, including a losing season.[27] Attracting and selecting talent is a major challenge for companies and for all levels of sport.[28] So we will be discussing how to attract talent.[29]

With jobs analyzed, the HR department typically recruits promising applicants, and line managers select candidates to fill positions. It is a good idea for you to understand the recruiting and selecting process because you will be interviewed during your career,

◀ **LEARNING OUTCOME 3**

State the two parts of the process of attracting employees.

What qualities are important to consider when recruiting new staff or star athletes?
© Stockbyte

and as a sport manager you will most likely conduct job interviews. This section discusses recruiting methods and the selection process; in the next section we teach you how to prepare for and conduct a job interview. Although our focus is on hiring, many nonprofits (NGOs) also have to attract volunteers who must be recruited and selected, especially for mega-events like the Olympic Games.

## Recruiting

**Recruiting** is the process of attracting qualified candidates to apply for job openings. For an organization to fill an opening, possible candidates must be made aware that the organization is seeking employees.[30] They must then be persuaded to apply for the jobs. Remember that recruiting is not about quantity,[31] it's about attracting qualified candidates;[32] you don't want to waste your time reviewing applications that don't meet your clear job specifications.[33] To be an effective recruiter, you need to select the right recruiting source for each position.[34] As the Rick Pitino case at the end of the chapter highlights, coaches need to be careful during recruitment! Their enthusiasm to recruit a star player may result in improperly offering gifts, money, and benefits that can jeopardize their coaching careers. Recruiting is conducted both internally and externally;[35] figure 7.2 lists possible recruiting sources.

General managers have to recruit players by selling unique factors to attract star athletes. GMs try to attract players by highlighting the nice weather, the large and enthusiastic fan base, the opportunity to live in a large urban city, and so on. When LeBron James of the Cleveland Cavaliers became a free agent in 2010, he became part of one of the most public recruitment processes in sport. James ultimately decided to play with the Miami Heat. James left his hometown, Cleveland, to be part of Miami's plan to start him, Dwyane Wade, and Chris Bosh, who was another free-agent acquisition. LeBron returned to Cleveland in 2014 and won the 2016 NBA Championship with the Cavaliers. However, LeBron became a Los Angeles Laker when he became a free agent again.[36] Even superstars like the feeling of being recruited and starting over in new cities.

NCAA teams, including football teams, also need effective recruiting. The University of Texas, USC, Alabama, Clemson, Florida State, Notre Dame, Georgia, LSU, Miami, Ohio State, and Oklahoma are known for having effective recruiting programs.

# Sample Job Description

## Division III College

### Position Description

#### Job Title: Athletic Director

Exempt (Y/N): Yes
Salary Level:
Department: Athletics
Supervisor: Vice President of Student Services
Approved:
Date:
Incumbent:
Status: Full-time, 12-month

#### General Responsibilities

The director is responsible for administering and developing the athletic programs and policies while supporting student-athletes and coaches. He or she is responsible for all areas of compliance as applied to a Division III program.

#### Specific Responsibilities

- Administer all athletic programs.
- Develop athletic programs that reflect the vision outlined by the college.
- Make recommendations for the quality of all athletic programs.
- Ensure consistency between athletic programs, college policies, and strategic plans.
- Monitor compliance as it applies to the student-athlete concept, the principles governing intercollegiate athletics, gender equity, NCAA Division III and conference regulations, and legislation.
- Develop marketing concepts in collaboration with the college marketing department.
- Develop and implement promotions and public relations programs in collaboration with the college marketing department.
- Plan and participate in fund-raising efforts.
- Work with the dean of academics and the dean of students to integrate and administer a high-quality athletics program.
- Supervise all summer sports camps for children.
- Manage and oversee department budgets.
- Lead and supervise direct reports.
- Develop and implement student-athlete recruiting strategies that are in agreement with the approach and philosophy of the admissions office.
- Monitor recruiting efforts by coaches, making adjustments as needed.
- Monitor coaching styles to reflect the college philosophy surrounding student-athletes, making adjustments as needed.
- Work collaboratively with the human resources office to ensure that college personnel policies and issues are handled with consistency.

These duties and responsibilities are required of this position. However, the list is not all-inclusive. Other responsibilities and duties may be assigned to meet mission or strategic plan requirements of the college, and cooperation of all personnel is expected.

#### Supervisory Responsibilities

- Administrative assistant
- Contest management

*(continued)*

Sample Job Description *(continued)*

- Director, sport information
- Athletic trainers
- Full-time and part-time coaches

### Qualifications and Requirements

### Education, Experience, Skills

The ideal candidate for this position will have demonstrated skills and experience in strategic leadership, written and oral communications, creative approaches, problem solving, operations, and administration management. Qualifications include a master's degree in athletic administration, sport management, physical education, or a related field; 5 years of related experience in a college athletic department; and conference, coaching, and NCAA experience.

### Standards of Performance

- Flexibility and adaptability: Is able and willing to support the strategic plan, mission, and vision of the college.
- Judgment and decision making: Demonstrates a proactive role in judgment and decision processes.
- Communication: Maintains effective internal and external communications.
- Planning and organizing: Demonstrates skills in managing all aspects of the athletic department.
- Procedural expertise: Adheres to the procedures and processes as established by the college.
- Management of projects: Demonstrates leadership skills in meeting desired outcomes and in oversight of projects.
- Goals and objectives: Develops and implements strategies that support the goals and objectives established by the athletic department and the college.
- Use of resources: Demonstrates a prudent use of all resources.
- Safety, security, environmental awareness: Consistently exhibits behavior and department oversight that promote the safety and security of people and facilities while ensuring responsible behavior for our environment, both on and off campus.
- Promotes the college's mission, purpose, and goals and understands the role of this position in achieving those goals.

### Physical Demands and Work Environment

The physical demands described here are representative of those that must be met by an employee to successfully perform the essential functions of this job. Reasonable accommodations may be made to enable individuals with disabilities to perform the essential functions. The incumbent is exposed to a typical, climate-controlled office environment and various weather-related conditions (extreme temperature ranges, rain), typical office equipment (computer, printer, fax machine, telephones), usual sport equipment, and associated items. This position requires sitting, standing, bending, reaching, vision (near, distance), walking, lifting, climbing stairs, and manual dexterity to perform essential job functions.

Reprinted by permission from Elms College.

## Internal Recruiting

Internal recruiting involves filling job openings with current employees or personal referrals. NCAA Division III teams have been criticized for doing too much internal recruiting of their own graduates and have been encouraged to expand their job searches.

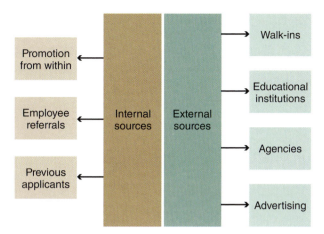

**FIGURE 7.2**  Recruiting sources.

- *Promotions from within/Internal mobility.* Horizontal (or lateral) transfers are common today, as are vertical promotions. The current term for horizontal and vertical moves is *internal mobility.*[37] Many organizations post job openings on bulletin boards, in company newsletters, and on their websites. Current employees can then apply or bid for the open positions.

- *Employee referrals.* When job openings are posted internally, employees may be encouraged to refer friends and relatives for the positions. Typically, employees refer only good candidates. This commonly used recruiting method[38] is based on *networking*, and more people get jobs through networking than all the other methods combined.[39] However, the U.S. government has stated that this referral method is not acceptable when current employees are predominantly white or male because it tends to perpetuate the present nondiversified composition of the workforce, which can result in discrimination.

### External Recruiting

The following are external recruiting sources:

- *Walk-ins.* Sometimes good candidates come to the organization "cold" (i.e., without an appointment) and ask for a job. However, professionals tend to send résumés and cover letters requesting an interview, which is good career advice.

- *Educational and other institutions.* Organizations recruit at high schools, vocational and technical schools, and colleges. Many schools offer career planning and placement services to aid students and potential employers. Take advantage of your career center. Educational institutions are good places to recruit people without prior experience. In addition to schools, professional associations, career conferences, and trade and job fairs are also used to recruit. Some professional and trade meetings and conferences have career services so that employers and applicants can hold job interviews.

- *Agencies.* There are three major types of agencies: (1) Temporary agencies, like Kelly Services, provide part- or full-time help for limited periods. They are useful for replacing employees who are out briefly or for supplementing the regular workforce during busy periods like game-day operations selling tickets, admitting and seating fans, and providing security. (2) Public agencies are government employment services in the United States that provide job candidates to employers at no, or very low, direct cost. (3) Private employment agencies charge a fee for their services. Agencies are good for recruiting people with experience. *Executive recruiters* are often referred to as "headhunters." They specialize in recruiting managers or those with high-level technical skills who are hard to recruit because they usually have a job. Headhunters tend to charge the employer a large fee.

- *Advertising/Internet.* It is important to use the appropriate media source to reach qualified candidates. A simple "Help Wanted" sign in the window may be appropriate for some positions, but newspaper and radio ads will reach a larger audience. Professional and trade magazines (print and online) are more suitable for specific skill categories. Some companies use direct mail and email to recruit from professional and trade members.

Technology is changing how organizations recruit and select employees. Employers now routinely advertise on the Internet. Numerous websites match applicants and job opportunities. Some good general websites for college students seeking career advice, part-time jobs, internships, and entry-level positions are www.internships.com, www.CollegeRecruiters.com, and www.CareerRookie.com. For more experienced workers, www.Indeed.com, www.CareerBuilder.com, and www.Monster.com are popular websites.

For a sport job search, you can use the following websites. Most require membership fees, but you can usually view job titles and descriptions without paying as part of your search for internships and jobs that you can apply for: www.JobsInSports.com, www.WorkInSports.com, www.SportsManagementWorldWide.com, www.IHireSportsandRecreation.com, www.SportsCareerFinder.com, www.SportsCareers.com, and www.TeamWorkOnline.com.

You may want to visit the website of specific companies, schools, colleges, and pro teams to find sport-related job openings because virtually every major organization's website has a link to career opportunities, with a list of job openings, most of which can be applied for online. You can find links to jobs and internships with the professional NBA, WNBA, NFL, NHL, and MLB websites.

At low or no cost, companies are also using social media, including LinkedIn, Facebook, and Foursquare, and they are even using Twitter to "tweet" job ads.[40] You most likely already have a Facebook account, but keep it professional because employers may look you up and refuse to hire you if they don't like what they see and read. If you don't have a LinkedIn account, career advice is to get one for networking opportunities with professionals.

**TIME-OUT 4** Identify the recruiting sources used to hire you both for your current job and for previous jobs.

---

## APPLYING THE CONCEPT 7.2

### Recruiting Sources

Select the recruiting source that would be most appropriate for the five job openings described.

- a. promotion from within
- b. employee referrals
- c. walk-ins
- d. educational institutions
- e. advertising
- f. agencies
- g. executive recruiters

_____ 11. You need a one-month replacement for Jason, who was hurt on the job manufacturing hockey skates.

_____ 12. Bonnie, a first-line supervisor in the fitness center, is retiring in two months.

_____ 13. You need an engineer to design new fitness equipment with very specific requirements. There are very few people with the qualifications you want.

_____ 14. Your sales manager likes to hire young people without experience in order to train them to sell insurance to athletes.

_____ 15. The maintenance department for your athletic center needs someone to perform routine cleaning services.

# Selection Process

**Selection** is the process of choosing the most qualified applicant recruited for a job. Although the speed of conducting business has increased, the speed of hiring new employees hasn't increased.[41] Hiring is time consuming and expensive;[42] you want to create equal opportunity and inclusion for everyone, while seeking diversity, without breaking antidiscrimination laws.[43]

Organizations don't follow a single universal sequence in their selection processes. Nor do they use the same selection process for different jobs. The selection process can be thought of as a hurdles race on the track. The applicant must jump every hurdle to win the job. That said, the typical selection process has six hurdles, which are presented in this section.

## Application Form

The first hurdle is usually the job application form or résumé. Today, even though résumés are requested, larger organizations commonly require online applications so that the job information is stored in the company's electronic *human resources information system (HRIS)* in a standard format to make it easier to compare candidates. The HRIS software scans application forms to compare the qualifications with the job specifications. However, the HR staff or line manager usually reviews the top candidates and selects the most qualified to continue to the next hurdle.[44]

The application gets you in the door so that you can convince the hiring interviewer that you are the best candidate for the job. If you are required to complete an application form, and you most likely will be, make sure you follow the instructions very carefully because the software doesn't deduct a few points from your grade for errors, it places your application in the rejection pile. Or you miss the hurdle and are out of the race.

## Screening Interview

HR department staff often conduct screening interviews to save managers' time—those candidates who they think are promising will continue in the selection process to the hiring line manager. Organizations such as Nike also now use computers to conduct screening interviews. In addition, to save time and travel expenses, companies conduct screening interviews via Skype, Voom, and similar programs.[45] With any of these options, the top candidates are brought to the organization for at least one personal interview. If this is the only interview, it is not a screening interview, it's the interview.

## Testing

Tests help employers to choose the best candidate for each job because tests can predict job success when they meet EEO guidelines for validity (candidates who score high on the test do well on the job, and those who score low do less well) and reliability (all candidates taking the same test on different days get approximately the same score each time).[46] Illegal tests can result in lawsuits. Tests of achievement, aptitude, personality, and interests have all been deemed appropriate, as have physical exams.

Many organizations are also testing for the use of illegal drugs. This type of testing is on the increase,[47] and candidates who fail are dropped from the search. Yes, marijuana is now legal in some states, but using it is still a federal crime. Many national and international companies follow national law, and they will not hire you, and they can legally fire you, if your test reveals marijuana in your system. Besides, if you are an athlete, why would you repeatedly put smoke in your lungs that will hurt your athletic performance?

An estimated 80 percent of major corporations in the United States use testing for some jobs,[48] and an estimated 60 to 70 percent of applicants take some form of online personality test.[49] A current trend is to have job candidates perform actual work for the organization for free as a type of test during the selection process. Unpaid internships can also serve as a type of test that can lead to a full-time job.[50]

Both internal and external candidates for management positions can be tested through assessment centers. **Assessment centers** are places where job applicants undergo a series of tests, interviews, and simulated experiences to determine their potential.

### Background and Reference Checks

Although references aren't given much weight in the selection because they are almost always positive,[51] carefully checking references to verify the information on a candidate's application form and résumé helps organizations to avoid poor hiring decisions. Unfortunately, around 10 percent of checks turn up inaccurate information.[52] Applicants caught lying in this way are dropped from consideration.

If you are not already aware, many organizations conduct an online search for job candidates, and if they find evidence for unprofessional behavior (like pictures of a sexual nature, drunkenness, or drug use), these candidates are eliminated.

### Interviewing

The interview is the most heavily weighted selection criterion and is usually the final hurdle in the selection process.[53] Interviews give candidates a chance to learn about the job and size up the organization firsthand (Is this a place where I want to work?). Interviews give managers a chance to subjectively size up candidates in ways that applications, tests, and references just don't.[54] (Does this candidate have the appearance, communication skills, personality, and motivation that match the job and fit within the organizational culture?)[55] Hiring managers are also including current employees in the interview process to help them decide on job and culture fit.[56] Because job interviewing is so important, in the next section we take you through the do's and don'ts of preparing for and conducting job interviews.

TIME-OUT 5

Create a simple table of the selection methods discussed in this section, and identify which ones were used for a job you were offered or for a position you were offered on a team you played for. If a test was used, specify the type of test.

### Hiring

After reviewing the information gathered, managers compare the candidates without bias and decide who is best suited for the job. Managers consider many criteria—among them qualifications, salary requirements, availability, and issues of diversity in the department or organization.[57] The chosen candidate is then contacted and offered the job. If the candidate doesn't accept the offer, or she accepts but leaves after a short period of time, the next best candidate is offered the job.

# Interviewing

Interviewing is a skill you will use over and over, both as an interviewer and as an interviewee. Study this section carefully, and complete Skill-Builder 7.1 in the web study guide. Figure 7.3 lists the types of interviews and the types of questions used in them.

## Choosing the Type of Interview

The three types of interviews are based on structure. (1) In *structured interviews*, interviewers use a list of prepared questions to ask all candidates. (2) In *unstructured interviews*, interviewers do not use preplanned questions or a preplanned sequence of topics. (3) In *semistructured interviews*, interviewers ask questions from a prepared list but also ask unplanned

## SELF-ASSESSMENT 7.1

### Are You Ready for a Sport Management Position?

The focus of this chapter is on hiring others. But let's take a few minutes to determine how ready you are to progress in your career.

Answer the questions on a scale from 1 to 5. Place the number (1-5) on the line before the question.

1 = not very descriptive of me

2 = somewhat descriptive of me

3 = neutral

4 = descriptive of me

5 = very descriptive of me

_____ 1. I know my strengths, and I can list several.

_____ 2. I can list several skills that I have to offer an employer.

_____ 3. I have career objectives.

_____ 4. I know the type of full-time job that I want next.

_____ 5. I have, or plan to get, part-time, summer, or internship experience related to my career objectives.

_____ 6. I have analyzed help-wanted ads and job descriptions and determined the most important skills I need to get the type of full-time job I want.

_____ 7. I know the proper terms to use on my résumé to help me get the job I want.

_____ 8. I understand how the strengths and skills I have developed in school or at work can be used in jobs I apply for.

_____ 9. I can give examples (on a résumé and during an interview) of how my strengths and skills can be used in the job I am applying for.

_____ 10. I can give examples (on a résumé and during an interview) of suggestions or contributions I have made that increased performance, reduced time or cost, increased sales, or changed a process.

_____ 11. If I have limited job experience, I focus more on the skills I developed than on giving job titles, stating how the skills relate to the job I am applying for.

_____ 12. If I have limited job experience, I give details of how my college education and the skills I developed in college relate to the job I am applying for.

_____ 13. I have a written job objective (preferably on a résumé) that clearly states the type of job I want and the skills I will use on the job.

_____ 14. I have, or plan to have, a résumé for every job I apply for (full-time, part-time, summer, or internship).

_____ 15. I plan to customize my résumé, changing the skills and ways in which they are transferable, to each job I apply for.

Add up your scores, place the number here _____, and put it on the following continuum.

|  |  |  |  | **Need** |  |  |
| **Career ready** |  |  |  | **career development** |  |  |
| 75 | 65 | 55 | 45 | 35 | 25 | 15 |

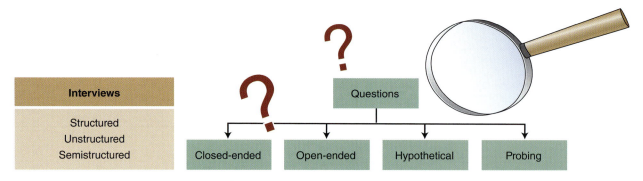

**FIGURE 7.3** Types of interviews and questions.

questions; that is, interviewers depart from their prepared questions when they believe it is appropriate. HR people generally prefer semistructured interviews because they help

TIME-OUT **6** What types of job interviews have you participated in?

prevent discrimination (the prepared questions are asked of all candidates), and they also give interviewers flexibility to pursue lines of questioning and conversation that give them accurate assessments of candidates' motivation and attitudes. At the same time, the standard set of questions makes it easier to compare candidates. The amount of structure you should use in interviews depends on your experience and on the situation. The less experienced you are, the more structure will help you conduct effective interviews.

## Formulating Questions

LEARNING OUTCOME 4 ▶

Explain how hypothetical questions and probing questions differ.

The questions you ask give you control over the interview; they allow you to dig out the information you need to make your decision. Make sure your questions all have a purpose and are job related. Ask all candidates for the same information.

Interviewers use four types of questions. (1) *Closed-ended questions* require a limited response, often a yes or no answer, and are appropriate for dealing with fixed aspects of the job. "Do you have a class I license, and can you produce it if hired?" (2) *Open-ended questions* allow for an unlimited response and are appropriate for determining abilities and motivation. "Why do you want to be a coach manager for our team?" "What do you see as a major strength you can bring to our team?" (3) *Hypothetical questions* require candidates to describe what they would do and say in a given situation; these questions help you assess capabilities. "What would you do if a free-agent baseball player wanted his own private locker room?" (4) *Probing questions* require candidates to clarify some aspect of their

background or some aspect brought up by the interviewer, and they help you to understand an issue or point. Probing questions are not planned. "What do you mean by 'it was tough'?" "What was the dollar increase your team achieved in ticket sales?"

TIME-OUT **7** List the types of questions you have been asked when you interviewed for jobs, and give an example of each one.

## Preparing for the Interview

Going through the formalized procedure shown in figure 7.4 will help you to improve your interviewing skills.

1. *Review the job description and specifications.* You cannot conduct an effective interview if you do not thoroughly understand the job for which you are assessing applicants. If the job description and job specifications are outdated or don't exist, conduct a job analysis.

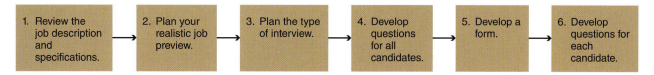

**FIGURE 7.4**   Preparing to interview.

2. *Plan your realistic job preview.* One of your jobs as interviewer is to help applicants understand what the job is and what they will be expected to do. They should know the job's good news and its bad news. Use the job description to plan this preview. It often helps to give candidates a tour of the work area and briefly meet people they will work with.

3. *Plan the type of interview.* What level of structure will you use? The interview should take place in a private, quiet place, without interruptions. It may be appropriate to begin in an office and then tour the facilities while asking questions. Plan when the tour will take place and what questions you will ask. Take your form with you if you intend to ask several questions.

4. *Develop questions for all candidates.* Use the job description and specifications to develop questions that relate to each job task and responsibility. Use a mixture of closed-ended, open-ended, and hypothetical questions. Don't be concerned about the order of questions; just write them down at this point. Now check that your questions are job related and nondiscriminatory. Ask them of all candidates.

5. *Develop a form.* Once you have a list of questions, determine the sequence. Start with the easy questions. One approach starts with closed-ended questions, moves to open-ended ones, and then moves to hypothetical ones, using probing questions as needed. Another approach structures the interview around the job description and specifications; the interviewer explains each and then asks questions relating to each responsibility.

Write your questions in sequence, leaving space for checking off closed-ended responses, for making notes on the responses to open-ended and hypothetical questions, and for writing follow-up questions. Add information gained from probing questions where appropriate. Recording the candidate's responses on this form will help guide you through the interview and help keep you on topic. Use a clean copy of the form for each candidate, and make a few extra copies to use when filling the same job in the future or to help you develop forms for other jobs.

6. *Develop questions for each candidate.* Review each candidate's application or résumé. You will most likely want to verify or clarify some of the candidate's information during the interview. "I noticed that you did not list any employment during 2012; were you unemployed during that time?" "On the application, you stated you had computer training; what types of computer software are you trained to operate?" Be sure that these individual questions are not discriminatory—for example, don't ask only women whether they can lift a specific amount of weight; ask every candidate this question.

You can note individual questions on the standard form, writing them in where they may be appropriate to ask, or you can add a list at the end of the form.

## Conducting the Interview

Following the steps in figure 7.5 will help make you an effective interviewer.

1. *Open the interview.* Try to develop rapport with applicants. Put them at ease by talking about some topic not related to the job. Maintain eye contact in a way that is comfortable for you and for them.

**FIGURE 7.5** Interviewing.

2. *Give your realistic job preview.* Be sure applicants understand the job requirements. Answer any questions they have about the job and the organization. If the job is not what they expected or want to do, allow applicants to disqualify themselves and close the interview at that point.

3. *Ask your questions.* Steps 2 and 3 can be combined if you like. To get the most out of a job interview, take notes on applicants' responses to your questions. Tell each applicant that you have prepared a list of questions and that you plan to take notes.

During the interview, applicants should do most of the talking. Give them a chance to think and respond. In addition to making sure the person fits the job requirements, you also need to determine whether the candidate fits the team, the company, and the culture.[58] If someone doesn't give you all the information you need, ask an unplanned probing question. However, if it's obvious that the person doesn't want to answer the question, don't force it. Go on to the next question or close the interview. End with a closing question such as, "I'm finished with my questions. Is there anything else you want to tell me about or ask me?"

4. *Introduce top candidates to coworkers.* Introduce top candidates to people with whom they will be working to get a sense of their interpersonal skills and overall attitude. Introductions can also give you a sense about whether the person is a team player.

5. *Close the interview.* Be honest without making a decision during the interview. Don't lead candidates on. Thank them for their time, and tell them about the next step in the interview process, if any. Tell candidates when you will contact them—be specific, and keep your word. You might say, "Thank you for coming in for this interview. I'll be interviewing over the next two days and will call [or email] you with my decision by Friday of this week."

Be sure that you make that call; simple courtesy demands that you give applicants closure. Also, you don't want job applicants to get a bad impression about your team or organization and tell their friends and relatives how you treated them poorly because you could lose fans and customers. After the interview, jot down general impressions not covered by specific questions.

TIME-OUT
8

Use figure 7.5 to analyze an interview in which you were the job seeker. Did your interviewer use all the steps we have examined? If not, why might the interviewer have skipped some steps?

## Avoiding Problems When Selecting

Sport managers often struggle with hiring decisions. After all interviews are completed, compare each candidate's qualifications with the job specifications to determine who will be best for the job and will fit with the organizational members and culture.[59] Gather coworkers' impressions of each candidate. Here are some tips for the selection process:

- Don't rush. Take your time—this is an important decision. Don't be pressured into hiring just any candidate. Find the best person available.

- Don't stereotype. Don't prejudge with assumptions, for example that overweight people are lazy. Don't leap to conclusions. Be objective and subjective; use analysis to match the best candidate to the job, but also trust your gut.

- Don't look for employees who are copies of you. Remember the tangible benefits of diversity (chapter 6). A department of your clones will not be an effective team. You want people with strengths that can offset your weaknesses.

- Don't look for "halos" and "horns." Don't judge a candidate on the basis of one or two favorable or unfavorable characteristics. Look at the total person and at the entire pool of candidates.

- Don't jump prematurely. Don't make your selection based solely on the person's application or résumé, and don't decide right after interviewing a candidate who impressed you. Don't compare candidates after each interview. The order in which you interview applicants can be strongly influential. Be open-minded during all interviews, and make a choice only after you have finished all interviews. Compare all candidates on each job specification.

# Developing Employees

After an organization has recruited and selected job candidates, it must develop its employees by orienting and training them and also by appraising their performance.[60] This is the third step in the HR process. If people are the organization's most important asset, they need to be developed.[61] Although it is expensive,[62] investing in developing employees will pay for itself in the long run by lowering the cost of attracting employees and increasing organizational performance.[63] The topic of this section is orienting and training; in the next section, we discuss appraising performance.

## Orientation

**Orientation** introduces new employees to the organization, its culture, and their jobs. Getting off to a good start affects individual and team success.[64] Orientation is about learning the ropes. Today orientation is commonly called *onboarding*.[65] Effective orientation reduces the time needed to get new hires up to speed, reduces their new-job jitters, and gives them an accurate idea of what is expected of them. Good orientation and training programs reduce turnover and improve attitudes and performance.[66] Allowing coworkers to help with orientation is a good method because new employees need to know whom to go to for information and help,[67] so they should have an informal mentor to help with onboarding.[68]

Today, newcomer socialization is the focus of orientation/onboarding.[69] Organizations socialize their members,[70] and they want to quickly create a sense of belonging for newcomers (see chapter 6).[71] *Newcomer socialization* refers to how new employees acquire the attitudes, knowledge, skills, and behaviors required to be productive on the job.[72]

Although orientation programs vary in formality and content, five elements are shared by effective programs:

1. Explaining what the organization does (products and services) and the department functions that the new person will be part of. Many organizations show videos to explain what the organization is all about.

2. Explaining what the new employee's job task and responsibilities are.

3. Going over the standing plans (policies, procedures, and rules) that need to be followed to get the job done.

4. Giving the new employee a tour of the facilities.

5. Introducing the new employee to coworkers.

Professional leagues such as the NBA conduct orientation programs with rookie players to highlight the complexities of being a professional player. The orientation includes discussions on the use of illegal drugs and fiscal responsibility.

◀ **LEARNING OUTCOME 5**
State the purposes of orientation and training and development.

? How would the Memphis Grizzlies' orientation program differ for its first-round draft pick compared with its new ticket sales manager?

**TIME-OUT 9** Describe an orientation you participated in recently. Which elements of effective programs did it include? Which ones did it exclude?

# Training and Development

Orientation and training often take place simultaneously. **Training** is about acquiring the skills necessary to perform a job. If you have diverse skills, you can perform a variety of tasks and jobs (recall our discussion of job expansion in chapter 5).[73] **Development** is ongoing education that improves skills for present and future jobs. Today, ongoing training and development are needed to keep up with the latest trends and skills. The G League is the NBA's official minor league for helping young players to develop their skills before they enter the NBA. Less technical than training, development is aimed at strengthening people skills, communication skills, conceptual abilities, and decision-making skills in managerial and professional employees; often these skills have no immediate application to the job.[74]

Let's focus on your development so far through this course. How many of the skills that you have learned and were able to develop through skill-building exercises are you currently using? As discussed in chapter 6, it's tough to implement new skills because we don't like to change our habits. Did you do Skill-Builder 6.3, New Habits? Have you actually developed any new habits?

Getting back to sports, some people complain that U.S. colleges and universities are training foreign athletes to compete against Americans in the Olympics. If you want to talk about cross-training, how about the fact that many of the workouts the NFL quarterbacks learn are straight from baseball, and that ex-MLB pitcher Tom House is teaching quarterbacks how to throw fastballs?

## Off the Job and On the Job

Off-the-job training is conducted away from the worksite, usually in a vocational classroom–type setting. A common method is **vestibule training**, which develops skills in a simulated setting. Vestibule training is used to teach job skills when teaching at the worksite is impractical. In preparation for the regular season, MLB baseball players attend spring training in Florida and Arizona every spring to practice before playing on their home fields. Big businesses conduct some training off the job,[75] whereas small businesses with limited budgets often use only on-the-job training.[76]

On-the-job training is conducted at the worksite with the same physical resources the employee uses to perform the job after being trained. With a proven track record based on evidence, job instructional training, discussed next, is a popular method used in both on- and off-the-job training around the world.[77]

## Job Instructional Training

**LEARNING OUTCOME 6 ▶**

Describe job instructional training.

Job instructional training (JIT) is composed of four steps (see figure 7.6). Remember that what *we* know well seems very simple to us, but new hires and athletes don't yet share this perspective, so take it slow.

1. *Preparation of the trainee.* Put trainees at ease as you create interest in the job and encourage questions. Explain the quantity and quality requirements and their importance.
2. *Presentation of the task by the trainer.* Perform the task yourself at a slow pace, explaining each step several times. Once trainees seem to have the steps memorized, have

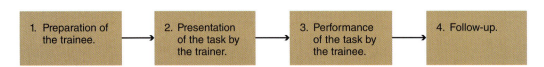

**FIGURE 7.6** Steps in job instructional training.

them explain each step as you perform the job at a slow pace. Write out complex tasks with multiple steps, and give trainees a copy.

3. *Performance of the task by the trainee.* Have trainees perform the task at a slow pace, explaining each step. Correct any errors and help them perform any difficult steps. Continue until they can perform the task proficiently.

4. *Follow-up.* Watch trainees perform the task, and correct any errors or faulty work procedures before they become a habit. Be patient and encouraging. Tell trainees whom to go to for help with questions or problems. Gradually leave them alone. Begin by checking quality and quantity often, and then decrease the amount of checking based on the trainee's skill level.

 **TIME-OUT 10** Identify which JIT steps your trainer used to teach you your current job. Was the training on or off the job?

## Training Cycle

Figure 7.7 shows the steps in the training cycle. Following these steps ensures that training is systematic and thus effective.

1. *Conduct a needs assessment.* Before you begin training, you must determine your staff's training needs. Based on your knowledge as a coach, what skills and plays do they need to work on?

2. *Set objectives.* Any training program should have well-defined, performance-based objectives. As with all plans, begin by determining the end result you want to achieve. Your objectives should meet the criteria discussed in chapter 4.

3. *Prepare for training.* Before conducting a training session, have written plans and all the necessary materials and equipment ready. If you have ever had an instructor come to class or a coach come to practice unprepared, you know why preparation before training is necessary for success.

    Selecting the training method is an important part of your preparation. You have already learned about JIT. Table 7.1 lists various training methods. Whatever method you develop, break the task into steps. Write down each step, and go through the steps yourself to make sure they work.

4. *Conduct the training.* Have your written plan with you, as well as any other materials you will need.

5. *Measure and evaluate training results.* Linking training outcomes and results will make you more effective as a trainer. During training and at the end of the program, measure and evaluate the results to determine whether you achieved your objectives. If you met your goals, training is over. If you didn't meet your goals, either continue the training until your objectives are met or take employees off the job if they cannot meet the standards. Revise and improve your written plans for future use.

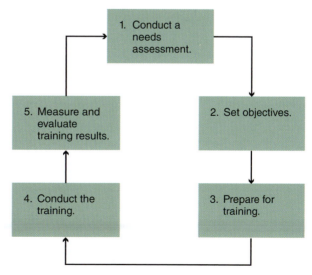

**FIGURE 7.7** The training cycle.

## TABLE 7.1  Training Methods

| Method | Definition | Skill developed |
|---|---|---|
| Written material | Trainees read manuals and books. | Technical |
| Lecture | Trainees listen to spoken instructions and class lectures. | Technical |
| Video | Trainees learn from television and class videos. | Technical |
| Question and answer | After using the other methods, the trainer asks the trainees questions about what they read, heard, and watched. | Technical |
| Discussion | A topic is presented and discussed. | Technical |
| Programmed learning | A computer or book is used to present material, followed by a question or problem. Trainees select a response and then are given feedback on their answers. Depending on the material presented, programmed learning may possibly develop people skills and conceptual skills. | Technical |
| Demonstration | Trainers show trainees how to perform the task. This is step 2 in JIT. Demonstrations can also be used to develop people skills and decision-making skills. | Technical |
| Job rotation | Employees learn to perform multiple jobs. | Technical and conceptual |
| Projects | Trainees learn via special assignments, such as developing a new product or a new team. Projects that require working with people and other departments also develop people skills and conceptual skills. | Technical |
| Role-playing | Trainees act out a possible job situation, such as handling a customer complaint, to develop skill at handling similar situations on the job. | People and communication |
| Behavior modeling | (1) Trainees observe how to perform the task correctly. This may be done via a live demonstration or a videotape. (2) Trainees role-play a situation using the observed skills. (3) Trainees receive feedback on how well they performed. (4) Trainees develop plans for using the new skills on the job. | People and communication |
| Cases | Trainees are presented with a situation and asked to diagnose and solve the problems involved. They are usually asked to answer questions. (Cases are included at the end of each chapter of this book.) | Conceptual and decision making |
| In-basket exercise | Trainees are given actual or simulated letters, memos, reports, and telephone messages typically found in the in-basket of a person holding the job they're being trained for. Trainees are asked what, if any, action they would take for each item and are told to assign priorities to the material. | Conceptual and decision making |
| Management games | Trainees manage a simulated company. They make decisions in small teams and get the results back, usually on a quarterly basis, over a period of several game "years." Teams are in an "industry" with several competitors. | Conceptual and decision making |
| Interactive video | Trainees sit at a computer and respond as directed. | Any of the skills |

## Training Methods

Table 7.1 lists the various training methods available, many of which can be used as part of JIT. The third column lists the primary skill developed. However, some of the technical methods can be combined. Technical skill also includes acquiring knowledge that can be tested.

When selecting a training method, keep in mind that people learn much more from what they use and do in real life. We learn more by doing. Unfortunately, there is a big gap between knowing and doing. Filling this gap is the foundation of this book's focus on learning concepts, applying them, and developing skills that can be used in your personal and professional lives. Again, are you applying what you learn and developing skills by using them?

The trend today is to keep training lessons short with the use of *microlearning*. Interactive video is commonly used in lessons that take around five minutes to complete and include a test. Trainees can complete any number of lessons independently whenever they want to access them online with a desktop computer, tablet, or smartphone.[78]

 **TIME-OUT 11** Describe the methods used to train you in your current job.

## APPLYING THE CONCEPT 7.3

### Training Methods

Select the most appropriate training method for the following situations.

a. written material

b. lecture

c. video

d. question-and-answer session

e. discussion

f. programmed learning

g. demonstration

h. job rotation

i. projects

j. role-playing

k. behavior modeling

l. management games

m. in-basket exercise

n. cases

o. interactive video

_____ 16. Your large department has a high turnover rate. Staff must know the rules and regulations in order to sell high-quality bicycles.

_____ 17. In the athletic center you manage, you occasionally need to teach new employees how to handle problems they face daily.

_____ 18. Your boss has requested a special report.

_____ 19. You need your staff to be able to cover for each other as lifeguards at the center's swimming pool.

_____ 20. Your staff must know how to handle customer complaints about weather conditions at the ski resort you manage.

# Performance Appraisals

Now that you have hired and trained, what's the next part of developing new employees? You need to assess how the new employees are working out.[79] Is their current performance outstanding or merely adequate,[80] and do they have the potential for advancement?[81] For hiring errors, you may need to dismiss them during the usual trial period. The HR department is responsible for helping develop performance appraisals, which is the topic for this section. Many workers and managers dread performance appraisals. A major reason is that they are not conducted effectively. But if you follow our guidelines here, you can do a good job.

**Performance appraisal** is the ongoing process of evaluating employee performance. Performance appraisals (PAs) are a critical part of understanding and managing people. Unfortunately, PA reviews are only conducted once a year by more than 75 percent of surveyed companies, when they should be ongoing throughout the review period, as our definition states.[82] PAs come in two types—developmental and evaluative. *Developmental PAs* are used to improve performance. *Evaluative PAs* are used to decide pay raises, transfers and promotions, and demotions and terminations. Evaluative PAs focus on the past, whereas developmental PAs focus on the future. However, developmental plans are always based on evaluative PAs. The primary purpose of both types is to help employees to continuously improve their performance. Most firms place the biggest emphasis on evaluation, which is a mistake because it doesn't develop employees.

When developmental and evaluative PAs are conducted together—which they commonly are—the developmental PA is often less effective, especially when an employee disagrees with the evaluation. Most managers are not good at both judging and coaching. Therefore, separate meetings make the two uses clear and make the process more productive for both employee and manager.

## Performance Appraisal Process

Figure 7.8 shows the connection between the organization's mission and objectives and the performance appraisal process. The feedback loop indicates the need to control performance. Employees' performance should be measured against their contribution to the achievement of the organization's mission and objectives (chapter 4).

1. *Analyze the job.* The PA method needs to be based on the job description because you can't assess performance if you don't know and understand what you are assessing. The responsibilities laid out in the job description should be ranked in order of importance and weighed accordingly.

2. *Develop standards and measurement methods.* After determining what it takes to do the job, you can develop standards and methods for measuring performance. (In the next section we describe several common measurement methods; we discuss how to set standards in chapter 13.)

3. *Carry out informal PAs through coaching and discipline.* Effective PA systems should be ongoing. We all benefit from regular informal feedback on our performance.[83] You most likely know how important good coaching is to athletic performance, but do you realize that it is just as important in sport management? Coaching involves giving praise for a job well done to maintain performance and taking corrective action when standards are not met.[84] Someone who is underperforming may need daily or weekly coaching or discipline to meet standards. In chapter 13, we examine coaching and discipline in more detail.

4. *Prepare for and conduct the formal PA.* Follow the steps in figure 7.9. Your success at conducting formal PAs doesn't come from the method or form you use once or twice a year; it comes from your ongoing coaching efforts so that your employees always know what the standards are and how they are doing.

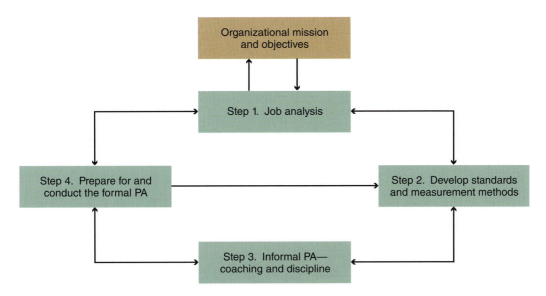

**FIGURE 7.8**   The performance appraisal process.

### Preparing for the PA

*Evaluative PA*

| 1. Make an appointment. | 2. Ask employee to perform a self-assessment. | 3. On a PA form, assess his/her performance using your notes and his/her SA. | 4. Identify his/her strengths and areas for improvement. | 5. Think about how he/she might react and how you can address his/her concerns. |

*Developmental PA*

| 1. Make an appointment. | 2. Ask employee to develop some objectives for improving his/her performance. | 3. Lay out objectives that you want the employee to accomplish. |

### Conducting the PA

*Evaluative PA*

| 1. Open the interview. | 2. Go over the PA form, inviting discussion and employee's responses. | 3. Agree on strengths and areas for improvement. | 4. Close the interview. |

*Developmental PA*

| 1. Open the interview. | 2. Agree on objectives together. | 3. Together, develop a plan for meeting the objectives. | 4. Make follow-up appointment(s) to check on how things are going. | 5. Close the interview. |

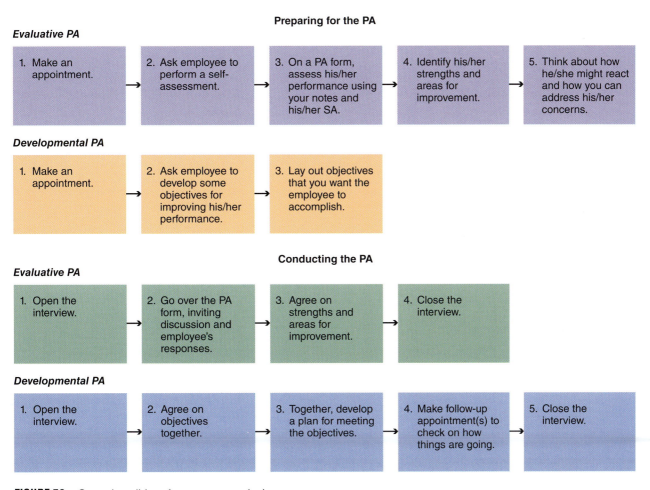

**FIGURE 7.9**   Steps in solid performance appraisals.

## Performance Standards

Your employees need to know what the job standards are and what your standards are.[85] Job performance standards must be defined precisely. As discussed in chapter 6, discrimination is common. Thus, although you will rely partly on intuition when you appraise performance, you must use objective standards that accurately measure performance so that you can avoid discrimination.[86]

If you give an employee an average rating rather than a good one, you must be able to clearly explain why. Otherwise, you may face allegations of discrimination. Employees also need to understand exactly what they can do during the next appraisal period to earn a higher rating. If your standards are clear and you are coaching effectively, there should be no surprises during the formal PA. In chapter 13, you will learn how to set standards in the areas of quantity, quality, time, cost, and behavior.

## You Get What You Reward

LEARNING OUTCOME 8 ▶

Explain the concept "You get what you reward."

All of us will do what we are rewarded for doing, and generally we will not do what we are punished for doing—such as breaking the law or the organization's rules. We seek information about what activities are rewarded and then we try to do (or at least pretend to do) those things, often to the exclusion of activities that are not rewarded. The extent to which this occurs depends on the attractiveness of the rewards.

If a professor distributes a list of readings but then tells the class (or the students realize without being told) that they will not discuss those readings in class or be tested on them, how many students will do the reading? How about if your professor tells that you A, B, and C from this chapter will be on the test, but X, Y, and Z will not? Would you spend equal time studying both groups?

In sport, actions speak louder than words. If you are a basketball coach who encourages teamwork and passing the ball, but then you ignore the players who pass and praise the high scorers, don't be surprised if you get ball hogs. You must clearly tell players and employees what you expect and then reward (or punish) accordingly.

## Measurement Methods

People giving formal PAs in larger organizations usually use a standard form (typically rating scales) developed by the HR department that is supposed to measure employee performance objectively.[87] Table 7.2 lists commonly used PA measurement methods. Which PA method is best? This depends on your objectives, on the type of people in your group, on the work being evaluated, and on your organization's culture. Combinations usually work better than any one method. For developmental PAs, critical incidents and management by objectives (MBO) work well because they are tailored to the individual. For evaluative PAs, ranking methods work well because they help you select the best.

The problem with most PA forms is that they include measures of non-performance-related stuff, like initiative, creativity, willingness to take responsibility, and promotability, which nobody really knows how to measure. As a result, employees try to please the boss rather than focus on results. Under these conditions, having a good relationship with your boss—not results—gets you ahead in the firm. Such measures are also very subjective. Successful PAs depend on your people skills as a manager and on your fair and objective analysis.

## Performance Appraisal Interviews

If you are a manager, part of the job is to evaluate the performance of your people or players. But you will also be evaluated by your boss. Here are some tips for both roles of evaluator and evaluatee.

## TABLE 7.2  Performance Appraisal Measurement Methods

| | |
|---|---|
| **Critical incidents file:** Managers note an employee's positive and negative performance behavior throughout the performance period. This form of documentation is particularly necessary in today's litigious environment. | **Ranking:** Managers rank employee performance from best to worst. That is, managers compare employees to each other, rather than comparing each person to a standard measurement. An offshoot of ranking is the forced distribution method, which resembles grading on a curve. A predetermined percentage of employees are placed in performance categories: for example, excellent—5%; above average—15%; average—60%; below average—15%; and poor—5%. |
| **Rating scale:** Managers simply check off the employee's level of performance. Typical areas evaluated include quantity of work, dependability, judgment, attitude, cooperation, and initiative. | **Management by objectives (MBO):** Managers and the employee jointly set objectives for the employee, periodically evaluate the person's performance, and reward according to the results (see chapter 4 for details). |
| **Behaviorally anchored rating scale (BARS):** This method combines rating and critical incidents. It is more objective and accurate than the two methods separately. Rather than using ratings like *excellent*, *good*, *average*, and *poor*, managers choose from several statements the one that best describes the employee's performance for the given task. A good BARS makes standards clear. | **Narrative:** Managers write a statement about the employee's performance. The system varies. Managers may be allowed to write whatever they want, or they may be required to answer specific questions about performance. Narratives are often combined with another method. |

### Evaluating Others

Always plan before you conduct PA interviews. Everybody comes out ahead when you are well prepared. Figure 7.9 gives you the steps you should follow in your all-important preparation and in the interview itself. When you conduct interviews, encourage employees to talk. You want them to feel free to talk and to share concerns; employees' feeling of freedom (or lack thereof) builds the trust (or distrust) that makes them more open (or closed) to viewing the evaluation objectively. Note that figure 7.9 presents the preparation and conduct of the evaluative and developmental PAs separately for better results.[88] We do this to show you how they differ and also how they resemble each other. Note the collaborative tone in the steps. Remember, you and your employees are on the same side—maximizing their potential is in the best interest of both of you.

### Being Evaluated

As an employee, you should relish a development conversation because it is your opportunity to improve your performance and thus get ahead in the organization. Be sure to leave your PA with a clear understanding of how to improve your performance for the next session, and continuously improve to get the highest rating. Sounds good, but it's not that easy if your boss is not doing a good job of coaching you. But don't tell your boss she has poor coaching skills.

What if you don't agree with your boss' assessment? First, remember that your supervisor's evaluation will affect your pay raises and promotions, so you don't want to make the situation worse. You can tell your boss you think he is wrong and why you think so, but it usually doesn't work because most managers will not admit to making a mistake. There is

## APPLYING THE CONCEPT 7.4

### Selecting Performance Appraisal Methods

Use table 7.2 to select the most appropriate PA method for the given situation.

a. critical incidents

b. rating scales

c. BARS

d. ranking

e. MBO

f. narrative

_____ 21. The roller-skating rink you started six years ago now has 10 employees. You're overworked, so you want to develop one PA form that you can use with every employee.

_____ 22. You've been promoted to middle management at Golf Balls Deluxe. You've been asked to select your replacement.

_____ 23. Winnie, who markets the new line of basketballs, isn't performing up to standard. You decide to talk to her about ways she can improve her performance.

_____ 24. You want to create a system for helping employees realize their potential.

_____ 25. Your roller-skating rink has grown to 50 employees. Some of them are concerned that the form you're using doesn't work well for the various jobs, so you've hired a professional to develop a PA system that is more objective and job specific. You have asked him to develop more focused PA forms.

also a good chance your boss will lose respect for you, and it will be hard to convince the boss you will change.

Here is some good advice about what not to do.[89] Try not to get angry and raise your voice; don't deny having made mistakes or having failed to meet the boss' performance expectations; don't make excuses and blame others. What should you do? Take responsibility for not meeting your boss' expectations, and schedule a separate developmental session with your boss to tell your boss you want to improve and get a higher-level assessment during your next PA. Get your boss to very clearly state exactly what you need to do to improve and how you will measure progress. Together, develop a plan to improve, and agree that if you meet the expectations you will get a higher assessment the next time. It helps to document your agreement in writing and to have both of you sign it. Also, follow up with your boss, keep a critical incidents file to document that you are meeting the standards, and use it during your next PA.

Here is an option to consider and only use if you really believe you will win: You can also complain to your boss' boss or to the HR department. But what are the odds that they will take your side? It occasionally works, but usually only if your supervisor already has a bad reputation. If you have a good working relationship with your subordinate, would you take sides against her to help a lower-level employee you may not even know? More likely than not, you will only anger your boss and make the situation worse.

## Retaining Employees

We have discussed the HR processes of planning, attracting, and developing employees, so now we present the fourth and last process—retaining employees. Organizations must have HR systems in place to retain good people and to separate (also called terminate) poor employees. An effectively trained, retained workforce does a better job and costs less.[90] High employee turnover rates reduce productivity and profitability.[91] Replacing a good employee is expensive.[92] To minimize this expense, organizations go to great lengths to keep the employees they have because it's the most effective way to save money.[93] If you became a manager of a Walmart sporting goods department, you'd face an 85 percent annual turnover rate of your staff. If you had 100 employees, 85 would have to be attracted and developed every year, so the organizing management function of interviewing and training would take up a lot of your time. In the nonprofit sector, retaining volunteers is also critical to many organizations, including the Olympic Games.

There are many strategies for retaining employees. But the bottom line is that you need to treat them well.[94] People who believe they are being justly rewarded tend to stay with an organization, but it's not just about pay.[95] A good work environment with strong, rewarding relationships between employees also keeps people.[96] So do challenging work and good feedback. And so does an informed and highly skilled HR department. Therefore, in this section we examine three areas that affect employee retention: compensation, health and safety, and labor relations. Because no company has 100% employee retention, we also discuss termination and outplacement.

# Compensation

**Compensation** is the total cost of pay and benefits to employees. Compensation is pivotal in both attracting and retaining employees.[97] Compensation schemes are also related to performance. An important strategic decision is the organization's pay level. Pay level refers to whether the organization aims at being a high-, medium-, or low-paying organization compared to other similar jobs. Low-paying firms may save money by low-balling wages, but such savings can be lost to the high cost of turnover as employees leave for better jobs. But good pay alone will not retain many disgruntled employees.

◀ **LEARNING OUTCOME 9**
State the two major components of compensation.

NCAA Division III colleges generally have less funding and thus can have more challenges in attracting and retaining coaches than do Division I schools. However, Division III colleges can offer coaches and sport managers an opportunity to work in a smaller educational system, often in a rural atmosphere.

As much as some people love to play sports and coach, it is extremely difficult to go pro, and it can be difficult to make a decent living as a coach. Thus, coaching often becomes a part-time job or volunteer position, especially coaching your own kids, which is very rewarding personally. I (Robert Lussier) never had a full-time coaching-only job. But I started as a teacher coaching high school for a year and moved up to college for three years (maybe making minimum wages on a per hour basis for the coaching part of my job), and I spent many years coaching one of my daughters and all three of my sons up to high school level. Although I stopped coaching, it's part of who I am today as a person and now a grandparent.

On a final note here, overall, as a sport manager, you need to be ethical and not discriminate when compensating employees. Everyone should be compensated based on their experience and ability to coach, not their gender, race, or any other reason.

## Pay Systems

Organizations can use any or all three pay systems: (1) Wages are paid on an hourly basis—hours worked times hourly wage. (2) Salary is figured weekly, monthly, or annually but does not take into account the number of hours worked. As a sport manager you will likely have a set salary, but you can work more than 40 hours a week without overtime. (3) Incentives are paid for performance, which can motivate employees to higher levels of performance. Incentives include piece rate (pay based on production), commissions (pay based on sales), merit raises (the more productive workers get paid more), and bonuses. Two common bonuses include a specific reward for reaching an objective and profit sharing, in which employees get a part of the profits. Pay for performance is also commonly used.

Professional athletes sometimes receive enormous salaries regardless of performance. MLB pitcher David Price signed a seven-year, $217 million contract with the Boston Red

Sox. He has an annual average salary of $31 million.[98] However, many athletes are paid a base amount and then get incentive pay if they perform well—that is, if they reach a certain number of hits, touchdowns, quarterback sacks, or games played. General managers believe that incentive pay motivates players to excel—to give it their all.

## Determining Pay

LEARNING OUTCOME 10 ▶

Describe how job analyses and job evaluations are used.

How much to pay each employee is a difficult decision that all organizations face. Some organizations use an external approach—they find out what other organizations pay for the same or similar jobs and set their pay based on that.[99] Other organizations use an internal approach that involves job evaluation. **Job evaluation** determines the worth of each job relative to other jobs in the organization. Organizations commonly group jobs into pay grades. The higher the worth or grade of the job, the higher the pay. The two approaches are often used together.

## Benefits

Benefits are the part of a compensation package that is not direct pay or merit based. Legally required benefits in the United States include workers' compensation to cover job-related injuries, unemployment compensation for when people are laid off or terminated, Medicare for health insurance in later years, and Social Security for retirement income. Employers match the amount the U.S. government takes out of each person's pay for Social Security. Most employers also must provide some time off for medical reasons and family care.

Benefits that are technically optional but that are offered in almost all large U.S. companies are health insurance; paid sick and personal days, holidays, and vacations; and pension plans. The costs of optional benefits (health insurance and pension plans) are commonly split between employee and employer or are paid completely by the employee. Other benefits less commonly offered include dental and life insurance, membership to fitness centers, membership in credit unions, and tuition reimbursement. Potentially, you could get a master's degree fully or partially paid for. Benefits such as elder care and child care are also on the increase as organizations focus on work–life issues.

The benefits portion of compensation packages has been increasing over the years, primarily attributable to the high cost of health insurance. The benefits portion varies with the level of job, but it has been

TIME-OUT 12 Describe the compensation package offered by your employer.

estimated that the average large U.S. employer spends 25 to 35 percent of total employee compensation on benefits.[100] When you look at full-time job opportunities, remember to compare total compensation, not just pay. One job that pays higher wages without benefits might offer less compensation than a lower-paying job with benefits—as can be the case with contract jobs for workers who are not actually employees. Consider that health insurance is very expensive; a family plan can cost more than $17,000 a year.[101]

Robert Lussier and David Kimball are college professors with salaries that include benefits. But as authors of this book, we are contract workers (without wages or salaries) who are paid by commissions (book sale royalties).

Let's take a personal view regarding retirement because many people don't realize how important it is and don't take full advantage of this benefit.[102] First, would you like to be a millionaire? You can be if you follow this advice and start saving young, preferably in your 20s. Think and start planning for *retirement*, right now.[103] Pay yourself first as your top payment priority.[104] If your employer offers a 401(k) or other plan, start one as soon as you can. If your employer offers to match your contribution, contribute the maximum to take advantage of this free money. Why pass up a matching dollar for dollar for a 100 percent return on your investment? Do talk to the HR department retirement person to make sure you understand your options and to set up the account—again, take maximum matching.

If you start putting away $2,000 a year (with or without a match) in your early 20s, in a low-fee account such as a stock index fund,[105] with competent professional help like TIAA or Fidelity, you can be a millionaire by the time you retire at age 67. If you start doing this with your first job, you will never miss the money, and less will be taken out of your pay for taxes because the retirement contribution is tax deferred. The general rule is to put away 10 to 15 percent of your gross income for retirement.[106] If you are thinking, "I can't afford to put money away today," replace that thought with, "I can't afford to lose compound savings and give away matching funds and give up being a millionaire."

## Health and Safety

The U.S. Occupational Safety and Health Act (OSHA) of 1970 requires U.S. employers to pursue workplace safety. Employers must meet OSHA safety standards, maintain records of injuries and deaths attributable to workplace accidents, and submit to on-site inspections. HR departments commonly are responsible for ensuring the health and safety of employees. They work closely with other departments and often conduct new-hire training and ongoing training in this area as well as maintaining health and safety records. A growing area of concern is workplace uncivil behavior and violence. To learn more about the U.S. Department of Labor's OSHA, visit www.osha.gov.

 Do you think an HR assistant for the Memphis Grizzlies has to be concerned with OSHA?

Coaches at all levels need to provide a safe environment that helps prevent accidents and injuries to athletes. With terrorist mass murders and fan violence occurring regularly around the world, event safety is a major concern every day, especially on game day. As a coach and sport manager, you must know the safety rules and procedures, make sure that your employees and volunteers know them, and enforce them to prevent accidents and injuries.

## Labor Relations

**Labor relations** are the interactions between management and unionized employees. Labor relations are also called *union–management relations* and *industrial relations*. There are many more U.S. organizations without unions than there are with unions. Therefore, not all organizations include labor relations as part of their HR systems. Unions are organizations that represent employees in collective bargaining with employers. They are also a source of recruitment. In the United States, the National Labor Relations Act (also known as the Wagner Act, after its sponsor) established the National Labor Relations Board (NLRB) in 1935; this board conducts unionization elections, hears unfair labor practice complaints, and issues injunctions against offending employers. (To learn more about the NLRB, visit www.nlrb.gov.)

There are typically five stages in forming a union, as figure 7.10 shows.

American MLB has outlasted panicky owners, spoiled players, scandal, and embarrassment for more than 100 years. America's national pastime thus provides a rich example of labor relations. Conflicts between baseball players and owners date back to the 1880s. Fans have endured five strikes since 1966, and the owners have locked players out three times. The last strike was from August 1994 to April 1995. The strike lasted 232 days, 938 games, including the entire playoffs and World Series.[107] Since 2002, there has been an ongoing investigation of the use of steroids in baseball. However, in terms of labor relations in baseball between owners and players, it has been a period of peaceful coexistence.

### Collective Bargaining

**Collective bargaining** is the process whereby unions and management negotiate a contract that covers employment conditions at the organization. Contracts typically stipulate compensation, including benefits, hours, and working conditions. Contracts can include other issues that both sides agree to include in the contract—job security is a hot issue for unions today.

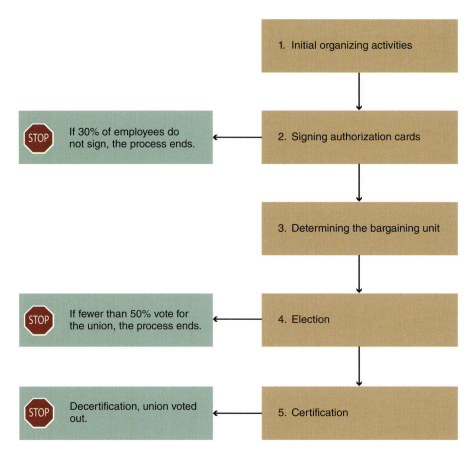

**FIGURE 7.10**   The union-organizing process.

To avoid a **strike** (employees refuse to go to work) or a **lockout** (management refuses to let employees in to work) and to handle grievances by either side, involved parties sometimes agree to use neutral third parties, called *mediators*, from the U.S. Federal Mediation and Conciliation Service (FMCS). (For more information about the FMCS, visit www.fmcs. gov.) Mediators are neutral parties who help management and labor settle disagreements. In cases in which the two parties are unwilling to compromise but still want to avoid a strike or lockout, they may choose to call in an arbitrator. *Arbitrators* differ from mediators in that arbitrators' decisions are binding (must be followed). Arbitrators more typically work to settle grievances; mediators deal with impasses in collective bargaining.

The NHL arbitration process pits the team management (which downplays a player's worth) against a player's agent (who plays up the player's value). An independent arbitrator selects a one- or two-year award no more than 48 hours later. A team then has 48 hours to accept the award or walk away from it. Does player performance increase, decrease, or remain the same after a free agent changes teams?

## Separating

The trend is to replace the word *termination* with *separation*—it sounds better, doesn't it? Although organizations want to retain good employees and keep turnover low, turnover will always be a challenge. Employees leave organizations in two ways: (1) voluntarily (for other jobs or for other reasons like retirement or health issues) and (2) involuntarily (because they are fired or are laid off). These employees usually need to be replaced.

Employees who separate voluntarily are often interviewed to find out why they are leaving. The exit interview, usually conducted by the HR department, helps identify problem areas that may be causing turnover. Involuntary termination occurs in one of two ways—firing (when employees break important rules or are otherwise found wanting) and layoffs (which often occur because of downturns in the economy, problems in the organization, or mergers and acquisitions).

As employees leave, turnover increases, and performance often decreases while the organization is replacing workers.[108] However, turnover also has a positive side—it brings in new, diverse employees who can improve organizational performance. Thus, there is ongoing research debate about what turnover levels are optimal. In any case, the HR department needs to manage turnover effectively.[109]

The Carlsbad-based golf equipment company TaylorMade-adidas Golf cut its workforce by 41. The cuts were the result of determining how well the company's workforce met its needs. When companies undergo layoffs, they sometimes offer *outplacement services* to help employees find new jobs. Why would companies bother? The reasons are simple—to help repay employees for service to the organization, for goodwill (they may want to hire those people back someday), and to avoid wrongful-termination lawsuits.

As we bring this chapter to a close, you should understand the HR process of planning (job analysis and the HR legal requirements), attracting employees (recruiting and selecting), developing employees (orientation, training and development, and performance appraisal), and retaining employees (compensation, health and safety, labor relations, termination, and outplacement).

## LEARNING AIDS

### CHAPTER SUMMARY

1. **Describe the four parts of HR management.**

    The four parts are (1) human resources planning, (2) attracting employees, (3) developing employees, and (4) retaining employees.

2. **Differentiate between a job description and a job specification, and explain why they are needed.**

    Job descriptions identify what a worker does on the job, whereas job specifications list the qualifications needed to do the job. Job analysis is an important basis for attracting, developing, and retaining employees.

3. **State the two parts of the process of attracting employees.**

    The two parts are recruiting and selecting. Recruiting is about persuading qualified candidates to apply for job openings. Selecting is about choosing the most qualified applicant recruited for a job.

4. **Explain how hypothetical questions and probing questions differ.**

    Hypothetical questions are planned; they require candidates to describe what they would do and say in a given situation. Probing questions are not planned and are used to clarify responses.

5. **State the purposes of orientation and training and development.**

    Orientation introduces new employees to the organization, its culture, and their jobs. Training and development help employees acquire new skills that they will use to perform present and future jobs.

6. **Describe job instructional training.**

    Job instructional training includes (1) preparation of the trainee, (2) presentation of the task, (3) performance of the task by the trainee, and (4) follow-up.

7. **Define the two types of performance appraisals.**

   Developmental PAs are used to improve performance. Evaluative PAs are used to determine pay raises, transfers and promotions, and demotions and terminations.

8. **Explain the concept "You get what you reward."**

   People seek information about what activities are rewarded and then try to do those things, often to the exclusion of activities that are not rewarded.

9. **State the two major components of compensation.**

   The two components are pay and benefits.

10. **Describe how job analyses and job evaluations are used.**

    Job analyses determine what the job should entail and the qualifications needed to staff the position. Job evaluations determine how to pay employees for their work.

## REVIEW AND DISCUSSION QUESTIONS

1. How do you feel about bona fide occupational qualifications?

2. What are the components of a job analysis?

3. What do you think about promoting from within for pro baseball teams? Why would this work or not work?

4. Should the interview be the primary criterion in selecting a coach? Why or why not?

5. What website helps people find jobs in sport?

6. Suppose the firm you work for has an HR department. What does this mean for you as a manager? What services will this department typically provide? What will you still need to do?

7. How does setting objectives affect measuring and evaluating training results for a general manager? For a coach? For an athlete?

8. How does compensation help attract and retain employees? Why do some organizations elect to be low-paying organizations whereas others elect to be high-paying ones?

9. Why don't most employees realize how expensive benefits are and how much they contribute to compensation cost?

10. Do players expect more than they are worth? Or do management and owners take too large a share of the profits for themselves? What do their stances imply for the future of pro sports?

11. What is the difference between mediators and arbitrators?

12. Curt Flood's name is often associated with free agency. But what other players followed Flood to help create the process of free agency?

13. What is the difference between a strike and a lockout?

14. How do you feel about the saying that it's not what you know but who you know that counts in getting a job? Is using connections to get a job a form of positive discrimination? To reduce discrimination, should using connections to get a job be illegal?

15. What is your view of performance appraisals? How can they be improved?

16. What pay system do you prefer? What compensation do you expect after graduation? State the pay and the benefits you expect. Add up the pay and benefits to get your compensation. If you can't estimate the cost of benefits, use 30 percent of your pay (multiply your pay times 0.30 [which is the cost of benefits] and add the result to your pay).

## Sport Management Professionals @ Work: KC Smurthwaite

We all like to win. In fact, we all LOVE to win. Winning comes in all forms, but the feeling is the same. Whether it is winning with a last-second touchdown in the two-minute offense, come-from-behind wins on the road, or making the game-saving play to seal the deal, winning is exhilarating. But these victories happen long before game day. The preparation to execute the two-minute offense started in two-a-days, the focus to perform in high-pressure situations came after countless hours of perfect practice reps. KC's sport management program was the perfect preparation and practice for his career in collegiate athletics. He took advantage of the classes, resources, and internships to graduate with both a résumé and a degree.

In KC's career, he has helped resurrect both a Division I softball and a junior college baseball program. Previously, both programs had a combined 35 straight losing seasons, but during his time as a coach, both teams turned in winning records. He credits much of this success to the lessons he learned in one classroom at Utah State University. His sport psychology classes taught him about creating a culture, teaching student-athletes (and all about himself!) to block out distractions amidst struggles, and keeping a team motivated. His motor-learning class taught him the correct way to enhance his coaching ability by teaching simply and directly, which allowed the players to find success even though they all learned in different ways.

His long-term goal is to become an athletic director. He now works on the administration side of athletics. He uses what he learned with his coaches, student-athletes, and their fan base. His master's program asked a lot from him, but he is grateful for the standard it held him to. It enabled him to recognize his personal strengths and weaknesses. The sport industry is fast-paced and ever-changing. You must always challenge the way you do things, or you will see the competition pass you. Leverage your time as a student by asking questions, doing research, and getting to know those who have been successful in the field. Years from now, KC hopes you can look back on your time in your program and say you wouldn't have done it any other way.

## Case Questions

1. KC leveraged his time as a student by reaching out to people in jobs similar to those he wanted. What type of job do you want after you graduate? Who can you contact for more information?

2. As a coach, KC tries to train his players to face high-pressure situations. What do you do to remain calm in high-pressure situations in school, work, or competition?

3. KC wants sport management students to know that homework never ends. What keeps you motivated to finish the task at hand?

## Coach Jekyll and Coach Hyde

The title of basketball coach Rick Pitino's book is *Born to Coach*. He must know what he is talking about; he has won 770 games and two national NCAA basketball championships, and his teams have made seven Final Four appearances. Pitino had successful college career stops at Boston University, Providence College, the University of Kentucky, and the University of Louisville. Pitino also coached in the NBA with the New York Knicks and the Boston Celtics. Unfortunately, Pitino has also faced some serious allegations, mostly during his time with Louisville, that question his leadership skills and ethics off the court.

In 2015, Katina Powell published a book titled *Breaking Cardinal Rules: Basketball and the Escort Queen*, which details sex-for-pay for 22 parties for Louisville recruits from 2010 to 2014 that she said she arranged at Billy Minardi Hall, which houses Cardinals basketball players.

In 2017, the FBI alleged an unnamed Louisville staffer worked with high-ranking Adidas representative Jim Gatto and others to lure an elite prospect to Louisville with a $100,000 bribe. According to the FBI's documentation, the player committed to the Cardinals almost immediately after the illicit bribe scheme.[110]

The University of Louisville was normally supportive of Pitino's antics because the basketball program was winning. But the university felt they had no choice but to fire Pitino three weeks after the program was implicated in the federal bribery and fraud investigation.[111]

Pitino's career is similar to what Bobby Knight experienced at Indiana University. Knight's coaching style was certainly not pretty—in fact, it was vocal, confrontational, and loaded with controversy.[112] Mention Bobby Knight, and chair throwing comes to mind (Indiana vs. Purdue, 1984-1985 season)—so does winning (Indiana was NCAA champion in 1976, 1981, and 1987).

Fans like winners, and Pitino and Knight are true basketball geniuses. Both built large and loyal basketball followings. Both were very successful at externally recruiting players. But there can be costs to winning, and sometimes those costs are just too high.

Since Pitino was fired, there have been whispers that many other college programs are interested in having him as their head coach. Pitino is a proven winner, and his name recognition will attract talented players to any campus. There is big money in college basketball. Another college may select Pitino to be their next coach and be the beneficiary of the money Pitino will attract from sponsors, ticket sales to fans, and media exposure.

Where was HR as Pitino's behavior began to deteriorate? Are some people above HR? Are some positions above the behavior parameters set for others? If so, is the organization still liable for unacceptable behavior from people in such positions? Did HR let Pitino and the university down? Did Pitino receive fair treatment? Was a program of progressive discipline or counseling undertaken before he was fired? Does he have a case against Louisville if he didn't receive counseling? Did the fact that Pitino brought fame and fortune to the Louisville campus enter into Louisville's winking at his behavior? Should it have?

Go to the web study guide to answer questions about this case study.

## @ TAKE IT TO THE NET

Please visit www.HumanKinetics.com/AppliedSportManagementSkills and go to this book's companion web study guide, where you will find the following:

A list of websites associated with the concepts in this chapter

Skill-Builder exercises, Sports and Social Media exercises, and a continuing Game Plan for Starting a Sport Business

Online versions of chapter exercises and end-of-chapter learning aids

An exercise that helps you define the Key Terms

# PART IV

Leading Controlling Planning Organizing Leading Controlling Planning Organizing Leading nning Organizing Leading Controlling Planning Organizing Leading Controlling Planning ling Controlling Planning Organizing Leading Controlling Planning Organizing Leading Controlling anizing Leading Controlling Planning Organizing Leading Controlling Planning Organizing Leading Planning Organizing Leading Controlling Planning Organizing Leading Controlling Planning ling Controlling Planning Organizing Leading Controlling Planning Organizing Leading Controlling

## Leading

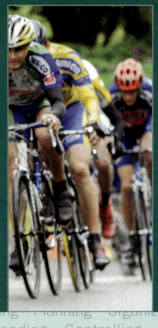

# Behavior in Organizations

## Power, Politics, Conflict, and Stress

### LEARNING OUTCOMES

After studying this chapter, you should be able to

1. describe the Big Five personality traits;

2. understand the perception process and the two factors on which it is based;

3. explain how personality, perception, and attitude are related and why they are important;

4. state what job satisfaction is and why it is important;

5. define power, and explain the difference between position and personal power;

6. explain how reward power, legitimate power, and referent power differ;

7. understand how power and politics are related;

8. explain what networking, reciprocity, and coalitions have in common;

9. describe the five conflict management styles;

10. use collaboration to resolve conflict; and

11. explain the stress tug-of-war analogy.

### KEY TERMS

| | | | |
|---|---|---|---|
| organizational behavior (OB) | Pygmalion effect | coalition | BCF statements |
| win–win situation | power | conflict | mediator |
| personality | politics | dysfunctional conflict | arbitrator |
| perception | networking | functional conflict | stress |
| attribution | reciprocity | initiators | stressors |
| attitudes | | | |

## DEVELOPING YOUR SKILLS

Effective leaders share at least one thing in common—they all have amazing people skills. People skills include understanding personality traits, perceptions, and attitudes and how they affect performance. In this chapter, you can develop your people skills by gaining and using power and organizational politics ethically. Models will also provide you with step-by-step guides so you can resolve conflicts and negotiate successfully to improve your performance. You can also develop your skill at recognizing the causes of stress and methods for reducing stress—fighting and winning the stress tug-of-war.

## REVIEWING THEIR GAME PLAN

### Applying Legitimate Power at the USADA

The United States Anti-Doping Agency (USADA) is the national anti-doping organization (NADO) in the United States for Olympic, Paralympic, Pan American, and Parapan American sport. The goal of the USADA is to preserve the integrity of Olympic sport, preserve the integrity of competition, and ensure the health of athletes.[1]

The USADA played an important part in finding bicyclist Lance Armstrong guilty of using banned drugs in his sport. As stated by USADA CEO Travis T. Tygart, "Lance Armstrong finally acknowledged that his cycling career was built on a powerful combination of doping and deceit. His admission that he doped throughout his career is a small step in the right direction."[2] Armstrong paid the United States government $5 million for using performance-enhancing drugs while the U.S. Postal Service was paying millions to sponsor his team.[3]

The USADA actually tries to help athletes in four ways: The first is to conduct research on substances that are prohibited. The second is to educate athletes about the dangers of using banned substances and about policies concerning banned substances. The third is to develop quality and consistency in testing in and out of competition. The fourth is to maintain an adjudication system that relies on arbitrations before the American Arbitration Association (AAA)/Court of Arbitration for Sport under modified AAA commercial rules, which have been agreed to by the relevant stakeholders.

The use of performance-enhancing drugs in sport still appears to be a problem. Maria Sharapova was banned from tennis for two years after failing a drug test at the Australian Open. Sharapova claimed she was using meldonium because it increases blood flow, which improves exercise capacity in athletes. Sharapova said she used the drug for 10 years because of a magnesium deficiency and family history of diabetes.[4]

Robinson Cano, potential Hall of Fame player for the MLB Seattle Mariners, was suspended 80 games of the 2018 season. Cano admitted to taking furosemide, a diuretic sometimes used to hide the presence of other banned substances. However, he also said it was a mistake and he had no intention of taking performance-enhancing drugs (PEDs). As Cano stated, "This substance was given to me by a licensed doctor in the Dominican Republic to treat a medical ailment," he said in a statement released by the Players Association. "While I did not realize at the time that I was given a medication that was banned, I obviously now wish that I had been more careful."[5]

Understanding the role that the USADA plays in Olympic sport is crucial for those who intend to pursue a career in sport administration. For more information about the USADA, visit www.usada.org.

# Organizational Behavior and Thoughts

Recall from chapter 1 that people skills are important to success and that recruiters want to hire employees with people skills.[6] In this chapter you will learn that the foundation of your people skills is organizational behavior (OB) skills.

OB has three levels of focus: individual, group, and organizational. In this chapter we examine individual behavior, and in chapter 9 we discuss group behavior. Organizational behavior was covered in chapter 5 (as organizational development).

OB has four foundational attributes that interact together through the systems effect: They are our (1) *thoughts*, (2) *personality*, (3) *perceptions*, and (4) *attitudes*.[7] Each OB foundation is discussed in the first four sections of this chapter. There are also several areas of OB, including power, politics, conflict, negotiation, collaboration, and stress management, that are discussed after the foundations in this chapter. In this first section, we define OB and thoughts because our behavior starts with thoughts.

## OB and Its Goals

Have you ever wondered why you do certain things and why teammates and coworkers behave the way they do? Our behavior consists of what we say and do—in a word, our actions. **Organizational behavior (OB)** is the study of actions that affect performance in the workplace. The goal of organizational behaviorists is to develop theories to explain and predict actions in the workplace and show how such actions affect performance.[8] The better you understand OB, the more effectively you will work with others in teams both as a manager and as a worker. Do you want to be able to better understand, predict, and influence peoples' behavior? You can if you implement the OB techniques you will learn in this chapter both in your workplace and in your private life.

Research highlights the importance of leaders' organizational behaviors to team performance. The goal of OB is to create win–win situations. **Win–win situations** occur when organizations and their employees get what they want. Note that it is similar to the stakeholders' approach to ethics (chapter 2).

## Thoughts

Virtually all of our behavior is preceded by our thoughts, and our thoughts affect our personality traits of self-esteem and self-confidence. We begin by discussing self-esteem and then how our thoughts affect our self-confidence and self-esteem. We end by explaining how to use thoughts and self-talk to improve our self-esteem and confidence.

### Self-Esteem

*Self-esteem* is our overall view of ourselves.[9] Clearly, your self-esteem affects your behavior.[10] Do you view and treat yourself as a winner or a loser?[11] We are not born with high or low self-esteem; it is influenced by our past experiences and our current thoughts. Don't compare yourself to others, and never put yourself down.[12] Focus on your own abilities and skills and your successes. If you are competing and start to feel pressure, it's because you are thinking about failing.

Forget your failures and move on, considering failure to be a part of progress, not a final outcome.[13] Legendary NBA star Michael Jordan had a lot of failure as a pro. MJ said, "I've missed more than 9,000 shots in my career. I've lost almost 300 games. Twenty-six times I've been trusted to take the game winning shot and missed. I've failed over and over and over again in my life. And that is why I succeed." As Winston Churchill said, "Success is the ability to go from failure to failure without losing your enthusiasm." You may have heard the old saying, "Winners never quit, and quitters never win." Are you persistent, or do you give up? Can you bounce back from failure and move forward to succeed like MJ?

### Self-Confidence

*Self-confidence* is believing you can or can't do a specific task; it is also called *self-efficacy* and *self-concept*.[14] To be successful, you need to project self-confidence.[15] Self-doubt leads to fear, failure, or not taking a risk—like taking the shot. *Self-doubt* is based on our negative thoughts,[16] and it holds us back more than our ability.[17]

An "I can do this" attitude is a quality of effective leadership and athletic performance.[18] You have to believe in your ability.[19] You have to overcome self-doubt[20] and gain the confidence to really believe in yourself to succeed.[21] But it needs to be based on realistic hard work in preparation for the task, experience, and skill, not irrational overconfidence.[22]

## Thoughts

Our *thoughts* determine most of our feelings and behavior, or our thoughts cause our behavior and performance, so stop the negative thoughts.[23] Science supports that what you think is what you get.[24] Or as Henry Ford said, if you think you will succeed or fail, you are correct. Have you ever shot a basketball at the hoop, or done something else, thinking you were going to miss? What usually happens? You can improve your self-esteem and confidence by using positive thoughts.[25] That's what you learn in this section. If you change your thoughts to be positive,[26] and make the new thoughts a habit,[27] you will change your self-esteem and your life.

Unlike pessimism, *optimism* helps to overcome self-doubt,[28] and it is a personality trait. Optimism and pessimism are on opposite ends of a continuum; most people aren't at either end, but they can be classified overall. Have you ever noticed that optimistic people believe that things will go well, they tend to be less stressed, are happier, more confident, and have higher levels of performance than pessimistic people? Are you more of an optimist or a pessimist? Optimism is based on positive thinking, and it increases performance.[29] That is why the Ohio State football team trains its players to use the power of positive thinking.[30]

Answer this important question: Are you a happy person? Do you want to be happier? Recall the last time you thought about the bad things that happen to you, and then recall the last positive thought you had about the good things that happen to you. Is your mind stuck in the past like a broken record repeating, rehearsing, rehashing, and reliving your hurts, the angry moments, and the disappointments over and over?[31] It's not unusual.[32] But it is self-destructive behavior, and you can change your thoughts. Former college football coach, now ESPN sports announcer Lou Holtz says, "You choose to be happy or sad" (and optimistic or pessimistic). "Happiness is nothing more than a poor memory of the bad things that happen to us."[33] So forgive people that hurt you; they are the jerks, not you. Forget the bad things, and think about the good things that happen in your life. Yes, it is easier said than done, but you can do it if you want to and work at it.

*Gratitude* also affects our happiness.[34] Grateful people are less stressed, healthier, and happier. Ungrateful people are never satisfied for long because no matter how much they get, it will never be enough.[35] Know any ungrateful people? Focus on the positive, and appreciate what you do have; don't be envious, and you will be happier.

## Improving With Self-Talk

If you use positive self-talk, you will improve your self-confidence and self-esteem, as well as performance. Self-talk is a way of thinking in which we make comments and give advice to ourselves.[36] You do self-talk, don't you? Motivational speaker and self-talk trainer Zig Ziglar said, "no Stinking Thinking."[37] As you may already know, successful athletes use positive self-talk and visualize success to psych themselves up and increase performance. Venus Williams says, "How you talk to people and how you talk to yourself has got to be positive both on and off the court."[38]

Effective self-talk is based on positive affirmation statements, never negatives. Call yourself by name rather than "I" or "you" because your thoughts will seem more objective and produce better results.[39] "Marylou, you enjoy going to class (work) and learning," not "I hate work (school)." "You can do this, Julio it's easy." "Take the shot, Henry, you are going to score."

Like with sports, you need to practice a new thought and self-talk over and over.[40] As with all the skills in this book, you need to practice every day until the skill becomes a habit. Here are a couple of simple ways to improve. You can use positive self-talk throughout the day, and especially as the task nears. Also, be aware of your thoughts, and if they turn negative or you start doubting yourself, stop and change to positive, optimistic thoughts.[41] To make positive thinking a *habit*, (1) the cue is negative thoughts, (2) the routine is changing to positive thoughts, and (3) the reward is feeling happier and more self-confident.[42] To develop your self-talk skills, complete Skill Builder 8.3.

Three other components—our personality, perception, and attitudes—drive our behavior. They are the foundations on which our behavior is built, and they are observable through our actions. Understanding how personality, perception, and attitude drive behavior gives you insight into how people will behave in certain situations. These are the topics of our next three sections.

# Personality

Look around you. You will see outgoing, shy, loud, quiet, warm, cold, aggressive, and passive people—we are diverse. These differences are what behaviorists call individual characteristics or traits.[43] **Personality** is the combination of traits that compose individuals. Our personality affects our behavior, our perceptions, and our attitudes,[44] including how we make decisions (chapter 3).[45] Take sport announcers. Quiet announcers—no matter how good their knowledge or skill—could hurt Monday Night Football on ESPN or NFL on Fox. Only extroverts need apply for announcer jobs. Think about Billy Packer, John Madden, Charles Barkley, and Deion Sanders—where would their viewership be if they didn't have lively on-air personalities? Personalities are pivotal in garnering viewership.

Our personalities are shaped by our genes and by the environment. Our genes we are born with; the environment that forms us is composed of our families, our friends, and our life experiences. Researchers have developed many ways to classify personality.[46] Two widely recognized ones are the single traits system and the Big Five personality traits,[47] our two topics of this section.

## Single Traits System of Personality

Key traits in the single traits system are locus of control, risk propensity, optimism, self-esteem, and self-efficacy. We have already discussed optimism, self-esteem, and self-efficacy, so here are locus of control and risk propensity.

### Locus of Control

This trait, which deals with who we believe controls our destiny, lies on a continuum with externalizers at one end and internalizers at the other. Externalizers believe that they have no control over their fate and that their behavior has little to do with their performance. Internalizers believe just the opposite—that they control their fate and that their behavior directly affects their performance. Internalizers obviously tend to perform better because they have high self-esteem and self-confidence.[48] Do you believe you can succeed if you work hard? Do you take responsibility for your actions, or do you blame others when things go wrong?

### Risk Propensity

This trait lies on a continuum between risk takers and risk avoiders. If you want to be successful, you have to take calculated risks.[49] If you don't try out for the team, you will not fail by not making it, but you can't play. Entrepreneurs have different risk propensity personality traits than managers.[50] It takes a lot of positive thoughts and self-esteem and self-confidence to start a business.[51] Entrepreneurs like Nike cofounder Phil Knight have a risk-taking propensity.[52] Organizational cultures are also risk takers or avoiders, and risk-avoiding cultures often lose market share and even go out of business because they do not innovate changes to stay ahead of their competitors.

## Big Five Personality Traits

**LEARNING OUTCOME 1** ▶

Describe the Big Five personality traits.

Before reading about the Big Five, complete Self-Assessment 8.1 to better understand your personality.

The use of the Big Five personality dimensions puts multiple traits together to form what is often called a personality profile.[53] It is said that all individual traits can be placed in one of the five dimensions.

The Big Five trait system is the most widely accepted way to classify personalities. The theory states that all our individual traits can be placed in one of the five dimensions, which give you your Big Five personality profile.[54] It is also known as the *Five-Factor Model*,[55] and its acronym is *OCEAN* (openness, conscientiousness, extroversion, agreeableness, and neuroticism).[56] The five personality traits, presented here, are also defined as continuums.

 **TIME-OUT 1** Use the five traits given in Self-Assessment 8.1 to characterize the personality of your current boss or coach.

- *Extroversion.* This trait lies on a continuum between extroverts and introverts. Are you outgoing or shy? Review your answers to the Self-Assessment 8.1 extroversion column for items 1, 6, 11, 16, and 21.

- *Agreeableness.* This trait lies on a continuum between easy and difficult to work with and cooperators and competitors. Do you cooperate and get along well with others, or are you overly competitive (a ball hog) and don't get along? The best teams tend to have cooperative teamwork with a focus on beating the external competitors, not each other. Review your answers to the Self-Assessment 8.1 agreeableness column for items 2, 7, 12, 17, and 22.

- *Emotionalism.* The continuum here is between emotionally stable and emotionally unstable. Stable people are calm, secure, and positive, whereas unstable people are nervous, insecure, and negative. Can you take trash talk during the game, or do you get emotional? Review your answers to the Self-Assessment 8.1 emotionalism column for items 3, 8, 13, 18, and 23. Note that the OCEAN acronym uses the word *neuroticism* instead of *emotionalism*, but it's the same trait.

- *Conscientiousness.* This continuum has responsible–dependable at one end and irresponsible–undependable at the other. Do you keep your word and promises? Can

## SELF-ASSESSMENT 8.1

### Your Big Five Personality Profile

There are no right or wrong answers, so be honest and you will really increase your self-awareness. Using the scale shown, rate each of the 25 statements according to how accurately it describes you. Place a number from 1 to 5 on the line before each statement.

1 = not very descriptive of me

2 = somewhat descriptive of me

3 = neutral

4 = descriptive of me

5 = very descriptive of me

_____ 1. I enjoy meeting new people.

_____ 2. I am concerned about getting along well with others.

_____ 3. I have good self-control; I don't get emotional or angry and yell.

_____ 4. I'm dependable; when I say I will do something, it's done well and on time.

_____ 5. I try to do things differently to improve my performance.

_____ 6. I feel comfortable speaking to diverse people (different age, race, gender, religion, and intelligence).

_____ 7. I enjoy having lots of friends and going to parties.

_____ 8. I perform well under pressure.

_____ 9. I work hard to be successful.

_____ 10. I go to new places and enjoy traveling.

_____ 11. I am outgoing and initiate conversations, rather than being shy and waiting for others to approach me.

_____ 12. I try to see things from other people's points of view.

_____ 13. I am an optimistic person who sees the positive side of situations (the glass is half full).

_____ 14. I am a well-organized person.

_____ 15. When I go to a new restaurant, I order foods I haven't tried.

_____ 16. I am willing to go talk to people to resolve conflicts, rather than say nothing.

_____ 17. I want other people to like me and to consider me to be very friendly.

_____ 18. I give people lots of praise and encouragement; I don't put people down and criticize.

_____ 19. I conform by following the rules of an organization.

_____ 20. I volunteer to be the first to learn and do new tasks at work.

_____ 21. I try to influence other people to get what I want.

_____ 22. I enjoy working with others more than working alone.

_____ 23. I view myself as being relaxed and secure rather than nervous and insecure.

_____ 24. I am considered to be credible because I do a good job and come through for people.

_____ 25. When people suggest doing things differently, I support them and help bring it about. I don't make statements like, "It won't work," "We've never done it before," "No one else has ever done it," or "We can't do it."

Next, use the following table to determine your personality profile: (1) In the blanks, place a number from 1 to 5 that represents your score for each statement. (2) Add up each column—your total should be a number from 5 to 25. (3) On the number scale to the right of each column, circle the number that is closest to your total score. Each column in the chart represents the specific personality dimension listed.

| 1. | 25 | 2. | 25 | 3. | 25 | 4. | 25 | 5. | 25 |
|---|---|---|---|---|---|---|---|---|---|
| 6. | 20 | 7. | 20 | 8. | 20 | 9. | 20 | 10. | 20 |
| 11. | 15 | 12. | 15 | 13. | 15 | 14. | 15 | 15. | 15 |
| 16. | 10 | 17. | 10 | 18. | 10 | 19. | 10 | 20. | 10 |
| 21. | 5 | 22. | 5 | 23. | 5 | 24. | 5 | 25. | 5 |
| Total | | Total | | Total | | Total | | Total | |

The higher the total number, the stronger the personality dimension that describes your personality. What are your strongest and weakest dimensions?

To see how others perceive you and how this fits with your perception of yourself—and to prepare for our next topic (perception)—have people who know you well assess your personality using this form. Do their scores agree with yours?

your family, team, and coworkers count on you to work hard and get the job done well? Review your answers to the Self-Assessment 8.1 conscientiousness column for items 4, 9, 14, 19, and 24.

• *Openness to experience.* This aspect varies from being very willing to try new things to being very afraid to try new things. Do you like change, or do you prefer routines? Review your answers to the Self-Assessment 8.1 openness to experience column for items 5, 10, 15, 20, and 25.

## Big Five at Work

From an individual perspective, there are no simple right and wrong ways to be, but from the organization's perspective, there are. Research supports the finding that personality is a reliable predictor of job performance.[57] Organizations therefore go to great lengths to recruit and retain people with positive personality traits. Many organizations give job applicants a personality test because the tests help to explain and predict job performance.[58]

Here are some of the traits organizations want. Personality and jobs need to match. Extroverts tend to do well in sales, whereas introverts don't. Firms want agreeable, cooperative team players who can regulate their behavior. Conscientious people tend to follow the rules, are more ethical, and outperform irresponsible people. Effective leaders are conscientious.[59] Dwayne "the Rock" Johnson says success isn't about greatness; it's about consistency—consistent hard work.[60] To realize your dreams and advance in your career, you need to work harder than others.[61] In today's quickly changing global economy, organizations want employees who are open to new experiences; they are more creative and innovative. Do you have the Big Five personality that organizations want?

The good news is that you very likely fall on the positive personality trait side. Why? Because people who score low in every trait don't get very far in life (e.g., extreme pessimists and externalizers don't have the determination to get into college, let alone succeed there). The bad news is that you're not perfect, so there are probably aspects of yourself that you need to work on. As you assess each trait in Self-Assessment 8.1, realize that you can change if you work at it every day throughout the day. First is the importance of positive thoughts, so use positive self-talk. To be more extroverted, reach out to others every day until it feels natural. If you get emotional, calm down rather than go with it. Make a greater effort to be conscientious every time you have something to do, and remember that meeting deadlines and doing more than you are asked to do is a key to career success. Be open to new experience; try new foods, play other sports or engage in other forms of recreation, go to new places, and volunteer for new assignments.

Your answers to the self-assessment are telling you something very important. This is the real you that you are looking at—do you really want to change? More importantly, are you willing to work at changing to continually improve in your profession and in your personal life?

# Perception

Your thoughts and personality affect how you perceive things, which also influences your behavior.[62] Why do some people believe, see, or experience the same thing differently, like whether a decision is ethical or not?[63] In this section, we answer this question by discussing the perception process and how bias in our perceptions influences behavior.

**LEARNING OUTCOME 2** ▶

Understand the perception process and the two factors on which it is based.

## Perception Process

Referees make mistakes, but why do some of us view a referee's videotaped decision as fair whereas others do not? We all see the same videotaped play, but we don't perceive it the same way. Why is it debated whether the USADA is doing a good job of managing doping issues in Olympic sport and if banning Russian athletes was a good decision? The answer is usually different perceptions.[64] Or our interpretation of reality is not the same, and it's biased.

**Perception** is the process through which we select, organize, and interpret information from the surrounding environment. Our behavior follows our perceptions of people, events, learning, work, and organizations. Because this perception process colors everything, no two people experience anything in exactly the same way.

## How Perception Influences Behavior

Perception is our individual interpretation of reality. Right or wrong, rational or irrational, it is the lens through which we view life. OB research makes it clear that understanding perception is not about the perception being right or wrong because either way the perception will affect behavior and performance.[65] Have you always perceived your level of athletic skill and your amount of playing time the same as your coach has? Ever played with or against athletes who think they are much better than they really are? If good athletes quit because they aren't getting the playing time warranted by their perceived skill level, or if they only perceive it incorrectly, the result is still the loss of good athletes.[66] So what people know or don't know isn't what counts—all that really matters is their perception.[67] To improve the accuracy of your perception, try to see things through the eyes of others.

How we select, organize, and interpret information is based on many factors—our personality, self-esteem, attitudes, intelligence, needs, and values. These make up the internal component of perception. Self-esteem comes by comparing our traits, abilities, goals, and performance with those of others. When you compare yourself with others, be realistic. Don't compare yourself with NBA star LeBron James; compare yourself with your peers. And never put yourself down. Everyone makes errors, but don't simply justify your mistakes; you need to learn from your mistakes and go on to improve. Do you consider yourself a valuable person or employee? Do you believe you are a capable person?

The second component of this process is the information itself—this is the external component of perception. The more accurate our information, the more closely our perception will resemble reality. Inaccurate information causes our perceptions to veer wildly from reality and can be a serious problem for organizations. The USADA must deal with all types of rumors (e.g., that lab technicians make errors, or that athletes are asked to inform on other athletes) and determine whether they are violations of USADA rules.

Others' perceptions of us, which build our reputation, are important to career progression. If your boss and higher-level managers perceive you as highly competent, you will advance, but if you get a bad reputation, you won't advance. Reputation explains why iconic athletes such as former NBA player Michael Jordan are highly paid to endorse products, whereas retired boxer Mike Tyson is not. In 2010, golfer Tiger Woods went from fan favorite to unloved after a series of extramarital affairs went public.

 Do you believe that the USADA should investigate an athlete based on rumors?

Customer and fan perception is also important to organizations, including teams. Perhaps nowhere are the topics of identity, image, and reputation more relevant than in the arena of sport. Teams with good reputations, often based on winning, tend to have high levels of fan support and attendance. Reputations and fan loyalty can change from season to season, again often based on winning, because people generally love a winner, and some like to hate a team like the MLB New York Yankees and NFL New England Patriots.

## Why We Attribute Reasons for Behavior

Attributions play an important role in perceptions because they affect behavior, but we can't observe perceptions.[68] So we see or hear about the behavior and make an attribution.[69] **Attribution** is the process of determining why we behave certain ways. Most of us continually try to find reasons behind behavior—our own behavior or that of those around us. The process (shown in figure 8.1) begins when we observe an act directly or learn of it indirectly (by reading or hearing about it). We want to know if the person's intent was

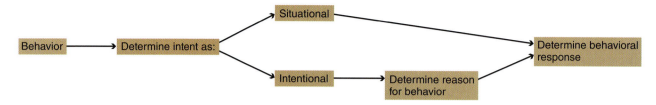

**FIGURE 8.1**   The attribution process.

situational (accidental or beyond the person's control) or intentional (within the person's control). We may not use these words, but this is what we are doing.

We judge intent, such as to do good or harm. We also look for reasons for the behavior, such as initiated or a response to a situation. Last, we decide on a response—we may perceive the behavior to be wrong, or we may be amused by it or even admire it. Or we may simply not care. All of these responses drive our behavior to take action or not. See figure 8.1 for the attribution process.

Attribution is how we determine reasons for our behavior and that of others. However, most of us spend more time mulling over why other people behave the way they do. When we do look at our own behavior, we tend to credit our successes to our intentions. Conversely, when we fail, we tend to blame the situation.[70] We also tend to reverse intention (Sally failed because she didn't practice enough) and situation (Jamal just got lucky) when we attribute reasons for other people's behavior. This is a classic example of perception differences.

If a teammate makes a negative remark to you, is it because the player doesn't like you and is putting you down, or is the person just kidding around in friendship? We sometimes misperceive motives and let them damage relationships; misunderstandings are common. So, when in doubt about why someone did something to offend you, talk to the person about it. Others may not even realize that their behavior bothers you. Later in this chapter, you will learn how to resolve conflicts without hurting relationships.

> **TIME-OUT 2** Explain how you used the attribution process (a) in a recent incident in professional sport and (b) in a recent incident at work.

## Bias in Our Perception

Why does each of us perceive the same behavior differently? In two words, personal bias. Bias in perception has several components—selectivity, frame of reference, stereotypes, expectation, and "like me" assumption—we are all subject to these biases.

### *Selectivity*

 Do you tend to select positive or negative information about USADA drug enforcement?

Selectivity is the manner in which we focus on information to favor the outcome we want. We often find information that supports our point of view yet ignore information that does not; or we only see and hear what we want to. Do you work harder and contribute more to your team than others? Maybe not—we tend to selectively see how hard we train and all the things we do, and we fail to see how hard others work and the contributions they make.[71] A related bias is the halo–horns effect, in which we judge others based on our perception of a single trait of theirs or simply whether we like or dislike them. (A person with a halo can do no wrong—a person with horns can do no right.)

### Frame of Reference

Our frame of reference is our bias for seeing things from our own point of view. Do you and your parents always agree? Managers and employees tend to have different perceptions. Do you and your boss or coach agree on how well you perform?

As a manager or coach, don't be surprised if your team doesn't perceive things the way you do. Try to see things from others' perspective, and give them effective coaching feedback so they can better align their perceptions of their skill level with yours. It also helps to explain to them why you make decisions, like benching a starter.

 Could athletes create a win–win situation by complying with USADA requirements?

### Stereotyping

Stereotyping happens when we project the characteristics or behavior of an individual onto a group. As discussed in chapter 2, women and minorities continue to be stereotyped in sport, and stereotyping leads to discrimination. Negatively stereotyping people can also hurt their self-perceptions and performance. Think about breakthrough athletes like MLB's Jackie Robinson or high school girls who wanted to compete on boys' teams. All faced stereotypes that charged (falsely) that they shouldn't play with other groups or couldn't be good at what they did. Don't let stereotyping get in your way of seeing true strengths and true weaknesses. Researchers hope that people in the sport industry can debunk stereotypical myths of what an ideally fit body should look like. Managers can then provide opportunities for nonstereotypical, qualified applicants. Keep an open mind when you are hiring sport employees and managers.

### Expectations

Read the phrase in figure 8.2.

Did you read the word *the* twice? Or, like most people, did you read what you expected to read, only one *the*? Our expectations also bias our perceptions. Many of us don't really listen to each other. We hear what we expect to hear.

**FIGURE 8.2**  Check your expectations.

### The "Like Me" Assumption

Another expectation bias is the "like me" assumption—that others perceive things as we do because they are like us. Don't expect others to behave as you do or perceive things the way you do, and don't judge others' behavior as wrong on the sole basis that it

| TIME-OUT 3 | Think about a misunderstanding that arose when you and another person perceived the same situation differently. Which perceptual biases do you think contributed to the misunderstanding? |
|---|---|

differs from yours. Remember to value diversity. As discussed in chapter 6, there are benefits to having cultural diversity in sport organizations.

## Attitude Formation and Behavior

**Attitudes** are positive or negative evaluations of people, things, and situations. Your evaluative judgments are based on your perceptions.[72] Putting our four OB foundations together through the systems effect, your *thoughts* and *personality* affect how you *perceive* things, which influences your *attitudes* and behavior.[73]

## The Importance of Attitudes

**LEARNING OUTCOME 3** ▶

Explain how personality, perception, and attitude are related and why they are important.

Our attitudes about others,[74] and their attitude toward us, often affect our behavior.[75] Don't you behave differently with people you like than you do with people you dislike? Do you try harder at the things you like to do than the things you don't like to do? Your success depends upon your attitude[76]—you have to maintain an upbeat attitude to succeed.[77]

## How Attitudes Are Formed

Our personalities, perceptions, and input from others (family, friends, teachers, coaches, coworkers, the mass media) form our attitudes. So our perceptions and attitudes are biased by others.[78] What were the primary factors that formed your present attitude toward sports and sport management? How was your interest influenced by your parents, by playing sports, by teammates, and by coaches? Attitudes are relatively stable, but they can and do change. Have you or any of your teammates dropped out of team athletics? Has your attitude toward this course and sport management become more positive or negative over time? Why?

Collective attitudes influence sport organization performance. Would you rather be on a team with athletes who have a positive, supportive attitude and help each other improve, or one with people who don't really care about doing their best and put others down with negative comments? Sport fans' attitudes influence attendance at events and merchandise purchases. Ever notice how many peoples' attitudes change and they become fans (watching and going to games and buying team merchandise) when their home team is winning and advances to the playoffs? And how their interest wanes when the team loses?

## The Self-Fulfilling Prophecy

You know that your thoughts affect your behavior. But do you realize that they also affect your attitudes? We tend to live up to or down to our attitudinal expectations of ourselves. When you go to bat (or any task) thinking "I'm going to strike out," doesn't your failing attitude tend to lead to a *self-fulfilling prophecy* of failure? After striking out, some people will think or actually say, "I told you so!"

Why is it so hard to get out of a slump? When we get into a slump (strike out a few times in a row, or miss a few shots), we tend to fear failure and think we will fail. So we live down to our attitudinal expectation. Has this ever happened to you or anyone you know? Try to think like this: My batting average is .333, so I get a hit every three times at bat. If I struck out the last three times, the odds of my getting a hit this time up are actually very high (not low, keeping me in a slump).

You should also understand that attitudes are contagious. Since we associate with others, we may take on their positive or negative attitudes.[79] Have you ever been around people who are always complaining about someone or something? Do you join in? Avoid being around downers as much as you can so they don't bring you down with them. If you catch yourself thinking like or being a complainer, stop and turn it around. Again, focus your thoughts on, and talk about, the positive things at work and in your life.

Getting back to sports, not only can athletes' attitudes have an effect on their own performance, but they can also have an effect on the performance of their team. When a star player or two go into a slump, so can the team. Ever seen a team with a big lead blow it? Now you have a better idea of why it happens. Michael Jordan had a positive winning attitude that rubbed off on his teammates. His positive attitude is still reflected in his talk and in the nice smile that has won the hearts of many people, and to this day endorsement contracts earn him millions.

A positive attitude is an important determinant of individual, team, and organizational performance. As an athlete, and more importantly as a coach or sport manager, maintain a "we can win" attitude. If some team members are habitual complainers, talk to them about it, and try to get them to realize how their attitude is affecting themselves and others. If they don't become more positive, coaches or managers should get them off the team or fire them to prevent their negativity from spreading. You may lose a competent athlete, but without that negativity, the rest of the team may step up and play better.

TIME-OUT 4 Relate incidents in which your attitude affected your workplace behavior negatively and positively.

## How the Attitudes of Management Affect Performance

Managers affect employee performance,[80] and coaches affect athletic performance. The **Pygmalion effect** has to do with how management's attitude toward workers, expectations of workers, and treatment of workers affect their performance. It's pretty simple—how you view your staff is what you get! That is, your attitude toward your staff directly affects the quality of their work.[81] There is much research to support this.[82] When you as a manager view your staff as competent and highly skilled (even though they might not be initially), they will rise to the occasion (it may happen slowly, but it will happen).[83] Likewise, when you don't believe your staff to be competent or trustworthy, guess what—they won't surprise you![84]

Coaches' and managers' attitudes become a self-fulfilling prophecy. In summary, then, your attitude is an essential part of your effectiveness as a manager. John Wooden, the legendary former basketball coach at UCLA, expected excellence from every player. The result was 10 NCAA national championships. Wooden constructed his "pyramid of success" (check it out at www.coachwooden.com) out of such concepts as "keep it simple" and "teamwork is not a preference, it's a necessity."[85]

With all this said about the Pygmalion effect and self-fulfilling prophecies, you as an employee or a manager are still responsible for your own actions. Others' attitudes can affect your behavior and performance, but only if you let them. Ignore negative comments, stay away from people with negative attitudes, and continue to get better at what you do. Look at a negative boss as a gift—you need to learn how to work with difficult people. Just don't let them defeat you. Show them you have what it takes to succeed.

TIME-OUT 5 Describe how expectations of you on the part of someone (a parent, friend, teacher, coach, or boss) strongly affected your success or failure.

## Attitudes and Job Satisfaction

Job satisfaction is our attitude, or how content we are (or are not), with our jobs. The continuum ranges from high satisfaction (positive attitude) to low satisfaction (negative attitude). Job attitudes and job performance are perhaps the two most central and enduring sets of constructs in individual-level organizational research.[86] Why? Because job satisfaction affects employee absenteeism, morale, performance, and turnover.[87] Thus organizations strive for high levels of employee job satisfaction because they lead to high levels of performance.[88] They measure job satisfaction in organizational development surveys (chapter 6) and create cultures to maintain and increase job satisfaction. A person has to fit the task (P–T fit) and the organization (P–O fit) to achieve job satisfaction.

Have you ever been unhappy on a team or at work because you just didn't fit in? P–O fit has a lot to do with finding a job that you like to perform and that you are also good at. Will you be happy performing a job you don't like or that you fail to do well? Were you happier as a star of the team or sitting on the bench? Were you happier playing on winning teams than on losing teams? Job satisfaction also affects our satisfaction with life—having a job that satisfies us affects the way we view our lives outside work.

What determines job satisfaction? According to management guru Ken Blanchard, the number-one indicator of job satisfaction is the relationship you have with your boss. But your boss is not the only determining factor. Do your relationships at work and other things affect your job satisfaction? To find out the others, complete Self-Assessment 8.2.

◀ **LEARNING OUTCOME 4**
State what job satisfaction is and why it is important.

223

Let's face it, your overall level of job satisfaction can be high because you enjoy key aspects of the job, but there are usually some aspects you don't enjoy. Often it's one part of the job that causes us to develop negative attitudes.[89] Because job satisfaction is based on personality and perception, it can be changed. If you work at being more positive by focusing on the good parts of your job and spend less time thinking about and especially complaining to others about your job, your job satisfaction will improve. Thus, managers need to recruit and retain employees with positive attitudes. If you ask job candidates about their previous jobs and they make negative statements, cannot think of anything good to say, or hesitate, they may have a negative personality and job attitude. Improving

# SELF-ASSESSMENT 8.2

## How Satisfied Are You With Your Job?

Select a present or past job or, if you prefer, a sport team. For each of the following determinants of job satisfaction, identify your level of satisfaction by placing a check on the continuum.

**Personality**
I have a negative self-esteem. _____ _____ _____ / _____ _____ _____ I have a positive self-esteem.
  1    2    3    4    5    6

**Work Itself**
I do not enjoy doing the tasks I perform. _____ _____ _____ / _____ _____ _____ I enjoy doing the tasks I perform.
  1    2    3    4    5    6

**Compensation**
I am not fairly compensated. _____ _____ _____ / _____ _____ _____ I am fairly compensated.
  1    2    3    4    5    6

**Growth and Upward Mobility**
I have the opportunity to learn new things and get better jobs. _____ _____ _____ / _____ _____ _____ I have no opportunity to learn new things and get better jobs.
  1    2    3    4    5    6

**Coworkers**
I like and enjoy working with my coworkers. _____ _____ _____ / _____ _____ _____ I do not like and enjoy working with my coworkers.
  1    2    3    4    5    6

**Management**
I'm happy with the working relationship I have with my boss. _____ _____ _____ / _____ _____ _____ I do not enjoy my working relationship with my boss.
  1    2    3    4    5    6

I believe that managers are doing a good job. _____ _____ _____ / _____ _____ _____ I do not believe managers are doing a good job.
  1    2    3    4    5    6

## Overall Job Satisfaction

When determining your overall job satisfaction, you cannot simply add up a score based on these six determinants because they most likely have differing importance to you. Thus, with the six factors in mind, rate your overall satisfaction level with your job. It is quite normal to have high job satisfaction and not like some aspects of your job.

**I am satisfied with my job (high level of satisfaction)**          **I am dissatisfied with my job (low level of satisfaction)**

6        5        4        3        2        1

your human relationship skills can help you get along better with coworkers and managers and increase your job satisfaction, as well as your chances for growth, advancement, and higher compensation.

## Moving from Internal OB Foundations to External OB Factors

Our four OB foundations (thoughts, personality, perception, and attitudes) that we have discussed are based on internal factors that are influenced by external factors. The rest of this chapter will help you to use your internal foundations to be successful at dealing with the external OB factors of power, organizational politics, conflict management, negotiation, collaboration, and stress. Each of these six factors will be discussed in the next six major sections of this chapter.

# Power

What are your thoughts and attitudes about power? Do you perceive power in organizations as good or bad?[90] People have different motivational needs for power[91] (you will learn this in chapter 11.) Is your personality type one that steps up to lead, which takes power, or do you avoid being in a position of power?[92] Either way, organizations have power structures,[93] and these structures give managers sources of power,[94] and colleges prepare students to be managers, which are positions of power.[95] The imbalance of power has constrained women and minorities in sport organizations. But the good news is that the trend is to be more inclusive and to give employees more power through shared leadership.[96]

To be effective in an organization, you need to understand how people gain power and how they use power. Power used properly enhances your job effectiveness and organizational performance. Therefore, in this section you will examine power—its importance, its bases, and its implications—so that you can use power wisely to help you achieve your objectives with the help of others.

◀ **LEARNING OUTCOME 5**
Define power, and explain the difference between position and personal power.

## A Positive View of Power

Power is often viewed as one's ability to make people do something or as one's ability to do something to people or for them. These definitions are valid, but they also cast power as manipulative, or even destructive, as does Lord Acton's saying, "Power corrupts, and absolute power corrupts absolutely." Unfortunately, some people abuse power and commit unethical acts.

Power in and of itself is neither good nor bad—only how it is used is. So, it is important to look at power as a constructive tool, as a way for you to organize action and get something done. For our purposes, then, **power** is the ability to influence the actions of others. Mark Emmert, president of the NCAA, is thus a powerful person, as is every effective coach and athletic director. FIFA is a powerful organization because of the influence it wields around the world.

Without power, organizations and managers cannot achieve objectives. Leadership and power go hand in hand. Employees are not influenced without a reason, and the reason is often the power a manager has over them. You don't always have to *use* your power to influence people. Often it is the perception of power, rather than the wielding of it, that influences others.

 How might the USADA use its power constructively to solve some of the troubling doping issues facing Olympic sport?

## Sources of Power

Power can be derived from one's position and from one's personal attributes. Management has the *position power* that is delegated down the chain of command through formal authority (chapter 5).[97] Recall that managers influence employee attitudes, behaviors, job satisfaction, and performance.[98] Position power is more effective when it is accompanied by personal power. The most effective leaders toggle between the two power sources.

You don't have to be a manager to have power; you can also have *personal power* based on your personality, abilities, and skill. Some athletes and employees actually have more influence over other teammates and employees than the coach and manager do. Have you and the team given power to the high-status star athletes?[99] Have you ever been influenced and motivated more by your teammates than by the coach? That's personal power.

Do you always do whatever others want to do, or do you try to get others to do what you want to do? Admit it—like the rest of us, you want personal power.[100] Don't we try to influence people off and on the job to get what we want every day? There is nothing wrong with looking out for your self-interest, so long as you don't use unethical behavior to get your way at the expense of others. Again, create win–win situations for all parties to have good relationships and happiness.

Just as it can be gained, every type of power can also be lost—think about what happened to Tiger Woods. Ask Pete Rose, all-time base hit champion, who was banned from the Baseball Hall of Fame for betting on baseball games. Power sometimes does shift in teams; new stars rise as others decline in performance.[101]

## Bases of Power

The seven bases of power, along with their two sources, are shown in figure 8.3. People who get results and who have good people skills are often granted power (either formally by promotion or informally by personal power). Note that building a power base does not necessarily mean taking power away from others. People who are willing to step forward and do the work are given power. However, having position power makes it much easier to have power.

### Coercive Power

Coercive power uses threats or punishment to achieve compliance. It gets its effectiveness from our fear of humiliation (in the form of reprimands, probation, suspension, or dismissal). Coercive power also uses verbal abuse and ostracism (both dramatic but not very productive). Abusive power leads to negative employee behavior and lower performance.[102] *Bullies* usually gain power for personal gain, and bullying is negative behavior.[103] Group members may use coercive power to enforce norms.[104] Coercion does have appropriate uses—for example, when employees or players break the rules. The USADA uses coercive power routinely, as do innumerable governing bodies.

 Should the USADA have coercive power over Olympic athletes?

### Connection Power

When people use their relationships with influential or important people to influence your behavior or attitudes, they are using connection power. When people know you are friendly with people in power, they tend to help you as a favor to their friend in power. Connections can help you find work and get the resources you need to succeed. What would you do if the boss' daughter asked you to do something for her? Networking is about developing relationships to increase connection power. We discuss networking in a later section.

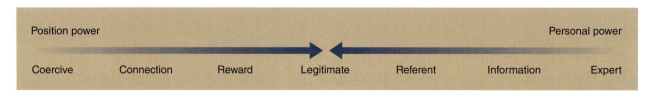

**FIGURE 8.3** Sources and bases of power.

## Reward Power

As a manager, you will have the ability to praise, recognize achievement, raise wages, and promote people. This is reward power—the ability to influence others by giving them something they value. As we noted in chapter 7, as a manager you will get what you reward. You will learn how to give praise that motivates in chapter 11. With teammates and coworkers, you can give compliments and help them.

◀ **LEARNING OUTCOME 6**
Explain how reward power, legitimate power, and referent power differ.

## Legitimate Power

Power given to people by organizations or by society is legitimate power.[105] Managers have legitimate power. So do police officers. (And both have coercive power as well.) When our boss asks us to do something, we typically think we should do it because it's a legitimate request that is part of our job, so we do the task.[106] If we don't think it is a legitimate request, for example if it seems unethical, we may try to get out of doing the task. Coaches and managers use legitimate power to get the job done every day.

## Referent Power

Referent power is about voluntarily giving someone power over you. Therefore, in your behavior you will refer to what you think the power holder would do or would want you to do. People using referent power don't give orders; they make relationship-related requests like "Please do this as a favor for me," and "Will you please do this for me?" Star athletes have referent power over their fans. This is personal power, of course. It is about the referent's charisma, interpersonal openness, and experience as someone older and wiser or more successful and more skilled. Managers gain this power when they are respected by their work group.

## Information Power

In this age of information, people who have knowledge or data that others need have information power because information is the important source of power, not money.[107] This is personal power, although sometimes it is also position power, because you happen to be in the right place (position) to acquire the knowledge or gather the data. As a manager, you will need to rely on information supplied by others. They will therefore have power over you because your work can be only as good as the information it is based on. You will also be a conveyer of information—to your staff and to your bosses—and as such will also have information power. You will improve your communication skills in chapter 10.

## Expert Power

People who have expertise or specialized skills that others need have expert power. This too is personal power. When you are an expert at something of value to others, they will come to you for your ideas and leadership.[108] NBA forward LeBron James has expert power that his team needs. The fewer the people who possess a particular expertise, the more power the expert has. The best managers and coaches are not always the ones with the most expertise. Expert power is essential to people who work with other departments and other organizations. They have no direct position power, but being seen as experts gives them credibility and standing.

# Gaining Power

Do you want to increase your power? Power is gained only with time, experience, success, and the increasing respect of your colleagues. To gain more bases of power, you can use coercion sparingly and only when necessary, network with people in power to gain

## APPLYING THE CONCEPT 8.1

### Using Power

Identify the appropriate power to use in each situation.

a. coercive

b. connection

c. reward or legitimate

d. referent

e. information or expert

_____ 1. Bridget, one of your top people, normally needs very little direction. However, recently her performance has faltered. You suspect that Bridget's personal problems are affecting her work.

_____ 2. You need a new computer to help you organize ticket sales more efficiently. Computers are allocated by a committee, which is very political in nature.

_____ 3. Jean, a promising assistant coach, wants a promotion. Jean has talked to you about getting ahead in sport management and has asked you to help prepare her for when the opportunity comes.

_____ 4. John, one of your worst players, has ignored one of your directives once again.

_____ 5. Whitney, who continually needs direction and encouragement, is not working to standard today. As she does occasionally, she claims that she doesn't feel well but can't afford to take time off. You have to get an important customer order for golf clubs shipped today.

connections, praise and reward others for a job well done using your people skills, make only legitimate requests of others, gain information about your field and organization, and develop your expertise so that others come to you.

TIME-OUT 6

Think about several bosses or coaches whom you are in a position to observe. Describe the types of power they have and the ones that they use. Do you think they use their power well? Why or why not?

If you are highly competent, have good people skills, and develop good relationships, you will gain power. Here are a couple of things you can do to increase your power. If you are willing to step up and take the lead and do the work, others will often give you the ball and let you run with it. Serve on committees to gain information and network connections. Take advantage of any training and development programs, and volunteer to be the first to take on new tasks.

# Politics in the Office and on the Field

**LEARNING OUTCOME 7** ▶

Understand how power and politics are related.

Before you read about the nature of politics at work, political behavior, and how to develop political skills, complete Self-Assessment 8.3.

## Nature of Politics in the Workplace

**Politics** is the efforts of groups or individuals with competing interests to obtain power and positions of leadership. Like power, organizational politics has a negative connotation

## SELF-ASSESSMENT 8.3

### How Political Are You?

Select the response that best describes your behavior on your job or team.

1 = rarely

2 = seldom

3 = occasionally

4 = frequently

5 = usually

_____ 1. I get along with everyone, even difficult teammates and coworkers.

_____ 2. I avoid giving my personal opinion on controversial issues, especially when I know others don't agree with me.

_____ 3. I try to make people feel important by complimenting them.

_____ 4. I often compromise when I work with others, and I also avoid telling people they are wrong.

_____ 5. I try to get to know key managers and find out what is going on in every department.

_____ 6. I dress the way the people in power dress and pursue the same interests (watch or play sports, join the same clubs) they do.

_____ 7. I network with higher-level managers so they will know who I am.

_____ 8. I seek recognition and visibility for my accomplishments.

_____ 9. I get others to help me get what I want.

_____ 10. I do favors for others and ask favors from them in return.

To determine your score, add your answers. The higher your score, the more political your behavior in the workplace or on a team. Place your score here _____ and on the continuum.

| Nonpolitical | 10 | 20 | 30 | 40 | 50 | Political |
|---|---|---|---|---|---|---|

because it can be manipulated and abused.[109] So we have to be ethical in using power and political behavior to help the organization achieve objectives.[110]

Do you have positive or negative thoughts, perceptions, and attitudes about politics? Either way, politics is used in virtually every organization, so it pays to have political skills.[111] You usually can't get your job done without the help of others, including people and departments within your firm and other organizations over which you have no authority, so you need to use political skills.[112] The real organization chart isn't the formal one on paper (chapter 5); it's knowing who to talk to and using political influence to get the job done.[113]

Here is a way of understanding politics at work. In the economy, the medium of exchange is money, but you don't use money to get what you want at work: You use politics. Politics is about give and take. Research supports the idea that successful managers spend more time using political behavior than average managers,[114] that you need to be political to climb the corporate ladder (or at least keep from being thrown off), and that the higher up you get, the more important politics becomes.[115]

## Political Behavior

**LEARNING OUTCOME 8** ▶

Explain what networking, reciprocity, and coalitions have in common.

Networking, reciprocating, and coalition building are important political skills. The goal is to build a net that works (networking) and helps you to develop useful relationships. Developing relationships is easier if you learn to use reciprocity and build solid coalitions.

### Networking

**Networking** is about developing relationships to gain social or business advantage. Networking is important to career success, and more people get jobs through networking than through all other methods combined. But networking is not just about you getting a job; successful networking is based on developing mutually beneficial relationships.[116] Many young people are good at using social media to network. However, some young people are not good at networking face-to-face, which is important on the job.

Many people develop networks by playing and talking about sports. People have been offered a job on the playing field. Many business deals have been made on the golf course. People network by taking up sports that their boss and people at other higher levels play and watch, even when they have no interest in the sport. Talk sports to those who are interested, but talk about other topics of interest to people who are not into sports.

### Reciprocating

Reciprocating is an element of *social exchange theory* that involves returning in kind.[117] **Reciprocity** thus involves using mutual dependence to accomplish objectives. Through work, you develop mutual obligation and reciprocity.[118] You can think of reciprocity as an unspoken "I owe you" (IOU). Have you heard the expressions "I owe you one" and "You owe me one"? When someone does something for you, you incur an obligation that the person may expect to be repaid in kind. Likewise, when you do something for someone, you create a debt that you may be able to collect later when you need a favor. Reciprocity is commonly used to get the job done.

Do you like people who take advantage of you for their own personal gain? Aren't your good personal and work relationships built on helping each other? Reciprocity is not all about getting others to help you. Helping others is the driver of your own success.[119] As motivational speaker Zig Ziglar said, "You can have everything in life you want, if you will just help enough other people get what they want."[120] Ever help anyone not expecting anything in return, but end up getting more than you gave?

### Coalition

A **coalition** is an alliance of people with similar objectives who have a better chance of achieving their objectives together than alone. It often takes a coalition to get changes that you want to make. Networking and reciprocity are work in continual progress. In contrast, coalitions often come together temporarily and then dissolve once their objectives are accomplished.

Most important decisions are made by coalitions outside of their formal meetings. Let's say you are on a team and the captain is selected by a nomination and vote of the team members. If you want to be captain, you can "politic" by asking close teammates who they will vote for and trying to get their votes, and if they are supportive, you can ask them to ask others to vote for you. If the majority of the team say they will vote for you, you have won the election before the coach even starts the meeting. If you don't get any support from your close teammates and others, you drop the effort to build a coalition, knowing that you will lose. This same coalition-building process is used to influence all types of decisions.

## Developing Political Skills

Do you believe managers always take a rational approach to decision making? If so, think again because many business decisions are nonrational, based primarily on emotions, power, and politics. If having a successful career climbing the corporate

TIME-OUT
7

Give examples of how your firm or team uses networking, reciprocity, and coalitions to achieve objectives.

ladder is your goal, political skills should be in your tool kit.[121] Review the statements in Self-Assessment 8.3 and strive to become comfortable with networking, reciprocating, and working with coalitions. Learn what it takes in the organization where you work as you follow the guidelines in figure 8.4.

### Learn the Organizational Culture of Success

By now, you know how important organizational culture is (chapter 6). Make sure you learn yours well—culture defines the ground rules for politicking at work, so watch how your managers use political behavior. It is very important to understand what it takes to succeed at your job and advance in the organization, so don't be afraid to ask. Unfortunately, both managers and staffers are often clueless about the ingredients for success. So, in addition to asking, observe the people who are advancing and figure out why, and learn to read between the lines. Promote yourself in politically acceptable and ethical ways without appearing to brag.

### Learn the Power Players

Power players are people who can help you in your career. Always remember that your coach or boss is the key power player for you. When you understand the power players in your group, department, and organization, you can tailor your presentations to meet their pet criteria. For example, some managers want details; others are impatient with the details and just want the big picture. Do things your boss' way, or convince the boss that your way is better and get support for your work so you stand out for advancement.

**FIGURE 8.4** Developing political skills.

## Develop a Good Working Relationship With Your Boss

Again, always remember that your coach or boss is a key player for you, regardless of your feelings toward him. His *perception* of you has a direct effect on your job and career success. To get playing time or raises and promotions, you need to have a good working relationship with your boss. A good relationship is not about socializing off the job, it's about your coach and manager perceiving you to be a reliable performer.

When the performance appraisal system is subjective, it doesn't objectively indicate ranking of performance; having a good relationship with your boss—not results—gets you ahead. And even with objective measures, if you want to get ahead, you need to have good working relationships with your managers. If you are not getting top performance evaluations, as we discussed in chapter 7, talk to your boss and develop a plan to get them. Here are some tips on how to succeed:

- Know what the boss expects from you and do it, and give more than asked for. Beating deadlines, arriving at work early and staying later when needed, and volunteering for more work are all ways to impress a boss and get top performance evaluations.

- Get your boss' advice and inclusion in your coalition when you think that forming a coalition is the best strategy.

- Give your boss the good news—and the bad news. Let the boss know early on if you're having a problem. No boss wants to find out about your problem from somebody else. Let your coach, manager, or customer know as early as possible if you are behind schedule, and set a new deadline.[122]

- Don't talk negatively about your boss behind her back, because she will likely find out, and it will hurt your chances of advancement. So follow the old rule—if you can't say something nice, don't say anything at all. Don't criticize your boss in public, even if asked to, because most bosses don't really want to hear anything negative about themselves. And don't show up a boss in public.

- Admit mistakes and apologize. If you make a work or political mistake that hurts your working relationship with your boss, there usually are negative consequences. But here is some damage control. We all make mistakes, so admit them to everyone, especially to your boss. Defending and justifying mistakes and behavior that hurts others damages relationships and can lead to lower performance evaluations. However, an apology to a boss is more than just saying "I'm sorry." You need to acknowledge what you've done, solve it for the future, then make some assurance that it won't happen again.[123] With colleagues, friends, and family, a sincere apology can go a long way in maintaining and repairing damaged relationships.[124] If you don't believe you did anything wrong, but your behavior hurt someone, an apology doesn't mean you need to accept blame, but that you are sorry for causing pain.[125] Saying "I'm sorry" helps maintain a relationship.[126] So apologize quickly and move on.

- Be very, very careful about going over your boss' head to complain. If your boss has a good relationship with the person higher up, you will lose, and your boss may take revenge on you.

- Again, if your boss doesn't give you excellent performance reviews, find out why and what it takes to get an excellent review—and do it if you want to get ahead.

- If you are not capable of meeting your boss' expectations or not willing to do so, consider looking for another job within the firm or at another organization. If you seek another job, don't complain about your boss; the manager you want to work for may think that you were the problem and not want to take a chance on you.

## Be an Honest Team Player

Secrecy breeds politics, so be open and honest. High-functioning organizations are built on respect, confidence, and trust. If you are caught lying or cheating, your boss and team

## APPLYING THE CONCEPT 8.2

### Political Behavior

Identify each behavior as (a) effective or (b) ineffective.

_____ 6. Jill is taking golf lessons so she can join the Saturday golf group that includes some higher-level managers.

_____ 7. Paul tells his boss' boss about mistakes his boss makes.

_____ 8. Sally avoids socializing so that she can be more productive on the job.

_____ 9. John sent a very positive performance report about himself to three higher-level managers to whom he does not report. They did not request copies.

_____ 10. Carlos has to drop off daily reports by noon. He brings them around 10 a.m. on Tuesday and Thursday so that he can run into some higher-level managers who meet at that time near the office where the report goes. On other days, Carlos drops the report off around noon on his way to lunch.

will not trust you. Self-discipline, teamwork, and fair play are great values on the playing field and in the office. Tell others the truth even when it is difficult.[127]

### Stay Tuned to the Networking Grapevine

The grapevine can be a good thing—it can help you learn your organization's culture and its key players. It can also let you know what is going on in the organization and what is coming up, such as job openings. Your grapevine should include people both inside and outside your organization. Be active in trade or professional associations to keep up in your field and increase your skills and knowledge.

### Resolve Conflicts

As you climb the corporate ladder, take care not to get thrown off. Choose your stands carefully. Avoid fights you can't win. If you find yourself suddenly out of the information loop, or if your boss or coworkers start treating you differently, find out why. Use your network or grapevine to find out whether someone is trying to undermine you and why. Understand where your enemies are coming from, how they operate, who's behind them, and what weapons they might use. Confront individuals or groups you suspect of instigating conflict. If you did something to offend a coworker, an apology from you may be in order. Admit mistakes; don't try to justify them. In any case, approach your adversary and try to resolve the conflict using the ideas in the next section.

 **TIME-OUT 8** Which suggestions for developing political skills feel least comfortable to you? Explain.

# Managing Conflict

A **conflict** exists whenever people disagree. That's right. It doesn't have to be a major disagreement. Every time someone says or does something you don't agree with, you are in opposition, and that is a conflict. Conflict occurs in every team and organization.[128] It exists in every relationship.[129] You are in conflict when you get aggravated at someone and when someone says or does something differently than you that bothers you.[130] You can't live and work without running into conflict. So you might as well learn to manage it effectively to maintain and improve relationships.[131] If you don't, you can hurt feelings, harm relationships, and hinder your career.[132] Thus, conflict management is an important skill to develop both at work and in your private life.[133] In this section, you will learn why people get into conflict, how conflict helps and hurts at work, and approaches to handling conflict.

## Ground Rules

Implicit in all of our interactions with others is a *psychological contract* that we'll call the ground rules. These are our—and others'—expectations.[134] At work, we all have a set of expectations about what we will contribute to the organization (effort, time, skills) and what this will provide us (compensation, job satisfaction, status). These are our unspoken, implicit ground rules, and we don't want them violated. We may believe that there is mutual agreement on the ground rules, when in fact this may not be true. And therein lies the problem.

We get into conflict because our ground rules get broken.[135] We fail to make explicit our own expectations, and we fail to inquire into the expectations of others. We further assume that others hold the same expectations we do.

As long as people meet our expectations and behave like we want them to, everything is fine. But when they don't, the result is conflict.[136] How can you expect others to meet your expectations when you don't tell them what they are? Sharing expectations, figuring out all the hidden agendas, and carefully negotiating explicit ground rules are key to avoiding conflicts.

Unfortunately, we often are not aware of our expectations until someone does something unexpected that we don't agree with. So if your expectations are not met, or if something unexpected that's bugging you comes up, you should start trying to resolve the conflict.[137] You can develop conflict resolution skills in the collaboration section.

## Functional and Dysfunctional Conflict

Mention conflict, and people tend to think of fighting and disruption,[138] but conflict can be either negative or positive.[139] **Dysfunctional conflict** prevents groups from achieving their objectives. **Functional conflict** fosters disagreement and opposition that actually help achieve a group's objectives. When the focus of the conflict is *innovative ideas*, the conflict can result in changes that improve performance (chapter 6)—functional conflict. Conversely, when it is a *personal conflict*, it tends to hurt relationships because people don't get along, and it usually hampers individual and team performance—dysfunctional conflict. In chapter 9, you will use your conflict skills in the context of teamwork. The challenge is to manage conflict so that it doesn't impair group functioning and so that it benefits the team's and the organization's performance.

Have you ever heard teammates or coworkers complain about each other's performance behind each other's back or to the coach? Well, this usually results in dysfunctional personal conflict. The NFL Seahawks don't do this. They developed a culture of confronting each other about performance on the field.[140] Tennis doubles players Bob and Mike Bryan say the key to their success is that they get mad and yell at each other about a bad play—and then get over it and act like nothing ever happened.[141] Confrontation can be difficult but effective if the focus is on improving performance, without any personal putdowns. Can you and your team do this?

The NCAA needs to resolve two very important but conflicting goals—the increasing commercialism of college sport and the development of young amateur athletes. If growing revenue through sponsorships and commercials becomes the NCAA's primary goal, it will be harder and harder to square this with keeping college athletes in amateur status. The NCAA has grappled with this dilemma for many years.

## Styles of Conflict Management

Conflict management is based on two dimensions (concern for others' needs and concern for your own needs), which result in three types of behavior (passive, aggressive, and assertive) and three win-lose situations. Taken together, these five components give us five different styles of conflict resolution to choose from, which are presented in figure 8.5 and discussed next.

◀ LEARNING OUTCOME 9
Describe the five conflict management styles.

As we will discuss, there is no one best style to use in every type of conflict; each has its own advantages and disadvantages. When selecting a conflict style, you should also consider that personality types affect how people respond to conflict. *Agreeable* personality types are usually more willing to work with you to resolve the conflict, whereas nonagreeable personality types are more likely to use force to get their way. When confronting *emotionally unstable* personality types, using logic and facts usually doesn't work. It's best to appeal to their emotional needs.

### Avoiding

Some people try to manage conflict by avoiding it. They refuse to take a stance, withdraw mentally, or simply leave. This approach is neither assertive nor cooperative, and it resolves nothing, as both sides tend to lose.

Be careful with avoiding because it can result in frustration, leading to passive-aggressive behavior—yelling arguments that never resolve the conflict.[142] So confront others early and stay calm.[143] Also, when people learn that you are an avoider, they will take advantage of you because they know you will not stand up to them. However, there are times when it is best to avoid an argument over a trivial matter that may hurt your relationship, and when you or the other person is overly emotional, or you don't have time, avoid until you have the correct emotional mindset and time to resolve the conflict.

### Accommodating

People who resolve conflict by passively giving in are managing conflict by accommodation. You satisfy the needs of others, but you neglect your own needs by letting others get their way by doing something you really don't want to do. The opposing party wins; you the accommodator lose.

**FIGURE 8.5** Styles of conflict management.

Avoidance and accommodation differ in one significant way. Avoiders basically do nothing, but accommodators have to do something they don't really want to do. You may like being a follower and preserving relationships by doing things other people's way, but it is counterproductive when you have a better solution. An overuse of accommodating tends to lead to people taking advantage of you, and the type of relationship you try to maintain is usually lost, anyway. We often must accommodate our bosses, especially when they use a forcing style. However, there are times when we should accommodate. Why not give in to others when it's not important to you, but it is to them, and you don't have time to resolve the conflict? Isn't doing things we don't want to do an important part of relationship reciprocity—friendship?

## Forcing

People who use aggression to get their way resolve conflict by forcing the other party to give them what they want. Forcers are uncooperative and aggressive—they do whatever it takes to satisfy their needs at the expense of others. Forcers threaten, intimidate, and call for majority rule when they know they will win. They also enjoy dealing with avoiders and accommodators because these are easy wins. Forcers win; everyone else loses.

Using force from personal power tends to result in poor relationships and resentment toward you. But when you know you have the better idea that will help the organization, push for it. From position power, the boss should enforce rules or confront open challenges to the manager's authority using force when needed. It may also be needed when unpopular action must be taken on important issues and resolving a conflict is urgent.

## Negotiating

People who resolve conflict through assertive give-and-take concessions are managing conflict by negotiation (also called compromise). Negotiators are both assertive and cooperative. Everyone wins some and loses some.

Compromise may result in suboptimal decisions and action through concessions. Continuing use of negotiation, such as bargaining over labor contracts, leads to asking for much more than expected to get closer to what each side wants. However, in true negotiation situations, it should be used. It is often the only resolution to a conflict when the issues are complex and critical and there is no simple, clear solution to resolve the conflict.

## Collaborating

People who jointly and assertively try to get to the best solution, one that all parties can buy into, resolve conflict by collaboration. Collaborators are problem solvers. They are both assertive and cooperative. Of the five styles, only collaborating focuses on finding the best solution. Avoiders and accommodators focus on avoiding conflict, and forcers focus on winning at all costs. Collaborators are willing to change positions if a better solution is presented. Negotiation is often based on secret information, whereas collaboration is based on open and honest communication. This is the only conflict management style in which all parties win.

Collaborating tends to lead to the optimal resolution to a conflict. However, it takes more skill, effort, and time to come to a resolution. There are situations in which it is difficult to come up with an agreeable solution, or when a forcer prevents its use.

## Selecting the Most Appropriate Conflict Style for the Situation

Again, there is no one best style for resolving conflict. The style we prefer personally may meet our needs but not the needs of the situation. If you wish to become a truly effective leader, you must become proficient at all five styles. And you must learn to judge a conflict and select the style that will best resolve it after considering the advantages and disadvan-

## APPLYING THE CONCEPT 8.3

### Selecting Conflict Management Styles

Identify the most appropriate conflict management style for each situation.

   a.  avoidance
   b.  accommodation
   c.  forcing
   d.  negotiation
   e.  collaboration

_____ 11.  While serving on a committee that allocates athletic funds for building a new football stadium, you make a recommendation that another member opposes quite aggressively. Your interest in what the committee does is low, although you can see quite clearly that yours is the better idea.

_____ 12.  The task force you've been assigned to has to select new fitness equipment. The four alternatives will all do the job. Members disagree on their brand, price, and service.

_____ 13.  You manage golf cart sales for the Hole in One stores. Beth, who makes a lot of the sales, is in the midst of closing the season's biggest sale, and you and she disagree on which strategy to use.

_____ 14.  You're late and on your way to an important meeting. As you leave your office, at the other end of the work area you see Chris, one of your employees, goofing off instead of working.

_____ 15.  You're over budget for labor this month. Work is slow, so you ask Kent, a part-time employee, to leave work early. Kent tells you he doesn't want to because he needs the money.

tages of each style discussed. Avoidance and accommodation are the easiest to learn for most people. If you have problems using these two styles when appropriate, work at giving in to others, and do things you don't want to do to help others meet their objectives. Most people find negotiation and collaboration the hardest to learn. Therefore, we explore negotiation and collaboration in more depth in the next two sections.

**TIME-OUT 9** Which style of conflict management does your current boss or coach use most often? Explain using a typical example.

**TIME-OUT 10** Which style of conflict management do you use most often? Why? Give several examples.

# Negotiation

Negotiating is about trying to get what you want, and you do it every day, even though you may not realize it. Good negotiators get better jobs with higher pay. Effective negotiation is not about being unethical;[144] it does not call for deceiving others to create an "I win and you lose" situation.[145] Negotiation is about building trust so that everyone gets a good deal.[146] Does this interest you? Negotiators try to hammer out agreements in which everyone gets something and everyone gives something. Negotiation is used to complete business deals, resolve disagreements, and reduce conflicts. Negotiation is appropriate and common in collective bargaining, buying and selling goods and services, and getting a job and raises. "Take it or leave it" situations, of course, leave no room for negotiation. Power, politics, and conflict management are important negotiating tools.

   *Negotiating* is a process in which two or more people in conflict try to come to an agreement or to make a deal. Negotiation often occurs in zero-sum conflicts, in which one party's gain is the other party's loss.[147] Each knockdown in price that athletic directors can negotiate for a new scoreboard is their gain and the seller's loss. Thus, negotiators must sell the other party on their ideas, or they must exchange something for what they want. For a deal to work over a period of time, all parties in the negotiation need to believe they got a good deal.[148] If a players' union believes that management won, player morale may dip, which could affect performance. Also, if fans (who are the nonrepresented third party in the wrangle between owners and the players' union) believe they got a bad deal, attendance might drop dramatically, as it has following past player strikes.

Are you a good negotiator? Following steps in the negotiation process that are evidence-based can help you develop your negotiation skills.[149] Let's now describe the four stages of the negotiation process presented in figure 8.6.[150] When you are negotiating, you may have to make slight changes during the process. Skill-Builder 8.1 in the web study guide gives you practice using the process.

## Planning for the Negotiation

Solid preparations, or lack thereof, can mean the difference between success and failure. Be clear about what it is you are negotiating—is it price or salary, options, delivery time, sales quantities, or all of these? Planning entails four steps:

1. Research the other party.

Know the key players, know the issues, know the context, and know what the deal is really worth to you and the other party.[151] Before you negotiate, try to find out what the other parties want and what they are and are not willing to give up.[152] Use your networking grapevine to size up negotiators' personalities and negotiation style. The more you know about the other side, the better your chances of reaching an agreement. Think about what worked and what did not work in previous negotiations with these parties. People often say that President Donald Trump moves quickly in negotiating deals, but he says the reason he moves fast is that he prepares himself thoroughly.

2. Set objectives.

Based on your research, what can you expect? Limit your goals. Focus on just a few important points that you actually might be able to get. Set objectives.[153] When you are looking for a job, you need to research what the common compensation range for the specific position is in the local area.

- Set a lower limit below which you will not accept. This lets you know when to walk away from a negotiation and not make a deal.

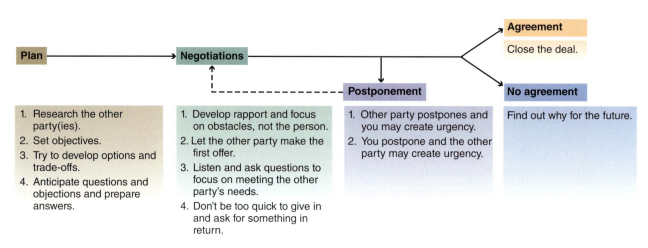

**FIGURE 8.6** The negotiation process.

- Set a target objective that you believe is fair.
- Set an objective for the opening offer that is higher than you expect to get.

The other party may be doing the same thing, so don't view their opening offer as final. The key to successful negotiations is for all parties to get between their minimum and their target. This is the "I win some, you win some" situation that negotiations strive to achieve. It is helpful to have "must" (if I don't get $50,000, no deal, I walk) and "want" (I want $50,000, but I will accept $45,000) criteria (chapter 3).

3. Try to develop options and trade-offs.

Suppose you are a free-agent NBA player. If you have multiple offers from other teams, you are in a strong power position to get your target salary. Remember context, however. If the job market is soft or you really want a particular job for whatever reason, dickering over salary may not be in your best interest. But don't shortchange yourself; explore your alternatives. If you have to give up something or cannot get exactly what you want, be prepared to ask for something else in return.[154] If you cannot get the salary or raise you want, ask for more days off, more in your retirement account, or something else in return for your concession.

4. Anticipate questions and objections, and prepare answers.

The other party may want to know why you are negotiating. Be prepared to answer the unasked question—what's in it for you? Don't focus on what you want but on how your deal will benefit the other team. Talk in terms of *you* and *we*, not *I*, unless you are telling others what you're going to do for them.

There is a good chance that the other side will raise objections—reasons why the negotiations won't result in agreement.[155] When agents ask for a raise, management typically says the team can't afford it. If, however, agents have done their homework, they strengthen their case by quoting profit numbers to prove their point. Unfortunately, parties don't always state their real objections. Thus, you need to listen and ask questions to find out what is preventing agreement.[156]

Make sure that you fully understand yourself, your position, and your deal and that you project confidence. If the other party doesn't trust you or believes the deal is not a good one, you won't reach an agreement. Thus, it's your job to convince the other parties that they are getting a good deal. When you are being interviewed for a job, you have to convince the manager that you can do the job.

# Negotiating

Now you are ready to negotiate the deal. Face-to-face negotiations are preferable because you can assess agreement or objections by observing the other party's nonverbal behavior (discussed in chapter 10). However, telephone and written negotiations can also be used. Again, know the other party's preference. Following the next four steps can help you to close the deal.

1. **Develop rapport and focus on obstacles, not the person.**

Building rapport is important because the first thing you have to sell is yourself. Smile and call the other party by name as you meet. A smile tells people you like them, are interested in them, and enjoy them. Open with some small talk. How much time to wait until you get down to business depends on the other party's style. Some people like to get right down to business, but others want to get to know you before they discuss business. However, you want the other party to make the first offer, so don't wait too long or you may have to make the first move.

Never attack people on the other side or put them down with negative statements like, "You're being unfair to ask for such a salary cut." The other party will become defensive, you will end up arguing, and prospects for agreement will dim if not disappear altogether.[157] Instead, ask questions like, "You think my salary request is too high?" Then state your competitive advantage in a positive way. If people perceive that you're pushing, threatening, or belittling, they won't trust you, and negotiations will stall or reach an impasse. Avoid the "take it or leave it" approach, and if others use it, ask why they are refusing a deal that you believe is fair. Use open-ended questions to keep the other side talking.

Stay calm even if the other person gets emotional and attacks you first.[158] Steve Jobs was known to get emotional and attack the other person to intimidate them during negotiations. Bill Gates knew this and said that when Steve started to yell insults, he stayed calm and closed a good deal for Microsoft and Apple.

2. **Let the other party make the first offer.**

There is always the possibility that the other party will offer you more than your target objective—you can then close the deal and be on your way.[159] On the other hand, if offered less than your target, you can work from the assumption that this is a lowball offer and negotiate up by asking questions like, "What is the salary range for this position?"

When others pressure you to make the first offer with questions like, "Give us your salary requirement, and we'll tell you whether we'll take it," put the ball back in their court by asking, "What do you expect to pay?" If things go well during steps 1 and 2, you simply close the deal—you agree to agree. If you're not close to agreement, all is not yet lost.

3. **Listen and ask questions to focus on meeting the other party's needs.**

Again, focus on what's in the deal for the other party, not you. Recall that when you give people what they want, they tend to give you what you want.[160] Create opportunities for revealing reservations and objections. If you go on and on about what you have to offer, you're not finding out what the other person is really interested in, and you may be killing the deal. Ask questions—"Is the salary out of the ballpark?" "Is it a reasonable amount?"—and then listen. Don't forget to listen and watch the nonverbal behavior. Perhaps the other person's objection involves a "want" criterion: Human resources wants to hire someone with two years of experience, and you have only one. Play up the features you have that are wanted, and you may get an agreement. If the objection is a "must" criterion that you cannot meet, at least you know, and you can stop chasing a deal that is not going to happen. Some people lie or withhold important information during negotiations; to help prevent this, you can ask questions like, "Is there something important that you know about this deal you haven't told me?"[161]

4. **Don't be too quick to give in—ask for something in return.**

Those who don't ask don't get. You want to satisfy the other party without giving up too much, and you want to get something in return. So, don't go below your minimum objective—if it is realistic, you may have to walk away. If you do walk away, you may or may not be called back; and if not, you still may be able to come back for the same low salary, but not always.

If the other side knows you are weakening and will accept a low agreement, they will be less likely to move from their stance. Think about "Must sell—need cash" signs. What type of price do you think they get? Don't let comments such as "are you kidding me, that's too much" intimidate you. Also, when you are not getting what you want, having other options in your bag—fallback positions—can give you bargaining power.

Avoid giving in quickly. Don't give something for nothing. When you give something, you ought to get something.[162] Recall and use your planned trade-offs.

# Postponing

When you are not making progress toward closing the deal, it is often better to postpone the negotiations. Be prepared to postpone and to deal with the other party's postponing.

## *They Postpone—You Create Urgency*

The other party says, "I'll get back to you." When you're not getting what you want, you can create urgency. When you are trying to close a deal, remember that people are more willing to avoid a loss than to score a win—for example, "This specific deal ends today." But don't be dishonest. The main reason negotiations work is that there is mutual trust and respect.

Establishing a relationship of trust is key to closing a deal. Indeed, honesty and integrity are the most important assets a negotiator can have. That doesn't mean you can't look at your options. Maybe you do have other job offers, in which case it's perfectly acceptable to say, "I've got another job offer pending. When will you let me know what you've decided?"

But what if urgency doesn't work and the other person says, "I'll think about it"? Your response? "That's a good idea." But you also should quickly review the parts of your deal that the other person does like. Leave them thinking about what they are walking away from. Putting them in the position of having second thoughts may keep the door open. If the other person doesn't appear to have second thoughts, then don't let the session end without pinning her down: "When can I expect to hear whether I get the job offer?" Ask for a specific time, and note that if you don't hear from her by that date, you will call. Follow up with a letter or email, thanking the other person for the time and highlighting what you have to offer.

When the other party becomes resistant, the hard sell won't work. Take the pressure off by backing off. Ask where he wants to go from here, but don't press for an answer. This is the place to leave things open-ended. Waiting and giving the other person some breathing room may keep the door open. This is where you say, "Why don't we think about it and discuss it some more later?" Learn to read between the lines. Some people will not come right out and tell you "no deal."

### You Postpone—They Create Urgency

Don't be hurried by others, and don't rush yourself. If you're not satisfied with the deal or you want to shop around, tell the other party that you want to think about it. You may also need to check with others for advice or approval (your boss) before you can finalize the deal. If the other party is creating urgency, be sure it is real. In many cases, you can get the same deal at a later date, so don't be pressured into making a deal you are not satisfied with or may regret later. If you do want to postpone, give a specific time that you will get back to the other person, and do so with more prepared negotiations, or simply say you cannot make an agreement.

## Agreeing or Not Agreeing

Negotiations eventually end up with or without making a deal.

### Agreeing

Once you've got an agreement, restate it. It is common to follow up an agreement with a letter or email of thanks that restates the agreement to ensure that the other parties have not changed their minds about the terms. After the deal is made, stop selling it. Change the subject to a nonbusiness one or leave, whichever is appropriate. The MLB and the Major League Baseball Players Association realized there was a drug problem in professional baseball. The two sides negotiated an agreement with a rigorous set of rules to try to stem the use of drugs in baseball.

### Failing to Agree

Not making an agreement is not necessarily a failure. Why should you settle for less than you deserve? It's not uncommon to lose one deal only to get a better one later. Refusal and failure happen to everyone—no one wins them all. The difference between also-rans and the stars often lies in how they respond to failure. Successful people keep trying, learn from their mistakes, and continue to work hard. Recall our example of Michael Jordan. If you cannot come to an agreement, analyze the situation, determine why the negotiation failed, and get it right the next time. Skill-Builder 8.1 in the web study guide allows you to practice negotiation skills that can help you come to an agreement.

# Collaboration

LEARNING OUTCOME 10 ▶

Use collaboration to resolve conflict.

When resolving a personal or innovative idea conflict, you can be *initiating*, *responding* to a resolution, or *mediating* a resolution between other people. In this section, we begin by presenting the BCF statement and then showing you how to use it to initiate a collaborative conflict resolution. We end with a discussion of how to mediate a conflict.

## Collaborative BCF Statements

Skillful **initiators** use short BCF statements and then get involved parties to respond in BCF statements. **BCF statements** describe conflicts in terms of specific behavior, consequences, and feelings. That is to say, when you do B (behavior), C (consequences) happens, and I feel F (feelings). Note that for personal conflicts the consequences are to you, not to the other party. An example of a BCF statement is, "When you don't shower after practice [behavior], it smells in our room and it makes me nauseous [consequence to you], and it frustrates me [feeling]." The sequence can be varied to fit the situation. "I fear [feeling] that the advertisement is not going to work [behavior] and that our hockey team will lose money [consequences]."

The idea is to resolve the conflict while maintaining the relationship. So try to keep people from becoming defensive. When we become defensive and justify ourselves, we go into behavior modes that are counterproductive and usually end in an argument without a resolution. So, to avoid making people defensive, use a short, specific BCF statement and follow these guidelines throughout the collaboration:

- *Be specific when stating the behavior; avoid generalities.*[163] Do you like to be told that you never/always/constantly do something? Don't say to a teammate, "You aren't giving it your best effort." Do say, "I saw the fullback run right by you and you didn't chase him."

- *Don't judge the behavior as being wrong.*[164] Be descriptive, not evaluative. Just state the specific behavior you'd like to have changed. When you tell someone they shouldn't do something, you are judging their behavior as wrong. Do you like to be told what you shouldn't do and that you are wrong? It's very common for people to get defensive and justify their behavior or to simply stop listening to you. If you say, "You shouldn't smoke," do you think that person is going to say, "You're right, I'm going to quit right now"? Don't say, "You shouldn't leave this place a mess." Do say, "This is the second time today that I saw you spill coffee and not clean it up."

- *Don't tell people what to do.* Do you like people telling you what to do? It goes along with judging because when you tell someone they shouldn't do something, you are telling them what to do. Telling people what to do may be a good solution, but don't have it in your opening BCF statement. Telling can come later after they respond to your BCF as step 3 of the model, asking for or giving alternative resolutions.

- *Don't assign blame about who is right or wrong.*[165] This goes along with judging. There are always two sides to every story. Your behavior may be directly or indirectly contributing to the conflict. Discussing who is right and wrong usually just ends in an argument and hurt relationships without resolving the conflict. Don't say, "This is all your fault."

- *Don't threaten the other person.*[166] How do you react to threats? Your opening BCF definitely should not include a threat. If used at all during the discussion, threats should be a last, not a first, option. Don't say, "If you do it again, I'm going to tell the boss on you." Clearly, threatening others will affect your relationships.

Now that you know what BCF statements are and how to develop them, you can use them to collaboratively resolve conflict. Figure 8.7 outlines the process of collaboration, and Skill-Builder 8.2 in the web study guide gives you practice using the process. Next, we focus on initiating resolution and mediating conflict.

| Initiating conflict resolution | Responding to conflict resolution | Mediating conflict resolution |
|---|---|---|
| **Step 1.** Plan a BCF statement that maintains ownership of the problem. | **Step 1.** Listen to and paraphrase the conflict using the BCF model. | **Step 1.** Have each party state the complaint using the BCF model. |
| **Step 2.** Present your BCF statement and agree on the conflict. | **Step 2.** Agree with some aspect of the complaint. | **Step 2.** Agree on the conflict problem(s). |
| **Step 3.** Ask for or give alternative conflict resolutions. | **Step 3.** Ask for or give alternative conflict resolutions. | **Step 3.** Develop alternative conflict resolutions. |
| **Step 4.** Make an agreement for change. | **Step 4.** Make an agreement for change. | **Step 4.** Make an agreement for change. |
| | | **Step 5.** Follow up to make sure the conflict is resolved. |

**FIGURE 8.7**    Resolving conflict by collaboration.

## Initiating Conflict Resolution

Do people ever say or do things that you disagree with or that annoy you?[167] Don't confront someone because you don't like his personality, because he cannot or will not change it for you—jerks will be jerks.[168] There really is no such thing as a personality conflict. However, there are specific things people do and say that bother you. Do you want to resolve such conflicts collaboratively without hurting relationships? The way you initiate a conflict resolution will influence perceptions and reactions, the way the process unfolds, and whether or not the conflict is resolved.[169] So, following the BCF statement guidelines and implementing the "Initiating conflict resolution" model presented in figure 8.7 will help you develop collaborative conflict skills. Here we present four evidence-based steps to successfully initiating a conflict resolution.[170]

1.  Plan a BCF statement that maintains your ownership of the problem.

First let's discuss what "ownership of the problem" means. Suppose you don't smoke, and someone who is visiting you starts smoking. Who "owns" this problem? The smoke bothers you, not your visitor, so it's your problem. Recall that BCF statements call on respondents to help you solve your problem, not to assess blame or evaluate the behavior. So, state the problem behavior clearly. Tell the person exactly what behavior bothers you. This approach reduces defensiveness and establishes an atmosphere of problem solving that keeps doors open. Telling the other person he is stupid to smoke and will get cancer will only make him defensive, and will likely start an argument rather than resolve the problem.

Think back to a conflict that wasn't handled well in a group you were a part of. How could the four steps to initiate a conflict resolution discussed here been implemented for a better outcome?

© Bananastock

Put yourself in the other person's position. What presentation would keep you most open to solutions? If possible, practice your BCF statement before you approach the other party—you don't want to lose your cool. Here's a BCF statement, "When you smoke in the locker room [behavior], I have trouble breathing and become nauseous [consequence], and I feel uncomfortable and irritated [feeling]."

2.  Present your BCF statement and agree on the conflict.

After you make your statement, let the other party respond. If they don't understand or refuse to acknowledge the problem, persist gently but firmly. You can't resolve a conflict if the other party won't acknowledge its existence. Explain the problem in different terms until you get an acknowledgment or realize that it's hopeless. But don't give up too easily.

3.  Ask for and give alternative conflict resolutions.

Ask the other party what she thinks can be done to resolve the conflict. If you agree, great; if not, offer your solution. The idea is to get to collaboration. If the other party acknowledges the problem but is not responsive to resolving it, appeal to common goals. Make her realize the benefits—to herself, to the team, and to the organization.

4.  Make an agreement for change.

Sometimes people don't realize that a specific behavior bothers you, but if you tell them about it using a good BCF statement, they may agree to change. Sometimes it's a two-way street, so find specific actions you can both take. Clearly state, or for complex agreements write down, the specific changes that all parties must make to resolve the conflict. People don't always live up to their agreements, so follow up to make sure the conflict is resolved.

TIME-OUT 11 Use figure 8.7 to outline how you could have resolved a conflict you recently faced.

## Responding to Conflict

Face it. There are times when you will say or do something that bothers someone, and they will confront you. As the responder, you have a responsibility to contribute to successful conflict resolution to solve a problem. You should follow the steps in the "Responding to conflict resolution" in the middle of figure 8.7. As you may know, some initiators will be emotional, but stay calm. Paraphrasing the conflict back to them using a good BCF statement and agreeing with something they say, even if you believe you did nothing wrong (you can at least say that you understand that your behavior upset them), can calm them and show that you understand the conflict. Asking for and giving alternative action can lead to a positive resolution.

## Mediating Conflict Resolution

Sometimes people in conflict cannot resolve their dispute alone. In these cases, mediators can be very helpful.[171] A **mediator** is a neutral third party who helps resolve conflict. In nonunionized organizations, managers are commonly the mediators. But some organizations have trained staff who are designated mediators. In unionized organizations, mediators are usually professionals from outside the organization. However, resolution should be sought internally first.

As a coach or sport manager, you may have to mediate a conflict between athletes or employees. Remember that you are a mediator, not a judge, and your job is to remain impartial, unless one party is breaking the rules. If one party says, "We cannot get along because of a personality conflict," focus on how the conflict is affecting their performance and the team. Ask them both to identify the specific behavior that bothers them using a BCF statement. Get the employees to resolve the conflict themselves if possible. Following the steps in the "Mediating conflict resolution" model in figure 8.7 will help resolve the conflict.

If the conflict is not resolved through mediation, an arbitrator may be used as a follow-up. An **arbitrator** is a neutral third party whose decisions are binding. Arbitrators commonly use negotiation. Arbitration should be kept to a minimum because it is not a collaborative style. Arbitration is more commonly used in sport than is mediation. The reason is that collective bargaining agreements in sport focus on arbitration instead of mediation.

# Stress

How we deal with power, politics, conflict, negotiation, and collaboration affects our level of stress.[172] Our lives today abound with tension caused by deadlines, traffic jams, long hours at work and school, the need to excel in an uncertain competitive climate, lack of time to fulfill our responsibilities—the list is seemingly endless. **Stress** is our body's internal reaction to external stimuli from the environment. Our emotional reactions drive our bodies' physical reactions. Stress is based on our perception of the situation. Your teammate may be very comfortable going up to bat or taking the shot under pressure to win the game, but you may be stressed. How well do you handle stress? In this section, you will learn about functional and dysfunctional stress, causes of stress, signs of stress, and, most important, how to manage stress and play the stress tug-of-war.

## Functional and Dysfunctional Stress

Stress is functional when it helps us perform better by challenging and motivating us to meet objectives. We all perform best under some pressure. When deadlines approach and the clock is ticking, our adrenaline flows, and we often rise to the occasion with better-than-usual performance. The operative word here is *some*: some pressure, but not too much. As you may know, you can overtrain or compete and burn out, which results in lower athletic performance.

Think of stress as existing on a bell-shaped curve. On one side, when you have too little stress, performance is lower; optimum stress (called *eustress*) is at the peak of the curve in the middle; too much stress moves you to the other side of the curve, which lowers your performance.[173] Or, think of a race car "stress-o-meter." In low gear you go slow; when the gauge is in the yellow zone, it's at its peak (time to shift), but going into the red can burn out the engine. What stresses you out?

Too much pressure is a serious problem in today's workplace. Excessive physical and mental stress can cause physical illness as well as mental and emotional problems. Too much stress increases appetite and cravings and leads to abdominal fat buildup and stomach problems; it can make you softer and heavier, disrupt your sleep, and leave you looking much older than you truly are. It can cause back, neck, shoulder and other pains, depression, ulcers, and heart disease.[174]

**Stressors** are situations in which people feel overwhelmed by anxiety, tension, and pressure. Stress that is constant, chronic, and severe can cause burnout. *Burnout* is the constant lack of interest and motivation to perform one's job because of too much stress.[175] From the organizational side, high stress results in job dissatisfaction, absenteeism, turnover, and lower levels of productivity.

## Causes of Stress

To overcome stress, it is important to understand what causes you stress. There are common job stressors. Before you read about them, complete Self-Assessment 8.4 to determine your stress personality type, which affects how you handle stress.

## SELF-ASSESSMENT 8.4

# What Is Your Stress Personality Type?

Identify how often each item applies to you at work or when you are playing on a team.

1 = rarely

2 = seldom

3 = occasionally

4 = frequently

5 = usually

_____ 1. I enjoy competition, and I work and play to win.

_____ 2. I skip meals or eat fast when there is a lot of work to do.

_____ 3. I'm in a hurry.

_____ 4. I do more than one thing at a time.

_____ 5. I'm aggravated and upset.

_____ 6. I get irritated or anxious when I have to wait.

_____ 7. I measure progress in terms of time and performance.

_____ 8. I push myself to work to the point of getting tired.

_____ 9. I work on days off.

_____ 10. I set short deadlines for myself.

_____ 11. I'm not satisfied with my accomplishments for very long.

_____ 12. I try to outperform others.

_____ 13. I'm not disturbed when my schedule has to be changed.

_____ 14. I consistently try to get more done in less time.

_____ 15. I take on more work when I already have plenty to do.

_____ 16. I enjoy work or school more than other activities.

_____ 17. I talk and walk fast.

_____ 18. I set high standards for myself and work hard to meet them.

_____ 19. I'm considered a hard worker.

_____ 20. I work at a leisurely pace.

_____ Total. Add up your scores (1-5) for all 20 items.

Your total score will fall between 20 and 100. Place an X on the following continuum that represents your score.

| Type A personality | 100 | 90 | 80 | 70 | 60 | 50 | 40 | 30 | 20 | Type B personality |
|---|---|---|---|---|---|---|---|---|---|---|

- *Type A, Type B personality.* Are you a type A or a type B personality? Type A personalities are characterized as fast moving, hard driving, time conscious, competitive, impatient, and preoccupied with work. Type B personalities are just the opposite of type A personalities. If you are a high type A personality, you may want to implement the stress management ideas presented here to offset the stress. There is also a type T thrill-seeking or risk-taking personality. People with type T personality find an outlet by participating in extreme sports. Are you an A or B, and should you make any changes?

- *Organizational culture and change.* The more type A the culture and the faster the rate of change, the more stress. What type of culture is a good fit for you?

- *Management's skill at managing.* Bad managers cause stress.[176] The more effectively managers supervise their employees, the less stress experienced by all. How much stress does your boss cause you and the rest of the team?

- *Work performed and time pressure.* Some work is more stressful than other work, and the time pressure of a deadline can help motivate you to complete the task,[177] but too much time pressure can be very stressful.[178] Part of our stress is determined by whether we enjoy our work. A secret to less stress and more success is to do the type of work you enjoy and that you are good at doing.

- *Human relations.* When people don't get along, stress increases. Our relationships with our coworkers are a very important factor in our job satisfaction. People who don't like their work but enjoy the people they work with can still be happy at work. Do you have good relationships with teammates and coworkers?

- *Smartphones.* Research shows that your phone is actually more of a time waster than a time saver; the average person stares at his phone 221 times per day. Repeatedly checking your phone, especially after work hours, can be stressful, which can cause long-term problems.[179] They are called cell phones because they make you prisoners in your little cell. How long can you go without checking your phone? Are you addicted to your phone? Should you make changes?

## Signs of Stress

It is important to understand when stress is coming on so that you can deal with it. Mild signs of stress include an increased breathing rate and an excessive amount of perspiration. When stress continues for a period of time, disillusionment, irritability, headaches and other body tension, a feeling of exhaustion, and stomach problems can result. When you continually feel pressured and fear that you aren't going to meet deadlines, you are experiencing stress. When you start to think about failing (missing that shot or striking out), you are feeling stress.

People under stress do many things to find relief. They watch TV, movies, or video games (too much); drink (too much) and take illegal drugs; eat (too much); sleep (too much); and turn to pornography and abusive sex. Do you do these things to relieve stress? Using these escapes for a short time to get through a bad situation may not have negative long-term effects. However, be careful, because these techniques can cause health problems over a longer period of time.

People who watch too much TV often lose their interest in exercising and playing sports; people who drink or take drugs can become addicted; people who overeat become overweight; and most miss out on experiencing life. Obesity is a major problem, and employee alcohol and drug use costs American businesses billions annually in lost production, absenteeism, and health costs. No one starts out thinking *I'm going to become inactive, fat, or addicted to substances*; it happens over time.

Besides, if you think about it, these techniques don't solve the problem that is stressing you, anyway. They are usually only a temporary escape from the stressor you have to face again. So now that we know what doesn't really work in dealing with stress, let's focus on what we can do to manage stress.

## Managing Your Stress

As already discussed, first you have to identify the stressors in your life. Next, you look at what's causing them and the consequences of living with them (and without them—maybe you really don't want to quit college!). Finally, you find ways to eliminate or decrease the stressors. Helping employees to stay fit increases productivity and is cost-effective; it improves the bottom line.[180] To combat the negative effects of stress, organizations are offering a variety of wellness programs. The stress management techniques we present here are widely effective, and you don't need to stress about using all of them or any that will cause you stress—pick the ones you will enjoy doing.

- *Manage your time.* Good time management skills can decrease job stress.[181] Chapter 14 gives details on time management.

- *Relax.* Start by getting enough rest to rejuvenate your body. Have some fun and laugh. Socialize with friends and family, listen to music, pray, meditate, find the ones that work for you. Going to practice and games relaxed, not stressed, will enhance your performance.

- *Use relaxation exercises.* Simple relaxation exercises can relieve stress. One of the most popular and simplest is deep breathing because it relaxes the entire body and can be done anywhere. Consciously relaxing your entire body from toe to head is another. Table 8.1 describes some relaxation exercises that you can do almost anywhere.

Deep breathing can be done during or between the other exercises. Simply take a slow, deep breath, preferably through your nose; hold it for a few seconds (count to five); then let it out slowly, preferably through lightly closed lips. Make sure that you inhale by expanding the stomach, not the chest. Breathe in without lifting your shoulders or expanding your chest. Think of your stomach as a balloon. Slowly fill it, and then empty it. As you inhale, visualize breathing in healing energy that makes you feel better, more energetic, and less pained. As you exhale, visualize breathing out tension, pain, illness, and other stress. Use this visualizing technique during the other relaxation exercises.

- *Sleep.* Sleep makes you more productive.[182] There is no magic number for everyone, but seven hours of sleep a night is recommended.[183] Hardworking athletes generally need more sleep than the average person to perform at the top of their game. Skimping on a full night's sleep, even by 20 minutes, impairs performance on and off the field and memory the next day,[184] and it also makes you more selfish, emotional, and more likely to get into arguments and hurt relationships.[185] Are you energetic, and do you recover sufficiently from your workouts?

- *Eat right.* Good health is essential to your performance on and off the field, and nutrition is a major factor in health. Stress often leads to overeating, and being overweight is itself stressful. Here's the short version to a healthy diet: Limit your intake of sugar and white flour (which most processed foods are full of); eat a good, high-protein breakfast; don't eat junk food; consume less fat (e.g., fried foods), caffeine, and salt; limit starchy carbohydrates (breads, grains, potatoes, rice, and so on); and eat more fruits and vegetables. You may like your soda and sport drinks (lots of sugar) and energy drinks (lots of caffeine), but they can cause health issues. Artificial sweeteners may not have sugar or calories, but they do increase your risk of weight gain, developing diabetes, and other health problems.[186] Consider drinking more water, which has health benefits.

- *Exercise.* You most likely already know how important exercise is to good health, and so do many organizations. But do you know that working out reduces the production of stress hormones, releasing stress?[187] Many firms pay all or part of gym memberships, and many have on-site exercise facilities and offer classes. More gyms leads to more sport management jobs. Exercising is an excellent way to break up your workday and release stress. Always check with a doctor before starting an exercise program. If you are on a competitive sport team, you are most likely exercising enough. If not, aerobic exercises that increase the heart rate for 30 minutes three or more times a week are generally recommended; interval training (faster and slower) is also recommended. The key is to pick an exercise you enjoy doing. If you hate to jog, how long will you stick with it?

## TABLE 8.1  Quick Tricks for Relaxation

| Muscles relaxed | Exercise |
|---|---|
| All | Take a deep breath, hold it for about five seconds, and then let it out slowly. See the text for details. Deep breathing may be performed during or between other relaxation methods. |
| Forehead | Wrinkle your forehead by trying to make your eyebrows touch your hairline for five seconds. Relax. |
| Eyes, nose | Close your eyes tightly for five seconds. Relax. |
| Lips, cheeks, jaw | Draw the corners of your mouth back tightly (grimace) for five seconds. Relax. |
| Neck | Drop your chin to your chest, and then slowly rotate your head without tilting it backward. Relax. |
| Shoulders | Lift your shoulders up toward your ears and tighten for five seconds. Relax. |
| Upper arms | Bend your elbows and tighten your upper arm muscles for five seconds. Relax. |
| Forearms | Extend your arms out against an invisible wall and push forward with your hands for five seconds. Relax. |
| Hands | Extend your arms in front of you and clench your fists tightly for five seconds. Relax. |
| Back | Lie on your back on the floor or on a bed and arch your back up off the floor while keeping your shoulders and buttocks on the floor. Tighten for five seconds. Relax. |
| Stomach | Suck in and tighten your stomach muscles for five seconds. Relax. Repeating this exercise several times throughout the day can help reduce the size of your waistline. |
| Hips, buttocks | Tighten buttocks for five seconds. Relax. |
| Thighs | Press your thighs together and tighten them for five seconds. |
| Feet, ankles | Flex your feet with toes pointing up as far as you can and tighten for five seconds, then point your feet down and tighten for five seconds. Relax. |
| Toes | Curl your toes under and tighten for five seconds, and then wiggle them. Relax. |

For all exercises, tighten your muscles as much as you can without straining, and perform as many tightening–relaxing repetitions as needed to feel relaxed without straining.

- *Think positively.* Optimistic personalities with positive attitudes experience less stress than pessimists because they focus on the positive, not on the negative.[188] Recall the importance of your thoughts; you become what you think, and you can become more positive. Get rid of your negative self-talk. Again, talk to yourself in the affirmative: "This is easy," or "I can do this." Repeat positive statements while doing deep breathing, but be realistic. Positive thinking doesn't guarantee that you will be free of stress headaches, but pessimism and negative self-talk push many people into headaches and various illnesses.

- *Don't procrastinate.* Procrastinating is stressful. When you procrastinate, you don't accomplish tasks that you're supposed to do. The resulting feeling of failure causes stress, and the longer you wait to do the task, the more stressed you get. Even if you eventually complete the task, the results will be poorer than they might have been had you not procrastinated. Follow Nike's advice and *Just Do It!* and you will avoid stress.

• *Don't be a perfectionist.* Striving for perfectionism is stressful. Here we are talking about work tasks, not athletic performance. Reworking something excessively usually isn't worth the time and effort, and it may make you rush through another task that is more important. Sometimes reworking actually makes things worse. Ever change a correct answer on an exam and gotten it wrong? Never change unless you are positive you are making an improvement. Define a job as done "perfectly enough," and stop.

• *Build a support network.* Talking to others about your stressful situation helps reduce stress. Talk to your friends, family, teammates, and coworkers—that's what they are there for. Don't be proud and clam up when things are getting you down. But don't continually complain and whine, either; you'll wear out the welcome mat. Be there for others in return; that's what networking relationships are all about.

> **TIME-OUT 12**
> Choose a major stressor in your life right now, and develop a plan to manage it, using the suggestions noted here or others that you think would work well for you.

> **TIME-OUT 13**
> Which of the stress management techniques noted here are you best at and worst at? Develop a plan to improve your weakest stress management skills.

• *Cut back smartphone checking.* Stop constantly checking your phone and going on social media. Set limits of frequency on checking it, such as only after you complete a certain amount of work, or every half hour. Even better, when you can, shut it off when you have a high-priority task to complete.[189]

## Stress Tug-of-War

**LEARNING OUTCOME 11** ▶

Explain the stress tug-of-war analogy.

View stress as a tug-of-war but with you in the center, as shown in figure 8.8 (or you are on a high wire act). On your left are ropes (causes of stress) pulling you to burnout (off balance). Stress that is too powerful will pull you off center (fall). On your right are ropes (stress management techniques) that you can use to pull yourself back to the center (keep your balance). The stress tug-of-war is an ongoing game. On easy days you move to the right, and on overly tough days you move to the left. Your objective in this game? Find

---

**APPLYING THE CONCEPT 8.4**

### Stress Management Techniques

Identify the technique being used in each statement.

    a. time management

    b. relaxation

    c. nutrition

    d. exercise

    e. positive thinking

    f. support network

_____ 16. I talk to myself to be more optimistic about my foul shooting.

_____ 17. I've set up a schedule for myself to meet season ticket sales goals.

_____ 18. I get up earlier and eat breakfast to improve my performance.

_____ 19. I'm talking to my partner about my problems in acquiring funding for our athletic department.

_____ 20. I pray.

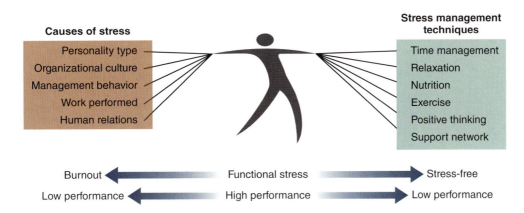

**FIGURE 8.8** The stress tug-of-war.

ways to stay centered (don't fall). But when you can't, it is also important to recover after being stressed out to avoid burnout.

Managing stress well doesn't mean that you have to use all the techniques. Use what works best for you, but be aware that taken together, the techniques add up to a pretty good definition of a healthy life. What if you are using these techniques and your stress levels are still off the charts? Consider getting out of the situation. Ask yourself two questions: "Is my long-term health important?" and "Is this situation worth hurting my health?" If you answered yes and no, in that order, it may be time to drop the ropes (climb back down) and walk away.

We've covered a lot in this chapter; you have learned about OB and creating win–win situations, about how your thoughts affect your behavior, the Big Five and your personality profile, about your attitudes and how they affect your performance and job satisfaction, how to use power and politics ethically to get what you want, how to manage conflicts, how to negotiate and collaborate, and how to manage your stress. Now it's time to apply this knowledge to develop the OB people skills that employers seek and to improve your quality of life and that of the people you interact with.

# LEARNING AIDS

## CHAPTER SUMMARY

1. **Describe the Big Five personality traits.**

   Five continuum traits exist: extrovert and introvert (the extroversion trait); cooperative and competitive (the agreeableness trait); stable and unstable (emotionalism); dependable and not dependable (conscientiousness); and willingness and unwillingness to try new things (openness to experience).

2. **Understand the perception process and the two factors on which it is based.**

   Perception is the process of selecting, organizing, and interpreting information from the external environment. How we do this is based on individual factors that include our personality and our attitudes. The second factor in the perception process is the information itself.

3. **Explain how personality, perception, and attitude are related and why they are important.**

   Our personalities affect our perceptions and our attitudes. Perception affects attitudes, and vice versa. Changing self-esteem and adjusting attitudes actually change single personality traits such as optimism. Personality, perception, and attitude are important because combined, they directly affect behavior and performance.

4. **State what job satisfaction is and why it is important.**

    Job satisfaction is a person's attitude toward her job. Job satisfaction is important because it has direct relationships with absenteeism, turnover, and performance.

5. **Define power, and explain the difference between position and personal power.**

    Power is the ability to influence others' behavior. Position power is derived from top management and delegated down the chain of command, whereas personal power is derived from the followers based on the individual's behavior.

6. **Explain how reward power, legitimate power, and referent power differ.**

    The difference is based on how the person with power influences others. Reward power is the user's ability to influence others with something of value to them. Legitimate power is given by the organization and is a type of position power. Referent power has to do with the user's personal power relationship with others.

7. **Understand how power and politics are related.**

    Power is the ability to influence the behavior of others. Politics is the process of gaining and using power. Therefore, political skills are a part of power.

8. **Explain what networking, reciprocity, and coalitions have in common.**

    Networking, reciprocity, and coalitions are all political behaviors. Networking is used to develop relationships to gain social or business advantage. Reciprocity is used to create obligations and develop alliances and then use them to accomplish objectives. Coalitions are alliances of people with similar objectives who together have a better chance of achieving their objectives.

9. **Describe the five conflict management styles.**

    Avoiders passively ignore conflict rather than resolve it. Accommodators resolve conflict by passively giving in to the other party. Forcers use aggressive behavior to get their own way. Negotiators resolve conflict through assertive give-and-take concessions. Collaborators resolve the conflict by finding the solution that is agreeable to all parties.

10. **Use collaboration to resolve conflict.**

    Collaboration involves (1) planning a BCF statement that maintains your ownership of the problem, (2) presenting your BCF statement, (3) agreeing on the conflict, (4) asking for or giving alternative solutions, (5) agreeing on change, and (6) following up to see whether the conflict was truly resolved.

11. **Explain the stress tug-of-war analogy.**

    The stress tug-of-war puts us between stressors that try to pull us off balance and stress management techniques that can keep us centered so that our stress is at functional levels and our performance is high. If the causes of stress pull us off center, we burn out, and our performance suffers.

## REVIEW AND DISCUSSION QUESTIONS

1. Are the conflicts that the USADA faces functional or dysfunctional?

2. How could the USADA use negotiation to solve some of its conflicts?

3. Could the USADA use mediation to solve some of its conflicts?

4. Can college athletes use stress management to improve their performance?

5. What are the Big Five personality traits?

6. What are the four biases in perception?

7. What factors determine job satisfaction? Are they of equal importance to everyone?

8. What are the seven bases of power?

9. Can management order the end of power and politics in the organization? Should it? Why or why not?

10. Why should you learn your organization's culture and identify power players where you work?

11. How do you know when you are in conflict?

12. What is the difference between functional and dysfunctional conflict, and how does each affect performance?

13. What is the primary reason for your personal conflicts? Your work conflicts?

14. What is meant by "ownership of the problem"?

15. How are BCF statements used?

16. What is the difference between a mediator and an arbitrator?

17. What are the characteristics of type A personalities?

18. What type T sports do you like to either participate in or watch on screen?

19. What are some stress management techniques?

20. Draw a simple diagram of John Wooden's pyramid of success. You can find it at the official Wooden website www.coachwooden.com/index2.html.

## CASES

### Sport Management Professionals @ Work: Nate Weissman

Nate Weissman is living his dream working in professional baseball. Nate went to college to pursue a sport management major with the goal of working in baseball.

Nate's journey started to kick into action during his internship, which was coordinated with the help of his instructors at Springfield College. Nate packed his bags, left home for the first time, and was fortunate to land an internship in the summer of 2017 in the front office of the Iowa Cubs, the Chicago Cubs' Triple A team.

Nate was also fortunate to work in baseball operations with Chatham of the Cape Cod League. The Cape Cod League is a collegiate summer league that has developed over 1,100 major league players, including over 250 current major leaguers.

Nate paid his own way to attend the Major League Baseball Winter Meetings. His goal was to make some more contacts in baseball. His hard work paid off, and he found a position as assistant director of operations for the Midland Rock Hounds, an Oakland A's affiliate in the Class AA Texas League.

Nate's job is to make sure everything about the game-day event is ready long before the first pitch is delivered. He works 16-hour days since he is also required to close up the stadium after the game is over.

Nate loves his job! He wants to work in baseball for the rest of his life.[190]

### Case Questions

1. What sport do you love that you would like to pursue?

2. What conventions or conferences can you attend to network with professionals in the sport you would like to work in?

3. Would you be willing to be a part of minor league baseball?

### A Tale of Two Athletic Directors: The Politics of Career Moves in College Sports

So, you still think being an athletic director (AD) for a major university is an easy job? Think again. For instance, scheduling games in all sports and at all divisions has become increasingly more complex. The need to have open dates to play in busy arenas, transportation costs for each team, referee availability, weather concerns, gasoline costs, and housing costs all make the process very complex. As an AD, even when you are successful, your career may suffer. On the other hand, you can lose the vast majority of the games you schedule and still score a big payday and promotion.

This case involves the scheduling of NCAA football games where one team is almost certain to lose. We look at how two teams, the University of Tennessee–Chattanooga and the University of Massachusetts–Amherst, schedule football games against various BCS opponents such as Alabama, LSU, and Florida State. These are games that both UTC and UMass were virtually guaranteed to lose. They are, from the higher-ranked team's perspective, cupcake games.[191] According to ESPN writer Darren Rovell, "Big Ten teams will pony up the most money in the so-called 'guarantee' games, which compensate smaller budget opponents for playing at the bigger opponent's stadium without returning to play at their stadium."[192] What are the costs and benefits from the UTC and UMass AD's perspective? What are the costs and benefits from a BCS team's perspective?

Why would Alabama want to play UTC? Why would Florida want to play UMass? Wouldn't they be able to make more money with a higher-ranked opponent? This appears to violate Rottenberg's uncertainty of outcome hypothesis, which states that sports fans value competitive contests. One study found that fans prefer their home team to win 60 to 70 percent of the time, meaning fan interest is greatest when this is the case. A league that becomes too unbalanced will lose fan support and the subsequent revenue brought by those fans.[193] The New York Yankees as well as the entire American League actually saw stagnation and decline in attendance over the course of the Yankees' incredible dominance in the 1950s.[194] In these cupcake games, the odds are closer to 99 percent that the home team with the big-time program will win.

So it might seem strange that big programs want to schedule these games at all. However, the games do make economic sense for the ADs in question. For some big schools, home games against top-tier opponents do not gain much revenue compared to games against teams from lesser conferences. The difference in revenue depends mostly on ticket prices because the best teams sell out their stadiums no matter who they are playing. In 2010, Ohio State's home schedule included a game against No. 12 Miami and, two weeks later, a game against Eastern Michigan, which would finish near the bottom of the Mid-American Conference. The Miami game earned Ohio State $959,672 more than the Eastern Michigan game. The total gate revenue in 2010 for seven home games was $42,181,260. So the loss was $959,672 compared to $42.2 million total season gate revenue, or about 2 percent. This has to be weighed against the much higher probability of losing a game to a tougher opponent and with that loss missing out on a higher-ranking bowl bid and perhaps a shot at the national title. Those bowl games offer significant payouts for the entire conference.[195] Playing a tough out-of-conference home game is a risky bet. Playing a UTC is not.

Through this year, UTC was on track to make $4.2 million on these games since 2010. UTC was happy to receive almost half a million dollars—$467,000—per game. The $467,000 average from those cupcake games was roughly double the entire athletic department's annual recruiting budget of $227,364 for all sports. UMass has done even better, pulling in $4 million in just four years between 2013 and 2016. "I think what it illustrates is what we said from the beginning—the income potentials at the Football Bowl Subdivision level are so significantly different than what they are at the Football Championship Subdivision level," UMass athletic director John McCutcheon said. "Yes, the expenses are higher, but your opportunities for income are exponentially higher.[196]

On April 20, 2011, UMass announced its move to the Football Bowl Subdivision (FBS) and the Mid-American Conference (MAC), and it said it would play a full FBS and MAC schedule beginning with the 2012 football season. Thus it wanted to develop a strong nonconference schedule that would help build its growing football program. University of Michigan athletic director Dave Brandon was looking for a game with a lower-tier opponent since Michigan had a difficult schedule against many college football powerhouses, such as Alabama, Notre Dame, and Nebraska.

In addition to the financial reward for UTC, there are other benefits to playing a game you know you will probably lose. "They are hard games," said Huesman, the Mocs' head coach. "When you play Alabama, you know that you're playing one of the best in the country and it's really not a fair playing field, obviously. But you just wanna compete, and that's what I tell our guys: 'Just compete, and go make plays.'"[197]

UTC was happy to receive $467,000 a year from cupcake games to help build its football program, and it was winning many games despite the guaranteed losses. The Mocs were Southern Conference Champions in 2013, 2014, and 2015. UMass, on the other hand, had a terrible record over the period. Between 2012 and 2015, UMass had a 7-25 record in the Mid-American Conference and 8-40 overall. While both UMass and UTC appear to have been very successful financially, the two athletic directors who guided these programs suffered very different fates.

In 2015 the UMass athletic director John McCutcheon landed the AD job at the University of California–Santa Barbara. McCutcheon was hired at UMass in 2004. Before that, he spent 13 years at California Polytechnic in San Luis Obispo from 1992 to 2004, and before that, he spent 12 years at Boston College. His last contract with UMass through 2016 paid him $259,338 per year.[198]

David Blackburn was the University of Tennessee–Chattanooga's athletic director from 2013 to 2017. He earned $185,000 a year. After a short four-year stint as AD and the three championships, he resigned amid speculation about the administration's unhappiness with his performance at UTC.[199]

Go to the web study guide to answer questions about this case study.

## @ TAKE IT TO THE NET

Please visit www.HumanKinetics.com/AppliedSportManagementSkills and go to this book's companion web study guide, where you will find the following:

A list of websites associated with the concepts in this chapter

Skill-Builder exercises, Sports and Social Media exercises, and a continuing Game Plan for Starting a Sport Business

Online versions of chapter exercises and end-of-chapter learning aids

An exercise that helps you define the Key Terms

# Team Development

## LEARNING OUTCOMES

After studying this chapter, you should be able to

1.  explain how groups and teams differ;

2.  explain the group performance model;

3.  categorize groups by their structure;

4.  define the three major roles group members play;

5.  explain how rules and norms differ;

6.  describe cohesiveness and why it is important to teams;

7.  describe the five major stages of group development and the leadership style appropriate for each stage;

8.  explain how group managers and team leaders differ; and

9.  lead a meeting.

## KEY TERMS

group

team

group performance model

group structure dimensions

group types

command groups

task groups

group composition

group process

group process dimensions

group roles

norms

group cohesiveness

status

stages of group development

## DEVELOPING YOUR SKILLS

For groups to maximize their performance, they must have effective organizational context, group structures, group process, and group development. In this chapter, the skills focus is on developing group process skills, analyzing the group's development stage, and selecting the leadership style appropriate to the stage. You can also develop your skills at leading and participating in meetings, including dealing with problem team members in meetings.

## REVIEWING THEIR GAME PLAN

### Getting Kids to Team Play

Playing together, learning together, working together: These activities start early in life and continue throughout our lives. They shape us in crucial and fundamental ways into functioning adults, functioning communities, and functioning societies. Set them up wrong and you can take the word *functioning* out of the preceding sentence. Our society tries in many ways to keep the next generation *functioning*. Groups like the Boys & Girls Clubs of America, the YMCA, Jewish Community Centers (JCCs), town sport leagues, and Little League Baseball—to name only a very few—all work to shape kids into team players and high-functioning adults.

The mission of the Boys & Girls Clubs of America is simple—to be available for kids. As the organization notes in its mission statement, "In every community, boys and girls are left to find their own recreation and companionship in the streets. An increasing number of children are at home with no adult care or supervision. Young people need to know that someone cares about them." Boys & Girls Clubs offer that and more. Club programs and services instill a sense of competence, usefulness, belonging, and influence. "Boys & Girls Clubs are a safe place to learn and grow—all while having fun. They are truly The Positive Place for Kids."[1]

The After School All-Stars can be found in Atlanta, Cleveland, Hawaii, Los Angeles, and many other locations. Their mission is to provide comprehensive after-school programs that keep children safe and help them succeed in school and in life. After School All-Stars offers *Sports as a Hook* with the idea that young people's participation in sports decreases the likelihood that they will engage in risky and violent behavior. Kids who form relationships with mentors, such as coaches, are 46 percent less likely to start using drugs and 27 percent less likely to start drinking alcohol.[2]

Whether leading basketball at the YMCA, coaching softball at the JCC, or leading a Boy Scout or Girl Scout troop, the men and women in these organizations devote their lives to helping kids and being positive role models. Their dream? That eventually the kids they coach will carry forward the torch of good sport conduct, integrity and hard work, and a love of sport as coaches, parents, teammates, teachers, and community leaders.

These organizations also need sport management students and alumni. Join them—it's time for you to take up the torch. You can either volunteer or look for careers helping these organizations. You will find that this is a boomerang endeavor. What you give away will come back in deep satisfaction, in surprising joy, in strength you never knew you had, and in wisdom you won't gain anywhere else. For example, the 2018 NBA All-Star Game in Los Angeles included events geared toward youth. The NBA, Under Armour, the Ross Initiative in Sports for Equality (RISE), and the Boys & Girls Clubs of Metro LA brought together local youth and Los Angeles Police Department officers. The program featured a combination of on-court basketball training and hands-on leadership activities developed by RISE and designed to inspire dialogue and build trust.[3]

For current information on local recreation centers, see www.afterschoolallstars.org/ programs/ for After School All-Stars, www.bgca.org for the Boys & Girls Clubs of America, www.ymca.net for the YMCA, and www.jcca.org for the JCC Association of North America.

# Importance of Teamwork to Performance

You might be familiar with the saying, There is no "I" in "team." On the other hand, managers have to be sure there is "team" in teamwork! Although there are great leaders, they know that success belongs to the team. You already understand the importance of teamwork to athletic performance. The same teamwork skills need to be applied to both athletics and sport management. Organizations are increasingly using team-based organizational structures to foster creativity and innovation (chapter 6).[4] Your teamwork skills are based on your ability to work well in teams (people skills, chapter 1), which is based on developing good relationships.[5] Thus, teamwork skills are becoming more important, and recruiters are looking to hire job candidates with the ability to work well within teams.[6]

Did you ever experience a great sense of teamwork when you belonged to a youth organization?

You have developed some teamwork skills that will help you get a job, so including team experience on your résumé is a sure winner. But in hiring sport managers, firms are seeking candidates with team leadership–related knowledge and skills, especially for dealing with team challenges. By reading this chapter, you can improve your teamwork skills, but more important to sport management, you can understand the factors that contribute to team performance, learn how to improve team performance, and develop some team leadership

## SELF-ASSESSMENT 9.1

### Are You an Individual or Team Player?

Answer the questions on a scale from 1 to 5. Place the number (1-5) on the line before the question.

1 = not very descriptive of me

2 = somewhat descriptive of me

3 = neutral

4 = descriptive of me

5 = very descriptive of me

_____  1. I focus on what I accomplish during team projects.

_____  2. Compromise comes easily to me.

_____  3. I depend on me to get things done.

_____  4. I prefer to work alone rather than in a group.

_____  5. I like to do things my way.

_____  6. I'm comfortable delegating work to others.

_____  7. I know that teams do better when each member has a separate job.

_____  8. I'm more productive when I work alone.

_____  9. I try to get things done my way when I work with others.

_____  10. It doesn't bother me if my team or group doesn't want to do things my way.

Add up your scores, place the number here _____ , and put it on the following continuum.

| Individual | | | Team player | |
|---|---|---|---|---|
| 10 | 20 | 30 | 40 | 50 |

There is no right or wrong here, but the manager's job is to get the work done through others. If you have a very high score, indicating individuality, you may want to work at being more of a team player. You may also consider seeking a professional job (e.g., sales) within the field of sport management rather than a supervisory position.

skills. Team skills are people skills,[7] so essentially all of the skills covered in other chapters will improve your teamwork.[8] But before reading on, complete Self-Assessment 9.1 to determine whether you are more of an individual player or a team player.

## Lessons of the Geese

Ever wondered why geese fly south for the winter in V formations? What scientists have found has implications that teams would do well to learn and apply.

- Each bird flapping its wings creates an uplift (thrust) for the bird following. Flying in a V adds 71 percent to the flying range compared to flying in disorganized clusters or flying alone.

   Lesson: Travel on each other's thrust (synergy). A common direction and a sense of community can get your team to the finish line faster and more easily.

- Falling out of formation causes individual birds to feel the sudden drag and the higher resistance of going it alone. This helps them to continually adjust their flying to keep the formation.

   Lesson: There is strength, power, and safety in members who travel in the same direction.

- When lead birds get tired, they rotate to the back of the formation, and another goose flies point.

   Lesson: Take turns doing the hard jobs.

- Geese at the back of the V honk to encourage front flyers to maintain their speed.

   Lesson: We all need to be reminded with active support and praise.

- When a goose gets sick or is wounded and falls out of the V, two geese follow it down to help and protect it. They stay with the downed goose until the crisis is resolved, and then they launch out on their own in a V formation to catch up with their group.

   Lesson: Stand by each other in times of need.

## There Are Groups and There Are Teams

**LEARNING OUTCOME 1** ▶

Explain how groups and teams differ.

Although we often use the words *group* and *team* interchangeably, they are different. All teams are groups, but not all groups are teams. **Groups** have a clear leader and two or more members who perform independent jobs with individual accountability, evaluation, and rewards. **Teams** are groups whose members share leadership and whose members perform interdependent jobs, with individual and group accountability, evaluation, and rewards. Team members tend to be more engaged than group members, which results in higher profits.[9] Table 9.1 and figure 9.1 further distinguish between groups and teams.

As table 9.1 and figure 9.1 show, it's not always easy to clearly distinguish when a group is also a team. The reason is that there are shades of team and group structures—they exist on a continuum—and most groups lie somewhere in between "extreme groups" (with little latitude in autonomy) and "extreme teams" (with great latitude in autonomy). Group managers are directive, and teams share leadership.[10] The terms *management directed*, *semiautonomous*, and *self-managed* (or *self-directed*) are commonly used to differentiate groups along this continuum. Management-directed groups are clearly groups, self-directed groups are clearly teams, and semi-autonomous groups are somewhere in between.

 **TIME-OUT 1** Describe a current work group or team you play for in terms of figure 9.1 and the six characteristics given in table 9.1. Use this group or team for the remaining Time-Outs in this chapter.

## TABLE 9.1 Differences Between Groups and Teams

| Characteristics | Groups | Teams |
|---|---|---|
| Size | Two or more; can be large. | Typically 5 to 12 members. |
| Leadership | One clear leader makes decisions. | Leadership is shared among members. |
| Jobs | Jobs are distinct and clear-cut; individual members do one independent part of the work. | Jobs are fluid and overlap in responsibility and tasks performed. Members perform many interdependent tasks with complementary skills; the team completes an entire task or project. |
| Accountability and evaluation | Leader evaluates each member's performance. | Members evaluate each other's individual performance and the group's performance. |
| Rewards | Rewards are based on individual performance. | Rewards are based on both individual and group performance. |
| Objectives | Set by the organization and group leader. | Objectives are set by the organization and the team. |

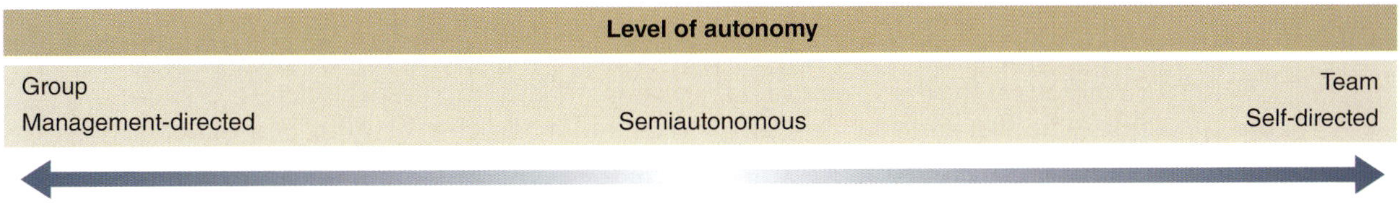

**Level of autonomy**

Group
Management-directed

Semiautonomous

Team
Self-directed

**FIGURE 9.1** Level of autonomy.

## APPLYING THE CONCEPT 9.1

### Is It a Group or Is It a Team?

Identify each statement as characteristic of (a) a group or (b) a team.

_____ 1. My boss conducts my performance appraisals, and I get good ratings.

_____ 2. We don't have departmental goals; we just do the best we can to accomplish our mission.

_____ 3. My compensation is based primarily on my club's performance.

_____ 4. I get the assembled tennis racket from Jean; then I paint it and send it to Tony for packaging.

_____ 5. There are about 30 people in my department.

# Group Performance Model

The performance of groups and teams is based on many variables that we sort into four key factors (as shown in figure 9.2).[11] In the **group performance model**, performance is a function of organizational context, group structure, group process, and group development stage. Groups and teams are affected by the systems effect (chapter 1): Each group or department's performance is affected by at least one other team, and each department affects the performance of the total organization.[12] Or, each factor is like a link on a chain; if any factor is weak, the team can fall apart. Before we get into the details of the four factors, read about pro team success next.

## High Performance and Evaluating Team Worth

Bill Belichick's phenomenal success in leading the New England Patriots to six Super Bowl victories is the stuff legends are made of. Belichick no doubt has other pro teams scratching their heads. The top Patriots players are willing to be paid less than market value to be part of a team with a strong chance of winning the Super Bowl again. How does he do it? Everyone on the team knows that star quarterback Tom Brady set an example of team behavior that any new players joining the team are expected to follow.[13]

What is the key to making teams in pro sport and in business work? Valuing everyone's contributions. This means that team members must understand and accept the idea that some players or workers are the stars and are key to the team's success. Of course, the flip (and equally important) side is that star players and star workers need to understand that they can't win alone—the team must work together seamlessly. This is especially true for the Patriots.

Determining the value of pro teams is a sport unto itself these days. *Forbes* rated the NFL Dallas Cowboys ($4.2 billion), the New England Patriots ($3.7 billion), and the New York Giants ($3.3 billion) as the three most valuable teams.[14] Why is this of such interest? Because pro sport teams are first and foremost businesses, and increasing the value of a franchise is good business (buy, make money, and sell higher). Building a strong team brand is a surefire way to increase the value of a franchise because each league can produce only one champion a year. Losing teams need to make money, too. Building fan trust in the team is more important than focusing too much on player identification, and it's more important in the long run than a short-term strategy of attracting star players.

## Organizational Context

A number of factors in the organization and the environment—called context—affect how groups function and their level of performance. We already discussed these factors in previ-

| Group performance | (f) | Organizational context | Group structure | Group process | Group development stage |
|---|---|---|---|---|---|
| High to low | | Environment<br>Mission<br>Strategy<br>Culture<br>Structure<br>Systems and processes | Type<br>Size<br>Composition<br>Leadership<br>Objectives | Roles<br>Norms<br>Cohesiveness<br>Status<br>Decision making<br>Conflict resolution | Orientation<br>Dissatisfaction<br>Resolution<br>Production<br>Termination |

(f) = a function of

**FIGURE 9.2** Group performance model.

ous chapters. So the next three major sections focus on group structure, group process, and stages of group development.

# Group Structure

**Group structure dimensions** include group leadership, type, size, composition, and objectives (see figure 9.3). These five dimensions of group structure are discussed in this section. A major challenge of teamwork is creating a group structure that effectively coordinates individual team members with teams and departments.[15]

## Group Leadership

To a large extent, leaders determine group structure, which can result in either success or failure.[16] The leader's relationships with team members differ, and these relationships affect team performance. Generally, better relationships lead to higher performance. Thus, your success and the fate of your teams will be determined by how effectively you lead them. Table 9.1 highlights the fact that the leadership requirements for groups and teams are different; team leaders share the leadership responsibility as they empower the team members.[17]

   **Sport Management Implications.** Leadership is often a response to environment, context, group size, composition, and objectives. Thus, team leadership is becoming increasingly important.[18] You will learn more about group leadership as a team member and as a manager throughout this chapter.

## Types of Groups

**Group types** can be formal or informal, functional or cross-functional, and command or task. We spend a great deal of our life working in groups. Thus, you need to understand the different types of groups that you will be part of during your career.

◀ LEARNING OUTCOME 3
Categorize groups by their structure.

### Formal or Informal

Formal groups, such as departments, are created by organizations as their official structures. Informal groups are not part of the organization's official structure; they are spontaneous creations that occur when members come together voluntarily because of similar interests, like sports.[19] You get a job in formal groups, and you develop informal relationships and

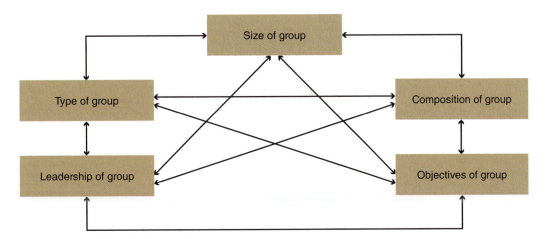

**FIGURE 9.3**   How groups are structured. The arrows indicate the effect that each dimension affects and is affected by (or systems interrelationship).

form informal groups, often through networking (chapter 8).[20] People join a formal team when they join a Little League Baseball or college intramural team. They join an informal team when they play a pickup game of baseball in their neighborhood, with their college friends, or at a Boys & Girls Club.

Do you recall having a better experience on formal or informal teams when you were younger?

## Functional or Cross-Functional

Groups organized by function (vertically) perform work of one type. Accounting, human resources, and sales departments are functional groups. Groups whose members come from different functional areas are cross-functional (horizontal) groups. Groups organized around projects are typically cross-functional groups. Managers coordinate activities between functional and cross-functional groups,[21] and thus they serve as links between them (see figure 9.4).[22] Rensis Likert called this the linking-pin role. Higher-level managers need to make important decisions across functional areas. The use of cross-functional groups is on the rise because of the need to coordinate functional areas.[23]

## Command or Task

**Command groups** consist of managers and their staffs, and they get the job done—whatever the job is. People are hired to be a part of a command group, such as a Formula 1 racing team. Command groups can be either functional or cross-functional. The president and vice presidents in an organization form a cross-functional command group; each vice president and her managers form a functional command group.

**Task groups** are composed of staff who work on specific objectives—that is, they are committees. There are two primary forms of task groups: task forces and standing committees.

*Task forces*, also called *ad hoc committees*, are temporary groups formed for a specific purpose. Project teams and ad hoc committees (chapter 5) are task groups in which members

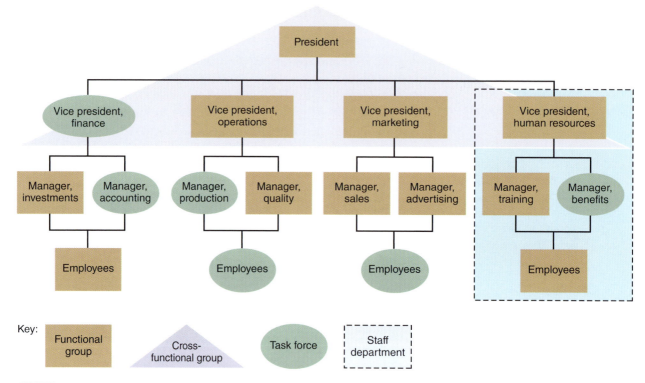

**FIGURE 9.4** Functional and cross-functional groups. Each manager serves as the linking pin between groups vertically and horizontally.

have a functional leader and work with cross-functional departments as needed. One person from each functional area involved in the work serves on the task force. Volunteers in sport organizations are often placed on task forces (temporary commit-

**TIME-OUT 2** Identify the task groups in the organization you work for or play for. Specify whether they are task forces or standing committees.

tees) to help with specific tasks. For instance, at the Olympics, volunteers coach, perform marketing activities, assist in medical situations, and distribute food and water at events.

*Standing committees* are permanent groups that work on ongoing organizational issues. Membership in standing committees is often rotated every year so that new ideas and fresh perspectives are brought in. For example, UMass tenure and promotion committee membership may be for three years, with one-third of the committee replaced every year. Some firms have budget committees and sport event committees.

Command groups and task groups differ in several ways. One difference is the membership. Command groups are usually (although not always) functional, whereas task groups are typically cross-functional. Another difference is in who belongs to which type of group. Everyone in an organization belongs to a command group, but employees often work for organizations for many years without ever serving on a task force or standing committee. Generally, the higher the level of management, the more time is spent serving in task groups.

With the advances in information and telecommunications technologies, there are new ways of structuring, processing, and distributing work and overcoming the barriers of distance and time.[24] Globalization has produced an increase in the use of global virtual teams. The members of *global virtual teams* are physically located in different places around the world, but they work together as a team. MNCs such as Nike are using virtual teams to develop new global products and are selling them online and by phone 24/7/365.

**Sport Management Implications.** As a team member, you will belong to various groups, and you can provide leadership. As a manager, you will lead a formal, functional command group. You will also participate in informal groups, and you may serve on global virtual teams, a task force, and standing committees using the skills you develop in this chapter and throughout the book.

## Group Size

There is no ideal group size. The sizes of groups vary depending on their purpose. But groups tend to be larger than teams.[25] Groups that are too small limit ideas and creativity and tend to be too cautious. Issues of overwork and burnout can also arise with small groups because the workload is not distributed among enough members. Conversely, groups that are too large tend to be slow;[26] individuals don't always get to contribute as much as they can in smaller groups,[27] and some members just sit back and let the others do all the work—these people are called *social loafers* or *free riders*.[28]

**Sport Management Implications.** Group size affects group process, so your leadership style must be tailored to the size of the group. The larger the group, the more formal or autocratic the leadership should be. Smaller groups need less formal and more participative management styles. Larger groups inhibit equal participation. Generally, participation is most equal in groups of around five. This is why teams are small. The larger the group, the more the members need support in the form of formal structured plans, policies, procedures, and rules.

Did you like smaller or larger groups in your youth?

As a manager, you usually don't select the size of your command group—your span of management (chapter 5).[29] However, as the manager of a large department, you can choose to organize your group into teams. Committee chairs can often select the group's size, and in doing so, you should keep the group size appropriate for the task and select the best group composition.[30] Although size should vary based on the task, having five to nine members generally provides the best relationships and performance.[31]

## Composing the Group

**Group composition** is the mix of members' skills and abilities. It doesn't matter what type and size team you lead; its performance will be affected by its composition,[32] and diversity provides group benefits (chapter 2).[33] Although some positions are more important than others, it takes an entire team to succeed. Having a great baseball pitching staff is important, but you can't win without hitters. Even a great NFL football quarterback like Tom Brady needs competent receivers to catch the ball and an offensive line to block so he has the time to execute the plays, not to mention an entire Patriots defensive squad to stop the other team from scoring more points.

Deciding whom to put on a project or a team is one of the biggest challenges facing a manager or team leader, and determining how to mix and match newcomers with old-timers to form new configurations is an important decision in designing teams. Coaches in the NFL, the NCAA, and high school face this decision every season. New England Patriots coach Bill Belichick is known for bringing in a few key players every year and bringing in a few complementary players at the same time. Belichick blends the acquisition of key star players and a few complementary players and stockpiles draft picks, a technique that has been used as a blueprint for many teams in the NFL.

**Sport Management Implications.** Attracting, selecting, and retaining the best people for the team or job are among the most important functions of a manager, and this really hits home when building teams. You need to select the right mix of skills and abilities for your team to win and for your organization to perform at high levels.[34] So, when assembling teams, choose people with complementary knowledge and skills, rather than people with the same skills, to maximize performance.[35]

## Objectives

In chapter 4, we explored the benefits of setting objectives. These benefits apply to both individuals and groups. In groups, objectives are commonly very broad—usually about

**?** Did you prefer to belong to competitive teams when you played sports as a youth? Were the teams you played on as a youth cohesive? Were they diversified?

How may a youth sport league face the same challenges to group composition as a NFL coach?

fulfilling the organization's mission. Teams often develop their own objectives. One reason teams often outperform groups is that having developed their objectives, they own them in a way that groups do not. A sport team might set goals to improve on

TIME-OUT
3

State the type of group or team you belong to and describe its size, composition, leadership, and objectives.

last year's win–loss record, to make the playoffs, or to win the championship. Recreational sport teams might emphasize teamwork and exercise. Work teams might set objectives to increase customer satisfaction, sales, or profits.

Setting and then achieving objectives lead to increased confidence, motivation, and job satisfaction. Motivational speaker, ESPN college football analyst, and former football coach Lou Holtz of the national championship winner University of Notre Dame and the University of South Carolina stated that "of all my experiences in managing people, the power of goal setting is the most incredible."[36]

**Sport Management Implications.** As a leader or as a member with leadership skills, be sure that the group or team has clear objectives. Be sure to use the setting objectives model: To + Action Verb + Specific and Measurable Result + Target Date. Following is an example of how W.L. Gore implements team structure.

W.L. Gore & Associates offers 124 products. You may wear clothing with GORE-TEX® (a waterproof, breathable, windproof fabric). The Gore organizational structure is a contemporary design with no rigid hierarchy; it is a team-based, networking, learning organization (chapter 5). Managers are called leaders who oversee teams. Teams in Gore's "*latticework*" structure set objectives and are responsible for achieving them. Team members select new members, and they evaluate each other, including ranking each other based on who is adding the most value to the company, which affects individual pay raises. In addition, Gore rewards all associates (they are not called employees) with good compensation, including profit sharing and stock options (chapter 7).

It is about how members get along, not how they do their work. **Group process dimensions** are *roles, norms, cohesiveness, status, decision making,* and *conflict resolution*. These components are discussed in the following section.

# Group Process

**Group process** is the patterns of interactions that emerge as group members work together. *Group dynamics* is another word for group process.[37] Dynamics are about how people work together (build relationships) as they get the work done, not how they do the work itself. It's important because relationships affect our behavioral interactions in teams,[38] and group process affects team performance.[39] Group process often changes over time, and it is not something most people figure out on their own. But careful and thoughtful training in group process like we offer here is crucial for teams to be effective.

The six group process dimensions are roles, norms, cohesiveness, status, decision making, and conflict resolution.

## Group Roles

*Job roles* are shared expectations of how group members will fulfill the requirements of their positions—what they do to get the job done—whereas group roles are the roles used through the group process—how members interact as they work.

Group roles are different from job roles;[40] group roles focus on how people interact as they do the job, and they can either help or hinder getting the job done. Roles do change with organizational changes (chapter 6).[41] For high levels of performance, job roles and group roles should be compatible.[42] **Group roles** are task, maintenance, and self-interest.

◄ LEARNING OUTCOME 4

Define the three major roles group members play.

### Three Group Roles

- Group members play *task roles* when they do and say things that help to accomplish the group's objectives.[43] Task roles are often described as structuring, job centered, production, task oriented, and directive.

- Group members play *maintenance roles* when they do and say things that shape and sustain the group process.[44] Maintenance roles are described as employee centered, relationship oriented, and supportive.

- Members play *self-interest roles* when they do and say things that help themselves but hurt the group. People with narcissistic personalities only focus on personal gain,[45] but self-centered people are less happy than those who look out for others.[46] Are you and your teammates and coworkers just looking out for yourselves or for the team?

### How Group Roles Affect Performance

To be effective, groups need their members to focus on both their task roles and their maintenance roles while minimizing self-interest roles. When members focus only on tasks, performance can suffer because maintenance roles not only help members deal with conflict effectively but also develop relationships.[47] Group process without maintenance roles may even become dysfunctional. Obviously, groups whose members focus solely on having a great time don't get the job done, and self-interest roles hamper team performance.

Group performance typically improves dramatically when members aren't concerned about who gets credit for specific accomplishments (e.g., when they demonstrate teamwork by passing the ball rather than letting one person try to score all the points). Pat Riley, an NBA Miami Heat executive and former head coach of five championship teams, said the most difficult thing for individuals on any team to do is to sacrifice, but without sacrifice the team will never reach its full potential. Sometimes you need to "take one for the team." Do you?

**TIME-OUT 4** State the primary group roles played in your current work group or team.

### Sport Management Implications

Savvy group leaders and members identify the roles being played in their groups and facilitate helping behaviors between members. If no other team member is playing the

---

## APPLYING THE CONCEPT 9.2

### Roles

Identify the role fulfilled in each statement.

a. task

b. maintenance

c. self-interest

_____ 6. Wait. We can't decide yet—we haven't heard Rodney's idea.

_____ 7. I don't understand. Could you explain why we're practicing our power play again?

_____ 8. We've tried that play before; it doesn't work. My play is much better.

_____ 9. What does "who's going to the dance?" have to do with the game tonight? We're getting sidetracked.

_____ 10. Ted's solution is much better than mine. Let's go with his idea.

task or maintenance role required for a given situation, you should play that role. As the manager, you should also make the group aware of the need to play these roles and the need to minimize self-interest roles to create a win–win situation by balancing personal and organizational interests.[48]

You should rein in members who put their self-interest ahead of the group's interest in order to be stars. In team sports like hockey, players who strive to score the most goals can cost the team goals because they don't pass to teammates who are in better positions to score. Even worse, they can lose the puck and even enable the other team to score. As the coach you need to take leadership action, such as talking to or benching the selfish player.

# Group Norms

Whether or not formal policies, procedures, and rules are in place to guide behavior, every group eventually develops group norms—unwritten and unspoken rules about expected behavior and how things are done.[49] **Norms** are the group's shared expectations of members' behavior. Rules are formally established by management or by the group itself,[50] whereas norms are not; they develop informally as members interact.[51] Norms can be thought of as informal, unspoken rules of a team that shape members' behavior and attitudes.[52]

## How Norms Develop

Groups spontaneously develop their own rules for what is acceptable and unacceptable in humor, socializing, ways of talking, and ways of letting new members know what the unwritten rules are. The list is endless and encompasses both subtle and obvious behaviors. These rules are arrived at without formal discussion and agreement. The U.S. military has the formal Uniform Code of Military Justice (UCMJ), Article 134, stating that indecent language should not be used. However, some military groups informally develop the norm of breaking the rule and swearing. Norms can change over time to meet the needs of the group.

◀ **LEARNING OUTCOME 5**
Explain how rules and norms differ.

## How Norms Are Enforced

Group peer pressure is a powerful influence for enforcing norms. Most people want to be liked and be part of the team, so they tend to follow group norms,[53] even when they disagree with the behavior.[54] Have you and others you know ever been peer-pressured to do something you didn't really want to do in order to fit in? Have you and others observed unethical or illegal behaviors and failed to try to stop it? If so, you have experienced and observed peer pressure.

 **TIME-OUT 5** Identify at least two norms in your current work group or team. How do you know these are norms? How does the group enforce these norms?

## Sport Management Implications

Group norms can help or hinder a group. Norms can promote healthy group process—helping each other, working hard, performing at one's best, and not being a prima donna are healthy group norms. Research supports the idea that positive norms—such as allowing everyone to contribute in meetings and to share ideas without being judged—are more important than who you put on a team.[55] Conversely, negative norms can sabotage performance, such as when bending the rules, heavy social drinking, using drugs, and underperforming are group norms.

Some fraternities, sororities, and sport teams require some type of initiation, which can be fun and can help form strong bonds between members. However, some initiations require dangerous behavior (some have resulted in deaths) that many members disagree with, but no one stops them. Watch for the natural tendency to follow team norms, and be careful not to be led into unethical and illegal behavior.

Rarely does any one person set an entirely new norm, but group leaders help perpetuate or shift norms. As a group leader or member, you should be aware of your group's norms. Be a positive role model of desired norms,[56] work to develop positive norms, and try to eliminate negative ones. Getting back to ethics (chapter 2), are you going to behave at the conventional level of moral development and follow the group norms even when you know the behavior is wrong, or are you willing to do the right thing on the postconventional level and challenge the team's unethical or illegal behavior?

## Group Cohesiveness

**LEARNING OUTCOME 6** ▶

Describe cohesiveness and why it is important to teams.

The extent to which individuals within a team follow and enforce its norms depends on its cohesiveness. **Group cohesiveness** is the extent to which members stick together. The more cohesive the team, the more it sticks together as a team. Members identify themselves with the group and want to be with the team. The more desirable membership in the group is, the more willing members will be to comply with the group's norms. In highly cohesive groups, all members follow the norms even when they don't agree with them. This doesn't happen in groups that have moderate or low cohesion. Cohesiveness is good when the norms are positive, but it can hurt when the norm is negative, like using illegal drugs.

### Factors Influencing Cohesiveness

Six factors influence cohesiveness:

1. *Objectives.* The stronger the agreement and commitment made to achieving the group's objectives, the higher the group's cohesiveness.

2. *Size.* The smaller the group, the higher the cohesiveness. Three to nine members appears to be a good group size for cohesiveness.

3. *Homogeneity.* Generally, the more similar the group members, the higher the group's cohesiveness. People tend to be attracted to people who are similar to themselves. The dilemma here is that you don't want to discriminate, and diverse groups often outperform homogeneous ones.

4. *Participation.* The more equal the member participation, the higher the group's cohesiveness.

5. *Competition.* If the group focuses on internal competition, members try to outdo each other, and low cohesiveness results. If the group focuses on external competition, members tend to pull together as a team to beat rivals.

6. *Success.* The more successful a group is at achieving its objectives, the more cohesive it becomes. Success breeds cohesiveness, which breeds more success. People want to be on a winning team.

### How Cohesiveness Affects Team Performance

There is a relationship between cohesiveness and team performance.[57] Cohesiveness is associated with performance in the following ways:

- Groups with the highest productivity were highly cohesive and accepted management's directives on productivity levels.

**TIME-OUT 6** Identify your work group's or team's cohesiveness as high, medium, or low. Support your assessment with examples.

- Groups with the lowest productivity were also highly cohesive but rejected management's directives on productivity levels; they set and enforced their own levels, which were below those of management. This can happen in organizations with unions that have an "us against them" attitude.

- Groups with intermediate productivity were low-cohesive groups, irrespective of their acceptance of management's directives. The widest variance in individuals' performance was in the groups with the lower cohesiveness. They tended to be more tolerant of nonconformity with group norms.

Three important factors contribute to team success.[58] They have a culture of having fun together. Everyone is included, and members like to be together and look out for each other. They are cooperative as they behave according to the group norms. So teams that stick together tend to play better together. Think about teams you played for. Did you push harder and play better with teammates you really liked and got along well with than when you didn't? Did the truly cohesive teams do better and enjoy playing more?

## *Sport Management Implications*

Your goal as a leader and team member is to develop cohesive groups that hold high productivity as a group norm. Remember to have fun, to help each other, and to cooperate to complete the task.[59] A participative management style helps groups to develop cohesiveness and builds agreement on, and commitment toward, objectives. All members need to be included (chapter 6) and feel as though they are part of the team; no one should be left out. There should be no cliques—you've experienced being in the in-group or the out-group, haven't you?[60] Coaching also encourages cohesiveness. Some intragroup competition may be helpful, but you should focus primarily on beating the competition. Winning teams become cohesive very naturally, which in turn motivates the group to higher levels of success. The trick is to develop a cohesive but diversified group.

# Status Within the Group

As group members interact, they develop respect for one another in many ways. Team members develop an unofficial hierarchy of status.[61] **Status** is the perceived ranking of one member relative to other members in the group. Status is based on several factors—one's performance, job title, salary, seniority, expertise, people skills, appearance, and education, among others.[62] In sports, the best athletes are generally the high-status members of the team, with the ball-hogging, bragging jerks being an exception—seen them?

**TIME-OUT 7**

List each member in your current work group or team, including you, and identify each person's status in the group. Support your assessment with reasons.

Members who conform to the group's norms typically have higher status than members who don't. Conversely, a group is more willing to listen to a high-status member who breaks the norms, but group leaders tend to conform to the group norms.

High-status members also have more influence on the development of norms and on decisions made by the group. Because members with less status often find their ideas ignored, they tend to copy high-status members' behavior. They also find acceptance by agreeing with the high-status members' suggestions.[63] When people need help and advice, they go to a person with high status. It's common for team members to compete and even fight for high status within the group.[64] Have you ever seen this and sought high status yourself?

## *How Status Affects Group Performance*

Status has a major positive or negative impact on a team's performance.[65] Managers are usually, but not always, the members with the highest status, and how they lead affects team performance. If high-status members support positive norms and high productivity, chances are the group will, too.

*Status congruence*, which is the acceptance and satisfaction that members receive from their status in the group, affects team performance. Members dissatisfied with their status may not participate as actively as they would if they were satisfied with their status.[66] Dissatisfied members may therefore physically or mentally escape from the group and not perform to their full potential. Worse, when they are not happy they may cause conflict between teammates, and they strive to gain status—seen it?

### Sport Management Implications

To be effective as a sport manager, you need high status.[67] Therefore, it benefits you to maintain good relations with the group, particularly with high-status informal leaders, and to be sure they endorse positive norms and objectives. You should also have good relationships with lower-status members to help them feel comfortable with their status as valued members of the team.[68] Compliment them for their contributions to the team's success. In addition, you should be aware of and work to prevent conflicts that may be the result of status incongruence.

## Decision Making and Conflict Resolution

Recall from chapter 3 that an organization's success is based on the decisions it makes. Organizations depend on teams to make important decisions, and how decisions are made by groups directly affects performance.[69]

Recall from chapter 8 that conflict is common in groups.[70] Conflicts of ideas can improve group performance, but personal conflicts tend to hurt relationships and performance because they cause members to withdraw from group participation, and they damage cohesiveness.

### Sport Management Implications

As discussed in chapter 3, participative decision making is the trend,[71] but the level of participation should be based on the type of decision and team members' ability to make such decisions. Guide the team to implement the decision-making model outlined in chapter 3 to improve team decisions. Lead in a manner that prevents disruptive conflicts, and work to resolve any existing conflicts to maintain productive working relationships.[72] In chapter 8, you developed your skills at resolving conflict, so use these skills as a team leader and member. Understanding and applying group processes will make you a more effective group and team member, leader, coach, and sport manager. Figure 9.5 summarizes the six group processes.

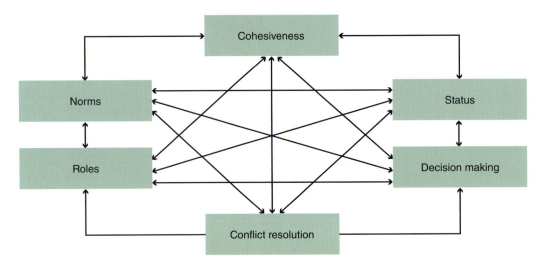

**FIGURE 9.5** Six group processes. The arrows indicate the effect that each dimension affects and is affected by (or systems interrelationship).

## APPLYING THE CONCEPT 9.3

### Group Process

Identify the group process operative in each statement.

   a. roles

   b. norms

   c. cohesiveness

   d. status

   e. decision making

   f. conflict resolution

_____ 11. Although we have occasional differences of opinion, we really get along well and enjoy playing together.

_____ 12. When you need advice on how to do things, go see Shirley—she knows the ropes around here better than anyone.

_____ 13. I'd have to say that Carlos is the peacemaker around here. Every time a disagreement occurs, he gets the players to work out the problem.

_____ 14. Kenady, you're late for the team meeting. Everyone else was on time, so we started without you.

_____ 15. What does fund-raising for a new scoreboard have to do with solving the problem? We're getting sidetracked.

# Stages of Group Development and Leadership Styles

As we have discussed, teams have organizational contexts, structures, and group processes. They also go through the same process or cycle,[73] commonly called developmental stages,[74] as they grow from a collection of individuals to a smoothly operating and effective team. The **stages of group development** are orientation, dissatisfaction, resolution, production, and termination. As teams develop, so does the most effective management style to use to lead the team to the next stage. See figure 9.6 for an illustration of the stages as you read about each stage in this section.

**◄ LEARNING OUTCOME 7**

Describe the five major stages of group development and the leadership style appropriate for each stage.

## Stage 1: Orientation–Autocratic Leadership Style

Command groups are rarely started with all new members. Therefore, the orientation stage is more characteristic of task groups that are clearly beginning anew. Orientation, also known as the *forming stage*, is characterized by low development (D1, high commitment and low competence). When people first form a group, they often come with a moderate to high commitment to it. However, because they haven't worked together, they lack competence as a team, even though they may be highly competent individuals.

During orientation, members must work out structure issues about leadership and group objectives. The size of the group and its composition are checked out. Members may be anxious about how they will fit in (status), what will be required of them (roles and norms), what the group will be like (cohesiveness), how decisions will be made, and how members will get along (conflict). These issues must be resolved if the group is to progress to the next developmental stage.

On athletic teams, it is common to start the season with newcomers replacing some players who have left the team due to age, graduation, or retirement, joining those who have

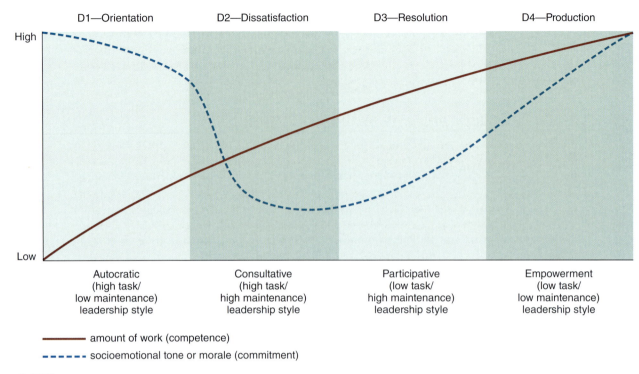

**FIGURE 9.6** Group development stages and leadership style.

stayed. Mixing and matching newcomers with old-timers is a big challenge for managers. A preseason training camp is an important mechanism not only for deciding which players will make the team but also for developing group norms and resolving orientation issues. Thus, a Ludlow Swim Team not only trains before school starts but also has social functions so that swimmers (and sometimes parents) can get to know each other.

**Autocratic Leadership Style.** The appropriate leadership style during orientation is autocratic (high task and low maintenance). When groups first come together, as a leader you need to focus on helping the group to clarify its objectives and provide clear expectations for members using task behavior. There is less focus on maintenance behavior. You can also establish a friendly tone that helps members start to get to know one another.

## Stage 2: Dissatisfaction–Consultative Leadership Style

This stage, also known as the *storming stage*, is characterized by a moderate development level (D2, lower commitment and some competence). After working together for a time, members typically become dissatisfied in some way with individuals or the group. Uncomfortable questions arise: Why am I a member? Are we ever going to win or accomplish anything? Why don't other members do what's expected of them? Often the task is more complex and difficult than anticipated; members mask their own feelings of incompetence with frustration. The group has developed some competence to perform the task, but not as much as members would like, so there is impatience as well.

Coaches in the swimming league may be frustrated with certain participants because they are trying to balance swim practice with another sport, and beginning swimmers may question whether they will ever get in shape and win any races. The individuals and the group need to resolve these dissatisfaction issues before they can progress to the next developmental stage. This is a dangerous stage because groups can get stuck in dissatisfaction and never progress to becoming fully functioning teams.

**Consultative Leadership Style.** The appropriate leadership style during the dissatisfaction stage is consultative (high task and high maintenance). When satisfaction drops, as a leader you need to focus on the maintenance role to encourage members to continue to work toward the objectives. At the same time, you must continue to focus on the task—improving the Ludlow swimming competencies.

## Stage 3: Resolution—Participative Leadership Style

Resolution, also called the *norming stage*, is characterized by a high development level (D3, variable commitment and high competence). With time, members often resolve the incongruence between their initial expectations and the realities that the objectives, tasks, and skills represent. As members develop competence, they typically grow more satisfied with the group. Relationships develop that satisfy group members' affiliation needs. Members learn to work together as they develop a structure and process with acceptable leadership, norms, status, cohesiveness, and decision-making styles. During periods of conflict or change, the group will return to resolve these issues yet again.

Commitment varies from time to time as the group interacts. If the group does not deal effectively with its process issues, it may regress to stage 2 (dissatisfaction), or it may plateau and stagnate in both commitment and competence. If the group succeeds at developing positive structures and processes, it will develop to the next stage. The Ludlow swimming team developed a series of organized practices that fit all of the swimmers' schedules. This resolution was not easy to achieve, but it made the team cohesive.

**Participative Leadership Style.** The appropriate leadership style during resolution is participative (low task and high maintenance). Once group members know what to do and how to do it, less time is needed to direct their task behavior. Groups in resolution need their leaders to focus on maintenance. When commitment varies, this is usually attributable to some problem in group process, such as a conflict. As a leader you should then focus on maintenance behavior to get groups through the issues they face. If you continue to over-manage task behavior, groups can become dissatisfied and regress or plateau at this level.

## Stage 4: Production—Empowerment Leadership Style

The production stage, also called the *performing stage*, is characterized by a high level of development (D4, high commitment and high competence). At this stage, commitment and competence don't fluctuate much. Groups function smoothly as teams with high levels of satisfaction. They maintain positive structures and processes. The fact that members are very productive further fuels positive feelings. Group structure and process may change with time, but issues are resolved quickly and easily; members are open with each other. The Ludlow Swim Team in our example moved into the production stage and routinely takes swimmers to state competitions.

**Empowerment Leadership Style.** The appropriate style during the production stage is empowerment (low task and low maintenance). Groups that achieve this stage play appropriate task and maintenance roles; by this stage, leaders don't need to play either role, unless there is a problem, because the group is effectively sharing leadership.

## Stage 5: Termination

Termination, also called the adjourning stage, is not reached in command groups unless there is some drastic reorganization. However, task groups do terminate, and sport team seasons end. During this stage, members experience feelings of loss as they face leaving the group. Closure is important. The Ludlow Swim Team's annual awards dinner, which carefully honors every team member, helps swimmers who are going on to college—and their parents—say good-bye to members who have become friends.

**Changing Competence and Commitment and Leadership Styles.** Competence and commitment identified through each stage of group development do not progress in the same manner. As figure 9.6 shows, competence continues to increase steadily through stages 1 to 4, whereas commitment fluctuates—it starts out high in stage 1, drops in stage 2, and then rises through stages 3 and 4. The success and failure of a team are often based on the coach or sport manager. Thus, managing with the appropriate leadership style is important. You will develop the skill of analyzing a team and selecting the appropriate leadership style to use in Skill-Builder 9.2 in the web study guide.

TIME-OUT 8

Identify your work group's or team's developmental stage and the leader's management style. Is his or her style appropriate for your group's stage? What could be done to improve your group's structure and process?

# Developing Groups Into Teams

LEARNING OUTCOME 8 ▶

Explain how group managers and team leaders differ.

As table 9.1 shows, groups and teams have differences. The trend is to empower groups to become teams because teams are more productive than groups.[75] As a coach or sport manager, it's your job to develop great teams,[76] but it's not easy to blend different skills and personalities into a successful team.[77] In this section, we examine training and the functions of management—planning, organizing and staffing, leading, and controlling teams—and how group managers and team leaders differ.

Large organizations have ongoing training to improve performance,[78] team skills are important,[79] and people are being trained to become better team players and leaders,[80] which is the objective of this chapter. OD programs, including team-building programs, as discussed in chapter 6, are also very helpful in turning groups into teams. HolacracyOne and other consulting firms have change agents who train employees to become teams.[81]

The management functions are handled differently in groups and teams. A major difference is that the old command-and-control method of telling employees what to do and closely watching has been replaced with shared leadership. Here we discuss how the manager's job changes with teams.

- *Planning.* Team members should set objectives, develop plans, and make the decisions. The manager's role is to involve and coach members, not to do the planning for the team. Use the setting objectives and decision-making models and planning skills you developed in chapters 3 and 4 to lead the team.

- *Organizing and staffing.* To lead teams, members participate in selecting, evaluating, and rewarding members. Jobs are more interchangeable and are assigned by members as they perform interdependent parts of the task. Use the organizing and human resource management skills developed in chapters 5 through 7 to lead the team.

- *Leading.* Most teams have a designated leader, but leadership is shared in teams. Effective team leaders are highly skilled in and focus on group process and team building. They lead the team to the production stage, and they change their leadership styles to address the team's developmental stage. Use the leadership skills you have developed so far and the ones you will learn in chapters 10 through 12.

- *Controlling.* Team members monitor their own progress, take corrective action when needed to achieve the objective, and perform quality control. These leaders don't spend much of their time checking on employees; instead, they spend time developing the leadership skills of all team members. Use the controlling skills you will develop in chapters 13 and 14 to lead the team.

In summary, the roles of group manager and team leader differ in significant ways.

TIME-OUT 9

State whether your current boss or coach is a group manager or a team leader. Give reasons for your choice.

Group managers perform the four functions of management. Team leaders empower members to perform the management functions and focus on shaping group structure and group process, and these leaders get the team to the mature developmental stage, that of production.

# Getting to Better Meetings

Teams operate through meetings.[82] With the increasing use of teams, meetings take up an increasing amount of time in organizations.[83] Estimates place the daily number of U.S. meetings at 11 million, and workers spend on average at least six hours per week in meetings.[84] Therefore, leading effective meetings is an important skill.[85] But people commonly complain that there are too many meetings,[86] they are too long, and that they are unproductive—a waste of time.[87] Committees have been known to keep minutes and waste hours. Do you dread going to meetings?[88] You need to avoid running bad meetings.[89] Do you know how to plan and conduct effective meetings and how to handle problem group members during meetings? In completing this section, you can improve your meeting management skills.

◀ LEARNING OUTCOME 9
Lead a meeting.

## Planning Meetings

Your preparations and those of your team are crucial for conducting effective meetings. Unprepared leaders conduct unproductive meetings. Planning is needed in at least five areas: (1) setting objectives, (2) selecting participants, (3) making assignments, (4) setting the agenda and the time and place for the meeting, and (5) leading the meeting. A written copy of the plan should be sent to members before the meeting (see the Meeting Plans sidebar).

### *Objectives*

Have an objective, or don't call a meeting. Amazing numbers of meetings are called without a clear purpose. Team members need to know why the meeting is important,[90] and objectives state what will be accomplished in a meeting. Clarifying the purpose of the meeting will ensure that all participants start the meeting with the same purpose and objective.

### *Participants and Assignments*

Before you call a meeting, decide who needs to attend. When too many people attend, your ability to complete the work slows down considerably.[91] Look at your objectives, decide who is affected by them and who should have input, and limit attendees on that basis.[92] Do you need an outside specialist to provide expertise? Participants should know in advance what is expected of them.[93] Give adequate notice if any preparation is required on their part (reading material, doing research, or writing a report). Make sure members are accountable for their assignments.

### *Agendas*

As the meeting leader, you select the agenda items, and members may also submit agenda items they want included. Before you call a meeting, identify the activities that will take place and list them in order by importance—this is your agenda, and it should be distributed before the meeting.[94] Place agenda items in order of priority; if the group doesn't get to every agenda item, the least important items will carry forward to the next meeting.[95]

Agendas tell people what is expected and how the meeting will progress.[96] Setting time limits for each item keeps everyone on task and avoids the needless (and endless) discussion and getting off topic that are so common at meetings.[97] When digression occurs, take the group back to the topic to keep your team on track to achieve the meeting objectives.[98] But be flexible and allow more time when it is really needed.

## Meeting Plans

### Content

- *Time.* List date, place, and time (both beginning and ending).
- *Objectives.* State the objectives and purpose of the meeting. The objectives can be listed with agenda items, as shown in the following example, rather than as a separate section. Make sure that objectives are specific (chapter 4).
- *Participation and assignments.* If all members have the same assignments, list them. If different members have different assignments, list their names and assignments. Assignments may be listed as agenda items, as shown for Ted and Karen in the example.
- *Agenda.* List each item to be covered in priority order with its approximate time limit. Accepting the minutes of the last meeting may be an agenda item.

### Example

**Boys Club Baseball Team Meeting**

December 15, 2020, Boys Club Central Office, 1 to 2 p.m.

*Participation and Assignments*

All members will attend and should have read the list of players available for each of the six teams before the meeting. Be ready to discuss your preferences for selecting players.

*Agenda*

Ted will lead a discussion of the process to be used in selecting players—15 minutes.

Karen will lead the process of selecting players—40 minutes.

Ted and Karen will present dates for teams to hold practice without discussion—5 minutes. Discussion will take place at the next meeting after you have given the possible practice dates some thought.

## Date, Place, and Time

To determine which days and times of the week are best for meetings, get members' input. People tend to be more alert early in the day before lunchtime.[99] When members work in close proximity, it is better to have more frequent, shorter meetings that focus on one or just a few items. However, when members have to travel, meetings must be fewer and longer. Select an adequate place for the group, and plan for their physical comfort. An important part of running effective meetings is starting and ending on time to avoid wasting everyone's time.[100]

A current trend is to hold important meetings at sport stadiums. Conference rooms in newer stadiums are often larger than those available at hotels. Holding a meeting at a sport stadium such as Yankee Stadium or at Madison Square Garden in New York City lends a lot of prestige to the event. Corporate rooms are also on the increase as an additional means of increasing sport team revenues.

## Leadership

Think about what leadership style best fits your objectives for the meeting to facilitate adequate discussion.[101] Each agenda item may need to be handled differently. Some items simply call for disseminating information; others may require a discussion, vote, or consensus; still other items require a simple, quick report from a member. Develop your team members' leadership skills by rotating meeting leaders.

### Technology

Email, teleconferences, and videoconferences have reduced the need for some in-person meetings. Team members are working together using Evernote, Google Keep, or Microsoft OneNote software file sharing for team projects and meetings.[102] The trend is to have more online meetings using more videoconferencing software, such as Skype and Voom.[103] These technologies save travel costs and time, and they may result in better and quicker decisions. Ongoing chat rooms and project sharing software tools can also take the place of meetings and are especially useful for virtual teams with global members in different time zones.[104]

Technology can help you plan, lead, and follow up on meetings, such as smartphone app Meeting Minutes Pro.[105] Digital dry-erase boards, such as SMART kapp, a new Bluetooth-connected board, can be used to instantly share meeting notes with team members. On the dark side, some meeting attendees bring smartphones to meetings, but they use them to do other things, which can distract members and reduce the effectiveness of the meeting (or class). Some organizations are banning their use during meetings (or classes).[106] For longer meetings, some leaders take a short tech break.

Tech helps facilitate the meeting, but successful meetings depend on the leader's skill at managing group process (people skills), not tech. Although the trend is to conduct more meetings via technology, they will never be as effective as interacting face-to-face,[107] so meet in person when feasible.

## Conducting Meetings

To conduct effective meetings, start and end on time.[108] An estimated 37 percent of meetings start or end late, which tends to put members in a bad mood that hurts creativity and performance.[109] Don't wait for late members because it penalizes the members who are on time and develops a *norm* for coming late. You also don't want to end late and make people late for their next important activity.

### First Meeting

At a group's first meeting, the group is in the orientation developmental stage. Therefore, develop objectives, but give members time to get to know one another. Introductions set the stage for subsequent interactions. A simple technique is to start with introductions and then move on to the group's purpose, its objectives, and members' jobs or assignments. Tell members you will be starting and ending meetings on time and that you will not spend meeting time catching up late members on what they missed.[110] Sometime during or following this procedure, take a break to enable members to interact informally. If members see that their social needs will not be met, dissatisfaction may occur more quickly.

### Effective Meetings Have Three Parts

1. Begin the meeting on time and identify objectives. Begin by reviewing progress to date, the group's objectives, and the meeting's purpose or objective. If minutes are recorded, they are usually approved at the beginning of the next meeting. For most meetings, a secretary should be appointed to record minutes.

2. Cover agenda items in priority order. Try to keep to the approximate times, but be flexible. However, if the discussion begins to digress or becomes a destructive argument, move on. Google Ventures uses a time clock that goes off when the time is up,[111] and you can use the timer on your smartphone.

3. Summarize and review assignments, and end the meeting on time. Whoever is leading the meeting should summarize what took place and whether the meeting's objectives were achieved.[112] Review the assignments given.[113] The secretary or leader should record all assignments. This sets up accountability and follow-up on assignments to ensure results.

Meeting leaders need to focus on group structure, process, and development. As already noted, leadership style needs change with the group's developmental level. Assess the stage your group is in as you decide how to lead meetings. Provide appropriate task or maintenance behavior only as it is needed, and avoid self-interest roles and problem members.

# Problem Members

Meeting members need to express opinions, concerns, or ideas that lead to improved work and group processes and innovation,[114] which is important to effective teamwork.[115] So encourage people to voice whatever is on their minds during meetings.[116] However, as groups and teams develop, certain personalities emerge that can cause the group to be less efficient. We call these personalities Silent Ones, Talkers, Wanderers, Arguers, the Bored, and the Social Loafer. Personality, position, and status affect meeting behavior.

## Silent Ones

In effective groups, every member participates. Silent Ones do not give the group the benefits of their input. Encourage Silent Ones to participate, without being obvious or overdoing it. One technique that works well is rotation, in which all members take turns giving input. Rotation is generally less threatening than being called on directly. However, rotation is not appropriate all the time. To build up the confidence of Silent Ones, call on them with questions they can easily answer.

Speaking at meetings is hard to do for many people.[117] If you have the personality of a Silent One,[118] push yourself to participate. Remind yourself that you have good ideas, too, and that others in the meeting feel as you do. Trust yourself, and assertively stand up for your ideas when you know they are as good as or better than others' views. Preparing what you will say before the meeting will give you confidence to speak up.

## Talkers

Talkers like to say something about everything. They dominate discussions and drown out other voices. Talkers can cause intragroup problems such as low cohesiveness and conflicts. Your job is to slow Talkers down, not to shut them up. But above all, don't let them dominate. Rotation works well here, too, because it limits Talkers' amount of "floor." When rotation isn't appropriate, gently interrupt Talkers and present your own ideas, or call on other members to present theirs.

Another type of talker is people who have a private conversation (crosstalking) during the meeting or class. To prevent this, you and your team could develop the Zappos rule of no-crosstalking, and interruptions are forbidden,[119] and you and the team members enforce the rule.

If you are a Talker, restrain yourself. Remember, powerful people listen. As a Talker, you are likely a leader, and thus it is your job to help others develop, so give them a chance to speak and do things for themselves.

## Wanderers

Wanderers are distracters. They digress, complain, joke too much, change the subject, and create roadblocks to getting things done. Your job is to keep the group on track, so keep to the agenda items. If Wanderers want to distract the team, cut them off. But be kind. Thank them for their contribution, and then ask a question to get the team back on topic.

If you are a Wanderer, you are likely high maintenance and low task oriented. Change your habits, and try to develop a balance between these two roles. Check your urge to stray from the topic, and pull your thoughts and comments back on track. Think about why you wander—are you subconsciously trying to sabotage the group?

## Arguers

Like Talkers, Arguers like to be the center of attention. For Arguers, arguing is an end in itself. Whether it is constructive or destructive doesn't concern them. They view everything as a win–lose situation, they argue that others' ideas are not as good as theirs, and they cannot stand losing.[120] Your job is to resolve conflict, but not in an argumentative way. Don't get into an argument with Arguers; that is exactly what they want. Should they start an argument, bring others into the discussion. If the argument gets personal, cut it off. Make it clear that you will not tolerate personal attacks. Keep the discussion moving, and keep it on target.

If you are an Arguer, practice backing off. Listen to others' ideas, and change positions and agree to do things their way when they have better ideas.[121] Even lose on purpose—it is not the end of the world. Think about why you have to be the center of attention. What makes you need to fight and win? Strive to change your win–lose view of life. (Win–win is much more pleasant.) Learn to convey your views assertively, not aggressively—by the way, this is good for your blood pressure! All of us get to be wrong. Learn to admit mistakes gracefully.

## The Bored

The Bored are not interested in the meeting, the group, or its objectives, so they are not engaged in the discussions.[122] Maybe they are preoccupied. Maybe they feel superior.[123] Whatever their reason, they don't pay attention and they don't participate. As attention spans shrink,[124] you need to involve members every few minutes or they will tune you out.[125] Assign the Bored tasks. Have them record ideas on the easel or record minutes. Call on the Bored; bring them into the group. Don't allow the Bored to sit back—boredom is contagious, and you don't want it to spread.

If you are one of the Bored, think about why. Should you change jobs? If not, then participate—you owe this to your team and to yourself. Remember, motivation comes from within. Take more of a leadership role. If you are on your smartphone multitasking during the meeting, others will perceive that you are disengaged even if you are paying attention. This behavior nonverbally says, "This person/text/email is more important than you." Some members, especially old ones, will believe you are being disrespectful and insulting them.[126] If you are addicted to your phone, you may want to shut it off and put it out of sight during the meeting. Shutting it off may even be required for this reason.[127] Again, for longer meetings you can take tech breaks.

## Social Loafers

This Social Loafer (or *free rider*) problem member doesn't want to take individual responsibility and do a fair share of the work.[128] Social Loafers tend to hurt team performance.[129] Following all the previously mentioned meeting guidelines helps prevent free riding, especially giving clear individual assignments. Don't let the group develop norms that allow social loafing, and use peer pressure to get people to do their work. Confront Social Loafers assertively using the conflict resolution model in chapter 8. When necessary, threaten to go to the boss. If these methods do not work, go to the supervisor (professor or boss) and explain the situation; specify the behavior that is lacking and explain that you and the group have tried to resolve the problem but that the Social Loafer refuses to perform her share of the work.

Do you want to be a member of an effective, successful team? If you are a Social Loafer, then step up to the plate and do your fair share of the work.

# Working With Problem Members

Here are the rules you do not want to break when working in a team and during meetings: Do not embarrass, do not belittle, do not intimidate, and do not argue with any members, no matter how much they push you. If you do, they will be martyrs and you will be a bully. Do get everyone to do their share of the work in a positive way, and don't allow others to behave negatively by breaking these rules.

If you have serious problem members who don't respond to the preceding techniques, talk with them individually outside the group. Review the BCF statements (behavior, consequences, feelings) in chapter 8, and maintain ownership of the problem. Be honest, be firm, and lay your cards on the table.

As we bring this chapter to a close, recall the importance of teamwork, the lessons of the geese, and the differences between groups and teams. Know the group performance model—group performance is a function of organizational context, group structure, group process, and group development. Develop effective group structure for the type of group; select the appropriate size, composition, and leadership style; and set objectives. Manage group process through group roles, set positive norms, develop cohesiveness, maintain status congruence, make good decisions, and resolve conflict. Analyze the group's development stage and use the appropriate leadership style, and bring groups to the production stage of development. Develop groups into teams by training and empowering your members to participate in management functions. Run effective meetings so you don't waste the group's time.

TIME-OUT 10

Recall a recent meeting you attended. Write a critique of the meeting, laying out what went well and why and what went wrong and why. Were there problem members? How did the leader handle them?

## APPLYING THE CONCEPT 9.4

### People Who Sabotage Meetings

Identify the problem personality described in each statement.

a. Silent one
b. Talker
c. Wanderer
d. Bored
e. Arguer
f. Social loafer

_____ 16. Charlie is always first or second to give his ideas. He elaborates and expounds and then elaborates again.

_____ 17. One of the usually active team members is sitting back quietly today for the first time. The other members are doing all the discussing and volunteering for assignments.

_____ 18. As the team discusses game strategy for next Saturday, Billy asks if they heard about the team owner and the mailroom clerk.

_____ 19. Eunice usually shrinks from giving her ideas. When asked to explain her position, she often changes her answers to agree with others in the group.

_____ 20. Dwayne loves to challenge members' ideas. He likes getting his own way. When someone doesn't agree with Dwayne, he makes wisecracks about the person's prior mistakes.

# LEARNING AIDS

## CHAPTER SUMMARY

1. **Explain how groups and teams differ.**

   Groups and teams differ by size, leadership, jobs, accountability and evaluation, rewards, and objectives. Groups have a clear leader and two or more (possibly many more) members who perform independent jobs with individual accountability, evaluation, and rewards. Teams typically have fewer members who share leadership and who perform interdependent jobs with both individual and group accountability, evaluation, and rewards.

2. **Explain the group performance model.**

   Group performance is a function of organizational context and the group's structure, process, and developmental stage.

3. **Categorize groups by their structure.**

   Groups can be structured as formal or informal, functional or cross-functional, and command or task. Formal groups are part of the organizational structure; informal groups are not. Functional group members come from one area; cross-functional members come from different areas. Command groups are composed of managers and their staff working to get the job done; task groups work on specific objectives. Task forces are temporary; standing committees are ongoing.

4. **Define the three major roles group members play.**

   Group task roles are played when members do and say things that directly aid in the accomplishment of the group's objectives. Group maintenance roles are played when members do and say things that develop and sustain the group process. Self-interest roles are played when members do and say things that help the individual but hurt the group.

5. **Explain how rules and norms differ.**

   Rules are formally established by management or by the group itself. Norms are the group's shared but unspoken expectations of its members' behavior. Norms develop spontaneously as members interact.

6. **Describe cohesiveness and why it is important to teams.**

   Group cohesiveness is the extent to which members stick together. Group cohesiveness is important because highly cohesive groups that accept management's directives for productivity levels perform better than groups with low levels of cohesiveness.

7. **Describe the five major stages of group development and the leadership style appropriate for each stage.**

   (1) Orientation is characterized by low development level (D1—high commitment and low competence), and the appropriate leadership style is autocratic. (2) Dissatisfaction is characterized by moderate development level (D2—lower commitment and some competence), and the appropriate leadership style is consultative. (3) Resolution is characterized by high development level (D3—variable commitment and high competence), and the appropriate leadership style is participative. (4) Production is characterized by outstanding development level (D4—high commitment and high competence), and the appropriate leadership style is empowerment. (5) Termination is not reached in command groups unless there is some drastic reorganization. However, task groups do terminate.

8. **Explain how group managers and team leaders differ.**

   The group manager takes responsibility for performing the four functions of management. The team leader empowers the members to take responsibility for performing the management functions and focuses on developing effective group structure, group process, and group development.

9. **Lead a meeting.**

Make sure the meeting has a purpose. Begin meetings by covering the objectives for the meeting. Cover agenda items in priority order. Keep people on track. Conclude with a summary of what took place and assignments to be completed for discussion at future meetings.

## REVIEW AND DISCUSSION QUESTIONS

1. Which are usually larger, groups or teams?

2. Give one reason the New England Patriots is a successful team.

3. One study found that NBA teams with a high shared experience and a low turnover tended to have significantly better win–loss records. Why?

4. Why is diversity important to group composition?

5. Why are objectives important to groups?

6. How do groups enforce norms?

7. Does member commitment to the group continue to increase through the first four stages of group development?

8. Are the four functions of management equally important to both groups and teams?

9. Why is it important to keep records of meeting assignments?

10. Describe the five types of problem members in meetings. How do they cause problems?

11. What are four reasons that volunteers gave for volunteering to work at the 2004 Athens Olympics?

12. Describe the team structure for a volunteering effort you have been involved with at your college.

13. Which lesson of the geese is most lacking and needed in teams today? Why?

14. Is it really worth making a distinction between groups and teams? Why or why not?

15. Which part of the group performance model is the most important to high levels of performance? Why?

16. Select any type of group (work, school, sport) that you belong to or have belonged to in the past. Explain how each of the group's five structure components affected its performance.

17. Select any type of group you belong to or have belonged to in the past. Explain how each of the group's six group process components affected its performance.

18. Based on your experience in meetings, and what you have read and heard from others, which part of planning a meeting is most lacking?

19. Which type of group problem member is most annoying to you? Why? How can you better work with this type in the future?

## CASES

### Sport Management Professionals @ Work: David McDaniel

David McDaniel was a fairly typical sport management student while he was in college. He played his favorite sport (basketball), didn't always like the core business classes he was required to complete, but enjoyed the sport management courses in his major. David was soft-spoken, even though he cut an imposing figure at six feet, five inches tall.

Like many college graduates, David had to learn quickly how to change from a college student to a full-time worker once he graduated. This process took a full two years while he conducted his first real career search.

The first step was to reexamine the résumé and cover letter he made during college. Although David stuck to one page, he made sure to reduce the amount of white space and to include more about himself on the résumé. Since he was short on work experience, like most recent college graduates, he added a section to his résumé on his volunteer work and his personal hobbies. David learned that interviewers were more interested in the two summer months he spent playing basketball in Greece than his grade point average (GPA) of 3.80. Employers considered David's travel an important skill since it showed he could handle a global work assignment.

At the same time, David learned that his cover letter had to be adapted to fit each job opening he used it for. The cover letter had to include some area that would catch the eye of the interviewer. It was critical to make sure the résumé and cover letter didn't have any spelling or grammatical errors!

David applied to be the assistant coach at his high school in the D.C. area. He had two successful years as the assistant before accepting the full-time coaching position. It looked like David would have a long career as a coach. David liked to have quite a few rules and policies in place since a well-organized team was more likely to win—in David's view!

However, the résumé and cover letter he sent to NBA headquarters in New York was selected by a computer software program to be a good match with a new position in league headquarters. David was thrilled to answer his cell phone when the NBA called right before the regular NBA season started.

David's calm and quiet demeanor was well received by the recruiters from the NBA. The league was looking for a recent college graduate. The NBA was also looking for someone with social media skills who would travel around the globe promoting basketball.

It was heart-wrenching to leave a high school basketball position coaching young people. But David could not turn down his dream job with the NBA. His new position, which was recently created by the NBA, was a league operations assistant. David monitors and records unusual statistics such as on-court issues, atypical events, and decorum, and he is a logger for NBA Hustle Stats.

## Case Questions

1. Would technical, people skills, or conceptual training most benefit David McDaniel at this stage of his career?

2. At the D.C. high school, was he primarily recruiting from internal or external sources?

3. What was unique about David's NBA job?

## DraftKings, FanDuel, and Legalized Gambling

Fantasy sports used to be called rotisserie baseball. In the 1980s, it was called roto for short. Fans play for entertainment, escape, competition, social interaction, and gambling.

What is really involved in building a fantasy team? The fantasy business has been growing rapidly, and fantasy sports have become popular with sport fans. Two main competitors have emerged: FanDuel and DraftKings. Both organizations have betting opportunities from a single game up to the entire season.

A league first needs to be formed. Many leagues use yahoo.com or espn.com as a platform for managing their teams. Owners need to be found to select players. In the early stages of selecting teams, owners do not usually know everybody who is selecting a team. Still, a date is selected and agreed upon by all owners.

Next, a commissioner, or leader, is selected to start the league on one of the sites. The owner of each team then drafts his team in a rotating sequence. Owners often have a sum of fantasy dollars to spend on their team. It takes great skill to build a team that performs to a high standard, is not injury prone, hits for home run power yet also for a high batting average, and so on.

But, how does an owner form a team? Does he pick players who work well together? Does he pick players on his favorite professional teams? Does he pick a few high-salaried players and fill in with a few extra players on the bench? Does he make trades with other owners in the league who he thinks are similar to him? What looks like an unorganized group of players is actually a well-orchestrated selection of players who work together like a team.

Owners look for a competitive advantage to find out how one player is statistically better than another player. The owners originally used traditional statistics such as home runs, batting average, and stolen bases. But the big data offered by sports such as baseball and football make it much more exciting to find new data to gain insights. Programs like Excel made it easier to make more sophisticated decisions using equations to calculate new statistics.

WAR is a recent term only added to baseball jargon in 2008. WAR stands for Wins Above Replacement. Although the calculation has six steps, it is easy to understand that a superstar player such as Mike Trout of the Los Angeles Angels is worth 8 to 10 more wins per year than an average player. Thus, Mike Trout has a WAR of 8-10, which means he helps his team to about 8 to 10 more wins than if he didn't play on the team.[130]

After selecting all their initial players, owners are beginning to know all the other owners in the league. They establish some normal behavior. For instance, all changes in a lineup have to be completed before game time. Injured players can be replaced from the pool of players who are not currently selected. One of the reasons fantasy baseball is addictive is that owners can add, delete, and trade players for most of the season. Owners like to have rules, since this helps to keep the league on track.

At the end of the regular season, the fantasy season also ends. A playoff takes place, and one team is crowned champion. In reality, the team of owners is disbanded until the new season begins next year.

However, the future of FanDuel, DraftKings, and fantasy sports might be quite different after a recent Supreme Court decision. In May 2018, the U.S. Supreme Court ruled to legalize sports betting in states. The Supreme Court struck down the 1992 federal law that prohibited most states from having sports betting. So, for the first time, states will be able to offer legalized gambling on professional sports such as the NFL, NBA, NHL, and MLB. Led by New Jersey, states are already preparing to authorize certain venues to offer sports betting.[131] Although it can take some time for states to process the venues where legal sports betting will take place and when, it is most likely going to be offered in states with existing casinos. DraftKings has already begun the process of working with casinos in Massachusetts. In Massachusetts, that includes MGM, Wynn Resorts, and Penn National Gaming.[132]

Go to the web study guide to answer questions about this case study.

## @ TAKE IT TO THE NET

Please visit www.HumanKinetics.com/AppliedSportManagementSkills and go to this book's companion web study guide, where you will find the following:

A list of websites associated with the concepts in this chapter

Skill-Builder exercises, Sports and Social Media exercises, and a continuing Game Plan for Starting a Sport Business

Online versions of chapter exercises and end-of-chapter learning aids

An exercise that helps you define the Key Terms

# Communicating for Results

## LEARNING OUTCOMES

After studying this chapter, you should be able to

1. understand how communication flows through organizations;

2. list the four steps in the communication process;

3. use transmission channels well;

4. communicate effectively in person;

5. select appropriate channels for your messages;

6. solicit feedback properly;

7. explain how we receive messages;

8. choose appropriate response styles; and

9. calm an emotional person.

## KEY TERMS

| | |
|---|---|
| communication | decode |
| vertical communication | nonverbal communication |
| horizontal communication | message-sending process |
| grapevine | feedback |
| communication process | paraphrasing |
| sender | message-receiving process |
| encode | listening |
| receiver | reflecting |
| transmit | empathy |

Organizing  Leading  Controlling  Planning  Organizing  Leading  Controlling  Planning  Organizi
ntrolling  Planning  Organizing  Leading  Controlling  Planning  Organizing  Leading  Controlling  Plann
Leading  Controlling  Planning  Organizing  Leading  Controlling  Planning  Organizing  Leading
Planning  Organizing  Leading  Controlling  Planning  Organizing  Leading  Controlling  Planning
ding  Controlling  Planning  Organizing  Leading  Controlling  Planning  Organizing  Leading  Control
Organizing  Leading

## DEVELOPING YOUR SKILLS

Humans are all about talk, and, frankly, the best managers talk better than the rest of us. They stay on target and get their messages across time and again to all manner of recipients, from staff to stockholders to the news media. Fortunately, this is a skill you can develop. In this chapter you will learn about the communication process and develop your skills at sending, receiving, and responding to messages through the use of models. You can also develop skills at dealing with emotional people and improve your ability to give and receive criticism.

## REVIEWING THEIR GAME PLAN

### Communication Is the Key to the Warriors' Success

Effective communication is often the key to winning. You can have the greatest player in the sport, but the team doesn't always win. Great communication requires the team to communicate from the owner, to the general manager, to the coach, and to the players on the field. Plus, you need to communicate with everyone else who isn't listed in the previous sentence.

The owner paves the way to success. An owner needs a vision to help set up the team for the future. The NBA Golden State Warriors have Joe Lacob, who has directed the organization to three of the last four NBA Championships. More importantly, with his wise investments (culled from Lacob's years in Silicon Valley assembling an all-star portfolio of companies at legendary venture capital firm Kleiner Perkins Caufield & Byers), they are primed for a lengthy run at the top of the NBA hierarchy.[1]

But the vision to turn around the perennially losing Golden State Warriors required a coach. Steve Kerr was hired away from broadcasting, with no head coaching experience, to become the coach. Kerr was a savvy communicator from his broadcasting experiences and playing days while winning championships with the Michael Jordan–led Chicago Bulls. Although health issues often require Kerr to miss some games, he is the unquestioned guru of game time communication and decisions.

Of course, the job has been easier since the Warriors also hired an unknown general manager and president of operations, Bob Myers. Myers said, "you need to find people who have a depth of desire." You also need to have a dose of authenticity in your communication when you are trying to lure a top-level free agent like Kevin Durant to want to play for your team for the next decade. "Our players have been hearing the voice of the coach for years now, and they've achieved success," Myers said. But after a while, it's easy to fall into a "heard-that-before" mentality. Sometimes you need to empower the team to take responsibility in order to stay fresh, Myers said. Letting the Warriors coach themselves was similar to parents asking their kids to cook dinner. "It empowers the team to take responsibility," even if they mess up.[2]

For more information, please visit their team page at www.nba.com/teams/warriors.

# Understanding the Importance of Good Communication

**Communication** is the process of transmitting information and meaning. Communication is the foundation of people skills (chapter 1),[3] and it is a transferable skill between the personal and professional spheres of your life.[4] The world of work revolves around communications. Unfortunately, miscommunication is common in organizations. This is why organizations rate communication skills as the most valuable knowledge, skill, or ability for career success.[5] But communication skills are lacking in many job applicants.[6] Personal and professional relationships are based on communications, as is networking. Think about the jerks you have to deal with. How would you rate their communication skills and success?[7] Work on developing your communication skills because they have a direct impact on your career success and personal relationships.[8] Developing your communication skills is the objective of this chapter.

How much time do you spend reading, listening to, and watching sport media? The communication industry is big business for sport. Owners, managers, athletes, and all the employees of a sport organization need to realize that their personal communications with the media, clients, fans, suppliers, and customers are part of an environment where the spoken and written word and actions can be transmitted instantly and globally via the Internet. And as you may already know, once something is put online (words, pictures, video) by you or anyone else, it is difficult to get it off.

Although there are lots of jobs in sport media, and we do discuss sport media briefly, we focus on communicating within sport organizations, which include ESPN and other media companies, throughout this chapter. For our purposes, there are two types of communication: organizational and interpersonal. Organizational communication takes place between organizations and between an organization's divisions, departments, projects, and teams. Interpersonal communication takes place between individuals. The next section presents organizational communications, and the rest of the chapter will focus on interpersonal communication skills.

# Using Organizational Communication

If an organization is to thrive, its mission, strategy, goals, and culture all must be communicated effectively within and outside the firm. To this end, sport managers develop communication strategies.

◀ **LEARNING OUTCOME 1**
Understand how communication flows through organizations.

Think about how communications flow through an organization. The first thing that comes to mind is the formal channels. These can be vertical—down from the top (from the CEO and corporate executives on down the chain of command) and up from the bottom (from staff at the front line on up the chain). Communications can also be horizontal—same-level communications between salespeople and between vice presidents, for example. Then there are the informal channels (the grapevine) that every organization has; these channels resemble the ricochet of bullets. So organizational communication flows up, down, and sideways;[9] formally in vertical and horizontal directions and informally through the grapevine.[10]

## APPLYING THE CONCEPT 10.1

### Communication Flow

Identify each communication as one of these types:

a. downward

b. upward

c. horizontal

d. grapevine

_____ 1. Hey, Carl, did you hear that our two linebackers, Tom and Frankie, were drinking at the prom last week?

_____ 2. Juanita, you know when you hand the baton off to me, you need to quickly move out of my way.

_____ 3. Dwayne, here's the team roster you needed. Check it, and I'll make changes.

_____ 4. Robin, I've got two new customers who want to set up charge accounts. Please rush the credit check so we can increase ticket sales.

_____ 5. Ted, please run this letter over to the athletic funding committee before noon.

## Formal Vertical and Horizontal Communication

**Vertical communication** is the downward and upward flow of information through the organization. The hierarchical chain of command (chapter 5) creates formal vertical communication.[11] Top management's strategies, policies, and rules are communicated down the chain of command to instruct employees.[12] The delegation process is downward communication.

Upward communication, on the other hand, involves staff sending information up through the different management levels. To facilitate upward communication, most organizations encourage open-door management styles and communications, with the idea of making people feel at ease talking to managers in order to improve results.[13]

> **TIME-OUT 1**
> Give examples of vertical communication and horizontal communication, and list a piece of information you got from your organization's grapevine.

*Can you provide an example of horizontal communication for a sport talk radio show you listen to?*

So when your coach or boss tells you what to do, it is vertical downward communication. Conversely, when you go and talk to your coach or boss, it is vertical upward communication. Any single conversation can have both upward and downward elements.

Coaches often meet with their teams when they are performing below par to get feedback from players on how the team can start winning. Depending on the issue, the coach's style, and the team's culture, the information flow is downward (the coach tells players what they need to do), upward (players tell the coach what needs to happen), or (ideally) both.

**Horizontal communication** *is the flow of information between colleagues and peers.* It is formal communication, but it does not follow the chain of command; instead, it is multidirectional. Horizontal communication is needed to coordinate within a department, between team members, and between different departments. When the manager of the marketing department communicates with the manager of the production department or other departments, horizontal communication takes place. Organizations are becoming flatter (chapter 5) and using more horizontal communications.[14]

## Informal Grapevine Communication

The **grapevine** *is the informal flow of information in any direction throughout an organization.* It is informal communication because it is not official or sanctioned by management. The information is often called rumors and gossip. Grapevine information can begin with anyone in the organization and can flow in any direction. Videogame company Valve, who created Half-Life and Portal, says that the grapevine tends to be used by, and contribute to, cliques.

Grapevines are a powerful means of communication. They can be useful, and they can be destructive.[15] Gossip has wrecked homes, friendships, and organizations. Organizations sometimes use grapevines to their advantage. Whole Foods CEO John Mackey says it uses the grapevine effectively. You should spread good news through the grapevine. But reining in rumors during times of uncertainty can be a daunting undertaking. When you hear false rumors, try to nip them in the bud. Effective managers provide formal information truthfully and quickly to prevent gossip and to correct errors spreading through the grapevine because transparency helps eliminate gossipy speculation.[16] How active are you in the grapevine at work? Do you spread accurate information? Are you being ethical?

# Using Interpersonal Communication

**LEARNING OUTCOME 2** ▶

List the four steps in the communication process.

You need to know how communication flows through organizations, but more important to employers are your interpersonal communication skills.[17] The **communication process** is the transmission of information, meaning, and intent. In this section, we discuss the interpersonal communication process with barriers to communication (see figure 10.1).

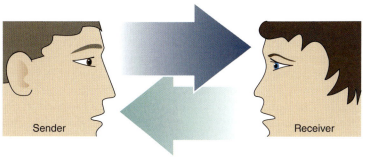

2. Message transmitted
through a channel.

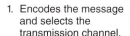
1. Encodes the message
and selects the
transmission channel.

Sender

3. Decodes the message
and decides if feedback
is needed.

Receiver

4. Feedback, response, or new message
may be transmitted through a channel.

The sender and receiver may continually change roles as they communicate.

**FIGURE 10.1**  The communication process.

1. A **sender** (the person doing the communicating) **encodes** the message (puts it into a form that the **receiver** of the message will understand).
2. The sender **transmits** the message by using a form of communication to send the message (by talking, texting, phoning, emailing) to the receiver.
3. The receiver **decodes** the message by translating the message into a meaningful form (interprets it).
4. The receiver may (or may not) give feedback.

## Encoding Your Message

When you send a message, you initiate the communication. Your message is the information, meaning, or intent that you want to get across to the receiver. It's your responsibility to make communication easy for the receiver.[18] Make sure you have a clear intent for your messages—if you don't have a clear idea of what you want to get across, neither will the receiver. Avoid the barriers discussed next that block communication (see figure 10.2).

### Words We Choose

When encoding, be careful about the words you select because they can get people to tune in to your message or tune out,[19] and poor wording results in costly miscommunication.[20] Through perception bias (chapter 8) we interpret messages differently,[21] and biases can lead

 What sort of audience do you think a sports radio host at a New York station would attract if they spoke with a British accent? A Texas drawl?

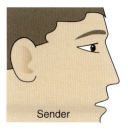

Sender

The words we choose
Information overload
Logic and order
The channel "shoe" doesn't fit
Trust and credibility
Failure to listen
Our emotions
Distortion

Receiver

**FIGURE 10.2**  Barriers to communication.

to miscommunication.[22] Semantics and jargon can be formidable barriers for your receivers— words can mean different things to different people (this is the subject of semantics), and jargon excludes people outside its originating group. Thus, the basketball achievement "triple double" is an expression that might confuse receivers who are unfamiliar with it.

To overcome problems of misinterpretation, consider what your receivers need in the way of language to understand your message. Don't use jargon with people who are not familiar with the terminology and especially with people from different cultures. Think for a moment about the many ways we use sport terms. Take the expressions "sure shot" (pool), "slam dunk" (basketball), and "tap in" (golf). Some people don't have a clue as to what these phrases mean. So watch your use of jargon, and if you need to, explain it.

### Information Overload

All of us have limits on the amount of information we can take in and process at any given time. New employees commonly experience information overload during their first few days at work because they are given so much new information. With so much information available so instantly via the Internet, we are often dazzled and overwhelmed and don't know what to do with it all. Overload is now the norm. We have reached the too-much-information age.

To minimize information overload, limit the information in your message to an amount the receiver can reasonably take in. If you talk too long, the receiver will become bored or will lose the thread of the message. Use two-way communication, checking periodically to be sure that the receiver is keeping up with you—job instructional training (chapter 7) helps.

**TIME-OUT 2** List three important messages you recently sent at work, on your team, or in your personal life and describe how you encoded them, how you transmitted them, and how they were received. State which barriers were operative and why. If there were no barriers, explain why. Now do this for a message your boss or coach sent you or someone else.

### Logic and Order

Make sure that your message makes sense. One of the simplest ways to do this is to check the order of your points. Outlines really help here. You want the receiver to be able to follow your message easily and not become confused. So instead of sending an important message off the top of your head, develop a well-planned message to overcome this barrier.

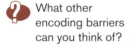 What other encoding barriers can you think of?

## Transmitting Your Message

After you encode your message, you must select the channel (oral or written, phone or text or email, video conference or face-to-face meeting) through which you will transmit the message.

Different channels work for different messages. The use of an inappropriate channel can kill a communication. Emails or cold calls just won't work in some situations. Using a phone call to clinch a deal with a star player isn't the same as meeting with him in person. Before you send an important message, give careful thought to which channel will help you get your message across. In the next section, we examine various channels in detail, so let's continue with barriers.

## Decoding the Message

Decoding occurs when receivers translate or interpret your message. They mix the content in your message with other ideas or information they have and with emotions they are feeling at the time, and they also look at your message through their own perceptual filters. All of these can be barriers (see figure 10.2) to receiving a message accurately.

### Trust and Credibility

Trust opens us to working and communicating effectively with others.[23] All of us as receivers consider whether we trust the sender and whether the sender has credibility. When we don't trust senders for whatever reason (they don't know what they're talking about, they don't have all the facts, they don't have good judgment, they've betrayed others before), we are reluctant to accept their messages at face value. Once doubt enters the equation, it is extremely difficult to rebuild trust.

Be honest and authentic in your communications. Know what you're talking about. Get the facts straight before you send your message.

### Failure to Listen

We are all guilty of not giving the sender our complete attention[24] when we are distracted by other things like our phones.[25] Our attention can wander; we may be more interested in how we're going to respond than in hearing what the sender is saying (we've thought of something clever to say, and we stop listening and start framing it). We want to get to the "end of the story"—we don't want to hear the details, or they bore us.

So help your receivers listen to you. Don't start your message until they stop what they are doing and give you their attention. Avoid distractions; ask them to put their phones away.[26] Question them in such a way that they must paraphrase your message and play it back to you. Stop during a long message and give receivers a chance to ask questions and to think about what you've just said. Ask for their thoughts on what you've said so far. Make your message interesting. If you are a problem talker (chapter 9), people will not listen to you. Later in this chapter we discuss how to be a better listener when receiving messages.

### Emotions

Getting emotional can cloud our judgment, so being calm helps communication. When we are angry, sad, or irrationally attached to an idea, concept, or person, we find it difficult to be objective and to hear (decode) the real message.

Take the receiver's emotions into consideration when you have to send a difficult message. Don't send messages when you are emotional, try not to get the person emotional, and stay calm throughout the discussion. Later in this chapter we give you ways to calm emotional people.

Can you think of a situation where a small group meeting would be better than a formal presentation of a new workplace guideline?
© laflor/iStock/Getty Images

**TIME-OUT 3**

Take three important messages you recently received at work, on your team, or in your personal life and tell how they were encoded and transmitted and how they were received. State which barriers were operative and why. If there were no barriers, tell why. Now do this for a message recently received by your boss or coach.

## APPLYING THE CONCEPT 10.2

### Barriers to Communication

Identify the barriers in the following messages or responses as

  a.  perceptual filter
  b.  information overload
  c.  wrong transmission channel
  d.  emotions
  e.  trust and credibility
  f.  distortion
  g.  failure to listen

_____  6.  Relax. You shouldn't be so upset that our young team didn't win the championship.

_____  7.  I don't have any questions. (Really thinking, "I was lost back on step one and don't know what to ask.")

_____  8.  We are right on schedule in building our new athletic facility. (Really thinking, "We are actually behind, but we'll catch up.")

_____  9.  I said I'd do it in a little while. It's only been 15 minutes. Why do you expect it to be done by now?

_____  10.  You don't know what you're talking about when you give your opinions on how to play defense. I think we will do it my way.

### *Distortion*

Distortion, or filtering, occurs when we alter information that we send and receive; it's a nice word for lying. We don't want to use the word "lying" because we may offend someone. We may do this for innumerable reasons. We don't like the truth, so we twist a message to fit our version of the incident and the "facts"—we believe what we want to believe. Tell the truth. Many people have said that things are going well only to get burned at the last minute when they can't deliver.

This results in lost trust and credibility; it's better to let people know of problems early because they may be able to help you. Likewise, when receiving messages, we hear what we want to hear. In these situations, you may have to repeat your message. You may have to reframe it. Asking for feedback helps you discern what the receivers are hearing. Listen carefully. Avoid having "yes" employees who filter out bad news—problems get solved only when they are faced honestly. Some executives build truth-telling cultures.

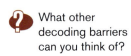 What other decoding barriers can you think of?

## Using the Channels

**LEARNING OUTCOME 3 ▶**

Use transmission channels well.

Sometimes the difference between failed communications and those that hit their mark is your choice of channel. When you are encoding a message, select the best channel.[27] The channels through which we transmit our messages are nonverbal, oral, written, and visual (see table 10.1).[28]

### Nonverbal Channels

Every time we talk to someone, we use words, but we also communicate nonverbally.[29] **Nonverbal communication** consists of the messages we send without words. It includes

## TABLE 10.1    Channels for Transmitting Messages

| Nonverbal | Oral | Written | Visual |
|---|---|---|---|
| Facial expressions (smile, frown; eye contact) | Face-to-face | Memos | Television |
| Vocal quality (emotional, emotionless, loud, quiet) | Meetings | Letters | Posters |
| Gestures (hand and body movements) | Presentations | Reports | Websites |
| Posture (sitting up, slouching) | Telephone | Bulletin boards | Skype/Zoom |
| Setting | Voice mail | Newsletters | Facetime |
| | | Electronic means (text messages, instant messages, emails, faxes, blogs, tweets) | Snapchat, Instagram, YouTube |

the setting (physical surroundings) and body language. Body language includes (1) facial expressions[30] (eye contact and a smile, or a dirty look), (2) vocal quality[31] (calmly or urgently, fast or slowly, softly or loudly), (3) gestures[32] (moving of hands, pointing, and nodding), and (4) posture[33] (sitting up straight or slouching, leaning back or forward, crossing arms or legs).

Use nonverbal communication effectively to project a calm, professional manner.[34] Smile, face the person, and use appropriate eye contact for three to five seconds; lean forward a bit and gesture often to convey that you are listening and are interested.[35] Do not cross your arms or legs (these are signs of being closed to communication), and speak in a pleasant, calm tone of voice.[36] Recall that Lou Holtz said that we choose to be happy or sad. Acting happy can make you and other people happier.[37]

Be aware of people's nonverbal communication because it reveals their feelings and attitudes toward you and the communication. Listen to what people say and don't say;[38] read between the lines. Do you consciously read nonverbal messages? Work on it. A major weakness of both writing (text/email) and speaking on the phone is that we lose most of the nonverbal communications that help convey meaning.[39]

The adage "Actions speak louder than words" is true. So be sure that your verbal message is consistent with your nonverbal signals because people tend to give more weight to the nonverbal communication. If you go to talk to your coach or boss about something important, and she says, "I'm really happy to talk to you," but she spends the entire time on her phone, will you believe the words or the actions? When you are speaking to people, show them that you care about them by giving them your complete attention; don't check your phone during the conversation.

Nonverbal communication can be more effective than verbal. Lovie Smith, former NFL Chicago Bears coach and current coach of the University of Illinois, doesn't yell at his players. When he gets mad, he stares straight ahead in silence. His players call it "the Lovie Look" and say it's more frightening—and more effective—than a torrent of angry words. Lovie Smith believes you can get a team to compete more fiercely and win more games by giving directives calmly and treating players with respect. Screaming managers are often resented and their messages ignored. Although there are exceptions, yelling in anger generally doesn't work well with females. Encouragement and positive behavior generally lead to better performance.

How you arrange your office sends nonverbal signals about your management style. If you want open communication, make your office conducive to open communication. Don't sit behind your desk and have the other person sit in front of the desk, unless you want to signal that you are in charge. Sitting side by side signals that you are willing to be open, that you are willing to meet the person halfway, and that you respect what they have to contribute.

# Oral Channels

**LEARNING OUTCOME 4** ▶

Communicate effectively in person.

We transmit messages orally by talking with each other. Using oral channels is easy and fast and allows for immediate feedback. The disadvantages are that such channels are often less accurate than other channels, and they may provide no record that the communication took place. Regardless of your career path, you will need to excel at presenting your ideas, be it face-to-face, in meetings, presentations, on the phone, or leaving a message. With increasing globalization, video communications via Skype and Zoom often replace face-to-face meetings and presentations.[40]

## Face-to-Face Communications

Face-to-face communications are appropriate for delegating tasks, disciplining, sharing information, answering questions, checking progress toward objectives, developing and maintaining rapport, and coaching[41] on the field and in the office. But don't be boring. Relationships are important,[42] and face-to-face conversations help develop and maintain relationships.[43] In the next section, you will learn a step-by-step process to follow when sending messages face-to-face.

## Meetings

Meetings are appropriate for coordinating team activities, delegating tasks to groups, and resolving conflicts. The most common meeting is the brief, informal get-together with a few athletes or employees. As you learned in chapter 9, with the increased use of teams, much more time is spent in meetings, and the ability to lead effective meetings is an important skill to acquire.

## Presentations

You present your ideas every day.[44] Whether you are talking sports, accepting an award, promoting a charity, or fulfilling sponsorship requirements, your ability to use words gracefully, lucidly, and accurately and to deliver them well is a sure way to garner positive attention from your colleagues and your bosses. Speaking skills are important because they are not used only for formal speeches.[45] The grace and confidence you gain from giving presentations are essential ingredients for working with others individually and in groups. Here are a few pointers.

Begin speeches with an attention-grabbing opener—a quote, a joke, or an interesting story that ignites interest in your topic. Following the opener, your presentations should have three parts: (1) a beginning—a purpose statement and an overview of the main points to be covered; (2) a middle—a discussion of the main points in enough detail to get the message across (but not so much detail that you lose your audience); and (3) an end—a summary of the purpose, main points, and any action required of the audience.[46] Stories are good at getting your message across, but they can't be boring. If you are uncomfortable giving presentations, practice. Then practice some more. Join your local Toastmasters club—these clubs have shaped many an effective speaker from the clay of pure terror. There are many books on giving effective presentations.

PowerPoint is a great presentation enhancer, and you should learn how to use it. To use it effectively, follow these two tips. First and foremost, don't just read your slides, unless you want to bore people senseless—"death by PowerPoint" is common. To avoid this, go easy on the text. Just use an outline to aid you in talking to your audience. If you can't talk to people, just show them your slides and let them read the slides for themselves. Second, the purpose of PowerPoint is to help you get your point across, so don't go crazy with special effects. They may be impressive, but they often distract from the point you are trying to make. Avoid laser pointers; they are distracting.

If you want to be good at giving presentations, it's the same as training for sports. You need to plan your workouts (develop PowerPoint slides), practice your skills (rehearse the presentation alone and in front of a few others), and win the competition (deliver a great speech). You also need to watch your nonverbal mannerisms, such as body movements and interjections like "um," so that they contribute to your message instead of distracting attention from it.[47]

### Telephone and Cell Phone Calls

The amount of time you spend on the phone will depend on your job. Phones are inappropriate for personnel matters (such as disciplining), but they are good for quick exchanges of information. They are especially useful for saving travel time. Although email and texting have gained in popularity, they are terrible for conversations, so use the phone and save time. If you prefer texting, recruiters say oral communications skills are more important.[48]

Here are a few pointers to keep in mind when you talk on a phone at work. Before making calls, set an objective and list what you plan to discuss. Use your list for jotting notes during the call. When receiving calls, determine the caller's purpose, and decide whether you or another person should handle it. When calls come in at inconvenient times, arrange to call the person back. Use your cell phone responsibly and politely. Other people (in restaurants, airports, and other public places) don't want to hear your business conversations. So step aside in private.

Mobile phones have evolved into personal assistants for many professionals. Phones can be used to schedule and organize your personal calendar, deliver and receive emails, browse the Web, and help you get to a meeting on time by providing guided directions. They give you an alarm clock for your hotel wake-up call; a calculator; and bar code scanning capabilities, replacing the need to carry credit cards. However, a mobile phone also means that your employer (if she has your phone number) can reach you at all times of the day.

On a personal note, although you may use your personal smartphone on the job, keep your personal use to a minimum while working. Privacy laws are not the same on and off the job. Companies have the technology and the legal right to listen to your personal calls on your own smartphone on their premises.[49] And avoid using your cell phone (especially texting) when you're driving—your life isn't the only one on the line.

### Voice Mail

If you call and don't get an answer, it is polite to leave a short message and request a call back or indicate when you will call back. Voice mail is also used for sending short messages containing information that doesn't need to be written, and texting is more popular today.

## Written Channels

Today, every time we text, email, post, tweet, or use social media, we are writing with technology constantly, and our words can last forever.[50] So organizations demand that their people have good writing skills.[51] Poorly written communications reveal your weaknesses more clearly (and more permanently!) than when you talk. Poor writing skills hinder your college performance, job search, and career development and advancement. Abbreviated jargon is fine for texting your friends but not for most formal business communications. So learn to write effectively.

Written communication allows time to ensure accuracy and precision, and it gives people time to think before they reply. It also provides an all-important record of what was communicated. But it often takes longer to text and email back and forth than it does to just pick up the phone and talk. You also lose the nonverbal part of communicating, and you get less feedback. And don't let social media exchanges take the place of face-to-face and phone communications for maintaining good working and social relationships with others.[52]

Here are the written channels you will continually use in your work.

1. Memos—commonly used to send intraorganizational messages
2. Letters
    1. "Snail mail" for getting your formal messages to people outside the organization, on company letterhead
    2. Faxes and scanning attachments for when the instant communication needs to be hard copy
3. Reports for formally conveying information, evaluations, analyses, and recommendations
4. Newsletters for conveying general information to the entire organization
5. Bulletin board notices for supplementing other channels and for wide dissemination of public information
6. Signs (or posters) for permanent reminders of important information, such as mission statements, safety instructions, and universal symbols such as a hexagonal stop sign with a line through the forbidden activity

Use written channels for all manner of communications—to send general information, to send specific and detailed information like facts and figures, to thank people, to send messages that require future action, or to send messages that affect several people, an entire team, or a department in a related way—to name but a few.

## Email, Texting, and Instant Messaging (IM)

Taken together, let's call these technologies e-comm. E-comm is commonly used for all of the written channels: to send memos, letters, reports, and newsletters, and to serve as a bulletin board and as a sign. E-comm is great for instant 24/7/365 communications (both formal and informal). E-comm has been called the greatest productivity tool of our time.

Conversely, some employees and friends complain that e-comm causes information overload, wastes work time, and is annoying. Personal e-comm takes up employees' work time, at great expense to employers. As a manager, don't let e-comm and talking on cell phones interfere with productivity on the job.

## Writing Tips

Here is a (very) short course for improving your writing. Before you write, organize your thoughts. Decide on the content that will help your audience understand your point—outlines are good for this. Check the message that you've laid out in your outline for focus. Weed out ideas and information that receivers don't need. Consider what you want your receivers to hear, to think, and to do. Now write from your outline in a way that makes it easy for the reader to understand your message, being brief and clear.[53]

As with effective presentations, effective written communications have a beginning (the purpose of the communication that encourages reading it),[54] a middle (support for the purpose—facts, figures, reasoning), and an end (a summary of the major points and a clear statement of conclusions or of action, if any, to be taken by you and the receivers).[55] When you get an email, respond with simple, direct answers.[56]

Write as though you are talking to the person. Write to communicate clearly, not to impress. Keep your message short and simple. Follow the 1-5-15 rule. Limit each paragraph to one topic, with an average of five sentences that average 15 words. Vary paragraph and sentence length, but never let paragraphs get too long because this discourages the person from reading your message. Write in the active voice ("I recommend . . . ") rather than the passive voice ("It is recommended . . .").[57]

Great writers use multiple drafts, and for important business issues, like your résumé, so can you. If you want your message to sizzle, reread it and edit it. Check your work for spelling and grammar errors. Have others edit your work. Do it again. If you are writing a paper or report, search out articles in the *Journal of Sport Management*, a leading journal in the field, and other sport journals.

### Press Releases

You could end up working in a sport information department (SID). Among many other responsibilities, SIDs are responsible for organizing and writing press releases. Press releases are crisply written letters that SIDs disseminate to local media about the sport teams, coaching staff, student-athletes, and the entire athletic department.

Many websites provide tips on writing a press release, such as the following: Make sure the information is newsworthy and substantial; tell the audience that the information is intended for them and why they should continue to read it; make sure the first 10 words of your press release are effective; avoid excessive use of adjectives and fancy language; deal with facts; provide as much contact information as possible; and make it as easy as possible for media representatives to do their jobs. See the example Springfield SLAMM news release.

## Visual Channels

Sporting event telecasts (on TV and increasingly on the Internet) are big business. Two notions dominate discussions of links between sport media and sport attendance. One side says that media use in sport both increases with and promotes event attendance. The

---

### Example of a Press Release

#### Springfield SLAMM Ready for 2020 Summer Pro-Am League

May 15, 2020
For Immediate Release
Media Relations Contact: Info@DrSteveSobel.com or 413-565-5000.

Head Coach Dr. Steve Sobel of Longmeadow announced that the Springfield SLAMM, one of the pro-am summer basketball teams in New England, will be playing in the 2020 Greater Hartford Pro-Am League this season and in selected appearances in the Greater Springfield area.

The team is NCAA sanctioned and approved for the inclusion of Division I basketball players. Former players include first-round NBA draft pick Jeremy Lamb, Deandre Daniels, and Ryan Boatright, all of the University of Connecticut. Additional former players include Missouri star Alex Oriakhi, Boston College graduate Joe Trapani, and the University of Vermont American East Player of the Year candidate Michael Trimboli.

The SLAMM reached the semifinals last year, and Sobel said he "is looking to make another significant run to the championship in August."

The coaching staff for the 2020 campaign include assistant coach Ethan Sobel.

The SLAMM players will also continue to visit hospitals to do clinics as they did last year at the Connecticut Children's Medical Center for Children and their Families. There will also be basketball shooting clinics for junior high and high school players of all ages on June 25 and 26.

The SLAMM's first game will take place on June 29 at the Mass Mutual Center.

Used with permission of Steve Sobel.

other side holds that media use can act as a recreational substitute for attendance. What do you think? If you aspire to work for NCAA Division IA or pro teams, you should realize that telecasting of games is big money for teams. You may also want to consider a career in sport media. There are lots of jobs behind the scenes, or should we say screens, of visual channel sports like ESPN.

Visuals are also critical to coaching in improving performance. Many teams watch game videos to identify strengths and areas to improve on for the next game. But watching video right after a performance is also important in coaching—for example, after a dive. Engineers from BMW (yes, the car people) developed a machine that not only videos long jumps; it spits out three crucial numbers: horizontal velocity, vertical velocity leaving the board, and angle of flight. Bryan Clay, two-time decathlon Olympic medalist, used it in preparation for tryouts and the Olympics. At the Olympic tryouts, he set the world record.

## Combining Channels

Repetition helps ensure that important messages are received and that their meaning is understood and remembered. This is where combining channels can be very useful; for example, to convey an important message, you might send a memo (sometimes several) and then follow up with personal visits or phone calls to see whether receivers have questions. There are times when you will want to formally document a face-to-face meeting, particularly in disciplinary situations. We discuss this more in chapter 13.

 Do you think broadcasting the *Mike Francesa* show on television reduces or enhances the normal communication process of radio?

Mike Francesa briefly left WFAN, only to return with an even larger communication plan. His WFAN radio show will also appear on an app for the show instead of using a TV simulcast. The radio show will be used as a generator of content to create more digital operations. Francesa missed communicating directly to his audience during his brief retirement.[58]

## Choosing Channels

**LEARNING OUTCOME 5** ▶

Select appropriate channels for your messages.

To choose the best channel for a given message, look at the media's richness. Media richness is the amount of information and meaning that the channel can transmit. The more information and meaning, the "richer" the channel. Face-to-face talk is therefore the richest channel because the full range of oral and nonverbal communication is available. Phone calls are less rich than face-to-face meetings because many nonverbal cues are lost. Written messages can be rich, but they must be very well written to qualify. Video is rich because body language is evident.

Key your channel choice to how difficult, complex, or important your message is.[59] Here are some general guidelines to follow: Use oral channels for sending difficult and unusual messages. Use written channels for transmitting simple and routine messages to several people or messages that contain facts or detailed instructions. Combine

**TIME-OUT 4** Identify the channel used for an oral message and a written one that you recently received at work or on your team. State whether the sender's choice of channel was effective and, if it was not, which channel would have been better and why.

channels for important messages that recipients need to understand and act upon. You can gain the benefits of nonverbal communication primarily in oral channels, but some does come through in writing, too. 😊

## APPLYING THE CONCEPT  10.3

### Choosing Channels

Select the most appropriate channel for transmitting the following messages (which haven't been encoded yet). When combined media will be most effective, indicate which ones.

a.  face-to-face

b.  meeting

c.  presentation

d.  phone call

e.  memo

f.  letter

g.  report

h.  bulletin board

i.  poster

j.  newsletter

_____ 11.  You want to know whether an important shipment of uniforms has arrived.

_____ 12.  You want staff and players to turn the lights off in the locker room when no one is in it.

_____ 13.  You need to explain the new community relations program to your team.

_____ 14.  John has come in late for work again; you want him to shape up.

_____ 15.  You've exceeded your ticket sales goals and want your boss to know about it because it should have a positive influence on your upcoming performance appraisal.

# Sending Messages

This section discusses the processes of planning and sending messages and how to properly check the receiver's understanding of the message.

Do you realize that every time you talk, you are sending messages?[60] An important part of a coach and sport manager's job is to give instructions. Sending a message might seem simple, but it's not easy. Did you ever hear a manager say, "This isn't what I asked for"? Well, it is usually the result of poor communication. To avoid miscommunications, take 100% of the responsibility for ensuring that your messages are transmitted accurately. Here's how: plan the message, send it effectively, and check understanding (get feedback). In this section, we discuss each of these three parts of sending messages.

## Planning the Message

Before you send a message that is difficult, unusual, or especially important, use this short checklist to make sure your message is on target: Ask yourself what, who, how, which, where, and when.

- What is my goal in this message? What do you want the end result of the communication to be?[61] Set an objective, and keep to it.

- Who should receive my message?

- How should I encode my message? Follow the guidelines discussed earlier.

- Which channel is appropriate for my message, my receivers, and the situation? Follow the guidelines discussed earlier.
- Where should I deliver my message? In your office, the locker room, or the receiver's workplace? Choose a place that keeps distractions to a minimum.
- When should I transmit my message? Timing is important, so think about your receiver and be considerate. Don't approach someone five minutes before quitting time. Make appointments when appropriate.

## Sending Oral Messages

Recall that oral channels are the richest, and face-to-face, oral communication is best when the message is difficult or complex. When sending a face-to-face message, follow these steps in the **message-sending process**: (1) develop rapport, (2) state your communication objective, (3) transmit your message, (4) check the receiver's understanding, and (5) get a commitment and follow up. The process steps are listed in figure 10.3 and are briefly discussed next.

*Step 1.* Develop rapport. Put the receiver at ease. It is usually appropriate to begin communication with small talk, like sports.

*Step 2.* State your communication objective. It is helpful for the receiver to know the purpose of the communication before you explain the details.

*Step 3.* Transmit your message. Tell the receiver the details of the message, such as using the job instructional training method (see chapter 7).

*Step 4.* Check the receiver's understanding. When giving information, ask direct questions or paraphrase. Simply asking "Do you have any questions?" does not check understanding. We describe how to check understanding later in this chapter.

*Step 5.* Get a commitment and follow up. If the message involves assigning a task, make sure that the message recipient can do the task and have it done by a certain time or date. When athletes and employees are reluctant to commit to the necessary action, coaches and managers can use persuasive power (chapter 8) within their authority (chapter 5). Follow up to ensure that the necessary action has been taken.

 **TIME-OUT 5** Think about a task your boss or coach recently assigned you. Note which of the message-sending process steps the boss took, which ones the boss didn't, and how the message could have been sent more effectively.

## Getting Receivers to Get It: Feedback

**LEARNING OUTCOME 6** ▶

Solicit feedback properly.

For communication to take place, after you transmit your message, you will need to know whether the receiver "gets it." This is where you check understanding by asking for feedback.[62] **Feedback** is the process of verifying messages. It literally feeds back to the sender the original information, meaning, or intent transmitted in the message.

**FIGURE 10.3**   The message-sending process.

Indeed, the most common reason that messages fail to communicate is a lack of feedback. Questioning, paraphrasing, and soliciting comments and suggestions are all ways you as the sender can check understanding through feedback. If the receiver of your message can answer your questions or paraphrase the message back to you accurately, you have successfully transmitted your message. If not, keep trying until you succeed. Before we discuss effective ways to solicit feedback, let's look at what can go wrong.

## *How Not to Solicit Feedback*

One sure way to block feedback is to send your entire message and then ask, "Do you have any questions?" Most of the time, you have very effectively killed any chances for discussion, because very few people will ask questions. Here is why they don't.

- *They feel ignorant.* No one wants to look like a dummy by asking a question.
- *They are ignorant.* Sometimes people don't know enough about the topic to ask questions. That is, they don't know whether the information given is complete, correct, or subject to interpretation.
- *They don't want to point out your ignorance.* Asking a question in this situation may suggest that you have done a poor job of preparing and sending the message or that you are wrong—do you really want to tell your boss you haven't got a clue about what he is talking about?

After senders ask whether there are questions (and thereby end the discussion), they often make yet another leap in the wrong direction. They assume that they are good at sending messages—that if there are no questions, the receivers have understood the message.[63] If only this were true! When receivers don't understand the message, they will act upon the message incorrectly (e.g., perform a task incorrectly). When this happens, the message has to be sent again; the task has to be done again; and time, materials, and effort are wasted in the meantime. Taking a few minutes to get feedback often saves hours of needless work.

## *How to Solicit Feedback*

Proper questioning and proper paraphrasing help ensure that when you send your message, your receivers get the message. In **paraphrasing**, receivers restate the message in their own words. Be sure to use your own words, to say it differently, because some people don't want you to parrot back what they said. Keep the following in mind when getting feedback.

- *There are no dumb questions.* Never sneer at a question (no matter how stupid you think it is). Always answer patiently and explain clearly. If people sense impatience in you, you've just stopped any question dead in its tracks. To encourage good questions, listen carefully and praise good questions.[64]
- *Tune in to your own nonverbals.* Match your walk to your talk. If your nonverbal messages are discouraging feedback, no amount of verbal pleading on your part will bring forth the harvest of questions you want. If you say, "ask me questions," but you look at them like they are stupid, or you behave impatiently, they won't ask questions.
- *Tune in to your receivers' nonverbals.* Seeing a lot of puzzled or blank looks out there? It's time to stop, backtrack, and clarify.
- *Ask your receivers questions.* If you ask good questions, you can get to good answers.[65] Ask anything (except, of course, "Do you have any questions?"). Ask direct questions for specific information you have given. If responses are off track or muddled, repeat the message, give more examples, or elaborate further. You can also ask indirect questions: "How do you feel about doing this task?" Ask "If you were me" questions (e.g., "If you were me, how would you solve our lack of focus during games?"). Ask third-party questions, such

as "How will players respond when they have to bring their grades up to stay on the team?" If you get receivers to talk, the feedback gates will open.

• *Have receivers paraphrase your message.* Paraphrasing is a valuable way to check understanding. Soliciting it gracefully is also an art. Clumsy soliciting of paraphrasing makes people feel stupid. Saying "Joan, tell me what I just said so that I can be sure

TIME-OUT
6

Think about an especially effective boss or coach you've had. Did he or she solicit feedback? If so, how? If not, why not?

you won't make a mistake, or so I will be sure you will do the job right" is not going to work—in fact, it's going to backfire big time! Have some paraphrasing questions worked out beforehand; with practice they will eventually roll off your tongue. "Now please tell me what you are going to do so that we will be sure we are in agreement on how you will complete this task." "Please tell me what you are going to do so that I can be sure that I explained the task clearly." This takes the pressure off them and puts it on you, where it belongs; you take 100 percent responsibility for sending your messages accurately.

# Receiving Messages

So far, we've discussed the communication process from the viewpoint of the sender. We are up to the third step in the communication process, which requires you as the receiver to decode the message into a meaningful form—interpreting it. Now it's time to become a good receiver, which begins with listening.[66] If someone asked you if you were a good listener, most likely you would say yes. But most of us are not good listeners,[67] because we don't remember what was said.[68] Unfortunately, the number-one thing lacking in new college grads is listening skills. Can you pay attention and listen effectively at school, in sport, and at work, and for how long? Complete Self-Assessment 10.1 to determine the level and quality of your listening skills. Be honest.

Before we sharpen your listening skills, consider how people receive messages, summarized in figure 10.4. The **message-receiving process** involves listening, analyzing, and checking understanding. To receive the real message the sender is transmitting, you have to do all three. Receiving doesn't end with good listening. By using the message-receiving process, you can become a better listener, which is covered in this section.

## Becoming a Listener

LEARNING OUTCOME 7 ▶

Explain how we receive messages.

Failure to listen is the killer of many an otherwise effective communication. Let's discuss some guidelines you can follow to improve your listening skills.

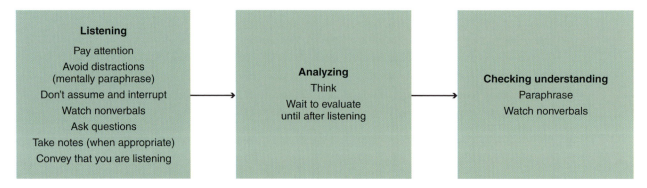

**Listening**

Pay attention

Avoid distractions (mentally paraphrase)

Don't assume and interrupt

Watch nonverbals

Ask questions

Take notes (when appropriate)

Convey that you are listening

**Analyzing**

Think

Wait to evaluate until after listening

**Checking understanding**

Paraphrase

Watch nonverbals

**FIGURE 10.4**  The message-receiving process.

# SELF-ASSESSMENT 10.1

## Are You a Good Listener?

Select the response that best describes the frequency of your behavior. This Self-Assessment is easiest to complete online.

A = almost always

U = usually

F = frequently

O = occasionally

S = seldom

_____ 1. To encourage others to talk, I show interest, ask them questions about themselves, and smile and nod.

_____ 2. I pay closer attention to people who are similar to me than to those who are different from me.

_____ 3. I evaluate people's words and nonverbal signals as they talk.

_____ 4. I avoid distractions; if it's noisy, I suggest moving to a quiet spot.

_____ 5. If people interrupt me when I'm doing something, I put what I was doing out of my mind and give them my complete attention.

_____ 6. When people are talking, I allow them time to finish. I don't interrupt them, anticipate what they're going to say, or jump to conclusions.

_____ 7. I tune out people who don't agree with me.

_____ 8. My mind wanders to personal topics when someone else is talking or when professors are lecturing.

_____ 9. I pay close attention to nonverbal signals to help me fully understand what the other person is really saying.

_____ 10. When the topic is difficult, I tune out and just pretend I understand.

_____ 11. When the other person is talking, I think about what I'm going to say in reply.

_____ 12. When I think something is missing or contradictory in a discussion, I ask questions to get the person to explain her ideas more fully.

_____ 13. I let the other person know when I don't understand something.

_____ 14. When listening to other people, I try to put myself in their place and see things from their perspective.

_____ 15. When someone gives me information or instructions, I repeat them in my own words and ask the sender whether I'm correct.

Have some of your friends fill out this assessment, giving their impressions of your listening habits.

**Scoring.** For statements 1, 4, 5, 6, 9, 12, 13, 14, and 15, give 5 points for an A answer; 4 for U; 3 for F; 2 for O; and 1 for S. For items 2, 3, 7, 8, 10, and 11, the score reverses: 5 points for S; 4 for O; 3 for F; 2 for U; and 1 for A. Place these scores on the lines next to your responses and add them to get your total. Your score should be between 15 and 75. Place your score on the following continuum.

| Poor listener | | | | | | | | | | | | Good listener |
|---|---|---|---|---|---|---|---|---|---|---|---|---|
| 15 | 20 | 25 | 30 | 35 | 40 | 45 | 50 | 55 | 60 | 65 | 70 | 75 |

### Retentive Listening

**Listening** is the process of giving the speaker your undivided attention (and we emphasize the word *undivided*). Our ability to comprehend words five times more quickly than speakers can talk results in—you guessed it—wandering minds. The result, of course, is that with all the background thoughts and sounds (bings and bongs of text/email), the sender's message loses out.

To listen, we have to hear what is said, which we can do, but it's not enough. *Retentive listening* results in remembering the message. How good is your listening memory?[69] Again, listening requires undivided attention and concentration. When managers send messages, they usually require us to take action to achieve an objective. But how can we take action if we don't understand or remember the message?

To understand and remember messages, you must concentrate. We remember what we see better than what we hear. You get distracted and lose your ability to pay attention and remember things when you separate the use of your eyes and your mind. When your eyes and ears are not working together as a team, you can't concentrate at all.[70] If you are listening to someone talking as you check your phone (or look somewhere else), you lose your concentration. Do you realize how multitasking kills concentration and memory? Think about it.

So, to listen with retention, you need to look the person in the eye and concentrate with your mind on what he says. If your eyes are looking but your mind is wandering or vice versa, bring them back together to work as a team. Next, let's go over some other listening guidelines that can improve your retentive listening skills.

### Listening Guidelines

- *Pay attention.* It's that simple and that hard—because paying attention *is* hard, or we would all be great listeners. Relax (quickly) and clear your mind, and then focus on the sender. This gets you on track right now. If you miss the first few words, you may miss the whole gist of the message. Practice this: The next time someone interrupts your work in order to talk, stop whatever you are doing (immediately, or ask for a minute to finish), and give the person your complete attention. Don't multitask when people want to talk to you; your nonverbals will be saying "Go away, I'm too busy to talk to you."

- *Avoid distractions.* Concentration is the key to listening, so shut off your phone and other distractions.[71] Keep your eyes on the speaker. Do not fiddle with pens, papers, your phone, or anything else. If the area is noisy or full of distractions, move to a quiet spot.

- *Stay tuned in, and repeat.* If your mind wanders to other topics (and it will), gently bring it back. Continue to bring it back every time you notice yourself straying. Don't tune out because you don't like something about the speaker or because you disagree with what is being said. Don't tune out because the topic is difficult—ask questions instead. Don't think about what you're going to say in reply. Stay tuned in by silently paraphrasing the message. The next time your mind wanders, repeat word for word what the person is saying; repeating really forces you to stay tuned in. Try it! It works.

- *Don't assume and don't interrupt.* Most mistakes in receiving messages are made when we hear the first few words of a sentence, think we know what is about to be said, finish it in our own minds, and then miss the real message. Listen to the entire message, without interrupting, because you really do not know what the speaker is going to say.

- *Watch nonverbals.* People sometimes say one thing and mean something else. Watch as you listen to be sure that the speaker's eyes, body, and face are in sync with the verbal message. If something seems out of sync, ask questions to clarify.

- *Ask questions.* Check your understanding. When you feel something's missing or contradictory, or you just don't understand, don't be afraid to ask for clarification. The speaker will be grateful, as will other listeners. If you don't understand a message, chances are they don't understand it, either.

- *Take notes.* Write down important things. This helps you concentrate on what is being said and helps you remember later. Always have something to write on and something to write with—you can use your smartphone. Taking notes also tells the sender nonverbally that you want to get the message right.

- *Convey that you are listening.* Active listeners use verbal cues ("You feel . . . ," "Yes," "I see," "I understand") and nonverbal cues (eye contact, nodding your head, leaning slightly forward) to indicate that they are interested and listening. Active listening also helps you concentrate and retain what you hear.

### Developing Listening Skills

Here is how to improve your listening skills. Work to change your behavior to become a better listener by following the listening guidelines, and review the 15 statements in Self-Assessment 10.1. Make a habit of doing items 1, 4, 5, 6, 9, 12, 13, 14, and 15. And avoid doing items 2, 3, 7, 8, 10, and 11.

Have you ever heard "Listen more and talk less,"[72] "You have two ears and one mouth because you should listen twice as much as you talk," "You learn more when your mouth is closed and your ears are open,"[73] or "Shut up and listen"?[74] Do you talk more often than you listen? Ask your teammates, coach, boss, coworkers, or friends, who will give you an honest answer. How about following the advice of listening more, at least for a week? Spend one week focusing on listening.

This is going to be a very quiet week for you. Talk as little as possible, and listen, listen, listen. When your attention wanders, bring it back. Get quiet. Take special pains to concentrate on what other people say and on the nonverbal signals they send. Note when verbal and nonverbal messages are particularly consistent and when they are blatantly out of sync. Note when nonverbal messages reinforce the speaker's words and when they detract from them. Talk only when necessary. (You can do this—it's just for a week! Try it.)

Once you've put in your week of listening, take some time and think about what it felt like to listen more than you talked. Was it hard? Now take Self-Assessment 10.1 again. Did your answers change? Do you still talk more than you listen? Regardless of how much and how well you listen, if you follow these guidelines, you will improve your conversational ability and become someone people want to talk to and listen to. To become an active listener, take responsibility for ensuring mutual understanding.

## Analyzing and Checking Understanding of the Message

Although listening is the most critical part of the message-receiving process, you also need to analyze and check understanding to ensure accurate communications.

### Analyzing the Message

When we analyze a message, we think about it, decode it, and evaluate it. Therefore, as speakers send their messages, you should be doing two things:

- *Thinking.* Use your excess capacity for comprehending to listen actively. Silently paraphrase, organize, summarize, review, and interpret often. When this is not working, repeat every word they say to yourself. This marshals all your forces for decoding the message.

- *Waiting to evaluate.* When we try to listen and evaluate what is said at the same time, we miss part or all of the message. So listen to the entire message, and then make your conclusions.[75] When you evaluate the message, base your conclusions on the facts presented rather than on perception bias and organizational politics (chapter 8).

### *Checking Understanding of the Message*

To ensure accurate communication, you need to check your understanding and give feedback. After you have listened to the message, or while listening if it's a long message, check mutual understanding in two ways:

**TIME-OUT 7** Now that you've listened for a week and have done Self-Assessment 10.1 twice, what do you think is your weakest listening skill? What are you going to do about it?

- *Paraphrasing.* When you are asked to do something, make sure you know exactly what needs to be done. As discussed earlier, give feedback by paraphrasing the message, and ask questions if you don't understand something.

- *Watch nonverbals.* During your conversation, watch the other person's nonverbal communication. If the person's verbal and nonverbal messages conflict, clarify the message to ensure mutual understanding. Use nonverbal active listening behavior to help the sender.

# Responding to Messages

**LEARNING OUTCOME 8** ▶

Choose appropriate response styles.

We are up to the fourth and last step of the interpersonal communication process—the receiver may (or may not) give feedback. Not every message requires a response, of course, but many do. With face-to-face and phone discussions, the role of sender and receiver flip throughout every conversation. So feedback needs to go both ways.

The way you respond to a message directly affects the way the communication process is completed. When you receive a message, you have five response styles from which to choose (see figure 10.5). There is no single best response type for all occasions, so we will discuss each style and when to use it. To demonstrate the different response styles, let's look at five responses to a rather confrontational message from a person on your team: "You supervise me so closely that I can't do my job—I have no breathing room."

## Advisor's Responses

Advisors: They evaluate, give their personal opinion, direct, or instruct. Advisors tend to close, limit, or redirect the flow of communication.

- Supervisor response: "You need my directions to do a good job; you lack experience." "I disagree. You need my instructions and you need for me to check your work." (Note that advice was not asked for, but it was given anyway.)

- When to give advice: Don't be too quick to give advice because you may stop people from discussing what is really on their minds, and they may not need or even want

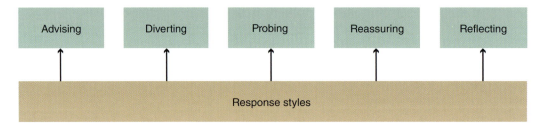

**FIGURE 10.5** Response styles.

your advice. So give advice when you are asked for it. Remember, however, that giving advice builds dependence. Developing your staff's ability to think things through and to make decisions is an important part of your job. When asked for advice by employees who you believe don't really need it, ask, "What do you think is the best way to handle this situation?" "What do you think we should do?"[76]

## Diverter's Responses

Diverters: They switch the focus to a new message—what we commonly call changing the subject. Diverters also tend to redirect, close, or limit the flow of communication. Diversions used early on in the conversation may cause senders to think that their message is not worth discussing or that the other party's message is more important.

- Supervisor response: "You've reminded me of Joe . . . Did you see the game last night?"
- When to divert: Diversion is appropriate when either party is uncomfortable with the topic. Diversion may be helpful when someone is sharing personal experiences or feelings but the other person wants to edge the conversation away from something too personal, too embarrassing, or too "close." Religious and political discussions rarely change people's minds but often end in arguments, so divert to another subject to avoid conflict.

## Prober's Responses

Probers ask the sender to give more information about some aspect of the message so the prober can better understand the situation.

- Supervisor response: "What did I do to make you say this to me?" (Not "Why do you feel this way?") "How long have you felt this way?"
- When to probe: Probe during the early stages of the message to ensure that you fully understand the situation. When probing, use good "what" questions rather than "why" questions.[77] After probing, you often may need to use some of the other response styles. Make sure you fully understand the situation before quickly giving advice.

## Reassurer's Responses

Reassurers make statements to reduce the intensity of the emotions associated with the message in order to build the sender's confidence.[78] They're saying, "Don't worry; everything will be OK."

- Supervisor response: "Don't worry, I won't do it for much longer." "Your work is improving, so I may be able to provide less direction soon."
- When to reassure: This technique works well when the other person lacks confidence because it can include giving praise to help people develop confidence. How often do you say something like "Don't worry, you will pass the test" or ". . . get a hit" or ". . . win the game" or ". . . get 'em next time"?

## Reflector's Responses

**Reflecting** paraphrases the message and communicates understanding and acceptance. When reflecting, do not use the sender's exact words; it is mimicking (and thus patronizing). When reflecting is used gracefully, senders feel listened to, understood, and free to explore the topic in more depth.

## APPLYING THE CONCEPT 10.4

### Identifying Response Styles

Identify each response to the given situation as

    a. advising

    b. diverting

    c. probing

    d. reassuring

    e. reflecting

Irate parent: Coach, do you have a minute to talk?

Coach: Sure, what's up?

Irate parent: Can you do something about all the swearing that players do on the team? It's disgusting. I'm surprised you haven't done anything.

Coach:

_____ 16. I didn't know anyone was swearing. I'll look into it.

_____ 17. You don't have to listen to it. Just ignore the swearing.

_____ 18. Are you feeling well today?

_____ 19. So you find this swearing offensive?

_____ 20. What words are they saying that offend you?

- "Checking up on you bugs you?" "You don't think I need to check up on you; is this what you mean?" (Note that these responses allow the person to express feelings and direct the path of the exchange.)

- When to reflect: Reflecting leads to the most effective communication and the best human relations.[79] It is generally a good idea to start a conversation with reflecting responses, and as the communication progresses, it may be appropriate to change to other response styles. But sometimes we just want someone to listen to us so we can get our frustration out. At these times, we don't want advice or lots of annoying questions, and we don't want someone to change the subject or say that everything is OK.[80] We just want a good listener with reflective responses. When you lose a close game after giving 100 percent, what do you want to hear from a friend? "You need to work harder." "Why didn't you pass the ball more?" "Don't worry; you will do better next time." "It was a tough game." Which response tells you that your friend is willing to listen to your frustration?

TIME-OUT 8

State two oral messages you received recently and your responses to them. Identify your response style for each message. Give two different responses using other styles, and state why each is appropriate or inappropriate.

# Dealing With Emotions and Criticism

In this section, we start by discussing how to deal with your own emotions and those of others and then how to take and give criticism.

## Dealing With Your Own and Others' Emotions

Emotions refer to feelings (anger, annoyance, boredom, disappointment, distrust, fear, happiness, sadness) that influence our behavior. Our brain can't be both rational and highly emotional at the same time—emotions win. We tend to make poor decisions when we are highly emotional and hurt our relationships.[81] It doesn't really matter what people think and what they know or don't know; they act on what they feel.[82] Someone you know personally or work with is going to start an emotional exchange with you—already been there? It is going to continue to happen throughout your life.

### Facts About Feelings

If you want to succeed both personally and professionally, understanding emotions and learning to deal with them (yours and others') will help.[83] Realize that feelings are

- subjective—they reveal people's attitudes and needs (they tell you if they are happy or sad),
- often disguised as factual statements ("It's hot in here" rather than "I feel hot." "This topic is boring" rather than "I'm feeling bored by this topic,"), and
- neither right nor wrong (so don't judge others' feelings or let them tell you how to feel).

### Acknowledge Your Feelings and Control Your Behavior

Ever been told to control your emotions? Actually, we cannot choose feelings or control the feelings themselves. Don't you feel the emotions when someone hurts you? Can you stop a painful feeling simply by saying, It doesn't bother me? However, we can control how we express our feelings.[84] We choose our behavioral responses (what we say and do). If I call you a hurtful name in anger (pick one that would upset you), you will feel it. The real question is how do you respond? Will you ignore me and walk away, shout a name back at me, hit me? How do you respond when players talk trash to you during the game—can you ignore them, or do you let your emotions hurt your game?

### Dealing With Your Emotions and Behavior

Let's discuss dealing with your emotions before getting into more details about helping calm others. Here are some guidelines to help you deal with your emotions.

- Sometimes no response is the best option. An alternative is to postpone a response until after you calm down.[85]
- Be aware of your feelings, and realize that it only takes seconds to say something that hurts others, but it can take years to heal the wounds your words and action cause others.
- If you get emotional and wish to reply in anger, consider that you may have misunderstood the behavior. The other person may not have meant it the way it sounds to you—*perception incongruence* and *attribution* (chapter 8). Have you ever been misunderstood?

- Realize that some people don't intend to upset you. The behavior that bothers you just comes out of their ignorance of good human relations. Others may not even realize their behavior upsets you.[86]

- Avoid being passive-aggressive.[87] Ever let something that upsets you happen several times without saying anything, and let it build to the point of getting angry and yelling about the behavior? And the person didn't know why you were upset or thought that you were overreacting?

- Do confront people early about their behavior that upsets you. But be calm,[88] and follow the steps for resolving conflicts in chapter 8.

- Getting upset and yelling don't help your relationship or fix the problem. Angry outbursts hurt your health,[89] you may regret responding in anger later, and your response will likely hurt your relationship.[90]

The lesson here? If you can control your negative emotional responses, you will have better relationships and be a more effective leader.[91] Each of us chooses our responses in emotional exchanges. Avoid getting caught up in others' emotions by responding emotionally. Staying calm when dealing with an emotional person works much better. We have a chance to shape these exchanges into something positive. In the name-calling scenario, you could make a calm, reflective statement—such as, "You must really be upset to call me that name." Don't let the competitors get into your head with trash talk and hurt your performance. Following are some specific do's and don'ts for dealing with emotional people that will also help prevent you from getting emotional.

## *Calming an Emotional Person*

LEARNING OUTCOME 9 ▶

Calm an emotional person.

If someone explodes at you in anger, what can you do? Fortunately, there are positive ways to handle the situation. But first, here is what you shouldn't do:

- Don't put the person down.
- Don't deny the anger (it's a judgment of the feeling).
- Don't accuse back (do you really want to fight?)
- Don't patronize the person (do you really want to fuel the anger?).
- Don't show who's boss (unless you are the boss and your authority is being challenged).

This means that the following statements should never be said (even if you are thinking them) because they escalate the feelings instead of calming the person:

- "It's no big deal." (Not to you, but it is to them.)
- "You shouldn't be angry." (Recall that feelings are neither right nor wrong, so don't judge feelings as wrong—using the word *should* results in a judgment.)
- "Don't be upset." (Too late—the person is already upset.)
- "You're acting like a baby." (Like this is going to get you somewhere?)
- "Just sit down and be quiet." (This may shut the person up, but it will fuel emotions. Think about it. If someone tells you to be quiet, will you calmly listen and agree to the lecture, admitting you are wrong and they are right?)
- "I know how you feel." (No, you don't. Recall the discussion of perceptions in chapter 8. No one, even someone who has experienced the same thing, knows how others feel.)

Can you list other statements that you should not make when you're trying to calm someone?

These statements only raise the temperature of the exchange. Belittlers cause emotional distress and undermine confidence. Contributing to a person's anger, fear, and panic hampers performance. So avoid emotional responses, which you often will regret later, anyway. Try to get away from an emotional exchange and get to communication.

First, you have to deal with the emotion, and then you can deal with the issue; you can't successfully deal with the issue when emotions are high. The best way to calm someone is to be an empathic listener.[92] That is, show empathy and acknowledge the feeling with open-ended, reflective responses. Let them express the feeling—let them vent. After emotions are calm, you can rationally discuss the issue. However, don't encourage people to vent about things that can't be changed because venting actually makes us angrier, and it is unhealthy.[93] Instead, focus on things that can be changed to solve problems; don't simply complain about them.

Fortunately, there are productive ways you can respond. For one thing, make sure you know chapter 8 inside and out. For another, learn to empathize. **Empathy** is the ability to understand and relate to someone else's situation and feelings. Empathic responders deal with feelings, content, and the underlying meaning expressed in the message.[94]

Empathic people are good listeners—in fact, with good listening comes empathy; they are natural by-products of each other. Exceptional leaders are empathic,[95] especially when they communicate bad news.[96] So remember to use good listening skills. Pay attention to what people are saying; don't assume and don't interrupt; let them know you are listening (honor their feelings, in other words); and withhold evaluative responses and advice.

Carefully reflect feelings back like this: "Were you hurt when you didn't get first-string position?" "You resent Charlie for not pulling his weight on the team—is that what you mean?" "Are you doubtful that the job's going to get done on time?" Very often, simply understanding the sender's feelings is the solution—only venting is wanted, not advice. Other times, solutions must be found. As emotions cool (and they will if you give them enough time), you can proceed to the crux of the problem and begin solving it. If emotions continue to run high, you may have to wait until a later time before you can consider solutions.

 **TIME-OUT 9** Recall an emotional exchange that you witnessed at work or on your team. Did the responder calm the person effectively? Write a paragraph about the exchange showing where the responder went right or went wrong.

# Giving and Receiving Criticism

You're going to give some criticism and you're going to get some. It's easier to give it than to get it, isn't it? In management as in sports, criticism is necessary for continuous improvement.[97] Some organizations develop a "culture of candor" that encourages criticism to improve everyone's performance.[98]

## *Giving Criticism*

Most managers dislike giving critical feedback to underperformers. This is part of the reason so many people don't do a good job.

**Effective Criticism**    The goal of criticism should be to improve performance. How you criticize will affect if the receiver will improve, both on and off the field. Keep in mind that criticism gets the best results when given with empathy in the spirit of helping others,[99] and when it is coming from a person who is trusted and respected.[100] Avoid personal criticism (no personal put-downs; focus on improving performance), and don't criticize things people can't change. It doesn't help to tell a player she dropped the ball; she knows it and most likely already feels bad about it. Don't waste time placing blame. The team wins or loses; saying it's someone's fault doesn't change anything in a positive way, but it will hurt cohesiveness. Never criticize someone publicly, especially your bosses.

Here are some guidelines for giving motivational criticism to improve performance. You will learn how to deal with problem employees and to discipline in chapter 13. Don't focus on the negative, and don't belittle someone. It isn't constructive; in fact, it often leads to lower performance. Avoid making judgments. Don't tell people they are wrong unless it is necessary—for example, when you are disciplining employees. When you tell people they are wrong, they tend to get defensive and become less open to change. Instead, get them to ask you for criticism.

TIME-OUT 10 — Think about what sorts of criticism you accept without getting emotional and defensive. Use this insight when you give criticism.

**Get People to Ask for Your Criticism** The best way to improve performance is to get others to ask you for your feedback without putting them down. Let them know you want to help them improve.[101] Try this approach: Don't say things like, "You're doing that wrong. Let me show you how to do it the right way." Do say things like, "Would you like me to show you a way to do that task better (faster/easier)?" How would you react to each of these messages? Which one would motivate you to improve your performance?

**Three Parts of Criticism** Now that the person has asked for your feedback, be sure it has these three parts:

1. State the *specific* behavior that can be improved.
2. *Specify* the improved behavior.
3. *Train* and *coach* as needed.

Receivers of criticism can't improve unless they know exactly what they can improve and how to improve. Often you will need to teach them how to perform the task more effectively and provide continuing coaching. Using job instructional training is an effective way to give criticism (see chapter 7).

## Getting Criticism

None of us enjoys being criticized, even when it is constructive, and many people detest criticism because the truth can cause emotional hurt.[102] Now that you know how to give criticism, you will be effective at it. But you're going to get some criticism, maybe lots of it, so you might as well learn to take it well. In fact, if you are wise, you will want constructive criticism. How else are you going to realize your full potential? View constructive criticism through the perceptual lens of wanting it. This will put you in a position to use it constructively and to see it not as a personal attack on you but as what it is—help, encouragement, and teaching. And taking criticism gracefully gives you power to continuously improve.

If you are overly sensitive and become defensive, people will avoid giving you the criticism you need if you are to grow. Think about it as "no pain, no gain," and consider how you will gain when you take the pain.[103] If your coach simply says "good game," which we love to hear, can you improve for the next game? Only if the coach or others criticize you with actionable feedback can you improve. Think of criticism as what it is—feedback to improve your performance.

During your formal performance appraisals, your boss will be giving you criticism. These interviews can be stressful, but they are the best way to find out how to improve your performance, which will lead to better performance reviews, raises, and promotions.[104] Go back to chapter 7 and review the Being Evaluated section for tips.

A big problem is that many people are so poor at giving criticism. Remember that even jerks can help you improve. So no matter how poorly the person gives criticism, don't get defensive.[105] Don't take the feedback as a personal put-down; instead, focus on how you can improve. Even when you disagree with it, there is usually some truth that can help you, so look for the nugget of value.[106] Stay calm (even when the other person is emotional), and don't get defensive, deny something you did, or blame others.[107] If you do (and it is hard not to when you feel attacked), your boss and others will stop giving you feedback that will help you improve your performance.

Take responsibility. Admit your mistakes, learn from them, and, most important, don't repeat them. Don't dwell on your mistakes, or you will make even more mistakes. If you drop the ball or miss a shot, get back out there with confidence and focus on getting it right. Even extraordinary talents get their share of criticism. If you watch sports, you see lots of coaches yelling.

## LEARNING AIDS

### CHAPTER SUMMARY

1. **Understand how communication flows through organizations.**

   Formal communication flows vertically (down and up through the chain of command) and horizontally (between coworkers). Informal communication flows through the grapevine in many directions.

2. **List the four steps in the communication process.**

   The sender (1) encodes a message and then (2) transmits it. (3) The receiver decodes the message. (4) The receiver decides whether feedback is needed and, if it is, encodes a message (a response) and transmits it—and the process begins again.

3. **Use transmission channels well.**

   Although oral communication is easy and fast and encourages feedback, it is also less accurate than other methods and provides no record. Written communication is more accurate and provides a record, but it also takes longer, and feedback is not immediate.

4. **Communicate effectively in person.**

   (1) Develop rapport. (2) State your message using a beginning, middle, and end. (3) Check the receiver's understanding. (4) Get a commitment, and follow up.

5. **Select appropriate channels for your messages.**

   As a general guide, use rich oral channels for sending difficult and unusual messages, written channels for transmitting simple and routine messages to several people, and combined channels for important messages.

6. **Solicit feedback properly.**

   Do not simply ask whether anyone has questions. Ask receivers to paraphrase your message. Ask them for specific information you have given. Ask indirect questions, "if you were me" questions, and third-party questions. Just get them talking.

7. **Explain how we receive messages.**

   To receive a message well, we listen (give the speaker our undivided attention), analyze (think about, decode, and evaluate the message), and check our understanding (often by giving feedback).

8. **Choose appropriate response styles.**

   Heated exchanges are best handled by advising, diverting, probing, reassuring, and reflecting, but not in this order. Depending on the exchange, reflecting, reassuring, or diverting is typically a good first response. Probing is appropriate later in the process, and advising is typically the last step if it is used at all.

9. **Calm an emotional person.**

Avoid statements that put the person down, patronize her, or show her who is boss. Instead, pay attention, don't assume, and don't interrupt; let her know you are listening (honor her feelings), and withhold your evaluation. Let her vent. Later, carefully reflect her feelings back to her.

## REVIEW AND DISCUSSION QUESTIONS

1. What are the differences between vertical, horizontal, and grapevine communications?

2. What is the difference between encoding and decoding?

3. What is distortion?

4. Give an example of nonverbal communication in baseball, in poker, and in soccer.

5. What forms of communication do you personally use to gather information about sports?

6. What is the 1-5-15 rule?

7. What is media richness?

8. What should you include when you send an oral message? A written one? What makes each effective, and why?

9. Which response style do you use most often?

10. When we calm emotional people, why don't we simply show them who is boss?

11. Visit your college library and find an article in the *Journal of Sport Management* that mentions communication. In what context is the term used?

12. What athletes can you name who received criticism in a professional manner? What athletes or coaches responded in an aggressive, reactionary manner?

13. Practice writing a press release for a local sporting team. You might also write a press release for a fantasy sport team (if you are part of a fantasy league) you manage.

14. Is the grapevine helpful or harmful to most organizations? Should managers try to stop grapevine communications? Why or why not?

15. Wireless phones and handheld devices are blurring work and home life. Is this positive or negative? Should people stay connected and work while on vacation?

16. Which communication barrier do you think is the most common, and which barrier do you believe has the most negative effects on communication?

17. Which message transmission channel do you use most often in your personal time, and which do you use most in your professional time? What is your strongest and weakest channel? How can you improve on your weakness?

18. When sending messages, how effective are you at checking the receiver's understanding? How can you improve?

19. When receiving messages, how effective are you at listening? How can you improve?

## CASES

### Sport Management Professionals @ Work: Spencer Kimball

It seems like there is always a new kid coming along who wants to work in sports. What happens when the new kid is your own relative? It was about 30 years ago when my nephew's interest in sports ranged from Worldwide Wrestling Federation (known today as WWE) to his idol, batting champion Tony Gwynn of the San Diego Padres in Major League Baseball.

Spencer completed his undergraduate major in communications from the University of Hartford. He might have picked sport management for his major, but sport management as a field and as a college major wasn't nearly as popular then as it is today. This is an important point since many professionals who work in a sport management capacity major in various fields of study. People who can write well and speak in front of audiences are in demand by all types of organizations.

Spencer went to law school and teaches political and sport communication courses at Emerson College. Spencer recently helped organize the bachelor of science degree in sport communication at Emerson, which is an immersive program that prepares students for a variety of careers in sports, from the emerging gaming entertainment field to esports. The program focuses on teaching the most important skill for success: a strong foundation in strategic communication. The curriculum is designed to strike a balance of core courses and electives with a digital focus, covering topics such as data analytics, social media, web design, and mobile communication. Emerson is also in the heart of Boston, and students can intern at famous locations such as Fenway Park. As you can see, Emerson focuses on the communication aspects of sport in its program.

For more information, you can visit the Emerson website at www.emerson.edu/academics/sports-communication-bs

## Case Questions

1. Research esports. What can you find in this emerging area of sports that has happened in the last 6 to 12 months? You can check teamworkonline.com for any job openings.

2. What courses are offered in the sport communication major as compared to the sport management major at your college?

3. With his law degree and a love of sport, what could Spencer do for a living if he were not pursuing his academic career?

## Klutch Sports Group Sports Management Speaks LeBron James' Language

Do you think you would be good at babysitting egos? Think you can handle the fickle media, long hours, and first-class seats on airplanes and at sporting events? Then become a sport agent—it's good work if you can get it. And life will never be dull. Some very large sport agencies—IMG and ProServ are two that come to mind—represent professional athletes in all sports. But many pro players use independent agents, and a growing number of these are lawyers.

Agents handle all or part of a professional athlete's business affairs, including contract negotiations, product endorsements, licensing arrangements, personal appearances, public relations, and financial counseling. Although agents don't like to reveal the commissions they get on the contracts they negotiate for their players, it appears that the average commission on players' contracts is between 3 and 5 percent—a good income when you consider how much some players earn.

Agents are regulated rather carefully because the opportunities to defraud players or to misrepresent them are legion. Regulators include state and federal governments, the agents themselves, the NCAA, and players' associations. All of these groups have, with varying success, adopted certification programs in attempts to monitor players' agents.[108] The best attempt so far has been spearheaded by the NCAA. The NCAA's endeavor to establish a uniform system for regulating athlete agents—the Uniform Athlete Agents Act (UAAA)— has been passed in the United States in 41 states, the District of Columbia, and the U.S. Virgin Islands. The act requires agents to register with a state authority to be able to act as an athlete agent in that state. The act was strengthened in 2015 to bar sports agents from illegally luring college athletes into contracts.[109]

Agents who represent MLB players must jump through a few hoops. To be certified by the players' association, agents must follow the rules set forth in 51 pages of the MLBPA Regulations Governing Player Agents (As Amended Effective December 8, 2017). The document can be accessed at http://reg.mlbpaagent.org/Documents/AgentForms/Agent%20 Regulations.pdf.[110] The association has more than 300 agents on record.

Why all the emphasis on regulating agents? It's because there are a lot of rules and regulations to comply with, and also because large amounts of money can tempt people to bend the rules. So unfortunately, there is too much monkey business in the business of sport agency. Agents are not supposed to communicate with college players, but some agents do this, anyway. And when they get caught, everyone pays—the athletes, the colleges, the sport programs, and the fans. In 2018, the FBI investigated corruption in college basketball. The agency showed that players from more than 20 of the nation's top collegiate basketball programs were implicated in possibly breaking NCAA rules. Edrice "Bam" Adebayo received a five-figure payout for his one year of playing at the University of Kentucky. Isaiah Whitehead received a five-figure payout while playing at Seton Hall.[111]

LeBron James is often considered the best basketball player in the world. He followed his convictions to help the Cleveland Cavaliers and the Miami Heat to multiple NBA championships. His announcements about what team he was considering playing for were front-page news on a daily basis.

LeBron uses his long-time friend, Rich Paul, to represent him in his contract negotiations. Paul represented James while he worked at the largest sports agency, CAA. Paul then started his own agency, Klutch Sports Group. James followed his long-time friend to be the key athlete at Klutch Sports Group. Klutch has continued to acquire talented basketball players such as John Wall and Tristan Thompson.[112]

Information about Klutch Sports Group and the sports agency industry can be found at www.forbes.com/companies/klutch-sports/

Go to the web study guide to answer questions about this case study.

## @ TAKE IT TO THE NET

Please visit www.HumanKinetics.com/AppliedSportManagementSkills and go to this book's companion web study guide, where you will find the following:

A list of websites associated with the concepts in this chapter

Skill-Builder exercises, Sports and Social Media exercises, and a continuing Game Plan for Starting a Sport Business

Online versions of chapter exercises and end-of-chapter learning aids

An exercise that helps you define the Key Terms

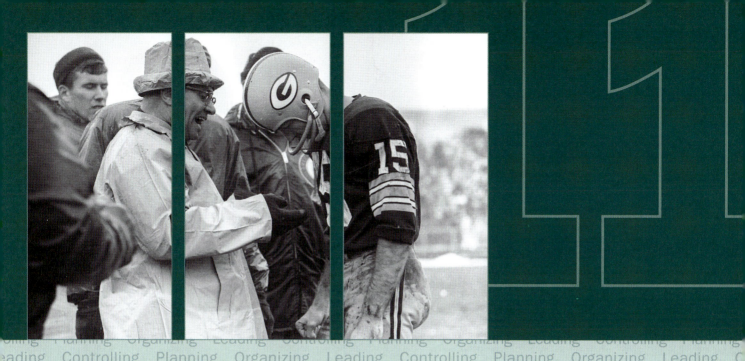

# Motivating to Win

## LEARNING OUTCOMES

After studying this chapter, you should be able to

1.  explain how motivation works;

2.  use the performance equation;

3.  discuss the four content-based motivation theories;

4.  discuss the three process-based motivation theories;

5.  discuss reinforcement theory; and

6.  compare content, process, and reinforcement theories.

## KEY TERMS

motivation

motivation process

performance equation

content-based motivation theories

hierarchy of needs theory

ERG theory

two-factor theory

acquired needs theory

process-based motivation theories

equity theory

goal-setting theory

expectancy theory

reinforcement theory

## DEVELOPING YOUR SKILLS

You can't win in business or sport without motivated players. In this chapter, you will learn about the motivation process, one reinforcement-based motivation theory, and four content-based and three process-based theories, and you will find tips on motivating with each theory. Giving praise is motivational and is not used nearly enough. You can develop this skill using a four-step model for giving praise.

## REVIEWING THEIR GAME PLAN

### Famous Motivational and Leadership Quotes

Sport coaches and athletes are known for their many memorable quotes about motivation and leadership. Vince Lombardi is well known for his amazing words of wisdom. We use a few of his quotes here to focus your attention on how exciting motivation can be.

#### Vince Lombardi

"It is essential to understand that battles are primarily won in the hearts of men."

"In great attempts, it is glorious even to fail."

"Leaders are made, they are not born. They are made by hard effort, which is the price which all of us must pay to achieve any goal that is worthwhile."

"The harder you work, the harder it is to surrender."

"It's not whether you get knocked down, it's whether you get up."

"The quality of a person's life is in direct proportion to their commitment to excellence, regardless of their chosen field of endeavor."

"There's only one way to succeed in anything, and that is to give it everything. I do, and I demand that my players do."

"If you aren't fired with enthusiasm, you'll be fired with enthusiasm."

"Once you learn to quit, it becomes a habit."

"Winning isn't everything—but wanting to win is."[1]

#### Special Olympics Motto

"Let me win, but if I cannot win, let me be brave in the attempt."[2]

#### Coach Darrell Royal

"Luck is what happens when preparation meets opportunity."[3]

#### Babe Didrikson Zaharias

"Luck? Sure. But only after long practice and only with the ability to think under pressure."[4]

# Motivation and Performance

**LEARNING OUTCOME 1** ▶

Explain how motivation works.

In chapter 8 we discussed how power, politics, and leadership are used to influence employees to achieve organizational objectives. Well, it takes motivated players and employees to work at achieving those objectives,[5] so good leaders are good motivators.[6] Great leaders motivate followers to achieve great things.[7] Organizations want great motivators, but they recruit self-starters,[8] with the skill of self-motivation and drive to succeed.[9] Do you need to be told what to do all the time, or are you a motivated self-starter?

In this chapter, you will read about what motivates you and others, and you will learn how to motivate others. Let's begin this section with an explanation of the motivation process, the role of expectations, the performance equation, and an overview of the motivation theories presented throughout this chapter.

## Motivation Process

Motivation is based on our feelings and needs. It is what drives us to satisfy our needs. **Motivation** is the willingness to achieve organizational objectives. Managers' behavior does influence employees' motivation to achieve objectives,[10] and managers strive to motivate employees to go above and beyond the minimum requirements of their jobs—called organizational citizenship behavior, or OCB[11]—because OCB results in increased employee productivity, customer satisfaction, and profitability.[12] Many firms are using the term *employee engagement* when referring to motivation for OCB.[13]

Motivation is also a process. Through the **motivation process**, people go from need to motive to behavior to consequence and finally to either satisfaction or dissatisfaction. Let's say you work up a powerful thirst (need) while working out and want some water (motive). You get a drink (behavior) that quenches (consequence) and thus satisfies your thirst. In many endeavors, our satisfaction is short-lived. For this reason, the motivation process loops back and begins anew as we continually strive to meet our needs (see figure 11.1).

Our needs and wants thus motivate every aspect of our behavior. Because our needs and wants are typically more complex than our thirst after a workout, we don't always know what they are and therefore don't always know why we do what we do. Ever done (or seen someone else do) something dumb and wonder why? Deep down the behavior was in some way supposed to make you happy, to meet a need. That is why organizational behaviorists study needs; understanding needs often explains behavior. We can't observe motives directly, but we can observe behavior and thereby infer motive. But humans are vastly trickier than this simple model. Different motives often drive the same behavior. Add to this the fact that we also strive to satisfy several needs at once, and you can see that motivation is complex.

Have you ever had a job that was fun? How did this affect your motivation?

## Role of Expectations

Both employee and manager expectations affect motivation and performance. Recall that you become what you think about; in chapter 8 we discussed the idea of the *self-fulfilling prophecy*, that our thoughts lead to self-confidence to perform a task. But we have to believe realistically based on hard work. You can't walk into a test or game unprepared and expect to do well. Hard work and practice give us the realistic confidence to believe we can succeed and even excel. And it takes motivation to work hard. Our relationship with our coach or boss also affects our motivation and performance.[14] We tend to put forth more effort when we believe we will succeed and have a good relationship with our coach or boss.

How managers treat employees also affects their behavior.[15] Remember the *Pygmalion effect* from chapter 8—your expectations and your treatment of people affect their motivation and hence their performance. Former college football coach and current ESPN commentator Lou Holtz said that you have to set a higher standard of expectations. We tend to be more motivated to put in the effort to live up to good coaches' and managers' beliefs in our ability to succeed. If you have high expectations for your staff and treat your workers as high achievers, you will get their best. Vince Lombardi treated his players as champions, and his players made history season after season. He said, "We would accomplish many more things if we did not think of them as impossible."

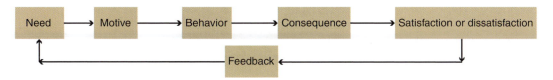

**FIGURE 11.1**   The motivation process loop.

You need to realize that what works to motivate you may not motivate others. Thus, rule number one is to know your people. Get to know them as individuals and learn what meets their unique and diverse needs. It is crucial to instill in them a self-perception of competence.

## Performance Equation

**LEARNING OUTCOME 2** ▶

Use the performance equation.

Motivated people try harder,[16] but this does not completely explain performance.[17] Motivation is one of the three parts of the **performance equation**:

$$\text{Performance} = \text{Ability} \times \text{Motivation} \times \text{Resources}$$

To get maximum performance, you need high levels of ability, motivation, and resources—it's that simple. It is also that complicated because this is not easy to pull off, as every manager knows all too well. What this equation does is focus your thinking. Is your group's performance suffering? Then examine what is missing from the equation and why. If your tennis player isn't winning any matches, is the reason lack of ability (we can't all be stars, no matter how much we practice), motivation (missing practice, not working hard, not following your coaching instruction), or resources (will a new racket help)?

Pat Riley, former coach of the two-time NBA champion Los Angeles Lakers and current president and head coach of the Miami Heat,[18] sets a standard of excellence. He is convinced that analyzing game video (a resource) in great detail improves motivation and ability in sport and gives his team the mental edge.

One of the frustrating parts of teaching, coaching, and managing is having motivated, hardworking people who just don't have the ability to make the cut. This takes us back

---

## APPLYING THE CONCEPT 11.1

### Performance Equation

Identify which part of the performance equation is operative in each situation.

  a.  ability

  b.  motivation

  c.  resources

_____  1. Calling on one of her golf club retailers, Latoya realizes belatedly that she has forgotten her product display book. No visuals—no interest. She loses the sale.

_____  2. Frank is definitely the team's slacker—as Coach says: Frank's got the goods, he just doesn't use them.

_____  3. I train longer and harder than they do, but Heather and Linda continually beat my times.

_____  4. Yeah, my grades could be better, but, hey, I made the team, so it's time to relax and have some fun.

_____  5. FIFA would be more efficient if it cut down on waste.

_____  6. Amateur athletes have to pinch pennies to pay for training.

_____  7. Our athletic director says we need money for the lacrosse program.

_____  8. When team cuts are going to be made, players train harder.

_____  9. Before Title IX, women did not enjoy equal opportunities to play collegiate sports.

_____ 10. Women's collegiate basketball teams have plenty of applicants now that WNBA pro basketball is an option after players finish school.

to our model of success. You need to find things that you are good at (ability) and enjoy (motivation) to do well and be satisfied.

It is also frustrating to lack resources. How many coaches and sport managers think, If we only had a bigger budget (more specifically, if we only had the court or field for more practice time, more assistant coaches, more money to attract better pros or more college scholarships, a new field), we could do a better job?

A third frustration is working with people who have ability but lack the motivation to reach their full potential. On the positive side of motivation, it has been said that ability is overrated and that a motivational passion translates to high performance;[19] if you do something you are passionate about, you will be successful.[20] That is the focus of this chapter. We teach you about budgeting in chapter 13, and if you develop your management skills, you will increase your ability to get more and better resources.

Only when you know what is missing can you develop strategies that will solve the problem. Coaches constantly look for ways to improve their team's performance equation. For instance, if a team's ability is not up to snuff, a coach needs to laser in on specifics, adjust training accordingly, and recruit to fix holes in the team. Great football coaches, such as Bill Belichick of the NFL New England Patriots, make adjustments to their offense and defense during the game.

When you apply the performance equation to the development of your career, you need to find things that you are good at (ability) and enjoy (motivation) and obtain the resources, such as a college degree, that you need to achieve your career goals. If you realize you can't be a pro athlete but you love sport and recreation and think you can be happy as a coach or sport manager, you are on the right track. Your next step is to narrow down your career path, but let's move on with motivation.

## Motivation Theories

How do we motivate our workers, our players, and ourselves to be our best? There is no single best way. However, keep in mind that the basic motivation is self-interest and that the pursuit of happiness is fundamental to human motivation. So if you want to motivate people, answer their often unasked question: "What's in it for me?" If you give people what they want, they will in turn give you what you want—creating win–win situations. This process is easier said than done, so it is the focus of this chapter. Self-awareness and introspection about what motivates you can help you to motivate yourself. To this end, we present two Self-Assessments to help you better understand what motivates you.

Nothing is as practical as a good theory, for theories help us to understand, explain, and predict behavior. So it's time for some theories. To get an overview, review table 11.1, and read about these motivation theories. In the following three sections you will learn how to motivate using content, process, and reinforcement theories, and in the last section you will learn how to put the theories together and motivate yourself.

# Content-Based Motivation Theories

According to content-based theorists, to create a satisfied workforce, organizations must meet their employees' needs.[21] **Content-based motivation theories** thus focus on identifying and understanding people's needs. The key to success is to meet the needs of the workforce and the objectives of the organization.[22] As you strive to create this win–win situation, you need to sell the benefits that meet the employees' needs. In this section, you will learn four content motivation theories: hierarchy of needs theory, ERG theory, two-factor theory, and acquired needs theory.

◀ **LEARNING OUTCOME 3**
Discuss the four content-based motivation theories.

## TABLE 11.1   Major Motivation Theories

| Classification of theories | Specific theories and types of reinforcement |
|---|---|
| 1. **Content-based theories**– The focus is on identifying and understanding people's needs. | **Hierarchy of needs**–People are motivated by five levels of needs: physiological, safety, social, esteem, and self-actualization (Maslow). |
| | **ERG**–People are motivated by three needs: existence, relatedness, and growth (Alderfer). |
| | **Two-factor theory**–Motivator factors (higher-level needs) are more important than maintenance factors (lower-level needs) (Herzberg). |
| | **Acquired needs**–People are motivated by their need for achievement, power, and affiliation (McClelland). |
| 2. **Process-based theories**– The focus is on how people choose behaviors to fulfill their needs. | **Equity**–People are motivated when their perceived inputs equal outputs (Adams). |
| | **Goal setting**–Difficult but achievable goals motivate people (Locke). |
| | **Expectancy**–People are motivated when they believe they can accomplish the task and when the rewards for doing so are worth the effort (Vroom). |
| 3. **Reinforcement theory**–The focus is on consequences for behavior (Skinner). | **Positive reinforcement**–Attractive consequences (rewards) for desirable performance encourage continued behavior. |
| | **Avoidance**–Negative consequences for poor performance encourage continued desirable behavior. |
| | **Extinction**–Withholding reinforcement for an undesirable behavior reduces or eliminates that behavior. |
| | **Punishment**–Undesirable consequences (punishment) for undesirable behavior prevent the behavior. |

# Hierarchy of Needs Theory

Abraham Maslow developed the hierarchy of needs theory in the 1940s, but it is still being researched today. The **hierarchy of needs theory** proposes that people are motivated by five levels of needs: physiological, safety, social, esteem, and self-actualization. Maslow operated under four major assumptions:[23] (1) Only unmet needs motivate. (2) People's needs are arranged hierarchically in order of importance. (3) People will not be motivated to satisfy a high-level need unless their lower-level needs have been somewhat satisfied. (4) People have five types of hierarchical needs (presented here and in figure 11.2 in order of importance from lowest to highest).

1. *Physiological needs.* Our primary or basic needs are air, water, food, shelter, sex, and relief from or avoidance of pain.
2. *Safety needs.* Our safety and security are our next level of need.
3. *Social needs.* Next, we look for love, friendship, and acceptance. MLB outfielder Stephen Piscotty was traded from the St. Louis Cardinals to the Oakland A's so he could be closer to his ailing mother. She had ALS, which is commonly called Lou Gehrig's disease. "It just really puts life in perspective," Piscotty said. "When I got the news it was a little tough to focus."[24]
4. *Esteem needs.* These include ego, status, self-respect, recognition for our accomplishments, and a feeling of self-confidence and prestige.
5. *Self-actualization needs.* This is our highest level of needs—our need to develop to our full potential.

**Motivating Employees with Hierarchy of Needs Theory.** Interestingly, decades before self-directed teams became popular in the 1990s, Maslow called for them, for this is a straightforward way to meet self-actualization needs. Today's young workers have grown up being told they are special, and they want to be treated as individuals, so managers need to be sensitive to meeting employees' needs.[25] You need to meet basic lower-level needs first and then focus on meeting higher-level needs. Figure 11.2 lists ways in which managers try to meet these five needs.

> **TIME-OUT 1** Where in the hierarchy of needs are you for a specific professional aspect of your life? For a specific aspect of a sport? Explain why you are at this level.

## ERG Theory

ERG simplified the hierarchy of needs. Psychologist Clayton Alderfer developed the **ERG theory** by reorganizing Maslow's needs hierarchy into three needs: existence (physiological and safety needs), relatedness (social), and growth (esteem and self-actualization). Alderfer agreed with Maslow that unsatisfied needs motivate people, but he disagreed that only one need level is active at a time.[26]

**Motivating Employees with ERG Theory.** To use this theory, first determine which needs have been met and which ones have not. Then work on meeting the unsatisfied needs and progress to growth needs.

**Self-actualization needs**
Develop workers' skills. Give them more control over their work. Encourage creativity. Expect achievement. Give them chances to grow.

**Esteem needs**
Help people excel at their work. Give merit pay raises. Recognize excellence. Design jobs to be challenging. Let people participate in decisions. Create opportunities for advancement.

**Social needs**
Design jobs so that people have opportunities to interact with others, to be accepted, and to make friends. Encourage togetherness through parties, picnics, trips, and sports teams.

**Safety needs**
Provide safe working conditions, salary increases to meet inflation, job security, and fringe benefits (medical insurance/sick pay/pensions).

**Physiological needs**
Pay a wage to provide employees with food and shelter.

**FIGURE 11.2**   How organizations satisfy the hierarchy of needs.

## Two-Factor Theory

Let's focus on you for a moment. What motivates you? Complete Self-Assessment 11.1 and find out before you learn about two-factor theory.

In the 1950s, Frederick Herzberg classified two sets of needs. Herzberg and his associates disagreed with the traditional view that satisfaction and dissatisfaction are at opposite ends of one continuum.[27] They proposed two continuums: One continuum is our satisfaction or dissatisfaction with the work environment; the other continuum is our satisfaction or dissatisfaction with the job itself. Herzberg called the first continuum the maintenance or hygiene factor (pay, job security, title, working conditions, fringe benefits, and relationships) and the second continuum the motivator factor (achievement, recognition, challenge, and advancement). In the **two-factor theory**, motivator factors, not maintenance factors, drive people to excel (see figure 11.3). Maintenance factors are also called extrinsic factors because they are outside the job itself. Motivators are intrinsic factors because they derive from the work itself.[28]

Herzberg contended that maintenance factors minimize or even prevent employee dissatisfaction, but they do not satisfy or motivate workers. Thus, dissatisfied employees who get a pay raise will, for a time, not fault their pay—they will be "not dissatisfied" for a while. Before long, however, they will grow accustomed to the pay, and dissatisfaction will creep back in. They will soon need another "fix" of money, which becomes a repeating cycle.

Herzberg's stance is that organizations must ensure that maintenance factors are adequate, but they do not have to go to excessive lengths. Once employees are no longer dissatisfied with their environment, the intrinsic factors in their jobs will kick in and motivate them. The current view of money as a motivator is that, yes, money matters, but money does not in and of itself motivate people to work harder. Recall from chapter 8 that people can experience overall job satisfaction without being satisfied with every determinant of job satisfaction, including pay.

Pro athletes are paid very well today; many people would argue that these athletes' compensation is excessive. Does David Price need $30 million or more per season to motivate him to pitch better for the Boston Red Sox? Do you think giving him a raise will get him to play any harder or better? Or would he be better motivated by such intrinsic factors as his reputation, setting records, and the chance to win the MLB World Series? You can see how intrinsic factors are important in the motivational equation.

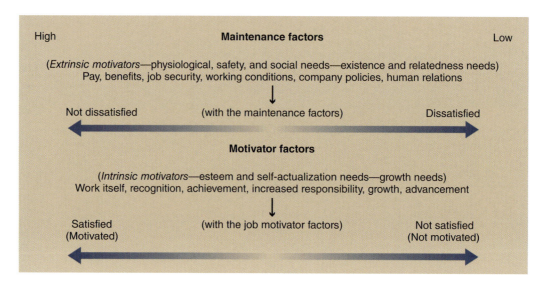

**FIGURE 11.3** Herzberg's two-factor theory.

## SELF-ASSESSMENT 11.1

# What Motivates You?

For the following 12 factors, rate how important each one is to you on a scale of 1 to 5.

1 = not important

2 = somewhat important

3 = neutral

4 = important

5 = very important

_____ 1. An interesting job I enjoy doing

_____ 2. A boss who treats everyone the same way, regardless of the circumstances

_____ 3. Getting praise, recognition, and appreciation for the work that I do

_____ 4. A job that has established procedures and not much change from day to day

_____ 5. A job where I have the opportunity for advancement

_____ 6. A prestigious job title regardless of the pay and work

_____ 7. A job that gives me the freedom to do things my way

_____ 8. Favorable working conditions (e.g., safe environment, cafeteria)

_____ 9. A job that gives me the opportunity to learn new things

_____ 10. An emphasis on following company rules, regulations, procedures, and policies

_____ 11. A job I can do well and can succeed at

_____ 12. Job security (the opportunity to stay with the same organization for my entire career)

Record your answer scores and total each column. Are motivator factors or maintenance factors more important to you?

**Motivator factors**

1. _____

3. _____

5. _____

7. _____

9. _____

11. _____

Total points _____

**Maintenance factors**

2. _____

4. _____

6. _____

8. _____

10. _____

12. _____

Total points _____

**Motivating Employees with Two-Factor Theory.** Two-factor theory implies that the best way to motivate employees is first to ensure that they are not dissatisfied with maintenance factors and then to focus on motivator factors. To get full, motivated effort, you and the team must be passionate about what you are doing: meaningful work.[29] This means building challenge and opportunity for achievement into the job itself. To motivate employees, you can make their jobs more interesting and challenging, give them more responsibility, provide them with opportunities for growth, and offer them recognition for a job well done. Job enrichment and delegation (chapter 5) are two methods of doing this. A trend of successful young companies is to create a culture of working hard at a fun place to work.[30]

TIME-OUT 2

List the maintenance and motivator factors in your current job or team, and rate your level of dissatisfaction or satisfaction in each continuum. Give reasons for your rating.

## Acquired Needs Theory

The **acquired needs theory** proposes that employees are motivated by their need for achievement, power, and affiliation. Henry Murray developed the original general needs theory; it was later adapted by John Atkinson and David McClelland, who developed a specific acquired needs theory. It is also called learned needs or three-needs theory.

McClelland did not classify lower-level needs.[31] His affiliation needs are the same as social and relatedness needs, and his power and achievement needs resemble esteem, self-actualization, and growth needs. Unlike Maslow, McClelland believed that our personality determines our needs, which are further developed as we interact with our environment. Personality does affect motivation.

All of us need some amount of achievement, power, and affiliation, just in varying degrees. One of the three needs tends to dominate in each of us and thus drives our behavior. Before we discuss the three needs in detail, complete Self-Assessment 11.2 to see which need drives you.

### Need for Achievement

People with high need for achievement (nAch) typically take personal responsibility for solving problems. They are goal oriented and set moderate, realistic, and attainable goals. They seek challenge and excellence and choose the road less traveled (i.e., they are often highly individualistic). They take calculated, moderate risks and want concrete feedback on their performance. They are willing to work hard.[32] High nAchs think about how they can do a better job, how they can accomplish something unusual or important, and how they can fast-forward their careers. They perform well in nonroutine, challenging, and competitive situations (in which low nAchs do not perform well).

McClelland's research showed that only about 10 percent of the U.S. population has a high dominant need for achievement. Evidence of a correlation exists between high achievement need and high performance. High nAchs tend to enjoy sales jobs and are often entrepreneurs. Olympic and other highly successful athletes have high nAch.

**Motivating High nAchs.** Don't get in their way—high nAchs motivate themselves! Assign them the nonroutine, challenging tasks that they crave. Give them frequent feedback on their performance. Increase their responsibility as they gain competence.

### Need for Power

People with a high need for power (nPow) typically like to control situations. They want influence or control over others; they enjoy competitions in which they can win (they do not like to lose), and they are willing to confront others. High nPows think about controlling situations and others, and they seek positions of authority and status. They tend to have a lower need for affiliation. See chapter 8 for more on power in organizations.

**Motivating High nPows.** Let them plan and control their jobs as much as possible. Try to include them in decision making, especially when the decision affects them. They tend to perform best alone rather than as team members. Try to assign them to a whole task rather than just part of a task.

## SELF-ASSESSMENT 11.2

### Which Acquired Need Drives You?

For the following 15 statements, rate how similar each one is to you on the following scale.

1 = not very descriptive of me

2 = somewhat descriptive of me

3 = neutral

4 = descriptive of me

5 = very descriptive of me

_____ 1. I enjoy working hard.

_____ 2. I like to compete, and I like to win.

_____ 3. I take good care of my friends.

_____ 4. I don't shrink from difficult challenges.

_____ 5. I usually end up deciding which movie or restaurant we'll go to.

_____ 6. I want other people to really like me.

_____ 7. I check on how I'm progressing as I complete tasks.

_____ 8. I confront people who do things I disagree with.

_____ 9. I love parties.

_____ 10. I go to great lengths to set and achieve realistic goals.

_____ 11. I try to influence other people to get my way.

_____ 12. I belong to lots of groups and organizations.

_____ 13. The satisfaction of completing a difficult task is as good as life gets.

_____ 14. I take charge when a group I'm in is floundering.

_____ 15. I prefer to work with others rather than alone.

Enter your scores here and total each column. The column with the highest score is your dominant or primary need.

| Achievement | | Power | | Affiliation | |
|---|---|---|---|---|---|
| _____ | 1. | _____ | 2. | _____ | 3. |
| _____ | 4. | _____ | 5. | _____ | 6. |
| _____ | 7. | _____ | 8. | _____ | 9. |
| _____ | 10. | _____ | 11. | _____ | 12. |
| _____ | 13. | _____ | 14. | _____ | 15. |
| _____ Total | | _____ Total | | _____ Total | |

### Need for Affiliation

People with high need for affiliation (nAff) seek close relationships with others. They very much want to be liked. They enjoy social activities and follow group norms (see chapter 9), and they tend to use organizational politics to fit in (see chapter 8). They join groups and organizations. High nAffs think in terms of friends and relationships. They enjoy developing, helping, and teaching others. They derive satisfaction from working with the group rather than from the task itself. They typically have low nPow.

Effective teams typically have some high nAffs. Very often the "heart" of great teams is nonstar players who are important because they are easy to get along with, develop relationships that make the team cohesive (chapter 9), and do whatever it takes to help the team.

TIME-OUT 3 — Explain how your need for achievement, power, or affiliation affects your behavior at your job or on your team.

**Motivating high nAffs.** Motivating them is important because you want nAffs on board—they will make your group effective. Make sure they are assigned to teams. Praise them and value them. Assign them the tasks of orienting and training new employees. They make great mentors. However, teams need a balance of all three types.

### Managerial Needs Profile

McClelland found that the common motivational needs profile of managers is highest for nPow, high for nAch, and low for nAff. Here are the reasons. People with a high nAff typically want to be one of the group, not the leader. They want everyone to like them, so they don't want to evaluate performance and discipline and fire employees. People with low nAch don't tend to strive to be managers, but people with high nPow and high nAch do.

Not everyone wants to be a manager. Do you? Promotion to manager is being refused by some.[33] Do you have the managerial needs profile? If you do, it doesn't guarantee success, but it helps. If you don't, you still can be a successful manager, especially if you work at it. Or you may want to consider other career paths. There are lots of great professional nonmanagement sport and recreation positions. Also, many people start out wanting to coach (not be a manager) but later in their career move to managerial positions, such as athletic director (AD).

Table 11.2 compares the four content-based theories of motivation.

### TABLE 11.2 A Comparison of Content-Based Motivation Theories

| Hierarchy of needs (Maslow) | ERG theory (Alderfer) | Two-factor theory (Herzberg) | Acquired needs theory (McClelland) |
|---|---|---|---|
| Self-actualization<br>Esteem<br>Social<br>Safety<br>Physiological | Growth<br>Relatedness<br>Existence | Motivators<br>Maintenance | Achievement and power<br>Affiliation<br>Not classified |
| **Notes** | | | |
| Needs must be met in a hierarchical order. | Needs at any level can be unmet simultaneously. | Maintenance factors do not motivate employees. | Motivating needs are developed through experience. |

# Process-Based Motivation Theories

**Process-based motivation theories** focus on understanding how and why employees choose behavior to fulfill their needs. Process-based theories are more complex than content-based theories. Content-based theories simply identify and then try to understand our needs. Process-based theories go a step further and try to understand several things: why we have different needs; how and why we choose to satisfy needs in different ways; the mental process we go through as we understand situations; how we evaluate how well we are satisfying our needs. In this section, you will learn how to motivate with equity theory, goal-setting theory, and expectancy theory.

◀ **LEARNING OUTCOME 4**

Discuss the three process-based motivation theories.

## Equity Theory

Equity theory, primarily J. Stacy Adams' motivation theory, proposes that we seek social equity in the rewards we receive (output) for our performance (input).[34] **Equity theory** proposes that employees are motivated when their perceived inputs equal outputs.

According to equity theory, all of us compare our inputs (effort, experience, seniority, status, intelligence) and outputs (praise, recognition, pay, benefits, promotions, increased status, supervisor's approval) with those of relevant others. A relevant other may be a coworker or a group of employees from the same or a different organization or even in a hypothetical situation. Notice that the definition says *perceived*, and not *actual*, in the comparison of inputs to outputs. Employees' perception (chapter 8) of being treated fairly affects their attitude and performance.[35] Equity may actually exist, but if we believe that inequity exists, we will change our behavior to create perceived equity. We need to perceive that we are being treated fairly relative to others. We know that we are not all equally competent at doing things, but don't you want to be treated fairly,[36] with rewarding relationships?[37]

Diversity (chapter 2) is a major issue facing sport managers, and you need to treat everyone fairly and justly. If you don't, you may face a lawsuit or a legislation issue. Title IX was passed because females were not given equality in sport. Even today, some girls are bringing lawsuits against schools that will not let them play on boys' teams. NCAA coaches and athletic directors struggle with fairness. Should resources be distributed equally based on program needs, or should they be distributed based on program contributions? Which do you perceive as fair?

Unfortunately, part of the problem with equity theory is that we are motivated by self-interest. What we perceive as fair to us is often not seen as fair to others. Many of us also tend to inflate our own efforts and performance when we compare ourselves with others. Have you ever seen players on teams who believe that they are much better than they really are? It's often the case that no one, not even their teammates, can convince them otherwise.

We also tend to overestimate what others earn. We may be very satisfied and motivated until we find out that a relevant other earns more for the same job or earns the same for less work. When we perceive inequity, we may try to reduce it by reducing input or by increasing output.

A comparison with relevant others leads to three conclusions: We are underrewarded, overrewarded, or equitably rewarded. When underrewarded, people try to create equity by doing things like less work, changing the situation (like getting a raise), or getting another job. Most people don't change behavior if they believe they are overrewarded, and with equity there is no problem.

Some pro athletes negotiate extremely lucrative contracts that suddenly become hard to fulfill because of injury, age, or declining skills. The athlete may still be motivated to excel, but physical ability no longer warrants his compensation. Management has to accept the responsibility of the large contract and find other ways to make the team competitive. In MLB, payment for a contract is fully guaranteed. NFL contracts are fulfilled only until the time a player is a cut from the team—the contracts are not fully guaranteed. Sometimes an NFL contract is announced, and it seems as if the player is being overrewarded—but only if he plays out the entire contract. In contrast, when an MLB contract is announced and it seems as if a player is being overrewarded, he just might be, because the contract is guaranteed.

People tend to be dissatisfied and unmotivated if they don't believe they are being treated fairly, rather than actually being motivated by equity. So don't expect people to work hard just because you are treating them fairly. Be ready to deal with perceptions of unfair treatment by you or by the organization. Also, be aware that when managers are unfair and abusive, they demotivate employees and hurt performance.[38] People who use unethical behavior sometimes justify their actions as a means of creating equity.[39]

**Motivating with Equity Theory.** Using equity theory in practice can be difficult because you as a manager don't necessarily know the employee's reference group, nor do you know her view of inputs and outcomes. Perceptions of inequity hurt attitudes, leading to lower individual, team, and organizational performance.[40] However, equity theory does offer some useful general recommendations:

1. Be aware that equity is based on perception, and perception may not be correct. Managers sometimes create equity and inequity by favoring certain workers.

2. Go to great lengths to make rewards equitable. When employees perceive that they are not treated fairly, morale and performance suffer. Employees who produce at the same level should be given equal rewards.

> **TIME-OUT 4**
> Give an example of how your perception of equity or inequity affected your motivation and performance in a job or team. Were you underrewarded, overrewarded, or equitably rewarded?

3. Reward excellence. Make sure employees understand the inputs needed to attain certain outputs. When using incentive pay, clearly specify what the employee must do to achieve the incentive. You should be able to objectively justify to others why one person got a high merit raise.

## Goal-Setting Theory

**Goal-setting theory** proposes that achievable but difficult goals motivate employees. Edwin Locke developed goal-setting motivation theory, and later with Gary Latham he validated that the theory does motivate people to higher levels of performance.[41] Goals influence the way we think, feel, and act;[42] so objectives help motivate us to achieve our goals.[43] Goal-setting complements Herzberg's and McClelland's theories because goals are motivators that meet higher-level needs.[44]

**Three Types of Goals.** There are three types of goals: easy, "do your best," and difficult but achievable, but only the latter is motivational.[45] Easy goals are not recommended because we tend to stop when we achieve the objective, performing below our

> **TIME-OUT 5**
> Give an example of how a goal affected your motivation and performance or that of someone with whom you work or play.

ability. The goal of just doing the best you can doesn't work for most people either; we tend to say we did the best we could when we really didn't. That leaves difficult but achievable goals as the best type because they push us. GE coined the term "stretch goals."[46] Latham said higher specific goals lead to higher levels of performance.[47] Lou Holtz said, "Of all my experiences in managing people, the power of goal setting is the most incredible."[48]

**Motivating with Goal-Setting Theory.** As in planning (chapter 4), the first step in motivation is developing objectives stating what you want to accomplish.[49] To have high levels of performance, you need to set difficult but achievable goals; having deadlines and measuring and evaluating performance based on objectives helps with motivation.[50] When setting individual and team goals, be sure to follow the guidelines and the model for setting objectives in chapter 4.

## Expectancy Theory

Expectancy theory is based on Victor Vroom's equation:[51]

$$\text{Motivation} = \text{Expectancy} \times \text{Instrumentality} \times \text{Valence}$$

**Expectancy theory** proposes that employees are motivated when they believe that they can accomplish the task, they will get the reward, and that the reward is worth the effort. Two important variables, expectancy and valence, must be met in order for people to be motivated.

*Expectancy* is our perception of our ability to accomplish an objective (i.e., the probability that we will succeed). Generally, the higher our expectancy, the better our chances of being motivated. When we don't believe we can achieve objectives, we stop trying. Also important is our perception of the relationship between performance and the outcome or reward (called *instrumentality*). Generally, the higher our expectancy of attaining the outcome or reward, the higher our motivation.

*Valence* is the value we place on the outcome or reward—that is, its importance. Generally, the more highly we value the outcome or reward, the higher our motivation. If we don't value the reward, we are less likely to work hard for it.

**Motivating with Expectancy Theory.** It does work. People are motivated when the following happen:

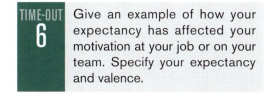

TIME-OUT 6 Give an example of how your expectancy has affected your motivation at your job or on your team. Specify your expectancy and valence.

1. Objectives are clearly defined and are doable (goal-setting theory).

2. Performance is tied to rewards, and high performance is rewarded.

3. Rewards have value to the employee.[52] (It thus helps with motivation when you know what makes your workers or players tick—yelling at one player may be motivational, while a look of disappointment may work better with another.)

4. Employees believe that you will give them the reward. (As we have noted many times, trust is a key to success.)

# Reinforcement Theory

B.F. Skinner affirmed that to motivate people we don't need to identify and understand their needs (content theories) or understand how they choose behaviors to fulfill their needs (process theories).

◀ LEARNING OUTCOME 5

Discuss reinforcement theory.

**Reinforcement theory** proposes that consequences for behavior cause people to behave in predetermined ways. The idea behind reinforcement is that we learn what is and is not desired behavior as a result of consequences for our behavior.[53] When you make a behavior more (or less) attractive, people will do more (or less) of it,[54] or people will do or not do what you want them to if you find the right incentives.[55] Because behavior is learned by experiencing positive and negative consequences, Skinner proposed three components, as shown in figure 11.4.

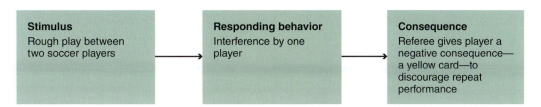

| **Stimulus** | **Responding behavior** | **Consequence** |
| Rough play between two soccer players | Interference by one player | Referee gives player a negative consequence—a yellow card—to discourage repeat performance |

**FIGURE 11.4** Skinner's three components of reinforcement theory.

So reinforcement is about getting people to do what we want them to do by answering their often unasked question, "What's in it for me?" In essence you are saying, "If you do this behavior [stimulus calling for response behavior], I will give you this reward—or this punishment if you don't [consequence, i.e., types of reinforcement]—and this is how often I will give you the reward or punishment [schedules of reinforcement]." In this section, we discuss different types of reinforcement done on schedules (operant conditioning), how to motivate with reinforcement, and giving praise to motivate employees.

## Types of Reinforcement

There are four types of reinforcement you can use to get your staff to do what you ask (positive, avoidance, extinction, and punishment). Deciding on the right time to use each type of reinforcement is an important step in producing the desired consequences. The ultimate goal is to use positive reinforcement as often as possible. However, certain situations might require the use of avoidance, extinction, or (unfortunately) punishment. Figure 11.5 illustrates the four types of reinforcement.

### Positive Reinforcement

You encourage desired behaviors and offer attractive consequences (*rewards*) for desirable performance. When an employee arrives on time for work or a meeting, he can be rewarded with thanks. The praise reinforces punctuality. Giving players a day off from practice after a well-played game is positive reinforcement. Many pro athletes get extra compensation when they win their division, make the playoffs, or win a championship. Recall from chapter 6 that to develop new habits, we have a cue, a routine, and a reward to reinforce the new behavior.[56] Other reinforcements include pay raises, promotions, time off, increased status—the list is endless.

If desirable behavior is not positively reinforced, it may decrease or even be eliminated (extinction). If an athlete makes good plays but is not praised by the coach, the athlete may stop making extra effort. In teams not given positive reinforcement, *social loafing* (see chapter 9) can occur.[57]

### Negative Reinforcement

This is the flip side of positive reinforcement. Positive encourages desirable behavior, whereas negative tends to discourage undesirable behavior. There are three types of negative reinforcement.

**Avoidance**   *Avoidance* works because we all prefer to avoid negative consequences. With avoidance, there is no actual punishment; instead, the threat of negative consequences controls our behavior. Standing plans, especially rules, are designed to make us avoid certain

| Employee behavior | Type of reinforcement | Manager action (consequence) | Employee behavior modification (future) |
|---|---|---|---|
| Improved performance | → Positive | → Praise improvements | → Repeat quality work |
| Improved performance | → Avoidance | → Do not give any reprimand | → Repeat quality work |
| Performance not improved | → Extinction | → Withhold praise/raise | → Do not repeat poor work |
| Performance not improved | → Punishment | → Discipline action, i.e., written warning | → Do not repeat poor work |

**FIGURE 11.5**   Types of reinforcement. Assuming that the employee improved performance, positive reinforcement is the best motivator.

behavior. We don't break the rules because we don't want to get punished. Employees see that breaking a rule, like being late, will cause them to miss rewards or to be punished, so they think twice about being late.

**Extinction**    *Extinction* is used to reduce or eliminate an undesirable behavior by withholding reinforcement when the behavior occurs; in other words, ignore the behavior and it will go away. This approach works sometimes, such as with an employee who wants attention. But ignoring bad behavior usually leads to more bad behavior, so in most cases, you need to take action. One action is to withhold a reward of value, such as a pay raise, until the employee performs to established standards. Another action, our next topic, is to punish the undesirable behavior. Managers can also inadvertently extinguish good performance if they do not reward it in some way.

**Punishment**    *Punishment* is an undesirable consequence and can thus be used to change undesirable behavior. If employees are reprimanded for being late, this may cause them to be on time. Punishments in the workplace include probation, fines, demotion, loss of privileges, and termination, to name but a few. Employees violating the company code of conduct, such as expectations regarding sexual harassment, need to be punished to send the message that the behavior is not acceptable and that it will be punished. Firms and sport teams are also punishing bad behavior off the job and field.

Punishment is the least effective way to motivate people. There are several reasons for this. We get accustomed to punishment (weird, but true!). Punishment can also cause other undesirable behaviors, such as lowered productivity (because of resentment or poor morale) and theft or sabotage.

 **TIME-OUT 7** Illustrate the four types of reinforcements with examples from your current job or team.

 What type of reinforcement do you believe Vince Lombardi used to motivate his players?

# Schedules of Reinforcement

The second consideration in modifying behavior is when to reinforce it. Behaviorists have developed two schedules: continuous reinforcement and intermittent reinforcement.

## *Continuous Reinforcement*

With continuous schedules, every time the desired behavior is completed, it is reinforced. Machines with automatic counters that display exactly how many units or sales have been produced or sold provide continuous reinforcement, as do pay-for-performance plans, piece rate pay for production workers, and commissions on every sale for salespeople. Reinforcement is also continuous when managers can discuss every customer complaint with employees.

## *Intermittent Reinforcement*

Intermittent schedules are of two types: time-based schedules, called interval schedules, and output-based schedules, called ratio schedules. Ratio schedules are generally better motivators than interval schedules. Either type can use a fixed interval or ratio or a variable interval or ratio. You may get paid a salary every two weeks regardless of the number of hours worked (fixed interval). A coach gives praise only for outstanding performance (variable ratio).

# You Get What You Reinforce

As discussed, people will do what is reinforced. If managers say that quality is important, but employees who do quality work are not rewarded and nothing happens to employees who do not do quality work, no one will be motivated to continue to do quality work. If a professor tells students to read this book but does not test them on the book (the reward or punishment is based on test performance), what percentage of students do you think will read and study this book?

**Motivating with Reinforcement.** Here are some guidelines:

1. Make sure people know exactly what is expected of them—the rules. Set clear objectives.
2. Select appropriate rewards. A reward to one person may not be to another. Know your employees' needs.
3. Use an appropriate reinforcement type and schedule for the situation.
4. Do not reward mediocre or poor performance.
5. Look for positive behavior and praise it; don't focus only on criticizing negative behavior. Use the Pygmalion effect (chapter 8)—make people feel good about themselves.
6. Make sure your praise is genuine and generously given—don't be miserly with your praise.
7. Focus on doing things *for* your employees (rewards), not *to* them (punishment).

TIME-OUT
8

Give examples of behavior at your current job or team that was modified by reinforcement. State the type of reinforcement and the schedule used.

Positive reinforcement should be a manager's first choice. Positive reinforcement creates win–win situations by meeting both employees' and the organization's needs. Avoidance and punishment create lose–win situations. Employees lose because they are punished. The organization or manager may win initially by forcing people to do (or not do) something, but the organization ultimately loses if highly skilled and trained people quit.

How can you tailor praise to an athlete's needs profile?
© digitalskillet/Getty Images/iStockphoto

# Recognition Praise

Let's discuss why recognition praise is a motivator, how to give praise, and why praise motivates better than reprimanding.

## *Our Need for Recognition*

From the 1940s to this day, research has revealed that people want appreciation for their work. Do you like to be criticized, ignored, taken for granted, or have someone else get credit for your work? Or do you want to be recognized for your good work and told you did a good job? Praise develops positive self-esteem and leads to better performance—the Pygmalion effect and self-fulfilling prophecy (see chapter 8) rolled into one tidy package. You can also use *altercasting*: characterizing someone as a certain type of person in order to encourage her to behave in a desired manner. "Collette, I know you're a good athlete and will play a good game today." People want to rise to the occasion.[58]

Older coaches and managers must realize that younger people coming to work today are an often-praised generation. They are used to being praised just for showing up in school, and their experience is that everyone on the team gets a trophy regardless of individual or team performance—they need praise. However, unearned praise is condescending and destructive; incentives become entitlements, and we've ruined our kids by celebrating mediocrity. So set a high standard with clear goals, and give praise when the goals are achieved. Start easy by praising a good effort, and then praise good performance.

Think about this: When was the last time your coach or boss thanked or praised you for a job well done? When was the last time your coach or boss complained about your performance? If you are a coach or manager, when was the last time you praised or criticized your players or employees? What is the ratio of the praise to criticism you use?

You don't have to be a coach or manager to give praise. When was the last time you told your coach or boss, a teammate or coworker, a friend or family member he did a good job? What is your personal praise-to-criticism ratio? Let's discuss the giving praise model you can use to give everyone effective motivational praise every day.

## *The Giving Praise Model*

Praise motivates because it meets our needs for esteem, self-actualization, growth, and achievement. Giving praise creates win–win situations. It is probably the most powerful, easiest to use, and least costly motivational technique for increasing performance—and yet it is underused.[59] Ken Blanchard and Spencer Johnson popularized praise through their best-selling book *The One-Minute Manager*, in which they showed how to give one minute of feedback in the form of praise. Figure 11.6 adapts their method.[60]

1. Tell the person exactly what was done correctly. Be sincere; look the person in the eye. (Eye contact shows sincerity and concern.) Be specific and descriptive. General statements such as "You're a good worker" are not effective. On the other hand, don't talk for too long, or the praise loses impact—keep the entire praise to less than a minute.

Jose: "Chris, I just watched you deal with that in-your-face reporter. Great job! You kept your cool; you were polite. That reporter came to the game angry and left happy."

2. Tell the person why the behavior is important. State (briefly) how everyone benefits from the action. Also, state how you feel about the behavior. Be specific and descriptive.

Jose: "Without reporters, we don't reach our fans. But one dissatisfied reporter can cost us fans. It really made my day seeing you handle that tough reporter the way you did."

3. Stop for a moment of silence. Stopping the praise to be silent is tough for many of us. The rationale for the silence is to give the person the chance to feel the impact of the praise. Think of this as "the pause that refreshes." When you are thirsty and take the first

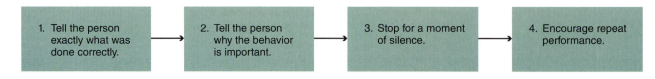

**FIGURE 11.6** Giving praise.

gulp of a refreshing drink, it's not until you stop and say "Ah" that you feel your thirst being quenched.

(Jose silently counts to 5.)

4. Encourage repeat performance. This reinforcement motivates the person to continue the desired behavior.

Jose: "Thanks, keep up the good work, Chris." (You can also use nonverbal communications, such as a handshake, high five, or thumbs-up.)

### Praise Rather Than Reprimand

Giving praise is a type of reward,[61] and it motivates much better than the punishment of negatively given criticism.[62] Giving praise is quick and easy, and it doesn't cost a penny. Managers who give praise genuinely and generously say it works wonders. It is also a better motivator than giving maintenance factors, such as monetary rewards.

Here's a true story of how to praise instead of reprimand to motivate for better performance. A manager noticed an employee who was taking his time stacking tennis ball cans on a display. The manager's first thought was to reprimanded the worker by saying something like, "Quit goofing off and get the job done." That statement would most likely result in a defensive response, such as "I'm not goofing off, I'm doing the best I can," and it would not motivate faster performance. However, it would have hurt human relations and could have ended in an argument with no improved performance.

Instead of being negative and criticizing, the manager was positive and looked for something to praise instead. The manager praised the employee for stacking the cans so straight, said good displays lead to increased sales, and encouraged him to continue doing a good job. The employee was so pleased with the praise that the display went up about 100 percent faster. Had the manager's praise not worked as intended, the manager could have then used another reinforcement method.

In today's global business world, you may never see people you work with face-to-face, but you can video conference or Skype or Voom them. Even with email, you can praise people following steps 1, 2, and 4. Plus, even now, the old-fashioned handwritten note of praise is considered a very powerful motivator.

# Putting Theory to Work Within the Motivational Process and Motivating Yourself

In this section, we illustrate how the motivation theories complement each other and how each of the motivation theories uses rewards. We then provide ideas on how you can motivate yourself to higher levels of performance.

## Putting the Theories Together

**LEARNING OUTCOME 6 ▶**

Compare content, process, and reinforcement theories.

Researchers seek an integration of motivation theories, which is the topic of this section. At this point, you're probably wondering, "Do all these theories fit together? Is one best? Or should I try to pick and choose for particular situations?" (The answers are yes, no, and yes.)

The theories fit together because each category of theories focuses on a different stage in the motivation process. They all answer different questions. Content-based theories address what needs people have that affect their motivation, or "What needs do people have that should be met on the job to motivate them?" Process-based theories address how people choose behavior to fulfill their needs, or "How do people go about fulfilling their needs?" Reinforcement theory addresses how managers can get employees to meet organizational objectives, or "How can I get people to behave the way I want them to?" Earlier in this chapter, we discussed how the motivation process progresses from need to motive to behavior to consequence and then to satisfaction or dissatisfaction. The motivation theories fit within the motivation process as shown in figure 11.7. Note the loop between step 4 and step 3; this occurs because behavior is learned through consequences of reinforcement. But step 4 does not loop back to steps 1 or 2 because reinforcement theory is not concerned with needs. The loop between step 5 and step 1 is always a given because meeting our needs is a never-ending process. Finally, note that according to two-factor theory, step 5 is two separate continuums (satisfied–not satisfied or dissatisfied–not dissatisfied), based on the need factor being met (motivator or maintenance). Refer to table 11.1 to review the motivation theories and figure 11.7 to put them together within the motivational process.

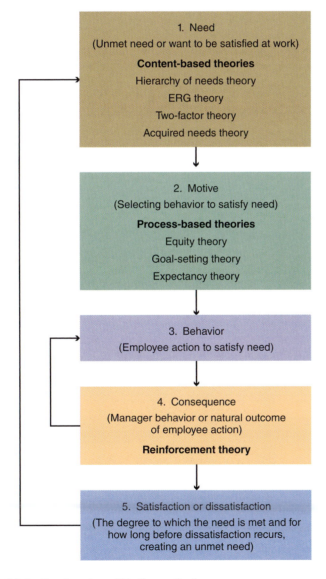

**FIGURE 11.7**   Motivation theories within the motivation process.

## How the Theories Motivate Using Rewards

Managers must act to motivate employees.[63] Yes, we have good theories, but it is not easy to motivate people. For one thing, what motivates one person will not motivate another, so it is important to know people as individuals in order to motivate them.[64] To answer the "What's in it for me?" question, organizations develop motivational systems that include rewards and recognition[65] that will create a motivational climate[66] and culture.[67] Here we cover how managers use rewards with each motivation theory.

Using *hierarchy of needs* and *ERG theories*, firms give financial rewards to meet the lower-level needs, but they use nonfinancial rewards to meet higher-level needs. With *two-factor theory*, maintenance needs are primarily met financially (like good working conditions and benefits), and motivators are met nonfinancially with rewarding work and recognition. *Acquired needs* rewards tend to vary with each need. High nAchs seek achievement and are often self-motivated to achieve objectives with both financial and nonfinancial rewards. The high nPows tend to be given both types of rewards because having power is a nonfinancial reward, but as people gain power, they often get pay raises. The nAffs' needs are met primarily through relationships in team-based positions.

People want *equity* in both their pay and their treatment, which includes recognition. Managers are expected to treat employees uniformly and consistently while considering individual needs and sometimes making exceptions. But making exceptions can be perceived as unfair organizational politics by others.[68] Managers use *goal-setting theory* by setting difficult but achievable goals and giving both financial and nonfinancial rewards for meeting goals. Using *expectancy theory* effectively is based on knowing what people value as rewards, which can be either financial or nonfinancial or both, depending on the individual, and always providing the reward.

With *reinforcement theory*, managers don't focus on meeting needs, and although the focus is on giving positive rewards, they also use negative reinforcement. Managers use avoidance by establishing standing plans, especially rules (chapter 4) to discourage specific behavior and punish violators, and they use extinction for undesirable behavior by withholding a reward. Reinforcement can be both financial and nonfinancial with either continuous or intermittent reinforcement, depending on the situation.

## Motivating Yourself

Keep in mind the performance equation (Performance = Ability × Motivation × Resources). Successful careers (performance) are usually based on doing what you are good at (ability), doing what you like to do (motivation), and getting the job you want (resources); resources include such things as a college degree, internships, and experience. Recall from chapter 8 how important your thoughts about yourself are because you become what you think about, or what you think is what you get.[69] To be self-motivated, you need to have a positive attitude about yourself and your job.

To be career self-motivated, decide what you need and want in a job (your content motivations) so that you can better understand what motivates you (process motivations) and how to get the job you want. Carefully read job descriptions and specifications. When you know your motivations, you make job decisions that better satisfy your needs.[70] Based on your needs and wants in a job, set objectives and develop new habits using cues, behavior changes, and rewards (reinforcement theory).[71]

Next we present a four-step model you can use to motivate yourself, followed by some other advice if you are not motivated and feel bored or trapped on the job. In either case, you have to take responsibility for motivating yourself and being happy.

### Set Objectives

First, you've got to know what you want—what your objectives are—and be willing to work hard to get whatever it is you want. What jobs and what career do you want? Develop objectives using the writing objectives model in chapter 4, table 4.2.

## APPLYING THE CONCEPT 11.2

### Motivation Theories

Identify the theory behind each statement.

a. hierarchy of needs

b. ERG theory

c. two-factor

d. acquired needs

e. equity

f. goal setting

g. expectancy

h. reinforcement

_____ 11. I make sure every job in our racket stores is interesting and challenging.

_____ 12. I treat everyone in our sporting goods store fairly.

_____ 13. I know Kate likes people, so I give her jobs in which she works with other employees.

_____ 14. Carl yelled at umpires because he knew it bothered me. So I decided to ignore his yelling, and he stopped.

_____ 15. I know my employees, what they like to do, and what about work excites them. And I know what sorts of rewards light a fire under their performance.

_____ 16. Our sporting goods company now offers good working conditions, salaries, and benefits, so we are working at developing employee camaraderie by having TGIF parties at 4 p.m. on Fridays.

_____ 17. Whenever my staff at the fitness center does a good job, I thank them.

_____ 18. I used to try to improve working conditions to motivate my staff. But I now focus on giving people more responsibility so they can grow and develop new skills.

_____ 19. I realize I tend to be autocratic because this fills my needs. I'm working at giving the team that makes baseball gloves more autonomy.

_____ 20. I focus on three needs and realize that needs can be unmet at more than one level at a time.

Although we all have limits to our abilities, drive and persistence are a key to success. A popular book some years ago stated that intelligence is overrated; the drive to win and persistence are better predictors of success. Are you willing to work hard and keep at it until you accomplish your difficult but achievable objectives?

### Develop Plans—Willpower Alone Fails

Why do so many people make New Year's resolutions and fail to keep them? The reason is that willpower or self-discipline alone, without a plan, doesn't work. What exactly are you going to do step by step to accomplish your objective? Do you need to improve your skills and qualifications, for example, by getting a college degree and passing a certification exam, getting internships, and getting job experience?

### Measure Results

Get feedback to know how you are progressing toward your objective. Compare your actual performance to your objective. For longer-term objectives, check regularly, not only at the end. How are you progressing—are we there yet? Chances are that you will not start out in your dream job as a head coach or high-level sport manager. It is common to start as an assistant coach or at an entry-level job and work your way up by gaining skill and experience and progressing to the position you really want.

## *Reinforce Results*

Be sure to use reinforcement theory on yourself. If you are missing the objective, consider punishing yourself; for example, if your weight is up, eat less next time. If you are on track to meet the objective, reward yourself in some way—have a special dessert.

Remember, what you think about is how you feel, and what you feel is how you behave. Recall that developing a new habit (see chapter 6) requires using cues to remind you of the new behavior, implementing the new behavior, and rewarding yourself to provide continuing motivation to develop the habit.[72] So develop a self-motivation objective; then plan, measure, and reinforce—and think about it and visualize yourself achieving the objective. The self-motivation model in figure 11.8 reviews the steps of self-motivation.

## *Bored or Feeling Trapped on the Job?*

If you are in these situations, you can keep things the same, or you can take responsibility and change the situation; you have two main choices. One, you can look for another job (within or outside the firm) following the four steps of the self-motivation model, which may require developing new skills, getting more education, or getting some type of certification. Two, you can think about how your job can be enriched or change the design.

With ideas in mind, talk to your boss about implementing ways to improve your job to make it more interesting and challenging, such as taking on new responsibilities. Taking over some of your boss' responsibility can help you develop new skills and give you experience to advance within the organization or to get a better job in another firm. You can also take any training programs offered at your organization and be the first to volunteer to learn new technology and tasks to expand your skills and experience for advancement.

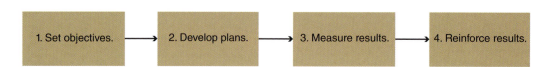

**FIGURE 11.8**   Self-motivation model.

## LEARNING AIDS

### CHAPTER SUMMARY

1. **Explain how motivation works.**

    People go through a five-step process to meet their needs. This is a circular process because needs recur.

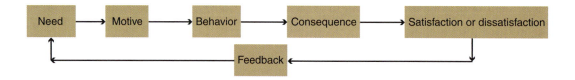

2. **Use the performance equation.**

   The performance equation states that

   $$\text{Performance} = \text{Ability} \times \text{Motivation} \times \text{Resources}$$

   A weakness in any one of these components will hamper performance. When performance declines, managers must determine which component of the equation is causing the problem and take action to correct it.

3. **Discuss the four content-based motivation theories.**

   All four content theories identify and then seek to understand people's needs. The theories identify similar needs but differ in how they are classified. Hierarchy of needs theory classifies needs as physiological, safety, social, esteem, and self-actualization. ERG theory classifies needs as existence, relatedness, and growth. Two-factor theory lists motivator factors and maintenance factors. Acquired needs theory uses achievement, power, and affiliation needs. (See table 11.1 and table 11.2 for a comparison of the four content-based theories.)

4. **Discuss the three process-based motivation theories.**

   All three process theories seek to understand how people choose behaviors to fulfill their needs. The process theories differ in their explanations of what motivates people. Equity theory proposes that motivation is based on the perception that inputs equal outputs. Goal-setting theory proposes that achievable but difficult goals are the driving factor in motivation. Expectancy theory proposes that motivation occurs when people believe they can accomplish the task and when the rewards for doing so are worth the effort.

5. **Discuss reinforcement theory.**

   Positive reinforcement rewards the person for performing the desired behavior. Avoidance reinforcement encourages the person to perform the desired behavior to avoid a negative consequence. Extinction reinforcement withholds a positive consequence to get the person to stop an undesirable behavior. Punishment reinforcement gives the person a direct negative consequence to get him to stop an undesirable behavior.

6. **Compare content, process, and reinforcement theories.**

   Content-based theories focus on identifying and understanding employees' needs. Process-based theories seek to understand how people choose behavior to fulfill their needs. Reinforcement theory is not concerned with need; it focuses on getting people to perform desirable behavior through consequences and reinforcement.

## REVIEW AND DISCUSSION QUESTIONS

1. What is motivation, and why is it important to know how to motivate employees?

2. Do managers' attitudes and expectations affect employee motivation and performance? Explain your answer.

3. Do you agree with the performance equation? Will you use it on the job?

4. Do people really have diverse needs?

5. Apply Maslow's hierarchy of needs to a sport organization you are familiar with.

6. Which of the three process-based motivation theories do you prefer? Why?

7. What reinforcements have been used to get you to go to work and to be on time?

8. True or false: Reinforcement theory is unethical because it is used to manipulate employees. Explain your reasoning.

9. What athletes in the past six months have been punished to discourage certain behavior? What was their punishment?

10. Which motivation theory do you plan to use on your job or as a coach? If you plan to use a hybrid, explain which parts of which theories you will emphasize.

11. Do you think that incentive-laden contracts motivate athletes to perform at their highest level?

12. What are the three major classes of motivation theories?

13. What are the four content motivation theories?

14. What are the two factors in two-factor theory?

15. What is the role of perception in equity theory?

16. What are the two parts of expectancy theory?

17. What are the two schedules of reinforcement?

18. What are the four steps of giving praise?

 **CASES**

### Sport Management Professionals @ Work: Dr. Eugene F. Asola

The study of sport management offers many benefits and career opportunities. The sports industry today is a growing and exciting field that calls for leaders who love and understand sports. A degree in sport management enabled me to combine my passion for sports with many other disciplines such as administration, marketing, and communications.

A sport management degree can position you for a high-level career in many of the specialized fields within the sports industry, including but not limited to professional sports, event and facility management, parks and recreation, intercollegiate and scholastic sports, equipment manufacturing, and sports agencies. I worked with the city of Boston as a field supervisor during the summers of 2003 and 2004 while in graduate school. I had the opportunity to combine theory with practical knowledge by being involved in the management of the summer tennis camps. I not only enjoyed it, but I learned a lot from my superiors. Experiential knowledge is spontaneous and very crucial for developing working skills in sport management. I will advise students in this area of study to look for such opportunities to develop in theory and practice.

Currently, my job as professor in higher education teacher preparation is facilitated by the knowledge I gained through sport management and other related courses. I teach both undergraduate and graduate students, and I teach management in sports administration, which is another facet of sport management in a broader sense. Please take a minute to reflect on your future career as you consider the following questions.

### Case Questions

1. Do I enjoy what I am doing now?

2. Five to ten years down the line, will I still enjoy doing what I do?

3. What passion do I derive from taking this course or related courses?

4. What then is my overall goal in the field of study I am currently pursuing?

### Living His Tennis Passion: Al Dunbar

Al Dunbar can normally be found at the Springfield, Massachusetts, Jewish Community Center (JCC) teaching the fine art of playing tennis. As a coach, he has a profound impact on youth. He is the father of two daughters and one son. When his girls were young, he would set up a tent on the grounds of the JCC for the girls so that he could teach and be a hands-on parent during the summer. As his own children grew up, Al went on to coach and train many other children in the skills of playing recreational, high school, and collegiate-level tennis. For his commitment, Al was voted a Key Players Ambassador. Key Players are noted for making a difference in children's lives.

However, Al is more than just a tennis instructor. He is truly passionate about tennis. He has been a member of the U.S. Tennis Association national board. He attends the U.S. Open, where the largest stadium is named after his late friend Arthur Ashe. He still plays tennis and often wins his age bracket.

Al is one of the tennis directors for the Shelly Rosenthal tournament held at Forest Park in Springfield. The tournament is often the first chance young players have to play in a competitive tennis event.[73]

Al has also been a schoolteacher all of his life. He started with a distinguished career teaching and coaching at a high school. After a short and restless retirement from teaching, Al returned as a media teacher in a different high school. As would be expected, he is also the tennis coach.

Al is very compassionate and loving with his junior players. His primary goal is for the players to love the game of tennis. He nurtures the students and helps them to learn more about the game and the famous players they watch on television. He often organizes trips to professional tennis matches so they can watch live events.

As his players get older, he instills in them a greater sense of competitiveness. As they enter high school with a competitive tennis team, he tells his players to be ready to practice hitting with the older students. At some point it will be their turn to play on their high school team, and they should be ready for either singles or doubles play.

On a good day (which can also be a cold, snowy day), you can find Al out coaching tennis to players of all ages. He motivates them with his passion for tennis.

Go to the web study guide to answer questions about this case study.

## @ TAKE IT TO THE NET

Please visit www.HumanKinetics.com/AppliedSportManagementSkills and go to this book's companion web study guide, where you will find the following:

A list of websites associated with the concepts in this chapter

Skill-Builder exercises, Sports and Social Media exercises, and a continuing Game Plan for Starting a Sport Business

Online versions of chapter exercises and end-of-chapter learning aids

An exercise that helps you define the Key Terms

# Leading to Victory

## LEARNING OUTCOMES

After studying this chapter, you should be able to

1. explain why managers are not always leaders;

2. compare the trait, behavioral, and contingency theories of leadership;

3. explain leadership trait theory;

4. contrast two-dimensional leaders and grid leaders;

5. identify the management levels where charismatic, transformational, transactional, and symbolic leaders work best;

6. contrast the various contingency models of leadership;

7. critique the continuum and the path–goal models; and

8. describe normative leaders.

## KEY TERMS

leaders

trait theorists

behavioral theorists

leadership style

two-dimensional leaders

Leadership Grid

charismatic leaders

transformational leaders

transactional leaders

symbolic leaders

contingency leaders

situational favorableness

continuum leaders

path–goal leaders

normative leaders

contingency managers

substitutes for leadership

Organizing Leading Controlling Planning Organizing Leading Controlling Planning Organizing
Controlling Planning Organizing Leading Controlling Planning Organizing Leading Controlling Planning
Leading Controlling Planning Organizing Leading Controlling Planning Organizing Leading
Planning Organizing Leading Controlling Planning Organizing Leading Controlling Planning
Leading Controlling Planning Organizing Leading Controlling Planning Organizing Leading Controlling
Organizing Leading

## DEVELOPING YOUR SKILLS

Leaders substantively affect the performance of organizations. Thus, organizations are increasingly looking for ways to train and develop leaders; one current focus is team leadership as more and more organizations turn to teams. The good news is that everyone has leadership potential. This means that you, too, can become an effective leader. In this chapter, you will learn about leadership traits, behavior, and contemporary and situational leadership theories. Through the use of the contingency management model, you can develop your ability to analyze employees' capabilities and choose the appropriate leadership style to maximize performance in a given situation.

## REVIEWING THEIR GAME PLAN

### Paul Fenton: Leading by Example

Paul Fenton was determined to be a hockey player in the NHL. Although he did play in the NHL from 1984 to 1992, his true success has come off the ice and in the boardroom. Fenton played for the Hartford Whalers, New York Rangers, Los Angeles Kings, Winnipeg Jets, Toronto Maple Leafs, and San Jose Sharks. He is considered the first American player to have scored 50 goals in a season, which he accomplished while playing for the Binghamton Whalers in the AHL.

But every professional athlete has to retire at some point—often before the age of 40. Paul was able to rely on a network of friends he had made during his lengthy journey through the NHL. His college coach at Boston College, Jack Parker, was his mentor as he entered the NHL. Former assistant general manager of the Whalers, Jack Ferreira, had coached Fenton when he was just 16 years old. Ultimately, Ferreira, as the general manager (GM) of the newly founded Anaheim Ducks, asked Fenton to take charge of the organization's professional scouting.

After five years in Anaheim with the Ducks, Fenton moved to the Nashville Predators, where he served as director of player personnel for eight years. Paul spent 15 seasons with the Predators and seven as the club's assistant general manager. Paul was in charge of all player acquisitions when he drafted Ryan Suter and Shea Weber in 2003. In 2012, Suter signed as a free agent with the Minnesota Wild for 13 years and $98 million. Weber decided to stay with the Predators after the Philadelphia Flyers offered a 14-year, $110 million offer sheet. Apparently, Paul is a good evaluator of talent.

Paul Fenton has a pleasant demeanor. He is quick with a smile and even quicker with an upbeat assessment of new young players he has scouted. These likable traits were evident even when Paul Fenton played Pee Wee and high school hockey. He always led by example. He wasn't the most graceful skater, but he worked hard, passed the puck to his teammates, and had a knack for scoring goals in bunches.

Early in Paul's career, a scout told him, "You're not Bobby Orr. You've got your degree, you should use it." Paul, though, showed determination and did have a successful playing career. Better yet, he parlayed that experience into a professional management career. His position as assistant GM required him to travel around the world scouting for talent. He was also involved in many day-to-day decisions to help the team run properly—he was not afraid to get his hands dirty and do some work around the Bridgestone Arena. Once again, his honesty and hard work paid off, and he was promoted through the Predator organization.

After being interviewed for many GM positions, Paul was finally signed to a multiyear contract by the Minnesota Wild to be their general manager of all hockey operations. As Wild owner Craig Leipold said, "Paul is uniquely suited for this job, having played 10 years of professional hockey and holding 25 years of management experience in the NHL. His gift of evaluating talent is obvious in Nashville's roster and recent success. My relationship with Paul goes back to my early days in Nashville, and I know that Wild hockey fans are going to love Paul's infectious passion for the game and unsurpassed work ethic. He's the right person to deliver a Stanley Cup to the State of Hockey."[1]

Paul Fenton continues to lead by example. The lessons here are many: Have a dream–yes; follow your dream–sure; but most of all, develop the ability to make it happen. You have to *work hard* to stay in the sport that you love.

For more information on Paul Fenton and the Minnesota Wild, go to www.nhl.com/wild.

# Leadership

Leadership is one of the most talked about, written about, and researched management topics.[2] If you search "leadership" on the website https://scholar.google.com, you will find about 3,900,000 articles on the subject.[3] Walk into a bookstore and you can find lots of books on the latest leadership gimmicks and fads,[4] but unfortunately, most are not based on scientific research like the theories you will learn in this chapter.

Why does leadership continue to be such a hot topic? Because good managers lead employees to organizational success.[5] Do you believe the NFL New England Patriots would have the winning record it has without its head coach Bill Belichick's leadership ability? This is why leadership is ranked in the top five skills companies want in all new hires.[6] In this section, you will learn that you can develop your leadership skills and that leaders and managers are different. We will also discuss the characteristics of good leaders according to the trait theory of leadership.

## Can Leadership Be Taught?

There are two common questions about leadership: "Are leaders made or born?" and "Can leadership skills be developed?" The answers: First, we are all born with leadership potential, but some of us have more natural ability than others. Second, research supports the idea that leadership skills can be developed.[7] If leadership skills can't be developed, why would colleges offer management and leadership courses, and why would companies spend millions on leadership training and development programs?[8] A common goal of sport management programs is to develop leadership skills. Learning the leadership theories in this chapter will help you to develop your leadership skills.[9] As Vince Lombardi said, "Leaders are made, they are not born. They are made by hard effort, which is the price which all of us must pay to achieve any goal that is worthwhile."[10] Are you willing to work on developing your leadership skills?

## Leaders Versus Managers

**Leaders** influence people to work to achieve the organization's objectives.

We often use the words *manager* and *leader* interchangeably. We shouldn't, because they are not necessarily the same.[11] Leading is a management function (remember, there are four—planning, organizing, leading, and controlling). Coaches and managers are given position power (chapter 8) that is broader in terms of responsibilities than leadership, but leadership is critical to organizational success.[12] Unfortunately, not all managers are leaders. And of course, there are leaders who are not managers. Many of us have been in situations in which one of our peers had more influence in the department or team than did the manager or coach.

◄**LEARNING OUTCOME 1**
Explain why managers are not always leaders.

Steve Jobs was viewed as a leader in his ability to influence others to make great Apple products, but he was not viewed as a good manager, and many employees left the company because of his offensive management style. His COO Tim Cook did most of the managing, and as CEO today, Cook is viewed as both a good manager and a good leader.[13] Tim Cook was called "The World's Greatest Leader" by *Fortune* in 2015.[14]

Recall from chapter 1 that leading is the process of influencing others to achieve objectives. You can be an influential leader without being a manager. You can be an informal leader or a peer leader, or you can play a leadership role in a team when you influence others to do something.[15] When we strive as a team to meet objectives, we influence each other;[16] team leadership is shared.[17] So anyone can be a leader within any group,[18] and regardless of your position, you are expected to share leadership because today leadership is a shared activity.[19] Unfortunately, new college grads lack the ability to manage and lead.[20] Fortunately, this book focuses on developing your sport management and leadership skills.

# Traits of Effective Leaders

**LEARNING OUTCOME 2** ▶

Compare the trait, behavioral, and contingency theories of leadership.

Researchers first formally studied leadership in the early 1900s. They wanted to identify a set of characteristics or traits that distinguished leaders from followers and effective leaders from ineffective ones. Their investigations of traits led to behavioral theories, and contingency perspectives, then to situational leadership theories. Here we discuss trait theory, and the other leadership theory classifications are presented in the following three major sections.

**LEARNING OUTCOME 3** ▶

Explain leadership trait theory.

Early leadership researchers assumed that leaders are born, not made. So **trait theorists** investigated characteristics that make leaders effective. Over 70 years in more than 300 studies, these theorists analyzed many physical and psychological qualities, such as appearance, aggressiveness, self-reliance, persuasiveness, and dominance, in an effort to identify a set of traits that successful leaders possess. The idea was that this list of traits would guide the promotion of the most promising candidates to managerial leadership positions.

## Personality Traits

Your personality is made up of traits (see chapter 8),[21] so personality is part of trait theory because your personality affects your leadership behavior.[22] Both extroverts and narcissists tend to seek leadership roles, as do people seeking power (chapter 8).[23] Recall that our discussion of the acquired needs motivation theory in chapter 11 described the management profile as having a strong need for power, whereas people with a high need for affiliation don't generally seek management careers. Does your personality match? Do you want to be a manager?

## Ghiselli's Study

Edwin Ghiselli conducted a study of leadership traits with more than 300 managers from 90 different U.S. businesses, and he published his results in 1971.[24] He concluded that certain traits are important to effective leadership, but you do not need all of them to succeed. Ghiselli identified the following six traits, in order of importance, as significant. Effective leaders generally have (1) supervisory ability (using the four functions of management—planning, organizing, leading, and controlling—that you learn in this course), (2) a need for occupational achievement, (3) intelligence, (4) decisiveness, (5) self-assurance, and (6) initiative. How many do you have?

Paul Fenton took the initiative to turn his experience as a professional hockey player into a lifetime career as an executive with the Nashville Predators and later as the general manager of the Minnesota Wild.

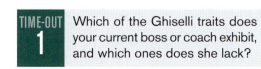

**TIME-OUT 1** Which of the Ghiselli traits does your current boss or coach exhibit, and which ones does she lack?

## Inconclusive Findings

The problem was that no one could create a list of traits that all successful leaders universally possess. There are always exceptions, or what we call inconclusive research findings. Researchers also couldn't determine whether traits such as assertiveness and self-confidence were developed before or after one became a manager. In addition, some people were successful managers in one position but not in another. The lesson here, of course, is that leaders are an extremely diverse lot.

### Current Research

Even though it is generally agreed that no universal set of leadership traits exists, researchers continue to study and write about leadership traits.[25] Why? Even though leaders don't universally possess the same qualities, a lot of leaders do possess certain qualities. And the good news is that these qualities can be learned. Fortune Senior Author Geoff Colvin said that the most important thing about a leader is traits, not skills.[26] You can teach and learn basic functional skills (accounting, operations), but it is difficult to develop traits. Also, recall that more organizations are giving personality tests (chapter 7). The contemporary perspectives of leadership are based on traits, which we will discuss.

### Ethics and Spirituality in the Workplace

Traits (personality, values, level of moral development) affect a leader's use of ethical or unethical behavior—this is called *moralized leadership*.[27] People want leaders with integrity.[28] Recall the importance of business ethics from chapter 2. Once again, we want to emphasize the importance of diversity and being inclusive and ethical with everyone, so develop an ethical culture.[29]

Related to ethics and values is spirituality at work. Some companies even have corporate chaplains. Consultants, including Edgewalkers International (https://edgewalkers.org) founded by Judi Neal, offer materials and packaged and custom programs to all types of organizations.[30] Former NBA coach Phil Jackson of the world champion Chicago Bulls and Los Angeles Lakers says that much of his outlook comes from his spiritual direction.[31]

The late Zig Ziglar, best-selling author and speaker who trained people to change their lives to be successful (his son Tom took over as CEO of Ziglar), said that proper emphasis on the spiritual aspects of life is extremely important to success. He quoted some hundred research studies conclusively finding that people who attend church regularly make more money, have better health, are happier with their jobs and family life, and have a much lower divorce rate than others. As Zig puts it, "In short, they get more of the things that money can buy and all of the things that money can't buy."[32] Of course, not all successful leaders are spiritual, but most are ethical.

# Behavior of Effective Leaders

By the late 1940s, most research into leadership had shifted from analyzing traits to analyzing what effective leaders do. To this end, researchers compared the behavior of effective and ineffective leaders in search of the one best leadership style. **Behavioral theorists** investigate the leadership style of effective leaders. Before we discuss the basic styles of leadership, two-dimensional leadership, and the Leadership Grid behavioral theories, complete Self-Assessment to determine your theory X, theory Y leadership style.

What leadership actions do you think create a winning sport program?

## SELF-ASSESSMENT 12.1

### Are You a Theory X or Theory Y Leader?

Note the frequency with which you do (or would do, if you have not yet held a position of leadership) each action. Be honest. There are no right or wrong answers. This Self-Assessment is easiest to complete online.

U = usually

F = frequently

O = occasionally

S = seldom

_____ 1. I set objectives for my department alone; I don't include staff input.

_____ 2. I allow staff members to develop their own plans rather than developing them myself.

_____ 3. I delegate to staff several of the tasks that I enjoy doing rather than doing them myself.

_____ 4. I allow staff members to solve problems they encounter rather than solving them myself.

_____ 5. I recruit and select new employees alone; I don't solicit input from staff.

_____ 6. I orient and train new employees myself rather than having members of my team do it.

_____ 7. I tell staff members only what they need to know rather than giving them access to anything they want to know.

_____ 8. I praise and recognize staff efforts; I don't just criticize.

_____ 9. I set controls for the team to ensure that objectives are met rather than allowing the team to set its own controls.

_____ 10. I often observe my group to ensure that it is working and meeting deadlines.

For items 1, 5, 6, 7, 9, and 10, give each U answer 1 point; F, 2 points; O, 3 points; and S, 4 points. For items 2, 3, 4, and 8, give each S answer 1 point; O, 2 points; F, 3 points; and U, 4 points. Total your score, which should be between 10 and 40.

You have just measured your theory X, theory Y behavior. This theory was developed by Douglas McGregor (1906-1964), who contrasted the two theories based on the assumptions managers make about workers. Theory X managers assume that people dislike work and need managers to plan, organize, and closely direct and control their work in order for them to perform at high levels. Theory Y managers assume people like to work and do not need close supervision. Place a check on the continuum that represents your score.

| Theory X Behavior | | Theory Y Behavior | |
|---|---|---|---|
| 10 | 20 | 30 | 40 |
| Autocratic | | Participative | |

The lower your score on this self-assessment, the more you tend toward theory X behavior; the higher your score, the more you tend toward theory Y behavior. A score of 20 to 30 shows a balance between the two extremes of the continuum. *Note:* Your score may or may not accurately reflect how you would behave in an actual job; however, it can help you understand your underlying attitudes.

## Basic Styles of Leadership

**Leadership style** is the combination of traits, skills, and behaviors that managers use to interact with employees. In the 1930s, even before behavioral theory became popular, researchers at the University of Iowa led by Kurt Lewin studied the leadership styles of managers and identified three basic styles:[33]

1. *Autocratic.* The manager makes the decisions, tells employees what to do, and closely supervises them—basically theory X behavior.

2. *Democratic.* The manager encourages employee participation in decisions, works with employees to determine what to do, and doesn't supervise them closely—theory Y behavior.

3. *Laissez-faire.* The manager lets employees go about their business without much input—that is, employees decide what to do and take action, and the manager does not follow up.

## Two-Dimensional Leaders

*Structuring and consideration styles.* In 1945, the Personnel Research Board of The Ohio State University began a study to determine effective leadership styles.[34] In the process, researchers developed an instrument known as the Leader Behavior Description Questionnaire (LBDQ). Respondents to the questionnaire perceived leaders' behavior on two distinct dimensions:

◄ LEARNING OUTCOME 4
Contrast two-dimensional leaders and grid leaders.

1. *Structuring*—the extent to which the leader takes charge to plan, organize, lead, and control as the employee performs the task. This dimension focuses on getting the job done.

2. *Consideration*—the extent to which the leader communicates to develop trust, friendship, support, and respect. This dimension focuses on developing relationships with employees.

*Job-centered and employee-centered styles.* At approximately the same time as the Ohio State studies began, the University of Michigan's Survey Research Center initiated its own leadership studies. This research identified the same two dimensions, or styles, of leadership behavior as the Ohio research. However, the Michigan researchers called the two styles *job centered* (analogous to structuring) and *employee centered* (analogous to consideration).

**Two-dimensional leaders** focus on job structure and employee considerations, a focus that results in four possible leadership styles. In 1945, Ralph Stogdill at Ohio State University and Rensis Likert at the University of Michigan began independent studies of leadership styles.[35] Although the research teams used different terminology, they identified the same two dimensions. UM's team called the two dimensions job centered and employee centered; OSU's team called them initiating structure and consideration. The OSU and UM leadership models also differed in structure: UM placed the two dimensions at opposite ends of the same continuum. OSU considered the two dimensions independent of one another. Both dimensions measure the manager's behavior when interacting with employees:

 **TIME-OUT 2** Which of the two-dimensional leadership styles does your coach or boss use? Describe his behavior using this model.

- Initiating structure, job centered: the extent to which managers take charge to plan, organize, lead, and control as employees perform tasks. This dimension focuses on getting the job done.

- Consideration, employee centered: the extent to which managers develop trust, friendship, support, and respect. This dimension focuses on developing rapport with employees.

In the two-dimensional model, managers get the job done by directing people and developing supportive relationships. Combinations of the two dimensions result in the four leadership styles shown in the OSU 2 × 2 matrix in figure 12.1 but only two leaderships styles in the UM model. Although the OSU and UM studies are now dated, they are still written about today, and they influence the current theories. The situational leadership theories extend the use of the two dimensions of leadership.

# Leadership Grid

In the 1960s, Robert Blake and Jane Mouton developed the Managerial Grid, which later became the **Leadership Grid**, developed by Blake and Anne Adams McCanse.[36] The Leadership Grid uses the same dimensions as the two-dimensional model; in the grid, these dimensions are called concern for production and concern for people (figure 12.2). The Leadership Grid identifies the ideal leadership style as having a high concern for both production and people. Because the grid measures the two dimensions on a scale from 1 to 9, 81 combinations are possible, from which Blake and McCanse categorized five major leadership styles:

- (1,1) Impoverished leaders show low concern for both production and people. They do the minimum required to remain employed.
- (9,1) Authority–compliance leaders show a high concern for production and a low concern for people. They focus on getting the job done by treating people like machines.
- (1,9) Country club leaders show a low concern for production and a high concern for people. They strive to maintain a friendly atmosphere without much regard for production.
- (5,5) Middle-of-the-road leaders balance their concerns for production and people. They strive for performance and morale levels that are minimally satisfactory.
- (9,9) Team leaders show a high concern for both production and people. They strive for maximum performance and maximum employee satisfaction.

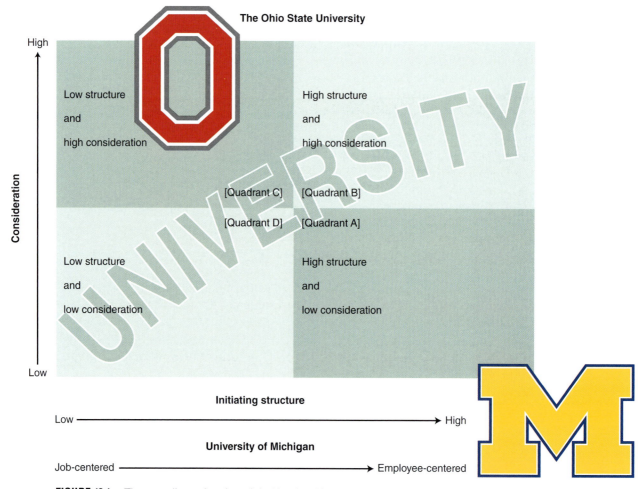

**FIGURE 12.1**   The two-dimensional model of leadership.

According to Blake, Mouton, and McCanse, the team leadership style (9,9) is the most appropriate style to use in all situations. However, most researchers disagreed; they concluded that there was no single style

TIME-OUT
**3**
Describe your boss' leadership style. Which of the Leadership Grid styles does your boss use?

that was best for all situations—that is, leadership is situational. So the research focus shifted from behavioral to situational leadership. However, contemporary perspectives on leadership are based on both traits and behaviors of leaders, as discussed in our next section.

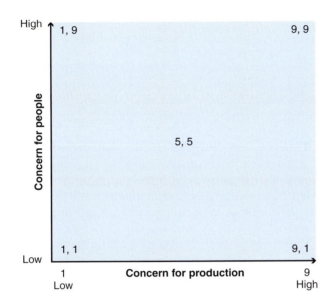

**FIGURE 12.2** The Leadership Grid.

## APPLYING THE CONCEPT 12.1

### Grid Leaders

Identify the five statements by leadership style.

a. 1,1 (impoverished)
b. 1,9 (country club)
c. 9,1 (authority–compliance)
d. 5,5 (middle-of-the-road)
e. 9,9 (team)

_____ 1. The marketing group's morale is high, and its members enjoy their work, but the department's productivity is one of the lowest in the company. The marketing manager is a people person but doesn't always get around to business.

_____ 2. The HR group's morale is adequate; its productivity is average. The HR manager is somewhat concerned about people and production.

_____ 3. The fitness center group's morale is at one of the lowest levels in the company, but this group is also one of the top performers. Its manager focuses on production but not on the needs of her staff.

_____ 4. The maintenance department is one of the lowest performers and has low morale. Its manager is not concerned with people or production.

_____ 5. The ticket sales group is a top performer in the company, and its morale is high. Its manager focuses on both people and production.

# Contemporary Behavioral Perspectives

Today, we know that a leader's behavior affects employees[37] and that leaders use different behavioral approaches to influence and motivate people.[38] Contemporary researchers focus on which behaviors make top-notch managers outstanding, even though the managers' individual leadership styles may vary dramatically. In this section, we discuss contemporary leadership theories with a heavy focus on leadership behavior.

## Leader–Member Exchange (LMX) Theory

**LEARNING OUTCOME 5** ▶

Identify the management levels where charismatic, transformational, transactional, and symbolic leaders work best.

Leader–member exchange (LMX) theory is based on the relationship between leaders and their followers.[39] LMX emphasizes the unique one-on-one relationships that develop between managers and each of their subordinates.[40] Effective *leader–member exchange (LMX) leaders* create a positive relationship with each person.[41] LMX theory says that relationships are important,[42] and leadership is about building relationships to influence all members of your team.[43] LMX is important because our personal and professional happiness and success are based on our relationships.

LMX research also identifies the effects of in- and out-groups. Have you ever been a member of a team and the coach liked you, and you were a member of the in-group (favorites, cliques)? Conversely, have you ever been in the out-group? Then you have experienced negative LMX grouping. Not surprisingly, the members of the in-group get better assignments, receive higher performance ratings, have greater job satisfaction, and often have higher-level performance—recall the Pygmalion effect (chapter 8).

Leadership should bring out the best in people,[44] but putting them in out-groups doesn't do that. In chapter 2, we discuss the importance of inclusion, and in chapter 9, we cover the importance of group process and team cohesiveness. Clearly, if you develop or allow in- and out-groups, you will not have group cohesiveness—they create status differences between members, which leads to conflict. LMX leadership usually results in the two groups fighting for power and using unethical politics. Again, you need to be inclusive in developing positive relationships with everyone without creating in- and out-groups.

The world champion NBA Golden State Warriors basketball team's success is based on inclusion. Although initially invited to the White House by President Trump, the team voted not to accept the invitation. "In lieu of a visit to the White House, we have decided that we'll constructively use our trip to the nation's capital in February to celebrate equality, diversity and inclusion—the values that we embrace as an organization."[45]

Recall from chapter 8 the importance of organizational politics. When you get a job, if there are in- and out-groups, your boss will usually start by believing you should be with the in-group. If there are clear-cut in- and out-groups, you should be able to recognize the members of each because the out-group tends to try to recruit new members to its coalition against the in-group. Belonging to the in-group has its career benefits. Recall that to advance, you need to get top evaluation ratings from your boss, so, figure out what you need to do to succeed (see chapters 7 and 8). Consultant Jack Welch says that it is important to know what the boss really thinks of you, but he says that only 5 to 10 percent of employees really know.[46] Are you willing to ask your boss? If you slip into the out-group based on performance, are you willing to confront your boss to agree on what it will take to get a top rating and then do it?

## Visionary and Charismatic Leaders

Visionary and charismatic leaders are top-level managers.[47] An executive can be both visionary and charismatic. These charismatic people develop strategic visions of future success and inspire others to achieve the vision.[48] Steve Jobs was a visionary leader who developed and improved disruptive, innovative products,[49] including the Apple Macintosh PC, the iPod, iTunes, the iPhone, and Pixar animated films. Jobs' success was largely attributed to his incredible charisma that inspired tremendous loyalty to create great products.[50] Jobs was called a pied piper of charisma by his frenemy Bill Gates of Microsoft.[51] But how many Steve Jobs are there? Most executives are neither visionary nor charismatic, and some are just one or the other. Let's discuss each separately.

*Visionary leaders* bring about innovative change and affect the future.[52] Visionaries create an image of the organization in the future. The vision creates shared purpose and provides direction for setting objectives and writing strategic plans.[53] Professor Russ Ackoff said that visionary leaders create opportunities. They envision a desirable future and invent ways of bringing it about.[54] Martin Luther King, Jr. had a vision of equality for all that was expressed with vivid imagery in his "I Have a Dream" speech.[55]

**Charismatic leaders** create enthusiasm to achieve objectives by developing strong relationships with followers they may not even know personally, producing strong loyalty that influences followers' behavior and performance.[56] Charisma is determined by the leader's personality traits and behavior. John F. Kennedy and Mother Teresa are often given as examples of charismatic leaders. NBA star LeBron James and NFL quarterback Tom Brady are sport examples. Charisma comes from having followers, but followers can also take it away; consider pro golfer Tiger Woods. Research supports the idea that charismatic leaders have a strong effect on performance and that charismatic leadership skills can be developed.[57]

## Transformational and Transactional Leaders

Transformational leaders are also top-level executives, and they are commonly compared against transactional leaders at lower levels of management.[58] However, some top-level managers are transactional. Both affect performance but do so differently, as discussed here.[59]

**Transformational leaders** emphasize continuous learning and making innovative changes. Many charismatic leaders are also visionary and transformational leaders, but few executives are all three.[60] Transformers gain acceptance of the objectives and motivate employees to go beyond (transcend) their own self-interest for the good of the team and the organization.[61] Jeff Bezos founded Amazon and transformed the way people buy books. Then, with his e-reader, he transformed how many people read books, and he also popularized tablets. Bezos has also made it possible to buy just about anything from Amazon through various electronic devices, include simply asking Alexa using Amazon Echo.[62]

Theo Epstein has been a transformational leader—twice! When he arrived, the Red Sox had not won a World Series since 1918. Epstein was brought in as the general manager to inspire the team and lead it to win. He succeeded by finding new players who were positive role models and who

 **TIME-OUT 4** Think about the top manager in your firm or team. Is she a charismatic leader or a transformational leader? Why or why not?

worked well together. The Red Sox won two World Series under Epstein's guidance. Epstein did it again when he switched to be the general manager of the Chicago Cubs. The Cubs had not won a World Series in 108 years. But Epstein assembled a strong minor league farm system that matured to win the 2016 World Series.[63]

**Transactional leaders** focus on stability as they implement change by creating standing plans (chapter 4) to standardize policies, procedures, and rules. Transactional leaders emphasize exchange. Exchange is about rewarding or punishing based on follower performance. The exchange process can be both constructive (promising rewards for performance) and corrective (correcting mistakes before or after they happen). Recall that LMX leadership is based on relationship exchanges,[64] organizational politics (chapter 8) is based on reciprocity,[65] and reinforcement theory motivates through rewards and punishments (chapter 11). Put them together and you can conclude that these relationships drive effective transactional leadership.

## Symbolic, Servant, and Authentic Leaders

People want leaders, but they reject self-serving, inauthentic leaders.[66] These three types of leaders focus on creating a helping environment so employees can meet objectives.

**Symbolic leaders** establish and maintain a strong organizational culture. An organization's workforce learns the organization's culture (shared values, beliefs, and assumptions about how workers should behave in the organization—see chapter 6) through its leadership. Symbolic leadership starts with top management and flows down to middle and first-line managers. Symbolic leaders go beyond looking out for their own self-interests and focus on meeting the needs of others. Do you believe that Paul Fenton is a charismatic, transformational, transactional, or symbolic leader, or some combination of these?

*Servant leaders* look out for the employees' and the organization's interests, rather than their own self-interest.[67] It's not all about you, it's about them.[68] Turn your hierarchical organizational chart upside down and report to your subordinates.[69] "What can I do to help you do your job? What do you need from me to succeed?" They try to create a win–win situation for everyone. Isn't this the foundation of effective relationships, true friendship, and happiness? Servant leaders create strong relationships that result in higher levels of performance.[70]

*Authentic leaders* develop open, honest, trusting relationships leading by example.[71] People often spot a phony,[72] such as when a narcissist is nice to you just to get something from you.[73] Ever seen it? The question is, are you being yourself, or are you putting on an act for others? Your inauthentic behavior may cause relationship problems and other kinds of problems.[74] You can only be on your best behavior, or put on an act, for so long before your true self comes through. Former NBA championship coach Phil Jackson says, "You have to be true to yourself as a leader."[75]

You should understand the need for unselfish servant-type, authentic behavior. But if you try too hard to be a serving authentic leader, you may come off as inauthentic.[76] Generally, as we age we care less about what others think of us and become more authentic. But don't be a jerk.

# Situational Leadership Theories and Models

The trait and behavioral theories tried to identify the one best leadership style for all situations—a one-size-fits-all approach. Researchers realized that there was no one best style, so the focus of research shifted to situational leadership. According to this approach, contingency leaders analyze the situation and use the leadership style most appropriate to the situation, and they are commonly called situational leaders.[77] Today's leaders need to get to know employees as individuals and motivate them to achieve objectives based on their situational needs.[78] In this section, we discuss five situational theories (see figure 12.7 later in chapter), which have models that identify the most appropriate leadership style for the situation.

## Contingency Leaders

**LEARNING OUTCOME 6** ▶

Contrast the various contingency models of leadership.

In the 1950s, Fred E. Fiedler began to develop the first situational leadership theory, the contingency theory of leader effectiveness, which he published in the 1960s.[79] Fiedler contended that our leadership style reflects our personality and remains fairly constant. That is, leaders do not change their styles; instead, they should change situations to match their leadership styles. **Contingency leaders** are task or relationship oriented, and their style should fit the situation.

## Leadership Style

First you determine whether your leadership style is task or relationship oriented by using the *Least Preferred Coworker Scale*, an instrument developed at the University of Washington. After determining your leadership style, you look at situational favorableness. Without completing the LPCS, would you say your leadership style is more task or relationship oriented?

## Situational Favorableness Variables

**Situational favorableness** is the degree to which a situation enables leaders to exert influence over followers. The three variables (shown in top row of figure 12.3), in order of importance, are as follows:

1. *Leader–member relations.* Is the relationship between the manager and subordinates good or poor? The better the relations, the more favorable the situation. Paul Fenton has a good relationship with the people who work for him. You can watch video on YouTube of Paul being comfortable in front of the media and in the locker room with the players.

2. *Task structure.* Is the task structured or unstructured? Do employees perform repetitive, routine, and standard tasks that are easily understood? The more repetitive the jobs, the more favorable the situation.

3. *Position power.* Is the manager's position power strong or weak to assign work, reward and punish, hire and fire, and give raises and promotions? The more power, the more favorable the situation.

## Using the Contingency Leadership Model

To determine whether a task or relationship orientation is appropriate, use the Fiedler contingency model and answer three questions (pertaining to situational favorableness) set up as a decision tree—figure 12.3 shows an adapted model. You answer question 1 and follow the decision tree to *Good* or *Poor* depending on your answer. After answering question 3, you end up in one of eight possible situations.

## Matching Your Style to the Situation

According to Fiedler, if your style matches the situation, you are using the appropriate style, so you do nothing. If your style doesn't match the situation, change either your relationships, the task repetitiveness, or your power so that your situation changes to match your preferred leadership style.

TIME-OUT
5

Is your current boss or coach task oriented or relationship oriented? Using figure 12.3, identify your boss' situation by number, and then identify the appropriate style to use for this situation. Does your boss use the appropriate style?

## Criticism

A major criticism of Fiedler's model concerns his view that leaders cannot change their style (a task versus a relationship style) and that if the leaders' style does not fit the situation, the leaders should change the situation to fit their style. It's usually difficult or impossible to change a situation to match your style. The other contingency researchers also theorize that leaders can and should change their leadership style to match the situation; change your leadership styles, not the situation. Do you believe you can or cannot change your leadership style?

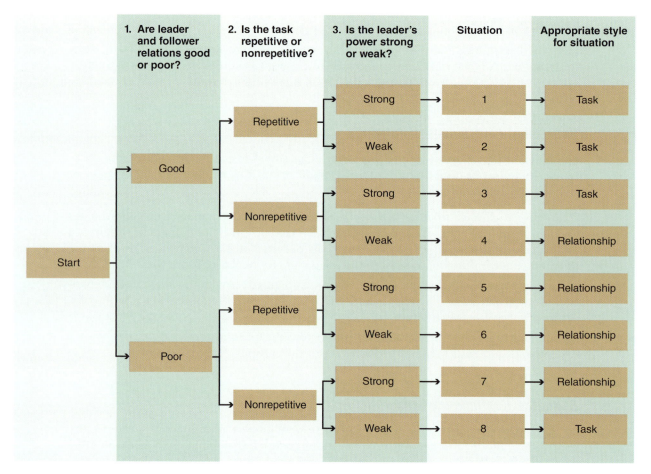

**FIGURE 12.3** The contingency model of leadership. If the manager's preferred leadership style matches the situation, the manager does nothing. If the preferred leadership style does not match the situation, the manager changes the situation to match her preferred leadership style.

## APPLYING THE CONCEPT 12.2

### Contingency Leaders

Use figure 12.3 to first identify which of the eight situations best fits the following descriptions, and then indicate whether the appropriate leadership style is (a) task oriented or (b) relationship oriented.

_____ 6. Saul oversees the assembly of mass-produced golf tees. He has the power to reward and punish. He is considered a hard-nosed boss.

_____ 7. Karen manages corporate event planning; she helps other departments plan events. She is viewed as a dreamer who doesn't understand the various departments. Employees are often rude to her.

_____ 8. Juan manages the processing of checks. He is well liked by his staff. Juan's boss enjoys hiring employees and evaluating their performance.

_____ 9. Sonia, the event manager, assigns dates and times for each event. The event-planning atmosphere is tense.

_____ 10. Louis owns a professional soccer team. He is highly regarded by volunteer members on the board of directors. The board members recommend ways to increase season ticket sales.

## Continuum Leaders

In Robert Tannenbaum and Warren Schmidt's model, developed in the 1960s, leadership occurs on a continuum from boss-centered (autocratic) to employee-centered (participative) leadership. Their model focuses on who makes the decisions.[80]

◀ LEARNING OUTCOME 7
Critique the continuum and the path–goal models.

### Leadership Styles and Model

Tannenbaum and Schmidt identified seven major styles from which leaders can choose. Figure 12.4, an adaptation of their model published in the 1970s, lists the seven styles. **Continuum leaders** choose their style based on a range between boss-centered (autocratic) or employee-centered (participative) leadership for the given situation.

TIME-OUT 6

Which leadership style (1-7) in figure 12.4 does your boss or coach use? Is it the most appropriate style? Why or why not?

### Situation Variables and Selecting the Leadership Style

Before selecting one of the seven styles, you consider the following three variables: (1) your preferred leadership style, (2) the subordinates' preferred style for your leadership, and (3) the situation. Based on the variables, which are not shown on the model, you select the appropriate leadership style for the situation.

### Criticism

Even though the continuum model was popular, a major criticism was that it was too subjective. Determining which leadership style to use is complex. You must determine the style you prefer to use, the one your subordinate wants you to use, and the one the situation calls for. Then you select one of the seven styles. No problem, right?

## Path–Goal Leaders

Robert House developed the path–goal leadership model in the 1970s. **Path–goal leaders** determine employee objectives and achieve them using one of four styles. The focus is on how leaders influence employees' perceptions of their goals and the paths they follow to attain them.[81] As shown in figure 12.5 (an adaptation of the model), House's model uses situational factors to determine which leadership style best achieves goals by influencing employee performance and satisfaction.

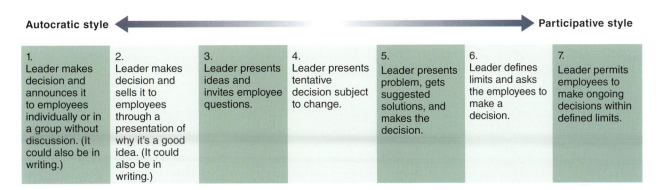

Autocratic style ◀————————————————————————▶ Participative style

| 1. | 2. | 3. | 4. | 5. | 6. | 7. |
|---|---|---|---|---|---|---|
| Leader makes decision and announces it to employees individually or in a group without discussion. (It could also be in writing.) | Leader makes decision and sells it to employees through a presentation of why it's a good idea. (It could also be in writing.) | Leader presents ideas and invites employee questions. | Leader presents tentative decision subject to change. | Leader presents problem, gets suggested solutions, and makes the decision. | Leader defines limits and asks the employees to make a decision. | Leader permits employees to make ongoing decisions within defined limits. |

**FIGURE 12.4** The continuum model of leadership.

## APPLYING THE CONCEPT 12.3

### Continuum Leaders

Use figure 12.4 to identify the continuum leadership style (1-7) implied in each statement.

_____ 11. Chuck, I recommended that you be transferred to the new public relations department, but you don't have to go if you don't want to.

_____ 12. Sam, go clean the tables in the stadium restaurant right away.

_____ 13. From now on, this is the way security at all games will be done. Does anyone have any questions about the procedure?

_____ 14. These are the two weeks in which we can schedule the high school basketball tournament. You select one.

_____ 15. I'd like your ideas on how to stop the bottleneck on the hockey puck production line. But I have the final say on the solution we implement.

### Situational Variables

*Subordinate situational characteristics* include (1) authoritarianism, the degree to which employees defer and want to be told what to do and how to do the job; (2) locus of control (see chapter 8), the extent to which employees believe they and not others control goal achievement (internal versus external locus of control); and (3) ability, the extent of employees' ability to perform tasks to achieve goals.

*Environmental situational factors* include (1) task structure, the degree of repetitiveness of the job; (2) formal authority, the extent of the leader's power; and (3) work group, the extent to which coworkers contribute to job satisfaction.

### Selecting the Leadership Style

After considering situational factors, managers choose the most appropriate leadership style by following these guidelines:

1. *Directive.* Leaders provide high structure and play task behavior roles (chapter 8). Directive leadership is appropriate when subordinates want authority, have external locus of control, and have low ability.

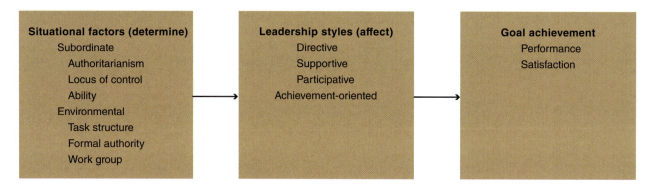

**FIGURE 12.5**   The path–goal model of leadership.

2. *Supportive.* Leaders provide high consideration and play maintenance behavior roles (chapter 8). Supportive leadership is appropriate when subordinates do not want autocratic leadership, have internal locus of control, and are highly competent and therefore do not need directives.

3. *Participative.* Managers solicit employee input with shared leadership. Participative leadership is appropriate when subordinates want to be involved, have internal locus of control, and are high in ability.

4. *Achievement-oriented.* Leaders set difficult but achievable goals, expect subordinates to perform at their highest level, and reward them for doing so. That is, leaders provide both high structure and high consideration. It's appropriate when

TIME-OUT 7

Which path–goal leadership style does your boss or coach use? Is this the most appropriate style for the situation? Explain.

subordinates are open to autocratic leadership, have external locus of control, and are high in ability.

### Criticism

Academics tend to like path–goal leadership because it is based on research. However, a major criticism from actual managers is that like continuum leadership, the path–goal model is too subjective and complex. The model lists the variables on the left and the leadership style in the center. But it doesn't provide practical guidance on how to use the variables to select the most appropriate style for achieving the goal (the right-hand box in figure 12.5).

## Normative Leaders

Yale University Professor Victor Vroom developed participative decision-making models during the 1960s, and with colleagues he revised the model that he presented in a 2000 publication.[82] His is a normative model because it provides a sequential set of questions that are rules (norms) to follow to determine the best decision style for a given situation.

◀ **LEARNING OUTCOME 8**

Describe normative leaders.

### Selecting the Leadership Style

To determine the appropriate style for a specific situation, users of the normative model answer seven questions (not discussed here), some of which may be skipped depending on prior answers. The questions are sequential and are presented in a decision-tree format similar to that of Fiedler's contingency model. So, unlike the leadership continuum and path–goal models, this model tells you which decision-making style to use. **Normative leaders** use one of five decision-making styles appropriate for the situation. Vroom identified the five leadership styles based on the level of participation of group members in the decision.

- *Decide.* The leader makes the decision alone without input from the group.
- *Consult individuals.* The leader describes the problem to individual group members, gets information and suggestions, and then makes the decision.
- *Consult group.* The leader holds a group meeting and describes the problem to the group, gets information and suggestions, and then makes the decision.
- *Facilitate.* The leader seeks participation from the group, debate, and consensus on the decision. However, the leader has the final say on the decision.
- *Delegate.* The leader lets the group diagnose the problem and make the decision within stated limits. The role of the leader is to answer questions and provide encouragement and resources.

TIME-OUT 8

Which normative leadership style does your boss or coach use? Is this the most appropriate style for the situation? Explain.

## Criticism

Vroom's model is popular with academics because it is based on research.[83] However, the model is not popular with managers, who find it too complex to select one of two models, then answer seven questions, and finally determine the appropriate leadership style. Because of this complexity, we don't show the two models with seven questions and five leadership styles. Vroom now has an electronic model.

# Contingency Management

The contingency models we have described so far are complex, making it difficult to determine which leadership style to use in what situations. In this section, we present the contingency management model developed by Robert N. Lussier.[84] **Contingency managers** analyze the employee capability level and select the autocratic, consultative, participative, or empowerment style for the situation. Lussier's model makes it relatively easy to select the appropriate style for a given situation. Before you learn how to be a contingency manager, complete Self-Assessment 12.2 to determine your preferred contingency management style.

## Analyzing the Employee Capability Level in a Given Situation

There are two distinct aspects of employee capability. Notice that to determine capability level, we are combining the first two dimensions of the performance formula discussed in chapter 11 (Performance = Ability × Motivation × Resources).

- *Ability.* Do employees have the knowledge, experience, education, skills, and training to do a particular task without direction?
- *Motivation.* Do employees have the confidence to do the task? Do they want to do the task? Are they committed to performing the task? Will they perform the task without encouragement and support?

Employee capability may be measured on a continuum from low to outstanding. As a manager, you assess each employee's capability level.

- *Low.* The employees can't do the task without detailed directions and close supervision. Employees in this category are either unable or unwilling to do the task.
- *Moderate.* The employees have moderate ability and need specific direction and support to get the task done properly. They may be highly motivated, but they still need direction.
- *High.* The employees have high ability but may lack the confidence to do the job. What they need most is support and encouragement to motivate them to get the task done.
- *Outstanding.* The employees are capable of doing the task without direction or support.

Most people perform a variety of tasks on the job, and employee capability may vary depending on the task. For example, a bank teller may handle routine transactions with great ease but falter when opening new or special accounts. Employees tend to start a new job with limited capabilities, and they need close direction. As their ability to do the job increases, managers can spend less of their time on close supervision and more on just being supportive. As a manager, you gradually develop your employees from low to outstanding levels over time.

# SELF-ASSESSMENT 12.2

## What Is Your Preferred Management Style?

Following are 12 situations. Select the alternative that most closely describes what you would do in each situation. Don't be concerned with trying to pick the right answer; select the alternative you would really use. Select *a*, *b*, *c*, or *d*. (Ignore the *C* preceding each situation and the *S* following each answer choice; these are explained in Skill-Builder 12.2 in the web study guide.)

1. C _____ Your rookie crew seems to be developing well. Their need for direction and close supervision is diminishing. What do you do?

    a. Stop directing and overseeing performance unless there is a problem. *S* _____

    b. Spend time getting to know the members personally, but make sure they maintain performance levels. *S* _____

    c. Make sure things keep going well; continue to direct and oversee closely. *S* _____

    d. Begin to discuss new tasks of interest to the crew members. *S* _____

2. C _____ You assigned Jill a task, specifying exactly how you wanted it done. Jill deliberately ignored your directions and did it her way. The job will not meet the customer's standards. This is not the first problem you've had with Jill. What do you decide to do?

    a. Listen to Jill's side, but be sure the job gets done right. *S* _____

    b. Tell Jill to do it again the right way, and closely supervise the job. *S* _____

    c. Tell her the customer will not accept the job, and let Jill handle it her way. *S* _____

    d. Discuss the problem and solutions to it. *S* _____

3. C _____ Your employees work well together and are a real team; the department is the top performer in the organization. Because of traffic problems, the president has approved staggered hours for departments. As a result, you can change your department's hours. Several of your workers are in favor of changing. What action do you take?

    a. Allow the group to decide the hours. *S* _____

    b. Decide on new hours, explain why you chose them, and invite questions. *S* _____

    c. Conduct a meeting to get the group members' ideas. Have them select new hours together, with your approval. *S* _____

    d. Send out a memo stating the hours you want. *S* _____

4. C _____ Bill, a new employee you hired, is not performing at the level expected after a month's training. Bill is trying, but he seems to be a slow learner. What do you decide to do?

    a. Clearly explain what needs to be done and oversee Bill's work. Discuss why the procedures are important; support and encourage him. *S* _____

    b. Tell Bill that his training is over and it's time to pull his own weight. *S* _____

    c. Review task procedures and supervise Bill's work closely. *S* _____

    d. Inform Bill that his training is over and that he should feel free to come to you if he has any problems. *S* _____

5. C _____ Helen has had an excellent performance record for the past five years. Recently you have noticed a drop in the quality and quantity of her work. She has a family problem. What do you do?

    a. Tell Helen to get back on track and closely supervise her. *S* _____

    b. Discuss the problem with Helen. Help her realize that her personal problem is affecting her work. Discuss ways to improve the situation. Be supportive and encourage her. *S* _____

    c. Tell Helen you're aware of her productivity slip and that you're sure she'll work it out soon. *S* _____

    d. Discuss the problem and solution with Helen and supervise her closely. *S* _____

*(continued)*

Self-Assessment 12.2 *(continued)*

6. *C* _____ Your organization does not allow smoking in certain areas. You just walked by a restricted area and saw Joan smoking. She has been with the organization for 10 years and is a very productive worker. Joan has never been caught smoking before. What action do you take?

   a. Ask her to put the cigarette out; then leave. *S* _____

   b. Discuss why she is smoking and what she intends to do about it. *S* _____

   c. Give her a lecture about not smoking and check up on her in the future. *S* _____

   d. Tell her to put the cigarette out, watch her do it, and tell her you will check on her in the future. *S* _____

7. *C* _____ Your employees usually work well together with little direction. But recently, a conflict between Sue and Tom has caused problems. What action do you take?

   a. Call Sue and Tom together and discuss how the conflict is affecting the department, how to resolve the conflict, and how you'll ensure it has been resolved. *S* _____

   b. Let the department resolve the conflict. *S* _____

   c. Have Sue and Tom sit down and discuss their conflict and how to resolve it. Support their efforts to implement a solution. *S* _____

   d. Tell Sue and Tom how to resolve their conflict, and closely supervise them. *S* _____

8. *C* _____ Jim usually does his share of the work with some encouragement and direction. However, he has migraine headaches occasionally and doesn't pull his weight when this happens. The others resent doing Jim's work. What do you decide to do?

   a. Discuss Jim's problem and help him come up with ideas for maintaining his work; be supportive. *S* _____

   b. Tell Jim to do his share of the work, and closely watch his output. *S* _____

   c. Inform Jim that he is creating a hardship for the others and that he should resolve the problem by himself. *S* _____

   d. Be supportive, but set minimum performance levels for Jim and ensure compliance. *S* _____

9. *C* _____ Barbara, your most experienced and productive worker, has come to you with a detailed idea that could increase your department's productivity at a very low cost. She can do her present job and this new assignment. You think it's an excellent idea. What do you do?

   a. Set some goals together. Encourage and support Barbara's efforts. *S* _____

   b. Set up goals for Barbara. Be sure she agrees with them and sees you as being supportive of her efforts. *S* _____

   c. Tell Barbara to keep you informed and to come to you if she needs any help. *S* _____

   d. Have Barbara check in with you frequently so that you can direct and supervise her activities. *S* _____

10. *C* _____ Your boss asked you for a special report. Frank, a very capable worker who usually needs no direction or support, has all the necessary skills to do the job. However, Frank is reluctant because he has never done a report. What do you do?

    a. Tell Frank he has to do it. Give him direction and supervise him closely. *S* _____

    b. Describe the project to Frank and let him do it his own way. *S* _____

    c. Describe the benefits to Frank. Get his ideas on how to do it and check his progress. *S* _____

    d. Discuss possible ways of doing the job. Be supportive and encourage Frank. *S* _____

11. *C* _____ Jean is the top producer in your department. However, her monthly reports are constantly late, and they contain errors. You are puzzled because she does everything else with no direction or support. What do you decide to do?

    a. Go over past reports, explaining to Jean exactly what is expected of her. Schedule a meeting so that you can review the next report with her. *S* _____

    b. Discuss the problem with Jean and ask her what can be done about it; be supportive. *S* _____

    c. Explain the importance of the report. Ask her what the problem is. Tell her that you expect the next report to be on time and error free. *S* _____

    d. Remind Jean to get the next report in on time without errors. *S* _____

12. *C* _____ Your workers are very effective and like to participate in decision making. A consultant was hired to develop a new method for your department using the latest technology in the field. What do you do?

    a. Explain the consultant's method and let the group decide how to implement it. *S* _____

    b. Teach the workers the new method and supervise them closely as they use it. *S* _____

    c. Explain to the workers the new method and the reasons it is important. Teach them the method and make sure the procedure is followed. Answer questions. *S* _____

    d. Explain the new method and get the group's input on ways to improve and implement it. *S* _____

To determine your preferred management style, circle the letter you selected for each situation.

|       | Autocratic | Consultative | Participative | Empowerment |
|-------|------------|--------------|---------------|-------------|
| 1     | C          | B            | D             | A           |
| 2     | B          | A            | D             | C           |
| 3     | D          | B            | C             | A           |
| 4     | C          | A            | D             | B           |
| 5     | A          | D            | B             | C           |
| 6     | D          | C            | B             | A           |
| 7     | D          | A            | C             | B           |
| 8     | B          | D            | A             | C           |
| 9     | D          | B            | A             | C           |
| 10    | A          | C            | D             | B           |
| 11    | A          | C            | B             | D           |
| 12    | B          | C            | D             | A           |
| Total |            |              |               |             |

Add up the number of circled items per column. The column with the most items circled suggests your preferred management style. Is this the style you tend to use most often? We will explain each style in this section.

Your management style flexibility is reflected in the distribution of your answers. The more evenly distributed the numbers, the more flexible your style. A total of 1 or 0 for any column may indicate a reluctance to use that style.

Note that there is no right or wrong preferred style. What we want to do is use the most appropriate management style for the situation. You will learn how to do that in this section.

Now that you have determined your preferred management style, you will learn how to determine the employee capability level and how to select the appropriate management style based on capability, followed by putting it all together in figure 12.6. We end by illustrating how to use the model in a hypothetical situation.

### Selecting the Appropriate Leadership Style in a Given Situation

As discussed earlier with reference to OSU's two-dimensional leadership model, when you interact with the employees you manage, your behavior can focus on directing or supporting employees.

- *Directive behavior.* The manager focuses on getting the task done by training, directing, and controlling behavior and closely oversees performance.
- *Supportive behavior.* The manager focuses on developing relationships by encouraging and motivating behavior without telling the employee what to do. The manager explains things and listens to employee views, helping employees make their own decisions by building confidence and self-esteem.

Based on the two dimensions of behavior (directive and supportive), four management styles have been described. The four contingency management styles are autocratic, consultative, participative, and empowerment. Which style to use is based on the employee capability level, as discussed next.

1. An *autocratic style* is highly directive and is little concerned with building relationships. The autocratic style is appropriate when you are interacting with low-capability employees. When interacting with such employees, give very detailed instructions describing exactly what the task is and when, where, and how to perform it. Closely oversee performance and give some support. Most of your time with the employees will be spent giving directions. Make decisions without input from the employees.

2. A *consultative style* involves highly directive and highly supportive behavior and is appropriate when you are interacting with moderately capable employees. Give specific instructions and oversee performance at all major stages of a task. At the same time, support the employees by explaining why the task should be performed as requested and answering their questions. Work on relationships as you explain the benefits of completing the task your way. Give fairly equal amounts of time to directing and supporting employees. When making decisions, you may consult with employees, but retain the final say. Once you make the decision, which can incorporate employees' ideas, direct and oversee their performance.

3. A *participative style* is characterized by less directive but still highly supportive behavior and is appropriate when you are interacting with highly capable employees. When interacting with such employees, spend a small amount of time giving general directions and a great deal of time giving encouragement. Spend limited time overseeing performance, letting employees do the task their way while focusing on the end result. Support the employees by encouraging them and building their self-confidence. If a task needs to be done, don't tell them how to do it; ask them how they will accomplish it. Make decisions together, or allow employees to make decisions subject to your limitations and approval.

4. An *empowerment style* requires providing very little direction or support for employees and is appropriate when you are interacting with outstanding employees. You should let them know what needs to be done and answer their questions, but it is not necessary to oversee their performance. Such employees are highly motivated and need little, if any, support. Allow them to make their own decisions, subject to your approval. Other terms for empowerment are *laissez-faire* and *hands off.* A manager who uses this style leaves employees alone to do their own thing.

### Contingency Management Model

The contingency management model puts the preceding information into an easy-to-use form. Note that figure 12.6 is somewhat similar to the group development and leadership style model seen in Skill-Builder 9.2 in the web study guide; figure 12.6 presents the same four management styles using the terms *directive* and *supportive* rather than *task* and *maintenance.*

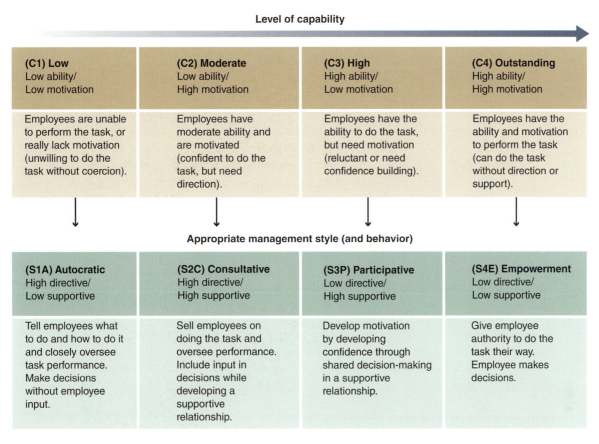

**Level of capability**

| **(C1) Low** Low ability/ Low motivation | **(C2) Moderate** Low ability/ High motivation | **(C3) High** High ability/ Low motivation | **(C4) Outstanding** High ability/ High motivation |
|---|---|---|---|
| Employees are unable to perform the task, or really lack motivation (unwilling to do the task without coercion). | Employees have moderate ability and are motivated (confident to do the task, but need direction). | Employees have the ability to do the task, but need motivation (reluctant or need confidence building). | Employees have the ability and motivation to perform the task (can do the task without direction or support). |

**Appropriate management style (and behavior)**

| **(S1A) Autocratic** High directive/ Low supportive | **(S2C) Consultative** High directive/ High supportive | **(S3P) Participative** Low directive/ High supportive | **(S4E) Empowerment** Low directive/ Low supportive |
|---|---|---|---|
| Tell employees what to do and how to do it and closely oversee task performance. Make decisions without employee input. | Sell employees on doing the task and oversee performance. Include input in decisions while developing a supportive relationship. | Develop motivation by developing confidence through shared decision-making in a supportive relationship. | Give employee authority to do the task their way. Employee makes decisions. |

**FIGURE 12.6**   The contingency management model.

## Using the Contingency Management Model

Let's take the first situation from Self-Assessment 12.2 and select the appropriate management style using figure 12.6. Follow the steps listed after you read the situation.

1. *C* _____ Your rookie crew seems to be developing well. Their need for direction and close supervision is diminishing. What do you do?

   a. Stop directing and overseeing performance, unless there is a problem. *S* _____

   b. Spend time getting to know the members personally, but make sure they maintain performance levels. *S* _____

   c. Make sure things keep going well; continue to direct and oversee closely. *S* _____

   d. Begin to discuss new tasks of interest to the crew members. *S* _____

Follow these steps:

1. Using figure 12.6, select the capability level. Put the number 1, 2, 3, or 4 after the *C* _____ preceding question 1.

2. Each alternative option (*a, b, c,* and *d*) is one of the four management styles. Place the management style letters (1A, 2C, 3P, 4E) illustrated for each alternative on the *S* _____ that follows each option.

3. Match the style to the capability by putting an *X* next to the most appropriate management behavior.

369

Here are the answers.

1. As a rookie crew, the employees' capability started at a low level, but they have now developed to the moderate level. Did you place a 2 after the *C*?

2. Alternative *a* is 4E, the empowerment style, involving low direction and support. Alternative *b* is 2C, the consultative style, involving both high direction and high support. Alternative *c* is 1A, the autocratic style, involving high direction but low support. Alternative *d* is 3P, the participative style, involving low direction and high support (in discussing employee interests). Did you get them all correct?

3. Based on C2 capability, the appropriate management style is S2C, consultative, which is option *b*. If you selected *b* as the management style that best matches the situation, you were correct.

In the business world, there is seldom only one way to handle a situation successfully. Therefore, you are given points based on how successful your behavior would be in each situation. In situation 1, *b* is the most successful alternative because it involves developing the employees gradually; answer *b* is worth 3 points. Alternative *c* is the next best alternative, followed by *d*. It is better to keep things the way they are now than to try to rush employee development, which would probably cause problems. So *c* is a 2-point answer, and *d* gets 1 point. Alternative *a* is the least effective because you are going from one extreme of supervision to the other. This is a 0-point answer because the odds are great that this approach will cause problems that will diminish your management success. The better you match your management style to employees' capabilities, the greater your chances of being a successful manager. You develop this ability in Skill-Builder 12.2 in the web study guide.

## When Leaders Are Not Necessary

The leadership theories we've presented thus far assume that some type of leadership style should be used in every situation. What happens when leaders are not what the situation requires? That is, Steven Kerr and John Jermier theorized that certain situational variables prevent leaders from affecting subordinates' attitudes and behaviors.[85] **Substitutes for leadership** eliminate the need for a leader. In certain circumstances, three characteristics can counteract or neutralize the efforts of leaders or render them unnecessary.

The following variables can substitute for or neutralize leadership because they provide the needed direction or support. (1) Characteristics of subordinates—because of their ability, knowledge, and experience, they don't need much supervision. (2) Characteristics of the task—because the job is routine, they don't need much supervision. (3) Characteristics of the organization—because of the structure, they don't need much supervision (for example, when teams share leadership).

TIME-OUT 9

Do the characteristics of your peers, the work you do, or your organization's culture eliminate the need for a designated leader? In other words, is your boss necessary? Explain.

# Getting to Your Personal Style of Leadership

You may be wondering, "Where do I start? Which style will work for me? How will I know which route to take in a given situation?" These are reasonable questions. And we have no nifty sound-bite responses for you. Masterful athletes, coaches, and leaders don't start out as masters—they all start out practicing, learning, and living the rules. Suffice it to say that you are not yet the manager or leader

TIME-OUT 10

State the leadership style you prefer and why.

you will be in the future. You will have many opportunities in your future jobs and teams to develop your own authentic leadership style to fit each situation, and the theories and models in this chapter can help.

As we bring this chapter to a close, to help you through this maze we've gathered the various behavior and situational leadership theories and models in figure 12.7. These theories and models are all based on two dimensions of leadership (OSU and UM), as shown in figure 12.1. However, different authors use different terms for what are essentially the same dimensions. Figure 12.7 provides a comparison of the behavioral and situational leadership models and uses *direction* and *support* to describe these two dimensions of leadership. The columns are headed "High direction/low support," "High direction/high support," "Low direction/high support," "Low direction/low support." The terms that appear below these headings have basically the same meanings as the column headings. Note that figure 12.7 doesn't include the contemporary perspectives (LMX; visionary and charismatic; transformational and transactional; symbolic, servant and authentic leadership) because they don't include specific leadership behavior. Study the leadership theories and models carefully. It will help you understand the similarities and differences in the approaches to leadership we've examined in this chapter.

| | High direction/ Low support | High direction/ High support | Low direction/ High support | Low direction/ Low support |
|---|---|---|---|---|
| **Behavioral leadership** | | | | |
| Basic leadership styles | Autocratic | Democratic | | Laissez-faire |
| The Ohio State University model (figure 12.1) | High structure/ Low consideration | High structure/ High consideration | Low structure/ High consideration | Low structure/ Low consideration |
| University of Michigan model (figure 12.1) | Job centered | | | Employee centered |
| Leadership Grid (figure 12.2) | Authority-compliance (9, 1) | Team (9, 9) | Country club (1, 9) | Impoverished (1,1) |
| | ← ——————————————— Middle of the road (5, 5) ——————————————— → | | | |
| **Situational leadership** | | | | |
| Contingency leadership (figure 12.3) | Task | | Relationship | |
| Leadership continuum (figure 12.4) | Style 1 | Styles 2 and 3 | Styles 4 and 5 | Styles 6 and 7 |
| Path–goal (figure 12.5) | Directive | Achievement oriented | Supportive | Participative |
| Normative leadership | Decide | Consult | Facilitate | Delegate |
| Contingency management (figure 12.6) | Autocratic | Consultative | Participative | Empowerment |

**FIGURE 12.7** A comparison of behavioral and situational leadership theories and models.

# LEARNING AIDS

## CHAPTER SUMMARY

1. **Explain why managers are not always leaders.**
   Just the fact that someone is a manager doesn't mean he understands how to lead people.

2. **Compare the trait, behavioral, and contingency theories of leadership.**
   Trait theorists look for distinctive characteristics of effective leaders. Behavioral theorists look at the behavior of effective leaders and try to find one leadership style that works for all situations. Contingency theorists try to fit leadership style to the situation.

3. **Explain leadership trait theory.**
   Trait theory assumes that certain characteristics make for effective leadership. According to Ghiselli, supervisory ability is the most important leadership trait. Supervisory ability is competence in the four management functions (planning, organizing, leading, and controlling).

4. **Contrast two-dimensional leaders and grid leaders.**
   These two types of leaders use the same two dimensions of leadership, but the two models describe and structure the dimensions somewhat differently. The two-dimensional model defines four leadership styles (high structure–low consideration, high structure–high consideration, low structure–high consideration, low structure–low consideration), whereas the Leadership Grid uses five leadership styles (1,1—impoverished; 9,1—authority-compliance; 1,9—country club; 5,5—middle-of-the-road; and 9,9—team).

5. **Identify the management levels where charismatic, transformational, transactional, and symbolic leaders work best.**
   Charismatic and transformational leaders are typically top-level managers. Transactional leaders are usually middle and first-line managers. Symbolic leaders work in top management, and, if successful, their vision flows down to middle and first-line management.

6. **Contrast the various contingency models of leadership.**
   Fiedler's contingency model recommends changing the situation, not the leadership style. The other contingency models recommend changing the leadership style, not the situation.

7. **Critique the continuum and the path–goal models.**
   Both models are subjective, making them difficult and cumbersome to use.

8. **Describe normative leaders.**
   Normative leaders use one of five decision-making styles, depending on the situation.

## REVIEW AND DISCUSSION QUESTIONS

1. What is leadership, and why is it important?

2. What traits do you think are important to leaders?

3. Based on your responses to Self-Assessment 12.1, are you a theory X or a theory Y leader?

4. Name several pro athletes who are charismatic leaders, and explain why.

5. What are the two dimensions of leadership and the four possible leadership styles?

6. Why do you think most sport management studies have focused on the leadership skills of coaches instead of those of athletic administrators?

7. Describe Phil Jackson's (Los Angeles Lakers) leadership style in terms of the Leadership Grid. Defend your answer.

8. Describe and compare the two leadership styles of the contingency model of leadership.

9. Describe and compare the two dimensions of the continuum model of leadership.

10. Describe and compare the four leadership styles of the path–goal model of leadership.

11. Give examples of MLB general managers who are transformational leaders.

12. What are three substitutes for leadership?

13. Do you believe that men and women lead differently?

14. Do you believe results differ when men coach women's college teams? What about women coaching men's college teams? Defend your answers.

15. Review the coaching examples provided in the discussion of Vroom and Yetton's normative model of leadership. Do you agree with our analysis of the leadership styles of these coaches? Why or why not?

16. Using "leadership" and "sport" as your key words, use www.scholar.google.com to search for the top five listed academic journal articles.

17. Find three additional leadership quotes attributed to Vince Lombardi at www. vincelombardi.com.

18. Which situational leadership model do you prefer? Why? Will you use it? Why or why not?

## CASES

### Sport Management Professionals @ Work: David Dubay

A professional scout told David Dubay that he was .05 seconds too slow to make it as a professional baseball player. However, he loved to play baseball, and he earned his bachelor's degree in sport management from Newbury College in Brookline, Massachusetts.

Since graduation, David has become a certified personal trainer and has received certifications in nutrition, speed, agility, balance, and coordination. He spent the last two years as the assistant varsity baseball coach at Hall High School in West Hartford, Connecticut, where he specialized in strength and conditioning along with catching and hitting mechanics.

David currently works at the Jewish Community Center. He can work with people of all ages on their training programs. David is building a client list of older members who like to schedule appointments in the morning. He also has a growing list of training appointments with high school athletes who like to work on strength and agility for the sports they play.

### Case Questions

1. What are the two jobs that David holds?

2. Why did David have to complete certification courses?

3. In what areas of fitness instruction is David qualified to teach?

## The New Leader of the Carolina Panthers

The battle for leadership was set. The Carolina Panthers, a valuable franchise in the NFL, was going to be up for sale. Jerry Richardson, the team's founder and only owner, announced he was selling the team after coming under investigation from the league for sexual and racial misconduct in the workplace.[86]

However, the battle for a new owner and leader never really occurred. David A. Tepper, a billionaire hedge fund owner, bought the team for a record-setting amount of at least $2.2 billion.

It is likely that other potential buyers offered slightly more to purchase the team. However, Tepper was already a minority owner of the Pittsburgh Steelers, so he was already vetted and virtually sure to be approved by the other NFL owners. Tepper will have to sell his portion of the Steelers to be able to purchase the Panthers. It didn't hurt that Tepper is worth somewhere around $11 billion, which will help him build the team once he owns it.

Tepper is often cited as the greatest hedge fund manager of our time. Tepper's Appaloosa Management hedge fund firm now manages some $17 billion and is based in Miami Beach, Florida. He is quoted as saying. "I am the animal at the head of the pack. I generally am. I either get eaten or I get the good grass."[87] You can watch Tepper's initial press conference as the owner of the Panthers at www.panthers.com/media-vault/videos/Watch-David-Teppers-full-press-conference/68eab818-ba0d-4869-bc7f-bdf7aaca9acd.

The case against Richardson was still pending at the time this case was written. However, it is important to note that even wealthy businessmen and NFL owners need to treat all of their employees with proper respect and professionalism.

Go to the web study guide to answer questions about this case study.

## @ TAKE IT TO THE NET

Please visit www.HumanKinetics.com/AppliedSportManagementSkills and go to this book's companion web study guide, where you will find the following:

A list of websites associated with the concepts in this chapter

Skill-Builder exercises, Sports and Social Media exercises, and a continuing Game Plan for Starting a Sport Business

Online versions of chapter exercises and end-of-chapter learning aids

An exercise that helps you define the Key Terms

# PART V

# Controlling

# Controlling Quality, Financials, and Productivity, and Managing People

## KEY TERMS

| | | |
|---|---|---|
| preliminary controls | damage controls | control frequencies |
| concurrent controls | standards | management audits |
| rework controls | critical success factors (CSFs) | budgets |

*(continued)*

| operating budgets | management counseling |
| capital budgets | employee assistance programs (EAPs) |
| financial statements | discipline |
| coaching | productivity |
| management by walking around (MBWA) | |

## DEVELOPING YOUR SKILLS

Every effective manager needs to be a pro at controlling. It is the only way you will know whether you and your department are on the right track. In this chapter, we present models for control systems and the control process to help develop your controlling skills. You will also learn about financial controls—budgeting and financial statements—and how to calculate productivity. Understanding accounting is vital because you won't be in business for long if you can't generate profits, and controlling is your key to making a profit. Take a least one course on accounting, often called the language of business. You will also develop your skills at getting the job done through others by using coaching and disciplining models to improve performance.

## REVIEWING THEIR GAME PLAN

### It Takes Three to Golf

In the story of The Ranch Golf Club in Southwick, Massachusetts, the three protagonists are a dairy family, a Jiffy Lube owner couple, and a few investors. The dairy family owned the dream, the Jiffy Lube couple owned the willingness, and the investors had more capital. How did this unlikely trio turn a dream into reality and a fledgling golf club into a four-star course in less than a year of operation? The answer is expertise—in this instance, in the form of Rowland Bates, a Realtor. The Hall family approached Bates with the idea that the family dairy farm was good turf for golf. The Halls would provide the land, and Bates would find the investors.

Enter Pete and Korby Clark, young part-owners of some 50 Jiffy Lubes in the northeastern United States, who had jingles in their pockets from a recent sale of most of their franchises and a desire to try something new. The Clarks had been looking at various ventures since 1991, but nothing much interested them until Rowland Bates approached them with his plan. What was different about Bates' proposal? Rowland offered the Clarks a hands-on deal—they would be in on the creation and management; he didn't want just their money.

The Clarks soon found that building a golf course requires money, and lots of it. And although banks were willing to loan them plenty of money if they built Jiffy Lubes, they could not borrow much for their golf course. Again, Bates' expertise, connections, and tireless beating of the investor bushes soon netted them enough investors to cut the deal. The final deal hammered out by Bates involved one-third ownership by the Halls, one-third by the Clarks, and one-third by other investors.

The idea from the beginning was to create a state-of-the-art, premier golf course. The trio had plenty of natural advantages to work with in the Halls' dairy land, which was rich in beauty, vistas, woods, and the all-important differing elevations. The owners hired California architect Damian Pascuzzo to design a grand golf course. And design one he did. The course boasts 7,100 yards (6,492 meters) in length and a 140 slope rating (a very good rating). Each golf car is equipped with a ParView GPS system that diagrams each hole and provides current yardage from the pin and other helpful facts and figures. Peak-season green fees are around $100; service is unsurpassed, similar to that in Arizona, where the Clarks played golf to learn about excellent service. On the course at all times, player assistants provide all types

378

of help, including golf tips, retrieval of left-behind clubs, and cool towels on hot days. The two massive 19th-century barns have been completely remodeled and painted their original and distinctive yellow color, and they now serve as clubhouse, restaurant and lounge, golf shop, and function facility.

The Clarks wanted to create a new business—they didn't necessarily want to be involved in its day-to-day operation, so they turned to Willowbend, a professional golf management team, for four reasons. (1) They needed expertise. (2) They had other things to do with their lives—a family to raise, community service they were keenly committed to, and coaching, among others. (Pete was the head baseball coach and assistant football coach for Agawam High School and has also coached for Trinity College.) (3) The mix was right—Pete and Korby oversaw the important strategic decisions and had input when they wanted, but Willowbend handled the day-to-day decisions. (4) The employees worked for Willowbend, which offered a good benefits package. The key to successful comanaging for the Clarks and Willowbend was clear, open communication of expectations.

However, in 2005 Willowbend stopped managing golf courses and sold the business. By now the Clarks had gained enough experience running The Ranch and no longer needed professional management. Peter Clark increased his management role to become the managing partner, overseeing day-to-day operations, and Korby works full-time, too. During the summer, 80 people work at The Ranch, and the professional staff gets benefits through the human resources function. The club has a sophisticated information system for its three departments—golf (greens and practice, tournaments and outings, golf shop), maintenance (the course and other facilities), and food and beverage (The Ranch Grille, bar, and functions)—that includes many performance measures. The partners also have a separate real estate business selling land and houses near the golf course.

The Ranch is striving to be the best golf club in New England. In less than a year, The Ranch earned a four-star course rating, one of only four in New England, and it has earned other awards over the years including awards from *Golf Digest* and *Golf World*.[1]

For current information on The Ranch Golf Club, visit www.theranchgolfclub.com, which features a virtual visit to the golf course.

# Quality and Control Systems

Recall from chapter 1 that all managers perform the four functions of management. Previous chapters have covered planning, organizing, and leading. We are now at the controlling function—establishing mechanisms to ensure that objectives are achieved. To achieve your objectives, you need to control.[2] Are you monitoring and measuring results and taking corrective action when needed to ensure that objectives are achieved?[3] In this section, we discuss quality and controlling from outside the firm, organizational systems control, and controlling functional areas.

## Quality and Controlling From the Outside

Recall from chapter 2 that quality involves comparing actual use to requirements in order to determine value, and that *total quality management (TQM)* is the process in which everyone in an organization focuses on the customer to continually improve value. Without continuous improvement, the firm will lose business to competitors. Clearly, effective control mechanisms are needed to ensure quality goods and services. Controlling to ensure high quality and productivity is what this chapter is all about. Government agencies such as the U.S. Food and Drug Administration (FDA) protect the health and safety of society with laws and regulations to control quality. Here we discuss some of the many organizations that set quality standards and award certifications.

## *International Organization for Standardization (ISO)*

ISO is the world's largest developer and publisher of voluntary international standards. Most multinational organizations have ISO certification, and they require suppliers they do business with to be certified to ensure quality. However, ISO doesn't provide certification or conformity assessment; external independent certification bodies provide the ISO certification.[4] To learn more about ISO and ISO certification, visit its website (www.iso.org).

## *American Society for Quality (ASQ)*

ASQ is the world's leading membership organization devoted to quality. ASQ is the global voice of quality; it provides education, training, and certification.[5] To learn more about ASQ, visit its website (https://asq.org).

## *Sport Governance*

Many sport organizations are also monitored and controlled by external bodies of governance, including most professional leagues. We have discussed many of these bodies: FIFA and its executive committee monitor all soccer activities; the IOC monitors all Olympic activities; the PGA is the regulating body for golf; each Jewish Community Center is monitored by the JCCA (JCC Association of North America); and each individual YMCA is governed by the rules of the World Alliance of YMCAs. College athletics are governed by the rules and policies set forth by the NCAA. These organizations establish rules and regulations that every member must follow, but sport authorities such as the IOC look out for the interests of all stakeholders. For more information on the IOC, visit its website (www.olympic.org).

> **TIME-OUT 1**
>
> Use figure 13.1 to identify the primary inputs, transformation, outputs, and customers of your firm or team. Also, identify the level of customer satisfaction. (Remember, customers can be fans, users of the golf course, buyers of your merchandise, players on your youth league soccer team, employees at your organization if your department is human resources, stockholders if you are the CEO, or suppliers of input to your company if you are the finance department that pays them. Employees, stockholders, and suppliers are also called stakeholders—stakeholders can thus be considered customers from certain viewpoints.)

# Organization Systems Control

**LEARNING OUTCOME 1 ▶**

Explain how controls function within the systems process.

Businesses of all sizes need control systems.[6] Because organizations are so diverse, the system must be tailored to each situation.[7] In chapter 2, we examined the systems process; now we examine how controls are used at each stage to ensure that objectives are met. Figure 13.1 shows how this works. Four different types of controls are needed in different parts of the systems process, which we discuss here.

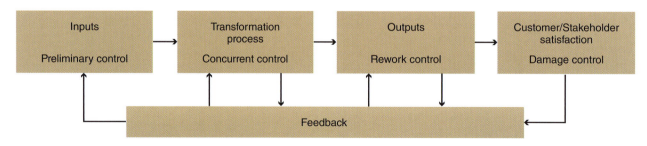

**FIGURE 13.1**　Controlling the systems process.

## Preliminary Controls

**Preliminary controls** anticipate and prevent possible problems. One major difference between successful and unsuccessful managers is their ability to anticipate and prevent problems rather than solve problems after they occur. If preliminary controls work, you don't need to fix a problem.

Effective planning and organizing are part of preliminary control, which is also called feedforward control. Standing plans (chapter 4) control employee behavior in recurring situations to prevent problems, and contingency plans tell employees what to do if problems occur.

A typical preliminary control is preventive maintenance. Many production departments and transportation companies or departments routinely tune up their machines and engines to prevent breakdowns. Purchase only quality inputs in order to prevent production problems. The practice area, golf cars, and tee times are the major inputs that require preliminary control at The Ranch.

## Concurrent Controls

**Concurrent controls** are actions taken during transformation to ensure that standards are met. The key to success here is quality control. In team sports, a preliminary control is assigning positions and practicing plays for the game. However, as the game is being played (transformation), concurrent controls are used to select who plays what position and which plays to run throughout the game to win. At The Ranch, the transformation is the actual playing of golf. A major concurrent control is player assistance out on the course. If players are not satisfied, player assistants know it early on and fix the problem before the game is over.

## Rework Controls

**Rework controls** are actions taken to fix output. You need to rework something when preliminary and concurrent controls fail. Most manufacturers inspect output before it is sold or sent as input to other departments in the organization. Sometimes rework is neither cost-effective nor possible, which can be costly. If Wilson Sporting Goods makes defective golf balls (outputs), it is too late; the company cannot change the past.

## Damage Controls

**Damage controls** are actions taken to minimize negative impacts on customers attributable to faulty output. When customers get a defective product, damage control is needed. Warranties require damage control that can be expensive. You must refund the purchase price, replace the product with a new one, fix the product, or reperform the service. The Ranch sells golf products through the Pro Shop and occasionally gets returns. Handling customer complaints is a controlling technique. When sport teams lose a lot of games, attendance tends to fall, and damage control is needed to try to get fans back to the venue.

 **TIME-OUT 2** Give examples of preliminary, concurrent, rework, and damage controls in your current organization or team.

## Feedback

Feedback helps organizations to continually increase customer satisfaction, so feedback is an important control and must be used at every stage of the system to continually improve performance. Many firms monitor often to increase performance and profits.[8]

Which of the four different types of controls would impact how much inventory you stock for your business/monitor customer satisfaction?

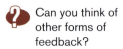 Can you think of other forms of feedback?

Customer evaluation cards are only one example of feedback. The Clarks spend much of their time at The Ranch talking to players about the service and looking for ways to improve the players' experience.

 **TIME-OUT 3** Describe the controls you personally use in your department.

### Preliminary and Concurrent Control Focus

Good coaches and sport managers know that the controls that lead to success are preliminary and concurrent, so that is where they spend more time and effort—which prevents the need for rework and damage control. Think about it. If you are not properly prepared for the game (preliminary) and are losing, you will not win (concurrent). After losing (although

## APPLYING THE CONCEPT 13.1

### Using Appropriate Controls

Choose the appropriate control for each situation.

    a. preliminary
    b. concurrent
    c. rework
    d. damage

_____ 1. The new golf shirt I bought today has a button missing.

_____ 2. I just got my monthly budget report telling me how much of its budget the marketing department spent.

_____ 3. Coach is reviewing the plays she will use in Sunday's big game.

_____ 4. As I was jogging in my new nylon shorts, they split down the side.

_____ 5. The manager uses the time management system on Fridays.

viewing game films and so on is helpful), you don't get a do-over (rework), and after you lose fans, it is hard to bring them back (damage).

## Controlling Functional Areas

Recall from chapter 5 that firms are commonly organized in some way into four functional areas: operations (makes the products), marketing (sells the products), human resources (manages employees), and finance (manages money). Information (manages information) is a fifth functional area; it can be a stand-alone department, part of finance, or part of another department. Organizations have other departments as well.

As shown in figure 13.2, all departments have a systems process based on the workflow.[9] Note that the marketing department product outputs go to external customers. The other

◀ **LEARNING OUTCOME 2**
Understand why feedback is a control.

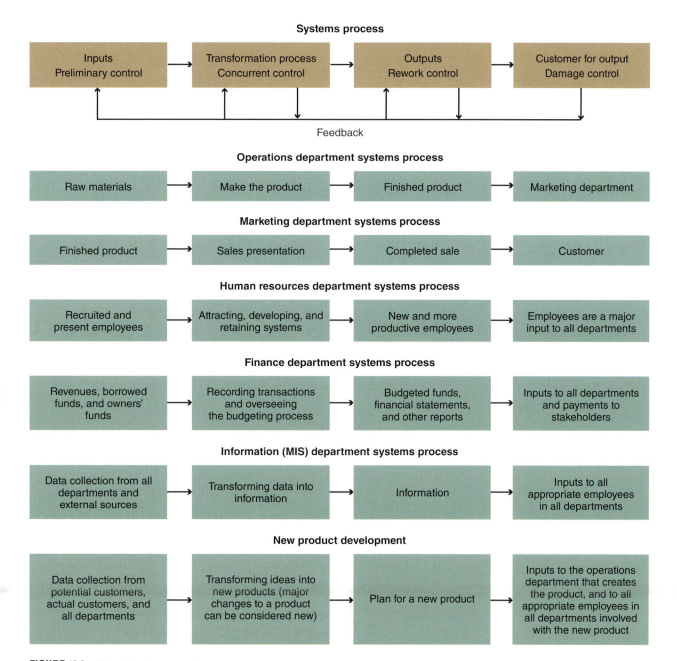

**FIGURE 13.2**  Functional-area systems processes.

department outputs stay within the organization and go to internal stakeholders. So internal damage control is needed within and between departments. Review each functional department in figure 13.2 to

TIME-OUT
4
Use figure 13.2 to diagram the systems process for the department you work in.

better understand its system process. You will learn more about operations in chapter 14.

Every employee in an organization transforms inputs into outputs in some way based on workflow.[10] A production worker makes a part of a Nike sneaker, which becomes input for the next person down the line, and so on until the footwear is completed. Every employee should therefore also use preliminary, concurrent, rework, and damage controls.

Feedback is essential if the system is to improve (see figure 13.3). Throughout the system, feedback circulating through all the functional areas improves inputs, transformations, and outputs while continually increasing customer satisfaction. Note that operations, marketing, finance, and human resources (HR) provide feedback to each other and to MIS as well.

At The Ranch, *operations* takes care of the golf course using a sophisticated scheduling system to seed, fertilize, water, and mow. It *markets* golf through word of mouth, TV ads, and print ads, and it has a professional website you can use to book a tee time. The Ranch *human resources* staff serves more than 80 seasonal employees. It also has top-flight *financial* software to conduct its financial transactions, including continuing measures of financial performance to stay within budget and make target profits. Its major departments have an integrated computerized *information system* to monitor the performance of the golf course, the restaurant and banquet facilities, and golf shop revenues and expenses, as well as unit sales for each.

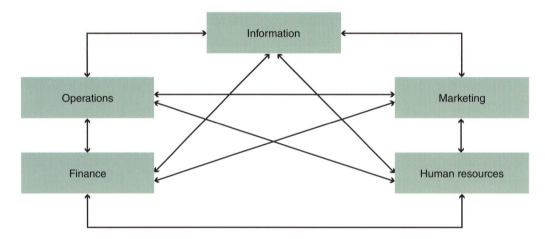

**FIGURE 13.3** The feedback process. The arrows represent the flow of feedback throughout the systems process.

# Control Process

**LEARNING OUTCOME 3** ▶

Describe the control process.

The control process involves the four steps shown in figure 13.4. The steps are the same whether the control is an organizationwide control or a functional-area control, even though the controls themselves may be very different. Effective control mechanisms provide knowledge for continuous improvement through the four phases of the control process.

1. *Step 1. Set objectives and standards.* The first step in the control process is the same as in planning, set objectives and standards (chapter 4).[11] Or, objectives and standards are the ends and the plans are the means.[12] Objectives (target dated) and standards (ongoing) are part of the input process and are forms of preliminary control.[13] Companies, including Nike and Dicks, want standardization in processes and products.[14]

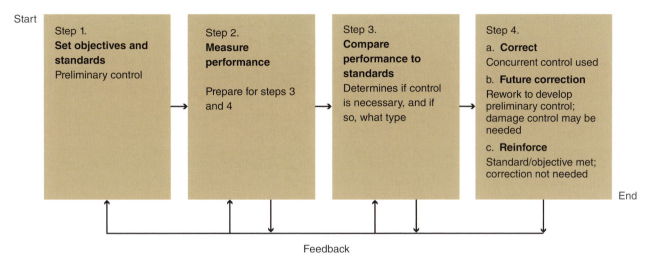

**FIGURE 13.4**   The control process.

To be comprehensive and complete, standards must address five criteria. **Standards** minimize negative impacts on customers attributable to faulty output by controlling quantity, quality, time, cost, and behavior. You need to measure performance,[15] because if you can't measure it, you can't manage it.[16] But be careful how you measure—that is, what *metrics* you use—with standards because incomplete standards often lead to negative unintended results.[17] Workers respond to what is measured and reinforced (chapter 11), so developing balanced standards drives team and business success.

- *Quantity.* How many units should employees produce to earn their pay?[18] Examples of quantitative standards include number of sales made, home runs hit, quarterback sacks made, or classes taught. Measuring performance quantitatively tends to be relatively clear-cut.

- *Quality.* How well must a job be completed to meet the standard? How many errors are acceptable? Quality can often be measured quantitatively, such as the number of defective products, interceptions thrown, coaching mistakes made in games, and poor teaching evaluations received from students. But other aspects of quality are often difficult to establish and measure.[19] How does an administrator determine how good the teachers are in a sport management program? It isn't easy, but quality must be measured and evaluated.

- *Time.* How fast and when should the task be completed? When you assign tasks, it is important to specify time frames. Deadlines are a time-honored, time-based standard. Performance is also measured against specific periods—goals scored per season, annual graduation rate, home runs in a season, or profits per quarter.

- *Cost.* How much should it cost to make the product? How much should employees be paid? Employee compensation (see chapter 7) is a major cost to many organizations, and firms around the world are increasing controls to help cut product and labor costs.[20] This is part of the budgeting function. In pro sports such as MLB, NFL, and NHL, the cost of athletes keeps going up; the cost is a major concern for team owners, and it is often passed on to the fans in the form of ticket prices and other costs (parking, food and drinks, merchandise) of attending the sport event.

- *Behavior.* Which behaviors are appropriate and which ones are not appropriate?[21] Standing plans, especially rules (chapter 5), guide and control the behaviors of workers.[22] Players are expected to be on time for practice and to behave morally on and off the field.[23]

2. *Step 2. Measure performance.* If you can't measure objectives and standards, you can't control them.[24] If you aren't measuring performance, how do you know if you are making progress and actually achieving the objective or not? Measuring also helps you

TIME-OUT 5

Give an example of a standard your organization or team uses that satisfies the five criteria for complete standards.

find ways to beat current performance and beat or match that of competitors. An important consideration in the control process is what to measure—what are the critical success factors—and how often to measure.

It is important to identify critical success factors. **Critical success factors (CSFs)** are pivotal areas in which satisfactory results will ensure successful achievement of the objective or standard. In other words, we cannot control everything, but as organizations, departments, teams, and individuals, we can identify the few most important objectives, goals, and standards without which we fail and with which we succeed. One important measure is customer satisfaction, because without customers you don't have a business. These are CSFs, and you must control them very carefully. Possible CSFs for the WNBA include improving team competitiveness, maintaining national television exposure, and improving marketing.

TIME-OUT 6

List several CSFs for your current job. Place them in order of importance, and explain why they are critical.

3. *Step 3. Compare performance with standards.* This performance evaluation step is relatively easy if the first two steps have been done correctly.[25] You are comparing what you want to happen to what is actually happening So far, are you getting the grade in this course to meet your objective or standard grade?

A performance or variance report, such as the one shown in table 13.1, is commonly used to measure performance. Performance reports typically show standards, actual performance, and deviations from the standards. In table 13.1, the golf club production results, although under the production goal and over cost, are good because they both deviate less than 1 percent from the standard. (To determine deviation, the variation is divided by the standard.) Managers need to be accountable for meeting the objectives and standards. When variances are significant, they should be examined carefully and fixed with rework and damage control. We discuss this in more detail later in this section.

4. *Step 4. Correct or reinforce.* The last step of the control process is to correct or reinforce. During the transformation process, concurrent controls are used to correct performance to meet standards. Or you take action to improve and meet the standard.[26] But when the job is done (the product is made or the service is delivered), if it is faulty and it is too late to correct the problem, then it is time to (1) figure out why the standard was not met, (2) use the information to develop new preliminary controls, and (3) implement the new controls so that the standard is met next time. When performance affects others, damage control may also be required. So learn from errors and mistakes by understanding their causes, and implement changes that will prevent future errors or reduce negative consequences when errors reoccur.

Of course, when the standard has been met, there is no need for corrective action. Keep things running smoothly. This does not mean that the control process ends here. It's time for a little gratitude—don't

TIME-OUT 7

Think about a situation in which you or your boss had to take corrective action to meet a standard. Describe the action taken.

forget to praise your team for a job well done and to give other rewards, such as bonuses (see chapter 11). Also, continue to find ways to increase performance.

**TABLE 13.1** **Operations Performance Report**

| Outputs and inputs | Standard or budgeted amount | Actual | Variance |
|---|---|---|---|
| Units produced (golf clubs–the outputs) | 100,000 | 99,920 | −80 |
| **Production cost (inputs)** | | | |
| Labor, including over-time | $700,000 | $698,950 | +$1,050 |
| Materials | $955,000 | $957,630 | −$2,630 |
| Supplies | $47,500 | $47,000 | +$500 |
| Totals | $1,702,500 | $1,703,580 | −$1,080 |

# Frequency of Controls

An important consideration in the control process is how often to measure performance.[27] Ten methods, which can be categorized by frequency of occurrence, are used to measure and control performance. **Control frequencies** are constant, periodic, and occasional.

◀ **LEARNING OUTCOME 4**

List which control methods are used with which frequency.

## Constant Controls

Constant controls are in continuous use and include self-control, clan control, and standing plans. The three I's that Pete Clark uses at The Ranch are constant controls, and so is the 10-foot rule: If you come within 10 feet (3.04 meters) of customers, you always greet them cheerfully and ask whether they need any assistance. (The three I's are detailed in the Coaching Corrective Action section later in this chapter.)

 How effective do you think the 10-foot rule is?

### Self-Control

A big question facing every coach and manager is, Will my staff do their job if they are not monitored closely?[28] The answer is that you must know your staff. Some groups need much less control than others. The issue here is one of balance—self-control (internal in employees) versus imposed control (external from managers).[29] Too much external control causes problems, and so does too little control. So, use contingency management (chapter 12).

### Clan Control

This control is about organizational culture and norms, which are powerful ways to shape desired behavior. Organizations that use teams often rely on clan control—peer pressure,[30] which helps prevent freeloaders.[31] See chapter 9 for details on group control (another term for clan control), norms, and enforcing norms. Self-control and clan control are used throughout the control process and in conjunction with the four control types.

### Standing Plans

Policies, procedures, and rules (chapter 4) exist to influence behavior in recurring predictable situations (chapter 3). Standards can be thought of as a type of standing plan.[32] When they are developed, they are preliminary controls. When they are implemented to solve problems, they become concurrent, rework, or damage controls. Standing plans are developed in sport by governing bodies, including the NCAA and IOC.

## Periodic Controls

Periodic controls are used on a regular, fixed basis, such as hourly, daily, weekly, monthly, quarterly, or annually. Periodic controls include regularly scheduled reports, budgets, and audits. The Ranch management team provides the owners with monthly reports. Together they develop annual and monthly budgets, and they have an annual audit performed.

### Scheduled Meetings and Reports

Oral reports in the form of daily, weekly, and monthly meetings to discuss progress and problems are common in all organizations. Written reports required on a schedule are also common, and they are typically sent via email. At Wilson Sporting Goods, the sales manager gets weekly sales reports. Vice presidents get monthly income statements. Regularly scheduled reports are designed as a preliminary control. But the report itself is used (when there is a problem) as a concurrent, rework, or damage control, depending on the situation.

Budgeting is one of the most widely used control tools. We discuss budgeting details in the next section of this chapter. The preparation of a new budget is a preliminary control. As the year progresses, the budget becomes a concurrent control. At year's end, it is reworked for the next year. A budget may require damage control if significant changes, such as overspending, take place for some reason.

### Budgets

Budgets are a common and essential control tool.[33] Budgets need to be constructed carefully, always with an eye on where costs can be cut even more, and actual costs must be measured against budgeted costs relentlessly. New budgets are preliminary controls. As the month and year progress, they become concurrent controls. At year end, they are reworked for the next year. A budget may also require damage control if significant changes, such as overspending, take place. You will learn more about budgeting in the Financial Controls section.

### Audits

Organizations use two types of audits: internal and external. Part of the accounting function is to maintain careful and extremely detailed records of the organization's transactions and assets. Large organizations maintain internal auditing departments whose responsibility it is to make sure assets are reported accurately. Internal auditors also serve as watchdogs to keep theft (embezzlement and fraud) to a minimum. Most large organizations hire outside certified public accounting (CPA) auditors to verify their financial statements.

There are two major types of audits: accounting and management. Part of the accounting function is to maintain records of the organization's transactions and assets. Most large organizations have an *internal auditing* person or department that checks periodically to make sure assets are reported accurately and to keep theft at a minimum. In addition to performing internal audits, many organizations hire a firm to verify the organization's financial statements through an *external accounting audit*. The **management audit** analyzes the organization's planning, organizing, leading, and controlling functions to look for improvements. The analysis focuses on the past, present, and future.

## Occasional Controls

Occasional controls are used on an as-needed basis. They include observation, the exception principle, special reports, and project controls. The management team comes in unannounced to observe operations at The Ranch to ensure that everything is up to standard. The Clarks provide special reports to managers to help them continually improve. Project controls are also in place for special golf events that involve corporate clients and other organizations.

## Observation

This is exactly what it sounds like—designated people, video cameras, and electronic devices observing work in progress, whether the work involves a professor giving a lecture, a pro athlete in training, or a machine making a golf ball. Observation is used with all four types of control. Management by walking around (MBWA) is an especially effective method of observation that we will examine in more detail later in this chapter.

## Exception Principle

This is about placing control in the hands of staff unless problems occur, in which case people go to their supervisors for help. Corrective action is then taken to get performance back to standard. However, people—be they production line workers or CEOs—often shrink from asking for help or reporting on poor performance until it is too late to take corrective action.

## Special Reports

When problems and especially opportunities are identified, management often requests special reports, which may be compiled by a single employee, a committee, or outside consultants. Reports can be verbal discussions. An employee can go to the boss to recommend an improvement; this is a form of reporting. So is a manager asking an employee what the problem is or asking for recommendations for improvements.

    With nonrecurring or unique projects, the project manager needs to develop a control system to ensure that the project is completed on time.

## Project Controls

With nonrecurring projects, project managers need to install controls to ensure that such projects are completed on time and on budget. Project controls are designed as preliminary controls, but they can be used with any of the other three types of controls when schedules are not being met. Because planning and controlling are so closely linked, the planning tools we will discuss in chapter 14 are project control methods.

    Organizations understand that controls are crucial to their success. Therefore, you should learn to use controls well to help you achieve your objectives. Table 13.2 summarizes controls. The types, frequency, and methods of control are listed separately because all four types of control may be

 **TIME-OUT 8** Give an example of a constant, a periodic, and an occasional control used by your organization or team. Explain why each control is classified as such.

## TABLE 13.2 The Control System

| Systems process (types of controls) | The control process | Frequency and methods of control | | |
|---|---|---|---|---|
| Inputs (preliminary) | 1. Set objectives and standards | *Constant controls* | *Periodic controls* | *Occasional controls* |
| Transformation (concurrent) | 2. Measure performance | Self | Scheduled reports | Observation |
| Outputs (rework) | 3. Compare performance to standards | Clan | Budgets | Exception principle |
| Customer satisfaction (damage) | 4. Correct or reinforce | Standing plans | Audits | Special reports |
| | | | | Project |

## APPLYING THE CONCEPT 13.2

### Control Methods

Identify the control method described in each situation.

**Constant**

a. self

b. clan

c. standing plans

**Periodic**

d. regularly scheduled reports

e. budgets

f. audits

**Occasional**

g. observation

h. exception principle

i. special reports

j. project

_____ 6. The boss asks the floor supervisor to meet with him to explain why the process of imprinting the current golf ball run with the corporate logo is behind schedule.

_____ 7. Posted signs state that helmets are to be worn throughout the factory—no exceptions.

_____ 8. The manager's desk faces the work floor.

_____ 9. Accounting staff members are working on supply contracts alone today because the boss is out of the office.

_____ 10. The manager assembles the monthly operations performance report.

used with any method. Recall how a budget changes its type of control over time and that more than one control method can be used at once. You need to be aware of which stage of the systems process you are in and of the most effective controls for that stage (see figure 13.1). Also, don't forget the four steps of the control process.

## Financial Controls

Budgets and financial statements are important control tools.[34] The information they contain is key to making decisions of all kinds, including athletic directors allocating money among teams and hiring coaches.[35] Therefore, you need to get very comfortable with budgets and financial statements. You may have to develop budgets and use spreadsheet software, such as Excel, to manage your team, department, or organization. Are you thinking about starting your own business or climbing the corporate ladder? You can't do it without being financially savvy because accounting is the language of business and, as such, is the bottom-line measure of business success.[36] Pro sport teams, including the NHL, MLB, NBA, WNBA, and NFL, are sports that entertain, but owners are in business to make money.

Some students fear budgeting because they believe they are not a good match for accounting. Don't fear, because the spreadsheet will do the math for you, and budgeting is not about a bunch of debits and credits. It is about figuring out how much it will cost you to run your team or department, usually for a season or a year, and in most cases you have a prior year's budget to use as a template, anyway. And until you make it to the top, someone will be helping you with and approving your budget. In this section, we discuss types of budgets and financial statements.

## Master Budget Process

Preparing and following budgets are every manager's business. **Budgets** are plans for allocating resources to specific activities. Notice that our definition does not refer to money. That is because organizations budget all types of resources—labor, machines, time, space, and, yes, funds. However, in the following discussion our focus is on financial budgets, the part of the picture that involves money.

To construct a master budget, organizations develop operating budgets and capital budgets; organizations then measure costs and revenue flow through the income statement, the balance sheet, and the statement of cash flow (see figure 13.5). Notice that information from two of the end products of the process, the income statement and the balance sheet, is used to construct future master budgets, because these two statements tell managers how much money they have to work with and therefore how much they may need to borrow to cover operating expenses and capital expenditures.

Budgets usually cover one year, broken down by month. The controller, the chief finance officer (CFO), oversees the budgeting process that results in the master budget. In other words, the master budget is the end result of the budgeting process. Although organizations commonly follow the three steps we noted previously, how each step is performed varies widely from organization to organization.

Each department submits a proposed budget to the controller or committee for approval. During the budgeting process, which by its very nature deals with limited fixed resources, power and politics usually come into play as managers defend their turf and their budgets. Budgeting is therefore also about negotiating (see chapter 8) and hard bargaining.

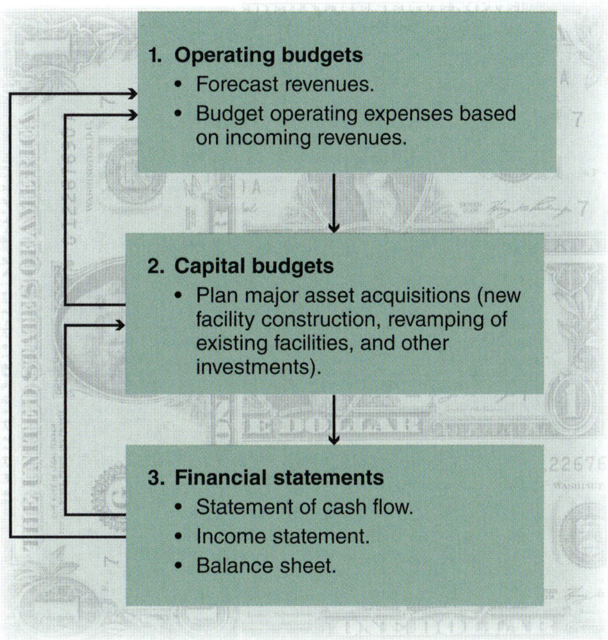

**FIGURE 13.5**   The master budget.

## Operating Budgets

Companies such as Adidas and Nike have to consider the cost to sponsor the Olympics. Adidas spent around $127 to $154 million to be a top sponsor for the 2012 London Olympics. Nike paid much less as a third-tier sponsor. However, Nike created more well-liked ads, and that company is remembered as the top-level sponsor.[37] By 2016 in Rio, Nike actually did become a top-level Olympic sponsor and paid more money—but its ads were not as well received.[38] **Operating budgets** use revenue forecasts to allocate funds to cover projected expenses. Only after organizations determine how much money they have, and expect to have, can they plan how it should be spent to make more money. Therefore, the first step in the master budgeting process is to forecast revenue, followed by the expense budget.

## Forecasting Revenue

This is the forecast of total income for the sport season or year. Before the season even begins, the team has to predict attendance revenues for the entire year and for the long term as well. The New York Yankees baseball team generated $276.9 million in revenue from regular-season tickets and luxury suites in 2015. However, ticket sales for the Yankees drooped considerably from 2009 to 2015, which is when the Yankees moved to a new stadium and lost star players to retirement.[39] By 2018 the Yankees had reloaded with stars, such as Giancarlo Stanton, who were expected to help increase ticket sales.

Although sales are the most common form of revenue, many organizations also have other forms of revenue. Some pro teams now make more on media deals than they do in ticket revenue. Pro football, America's most popular and profitable sport, has rising media revenues but has been trying to tackle a decrease in game attendance. Ticket sales have been down every year since 2007.

Here are some other forms of sport revenues. MLB, WNBA, and other pro sport teams have sales revenues (tickets, luxury boxes, concessions, and logo product sales, plus sponsor advertising); they also have revenue sharing and TV and cable revenue. College athletic programs and high school programs commonly have sales, school funding, donations, and fund-raising. Research supports the idea that good athletic programs lead to increased athletic donations and increased academic support.

Some teams, primarily large NCAA Division IA teams, get to enjoy large sums of money from TV and cable broadcasting and merchandise sales. The University of Notre Dame receives millions a year in television revenues from NBC to broadcast its football games. The University of Texas is regularly counted as the most valuable college franchise. You may think there is big money to be made in college sports, but the reality is that only about 22 of 337 Division I colleges (6.5 percent) make a profit.[40] Even if one or two teams are making money, they have to support all the teams that lose lots of money. So thousands of college athletic department budgets are very heavily subsidized with funds from outside the athletic department. Most sports teams are a recruiting tool to get students to attend the college and pay the tuition to cover the cost of teams.

Revenue forecasts project and then total all sources of income. Marketing commonly provides revenue figures for the entire firm. Revenue forecasts are therefore primarily built on sales forecasts (chapter 14). In one sense, the sales forecast is the building block on which all budgets are based. Major sources of revenue at The Ranch, by department, include membership, golf green and practice fees, restaurant, pub, functions, and golf shop.

## Budgeting Expenses

Operating budgets use expense projections to allocate total operating spending for the season or year. It is true, of course, that controlling expenses and cutting them is important.[41] Each functional-area department has an operating budget. Because of the systems effect, every functional-area budget affects the others. The operations department needs sales forecasts to determine how many products or services to produce (and to estimate the related expenses of doing so). The HR department needs staffing requirements before it can determine how many people it needs to hire (and to estimate the related expenses of doing so). And so it goes through every functional area and every department. Therefore, it is imperative that managers share information.

Things can happen that increase expenses dramatically. Free agency in the NHL, NFL, and MLB increased the cost of players, a cost that was passed on to fans through increased ticket and concession prices. A large, unexpected jump in energy cost can ruin a budget.

Ticket scalping has cost teams and fans who buy tickets. Major expenses at The Ranch include golf course maintenance, building maintenance, purchasing for all departments (fertilizer and chemicals, food and beverages, clothes and golf equipment), management and administrative expenses, employee compensation, and energy.

## Types of Operating Budgets

Two costs are important in operating budgets. *Fixed costs* are costs that don't change as business activity fluctuates. The rent remains the same regardless of whether the facility is used once a year or every day. *Variable costs*, however, do change as business activity fluctuates. The total cost of sales catalogs and mailing increases or decreases as the number printed and mailed changes.

◀ **LEARNING OUTCOME 5**

Differentiate between static and flexible budgets and between incremental and zero-based budgets.

### Static Versus Flexible Budgets

*Static budgets* have only one set of expenses, whereas *flexible budgets* have a series of expenses for a range of activities. Static budgets are appropriate in stable environments in which demand for the product is unchanging. Flexible budgets are appropriate in turbulent environments in which demand for the product varies dramatically. With spreadsheet software, it is easy to make flexible budgets because as you change the "what-if" scenarios, all the calculations change for you. The Ranch has a static budget for each month, which it tries hard to meet.

### Incremental Versus Zero-Based Budgets

These two types of budgets differ in how allocations are justified. With *incremental budgeting*, justification of funds from past budget periods and approval of previously allocated expenses are not required; only new expenses are justified and approved. With *zero-based budgeting (ZBB)*, all expenses are justified and approved with each new budget. That is, ZBB assumes that the previous year's budget should not be the base on which next year's budget is constructed. Zero-based budgets focus on the organization's mission and objectives and what it will cost to achieve them. ZBB is especially appropriate in turbulent environments in which some departmental activities or products are increasing dramatically and others are decreasing.

### Activity-Based Cost Accounting

*Activity-based cost accounting (ABC)* allocates costs by tasks performed and resources used. ABC is not as widely used as the preceding approaches. However, it is particularly

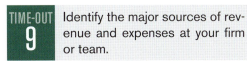

**TIME-OUT 9** Identify the major sources of revenue and expenses at your firm or team.

useful to organizations that produce many goods and services whose production requires a wide diversity of tasks and resources. Recreation facilities offer a variety of services. Some are simple activities that use few resources and take little time (such as a weekly exercise class for 10 adults—about three hours a week). Others use many resources and take a lot of time (such as a sport camp for 300 campers—an all-summer endeavor). How does the facility calculate the cost of these two services? Eight times the cost of the weekly exercise class does not accurately reflect the expenses that will be incurred in the more complex summer camp.

## Capital Budgets

An important part of the master budget process is to estimate funds for capital expenditures. **Capital budgets** allocate funds for improvements. It takes money to make money; that is what capital budgeting is all about.

◀ **LEARNING OUTCOME 6**

Explain how capital budgets and operating budgets differ.

Capital expenditures are investments to purchase or improve long-term assets. These are the assets from which the organization expects to receive benefits for several years, that are paid for over several years, and that are depreciated over several years. They include land, new buildings, new stadiums and arenas, and—today—existing companies that the organization acquires. They also include replacements for expensive machinery and equipment or for outmoded arenas that must be updated if the organization is to remain competitive. In every case, the objective is to earn a satisfactory return on invested funds. Raising money to buy capital assets is an important function of finance. Turning a farm into The Ranch was a very expensive project that needed funds from investors and years to get a payback.

Building new sport stadiums is a capital budget decision. Many professional teams want the city to pay for all or part of the cost of stadiums and arenas. Unfortunately, public financing of sport stadiums can be a cost that exceeds the benefits. The New York Yankees built a new stadium and expected the increase in revenue to pay off; many figured it would be a gold mine that would dramatically improve the team's value should it be sold. The Yankees paid the entire $800 million cost of construction; New York State and New York City kicked in the remaining $400 million in the form of land acquisition, infrastructure improvements, and tax breaks. At times, the economic recession and high ticket prices at the new Yankee Stadium resulted in management's having to lower prices on premium seats. So the Yankees are hard at work with capital budgeting.

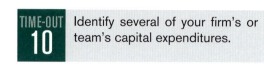

TIME-OUT 10 Identify several of your firm's or team's capital expenditures.

## Financial Statements

LEARNING OUTCOME 7 ▶

State what the three basic financial statements entail.

The last step in the master budgeting process is preparation of the projected (or pro forma) financial statements. After the other budgets are complete, the accountants put it all together to predict the financial status of the organization after a year of projected operations. In developing pro forma financial statements, accountants and managers may change other budgets, for example by cutting expenses or capital investments, to ensure financial stability in the long run. However, it is often a good decision to forgo short-term profits or even to take a short-term loss in preparation for long-term growth and profits—for example, by increasing capital investments to take on debt that will eventually pay off. The pro forma statements are not shown to the public; only the actual statements are made public.

The financial statements lay out, for the world to see, the organization's financial health or lack of health. Don't be afraid of the numbers;[42] being able to read financial statements will let you understand how the organization is doing and help you to make better decisions.[43] Financial statements are used both internally (as the organization monitors its own health) and externally (as investors decide whether they will invest in the firm, creditors decide whether they will lend it money, and suppliers decide whether the firm will stand good on its credit line). As you can see, financial statements are important pieces of paper. When well done, they are transparent and allow stakeholders (investors, credit markets, and suppliers) to evaluate a company's performance, its growth rate, and its reserve funds. The Ranch prepares a budget and pro forma statements for the year, and each month the budget is compared to actual financial statements as all departments work hard to meet the budget. The regularly scheduled meetings devote time to budgets and financial statements.

The three **financial statements** are the income statement, the balance sheet, and the statement of cash flow. We present them in the usual order in which they appear in companies' annual reports.

### Income Statement

The income statement shows the company's revenues and expenses and its profit or loss for the stated period. In annual reports, income statements show year-to-year figures. Why?

Because a $10 million profit is meaningless unless you know that the company made $5 million last year and $20 million the year before that. (Stakeholders need a context, and year-to-year numbers give them this context so that they can identify trends.) Organizations also use monthly and quarterly income statements to measure interim performance and to catch performance problems early on. Table 13.3 shows an abbreviated income statement and balance sheet for an example golf company.

What are the two primary ways organizations increase net income? They increase revenues or they decrease expenses. Unfortunately, this is more easily said than done. Capital expenditures are one way in which companies try to increase revenues; they use operating budgets to see where they can decrease costs.

## TABLE 13.3  Income Statement and Balance Sheet for the Golf Company

### The Golf Company Income Statement

|  | Dec 2020 | Dec 2019 | Dec 2018 |
|---|---|---|---|
| Revenue | 886.5 | 967.7 | 950.8 |
| – Cost of goods sold | 575.2 | 602.2 | 607.0 |
| Gross profit | 311.3 | 365.5 | 343.8 |
| Gross profit margin | 35.1% | 37.8% | 36.2% |
| **Expenses** |  |  |  |
| SG&A expense | 358.1 | 348.2 | 342.1 |
| Depreciation & amortization | 38.6 | 40.9 | 40.7 |
| Income before taxes | (90.3) | (35.6) | (29.6) |
| Income taxes | 81.6 | (16.8) | (14.3) |
| Net income after taxes | (171.8) | (18.8) | (15.3) |
| Net profit margin | −19.4% | −1.9% | −1.6% |

### The Golf Company Balance Sheet

| Assets | Dec 2020 | Dec 2019 | Dec 2018 |
|---|---|---|---|
| Cash | 43.0 | 50.7 | 46.2 |
| Account receivables | 19.3 | 23.8 | 21.9 |
| Inventories | 133.1 | 172.4 | 158.3 |
| Supplies | 23.9 | 33.1 | 31.8 |
| Facilities | 507.8 | 507.8 | 507.8 |
| **Total assets** | **727.1** | **787.8** | **766.0** |
| **Liabilities and stockholder equity** | **Dec 2020** | **Dec 2019** | **Dec 2018** |
| *Liabilities* |  |  |  |
| Accounts payable | 39.0 | 46.4 | 45.1 |
| Facilities long-term loan | 178.1 | 180.6 | 182.7 |
| **Total liabilities** | **217.1** | **227.0** | **227.8** |
| *Stockholder's equity* |  |  |  |
| Common stock | 450.0 | 450.0 | 450.0 |
| Retained earnings | 60.0 | 110.8 | 88.2 |
| **Total equity** | **510.0** | **560.8** | **538.2** |
| **Total liabilities and equity** | **727.1** | **787.8** | **766.0** |

All amounts (except percentages) are in millions of U.S. dollars.

Profit is not the same as cash. In fact, a company can be earning substantial profits and still need to borrow cash to operate. Cash therefore does not appear on the income statement; it appears on the balance sheet and the statement of cash flow. When you make a sale, you increase assets (cash—debit—balance sheet) and increase sales (revenues—credit—income statement).

## Balance Sheet

The balance sheet lists assets, liabilities, and owners' equity. Assets are what the organization owns. Liabilities are what it owes to others. Subtract the organization's liabilities from its assets and you have the owners' or stockholders' equity (that share of the assets owned free and clear). This statement is called a balance sheet because assets always equal liabilities plus owners' equity at a particular point in time (see table 13.3).

Operating costs affect current (less than a year) assets and liabilities. Capital expenditures affect long-term assets and liabilities in the form of property or plant and equipment. Long-term liabilities are the payments (such as mortgage payments and bond debt) that the organization has contracted for in order to purchase major assets (capital budget).

## Statement of Cash Flow

This statement shows cash receipts (including checks and debit transactions) and payments for the stated period. You can't pay your bills without cash flowing into the firm, and you can't get credit and bank loans without showing steady cash flow. So you need to keep tabs on cash flow.

This statement commonly has two sections: operating and financial activities. Statements of cash flow typically cover one year. However, monthly and quarterly statements of cash flow are also computed to measure interim performance and to stop cash flow problems. Operating costs and capital expenditures affect the statement of cash flow as revenue is received and cash expenditures are paid for. It is not unusual for firms to have uneven cash flow. NHL and WNBA teams take in most of their money during their playing seasons, but they have to pay the bills in the off-season with cash. Some companies need to borrow money during their off-season, which they pay back during the season.

## Bonds Versus Stocks

A company with a growth strategy needs money to expand. Two commonly used options for large corporations are to sell bonds and to sell stock. The sale of bonds and stocks doesn't affect the income statement, but it affects the balance sheet and cash flow statements. So what's the difference between bonds and stock? Let's say the company wants to raise $1 million for a capital investment.

**Bonds**  If the company sells bonds, it must pay back the bondholders plus the rate of interest specified. It's essentially a loan. The firm increases its assets of cash and its liabilities by $1 million. No ownership in the company has been given away. Bonds have been sold to raise money for sport stadiums.

**Stock**  If the company sells stock, it never has to pay back the stockholders because they become owners of the company. The firm increases its assets of cash and its owners' equity by $1 million. So if you buy stock, you hope that the value of the stock goes up and that the company will pay dividends, but you can lose money if you sell the stock for less than you paid for it. The Ranch has three ownership groups: the Clarks, Halls, and other investors. Be careful not to give away too much ownership (that is, sell too much stock), because you can lose control of your company and even get fired, like Steve Jobs at Apple. Mark Zuckerberg avoided this by creating a new class of nonvoting shares that would allow him to maintain control of Facebook.[44]

Investor owners in pro sport teams want to make a yearly profit, but they want to see the valuation of the team increase for capital gains. Michael Jordan (MJ) still dominates

## Personal Finance

On a personal note, two critically important financial areas to focus on are managing your credit prudently and saving for retirement. Learn to live within your income—that is, spend less than you make—as soon as you can. Having credit cards makes it easy and very tempting to buy things you don't really need that you can't really afford. However, using credit cards wisely is a good way to build a good credit history; this history determines your credit score, and a good credit score offers such potential benefits as lower insurance and mortgage interest rates.

One or two credit cards should be enough. When you select a credit card, be aware that offers you get in the mail are often not good deals. Go to websites such as www.creditcards.com and www.rewardscards.com to see side-by-side comparisons of various card options. It is usually better not to pay any fees simply for having a credit card account.

Before you select a credit card, an important consideration is whether you can pay off the entire balance every month. If you are spending more than you are making, you will have to pay interest on the outstanding balance, and this is very expensive. If this is your situation, select a credit card that has the lowest interest rate. Also, try to get a card that offers no interest payments for a set time, like six months. However, understand that this is a card company's way of getting you to build up a large balance so that when the grace period ends, you will begin to pay a high interest rate on that balance. Still, this type of card is a good option if you make a large purchase knowing that you can pay it off before the interest charges begin.

If you can pay off your entire credit card balance every month, you will pay no interest on your purchases. You can select a card that offers rewards, such as travel and money back. Rewards cards usually have higher interest rates to offset the rewards offered. With rewards cards, charge as much as you can, such as rent, food, and gas. But be sure to pay off the debt on time and in full to avoid late fees and to avoid paying interest charges to carry high balances.

Start planning your retirement right now, no matter how young you are.[46] You can start to implement your plan when you graduate and have a job. An important benefit is a retirement 401(k) program. As stated in chapter 7, never refuse free money—put enough money into your retirement fund to get the full match of any retirement plan. Start young (in your 20s if you can) and you can become a millionaire.

Nike basketball shoe sales. MJ is the first athlete to become a professional team owner and billionaire. In 2010, MJ acquired a majority stake of the NBA's Charlotte Hornets for $175 million, and in 2013, he increased his share of ownership to 90 percent. MJ is also part owner of Sportrader, a company that feeds data to sports-betting platforms. He splits his time jetting in his custom-designed Gulfstream G450 between Charlotte and Florida.[45]

Note that the only time the company gets any money is when it first sells the stock—an initial public offering (IPO). When a stockholder sells the shares to another person, the company gets nothing and has to record the new owner of the stock. Stockbrokers make their money in commissions by buying and selling stocks for their client investors.

The financial statements are prepared last because they use information from the operating and capital budgets. The cash flow statement is prepared first because it is used to prepare the other two statements. The income statement is prepared next because this information is used on the balance sheet. If the financial statements do not meet expectations, next year's capital budget and operating budgets will need to be revised—hence the feedback loop in the master budget process in figure 13.5. Revisions are common when a net loss is projected.

**TIME-OUT 11** Does your organization make its financial statements available to the public? If so, get a copy and review them. Also, does it develop operating and capital budgets? Try to get copies of those as well. If you are not sure, ask your boss.

# Managing People

An important part of your leadership role is to manage people.[47] Because they are your most valuable resource, you work with each of them to meet their full potential.[48] To manage people well, you need control systems with objectives and standards and rules.[49] How well you manage people will determine your success as a leader.[50] This section covers the roles of properly coaching employees, providing positive feedback, and using the proper corrective actions when monitoring employee performance.

## Coaching

**LEARNING OUTCOME 8** ▶

Use motivational feedback.

Many people who hear the word *coaching* immediately think of athletes, but coaching is also an important sport management skill.[51] Effective coaches can identify any laggards and prevent free riding (chapter 9).[52] So coaching is also a key focus of business,[53] and companies are training managers to improve their coaching skills.[54] A great boss, like a sport coach, can inspire employees to new heights.[55] Before reading about coaching, complete Self-Assessment 13.1 on coaching to determine how well you do or can coach people to improve performance.

**Coaching** involves giving motivational feedback to maintain and improve performance. If you have ever had a good coach, think about what he did to maintain and improve your performance and that of other team members. The next time you watch a sporting event, keep an eye on the coaches and watch their technique.

The Ranch's approach to motivation is a coaching approach. Each employee goes through an extensive orientation and training program. Managers continue to motivate staff by working on the basics to continually improve performance through (coach) Pete Clark's three I's.

### Importance of Motivational Feedback

Feedback is the foundation of coaching,[56] and it should be continuous, motivational, and developmental.[57] The idea is to give more positive feedback than negative feedback. A culture of positive feedback creates an abundance of enthusiasm and energy in teams and organizations. Cheer your people on with an immediate response to their excellent work.[58] When athletes make good plays, the coach and team cheer them on—the same technique motivates people in the workplace.

Ineffective and frustrated managers spend more time criticizing than praising. Managers who only criticize staff undermine their motivation. Unmotivated workers play it safe, do the minimum, focus on not making errors, and cover up errors to avoid criticism—not exactly the way you want your team to work. If you find yourself criticizing (chapter 10) more often than praising (chapter 11), it's time to consider what you are doing.

Now think about your best and worst bosses and coaches. Who gave you more positive feedback? For whom did you do your best work? (We think we already know the answer.) Remember the Pygmalion effect, and give praise following the giving praise model (figure 11.6, chapter 11). Use this coaching technique daily.

### Coaching Corrective Action

Coaching is needed when performance falls below standards or aspiration levels.

Remember the performance equation (chapter 11)? Use it to analyze the situation: Performance = Ability × Motivation × Resources.

- *Ability.* When the person doesn't have the ability to meet the standard, provide training. If she still can't meet the standard, she needs to be let go and replaced.
- *Motivation.* When motivation is lacking, find out why. Talk to the person to gain some insight, and develop a plan together using motivational techniques (chapter 11). If you can't motivate him, you may have to use discipline, which we discuss later.
- *Resources.* When the employee doesn't have the necessary resources, work to obtain them.

## SELF-ASSESSMENT 13.1

### Your Coaching Skills

For each of the following 15 statements, select the response that best describes your actual behavior or what you would do when coaching others to improve their performance. Place the number 5, 4, 3, 2, or 1 on the line before each statement.

1 = does not describe my behavior

2 = somewhat describes my behavior

3 = not sure

4 = describes my behavior

5 = strongly describes my behavior

_____ 1. I know when to coach, counsel, and discipline people.

_____ 2. I don't try to be a psychological counselor or offer advice to solve personal problems, but I do refer people who need help to professionals.

_____ 3. I deal with mistakes as learning opportunities rather than as reasons to place blame and punish.

_____ 4. I make sure people are clear about my expectations rather than forcing them to guess what my expectations are.

_____ 5. I take action to make sure people do at least the minimum rather than letting them perform below standard.

_____ 6. I maintain a relationship with people when I coach them; I do not let coaching hurt our relationship.

_____ 7. I coach soon after an incident rather than waiting for a later time to talk about it.

_____ 8. I focus on showing concern for people and helping them to improve performance for their own benefit rather than to get what I want done.

_____ 9. I show people how they can benefit by taking the action I suggest rather than just telling them what to do.

_____ 10. I offer very specific suggestions for improvement rather than making general comments like "You're not doing a good job" or "You need to do better."

_____ 11. I don't use words like "always" and "never" when talking about what the person does that needs to be improved. For example, I would say, "You were late twice this week," not "You're always late" or "You're never on time."

_____ 12. I focus on the behavior that needs to be improved rather than on the person. For example, I would say, "Why not set an earlier time to get to work—say, 7:45 instead of 8:00?" not "Why can't you be on time?"

_____ 13. I walk around and talk to people to help them improve rather than waiting for them to come to me.

_____ 14. I feel comfortable giving people feedback; it is not uncomfortable or awkward for me.

_____ 15. I coach differently depending on the problem rather than always in the same way.

_____ Total score

To determine your coaching score, add up the numbers for your 15 answers (between 15 and 75) and place the score on the total score line and on the following continuum.

| Ineffective coaching | | | | | | Effective coaching |
|---|---|---|---|---|---|---|
| 15 | 25 | 35 | 45 | 55 | 65 | 75 |

Pete Clark has spent several years coaching football and baseball, managing a Jiffy Lube, and managing The Ranch Golf Club. He says there are more similarities than differences between coaching, business management, and sport management. You must treat the player or employee right. Pete uses the same three I's coaching philosophy at all three: You need *intensity* (to be prepared to do the job right), *integrity* (to do the right thing when no one is watching), and *intimacy* (to be a team player). If anyone does not do the job right, everyone is negatively affected. You need to strive to be the best in sports and in business. Pete strongly believes in being positive and developing supportive working relationships. Pete takes the time to sit down to talk and really listen to his players and employees.

Management by walking around (discussed soon in this section) increases your knowledge and thus will give you ideas for possible solutions, whether they are resource problems or ability or motivation problems.

## The Coaching Model

What do managers often shrink from doing? In three words, advising problematic employees. Managers all too often hesitate to work with employees who are not meeting standards. They hope that the employees will somehow turn around on their own, but they find that the situation often worsens. When you see that an employee is having problems meeting standards, you need to take corrective action quickly. Part of the problem is that many managers don't know how to coach. Coaching is easier if you view it as a way to provide ongoing feedback to help people improve their performance—and if you follow the steps in the coaching model in figure 13.6.

 **TIME-OUT 12** Rate your current boss' coaching ability using specific incidents to defend your answer.

1. Describe current performance. Using specific examples, describe the current performance that needs to be changed. Tell people, in a positive way, exactly what they are doing that needs to be improved.

- *Don't say:* "You're always late for work."
- *Do say:* "Billie, this is the second time this month that you have been late for work."

2. Describe desired performance. Tell people in detail exactly what the desired performance is. Explain how they will benefit from following your advice. If the problem is ability related—that is, lack of knowledge or experience—demonstrate the proper way. If the problem is motivational, simply describe the desired behavior and ask the person to state why the behavior is important.

- *Ability:* "Is there some good explanation as to why you are late for work? I understand, but you need to figure out a way to be on time."
- *Motivation:* "Why is it important to be on time for work?"

3. Get a commitment to the change. When the issue is ability, it usually isn't necessary to get a verbal commitment to the change if the person seems willing to make it. However, if the person defends the action and you're sure it's not effective, explain why your proposed way is better. If you cannot get the person to understand and agree, get a verbal commitment. This step is also important if the issue is motivation; if employees are not willing to commit to a change, they will most likely not make the change.[59]

- *Ability and motivation:* "Will you be on time for work in the future?"

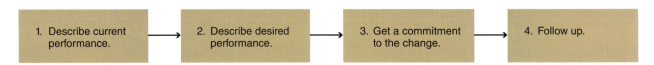

**FIGURE 13.6** The coaching model.

4. Follow up. Remember, most employees will do what managers inspect (imposed control), not what they expect. Therefore, you're doing both yourself and the employee a favor by following up to ensure that change is occurring as desired. In ability situations (and if the person was receptive in step 3), say nothing—just watch to be sure the task is done correctly in the future. Coach again, if necessary. In motivation situations, clearly state that you will follow up and that there are consequences if performance doesn't improve.

- *Ability and motivation:* "Billie, if you are late again, I will take disciplinary action."

## Management by Walking Around

Coaching focuses on helping employees to succeed by monitoring their performance, giving feedback to praise progress, and redirecting inappropriate behavior. You can extend coaching with management by walking around.[60] **Management by walking around (MBWA)** is about listening, teaching, and facilitating.

- *Listening.* If you want to find out what's going on, listen more than you talk, and be open to feedback. Learn to talk last, not first. Open with a simple question like, "How are things going?" Then use the communication skills you developed in chapter 10 as you pry useful information out of everyone.

- *Teaching.* It is not about telling people what to do—it's about training (chapter 7), so use job instructional training when needed. Teaching is also about development by empowering employees to solve their own problems. Therefore, coaches say, "What do you think should be done?" and "How can we improve?"

- *Facilitating.* It is about taking action that helps people to do their jobs and to satisfy customers. The focus is on improving the system. Your team members know their jobs, and they know (often all too well) the stumbling blocks because they deal with them every day. Your job is to run interference and to remove stumbling blocks so that the team can get on with its business.

Now it's your turn to give feedback. Tell the team what is going to be done about the problem—if anything—and when. If you listen but don't facilitate, your staff will stop talking, and you will lose your most important resource for improving the system. The Clarks and their managers are classic MBWA-ers. They are constantly around and following the three steps of MBWA with both employees and golfers. The result? A four-star golf course almost from the get-go and a highly motivated staff.

## Managing Problem Employees

Coaching is about fine-tuning the performance of someone who wants to improve. When you counsel and discipline, you are dealing with a problem employee who is not performing to standard or who is violating standing plans. Discipline can make both parties uncomfortable, but it is a necessary part of being a manager.

Who are the problem employees? Problem employees have negative attitudes, and their behavior has negative effects at work. They do poor quality work, don't get along with coworkers, come to work late, and don't show up. They fall into four categories:

 **TIME-OUT 13** Think about a problem employee or teammate. Describe how the person affected your department's or team's performance.

1. Employees who do not have the *ability* to meet the job performance standards. This is an unfortunate situation, but after training reveals that such employees cannot do a good job, they should be dismissed. Many employees are hired on a trial basis; this is the time to say, "Sorry, but you have to go." It's tough for pro athletes to retire,

and it's tough for coaches to cut those whose performance declines with age and those who play hard but not well enough to make the team.

2. Employees who do not have the *motivation* to meet job performance standards. These employees often need discipline to get them to do a good job.

3. Employees who intentionally *violate standing plans*. As a manager, it is your job to enforce the rules through disciplinary action.

4. Employees with *problems*. These employees may have the ability, but they have a problem that affects job performance. The problem may not be related to the job. It is common for personal problems, such as child care and relationship or marital problems, to affect job performance. Employees with problems should be counseled before they are disciplined.

Review the list of problem employees you may encounter. It is not always easy to distinguish between the types of problem employees. Therefore, it is often advisable to start with coaching, then move to counseling when appropriate, and finally change to discipline if the problem persists.

## Management Counseling

LEARNING OUTCOME 9 ▶

Understand the role of EAP staff.

Organizations realize that part of their job is to help employees deal with their problems. When most people hear the term *counseling*, they think of professional therapy. People who are not professional counselors—and that includes managers—should not attempt this level of help.[61] Management counseling is something very different; it consists solely of recognition and referral.

**Management counseling** helps employees to recognize that they have a problem that is affecting their job performance and then refers them to the employee assistance program. **Employee assistance programs (EAPs)** help employees to get professional assistance in solving their problems. EAP professional help has a cost, but it also improves performance, making it more of an investment in human capital than an expense.[62]

More and more companies are offering EAPs because they improve employee retention and productivity. The San Francisco Giants have one of the best-organized EAP programs in professional sport. The program provides work-life and wellness services for ballplayers and full-time, year-round employees, including managers, coaches, scouts, retirees, game-day workers, and family members. The EAP is helping them with wellness programs, legal and financial referrals, mental health and substance-abuse crisis interventions, and informal consultations.

Management counseling is not about delving into someone's personal life. There is a line here that must not be crossed—for the employee's sake and also for yours. You

 **TIME-OUT 14** Explain the manager's role in counseling.

don't need to know the details; in fact, it is better that you not know them. Knowing too much can hurt your effectiveness as a manager, and it is not your job. Issues of privacy play a big role in these situations; that's why your organization has a separate department—the EAP.

So don't give advice. If you do, you are putting both yourself and your organization at risk for litigation. To make the referral, you can say, "Are you aware of our EAP? Would you like me to set up an appointment with Jean in HR to see if she can help?" If job performance continues to suffer, then discipline becomes an appropriate choice.

Remember, your first obligation is to your organization—it is not to individual employees. Not taking action because you feel uncomfortable approaching people, because you feel sorry for them, or because you like them helps neither you nor the employees. Don't

## Problem Employees

- The late employee
- The absent employee
- The dishonest employee
- The violent or destructive employee
- The alcoholic or drug user
- The nonconformist
- The employee with a family problem

- The insubordinate employee
- The employee who steals
- The sexual or racial harasser
- The safety violator
- The sick employee
- The employee who's often socializing or doing personal work

forget that problem employees have negative effects on performance, causing more work for you and for the rest of the team. This is not good for morale. Taking action is the right thing to do; just make sure it is the right action.

# Discipline

Coaching, which includes counseling, should generally be the first step in dealing with a problem employee. However, if an employee is unwilling or unable to change, a rule has been broken, or there is misconduct, discipline is necessary.

You've taken the coaching route. You've taught and facilitated and fed back positive reinforcements. And you've been down the EAP road. Nothing has worked. Now what do you do? You take disciplinary action.[63] **Discipline** is corrective action to get employees to meet standards and to follow the rules. Discipline can be effective if it makes the person realize the seriousness of the situation. The primary objective of discipline is to change behavior.[64] Other objectives include letting athletes and employees know that action will be taken when rules are broken or performance standards are not met, and maintaining your authority when challenged.[65]

When you find yourself having to take disciplinary action, it's usually time to involve your boss and the HR department to make sure you discipline appropriately without violating any company policies or laws. HR procedures outline grounds for specific sanctions and dismissal based on the violation of the employee (see the Problem Employees list). See the Guidelines for Legal and Effective Discipline.

## *Progressive Discipline*

Punishment varies with the violation.[66] Some actions, such as theft and sexual or racial harassment, result in automatic firing. Many organizations use a series of escalating actions for less serious behavior,[67] such as being late for work, excessive absenteeism, and below-standard levels of work.[68] Progressive discipline typically occurs in this order: (1) oral warning, (2) written warning, (3) suspension, and finally (4) dismissal to avoid more problems.[69] Documenting each step is extremely important.[70] At The Ranch, employees are well trained and clearly informed of expectations. Employees who do not meet the standards are warned and terminated if they don't perform to standard. The managers, with the Clarks, are involved in performance appraisals, discipline, and termination.

---

## Guidelines for Legal and Effective Discipline

- Clearly communicate the standards and standing plans to all employees.
- Be sure that the punishment fits the violation.
- Follow the standing plans yourself.
- Take consistent, impartial action when the rules are broken.
- Discipline immediately, but stay calm and get all the necessary facts before you discipline.
- Discipline in private.
- Document discipline.
- When the discipline is over, resume normal relations with the employee.

---

### When You Have to Discipline Someone, Follow the Disciplining Model

The steps shown in figure 13.7 set up an effective model for you to use to discipline an employee. These steps would also serve a team well when faced with low performance by a team member.

1. Refer to past feedback. Begin by refreshing the employee's memory. Refer to the coaching or counseling the person has received or to the fact that the person has been warned about breaking the rule in question.

Prior coaching: "Billie, remember our discussing your being late for work?"

2. Ask why the undesired behavior was used. Giving the employee a chance to explain the behavior is part of getting all the necessary facts before you discipline. The employee may or may not have justification for the behavior.

"Two days ago you agreed to be on time. Is there a good reason you're late again today?"

3. Give the discipline. Review the guidelines set up by your HR department and follow them carefully. If there is no good reason for the undesirable behavior, or excuses are not accepted for the behavior, give the discipline based on the stage in the disciplinary progression.

"I'm giving you a verbal warning." (first discipline)

## APPLYING THE CONCEPT 13.3

### Guidelines for Effective and Legal Discipline

Use the Guidelines for Legal and Effective Discipline to identify which guideline is or is not being followed in each situation.

_____ 11. To yell that loudly, the coach must have been very upset about our not trying hard enough.

_____ 12. It's not fair. The star players come back from winter break late all the time; why can't I?

_____ 13. When I miss my defensive assignment, coach reprimands me. When Chris does it, nothing is ever said.

_____ 14. Coach gave me a verbal warning for smoking inside the locker room, which is a restricted area, and placed a note in my file.

_____ 15. I want you to come into my office so that we can discuss this matter.

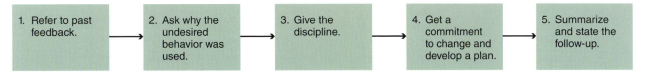

| 1. Refer to past feedback. | 2. Ask why the undesired behavior was used. | 3. Give the discipline. | 4. Get a commitment to change and develop a plan. | 5. Summarize and state the follow-up. |

**FIGURE 13.7** The disciplining model.

4. Get a commitment to change, and develop a plan. Ask the employee to state that she commits to changing the behavior. If she will not commit to changing, move to step 5. If she agrees to change and a plan was developed in the past, review it with her, discuss what changes might make the plan more useful, and ask her to commit to it again. Offer recommendations for change and develop a new plan, if necessary. Statements like "Your previous attempt didn't work; there must be a better way" are often helpful. With a personal problem, offer professional help again.

"Do you agree to be on time for work?"

5. Summarize and state the follow-up. Part of your follow-up is to document the discipline given. If a warning or suspension has been triggered, get the employee's signature to document that the employee was warned and knows the consequences if the behavior doesn't change. If the employee will not commit to changing, document the refusal.

"To recap our discipline session, you agree to be on time for work. I've given you a verbal warning. If you are late again, you will be given a written warning, which is followed by a suspension, and you will be fired if necessary. I want you to sign this document summarizing our discipline session that will be placed in your personnel file."

**TIME-OUT 15** Think about a situation you are aware of in which discipline was required. Which steps in figure 13.7 did your boss or coach follow? Which ones did he or she not use? Was the discipline meted out effectively? Why or why not? Did the discipline bring about the desired change?

# Productivity

When America increases productivity, it drives wages and raises living standards.[71] All of us would like to get paid more. However, if we are paid more without producing more, the only way for the company to maintain profits is to cut costs or raise prices to offset the increased wage cost. Not only does this cause inflation, but cutting costs often leads to layoffs, and increased prices damage an organization's competitiveness. As pro athlete salaries increase, so does the cost of tickets and other expenses of attending the game and buying food, drinks, and apparel. Some fans come to fewer games or stop coming. And many people who are laid off can't afford to attend pro sports. With TV, fans can stay home to watch the games.

Have you heard people complain that technology is taking away jobs? The fact is that technology creates more jobs than it eliminates.[72] What changes jobs is innovation and productivity.[73] What happens is that technology creates new, higher-skill-level jobs and eliminates less-skilled jobs. The people losing their jobs aren't qualified to take the new jobs without education and training, so they often end up in lower-paying jobs than they had. Companies invest in technology to increase productivity,[74] and they tend to replace employees as wages go up, which occurs with an increase in the minimum wage, especially in global markets that include low-wage countries. So the only real way to increase our income and standard of living is to increase our productivity.[75] Employment is up, but unfortunately productivity declined in 2016.[76]

Personal productivity isn't about how many hours you work. It's about getting more done in less time or with fewer resources, and this requires being mentally alert and focused when working.[77] Recall from chapter 5 that multitasking is distracting and actually decreases your productivity.[78] Recall the importance of setting priorities and getting the important tasks done (chapter 6). Is your smartphone keeping you busy and preventing you from getting your important tasks done? How is your personal productivity?[79]

# Measuring and Increasing Productivity

You can improve only what you measure. Measuring productivity can be complex, but it doesn't have to be. Keeping it relatively simple, productivity can be measured by how much is produced in an hour of work, and it can be the output per hour of labor.[80] In this section, we outline a simple yet realistic approach that you can use on the job to measure and increase productivity.

**Productivity** measures performance by dividing outputs by inputs.

$$\frac{\text{Outputs}}{\text{Inputs}} = \text{Productivity}$$

Let's say ExxonMobil wants to know the productivity of its new Formula One racing fuel. In this test, the Formula One car traveled 1,000 miles (1,609 kilometers) and used 100 gallons (378.5 liters) of the new fuel. Its productivity was 10 miles to the gallon (16 kilometers/3.78 liters):

$$\text{Productivity} = \frac{\text{Output (1,000 miles traveled)}}{\text{Input (100 gallons of fuel)}} = 10 \text{ miles per gallon}$$

Now let's say a Wilson Sporting Goods manufacturer wants to know the weekly productivity of its accounts payable department. We are going to simplify things here a bit, but this example will give you an idea of how to get a realistic idea of your group's productivity rate.

1.  Select a time period, such as an hour, a day, a week, a month, a quarter, or a year. In this example, the accounts payable manager decides to look at a week.

2.  Determine how many bills (outputs) were sent out during that period. The manager checks the records and finds out that the three-person department sent out 800 bills last week.

3.  Determine the "quick cost" of sending out the bills (inputs). Determining costs can be complicated if you determine total cost, which includes overhead, depreciation, and many other variables. In this instance, our manager uses only direct labor charges for the three employees, who are each paid $10 an hour. They all worked 40 hours during the week in question for a total of 120 hours. The total quick cost then is $10 an hour × 120 hours, or $1,200.

4.  Dividing the number of outputs (bills sent out) by the inputs (direct labor charges) gives the productivity ratio, 0.67 (800/$1,200 = 0.666), which of course can be expressed as a percentage (67 percent). It can also be stated as labor cost per unit. To determine labor cost per unit, simply reverse the process and divide inputs by outputs ($1,200/800). It thus cost $1.50 to send out each bill.

## *Calculating Productivity Rate Changes*

Our manager now sets the 0.67 productivity rate as the base or standard rate. In the next week, the accounting department again sends out 800 bills, but because of computer problems, the three employees have to work overtime at an additional cost of $100. The productivity rate thus decreases to 0.62 (800/$1,300). The labor cost per unit goes up to $1.63 ($1,300/800). To determine the percentage change, use the following formula:

Current productivity rate (62%) – Base productivity rate (67%) = Change (5%)

Change/Base productivity rate (5/67) = 0.0746, or a 7.46 percent decrease in productivity

### Production Versus Productivity

Be aware that productivity can decrease even though output increases. Suppose Wilson's accounts payable department sends out 850 bills, but doing so requires 10 hours of overtime (time-and-a-half at $15 an hour × 10 hours = $150)—productivity has decreased to 63 percent, which is below the 67 percent standard (850/1,350). So if you measure only output and it increases, you will be fooled into thinking you are improving when in fact you're doing worse.

### Increasing Productivity

Productivity can be increased.[81] Here are three ways to increase productivity:

- Increase output value and maintain input value ($\uparrow$ O $\leftrightarrow$ I).
- Maintain output value and decrease input value ($\leftrightarrow$ O $\downarrow$ I).
- Increase output value and decrease input value ($\uparrow$ O $\downarrow$ I).

◀ LEARNING OUTCOME 10
State three ways to increase productivity.

Always compare your productivity to the standard, and compare productivity during one period to that of previous periods; productivity during any single period by itself is meaningless. What is important is whether productivity is changing for the better or worse or whether it is stagnating. Unfortunately, as your level of productivity increases, it often becomes increasingly difficult to continuously improve it.

TaylorMade has been successful in a perpetual race to increase the distance (productivity) people can hit a golf ball with its golf clubs.[82] Pepsi's Gatorade has a Sports Science Institute to improve Gatorade drinks so that they better enhance athletes' performance. It uses this slogan: "Studied. Tested. Proven." It developed G Sport Drinks and more recently protein powders and drinks, bars and chews, and endurance products.[83] The Ranch maintains productivity by keeping players to average game-completion times. Slow players or parties hold up players in the pipeline and can hurt customer satisfaction. The golf cars' GPS systems tell the players if they are on schedule, and player assistants help players stay on schedule.

## Measuring Functional-Area Productivity

Productivity measures are important for another reason—they indicate how well an organization is being managed. Therefore, you should measure functional-area productivity as you strive to drive down costs. Table 13.4 lists the ratios that are used to measure functional areas. The numbers used to calculate the financial ratios are taken from the income statement and balance sheet (examples of which are shown in table 13.3). As indicated in table 13.4, these ratios are easy to calculate and understand, and they are used commonly as controls. To make meaningful year-to-year comparisons, analysts commonly use three to five years of data.

### Measuring the Organization's Overall Performance

Financial ratios indicate the organization's overall performance; they do not measure the performance of the finance area itself. The profitability ratios are based heavily on sales, which is a marketing function. However, the performance of the other functional areas is affected by how well finance does its job. Finance controls the budget, which helps (or

## APPLYING THE CONCEPT 13.4

## Measuring Productivity

The standard monthly productivity rate in the golf club department is as follows:

Productivity = Outputs / Inputs = 6,000 units / $9,000 cost = 0.67, or 67 percent

Calculate the current productivity rate for each month and show it as both a ratio and a percentage. Then calculate the percentage productivity change compared to the standard, stating whether it was an increase or a decrease.

16. January: outputs = 5,900; inputs = $9,000

    ratio: _____; percent: _____; change: _____ %

    _____

17. February: outputs = 6,200; inputs = $9,000

    ratio: _____; percent: _____; change: _____ %

    _____

18. March: outputs = 6,000; inputs = $9,300

    ratio: _____; percent: _____; change: _____ %

    _____

19. April: outputs = 6,300; inputs = $9,000

    ratio: _____; percent: _____; change: _____ %

    _____

20. May: outputs = 6,300; inputs = $8,800

    ratio: _____; percent: _____; change: _____ %

    _____

hinders) the other functional areas. Marketing sells the products on credit, and finance (through its accounting function) collects the payments and pays for purchases made throughout the organization. The Ranch managers use a variety of financial ratios and percentages to measure performance monthly, and performance is discussed during regular meetings. With decreases in performance, additional meetings occur and corrective action is taken to ensure standards are met.

### Measuring Productivity in Marketing and Operations

Marketing and operations in an organization can be likened to the heart and lungs in the body. The key to business success is for these two areas, with the aid of the other functional areas, to continually increase customer value. If marketing and operations do not work well and do not work well together, the organization may fail to thrive. Gross profit margin and net profit margin are also considered marketing ratios because they are based on sales.

Inventory turnover is primarily the responsibility of operations. However, the operations department depends on marketing's sales forecasts, which it uses to decide how much product to produce. If sales forecasts are too optimistic, operations will produce too much product, which will sit in inventory, which decreases the turnover rate.

**TABLE 13.4** **Financial Ratios**

| Functional area | Ratio | Calculation | Information |
|---|---|---|---|
| Accounting<br>Profitability | Gross profit margin | Sales–COGS<br>Sales | Measures efficiency of operations and product pricing. |
| | Net profit margin | Net profit and income<br>Sales | Measures product profitability. |
| | Return on investment | Net profit and income<br>Total assets | Measures return on total capital expenditures or ability of assets to generate a profit. |
| Liquidity | Current ratio | Current assets<br>Current liabilities | Measures ability to pay short-term debt. |
| | Quick ratio | Current assets–inventory<br>Current liabilities | This is a stronger measure of bill-paying ability because inventory may be slow to sell for cash. |
| Leverage | Debt to equity | Total liabilities<br>Owners' equity | Shows proportion of the assets owned by the organization. |
| Operations | Inventory turnover | COGS<br>Average inventory | Shows how efficient the organization is in controlling its investment in inventory. The larger the number the better, because this means that products are being sold faster. |
| Marketing | Market share | Company sales<br>Total industry sales | Measures the organization's competitive position. The larger, the better, because this means the organization is outselling its competitors. |
| | Sales to presentations | Sales completed<br>Sales presentations made | Shows how many presentations it takes to make a sale. |
| Human resources | Absenteeism | Number of absent employees<br>Total number of employees | Shows the ratio of employees not at work for a given time period. |
| | Turnover | Number of employees leaving<br>Total number of employees | Shows the ratio of employees who must be replaced for a given period (usually one year). |
| | Workforce composition | Number of a specific group<br>Total number of employees | Shows the ratio of women, Hispanics, African Americans, and so on in the organization's workforce. |

COGS = cost of goods sold.

As we bring this chapter to a close, you need to understand types of controls, the control process, and frequencies and methods of controls; see table 13.2 for a review. Budgeting is also important. The master budget includes operating budgets, capital budgets, and financial statements; see figure 13.5 for a review. You should develop your coaching skills and improve your ability to handle problem employees with management counseling and discipline when needed; learn figures 13.6 and 13.7. Lastly, you should be able to measure productivity and know how to increase it.

# LEARNING AIDS

## CHAPTER SUMMARY

1. **Explain how controls function within the systems process.**

   The first stage of the systems process is inputs. Preliminary controls are designed to anticipate and prevent possible problems. The second stage is the transformation process. Concurrent controls are actions taken during the transformation to ensure that standards are met. The third stage is outputs. Rework controls are actions taken to fix an output. The fourth stage is customer or stakeholder satisfaction. Damage controls are actions taken to minimize negative impacts on customers attributable to faulty outputs. Feedback is used at each stage to improve the process to continually increase customer satisfaction.

2. **Understand why feedback is a control.**

   Feedback is circulated through all the functional areas to improve organizational performance in the input, transformation, and output processes and to continually increase customer satisfaction.

3. **Describe the control process.**

   The four steps in the control process are (1) set objectives and standards; (2) measure performance; (3) compare performance to standards; and (4) correct or reinforce, with a feedback loop for continuous improvement.

4. **List which control methods are used with which frequency.**

   Self-control, clan control, and standing plans are used constantly (continuously). Routine reports, budgets, and audits are used periodically. Observation, the exception principle, special reports, and project controls are used occasionally.

5. **Differentiate between static and flexible budgets and between incremental and zero-based budgets.**

   A static budget has only one set of expenses, whereas a flexible budget has a series of expenses for a range of activities. With incremental budgeting, past funds are allocated with only new expenses being justified and approved. With zero-based budgeting, all funds must be justified each year.

6. **Explain how capital budgets and operating budgets differ.**

   The capital expenditures budget includes all planned major asset investments. It consists of funds allocated for investments in major assets that will last, and be paid for, over several years. The expense budget contains funds allocated to pay for operating costs during the budgeting year. With expense budgets, the focus is on cost control. With capital expenditures, the focus is on the more important role of developing ways to bring in additional revenues through new and improved products and projects that will create customer value.

7. **State what the three basic financial statements entail.**

   The income statement details revenue and expenses and the profit or loss for the stated time period. The balance sheet presents assets, liabilities, and owners' equity. The statement of cash flow presents the cash receipts and payments for the stated time period.

8. **Use motivational feedback.**

   The objective of coaching is to improve performance. Positive feedback, such as giving praise, motivates employees to maintain and improve their performance.

9. **Understand the role of EAP staff.**

   The manager's role in counseling is to recognize that an employee has a problem and to refer that person to the employee assistance program. EAP staff members then help employees get professional help to solve their problems.

10. **State three ways to increase productivity.**

    To measure productivity, outputs are divided by inputs. Productivity is increased by (1) increasing output value while maintaining input value; (2) maintaining output value while decreasing input value; and (3) increasing output value while decreasing input value.

## REVIEW AND DISCUSSION QUESTIONS

1. Why is damage control important?

2. Name five sport governing bodies.

3. Discuss the role of governing bodies in managing and controlling their sports.

4. Who are the primary customers or stakeholders for the outputs of operations, marketing, human resources, finance, and MIS departments?

5. Why do organizations measure performance?

6. What is shown in a performance report?

7. What is the role of reinforcement in the control process?

8. List the three constant-control methods, the three periodic-control methods, and the four occasional-control methods.

9. What are the three steps in the master budgeting process?

10. Why is the capital budget the most important budget?

11. State what the three financial statements show.

12. What is the objective of coaching?

13. How do managers commonly undermine employees' motivation?

14. What is the performance equation, and how is it used with coaching?

15. What are the three activities of management by walking around, and what is the role of facilitating?

16. How do coaching, counseling, and disciplining differ?

17. Which of the eight discipline guidelines is most relevant to you personally? Explain.

18. Name the major ratio measures in finance, marketing, and human resources, and explain what they measure.

19. Do you agree with the ASQ study that determined Reebok had a better quality score than Nike?

## CASES

### Sport Management Professionals @ Work: Anika Goodhue

Anika's passion for coaching began in high school with the urge to share her knowledge by hosting youth clinics. After graduating from Smith College, Anika returned to coach field hockey at Mount Anthony Union High School, her alma mater, and she helped lead the squad to four Vermont State semifinal appearances in five seasons. Anika was a four-year player for the Smith College field hockey program, and she served as a team captain during her senior season. During a versatile career where she played offense, defense, and midfield, Anika registered five goals, 18 assists, and one defensive save. In addition to collegiate athletics, Anika has played internationally in five different countries, including a six-month stint in Australia, where she was a key performer for the University of Melbourne Hockey Club.

Anika is currently in her third year as head coach of the Elms College field hockey program. She was previously the assistant field hockey coach at Connecticut College. She also assisted at Westfield State University during their spring seasons in 2014 and 2015.

Anika is passionate about teaching field hockey! "It is my vision to become a smarter and more cohesive team with everyone working hard for each other and really embracing their passion for field hockey," she said. "If every member of the team is enjoying what they are doing, understanding how important their contributions are, and achieving both individual and team goals, the rest of it will come easy."

Anika founded Evolution Field Hockey Club to help stimulate growth and knowledge of field hockey in her hometown. While she mainly focuses on youth development, Anika has also created opportunities for adults to play after graduation, and she developed a young coaches program that mentored interested high school athletes in coaching. In her spare time (if she has any), Anika has her own freelance photography business, and she often takes pictures at Elms College games.

## Case Questions

1. What can you learn from this case to help build your own coaching career?

2. How does Anika express her passion for field hockey in a way that is attractive to colleges when they hire her to coach?

3. What type of leader is Anika based on the theories you have learned about in this book?

## Lean and Mean Manufacturing at Nike

Nike has been careful about manufacturing ever since the company was accused of using sweatshops to manufacture its products in the 1970s. Nike has since been a leading proponent of the establishment of the Fair Labour Association.[84]

Nike has used lean manufacturing to help its suppliers to become more oriented toward continuous improvement. One of the main principles of lean manufacturing is that quality should be built into the products while they are being manufactured. Just like automobiles, sporting goods need to meet the highest of expectations since athletes rely on them for performance and protection. Consumers typically know Nike for its splashy advertisements that pull customers into retail outlets to buy the latest sporting good styles. But Nike is just as serious about focusing on continually improving cost, quality, delivery, and innovation.

Another major goal of lean manufacturing might be summarized as the elimination of waste throughout an organization's entire supply chain. Waste needs to be eliminated not only in the production process but also in the way the managers forecast customer demand, schedule the facilities, and program the operations.

At Nike, the entire process was measured, and improvement was noticeable. The manufacturing shop employees received extensive training. Setup time for machines was cut in half. Managers walked around the manufacturing facility and mapped the flow of materials through the process. Job functions were timed. Bottlenecks were removed. It took at least 18 months for employees to become familiar with the new methods.

One of the keys to the process was balancing supply and demand. Lean manufacturing relies on an older Japanese method of just-in-time inventory to keep inventories down and yet have sporting goods available just when customers need them. Sales, marketing, operations, and product development had to learn to communicate with each other better to improve their own knowledge of the supply and demand cycle. Nike has learned to Make Today Better (lean) and Design the Future (innovate).[85]

Mark Parker, CEO and president of Nike, included lean manufacturing in his statement about improving Nike's role in sustainability:

Sustainability at Nike means being laser-focused on evolving our business model to deliver profitable growth while leveraging the efficiencies of lean manufacturing, minimizing our environmental impact and using the tools available to us to bring about positive change across our entire supply chain. We've made significant progress in these areas. But as we all know at Nike, there is no finish line.[86]

To learn more about the company, you can watch the founder, Phillip Knight, talk about the 11 Maxims at Nike. www.youtube.com/watch?v=DiRml0uRnrg.

Go to the web study guide to answer questions about this case study.

## @ TAKE IT TO THE NET

Please visit www.HumanKinetics.com/AppliedSportManagementSkills and go to this book's companion web study guide, where you will find the following:

A list of websites associated with the concepts in this chapter

Skill-Builder exercises, Sports and Social Media exercises, and a continuing Game Plan for Starting a Sport Business

Online versions of chapter exercises and end-of-chapter learning aids

An exercise that helps you define the Key Terms

# Facilities and Events Management

## DEVELOPING YOUR SKILLS

If you want to manage a sport facility or work as an athletic director, you're going to plan and control events at one time or another. In this chapter, you will learn about dimensions of plans and how to use scheduling tools: the planning sheet, Gantt charts, and PERT. You will also learn the methods for forecasting sales for events and ongoing business such as ticket, concession, and apparel sales. In addition, you can use the time management system and 50 tips to improve your time management skills so that you can become a skillful planner and controller of facilities and events.

## REVIEWING THEIR GAME PLAN

### Making the JCC Maccabi Games a Hit

Sport events don't just happen. Events that come off without a hitch mean that a whole team of event planners have been at work behind the scenes, scrambling, smoothing, and problem-solving for months, if not years. Events like the Senior Olympics, the Goodwill Games, and the Maccabi Games, which have dramatically expanded opportunities for people of all ages and all walks of life to participate in sport, exemplify event planning at its best. An offspring of the Israeli Maccabiah Games—the "Jewish Olympics" held in Israel—the U.S. JCC Maccabi Games attract thousands of young athletes aged 13 to 16 to compete at different sites in the United States. The games have helped to develop top Jewish athletes, many of whom (Mark Spitz, 1968 and 1972 Olympics; Mitch Gaylord, 1984 Olympics; and Lenny Krayzelburg, 2000 Olympics, to name a few) went on to achieve fame in the Olympics.[1]

Emily Shotland is the new Maccabi Games director for the Springfield Jewish Community Center. As in any case when a job is passed to another person upon retirement, Emily has the big shoes of Stuart Greene to fill. Stu was the games director for the 2002 and the 2011 U.S. JCC Maccabi Games in Springfield, Massachusetts. He also helped organize games in many communities across the United States all the way up to his retirement in 2017. He worked hard to make sure that each event, which takes more than a year to plan, was a success. First on his agenda was securing a host community center. Greene negotiated with the management of potential host centers, alerted local governments so they could prepare for the influx of people, organized volunteers, found homes for the participants to stay in during the games, and secured sites at local colleges where games such as soccer and volleyball could be played. He had his committees in place by August of the previous year, a kickoff campaign ready two months later in October, and host families selected at least six months before the start of the games. Greene also helped raise nearly $500,000 in donations and products to support the games.

The umbrella organization, the Maccabi World Union, was of great assistance to Greene in these endeavors. The organization circulates a yearly planning calendar to assist in the design of the games.

Since Stu retired after a stellar career, fielding a Maccabi team each year is now under Emily's direction. As a former Maccabi athlete, she understands the mission of the organization is to give youth a sport and cultural experience. She also has led a team of athletes at the New Jersey JCC to different Maccabi events. Emily has the passion, experience, and energy to manage the Maccabi events for the next 30 years!

For current information on the JCC Maccabi Games in your area, visit www.jccmaccabi.org.

# Sport Facilities and Event Management

In this opening section, we discuss the difference between facilities and event management, and careers in these sport management areas.

## Sport Facilities and Event Management Differences

Let's start by defining some important terms. *Facilities* are something built, installed, or established to serve a purpose. An *event* is a contest in a program or sport, often called a game. The *venue* is the place where the event takes place within facilities, and one main event like the Olympics has several venues for various event competitions. So, you could manage the facilities or the actual event. No matter how large or small the facility and its events, without effective facilities and event sport management, you can't have a safe and enjoyable environment. We discuss facilities and event management in separate sections.

In chapter 4, we examined strategic planning, which focuses on the long term. In this chapter we examine operational planning (also called short-term action planning) and controlling issues. We discuss planning and controlling together because they are inseparable. When you plan, you also need to build in controls because without controls, the plans will not meet the objective. This chapter focuses on events and facilities because most high-level sport managers at one time or another manage (plan and control) a facility and put on events. For example, your college or university might ask you to plan a three-on-three basketball tournament or road race for charity, host a sport-related event for Special Olympics, or manage the daily operation of the fitness center on your campus.

## Sport Management Facilities and Event Careers

The value of sport in each case depends on the ways in which sport is managed, and without facilities and events, there is no sport. There are many jobs related to sport management, including planning, designing, and constructing and financing facilities. You may also work with facility operations, schedule events, manage a facility finance budget, equip facilities with TV and video connections, oversee maintenance and custodial services, conduct facility marketing and promotions, engage in event merchandising, or direct risk management services, user agreements, and insurance—and jobs in sport facility security have increased in importance since September 11, 2001.[2]

Sport management professionals often find careers in managing various types of facilities and events. Such work includes managing private Gold's Gym health clubs, hotel fitness centers, YMCA or JCC athletic facilities; monitoring the manufacture of sporting apparel such as uniforms, footwear, and baseball caps; and managing anything from indoor sporting centers to entire stadiums.

You can build a career working in facilities and events in the sport about which you are passionate. Have you noticed that sport and entertainment are merging? Most professional teams realize that sport is a form of entertainment; you can be doing lots of other things besides watching a sport competition. Think about half-time entertainment and especially the NFL Super Bowl half-time show. Managing sport and entertainment facilities requires the same skill set. In this chapter, we don't expect to make you an expert in facilities and event management. Your college or university may offer one or more courses related to facilities and events.

If you are interest in a facilities or event career, you must read the job descriptions carefully because the same job title can have very different responsibilities and duties in different organizations. You may want to consider doing an internship in these areas.

# Sport Facilities Management

In order to host different types of sporting events, you need facilities. You can build new facilities or renovate existing facilities to accommodate the sporting event, and you need to effectively manage the facilities. Facilities can be managed internally, or they can be managed externally by hiring professional facility management firms.

# Types of Sport Facilities

LEARNING OUTCOME 1 ▶

Describe what managing a sport facility entails.

There are different types of facilities based on their purpose and events they host.

## Single- and Multipurpose Facilities

Single-purpose facilities are used for one sport or activity. Bowling alleys, golf courses, ski areas, motorsport tracks, ice arenas, and swimming pools are single purpose. However, you can use the same facility for similar activities. The ice arena can provide a venue for competitive hockey teams, figure-skating competitions, and recreational ice skating. The swimming pool can provide a venue for swimming and diving competition, as well as swim lessons and recreational swimming.

Multipurpose facilities provide a venue for multiple events. Many stadiums are venues for multiple pro or college teams, concerts, truck pulls, motocross races, home and garden shows, recreational vehicle shows, and college graduations. Your high school gymnasium most likely hosted both physical education classes and other events like dances. It is more common for multipurpose facilities to be larger so that they can host larger venues, but the size of the facilities doesn't necessarily vary with the type of facility.

Also, many of these facilities have party event room venues. Attendees can skate, swim, or bowl and have a party, often celebrating a kid's birthday. Pro teams have corporate boxes where managers reward employees and customers with snacks, drinks, meals, and a game while also hosting prospective customers for new business deals. Someone has to market, sell, schedule, plan, and run these events.

## Stadiums, Arenas, and Centers

There are two major types of single-purpose or multipurpose facilities that can serve as sport venues: stadiums and arenas.

- *Stadiums.* These are the facilities commonly used for outdoor sports played on a field, including soccer, football, baseball, and cricket.
- *Arenas.* These are the facilities commonly used for indoor sports, including basketball, ice hockey, volleyball, boxing, and wrestling. Notice that stadiums tend to be longer and more rectangular and arenas are more circular or oval shapes.
- *Centers.* Some arenas are called centers, especially when they host a variety of events. The Barclays Center is home for the Brookland Nets basketball and New York Islanders hockey teams, but it also hosts several concerts and other types of events each year and some college games as well.
- There are exceptions to the commonly used terms; Duke University's home basketball venue qualifies as an arena, but the facility is called Cameron Indoor Stadium.

# Renovating and New Facilities

At the youth, high school, college, and pro levels, facilities and event management is critical to an athletic program's success. Recall the performance equation (chapter 11, $P = A \times M \times R$). Resources include facilities. Teams with the best facilities may not always win, but having excellent facilities helps. Facilities wear out, get dated, and are constantly being fixed and improved. However, facilities eventually get to the point of needing a major renovation or replacement. Many colleges and universities have renovated and built new athletic facilities to attract top athletes, to appeal to students who want to work out, and to get more media coverage.

## Renovating Facilities

If an existing facility is not adequate and another one is not available, facility management may decide to renovate the existing facility to fit their criteria. Virtually all the MLB Boston Red Sox home games sell out, and the team would like to have a new stadium, but it wants to stay in Boston, where little land is available. To help sell more tickets, the team renovated the stadium to add more seats and boxes, but it hasn't solved the problem of constantly sold-out games and disappointed fans.

## New Facilities

When facilities are not adequate, the firm may decide that moving to another existing facility is more cost efficient. Twenty years ago, the Naismith Memorial Basketball Hall of Fame in Springfield, Massachusetts, moved from a small building on the Springfield College (SC) campus (the actual birthplace of basketball—SC alumnus and professor James Naismith invented basketball in his physical education class held at the YMCA in 1891 in a building owned by SC in downtown Springfield).[3] The collection eventually outgrew the downtown facility, and in 2002 a brand-new Basketball Hall of Fame almost twice the size of the original facility opened its doors. The Volleyball Hall of Fame in Holyoke, Massachusetts (the birthplace of volleyball—invented in 1895 by SC alumnus William G. Morgan at the Holyoke YMCA), opened in 1987 and has had renovations over the years.

## Public Financing

At the city recreational, youth sport, high school, and public college levels, most of the sport funding comes from public expenditures (government funds) in sport facilities. Hosting the Olympics requires expensive public funding and other resources (such as land), which are commonly used for local sports after the Games.

At the professional level, facilities help to attract attendance, and stadium capacity is important. Economic development has provided large numbers of people with access to sport facilities. Teams constantly look for public financing of facilities, and a lot of political maneuvering is involved in getting large public expenditures for stadiums and arenas.

We discussed earlier that the New York Yankees built a new stadium, ready for the 2009 season, paying the $800 million cost of construction, with $400 million kicked in by New York State and New York City in the form of land acquisition, infrastructure improvements, and tax breaks. The cross-town New York Mets also built a new stadium.

Since the early 1980s, more than a dozen NFL, MLB, NBA, and NHL franchises relocated to new cities, and an important part of the reason for moving was facilities. Most pro teams need a substantial investment in the new facility, and it is increasingly being partly paid for by corporate sponsors who put their names on the facility, such as Tropicana (juice) Field, home of the MLB Tampa Bay Rays and the MassMutual Center (insurance), home of the AHL Thunderbirds. Both are multipurpose facilities that hold other events.

Many steps are needed in facility planning. Feasibility assessments must be conducted to determine the need and the demand of the marketplace for such a building. Funding needs to be addressed. An architect must be selected to draw a detailed conceptual design. An operational plan will be needed to implement the stages of construction. Facility audits will have to be prepared to ensure that all areas of construction are abiding by safety regulations. These are only some of the steps required to plan a facility, and the process is a huge undertaking. However, being part of a committee overseeing the development of a modern athletic building can be very exciting and rewarding.

## Managing Facilities

Once an athletic or recreational facility is open for business, you begin the continuing process of managing and training the people who will run it. Planning daily operations also includes soliciting and scheduling events to keep the facility's calendar full and revenues coming in. With multiple events to plan for, project management skills are a must.

Facility managers face daily challenges in this growing industry. Managers are involved in scheduling and promoting events, arranging for transportation, setting up and taking down event facilities, managing event security, and making sure food concessions are ready for game time.

The number of sport facility managers varies, as do their job titles and duties, depending on the size and purpose of each facility. However, there are two common levels in most larger facilities.[4]

- *Facility manager (director or CEO).* These top-level managers have overall responsibility for the entire facility.
- *Facility operations manager.* These managers report to the director; they mainly oversee the facility staff, policies and procedures, daily activities, and coordination of resources.
- *Event manager (or coordinator).* Event managers also report to the director. They are responsible for the individual events held in the facility. We will discuss their responsibilities in the Sport Event Management section.

Joe Esile (who was featured in chapter 1) was the athletics facilities and game operations coordinator for three years at the University of Pittsburgh. His responsibilities included coordinating all projects and routine inspections with the trade labor department for five athletic facilities regarding carpentry, plumbing, painting, and cleaning. He was also responsible for many renovation projects, such as technology upgrades, turf installation, carpet installation, furniture replacement, and field maintenance.

Joe is currently the athletic facilities and events director for the University of California, Berkeley.[5]

## Hiring Professional Facility Management Firms

This means that the owners pay a firm to manage the facility and event operations. Recall that The Ranch Golf Club initially hired the professional golf management team Willowbend. In 1976, the Louisiana Superdome became the first major sporting facility to use outside professionals, the Sport Management Group (SMG—now SMG Worldwide), to manage its operations. In the aftermath of Hurricane Katrina, SMG spent nearly a year literally rebuilding and updating the Superdome.[6]

Today, SMG is a world leader in event and facility management, with more than 65 million guests at its venues in more than 240 stadiums, arenas, theaters, and exhibition and convention centers in eight countries. In addition, it offers food services and has three other service departments: sport and entertainment booking, design and pre-opening, and impression networks. SMG has more than 5,000 employees. For internship and job opportunities, visit its website at www.smgworld.com.[7]

## Sport Event Management

LEARNING OUTCOME 2 ▶

Describe what is involved in event planning.

Sport managers plan and host many types of events. They coordinate games, provide food for teams, arrange team transportation, hire officials, manage ticket sales, plan and monitor concession sales, schedule the various leagues, and organize tournaments.

Every event is a product that has a systems process (chapter 13) of *inputs* (resources and plans for the event), *transformation* (actual event/game), *output* (result of the event), and hopefully customer and fan satisfaction with the event. In this section, we discuss the event management team, pre-event tasks (inputs), managing the event (transformation and outputs), and post-event tasks (satisfaction).

## Event Management Team

Event management is a team-based task. The size of the management team varies with the size of the venue and the specific event. For high school and college-level sports, the AD and staff are usually responsible for scheduling and managing home events in coordination with the facilities staff.

For the pros in multipurpose stadiums and arenas like the TD Garden, the facility manager is responsible for the entire facility and may be involved in the planning and scheduling of individual events. Both the NHL Boston Bruins and NBA Boston Celtics play home games in the TD Garden. The facility manager and event manager must work together to set up the facilities for the different sports and other events.

In chapter 1 we learned that sport managers *plan*, *organize*, *lead*, and *control*. Planning begins with setting an objective and determining in advance how it will be accomplished. The objective is to host an event, and the event management team develops the plans and organizes the resources (human, physical facilities, finances, and information) with control systems to lead the facilities team in staging the event.

## Pre-Event Tasks

There is a direct relationship between planning with preliminary controls and event success. Here are some of the important pre-event tasks. Note that this is not a simple linear step-by-step process; multiple tasks may be completed simultaneously, and you may need to go back and change previous tasks.

What are some challenges an event planning team would face in planning and staffing events in large multipurpose stadiums versus single event venues?

© Mary Knudson/fotolia.com

### Profitability and Budgeting

In a for-profit business, the first decision is to determine if the event will make any money or at least pay for itself. Each profit or nonprofit event should have its own budget. As discussed in chapter 13, you start by determining the revenues, such as ticket sales, concession and merchandise sales, sponsors' in-kind support with goods (free or low-cost facilities, T-shirts for your road racers), services (drinks and food for athletes and concession sales), and financial donations. We will discuss sales forecasting methods later in this chapter. Then you project the expenses for hosting the event. Again, revenues minus expenses equals a profit or loss for the event. Also, can you get the team or entertainers and their staff to host the event?

### Negotiating the Event

You may have to negotiate things like renting an actual venue, equipment and supplies for the event, police security staff, the cost of entertainment, and so on. You can also negotiate to split any sources of revenues, such as ticket sales and merchandise revenues, with entertainers, concessionaires, and merchandisers. It is common to have formal written contracts with parties in these negotiations, and there are boilerplate fill-in-the blank forms that can be used. Use the negotiation skills you developed in chapter 8.

### Scheduling the Event

Scheduling the event is about making reservations or booking the event. Scheduling includes the date, time, and place of the event, which may be decided before negotiation or during the negotiations. You can rent facilities on your own or have an event planner plan and stage the event for you. However, you also need to schedule various activities in preparation for the event using schedules with checklists. You will learn how to schedule in the Scheduling Tools section.

### Planning the Event

With the event date, you can set your objective and plan how to achieve it. Here is a Springfield College (SC) objective: "To host the annual Naismith Memorial Basketball Hall of Fame Spalding Hoophall Classic January 11-15, 2020." This tournament attracts more than 50 top-ranked high school basketball teams from all over the United States. Several colleges send scouts to SC to recruit players. Duke University Coach K and others have attended themselves to see specific players on the court. This is a large event requiring lots of planning. The tournament gives SC students real-world experience at facility and event management. We will discuss details of planning in the Planning and Controlling Sports section.

### Coordinating the Event

With the venue established, you often need various types of equipment to host the event, which may require rental, purchase, and storage. The event manager often needs to transport, assemble, erect, and store equipment. You may need to coordinate with facilities managers to have them perform some of these tasks for your event. They are usually responsible for warehouse areas for equipment storage and distribution and for control systems for venues and equipment. They may also provide logistics in areas such as inventory management, storage, transportation, and equipment setup, and they may set up in-house stages, audio-visual equipment, and seating.

## Training

To host a safe, successful event without problems, you need an adequate number of competent people. You may need to provide training to some staff members, especially to new volunteers. Part of this training should include a rehearsal or walk-through to ensure that everyone and everything is coordinated and goes off as planned. Use the training knowledge and skills you developed in chapter 7.

## Promoting the Event

For a larger event that is open to the public, you need to promote it. You can get free word of mouth and social media ads, and you may be able to get local news media coverage. But your budget should include promotion expenses, even if you only have printed flyers and programs for the event. You may get professional help and take a marketing class to help you with your event using the four Ps of marketing: (1) product—the event, (2) place—the venue, (3) price—ticket price, (4) promotion—select it for the specific event.

Table 14.1 gives a partial list of the activities involved in planning the Maccabi Games for 1,000 athletes. The event management team must accomplish the following:

- Create an event budget in line with the overall budget allowances for events. For instance, how much money will be spent buying ping-pong tables or preparing the gymnasium floor for volleyball games?
- Find out whether the caterers being considered are licensed and insured. The caterer must be able to serve 1,000 athletes and provide foods that will appeal to teens. Also, the caterer must serve food quickly because the athletes have a very busy schedule.

## TABLE 14.1   Typical Activities in Planning the Maccabi Games

| People activities | Athletic activities | Financial activities |
|---|---|---|
| Forming an administrative games management team (games director, assistant games director) | Training coaches and players on the rules of compassion for other coaches, athletes, and spectators | Securing sponsorship from businesses and individuals—sponsorship at the game sponsor level (top sponsors) and the gold, silver, bronze, or patron sponsor levels |
| Forming operations committees to organize food, water, opening and closing ceremonies, transportation, and security | Conducting tryouts for teams | Developing budgets for all the administrative functions and athletic events |
| Recruiting coaches for each sport | Recruiting athletes for sports that do not have enough players | Managing cash activities that range from collecting entrance fees from the athletes to paying suppliers (such as the bus company and security forces) |
| Developing public relations material (optional—only if you want the games to have media exposure) | Organizing a caring-and-sharing event to allow athletes to take time out from competition to volunteer within their community | Determining final revenue and cost comparison after the games have ended and the athletes have returned home |

- Ask the caterer for a list of past clients, and check with those clients to make sure the caterer is reliable.
- Find out whether the caterer can accommodate various dietary restrictions. For instance, the Maccabi Games need to have kosher foods available for athletes who follow Jewish dietary laws.
- Plan evening social activities. Visiting local amusement parks, museums, and dance clubs costs money and requires security and transportation.
- Arrange for security. Police escorts to all events are required. Security at sporting events is monitored by having all athletes, coaches, and friends wear credentials around their necks at all times.
- Develop transportation networks to move all the athletes and coaches from venue to venue. All buses should be coordinated at a hub. Jewish Community Center buses need to run on tight schedules to ensure that athletes arrive at their events on time.

*What activities do you think are involved in planning for parking at a Maccabi event?*

## Managing the Event and Crowd Control

As discussed in chapter 13, if you have good plans with preliminary controls, the event should go well for *game-day operations*. Setup, including having everything everyone needs for the event, is an important part of staging a memorable event. It's time to park the cars, open the doors or gates, let the crowd enter the facility, and start the event. Crowd control is an important part of game-day operations.

Getting people into and out of the event must proceed as quickly and safely as possible, especially at large facilities such as pro sport stadiums and the Indianapolis Motor Speedway, which can accommodate 250,000 people. Moving people within the event venues is critical for some events, like Disney theme parks and Olympic Games.

Your success in managing the crowd is based on several factors that should be carried out according to your plans for the event. Your preliminary controls are now replaced by your concurrent controls to ensure that corrective action is taken quickly to solve any problems (chapter 13).

- *Training.* As stated, all the staff need to be well trained.
- *Communication.* The event manager needs to know what is going on at all times to quickly solve any problems. Having a central area helps coordinate people and activities.
- *Signs.* Informational signs, such as alcohol policies and prohibited items, let people know the rules before entering the venue. Directional road and parking signs get people to the venue. Signs tell people where to buy tickets, which entrance to use, where to find their seats, and where to exit. Other signs tell them where to find restrooms, concession stands, and first aid stations.
- *Seating and ADA.* Seating arrangements are based on ticket sales before and on the day of the event and can be reserved seat or open seating. Managing this function includes helping people to enter the venue and find their seats, and for this, large signs help. Special seating areas and facility accommodations must meet the Americans with Disabilities Act (ADA) requirements.
- *Disruptive people.* Event managers want a safe and enjoyable event for everyone, so disruptive people need to be dealt with correctly. Mishandling disruptive people can result in violence, damage, and even a lawsuit. During large events, only trained professionals (police and security guards) should confront and eject disruptive, unruly people who may be under the influence of alcohol or drugs.
- *Emergency planning.* You need to be ready to mitigate the effects of an emergency quickly. Hopefully, you will not have to deal with a power loss, severe weather, medical problems, natural disasters, fires, bomb threats, or terrorist activities.

## Post-Event Tasks

Well, the event is over, but your work as a facility or event manager isn't. Here are some of the post-event tasks.

- *Crowd control.* You need to get people out of the venue as quickly and safely as possible, and signs help. This may include car crowd control out of the parking lot.
- *Breakdown.* Anything set up for the event, including signs and banners, audio and video equipment, stages, and extra seats, must be taken down and moved before the next event can be set up and staged. Any rented items must be returned on time to avoid going over budget with extra charges.
- *Cleanup.* If you've been to a pro game or major event, you've seen the concession stand papers and containers everywhere. If you use a professional cleaning service, it should be in the budget.
- *Evaluation.* The management team assesses how well the event went according to plans. Plans for improvement and plans to avoid repeating the same problems are documented and implemented in the planning of the next event.
- *Financials.* Revenues and expenses are calculated to determine the profits or losses from the event. Any revenue sharing or expense payments take place in a timely manner in compliance with contractual obligations.

We don't expect you to become an expert facilities and event manager just by reading about it, but you should now have a better understanding of what it takes to plan and manage a large event. There is a good chance that part of your sport management career will include some type of facilities and event management. There are lots of internship and job opportunities in this field.

Now that you have an overview of facilities and events, let's get into some of the details of how to plan and control sports events, forecast revenues, and use scheduling tools. We end the chapter with suggestions for time management systems and techniques to help you get more done in less time with better results.

# Planning and Controlling Sports

There is an old saying, "When you fail to plan, you plan to fail." It is also said that setting objectives improves performance.[8] Research supports both of these statements;[9] there is a link between planning and performance.[10] With regard to facility and event management, in this section we discuss planning dimensions, standing plans and single-use plans, contingency plans, why managers don't plan and control, and flags that indicate poor planning and controlling.

## Planning Dimensions

Plans are characterized by five dimensions, as shown in table 14.2. Chapter 4 covered the first four dimensions; here we cover the operational repetitiveness dimension. Note that upper-level managers use single-use planning more often than do first-level and middle

### TABLE 14.2 The Five Dimensions of Plans

| Management level | Type of plan | Scope | Time | Repetitiveness |
|---|---|---|---|---|
| Upper and middle | Strategic | Broad | Long range | Single-use plan |
| Middle and lower | Operational | Narrow | Short range | Standing plan |

managers, who typically use standing plans. So the facility and event management team focuses on single-use plans (programs and budgets) for the one-time event, and the operations managers implement the plan on game day through their staff using standing plans (policies, procedures, and rules) related to all events.

## Standing Plans and Single-Use Plans

Plans are either standing plans, which are designed to be used repeatedly, or single-use plans, which are designed to be used just once. Figure 14.1 gives the different uses for standing and single-use plans.

### Standing Plans

**Standing plans** are the policies, procedures, and rules for handling routine issues or situations that arise repeatedly.[11] These plans save everyone involved valuable time because the plans are used over and over, and they guide future decision making.

**Policies** are general guidelines for decision making. Managers develop policies to help the organization to achieve its mission and objectives;[12] policies guide employee behavior as they interact with other employees, customers and fans, and other stakeholders.[13] External groups such as governments, labor unions, and accrediting associations also dictate certain policies. Examples of typical policy statements are, "We create a fun, enjoyable environment for our fans" and "Our ticketing, sport merchandise, and concessions staff provide quality, friendly service." Notice that policy statements are intentionally general—managers have much discretion in how they implement policy. As a manager, your daily decisions will be guided by policies. It will be your job to interpret, apply, and explain company policies to your team.

**Procedures** (also called standard operating procedures and methods) are sequences of actions to be followed to achieve an objective. Procedures are more specific than policies;[14] they entail a series of steps for completing a task.[15] Procedures ensure that recurring, routine situations are handled in a consistent, predetermined manner while saving time.[16] Large sport organizations typically develop procedures for setting up for game day, such as changing over the hockey rink to the basketball court. Ticket sales, merchandise purchasing and inventory, grievances, and other regular activities follow set procedures.

**Rules** state exactly what should or should not be done. Rules and regulations are set to govern employee, customer, and fan behavior.[17] In addition to the company, the government and sport organizations such as the NCAA develop rules. As you can see from the following examples, rules do not allow for discretion or leeway:[18] "No shoes on the ice." "No smoking or eating in the locker room." "Helmets are required on the field." Rule violations require disciplinary action.[19]

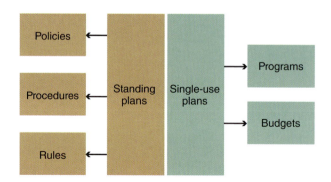

**FIGURE 14.1**  Uses for standing and single-use plans.

It is important that you distinguish between the three types of standing plans so that you know when you can do something your way and when you cannot. As a sport manager, you will be responsible for

**TIME-OUT 1** Give an example of a policy, procedure, and rule from an organization you work for or play for.

establishing policies and enforcing procedures and rules consistently. Standing plans are especially important in facility and event management. So treat everyone fairly with consistent behavior.[20] Use the coaching and disciplining skills you developed in chapter 13.

### Single-Use Plans

**Single-use plans** include programs and budgets that address nonrepetitive situations. Single-use plans, unlike standing plans, are developed for a specific purpose and most likely will not be used again in the same form. However, an effective single-use plan may become a model for future events, programs, budgets, or contracts. The plan for building the new Yankee Stadium was a single-use plan, which also required controls.

College teams making it to March Madness Sweet 16 and pro teams getting into the playoffs and the NFL Super Bowl build up their merchandise inventories so they can increase sales. Nike plans for the Olympics by increasing its inventory of selected special items. But these plans for the one-time events are often based on prior experience.

A **program** describes a set of activities designed to accomplish an objective over a specified period, which can be short (days, weeks, months) or long (years, decades); an event is a type of program. Programs are set

What sorts of planning activities might Stu Greene have engaged in to accomplish his objectives?

**TIME-OUT 2** Give an example of a program your firm or team has in place, and assess whether it was set up following the guidelines we have described.

up for objectives as varied as hosting events, developing products, expanding facilities, and taking advantage of new opportunities in the environment. We will discuss methods you can use to develop programs, including events, in the Scheduling Tools section.

We examined **budgets** in detail in chapter 13. Budgets are the funds allocated to operate a department or program for a fixed period, including an event. Budgets are crucial tools in both planning (they help you to develop realistic plans) and control (they help you assess how implementation is going), and you need to operate within your budget. One year's or one event's budget is the foundation for the next. One of Emily Shotland's most important responsibilities is going to be to ensure that the Maccabi Games are held within their budget.

## Contingency Plans

You develop a great event plan. Guess what? There will be times when things go wrong that are out of your control and that prevent you from achieving your objectives.[21] Maybe the computer on which all the ticket information is stored goes down, or your star player is sidelined for the season because of injuries. Just the fact that something is uncontrollable doesn't mean it is not foreseeable. Effective managers have contingency plans for just such situations. **Contingency plans** are alternative plans that can be implemented if uncontrollable events occur. They are also called *scenario plans*—if this happens, we will do that.

**◄ LEARNING OUTCOME 4**

Explain when, and why, contingency plans are necessary.

Outdoor events are often contingent on the weather, and games are delayed or canceled. Wise coaches and managers take great pains to develop backup players and employees who will be ready to step in should a first-string player or employee be sidelined for any reason. MLB managers keep close tabs on promising minor league players who are their contingency plans for sidelined players.

To develop a contingency plan for your department or team, answer these three questions:

1. What might go wrong?
2. How can I prevent it from happening?
3. If it does occur, what can I do to minimize its effect?

Pose questions 1 and 2 to everyone involved. Your answer to question 3 is your contingency plan. It is also a good idea to talk to others both inside and outside your organization who have implemented similar facility and event plans. They may

**TIME-OUT 3**

Describe a situation in which a contingency plan is appropriate, and then briefly describe a possible plan for it.

have encountered problems you haven't thought of, and their contingency plans can serve as models for yours.

## Planning and Controlling Paradox

Although we know the importance of planning and controlling, managers don't always take the time to develop effective plans and controls. Why? And what are the signs and consequences of poor planning and controlling?

### Why Managers Don't Plan and Control

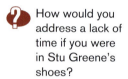

How would you address a lack of time if you were in Stu Greene's shoes?

Stu Greene notes that by far the most common reason managers don't plan is that they don't have time to plan. It's a catch-22 because many crises can be avoided, or controlled, if you carve out time for planning. Why do so many managers find time to do a job over but don't find the time to do it right in the first place (plan and control, in other words)? Managers who don't plan find themselves scrambling from one fire to the next.

Managers who plan have fewer crises; they are in better control of their teams and departments. Planning is a continuous activity, and plans don't have to be complicated or take lots of your time. Developing good standing and contingency plans really helps.

## APPLYING THE CONCEPT 14.1

### Categorizing Plans

Categorize each of the following items or statements as follows:

a. objective
b. policy
c. procedure
d. rule
e. program
f. budget

_____ 1. Programs should build a healthy spirit, mind, and body for all (YMCA).

_____ 2. An athletic director has a plan to improve the performance of the college's women's swim team.

_____ 3. We will increase our attendance by 10 percent next year.

_____ 4. Employees will be given a two-month maternity leave after the birth of a child.

_____ 5. This is the cost to operate your department next month.

_____ 6. Safety glasses are required for touring the new sport arena's construction site.

_____ 7. Leaves of absence must be approved by the manager and the forms submitted to the personnel office one month in advance of their effective dates.

_____ 8. Keep the reject rate on sneakers under 1 percent.

_____ 9. One thousand dollars has been allotted for conducting a facilities management seminar.

If you are tempted to skip the planning stage, remember the adage, "When you fail to plan, you plan to fail." Emily Shotland agrees, so she makes sure to allot time for this all-important activity. Learning to plan is a part of time management, as we will see in the last section of this chapter.

### *Flags That Indicate Poor Planning and Controlling*

Have you ever had a teacher, coach, or boss show up late or without a plan and waste your time while they figured out what you and the others were going to do? Signs of poor planning you may have encountered and the negative consequences include the following:

- Unmet objectives: Deadlines, delivery dates, and schedules are not met.
- Continual crises: Every job is a rush job, and overtime is overused to complete jobs.
- Idle resources: Physical resources are idle, financial resources are accumulating interest and not being put to immediate use, or staff are kept waiting for the manager to assign tasks. Coach Lussier's philosophy is that every athlete should be actively practicing, not sitting around waiting or fooling around.
- Lack of resources: Resources are not available when needed.
- Duplication: The same task is done more than once.

**TIME-OUT 4** How would you rate the planning ability of a current or past boss or coach? Give examples of inadequate planning.

# Sales Forecasting Techniques

Forecasting is the process of predicting what will happen in the future. Managers pay particular attention to sales forecasts to predict consumer expenditures on sport, as does Nike in predicting extra sales for the Olympics. It is generally easier to accurately predict sales for regularly scheduled games than for special events. In this section, we discuss qualitative and quantitative sales forecasting techniques.

◀ **LEARNING OUTCOME 5**
Discuss how sales forecasts shape strategy.

A **sales forecast** predicts the dollar amount of product that will be sold during a specified period. Accurate sales forecasts are crucial in planning because many activities hinge on them—staffing and laying off workers, ordering in adequate supplies to meet production needs, and avoiding under- and overstocking. Marketing departments typically forecast short-term sales a year out. The forecasts are reviewed by the sales manager, who submits them for approval and possible adjustment by upper management. Marketing then uses the forecasts to set sales quotas.

The operations department uses the forecasts to decide how much product or service to produce. Marketing also monitors inventory levels (production and customer) to adjust the forecasts as needed. Finance uses forecasts to determine how much money the organization will take in so that the finance team can budget expenditures, and also to determine how much money the organization will need to borrow to cover short-term and long-term expenses. The human resources department uses the forecasts to increase staffing or plan for layoffs. The pro team will use the ticket sales number to forecast its net revenues (which will also include advertising and media sales forecasts and team merchandise sales forecasts). Revenue forecasts help the team to determine its budget for acquiring new talent.

Companies use total industry sales to calculate their market share. **Market share** is the organization's percentage of total industry sales. Nike has the largest share of the global market for athletic shoe sales. Professional and trade publications forecast industry sales numbers to help organizations analyze the environment and forecast their own sales.

Organizations also take local conditions, especially local competition, into account when they forecast sales.

Sales forecasting techniques are either qualitative or quantitative. **Qualitative forecasting techniques** primarily use subjective judgment, intuition, experience, and opinion to predict sales. (Some math is also used.) **Quantitative forecasting techniques** use objective, mathematical techniques and past sales data to predict sales. Organizations typically combine quantitative and qualitative techniques to increase accuracy.

## Qualitative Sales Forecasting

As table 14.3 shows, qualitative techniques include individual opinion, a jury of executive opinion, sales force composites, customer composites, operating unit composites, and surveys. Only qualitative techniques can be used for new products or by new companies because no past sales data exist on which to base a quantitative forecast (although new companies can be influenced by all sorts of quantitative data if they are going into an established industry).

- *Individual opinion.* We all use our personal experience, intuition, and past events to predict what we think will happen in the future. A person starting a new business alone has no option but to form an educated (based on industry analysis), individual opinion.
- *Jury of executive opinion.* A group of managers or experts pool their opinions to forecast sales. A typical example is a group meeting in which ideas are shared and an attempt is made to reach consensus on the sales forecast. It is often used in business partnerships, which is the form of ownership of some professional franchises.
- *Sales force composite.* This approach combines forecasts made by each sales rep; these are then totaled to give the composite forecast. Managers often balance the composite with other forecast techniques. Sales force composites work well when sales reps sell relatively expensive products (or total orders) with a clear-cut customer base or territory.
- *Customer composite.* The purchase forecasts of major customers are combined. Managers often balance the customer composite with other forecast techniques. It works well when an organization has relatively few customers with large-volume sales.
- *Operating unit composite.* Businesses with multiple operating units, such as chain stores like Dick's and Modell's, commonly predict the sales for each store and then add them to forecast total composite company sales. A business with multiple departments or products (such as golf, baseball, soccer, and clothing departments) can treat each department or product as an operating unit and combine them to create a total forecast.

 In what situations do you think the Maccabi Games staff would use qualitative forecasting techniques?

TIME-OUT 5 — Describe a situation in which your firm or team might forecast sales or team growth using qualitative techniques.

## TABLE 14.3  Summary of Common Sales Forecasting

| Qualitative (subjective) | Quantitative (objective) |
| --- | --- |
| Individual opinion | Past sales |
| Jury of executive opinion | Time series |
| Sales force composite | Regression |
| Customer composite | |
| Operating unit composite | |
| Survey | |

• *Survey.* This technique uses mail or email questionnaires or telephone or personal interviews to predict future purchases. A sample of a population is surveyed, and a forecast for the entire population is made based on the responses. Questionnaire data collected are often used for statistical quantitative analysis.

Stu and the administrative committee of the Maccabi Games interviewed the leaders of a local community to gauge their interest in hosting the games. The interview results indicated that the community leaders weren't sure if their community was large enough to host an event of this magnitude. From this information, Stu determined that his strategy would be to convince the community that by working together they would be able to properly host the games.

## Quantitative Sales Forecasting

Quantitative techniques include past sales, time series, and regression. Qualitative techniques can be combined with quantitative ones as long as the products and companies have existed long enough to accrue an adequate database for sales. Time series and regression techniques require at least a year of data, and a longer period will give better results. This technique amounts to business forecasting by data, and although numbers can't tell the future, data do help.

◀ **LEARNING OUTCOME 8**
Explain how past sales and time series forecasting techniques differ.

• *Past sales.* This technique assumes that past sales will be repeated or can be subjectively adjusted for environmental factors. The Red Sox have sold around two million tickets annually for the past 20 years no matter how well the team has been performing on the field. Slight structural changes to venerable Fenway Park facilities allowed the team to increase sales and to continue to consistently sell out each game. The Sox's past sales therefore indicated a strong likelihood that this pattern would continue.

• *Time series.* **Time series** predict future sales by extending the trend line of past sales into the future. Sales data are collected weekly, monthly, quarterly, or yearly and then plotted to show the trend. The trend line can be extended by hand (an upward-trending line implies increasing sales, a horizontal line implies flat sales, and a downward-trending line implies decreasing sales) and the sales estimated manually, but computer time series programs are much more accurate. Time series are also used to plot seasonal trends. With time series, adjustments for environmental factors are still made, but they are more objective.

• *Regression.* Regression (using line of best fit), which is beyond the scope of this book, is a mathematical modeling technique that helps you to minimize error as you find a line that best fits your sales data. Regression analysis therefore makes forecasts more accurate. As a manager, you will find regression analysis very useful (simple regression analysis is not especially difficult); make sure you master it in your statistics classes. A regression forecasting model is used to predict Minor League Baseball (MiLB) teams' ability to capture attendance and the long-term viability of a franchise.

 In what situations do you think Maccabi Games staff would use quantitative forecasting techniques?

Sport managers are combining forecasting techniques. Emily Shotland uses her experience at previous Maccabi Games to forecast what will be needed at upcoming games. For instance, you can use past data on the number of athletes at previous games and the amounts of food, housing, and security and the number of venues that were used. You can adjust these figures based on the number of athletes who will be competing in upcoming games.

 **TIME-OUT 6** Describe a situation in which your team might forecast sales or team growth using quantitative techniques.

### Sales Forecasting Techniques

Choose the most appropriate forecast techniques for the following organizations:

- a. individual opinion
- b. jury of executive opinion
- c. sales force composite
- d. customer composite
- e. operating unit composite
- f. survey
- g. past sales
- h. time series analysis
- i. regression analysis

_____ 10. Dick's Sporting Goods footwear chain

_____ 11. AND1 sports apparel with a sales force that calls on specific stores in the sales area

_____ 12. A sole proprietor who sells her own new, very different sport cream for pain

_____ 13. Jim and Betty's mom-and-pop sport store

_____ 14. Nike sneakers

_____ 15. Ticket sales to a game between your championship team and last year's second-place finisher

# Scheduling Tools

**LEARNING OUTCOME 9** ▶

Know when to use planning sheets, Gantt charts, and PERT diagrams.

**Scheduling** is the process of listing essential activities in sequence with the time needed to complete each activity. Effective schedulers define the objective to be accomplished, break it into finite, doable tasks, and make sure resources are available when needed. The details of the schedule answer the "what," "when," "where," "how," and "who" questions. Emily needs to schedule a number of things for the Maccabi Games. When will the games take place (exact dates and times)? Where are the venues located? What size buses will be needed? Who will greet the athletes and make sure they are picked up and dropped off properly?

All managers schedule resources, including their time. So, let's start with two simple, fundamental time management tools you can use to schedule your daily activities—your *calendars* and *to-do lists*. Don't underestimate their value in maximizing your efficiency. Planning calendars can be bought in every office supply store; a to-do list is as close as a scrap of paper; and as you know, you can use your smartphone, and there are plenty of apps to help you. Use them.

A wide variety of business scheduling software is available but is beyond the scope of this book. Keeping it simple, we will explore planning sheets, Gantt charts, and PERT diagrams using the old-fashioned paper and pencil in this section. Part of the benefit of using these visual tools is that we remember what we see better than what we hear.[22]

## Planning Sheets

**Planning sheets** state an objective and list the sequence of activities, when each activity will begin and end, and who will complete each activity to meet the objective. The Maccabi Operational Plan shows a planning sheet for a monthly marketing letter developed by Stu for staff and volunteers involved in the Maccabi Games. Before continuing, review the operational plan and identify the five planning dimensions involved in this plan (table 14.2). (The answers are at the bottom of the plan.) Planning sheets work best with single activities that are fairly simple, and they are accomplished in independent, sequential steps.

- Use the Maccabi Operational Plan as a template for the planning sheets you use. Note that you start with a clear objective (chapter 4). Then you fill in who will be responsible for achieving the objective, the starting and ending dates, the priority, and the control checkpoints for monitoring progress.

- Next, list the sequence of activities in stating what, where, how, resources needed, and so on in the first column of the planning sheet. In the second and third columns, place the start and end time for each step. The fourth column indicates the person responsible for each step.

TIME-OUT 7 Give an example of one of your firm's or team's plans that could be effectively tracked by a planning sheet.

---

## Maccabi Operational Plan

Objective: To mail a personalized letter to everybody involved in the Maccabi Games by the 15th of each month

- Person responsible: Joel
- Starting date: 1st of each month
- Due date: 15th of each month
- Priority: High
- Control checkpoints: 7th and 12th of each month

| Activities | Start | End | Who |
|---|---|---|---|
| 1. Write letter | 1st | 2nd | Stu |
| 2. Email letter for mass production | 3rd or 4th | | Stu |
| 3. Print letters on Maccabi stationery using computer's mail merge feature to print names and addresses on letters and envelopes | 5th | 9th | Joel |
| 4. Put Stu's stamped signature on each letter for a personal look | 10th | 11th | Joel |
| 5. Stuff envelopes | 10th | 11th | Joel |
| 6. Bundle to meet bulk-mailing specifications | 12th | 13th | Joel |
| 7. Deliver to U.S. Postal Bulk Mail Center | 13th | | Joel |
| 8. Mail letters | 14th or 15th | | U.S. Postal Service |

Five planning dimensions are used as follows: (1) This plan was developed by Stuart. Stuart is the top-level manager who works closely with Maccabi headquarters in New York. (2) Plan type—operational. (3) Plan scope—narrow. (4) Time frame—short range. (5) Repetitiveness—standing plan.

---

## Gantt Charts

Popularized by Henry Gantt in the early 1900s, **Gantt charts** use bar graphs to illustrate progress on a project. Activities are shown vertically, and time is shown horizontally. The resources to be allocated, such as people or machines, are shown on the vertical axis. Alternatively, a variety of department projects can be shown on the same chart. Gantt charts, like planning sheets, are appropriate for plans with independent, sequential steps. Two advantages of Gantt charts over planning sheets are that the chart's control is built in (progress can be seen at a glance) and you can view multiple projects on one chart. This is very helpful when you are prioritizing and scheduling activities that use the same resources.

TIME-OUT 8 Give an example of one of your team's plans that could be tracked effectively using a Gantt chart.

Figure 14.2 is a hypothetical Gantt chart for multiple orders at a manufacturing company in its operations department. Each bar represents the start-to-end time, and the filled-in part represents order completion to date. The chart shows at a glance how orders are progressing. Knowing instantly when a project is behind schedule is crucial for taking corrective action. Assume that "today" is day 1 of week 3 in May (the end of the dark color of the bar should be directly under the 3 to be on schedule). What is the status of each of the four projects on the chart in figure 14.2? The answer is in the figure caption.

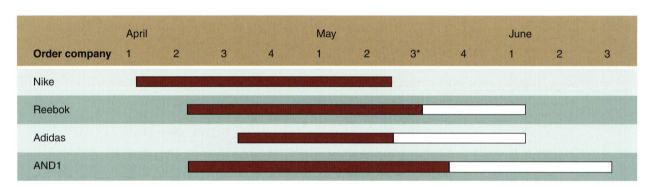

**FIGURE 14.2** Multiple-project Gantt chart (order by week). *Today. The Nike project is done; Reebok is on schedule to be completed in June; Adidas is behind schedule and needs to become a high priority; AND1 is ahead of schedule.

## Performance Evaluation and Review Technique (PERT)

PERT is more complex because it includes two types of activities. Independent activities can be performed simultaneously, whereas dependent activities cannot begin until a preceding activity has been completed. The planning sheet and Gantt chart are useful tools when the activities follow each other in a dependent series. However, when activities are both dependent on and independent of each other, and the event is more complex, PERT diagrams are more appropriate. **PERT (Performance Evaluation and Review Technique) diagrams** highlight the interdependence of activities by diagramming their "network." Figure 14.3 shows a PERT diagram.

As shown in figure 14.3, the PERT diagram includes activities, time, arrows, and the critical path.

- *Activities.* There are 10 activities labeled A to J to be completed for this event.
- *Time.* It is measured in days; activity A will take two days (A-2), for example.
- *Arrows.* These show the sequence of activities that must be followed to the end of the event numbered 1-9.

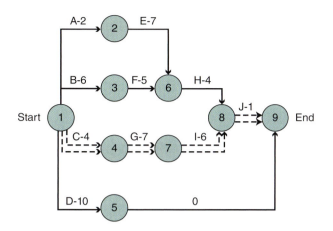

**FIGURE 14.3** PERT diagram.

- *Critical path.* The **critical path** tracks the most time-consuming series of activities and therefore determines the length of time it will take to complete a project. The double arrows show this project should take 18 days to complete. Any delay in completing the critical path delays the entire project.

Many organizations focus on shortening the time it takes to complete each activity (time-based competition). The cost for each activity can also be tracked in a PERT diagram.

 **TIME-OUT 9** Give an example of one of your team's plans that could be tracked effectively using a PERT diagram.

Let's compare the three scheduling tools. Gantt is the only one that diagrams multiple activities. The planning sheets and Gantt charts are typically used to develop procedures for routine standing plans, whereas PERT diagrams are more commonly used with single-use plans for complex projects with dependent activities. However, all three can be used for standing and single-use plans. Multiple tools can be used for the same complex event. The Maccabi Games could use a PERT diagram for the overall event, but it could also include several planning sheets, like the one included to mail a letter, for various activities.

You can develop a template for planning sheets, and there are computerized versions of Gantt charts and PERT diagrams. Skill-Builder 14.1 in the web study guide gives you practice in constructing a Gantt chart and a PERT diagram by hand.

## APPLYING THE CONCEPT 14.3

### Scheduling Tools

Select the most appropriate scheduling tool for each situation:

a. planning sheet
b. Gantt chart
c. PERT diagram

_____ 16. A high school with six teams and three practice fields

_____ 17. Planning the construction of a new sport arena

_____ 18. Developing procedures for a new way to track ticket sales

_____ 19. A plan to restructure the athletic department at a university

_____ 20. Scheduling the use of the YMCA's weight training rooms and courses

# Time Management

How often do you have so much to do that you feel like there isn't enough time?[23] Time is valuable, but we tend to waste it, on average an hour a day.[24] Time is measured objectively—we all have the same amount of time—but how we spend it is subjective. How much of your time can you devote to playing and watching sports and all of your other activities?

**Time management** enables people to get more done in less time with better results. Time management skills have a direct effect on your productivity and on your career.[25] The idea is to work smarter, not harder, or to work less and do more. The good news is that time management skills can be developed. This section is all about time, and it shows you how to analyze your use of time, learn a time management system, and select from 50 time management techniques to improve your time management skills.

## Analyzing Your Use of Time

**LEARNING OUTCOME 10** ▶

Use a time log.

The first step in controlling your time is to figure out how you spend (and waste) time.[26] Most people who keep a time log confess that they didn't realize how much time they waste.[27]

### Keep a Time Log

The time log tracks your daily activities and helps you figure out "where all the time goes." You can use figure 14.4 as a template for creating your own time logs. Track your time every day for one or two weeks. (Make sure these are typical weeks. Tracking atypical weeks won't be of much use.) Take the time log with you throughout the day, and fill in each 15-minute time slot, if possible.

Try to keep the time log with you throughout the day. Fill in the Description column for each 15-minute time slot, if possible, describing what you did. If you are technically inclined, there are software programs for PCs and apps for smartphones that will track the amount of time you use these devices.[28]

If you use a computer much of the day, there are services you can purchase for a low monthly fee or download for free. Tools such as those available at www.slifeweb.com, www.rescuetime.com, https://manictime.com, and http://getklok.com/ will help you keep track of your time on the computer and improve your time management. Just knowing that the lengths of their sessions on Facebook or other websites are going to be recorded makes people think twice about the visit.

### Analyze It

After logging your time, you need to analyze your data. Using the following evaluation list and the abbreviations noted in parentheses, review your logs and answer the questions. We give you ideas for solutions in the following discussion, but first take a moment and annotate your time logs.

- How did you spend most of your time? Note how much time you spent on your high priorities (HP) and on your low priorities (LP).
- Where did you spend too much time (TT)?
- Where could you have spent more time? That is, where did you not spend enough time (NT)?
- What major interruptions (I) kept you from doing what you wanted to get done? Do you interrupt yourself by constantly checking your phone and email and getting sidetracked doing unimportant things, rather than staying with important things until they are done? Unnecessary interruptions cost the U.S. economy more than $997 billion a year.[29] Also, recall that multitasking slows you down when each task requires you to think. Why not turn off all the electronic devices you don't need (and

| Daily time log for: Day _____ Date _____ | | |
|---|---|---|
| **Starting time** | **Description** | **Evaluation of time use** |
| 8:00<br><br>8:15<br><br>8:30<br><br>8:45 | | |
| 9:00<br><br>9:15<br><br>9:30<br><br>9:45 | | |
| 10:00<br>(etc., to<br>ending time) | | |

**FIGURE 14.4**   Daily time log.

the noises they make) until you complete important tasks?[30] What tasks could you delegate to someone else (D)? To whom can you delegate these tasks? (You learned about developing delegation skills in chapter 5.)

- How much time does your boss control (B)? How much time do your employees control (E)? How much time do others outside your department control (O)? How much time do you actually control (M)?

- How can you gain more control of your own time?

- Look for crisis situations (C). Were they caused by something you did or did not do? Do you have recurring crises? What changes can you make to help eliminate recurring crises? Do you have effective contingency plans?

- Look for habits, patterns, and tendencies. Do they help you get the job done or prevent you from getting the job done? How can you change them to your advantage?

TIME-OUT **10** Use your time log data to identify your three biggest time wasters. Read the following discussion, and develop some strategies for minimizing them.

- List three to five of your biggest time wasters (W). What can you do to eliminate them?

- Ask yourself, "How can I manage my time more efficiently?"

## A Time Management System

Are you accomplishing all the important things you need to get done? If not, the time management system we present here has a proven track record with thousands of managers. Try it for three weeks. After that, you can tailor it to your own needs.

◀ **LEARNING OUTCOME 11**

Manage your time better.

### The Four Foundations of Effective Time Management

The problem we all face is not a shortage of time—we all have the same 24 hours in a day—but rather the ineffective use of our time. Here are four things you can do to improve your time management skills.

- *Prioritize.* Seldom, if ever, do we have enough time to do everything we want to do. However, there is usually enough time to do what's really important. Employees confess to wasting time at work doing unimportant and irrelevant activities, like spending time on Facebook.[31] Don't confuse being busy with time-wasting activities with accomplishing important priorities.[32] Do your most important priorities well,[33] and eliminate time wasters.[34] Make it a rule to assign a priority to each task, and do the most important thing first (without unnecessary interruptions).[35] Work on getting at least 90 minutes of uninterrupted time a day to accomplish top priorities.[36]

- *Set objectives.* We've been here before (see chapter 4), but it's important because we should know the end result we want before we try to complete a task. People who get things done set objectives. Write down your objectives—the important things you need to accomplish.

- *Plan.* Plan how you are going to get your objectives done before taking action to complete a task. Don't skip this step.

- *Schedule.* Make a schedule each week and workday, and complete your scheduled priorities.[37]

### A Three-Step Time Management System

Time management systems all boil down to two things—develop a game plan and stick to it. **Time management systems** involve planning each week, scheduling each week, and scheduling each day.

1. *Plan each week.* Ideally, you will plan the coming week on the last day of the current week before you leave for the day so that on Monday, you will be ready to go. However, some jobs require that you plan the week on the first day of the week. Using figure 14.5 as a template, think about your objectives, and list the ones you think you can accomplish in the week. Focus on important nonroutine tasks, not routine ones you do weekly or daily.

Plan for the week of: _____

Objectives:

| Activities | Priority | Time needed | Day to schedule |
|---|---|---|---|
| Total time for the week | | | |

**FIGURE 14.5** Weekly planner.

After setting a few major objectives, list the activities you need to accomplish for each objective in column 1. If an objective calls for multiple activities, use one of the three scheduling tools given earlier. Prioritize each activity. High priorities must be done first (see chapter 5 on setting priorities).

In the last two columns, fill in the time you think you will need and the most promising day to do each task. Total the time you have allotted for your objectives for the week. Is this time realistic given that you still need to do routine tasks and deal with unexpected events? With experience, you will become more accurate about what you can and cannot accomplish in a given week. Planning to do more than you can actually get done is not only frustrating—it guarantees failure, so focus on the important things you get done, not what is left to do that is less important, anyway.[38] Not planning enough activities, of course, gives you time to waste.

2. *Schedule each week.* Scheduling your work is critical because it gets you organized and focused on completing your priorities.[39] Make your schedule as you plan your week or do it afterward, whichever you prefer. These two tasks should take 30 minutes or less. Using figure 14.6, fill in time slots that are already spoken for, such as standing weekly meetings. Next, schedule events over which you have control, like performance appraisals and classwork. Most managers leave about 50 percent of their week unscheduled to deal with unexpected events. Your job and classwork may require more or less unscheduled time. With practice, you will find the balance that works for you.

The key to time management is not to prioritize your schedule but to schedule your priorities. In other words, control your schedule; don't let it control you. Allocate time to get your important objectives accomplished, and don't get diverted with less important activities.

3. *Schedule each day.* At the end of each day, schedule the following day. Or you can schedule your day first thing in the morning. This should take 15 minutes or less. Base the day's schedule on your plan and schedule for the week, using figure 14.7 as a template. Daily schedules are in essence your to-do list for each day, and they help you to adjust for unplanned events. Pencil in already scheduled activities like meetings. As we noted earlier, be flexible, leaving time for unscheduled and unexpected events. Here are some other scheduling tips:

- Don't be too optimistic; schedule enough time to do each task. Many managers find that doubling their initial estimate works well. Don't despair; you will improve with practice.

Schedule for the week of: _____

| Time | Mon. | Tues. | Wed. | Thurs. | Fri. |
|------|------|-------|------|--------|------|
| 8:00 | | | | | |
| 8:15 | | | | | |
| 8:30 | | | | | |
| 8:45 | | | | | |
| 9:00 (etc., to ending time) | | | | | |

**FIGURE 14.6**   Weekly schedule.

| Schedule for the day of: _____ |
| **Time** |
| 8:00 |
| 8:15 |
| 8:30 |
| 8:45 |
| 9:00 |
| (etc., to ending time) |

**FIGURE 14.7**  Daily schedule.

- Don't procrastinate. It usually leads to more stress and results in lower-quality work completed at the last minute or late. Procrastinating can also cause problems in your relationships, jobs, finances, and health.[40] So, as Nike says, "Just Do It!" Complete only one thinking task at a time. Don't *multitask* because it's a time waster;[41] we explain why in the next section. Some people seem to get an incredible number of things done—but as the late great Peter Drucker said, if you watch them closely, you will see they have the discipline to laser in on one task at a time. So, tackle one task at a time in priority sequence.

- Schedule high-priority items during your "prime time," the time when you are at your best. For most people this is early in the morning. Others start slow and build momentum throughout the day. Figure out your own prime time, and use it to work on tasks that require your full attention. Do routine tasks, such as checking your mail, at other times.

- Try to schedule a time for unexpected events. Tell employees to see you with routine matters during a set time, such as 3 p.m. Have people call you, and plan to call them, during this set time. Depending on your job, don't be checking your phone and email constantly; do so at set times to avoid interruptions in getting your high-priority items done.

- Don't perform an unscheduled task without determining its priority. If you are working on a high-priority item and a medium-priority matter arises, let it wait. Even so-called urgent matters can often wait.

Time management works well for managers whose jobs entail a variety of nonrecurring tasks. For managers and employees who deal primarily with routine tasks, the time management system we've outlined here may not be necessary. If you are in a routine situation, a good to-do list that prioritizes items (shown in chapter 5) may be all you need. Skill-Builder 14.2 in the web study guide helps you to analyze your time use. Forms similar to those in figures 14.4 through 14.7 can be purchased in pad, book, and even computer versions. You can also copy these examples.

## Multitasking

Before we discuss multitasking, complete Self-Assessment 14.1 to determine how it affects you. Now, regardless of your multitasking score, we discuss why multitasking slows you down, your attention span and concentration, smartphones, and how to effectively multitask.

## SELF-ASSESSMENT 14.1

### Are You a Multitasker?

Identify how often you experience each statement.

1 = infrequently
2 = occasionally
3 = sometimes
4 = frequently
5 = most of the time

\_\_\_\_\_ 1. I'm bored.

\_\_\_\_\_ 2. I check my smartphone or other screens while working or doing schoolwork.

\_\_\_\_\_ 3. My mind wanders when I'm trying to pay attention to someone or reading.

\_\_\_\_\_ 4. I do more than one work task or schoolwork assignment at the same time.

\_\_\_\_\_ 5. I have a hard time concentrating on one task for an hour.

\_\_\_\_\_ 6. I get distracted or interrupted while working or doing schoolwork.

Add up your score and place it here (6 to 30): _____. The higher your score, the more you are negatively affected by multitasking. If your score is high, you may want to change some of your habits to improve your time management.

### How Multitasking Slows You Down

First, as supported by research, although you may not want to believe it, the human mind is not capable of doing more than one thinking task at a time.[42] Think of it like a single-screen TV; you can't watch more than one show at a time. However, you can watch two shows during the same half hour by flipping back and forth between channels. You will get the gist of both shows, but you will lose some of the details that could be important. This is what happens every time you multitask.

Secondly, when you multitask things that require thinking, errors go way up, and it takes far longer to get the jobs done than if they were done sequentially.[43] You may think you are accomplishing two tasks at once, but you're not because you are switching back and forth. Each time you switch, it takes time to figure out where you left off on the last task, slowing your speed at completing each task, and the time loss increases with the complexity of the task, by 50 percent or more.[44]

### Your Attention Spans and Concentration When Multitasking

The ability to pay attention and concentrate are important skills for completing high-priority tasks with high levels of performance. Unfortunately, employers today complain that young college grads have short attention spans and can't concentrate for very long, so they can't follow instructions. Why? One of the problems is multitasking because it attacks our attention span by decreasing our ability to concentrate for long. With things binging and bonging and tweeting at you, you can't concentrate and think clearly.

Daily workplace interruptions and distractions, such as texts, phone calls, apps, or the arrival of email or social media alerts kill your ability to pay attention for very long.[45] Recall from chapter 10 that a major reason you get distracted and lose your concentration is the separation of your eyes and mind; they need to work together to concentrate at all.[46] Looking at your phone while receiving instructions doesn't work. Again, multitasking slows you down, but it also hurts your performance.

### Smartphones

Smartphones were praised as a revolutionary new productivity tool because they were supposed to save time, but they actually prove to do the opposite. Why? Because they lead to unproductive multitasking. Researchers found that on average, people look at their smartphones 221 times per day, or a total of over three hours—that's about once every four minutes.[47] How long can you go without looking at your smartphone? Try timing yourself, including incoming texts. If you really want to get those important priorities completed faster and more accurately, avoid multitasking.[48] Shut off your phone, stop or minimize other distractions, and do one important priority task at a time.[49]

### Effective Multitasking

I know you most likely can't give up multitasking. So, let's discuss how you can multitask effectively. First, realize that multitasking is a form of time management.[50] Here are some guidelines.

- *Know when it is not appropriate.* Thinking tasks, like reading, require your undivided attention. So don't multitask when your full attention should be on a single complex or important task because it will affect the quality of your work.

- *Limit interruptions.* Of all our interruptions, we interrupt ourselves around 45 percent of the time, such as checking our phone or social media.[51] Face it, most of those bings and bongs telling you to check your texts or email are usually less important than the high-priority task you are working on, and they can wait. If your job allows it, turn off all the electronics you don't need to perform a high-priority task.[52] Stay on the high-priority task for a set amount of time, say a half hour or a full hour. Only after the set time can you interrupt yourself by checking texts, emails, and so forth.

- *Limit distractions.* Like with the TV example, your mind can't listen to music and another thinking task at the same time. Your mind is either listening to the music or reading and bouncing back and forth. So music you like to listen to and especially TV are distracting. If you need background white noise sounds to overcome distractions, try music that you don't really like much so that you can ignore it, like classical instrumental music or ocean sounds. Or you can wear noise-canceling headphones.

- *Know when to use multitasking.* Save multitasking for simple tasks that do not require much thinking. Listen to music while checking your routine email and similar tasks. Checking texts, emails, and social media only after completing a high-priority task, or after a set amount of time, is effective multitasking. While watching an intermittent action sport, like football or baseball, pay attention to the game during the action. During the ads and between plays, don't read a chapter of this textbook, but do review your course notes and test yourself for exams (making three-by-five cards and testing yourself with them works great). Even if you miss the live play, you can watch the replay.

## Time Management Techniques

Self-Assessment 14.2 contains 50 time management techniques, many of which can be applied to multitasking—especially stopping interruptions and distractions. The techniques are arranged by management function. Planning and controlling are placed together because they are so closely related. Organizing and leading are separated.

 **TIME-OUT 11** Using your answers from Self-Assessment 14.2, choose the three most important techniques you should use. Explain how you will implement each technique.

## SELF-ASSESSMENT 14.2

# Time Management Techniques

Here are 50 ideas that you can use to improve your time management skills. Check the appropriate box for each idea.

| Time management techniques | Should do | Could do | Do not do | Does not apply to me |
|---|---|---|---|---|
| **Planning and controlling management functions** | | | | |
| 1. I use the time management system presented in the text. | ☐ | ☐ | ☐ | ☐ |
| 2. I use a to-do list and prioritize items on it. I do the important things rather than the "urgent" ones. | ☐ | ☐ | ☐ | ☐ |
| 3. I get an early and productive start on my top-priority items. | ☐ | ☐ | ☐ | ☐ |
| 4. I do only high-priority items and unpleasant or difficult tasks during my prime time. | ☐ | ☐ | ☐ | ☐ |
| 5. I don't spend time on unproductive activities to avoid or escape job-related anxiety. I get the job done. | ☐ | ☐ | ☐ | ☐ |
| 6. Throughout the day I ask myself, "Should I be doing this now?" | ☐ | ☐ | ☐ | ☐ |
| 7. I plan before I act. | ☐ | ☐ | ☐ | ☐ |
| 8. I do contingency planning—that is, I have plans in place for recurring crises. | ☐ | ☐ | ☐ | ☐ |
| 9. I am decisive. It is better to make a wrong decision than none at all. | ☐ | ☐ | ☐ | ☐ |
| 10. I schedule enough time to do the job right the first time. I try to be realistic about the amount of time it takes to do a job. | ☐ | ☐ | ☐ | ☐ |
| 11. I schedule a quiet hour during which my staff interrupts me only for true emergencies. I have someone take messages, or I ask people to call me back. | ☐ | ☐ | ☐ | ☐ |
| 12. I've established a quiet time for my team. I've found that the first hour of the day works best. | ☐ | ☐ | ☐ | ☐ |
| 13. I schedule large blocks of uninterrupted (emergencies only) time for projects. | ☐ | ☐ | ☐ | ☐ |
| 14. If this doesn't work, I hide somewhere. | ☐ | ☐ | ☐ | ☐ |
| 15. I break big tasks into smaller, more doable tasks. | ☐ | ☐ | ☐ | ☐ |
| 16. Before I stop work on a scheduled item to do something unscheduled, I ask, "Is doing this unscheduled task more important than the scheduled event?" | ☐ | ☐ | ☐ | ☐ |
| 17. I schedule a time for doing similar activities (making and returning calls, writing letters and memos). | ☐ | ☐ | ☐ | ☐ |
| **Organizing management function** | | | | |
| 18. I schedule time for unexpected events (my "office hours") and let people know when I'm open for calls and questions. I ask people to see me or call me during those hours, unless it's an emergency. I answer mail and do other routine tasks during this time. If people ask to see me—"Got a minute?"—I ask them whether it can wait until my office hours. | ☐ | ☐ | ☐ | ☐ |
| 19. I schedule a time, set up an agenda, set a time limit for all visitors, and keep on topic. | ☐ | ☐ | ☐ | ☐ |
| 20. I keep a clean, well-organized work area and desk. | ☐ | ☐ | ☐ | ☐ |
| 21. I remove all non-work-related or distracting objects from my work area and desk. | ☐ | ☐ | ☐ | ☐ |

*(continued)*

| Time management techniques | Should do | Could do | Do not do | Does not apply to me |
|---|---|---|---|---|
| **Organizing management function** *(continued)* | | | | |
| 22. I do one task at a time. | ☐ | ☐ | ☐ | ☐ |
| 23. With paperwork, I make a decision at once. I don't reread it later and decide later. | ☐ | ☐ | ☐ | ☐ |
| 24. My files are systematically arranged and labeled as active or inactive. When I file an item, I note a throwaway date on it. | ☐ | ☐ | ☐ | ☐ |
| 25. When appropriate, I call rather than write or visit. | ☐ | ☐ | ☐ | ☐ |
| 26. I delegate appropriate tasks when I can. | ☐ | ☐ | ☐ | ☐ |
| 27. I use form letters and a word processor. | ☐ | ☐ | ☐ | ☐ |
| 28. I answer letters or memos on the letter itself. | ☐ | ☐ | ☐ | ☐ |
| 29. I have someone read and summarize appropriate things for me. | ☐ | ☐ | ☐ | ☐ |
| 30. I divide reading requirements with others and share summaries. | ☐ | ☐ | ☐ | ☐ |
| 31. I have calls screened to make sure the right person handles them. | ☐ | ☐ | ☐ | ☐ |
| 32. I plan before I call. I have an agenda and all pertinent information handy, and I take notes on the agenda. | ☐ | ☐ | ☐ | ☐ |
| 33. I ask people to call me back during my office hours. I also ask about the best time to call them. | ☐ | ☐ | ☐ | ☐ |
| 34. I have a specific objective or purpose for every meeting I conduct. If I can't state the meeting's purpose, I don't have the meeting. | ☐ | ☐ | ☐ | ☐ |
| 35. When I do hold meetings, I invite only the necessary participants, and I keep them only as long as needed. | ☐ | ☐ | ☐ | ☐ |
| 36. I always have an agenda for a meeting, and I stick to it. I start and end as scheduled. | ☐ | ☐ | ☐ | ☐ |
| 37. I set objectives for travel. I list everyone I will meet with, and I email them agendas. I have a file folder for each person with all the necessary data for our meeting. | ☐ | ☐ | ☐ | ☐ |
| 38. I combine and modify activities to save time. | ☐ | ☐ | ☐ | ☐ |
| **Leading management function** | | | | |
| 39. I set clear objectives for my staff with built-in accountability; I give them feedback often. | ☐ | ☐ | ☐ | ☐ |
| 40. I don't waste others' time. I don't make my team wait idly for decisions, instructions, or materials in meetings. I wait for a convenient time—I don't interrupt team members or others and waste their time. | ☐ | ☐ | ☐ | ☐ |
| 41. I train my staff carefully. I don't do their work for them. | ☐ | ☐ | ☐ | ☐ |
| 42. I delegate activities in which I don't need to be personally involved. | ☐ | ☐ | ☐ | ☐ |
| 43. I set deadlines earlier than the actual deadline. | ☐ | ☐ | ☐ | ☐ |
| 44. I use the input of my staff. I don't try to reinvent the wheel. | ☐ | ☐ | ☐ | ☐ |
| 45. I teach time management skills to my team. | ☐ | ☐ | ☐ | ☐ |
| 46. I don't procrastinate; I do it. | ☐ | ☐ | ☐ | ☐ |
| 47. I'm not a perfectionist—I define what is acceptable and stop there. | ☐ | ☐ | ☐ | ☐ |
| 48. I try to stay calm. Getting emotional only causes more problems. | ☐ | ☐ | ☐ | ☐ |
| 49. I've found ways to reduce socializing without rocking the team spirit. | ☐ | ☐ | ☐ | ☐ |
| 50. I communicate well. I don't confuse my staff with vague, poorly planned directives. | ☐ | ☐ | ☐ | ☐ |

After you have completed the Self-Assessment, implement your "Should do" items. Next, work on your "Could do" items. Try to keep a mind-set of continually improving your time management skills. Once in a while, reread the "Does not apply to me" column to see if any of these items apply now.

As we bring this chapter to a close, you should understand the important role of facilities and event management. Facilities and event management includes developing the sales forecast to predict attendance and profitability and scheduling to plan and control activities. You should have ideas on how to improve your time management skills.

As we bring this text to a close, complete Self-Assessment 14.3 to review your prior course self-assessment exercises.

## SELF-ASSESSMENT 14.3

### Your Course Self-Assessment

This last self-assessment uses the prior self-assessments, so go back and review them from each chapter and then write down a few things you have learned about yourself, focusing on strengths and areas for improvement.

Chapter 1, Self-Assessment 1.1, What Are Your Management Traits? p. 9

_____
_____

Chapter 2, Self-Assessment 2.1, Sport Ethics, pp. 38-39

_____
_____

Chapter 3, Self-Assessment 3.1, What Is Your Decision Style? p. 60

_____
_____

Chapter 4, Self-Assessment 4.1, Are You an Effective Planner? p. 82

_____
_____

Chapter 4, Self-Assessment 4.2, Do You Have Entrepreneurial Traits? p. 98

_____
_____

Chapter 5, Self-Assessment 5.1, What Are Your Personal Priorities? pp. 131-132

_____
_____

Chapter 6, Self-Assessment 6.1, Attitudes About Women in the Workplace, p. 161

_____
_____

Chapter 7, Self-Assessment 7.1, Are You Ready for a Sport Management Position? p. 187

_____
_____

Chapter 8, Self-Assessment 8.1, Your Big Five Personality Profile, pp. 216-217

_____
_____

Chapter 8, Self-Assessment 8.2, How Satisfied Are You With Your Job? p. 224

_____
_____

*(continued)*

Self-Assessment 14.3 *(continued)*

Chapter 8, Self-Assessment 8.3, How Political Are You? p. 229

_____

_____

Chapter 8, Self-Assessment 8.4, What Is Your Stress Personality Type? p. 246

_____

_____

Chapter 9, Self-Assessment 9.1, Are You an Individual or Team Player? p. 259

_____

_____

Chapter 10, Self-Assessment 10.1, Are You a Good Listener? p. 305

_____

_____

Chapter 11, Self-Assessment 11.1, What Motivates You? p. 327

_____

_____

Chapter 11, Self-Assessment 11.2, Which Acquired Need Drives You? p. 329

_____

_____

Chapter 12, Self-Assessment 12.1, Are You a Theory X or Theory Y Leader? p. 352

_____

_____

Chapter 12, Self-Assessment 12.2, What Is Your Preferred Management Style? pp. 365-367

_____

_____

Chapter 13, Self-Assessment 13.1, Your Coaching Skills, p. 399

_____

_____

Chapter 14, Self-Assessment 14.1, Are You a Multitasker? p. 441

_____

_____

Chapter 14, Self-Assessment 14.2, Time Management Techniques, pp. 443-444

_____

_____

Now it's time to use this self-knowledge to help you in your sport career development. Write some objectives (chapter 4), and then plan how you will apply this self-knowledge in both your profession and in private life to meet your objectives. What specific areas will you work on improving? How will you improve? How will you know if you have improved?

# LEARNING AIDS

## CHAPTER SUMMARY

1. **Describe what managing a sport facility entails.**

   Sport management personnel often help plan, design, and manage new facilities. A crucial part of their job is to generate interest in the organization or the local community for the new facility. Forming a committee of interested people early in the process ensures doing the right job. Once the facility is open for business, the job shifts to managing and training staff to run the facility on a day-to-day basis.

2. **Describe what is involved in event planning.**

   Sport managers plan many types of events. They coordinate games, provide food for teams, arrange team transportation, hire officials, manage ticket sales, plan and monitor concession sales, juggle league schedules, and organize tournaments.

3. **Explain how standing plans and single-use plans differ.**

   They differ in repetitiveness. Standing plans are policies, procedures, and rules for handling repetitive situations. Single-use plans are programs and budgets for handling nonrepetitive situations.

4. **Explain when, and why, contingency plans are necessary.**

   Contingency plans are plans that may need to be implemented if uncontrollable events occur. There are many events managers cannot control that can prevent achievement of objectives. By identifying what can go wrong and planning how to handle it, managers increase their chances of achieving objectives.

5. **Discuss how sales forecasts shape strategy.**

   Sales forecasts sometimes determine strategy. If forecasts indicate a slowdown in the economy (environment), companies can elect to defend market share. If forecasts indicate stable demand for a product or service, companies may choose to use a cash cow to fund new products. If sales forecasts indicate that the economy is turning up, companies may choose to market aggressively to open up new markets.

6. **Explain how qualitative and quantitative forecasting techniques differ.**

   Qualitative forecast techniques use subjective judgment, intuition, experience, and opinion, with some math. Quantitative techniques use past sales data and mathematical (objective) analysis to predict sales. However, the two methods are often used in combination to improve forecasting.

7. **Explain how the jury of executive opinion and the three sales composites differ.**

   The jury of executive opinion seeks a consensus from managers or experts. Composite sales methods combine the independent forecasts of salespeople, customers, or operating units to predict total company sales without reaching consensus. The composite techniques are more objective than the jury of executive opinion.

8. **Explain how past sales and time series forecasting techniques differ.**

   With past sales, future sales are predicted to be the same or are subjectively adjusted for environmental factors. With time series, future sales are predicted by extending the trend line over time.

9. **Know when to use planning sheets, Gantt charts, and PERT diagrams.**

   Planning sheets and Gantt charts work best for plans with independent, sequential activities. Gantt charts have two advantages over planning sheets: They show progress directly on the chart, and they can show multiple projects on one chart. PERT diagrams are more appropriate when activities are dependent on each other.

10. **Use a time log.**

    A time log is a daily diary that shows how we use our time. It identifies areas to work on to improve time use.

11. **Manage your time better.**

    The basic steps in the time management system are (1) plan each week, (2) schedule each week, and (3) schedule each day.

## REVIEW AND DISCUSSION QUESTIONS

1. What are the five planning dimensions?

2. What is the difference between a policy, a procedure, and a rule?

3. Why do some sport managers fail to plan?

4. Why is sales forecasting important?

5. What are some of the activities involved in planning a youth Olympics-style games?

6. What types of events do sport managers plan?

7. What is the mission of the University of Southern Mississippi National Center for Spectator Sports Safety and Security?

8. When would you use a PERT diagram rather than a Gantt chart?

9. Why are time management skills important to a team manager?

10. What does a time log show?

11. What are the four key components of the time management system?

12. What are the most likely major opportunities and threats to be concerned about in sport management in the next few years?

13. What do you believe is the most important issue facing sport management today?

14. What is your vision of the future of sport management?

## CASES

### Sport Management Professionals @ Work: Trevor Lininger

Trevor Lininger is currently the ticket analyst coordinator for the Kansas City Royals. Trevor's path is interesting because he is a good example for students of how analytics is becoming more prominent in strategic decision making and marketing in sport. Trevor gathers and analyzes the ticket sales data for the Royals games. He looks for trends in the ticket sales data at Kauffman Stadium: How do the attendance data differ between day games and night games? Are group ticket sales to businesses, groups, and other organizations trending up or down? Does gender play a role in ticket sales?

Trevor also used his networking skills well to get an interview by following up with a professional after seeing her at a guest speaking event on the Baker University campus. He polished up his résumé and interview skills and got the job.

Trevor's career started by completing a B.S. in sports administration from Baker University from 2013 to 2017. He was active on campus with the baseball team and the Sports Administration Club.

Trevor completed a sports information internship in the athletic department on the Baker University campus. A second internship was completed at the offices of the National Association of Intercollegiate Athletics as the athletics communication and sports media intern.

The two internships helped Trevor to get the experience that he needed to land the Kansas City Royals job in January 2018. At Baker University, the sports programs try to supplement classes with guest speakers to broaden students' perspective and inspire thought about their career options. In the case of Trevor Lininger, it worked. He now works in Major League Baseball!

## Case Questions

1. Identify two guest speakers who have visited your sports courses at college. Can you remember their names? Where do they work?

2. Are you interested in arranging two internships for yourself? What are two places where you would like to complete an internship?

3. Research using the Internet the role of a ticket analyst coordinator. Start by researching ticket sales openings at teamworkonline.com.

## Controlling Risks at Professional Sporting Events

The number-one issue facing sports events and operations is increased security. Terrorist attacks in the streets of England and France in recent years have increased the need to assess security. The horrible lone-gunman shootings at schools in the United States, along with the terrible 2017 mass shooting in Las Vegas at the Jason Aldean concert, has made security the number-one concern for event managers. New security measures, such as using drones to provide surveillance around stadiums, will become standard operations. Radiation monitors were used at Rio for the 2016 Olympics, including portable scanners to detect traces of radioactive material.[53] Increasingly sophisticated technology will be used to help keep sporting events safer.

Event planners need to determine security objectives before the event, implement the security plan, monitor and control the actual event, and then have a post-event security meeting. You can be proactive and plan for potential problems before they happen. Security considerations include perimeter security around the outside of the civic center, field, or stadium, and training for security personnel. A post-event analysis helps you to better plan for future events. The 2013 Super Bowl experienced a power outage for nearly 35 minutes in the second half of the game. A complete post-event analysis between SMG, which manages the Superdome, the local utility company Entergy Services, and the NFL was conducted to determine why the power outage occurred during the biggest sport event of the year.[54]

Unfortunately, examples of rowdy fan behavior are also common and need to be assessed. For instance, fans were warned to behave properly at the Euro 2012 football tournament. However, 183 fans of Poland and Russia were arrested when they clashed. Water cannons, tear gas, and rubber bullets were used to disperse a mob, while fireworks, bottles, and other makeshift missiles were thrown by fans on both sides.[55]

In 2011, four San Francisco Giants baseball fans took a road trip to Los Angeles to watch the opening day game between the Giants and the Dodgers. The four Giants fans wore their Giants clothing to the game in L.A. After the game, they were attacked in the parking lot. Giants fan Bryan Stow was seriously injured and ended up permanently disabled; he was unable to return to his work as a paramedic.[56]

Measures to reduce hooliganism (causing game-time trouble) at soccer games include providing family enclosures; trying to reduce racist chanting and remarks; promoting cooperation between clubs, police, and media in finding and prosecuting hooligans; and making sure that banned hooligans are not allowed at games. Standing plans can be used to improve efficiency through the development of some regular steps and procedures to implement at all events.

Fans want a safe environment in which to watch a game. When Barry Bonds hit his historic home run to break Hank Aaron's home run record, the resulting scrum to claim the ball looked quite dangerous. However, police personnel were strategically placed around the ballpark to control the situation. Two police officers did help a lucky fan to catch the ball, and the only real harm was that his New York Mets shirt was torn. Proactive planning eliminated a potential chaotic situation and instead created a positive moment for all fans.[57]

For information about the legal side of event management security, you can watch this video www.youtube.com/watch?v=QwBUzVXCY3I led by Orange County Assistant Sheriff Michael Hillmann.

Go to the web study guide to answer questions about this case study.

# @ TAKE IT TO THE NET

Please visit www.HumanKinetics.com/AppliedSportManagementSkills and go to this book's companion web study guide, where you will find the following:

A list of websites associated with the concepts in this chapter

Skill-Builder exercises, Sports and Social Media exercises, and a continuing Game Plan for Starting a Sport Business

Online versions of chapter exercises and end-of-chapter learning aids

An exercise that helps you define the Key Terms

# The Future of Balance in Sport

As we near the close of this book, we would like to present our own version of a balanced report on some of the problems and opportunities facing professional sport management. Not coincidentally, this discussion integrates many of the important issues we have discussed throughout the text.

## Increased Security and Other Issues at Sporting Events

Terrorists and lone gunmen have changed the nature of all events that are held as public displays of sport and entertainment. Technology will be used to help facilitate safety measures at arenas and stadiums. Stadiums also need to improve in the area of sustainability: they will pursue more measures to reduce waste, offering recyclable or compostable food and drink containers and utensils. Digital ticketing will allow fans to show their tickets using their cell phones, and this will also help build large digital databases to enable sport managers to analyze customer behavior. Fans will expect to have at least as much access to the Internet, team apps, interactive contests, etc. at the games as they have at home.[1]

## Personal Ethics and Honesty

Sports are one of the true forms of mass entertainment. Like rock singers and movie stars, athletes are constantly followed by the media. When star athletes do something wrong, their actions are major news on cable TV (ESPN, CBSSports, NBCSports) and online (Twitter, Facebook, TMZ). Fans carry their own cameras in their cell phones and can post pictures online as situations involving athletes occur.

Athletes are not alone in the need to improve ethical behavior. Coaches, athletic directors, and all administrators need to act ethically when they recruit new student-athletes. As we discuss in the text, the NCAA found that a former Louisville University director of basketball operations acted unethically when he arranged striptease dances and sex acts for prospects, student-athletes, and others and did not cooperate with the NCAA's investigation, according to a Division I Committee on Infractions panel. The head men's basketball coach, Rick Pitino, violated NCAA head coach responsibility rules when he did not monitor the activities of his former operations director.[2]

Organizations that hire medical personnel to check the health of their employees need to be extremely careful about the doctors who perform the exams. "After a remarkable hearing that featured gut-wrenching statements from 156 of his accusers and an apology that the judge said rang hollow, former Olympic gymnastics doctor Larry Nassar was sentenced to 40 to 175 years in prison for molesting young girls under the guise of treatment."[3] The bravery the Olympic gymnasts and other young women showed in reporting abuses should be applauded and encouraged. Sport management professionals need to make sure that athletes are always safe.

## Steroid Use and Drug Testing

The use of illegal drugs in sport will need to be continually monitored. The legacy of the use of illegal drugs in baseball has meant that notable athletes such as Barry Bonds, Mark McGwire, and Roger Clemens have been excluded from the Baseball Hall of Fame. MLB star Robinson Cano was suspended in May 2018 for 80 games for using illegal drugs.[4]

Twenty-eight Russian athletes were banned from the Olympic Winter Games in Pyeongchang, South Korea, in 2018. However, the Court for Arbitration in Sport allowed the athletes back into the Games days before they started because of insufficient evidence.[5] The doping scandal involving the Russian Olympic Committee goes back to at least the 2016 Rio Olympics. One 2017 study found that doping appears remarkably widespread among elite athletes, and it remains largely unchecked despite current biological testing.[6]

## The Impact of Esports and Technology on Traditional Sports

Will Millennials watch real sports as much as previous generations do? Wealthy investors, including Patriots owner Robert Kraft, have bought franchises in esports. Professional gaming is leading to careers for those players who are most adept at playing sports on computers.

The NHL sponsored the 2018 NHL Gaming World Championship so they could stay ahead of the curve in regard to the future growth of online sporting events.[7] Sport management graduates will be at the cutting edge of the growth in esports.

## Future of Sport Management

As a student of sport management and as a future manager, you must ask questions that people in the industry should be asking themselves: What are the bad management decisions being made? What do these issues portend for the future of pro sports? What ripple effects might result from a severe recession in the pro sport team industry? How would it affect the industries that depend on the financial health of pro sport teams? The sport industry is an odd-duck industry—by its very nature, it will always have winning teams and losing teams. How can they all win at the biggest game of all—the bottom-line game?

The good news is that America's love affair with sport has lost none of its bloom. Look around you: There are fencing teams, dance studios, soccer teams, and figure skating clubs. The list is long and diverse, and people from all walks of life build their free time around sports—doing them, watching them, teaching them, and traveling great distances to participate in them. The future of sport management is bigger, brighter, and more diverse than it has ever been.

Whereas pro sport teams have some serious white water directly ahead that they badly need to find ways to negotiate, sports are thriving in America and around the world. Managers trained in sport management are in great demand. Opportunities abound in managing sporting goods stores; organizing athletic departments at educational institutions; shaping the future of sports in governing bodies such as FIFA, the NCAA, and the IOC; planning events; working in local community recreation centers and youth leagues; officiating; coaching; broadcasting; and working in numerous professional leagues. Maybe you took this course because you want to work for a professional team. However, we hope this book has helped you see just how many different sport organizations need great managers. (See the appendix for a discussion of careers in sport management over the next few years.)

Organizational success is not just about focusing on profits. Be aware of issues and the future of sport management, keep up with the latest issues in your field, and keep networking throughout your career.

# APPENDIX

# Careers in Sport Management

A wide array of career opportunities is available to you in the field of sport management. In this appendix, we offer tips for the job search and suggest ways to gain valuable work experience. We also describe various resources that may be helpful as you begin to investigate your career options.

## Career Search

A career search in sport management is no different than any other career search. A wise man who taught with us once said, "Nobody who completes a job search ends up without a job." The central idea is that any career management process requires a good understanding of yourself, your personal goals, your interests, your salary and benefits requirements, and your willingness to travel extensively for business. Any job in the field that interests you can, and should, lead to more responsible, higher-paying work later in your career. However, you typically have to start at the bottom and work your way up the organization.

Many career books are available to help you learn about conducting a job search. Our favorite career management book has been on the market for 40 years: *What Color Is Your Parachute?* by Richard Nelson Bolles is an annual best-seller. Bolles asks two basic career questions: What do you want to do? Where do you want to do it? We add, What are you good at doing? The book helps you answer these questions.

## Specific Fields in Sport Management

Chapter 1 provides an overview of the field of sport management. Review the various careers you can enter, which are outlined in that chapter. These careers include such areas as sport broadcasting, athletic administration, coaching, officiating, fitness center management, retail sport management, sporting goods manufacturing, and recreation and youth centers, and from chapter 14, careers in facilities and events management. In addition, the cases provided in this book cover different areas within sport in which you might like to find a job and build a career.

## Internships

As the people profiled in the Sport Management Professionals @ Work often said, internships often led to actual jobs in the organization. Internships are a valuable way to gain on-the-job experience that can either lead to a full-time position with the same organization or help you get a job in another organization. Pick your internship wisely by selecting an organization you can see yourself with for a long time. If you like facility management or event planning, contact the arenas and stadiums in your area. If you like recreation management, contact the YMCA or JCC in your area. Retail sporting goods stores are also good places to contact because you will find this type of store most everywhere. A recent sport management student just completed an internship with Dream Bat Company in the small town of Somers, Connecticut. The intern is now a product representative for the company and will receive a commission on all the Dream Bats that he sells.

Some students are fortunate enough to land paid internship positions. However, most internships are unpaid and call for 120 to 150 hours to fulfill academic requirements. Most internships require the student to write a paper or complete a journal of the experience. We have found that students who develop an interesting PowerPoint presentation on their sport internship can show future employers what they actually did during that experience.

# Networking

More people get jobs through networking than all other methods combined. Many jobs open but are never advertised because they are quietly filled through networks. Recall from chapter 7 that employee referral is a common method of job recruiting. So when you are looking for an internship or job, tell everyone you know, and you may get a referral.

Most students underestimate the power of networking. They think it sounds easy and that they understand it because they have so many friends on Facebook. However, the reality is that social networking and career networking are different. Career networking is a learned skill that just about everyone struggles with at one time or another.

We take the word "networking" for granted, but think about it. It is really two words— "net" and "working." Is your net working? Do you know people in the sport field? Did you ever try to contact a sport administrator at your local sport arena? Fitness center? Recreation center? Television station? Newspaper? In the electronic age, it is possible to email these people and begin a relationship. Often, you can find their email addresses at the end of an article in the newspaper or on their organization's website. Be polite, and make sure to tell the professional that you are a student looking for assistance in your quest to understand the field of sport management. These people are often very supportive of students' efforts to learn about their business. Keep a log of the people you meet in your networking endeavors. Add their email addresses to your Internet address book. Send them quick notes on events you attended at their organization, and tell them how you enjoyed the experience. Building a good network is not about finding a job right away but rather about developing a long-lasting relationship that is beneficial to both parties. Networking is not exactly about who you know. It is more about whether the sport professional knows you. So you need to make sure these professionals learn about you. Identify important sport leaders in industries where you want to work and send them an email, a Facebook message, a LinkedIn invitation, or a Twitter tweet. Live the journey!

# The Networking Process

In addition to the general advice we just gave you, there is a five-step networking process you can use.

1. *Perform a self-assessment and set objectives.* Perform a self-assessment to better understand what jobs you want in your career. What do you like to do that you are good at? One thing that really helps you select jobs is to visit websites (there is a list in the last section of this appendix) and read job descriptions to find out what you will do on the job and the qualifications you need to get the job. The book *What Color Is Your Parachute?* can help you. Based on your self-assessment, in networking, you set narrower objectives, such as to "get a mentor," "determine the expertise, skills, and requirements needed for [a specific job]," and "get feedback on my résumé and job or career preparation so that I can be ready to move into [a specific job]."

2. *Create your one-minute self-sell.* Create a brief statement about yourself to help you accomplish your networking objective. We'll tell you how to develop one in the next section.

3. *List your potential network contacts.* You should build a network before you need it, so start today. Chances are you have already been involved in networking with Facebook or

other websites (and don't forget to develop a profile at LinkedIn or another professional website), so use it along with other networking methods to get a job. Begin with who you know, your primary contacts; look through your email contact address book. It is a good idea to set up a separate email account for professional networking.

4. *Conduct networking interviews.* Consult your list of potential network contacts and set up a networking interview to begin meeting your objective. It may take many interviews to meet a goal, such as getting a job. You may have to begin with an informational interview—a phone call or (preferably) a meeting that you initiate to gain information from a contact who has hands-on experience in your field of interest. In such a situation (in contrast to a job interview), you are the interviewer, so you need to be prepared with specific questions to ask the contact about your targeted career or industry.

5. *Maintain your network.* It is important to keep members of your network informed about your career progress. Saying thank you to those who helped you along the way will strengthen your business relationships; providing updated information about yourself will increase the likelihood of getting help in the future. It is also a good idea to notify every-one in your network that you are in a new position and to provide contact information. Networking doesn't stop once you've made a career change. Make a personal commitment to continue networking in order to be in charge of your career development. Go to conven-tions, make business contacts, and continue to update, correct, and add to your network list. Computer software is available that can help you manage your networking.

Reid Hoffman, founder of LinkedIn, is the guru of networking, and he is in constant contact with his network he calls his tribe. He wrote the book on networking, with Ben Casnocha, *The Start-Up of You* (Crown, 2012), and there are great excerpts in "The Real Way to Network" and "Three Degrees of Reid Hoffman"; both articles are in *Fortune* (February 6, 2012, pp. 23–32).

## Your One-Minute Self-Sell

To network, you should have a good pitch, like on *Shark Tank*. Create a brief statement about yourself to help you accomplish your objective. A *one-minute self-sell* is an opening statement used in networking that quickly summarizes your history and career plan and asks a question. It should take 60 seconds or less, so it must be concise, but it also needs to be clear and compelling. It gives the listener a sense of your background, identifies your career field and a key result you've achieved, and tells the listener what you plan to do next and why. It also should stimulate conversation.

- *History.* Start with a summary of the highlights of your career to date. Briefly describe the jobs or internships you've held and any relevant courses, certifications, and other qualifications you have.

- *Plans.* Identify the career you are seeking, the industry you prefer, and a specific function or role. You can also mention names of organizations you are targeting and state why you are looking for work.

- *Question.* Finally, ask a question to encourage two-way communication. The question will vary, depending on the person you hope to network with and the goal of your one-minute self-sell. For example, you might ask one of the following questions:

  "What areas might offer opportunities for a person with my experience?" "In what other fields can I use these skills or this degree?" "Are there other positions in your organization where my skills could be used?" "What do you think of my career goals? Are they realistic, given my education and skills?" "Do you know of any job openings in my field?"

In your one-minute self-sell, be sure to clearly separate your history, your plans, and your question, and customize your question based on the contact you are talking to. Consider the following example:

> Hello. My name is Will Smith. I am a senior at Springfield College, graduating in May with a degree in sport management. I have small-college event management experience at SC, and I completed an internship in the athletic department at Connecticut College. I'm seeking a job in the athletic department of a large university. Can you give me some ideas of the types of specialized positions available in large universities like UMass?

# Websites for Sport Careers

The best way for us to help you find specific jobs in sport is to tell you about websites that are geared toward this goal. These sites are excellent sources of information about jobs in sport, although some sites provide more information than others. Some sites are more interested in having people sign up for their monthly service; others provide job titles, short descriptions, and addresses to which you can send a resume and cover letter. It is a good idea to visit multiple websites because some list jobs that others don't. Again, reading the job description and specifications can help you select jobs that meet your interest, abilities, and qualifications.

The people profiled in the Sport Management Professionals @ Work all indicated that teamworkonline.com was the site they used to apply for jobs in sport management. New job openings are constantly listed on the site from leagues such as the NFL, NHL, MLB, and the minor league teams throughout the country.

Higheredjobs.com is also a very useful site for quickly finding sports jobs that are open on college campuses. You can use the search box to enter "sports" or you can pick your favorite sport such as "softball" or "field hockey," and you will quickly find many good jobs in sports at the collegiate level.

Another useful site is https://ncaamarket.ncaa.org/jobs. This site will immediately bring up all the open jobs in colleges and universities. The site is also useful for finding out what job experience and degree is required for different positions.

Also, if you know you want to work for a specific team, college, or organization, visit its website. Most will have some type of link from the home page, such as Job Opportunities.

**acquired needs theory**—Proposes that employees are motivated by their need for achievement, power, and affiliation.

**acquisition**—Occurs when one business buys all or part of another business.

**adaptive strategies**—Prospecting, defending, and analyzing.

**arbitrator**—Neutral third party whose decisions are binding.

**assessment centers**—Places where job applicants undergo a series of tests, interviews, and simulated experiences to determine their managerial potential.

**attitudes**—Positive or negative evaluations of people, things, and situations.

**attribution**—The process of determining why people behave in certain ways.

**authority**—The right to make decisions, issue orders, and use resources.

**BCF statements**—Statements that describe conflicts in terms of behavior, consequences, and feelings.

**behavioral theorists**—Theorists who look at the leadership style of effective leaders.

**bona fide occupational qualification (BFOQ)**—Allows discrimination where it is reasonably necessary to normal operation of a particular organization.

**brainstorming**—The process of suggesting many possible alternatives without evaluation.

**budgets**—Plans for allocating resources to specific activities.

**business portfolio analysis**—The corporate process of determining which lines of business the corporation will be in and how it will allocate resources among them.

**capital budgets**—Budgets that allocate funds for improvements.

**centralized authority**—Important decisions are made by top managers.

**charismatic leaders**—Inspire loyalty, enthusiasm, and high levels of performance.

**coaching**—Giving motivational feedback to maintain and improve performance.

**coalition**—An alliance of people with similar objectives who have a better chance of achieving their objectives when they work together versus separately.

**collective bargaining**—The negotiation process resulting in a contract that covers employment conditions at the organization.

**command groups**—Consist of managers and their staffs.

**communication**—The process of transmitting information and meaning.

**communication process**—The transmission of information, meaning, and intent.

**communication skills**—The ability to get your ideas across clearly and effectively.

**comparable worth**—Jobs that are distinctly different but that require similar levels of ability, responsibility, skills, and working conditions are valued equally and paid equally.

**compensation**—The total cost of pay and benefits to employees.

**competitive advantage**—Specifies how the organization offers unique customer value.

**components of culture**—Behavior, values and beliefs, and assumptions.

**conceptual skills**—The ability to understand abstract ideas.

**concurrent controls**—Actions taken during transformation to ensure that standards are met.

**conflict**—Exists whenever disagreement becomes antagonistic.

**consensus mapping**—The process of developing group agreement on a solution to a problem.

**consistent decision style**—Taking time but not wasting time; knowing when more information is needed and when enough analysis has been done.

**content-based motivation theories**—Focus on identifying and understanding people's needs.

**contingency leaders**—Are task or relationship oriented, and their style should fit the situation.

**contingency managers**—Contingency managers analyze employee capability level and select the autocratic, consultative, participative, or empowerment style for the situation.

**contingency plans**—Alternative plans that can be implemented if unpredictable events occur.

**continuum leaders**—Choose their style based on boss-centered or employee-centered leadership.

**control frequencies**—Constant, periodic, and occasional.

**controlling**—The process of establishing and implementing mechanisms to ensure that objectives are achieved.

**core values of TQM**—A companywide focus on (1) delivering customer value and (2) continuously improving the system and its processes.

**corporate growth strategies**—Concentration, backward and forward integration, and related and unrelated diversification.

**creative process**—The three stages are (1) preparation, (2) incubation and illumination, and (3) evaluation.

**creativity**—A way of thinking that generates new ideas.

**criteria**—The standards that must be met to accomplish an objective.

**critical path**—The most time-consuming series of activities in a PERT network.

**critical success factors (CSFs)**—Pivotal areas in which satisfactory results will ensure successful achievement of the objective or standard.

**customer value**—The purchasing benefits used by customers to determine whether to buy a product.

**damage controls**—Actions taken to minimize negative impacts on customers caused by faulty output.

**decentralized authority**—Important decisions are made by middle and first-level managers.

**decision making**—The process of selecting an alternative course of action that will solve a problem.

**decision-making conditions**—Certainty, risk, and uncertainty.

**decision-making skills**—The ability to select alternatives to solve problems.

**decode**—The receiver's process of translating a message into a meaningful form.

**delegation**—The process of assigning responsibility and authority for accomplishing objectives.

**delegation model**—Steps are to (1) explain the need for delegating and the reasons for selecting the employee; (2) set objectives that define responsibility, the level of authority, and the deadline; (3) develop a plan; and (4) establish control checkpoints and hold employees accountable.

**departmentalization**—The grouping of related activities into work units.

**development**—Ongoing education that improves skills for present and future jobs.

**devil's advocate**—Group members defend the idea while others try to come up with reasons why the idea won't work.

**direct investment**—Occurs when a company builds or purchases operating facilities (subsidiaries) in a foreign country.

**discipline**—Corrective action to get employees to meet standards and to follow the rules.

**dysfunctional conflict**—Conflict that prevents groups from achieving their objectives.

**empathy**—The ability to understand and relate to someone else's situation and feelings.

**employee assistance programs (EAPs)**—Programs that help employees get professional assistance in solving their problems.

**encode**—The sender's process of putting a message into a form that the receiver will understand.

**equity theory**—Proposes that employees are motivated when their perceived inputs equal outputs.

**ERG theory**—Proposes that people are motivated by three needs: existence, relatedness, and growth.

**ethics**—Standards of right and wrong that influence behavior.

**expectancy theory**—Proposes that employees are motivated when they believe they can accomplish the task and the rewards for doing so are worth the effort.

**external environment**—The factors that affect an organization's performance from outside its boundaries.

**feedback**—The process of verifying messages.

**financial statements**—The income statement, the balance sheet, and the statement of cash flow.

**force-field analysis**—Assesses current performance and then identifies the forces hindering change and those driving it.

**free agent**—A player who is free to negotiate a contract with any team.

**functional conflict**—Disagreement and opposition that help achieve a group's objectives.

**Gantt charts**—Charts that use bars to graphically illustrate progress on a project.

**global sourcing**—The use of worldwide resources for inputs and transformation.

**goals**—General targets to be accomplished.

**goal-setting theory**—Proposes that achievable but difficult goals motivate employees.

**grand strategies**—The corporate strategies for growth, stability, turnaround, and retrenchment, or a combination thereof.

**grapevine**—The flow of information through informal channels.

**group**—Two or more members with a clear leader who perform independent jobs with individual accountability, evaluation, and rewards.

**group cohesiveness**—The extent to which members stick together.

**group composition**—The mix of group members' skills and abilities.

**group performance model**—Group performance is a function of organizational context, group structure, group process, and group development stage.

**group process**—The patterns of interactions that emerge as group members work together.

**group process dimensions**—Include roles, norms, cohesiveness, status, decision making, and conflict resolution.

**group roles**—Expectations shared by the group of how members will fulfill the requirements of their various positions.

**group structure dimensions**—Include group type, size, composition, leadership, and objectives.

**group types**—Formal or informal, functional or cross-functional, and command or task.

**hierarchy of needs theory**—Proposes that people are motivated by the five levels of needs: physiological, safety, social, esteem, and self-actualization.

**horizontal communication**—Information shared between peers.

**human resources management**—Planning, attracting, developing, and retaining employees.

**initiators**—People who approach other parties to resolve conflicts.

**innovation**—The implementation of a new idea.

**internal environment**—Factors that affect an organization's performance from within its boundaries.

**international business**—A business primarily based in one country that transacts business in other countries.

**job characteristics model**—Comprises core job dimensions, critical psychological states, and employee growth-need strength to improve quality of working life for employees and productivity for the organization.

**job description**—Identifies the tasks and responsibilities of a position.

**job design**—The process of combining tasks that each employee is responsible for completing.

**job enrichment**—The process of building motivators into a job by making it more interesting and challenging.

**job evaluation**—The process of determining the worth of each job relative to other jobs in the organization.

**job specifications**—Qualifications needed to staff a position.

**joint venture**—Created when firms share ownership (partnership) of a new enterprise.

**labor relations**—Interactions between management and unionized employees.

**leaders**—Influence employees to work to achieve the organization's objectives.

**Leadership Grid**—Identifies the ideal leadership style as having a high concern for both production and people.

**leadership style**—The combination of traits, skills, and behaviors that managers use to interact with employees.

**leading**—The process of influencing employees to work toward achieving objectives.

**learning organization**—An organization that learns, adapts, and changes as its environment changes to continuously increase customer value.

**levels of authority**—Inform, recommend, report, and full.

**levels of management**—Top, middle, and first-line.

**line authority**—The responsibility to make decisions and issue orders down the chain of command.

**listening**—The process of giving the speaker your undivided attention.

**lockout**—When management refuses to let employees work.

**management audits**—Look at ways to improve the organization's planning, organizing, leading, and controlling functions.

**management by objectives (MBO)**—The process by which managers and their teams jointly set objectives, periodically evaluate performance, and reward according to the results.

**management by walking around (MBWA)**—Is about listening, teaching, and facilitating.

**management counseling**—Helps employees recognize that they have a problem and then refers them to the employee assistance program.

**management functions**—The activities all managers perform, such as planning, organizing, leading, and controlling.

**management information systems (MISs)**—Formal systems for collecting, processing, and disseminating information that aids managers in decision making.

**management roles**—The roles managers undertake to accomplish the management function, including interpersonal, informational, and decisional.

**management skills**—Include (1) technical skills, (2) people skills, (3) communication skills, (4) conceptual skills, and (5) decision-making skills.

**manager's resources**—Include human, financial, physical, and informational resources.

**market share**—An organization's percentage of total industry sales.

**mediator**—Neutral third party who helps resolve conflict.

**merger**—Occurs when two companies form one corporation.

**message-receiving process**—Includes listening, analyzing, and checking understanding.

**message-sending process**—(1) develop rapport, (2) state your communication objective, (3) transmit your message, (4) check the receiver's understanding, (5) get a commitment and follow up.

**mission**—An organization's purpose or reason for being.

**motivation**—The willingness to achieve organizational objectives.

**motivation process**—Process through which people go from need to motive to behavior to consequence and finally to either satisfaction or dissatisfaction.

**multinational corporation (MNC)**—A business with significant operations in more than one country.

**networking**—Developing relationships to gain social or business advantage.

**nominal grouping**—The process of generating and evaluating alternatives using a structured voting method.

**nonprogrammed decisions**—With significant and nonrecurring and nonroutine situations, the decision maker should use the decision-making model.

**nonverbal communications**—Messages sent without words.

**normative leaders**—Use one of five decision-making styles appropriate for the situation.

**norms**—The group's shared expectations of members' behavior.

**objectives**—State what is to be accomplished in specific and measurable terms by a certain target date.

**OD interventions**—Specific actions taken to implement specific changes.

**operating budgets**—Use revenue forecasts to allocate funds to cover projected expenses.

**operational planning**—The process of setting short-term objectives and determining in advance how they will be accomplished.

**operational strategies**—Strategies used by every functional-level department to achieve corporate- and business-level objectives.

**organizational behavior (OB)**—The study of actions that affect performance in the workplace.

**organizational culture**—The shared values, beliefs, and standards for acceptable behavior.

**organizational development (OD)**—The ongoing planned change process that organizations use to improve performance.

**organization chart**—A graphic illustration of the organization's management hierarchy and departments and their working relationships.

**organizing**—The process of delegating and coordinating tasks and resources to achieve objectives.

**orientation**—Introduces new employees to the organization, its culture, and their jobs.

**paraphrasing**—The process of having receivers restate the message in their own words.

**path–goal leaders**—Determine employee objectives and achieve them using one of four styles.

**people skills**—The ability to work well with people.

**perception**—The process through which we select, organize, and interpret information from the surrounding environment.

**performance**—A measure of how well managers achieve organizational objectives.

**performance appraisal**—The ongoing process of evaluating employee performance.

**performance equation**—Performance = Ability × Motivation × Resources.

**personality**—The combination of traits that characterizes individuals.

**PERT (Performance Evaluation and Review Technique) diagrams**—These diagrams highlight the interdependence of activities by diagramming their network.

**planning**—The process of setting objectives and determining in advance exactly how the objectives will be met.

**planning sheets**—State an objective and list the sequence of activities, when each activity will begin and end, and who will complete each activity to meet the objective.

**policies**—General guidelines for decision making.

**politics**—The efforts of groups or individuals with competing interests to obtain power and positions of leadership.

**power**—The ability to influence the actions of others.

**preliminary controls**—Anticipate and prevent possible problems.

**problem**—Exists whenever objectives are not being met.

**problem solving**—The process of taking corrective action to meet objectives.

**procedures**—Sequences of actions to be followed in order to achieve an objective.

**process-based motivation theories**—Focus on understanding how employees choose behavior to fulfill their needs.

**process consultation**—An OD intervention designed to improve team dynamics.

**productivity**—Measures performance by dividing outputs by inputs.

**programmed decisions**—With recurring or routine situations, the decision maker should use decision rules or organizational policies and procedures to make the decision.

**Pygmalion effect**—Manager's attitudes and expectations of employees and how the manager treats employees affect their performance.

**qualitative forecasting techniques**—Use subjective judgment, intuition, experience, and opinion to predict sales.

**quality**—Actual use is compared to requirements to determine value.

**quantitative forecasting techniques**—Use objective, mathematical techniques and past sales data to predict sales.

**receiver**—The person to whom the message is sent.

**reciprocity**—Using mutual dependence to accomplish objectives.

**recruiting**—The process of attracting qualified candidates to apply for job openings.

**reflecting**—Paraphrasing the message and communicating understanding and acceptance to the sender.

**reflective decision style**—Taking plenty of time to decide, gathering considerable information, and analyzing numerous alternatives.

**reflexive decision style**—Making snap decisions without taking time to get all the information needed and without considering alternatives.

**reinforcement theory**—Proposes that consequences for behavior cause people to behave in predetermined ways.

**responsibility**—The obligation to achieve objectives by performing required activities.

**rework controls**—Actions taken to fix output.

**rules**—State exactly what should or should not be done.

**salary caps**—The maximum amount of money a team can spend on players.

**sales forecast**—Predicts the dollar amount of a product that will be sold during a specified period.

**scheduling**—The process of listing essential activities in sequence with the time needed to complete each activity.

**selection**—The process of choosing the most qualified applicant recruited for a job.

**sender**—Initiates communication by encoding and transmitting a message.

**single-use plans**—Programs and budgets developed for handling nonrepetitive situations.

**situational favorableness**—The degree to which a situation enables leaders to exert influence over followers.

**situation analysis**—Draws out those features in a company's environment that most directly frame its strategic window of options and opportunities.

**social responsibility**—The conscious effort to operate in a manner that creates a win–win situation for all stakeholders.

**span of management**—The number of employees reporting to a manager.

**sport management**—A multidisciplinary field that integrates the sport industry and management.

**sport manager**—The person responsible for achieving the sport organization's objectives through efficient and effective utilization of resources.

**staff authority**—The responsibility to advise and assist other personnel.

**stages in the change process**—Denial, resistance, exploration, and commitment.

**stages of group development**—Orientation, dissatisfaction, resolution, production, and termination.

**stakeholders**—People whose interests are affected by organizational behavior.

**stakeholders' approach to ethics**—Creating a win–win situation for all stakeholders so that everyone benefits from the decision.

**standards**—Minimize negative impacts on customers attributable to faulty output by controlling quantity, quality, time, cost, and behavior.

**standing plans**—Policies, procedures, and rules for handling situations that arise repeatedly.

**status**—The perceived ranking of one member relative to other members in the group.

**strategic human resources planning**—The process of staffing an organization to meet its objectives.

**strategic planning**—The process of developing a mission and long-term objectives and determining how they will be accomplished.

**strategic process**—In this process, managers develop the mission, analyze the environment, set objectives, develop strategies, and implement and control the strategies.

**strategy**—A plan for pursuing the mission and achieving objectives.

**stress**—Our body's internal reaction to external stimuli coming from the environment.

**stressors**—Situations in which people feel overwhelmed by anxiety, tension, and pressure.

**strike**—When employees collectively refuse to go to work.

**structure**—The way in which an organization groups its resources to accomplish its mission.

**substitutes for leadership**—Eliminate the need for a leader.

**survey feedback**—An OD technique that uses a questionnaire to gather data to use as the basis for change.

**SWOT analysis**—Used to assess strengths and weaknesses in the internal environment and opportunities and threats in the external environment.

**symbolic leaders**—Establish and maintain a strong organizational culture.

**synectics**—The process of generating novel alternatives through role-playing and fantasizing.

**systems process**—The method used to transform inputs into outputs.

**task groups**—Consist of employees who work on a specific objective.

**team**—A group with shared leadership whose members perform interdependent jobs with both individual and group accountability, evaluation, and rewards.

**team building**—Helps work groups increase structural and team dynamics performance.

**technical skills**—The ability to use methods and techniques to perform a task.

**three levels of strategies**—Corporate, business, and functional.

**time management**—Techniques that enable people to get more done in less time with better results.

**time management systems**—Planning each week, scheduling each week, and scheduling each day.

**time series**—Predicts future sales by extending the trend line of past sales into the future.

**total quality management (TQM)**—The process by which everyone in the organization focuses on the customer to continually improve product value.

**training**—Acquiring the skills necessary to perform a job.

**trait theorists**—Look for characteristics that make leaders effective.

**transactional leaders**—Emphasize exchange.

**transformational leaders**—Emphasize change, innovation, and entrepreneurship as they continually take their organization through three acts.

**transmit**—Use a form of communication to send a message.

**two-dimensional leaders**—Focus on job structure and employee considerations, which results in four possible leadership styles.

**two-factor theory**—Proposes that motivator factors, not maintenance factors, are what drive people to excel.

**types of managers**—General, functional, and project.

**variables of change**—Strategy, structure, technology, and people.

**vertical communication**—The downward and upward flow of information through an organization.

**vestibule training**—Develops skills in a simulated setting.

**win–win situation**—A situation in which both parties get what they want.

# REFERENCES

## CHAPTER 1

1. L. Thomas, "Retail Is in 'Panic Mode,' Says Dick's Sporting Goods CEO," CNBC.com (August 15, 2017).

2. Society of Health and Physical Educators, SHAPE America, www.shapeamerica.org (accessed October 26, 2017).

3. H. Mintzberg, Quoted in "From the Guest Editors: Change the World: Teach Evidence-Based Practices!" *Academy of Management Learning & Education* 13, no. 3 (2014): 319.

4. R. McCammon, "Do Me a Solid," *Entrepreneur* (March 2014): 32-33.

5. W.L. Bedwell, S.M. Fiore, and E. Salas, "Developing the Future Workforce: An Approach for Integrating Interpersonal Skills Into the MBA Classroom," *Academy of Management Learning & Education* 13, no. 2 (2014): 171-186.

6. Y. Zhang, D.A. Waldman, Y.L. Han, and X. Li, "Paradoxical Leader Behaviors in People Management: Antecedents and Consequences," *Academy of Management Journal* 58, no. 2 (2015): 538-566.

7. North American Society for Sport Management, www.nassm.org (accessed October 26, 2017).

8. N.J. Fast, E.R. Burris, and C.A. Bartel, "Managing to Stay in the Dark: Managerial Self-Efficacy, Ego Defensiveness, and the Aversion to Employee Voice," *Academy of Management Journal* 57, no. 4 (2014): 1013-1034.

9. J. Naisbitt, "On Power," *Forbes* (November 23, 2015): 160.

10. G. Colvin, "The Benefit of Baring It All," *Fortune* (December 2015): 34.

11. B. Beane, "Data by Billy Beane," *Forbes* (September 28, 2017): 128.

12. *The Wall Street Journal* (November 14, 1980): 33.

13. D.R. Ames and A.S. Wazlawek, "How to Tell If You're a Jerk in the Office," *The Wall Street Journal* (February 23, 2015): R2.

14. E. Holmes, "The Charisma Boot Camp," *The Wall Street Journal* (August 6, 2014): D1, D3.

15. The self-assessment questions are based on the three management traits identified in a *Wall Street Journal* Gallup survey, published in *The Wall Street Journal* (November 14, 1980): 33.

16. K. Davidson, "Hard to Find: Workers with Good 'Soft Skills,'" *The Wall Street Journal* (August 31, 2016): B1, B6.

17. G. Colvin, "Humans Are Underrated," *Fortune* (August 1, 2015): 100-113.

18. K.E. Brink and R.D. Costigan, "Oral Communication Skills: Are the Priorities of the Workplace and AACSB-Accredited Business Programs Aligned?" *Academy of Management Learning & Education* 14, no. 2 (2015): 205-221.

19. G. Colvin, "Heavy Hitters Travel Light," *Fortune* (February 1, 2016): 20.

20. A.M. Kleinbaum and T. E. Stuart, "Network Responsiveness: The Social Structural Microfoundations of Dynamic Capabilities," *Academy of Management Perspectives* 28, no. 4 (2014): 353-367.

21. G. Colvin, "Ignore These Leadership Lessons at Your Peril," *Fortune* (October 28, 2013): 85.

22. K.J. Lovelace, F. Eggers, and L.R. Dyck, "I Do and I Understand: Assessing the Utility of Web-Based Management Simulations to Develop Critical Thinking Skills," *Academy of Management Learning & Education* 15, no. 1 (2016): 100-121.

23. A. Lim, D.C.J. Qing, and A.R. Eyring, "Netting the Evidence: A Review of On-Line Resources," *Academy of Management Learning & Education* 13, no. 3 (2014): 495-503.

24. North American Society for Sport Management, www.nassm.org (accessed November 1, 2017).

25. The Commission on Sport Management Accreditation website, www.cosmaweb.org (accessed November 19, 2018).

26. E. Ghiselli, *Explorations in Management Talent*, Santa Monica, CA: Goodyear, 1971.

27. H. Mitchell, "What's the Best Way to Stick with a Resolution?" *The Wall Street Journal* (December 23, 2014): D1, D2.

28. M.L. Verreynne, D. Meyer, and P. Liesch, "Beyond the Formal-Informal Dichotomy of Small Firm Strategy-Making in Stable and Dynamic Environments," *Journal of Small Business Management* 54, no. 2 (2016): 420-444.

29. R. Bachman, "The Week Resolutions Die," *The Wall Street Journal* (January 20, 2015): D1, D4.

30. A. Chatterji and A. Patro, "Dynamic Capabilities and Managing Human Capital," *Academy of Management Perspectives* 28, no. 4 (2014): 395-408.

31. R. Lussier and J. Hendon, *Human Resource Management*, 2nd ed. (Thousand Oaks, CA: Sage, 2016).

32. B.R. Spisak, M.J. O'Brien, N. Nicholson, and M. Van Vugt, "Niche Construction and the Evolution of

Leadership," *Academy of Management Review* 40, no. 2 (2015): 291-306.

33. CEO Survey, "Bosses Are Creating a New Generation of Leaders," *INC.* (September 2014): 76.

34. CEO Survey, "Bosses Are Creating a New Generation."

35. McCammon, "Do Me a Solid."

36. Zhang et al., "Paradoxical Leader Behaviors"; D. A. Waldman and R. M. Balven, "Responsible Leadership: Theoretical Issues and Research Directions," *Academy of Management Perspectives* 28, no. 3 (2014): 224-234.

37. A. Murray, "Should Leaders Be Modest?" *Fortune* (September 15,2015): 28; C. Hann, "Dedicated to You," *Entrepreneur* (September 2013): 24.

38. R. Krause and G. Brunton, "Who Does the Monitoring?" *Academy of Management Review* 39, no. 1 (2014): 111-112.

39. Staff, "Jargon," *Entrepreneur* (August 2015): 30.

40. L.B. Belker, J. McCormick, and G.S. Topchik, *The First-Time Manager* (New York: AMACOM, 2012).

41. M. Weber, "Culture Matters: 7 Ways of Great Leaders," *Forbes* (October 20, 2014): 113.

42. Zhang et al., "Paradoxical Leader Behaviors."

43. F.P. Morgeson, T.R. Mitchell, and D. Liu, "Event System Theory: An Event-Oriented Approach to the Organizational Sciences," *Academy of Management Review* 40, no. 4 (2015): 515-537.

44. H. Mintzberg, *The Nature of Managerial Work* (New York: Harper & Row, 1973).

45. A.M. Grant, J.M. Berg, and D.M. Cable, "Job Titles as Identity Badges: How Self-Reflective Titles Can Reduce Emotional Exhaustion," *Academy of Management Journal* 57, no. 4 (2014): 1201-1225.

46. N. Li, B.L. Kirkman, and C.O.H. Porter, "Toward a Model of Work Team Altruism," *Academy of Management Review* 39, no. 4 (2014): 541-565.

47. T.A. De Vries, F. Walter, G.S. Van Der Vegt, and P.J.M.D. Essens, "Antecedents of Individuals' Interteam Coordination: Broad Functional Experiences as a Mixed Blessing," *Academy of Management Journal* 57, no. 5 (2014): 1334-1359.

48. Small Business Administration, www.sba.gov/sites/default/files/FAQ_Sept_2012.pdf (accessed January 26, 2018).

49. Colvin, "Humans Are Underrated."

50. S.D. Parks, *Leadership Can Be Taught* (Boston: Harvard Business School Press, 2005).

51. www.linkedin.com/in/joseph-esile-1765917b

52. S. Overly, "Partnership with Under Armour Gets Attention for U-Md's Football Teams," *Washington Post* (September 1, 2001).

53. L. Mirabella, "Under Armour CEO Kevin Plank Responds to Trump Tempest with Letter to Baltimore," *Baltimore Sun* (February 15, 2017).

54. C. Morency, "The Trouble With Under Armour," *Business of Fashion* (November 3, 2017).

## CHAPTER 2

1. http://m.mlb.com/news/article/66923096/masahiro-tanaka-signs-seven-year-155-million-contract-with-new-york-yankees/

2. Dinitto, Marcus, "Two-Way Japanese Star Shohei Ohtani to Sign With Angels," *Sporting News* (December 8, 2007).

3. R. Blum, "MLB Approves Deal to Allow Shohei Ohtani Bids, Starting a 21-Day Window," *Chicago Tribune* (December 1, 2017).

4. Definition recommended by a reviewer from Ohio University, March 30, 2015.

5. R. Karlgaard, "Vivid Vision for Success," *Forbes* (January 19, 2015): 28.

6. D. Albert, M. Kreutzer, and C. Lechner, "Resolving the Paradox of Interdependency and Strategic Renewal in Activity Systems," *Academy of Management Review* 40, no. 2 (2015): 210-234.

7. Editors, "Reputation and Status: Expanding the Role of Social Evaluations in Management Research," *Academy of Management Journal* 59, no. 1 (2016): 1-13.

8. W. Su and E.W.K. Tsang, "Product Diversification and Financial Performance: The Moderating Role of Secondary Stakeholders," *Academy of Management Journal* 58, no. 4 (2015): 1128-1148.

9. V.F. Misangyi and A.G. Acharya, "Substitutes or Complements? A Configurational Examination of Corporate Governance Mechanisms," *Academy of Management Journal* 57, no. 6 (2014): 1681-1705.

10. A. Murray, "The Pinnacles and Pitfalls of Corporate Culture," *Fortune* (March 15, 2016): 14.

11. Information taken from the Springfield College website, https://springfield.edu/about/philosophyhttp (accessed January 29, 2018).

12. North American Society for Sport Management, www.nassm.org (accessed January 24, 2018).

13. D. Baden and M. Higgs, "Challenging the Perceived Wisdom of Management Theories and Practice," *Academy of Management Learning & Education* 14, no. 4 (2015): 539-555.

14. Murray, "Pinnacles and Pitfalls."

15. S. Sonenshein, "How Organizations Foster the Creative Use of Resources," *Academy of Management Journal* 57, no. 3 (2014): 814-848.

16. Albert et al., "Resolving the Paradox."

17. S. Sonenshein, "How Organizations Foster."

18. Albert et al., "Resolving the Paradox."

19. G. Golvin, "A CEO's Plan to Defy Disruption," *Fortune* (November 17, 2014): 36.

20. www.statista.com/statistics/207458/per-game-attendance-of-major-us-sports-leagues/ (accessed January 24, 2018).

21. Y. Kubota, "Honda CEO Rethinks Car Maker's Priorities," *The Wall Street Journal* (December 3, 2014): B1, B2.

22. J.P. Doh and N.R. Quigley, "Responsible Leadership and Stakeholder Management: Influence Pathways and Organizational Outcomes," *Academy of Management Perspectives* 28, no. 3 (2014): 255-274.

23. K. Stock, "Briefs," *BusinessWeek* (November 2-8, 2015): 26; J. Reinsdorf, "Newcomer Michael Jordan," *Forbes* (March 23, 2015): 151; S. Gummer, "Michael Jordan," *Fortune* (June 13, 2011): 38.

24. Associated Press, "Jeter 4 Percent Stake in Marlins, Who Will Have $400M Debt," *USAToday* (September 28, 2017).

25. Staff, "The Most Entrepreneurial Athletes of 2017," *Entrepreneur* (January/February 2018): 28.

26. D. Chandler, "Morals, Markets, and Values-Based Business," *Academy of Management Review* 39, no. 3 (2014): 396-397.

27. North American Society for Sport Management, www.nassm.org (accessed November 14, 2017).

28. A.H. Bowers, H.R. Greve, H. Mitsuhashi, and J.A.C. Baum, "Competitive Parity, Status Disparity, and Mutual Forebearance: Securities Analysts' Competition for Investor Attention," *Academy of Management Journal* 57, no. 1 (2014): 38-62.

29. D. Roberts, "Flight of Fantasy," *Fortune* (October 1, 2015): 80-84.

30. R.J. Reichard, S.A. Serrano, M. Condren, N. Wilder, M. Dollwet, and W. Wang, "Engaging in Cultural Trigger Events in the Development of Cultural Competence," *Academy of Management Learning & Education* 14, no. 4 (2015): 461-481.

31. O.E. Varela and R.G. Watts, "The Development of the Global Manager: An Empirical Study on the Role of Academic International Sojourns," *Academy of Management Learning & Education* 13, no. 2 (2014): 187-207.

32. A. Murray, "The Hard Truths of Globalization," *Fortune* (August 1, 2016): 6.

33. M.L. Turner, "Remote Control," *Entrepreneur* (January 2016): 75-79.

34. North American Society for Sport Management, www.nassm.org (accessed November 14, 2017).

35. North American Society for Sport Management, www.nassm.org (accessed November 14, 2017).

36. Gold's Gym, www.goldsgym.com (accessed November 14, 2017).

37. A. Chuang, R.S. Hsu, A.C. Wang, and T.A. Judge, "Does West Fit with East? In Search of a Chinese Model of Person-Environment Fit," *Academy of Management Journal* 58, no. 2 (2015): 480-510.

38. C. Hardy and D. Tolhurst, "Epistemological Beliefs and Cultural Diversity Matters in Management Education and Learning," *Academy of Management Learning & Education* 13, no. 2 (2014): 265-289.

39. Call for papers, *Academy of Management Review* 40, no. 4 (2015): 669-670.

40. Baden and Higgs, "Challenging the Perceived Wisdom."

41. H.G. Barkema, X.P. Chen, G. George, Y. Luo, and A.S. Tsut, "West Meets East: New Concepts and Theories," *Academy of Management Journal* 58, no. 2 (2015): 460-479.

42. Adapted from M. Javidon and R. J. House, "Cultural Acumen for the Global Manager: Lessons from Project GLOBE," *Organizational Dynamics* 29, no. 4 (2001): 289-305.

43. P.J. Buckley and R. Strange, "The Governance of the Global Factory: Location and Control of World Economic Activity," *Academy of Management Perspectives* 29, no. 2 (2015): 237-249.

44. Ryder Ad, "Outsourcing Solves Business Problems," *INC.* ryder.com (accessed January 4, 2017).

45. V. Harnish, "Five Reasons to Escape Overseas," *Fortune* (August 11, 2014): 34.

46. A. Busch, "IMG, Mandaly Sports Media Partner on Feature Slate, First Project Chosen," *Deadline Hollwood* (May 2, 2017).

47. Ad, "Made in India," *Fortune* (October 1, 2015): 29.

48. M. Ayyagari, L.A. Dau, and J. Spencer, "Strategic Responses to FDI in Emerging Markets: Are Core Members More Responsive than Peripheral Members of Business Groups?" *Academy of Management Journal* 58, no. 6 (2015): 1869-1894.

49. A. Breer, "London Team by 2022? NFL Continues to Forge Forward in U.K.," www.nfl.com (October 2, 2015).

50. Baden and Higgs, "Challenging the Perceived Wisdom."

51. I. Bremmer, "These Are the 5 Facts That Explain the FIFA Scandal," Time.com (June 4, 2015).

52. R. Noe, "Pro Racing Cyclist Caught With Motor Hidden Inside Bike. Here's How She (Probably) Did It," Core777.com (February 4, 2016).

53. B. Oliver, "Record Level of Anti-Doping Tests for 2017 IWF World Championships," Inside The Games.com (October 16, 2017).

54. M. Tracy, "Rick Pitino Is Out at Louisville Amid F.B.I. Investigation," *The New York Times* (September 27, 2017).

55. L. Schnell, "Scandal Finally, Correctly, Finishes Rick Pitino at Louisville, but His Legacy Is Set," *USA Today* (September 27, 2017).

56. H. Keyser, "Rick Pitino Denies Responsibility for Louisville Prostitution Scandal, Once Again Invokes 9/11," *Deadspin* (October 20, 2016).

57. R. Bort, "The St. Louis Cardinals Deserve Harsh Punishment for Hacking the Houston Astros," *USA Today Sports* (July 19, 2016).

58. C. Bonanos, "The Lies We Tell at Work," *BusinessWeek* (February 4-10, 2013): 71-73.

59. G. O'Brien, "Honesty Policies," *Entrepreneur* (October 2014): 34.

60. G. Colvin, "Personal Bests," *Fortune* (March 15, 2015): 106-110.

61. W.L. Bedwell, S.M. Fiore, and E. Salas, "Developing the Future Workforce: An Approach for Integrating Interpersonal Skills Into the MBA Classroom," *Academy of Management Learning & Education* 13, no. 2 (2014): 171-186.

62. C. Carr, "Stress to Impress," *Costco Connection* (February 2015): 13.

63. K. Leavitt and D.M. Sluss, "Lying for Who We Are: An Identity-Based Model of Workplace Dishonesty," *Academy of Management Review* 40, no. 4 (2015): 587-610.

64. A.C. Cosper, "Meeting Fear's Antidote: Hope," *Entrepreneur* (January 2016): 10.

65. S. Bing, "Does the Truth Matter?" *Fortune* (May 1, 2016): 136.

66. D. Ariely, "Why We Lie," *The Wall Street Journal* (May 26-27, 2012): C1-C2.

67. S.D. Levitt and S.J. Dubner, "SuperFreakonomics: Global Cooling, Patriotic Prostitutes, and Why Suicide Bombers Should Buy Life Insurance," *Academy of Management Perspectives* 25, no. 2 (2011): 86-87.

68. Leavitt and Sluss, "Lying for Who We Are."

69. G. O'Brien, "Sparring Partners," *Entrepreneur* (August 2015): 32.

70. Bonanos, "The Lies We Tell."

71. S.S. Wiltermuth, "Power, Moral Clarity, and Punishment in the Workplace," *Academy of Management Journal* 56, no. 4 (2013): 1002-1023.

72. D.T. Welsh and L.D. Ordonez, "Conscience Without Cognition: The Effects of Subconscious Priming on Ethical Behavior," *Academy of Management Journal* 57, no. 3 (2014): 723-742.

73. Ariely, "Why We Lie."

74. D.T. Kong, K.T. Dirks, and D.L. Ferrin, "Interpersonal Trust Within Negotiations: Meta-Analytic Evidence, Critical Contingencies, and Directions for Further Research," *Academy of Management Journal* 57, no. 5 (2014): 1235-1255.

75. R. Wilson, "Joe Montana on Patriots: 'If You Ain't Cheating, You Ain't Trying,'" CBSSports.com (October 16, 2015).

76. Ariely, "Why We Lie."

77. R. Whelan, "Lawsuit: Schorsch Told Us to Lie," *The Wall Street Journal* (December 19, 2014): C1.

78. R. Fehr, K.C. Yam, and C. Dang, "Moralized Leadership: The Construction and Consequences of Ethical Leader Perceptions," *Academy of Management Review* 40, no. 2 (2015): 182-209.

79. K.Y. Hsieh, W. Tsai, and M.J. Chen, "If They Can Do It, Why Not Us? Competitors as Reference Points for Justifying Escalation of Commitment," *Academy of Management Journal* 56, no. 1 (2015): 38-58.

80. Ariely, "Why We Lie."

81. H. Willmott, "Reflections on the Darker Side of Conventional Power Analytics," *Academy of Management Perspectives* 27, no. 4 (2013): 281-286.

82. D. Baden, "Look on the Bright Side: A Comparison of Positive and Negative Role Models in Business Ethics Education," *Academy of Management Learning & Education* 13, no. 2 (2014): 154-170.

83. News story, National Public Radio (aired September 7, 2016).

84. M. Kelly, *Rediscovering Catholicism* (New York: Beacon, 2010).

85. News story, National Public Radio (aired September 7, 2016).

86. R. McCammon, "So, Here's the Bad News . . ." *Entrepreneur* (July 2015): 24-25.

87. C. Hann, "Truth Time," *Entrepreneur* (March 2016): 24.

88. L. Daskal, "4 Pieces of Advice Most People Ignore," *INC.* (July/August 2016): 8.

89. From the Editors, "Organizations With Purpose," *Academy of Management Journal* 57, no. 5 (2014): 1227-1234.

90. L.J. Christensen, A. Mackey, and D. Whetten, "Taking Responsibility for Corporate Social Responsibility: The Role of Leaders in Creating, Implementing, Sustaining, or Avoiding Socially Responsible Firm Behavior," *Academy of Management Perspectives* 28, no. 2 (2014): 164-178.

91. Daskal, "4 Pieces of Advice."

92. P. Jackson, "Conversation With Phil Jackson," *AARP Bulletin* (January–February 2014): 10.

93. "Infractions Appeals Committee Upholds Findings, Penalties of Former Head Women's Basketball Coach at Howard University," www.ncaa.org (accessed January 4, 2018).

94. D. Crilly, M. Hansen, and M. Zollo, "The Grammar of Decoupling: A Cognitive-Linguistic Perspective on Firms' Sustainability Claims and Stakeholder' Interpretation," *Academy of Management Journal* 59, no. 2 (2016): 705-729.

95. M. Langley, "The Many Stakeholders of Salesforce.com," *The Wall Street Journal* (October 27, 2015): R2.

96. Contents page statement, *BusinessWeek* (September 7-13, 2015): 3.

97. Ariely, "Why We Lie."

98. E. Grijalva and P.D. Harms, "Narcissism: An Integrative Synthesis and Dominance Complementarity Model," *Academy of Management Perspectives* 28, no. 2 (2014): 108-127.

99. Welsh and Ordonez, "Conscience Without Cognition."

100. National Federation of High School Officials (NFHS), https://www.nfhs.org/nfhs-for-you/officials/officials-code-of-ethics/ (accessed November 23, 2018).

101. Fehr et al., "Moralized Leadership."

102. Christensen et al., "Taking Responsibility."

103. Oliver, "Record Level of Anti-Doping Tests."

104. S. Foy, "Can Physical Educators Do More to Teach Ethical Behavior in Sports?" *Journal of Physical Education, Recreation and Dance* 72, no. 5 (2000): 12.

105. Ariely, "Why We Lie."

106. S.S. Wiltermuth, "Power, Moral Clarity, and Punishment in the Workplace," *Academy of Management Journal* 56, no. 4 (2013): 1002-1023.

107. C.C. Manz, "Taking the Self-Leadership High Road: Smooth Surface or Potholes Ahead?" *Academy of Management Perspectives* 29, no. 1 (2015): 132-151.

108. M. Washburn and P. Bromiley, "Managers and Analysts: An Examination of Mutual Influence," *Academy of Management Journal* 56, no. 4 (2013): 1002-1023.

109. D.A. Waldman and R.M. Balven, "Responsible Leadership: Theoretical Issues and Research Directions," *Academy of Management Perspectives* 28, no. 3 (2014): 224-234.

110. C.L. Pearce, C.L. Wassenaar, and C.C. Manz, "Is Shared Leadership the Key to Responsible Leadership?" *Academy of Management Perspectives* 28, no. 3 (2014): 275-288.

111. T. Hahn, L. Preuss, J. Pinkse, and F. Figge, "Cognitive Frames in Corporate Sustainability: Managerial Sensemaking with Paradoxical and Business Case Frames," *Academy of Management Review* 39, no. 4 (2014): 463-487.

112. M.E. Porter and M.R. Kramer, "Profiting the Planet," *Fortune* (September 1, 2015): 64-65.

113. R.M. Kanter, "Why Global Companies Will Behave More and More Alike," *The Wall Street Journal* (July 8, 2014): R8.

114. D.S. Siegel, "Responsible Leadership," *Academy of Management Perspectives* 28, no. 3 (2014): 221-223.

115. Doh and Quigley, "Responsible Leadership."

116. S. Schaefer, "The Just 100: America's Best Corporate Citizens," *Forbes* (December 20, 2016): 82.

117. B Corp website, "About B Corps," www.bcorporation.net (accessed November 19, 2018).

118. B Corp website, www.bcorporation.net (accessed November 19, 2018).

119. Staff, "Corporate Social Responsibility: Good Citizenship or Investor Rip-off?" *The Wall Street Journal* (January 9, 2006): R6.

120. Tracy, "Rick Pitino Is Out."

121. R. Karlgaard, "Society's Lottery Winners," *Forbes* (June 15, 2015): 30.

122. D. Bennet and D. Gambrell, "How CVS Quit Smoking," *BusinessWeek* (December 29, 2014–January 11, 2015): 58.

123. L. Buchanan, "Call to Action: Make a Profit, Change the World," *INC.* (October 2014): 46-50.

124. P. Schreck, "Reviewing the Business Case for Corporate Social Responsibility: New Evidence and Analysis," *Journal of Business Ethics* 103, no. 2 (2011): 167-188.

125. J. Welch and S. Welch, "Giving in an Unforgiving Time," *BusinessWeek* (June 1, 2009): 80.

126. Definition developed by the Brundtland Commission.

127. A.A. Marcus and A.R. Fremeth, "Green Management Matters Regardless," *Academy of Management Perspectives* 23, no. 3 (2009): 17-26.

128. M.P. Johnson and S. Schaltegger, "Two Decades of Sustainability Management Tools for SMEs: How Far Have We come?" *Journal of Small Business Management* 54, no. 4 (2016): 481-505.

129. Pearce et al., "Is Shared Leadership the Key?"

130. Siegel, "Responsible Leadership."

131. A. Nadim and R.N. Lussier, "Sustainability as a Small Business Competitive Strategy," *Journal of Small Strategy* 21, no. 2 (2012): 79-95.

132. R. Karlgaard, "Riches From the Disruptive Dozen," *Forbes* (October 19, 2015): 38.

133. Ad, "Green Building U.S.A." *Fortune* (November 1, 2015).

134. Hahn et al., "Cognitive Frames."

135. L. Lorenzetti, "Southwest Airlines Is Flying High," *Fortune* (October 27, 2014): 38.

136. Crilly et al., "Grammar of Decoupling."

137. J.A.A. Correa, A. Marcus, and N.H. Torres, "The Natural Environmental Strategies of International Firms: Old Controversies and New Evidence on Performance and Disclosure," *Academy of Management Perspectives* 30, no. 1 (2016): 24-39.

138. Nadim and Lussier, "Sustainability as a Small Business Competitive Strategy."

139. P. French, "Boeing 2008 – China's Olympic reputation risk," www.ethicalcorp.com

140. D. Owen, "New Olympic Committee Chief Plans Reform, www.ft.com (July 17, 2001).

141. J. Macar and E. Pfanner, "London Rioting Prompts Fear Over Soccer and Olympics," www.nytimes.com (August 9, 2011).

142. T. Waldron, "Everything Is Going Wrong in Brazil Ahead of the Olympics," *HuffPost* (July 26, 2016).

143. M. Hazlett, "Ryan Lochte: Will Brazil Press Charges Against Him?" Reuters (August 18, 2016).

144. BBC News, "Olympic Ticket Scandal: Pat Hickey Formally Charged by Judge in Brazil," BBC Europe (September 10, 2016).

145. B. Henderson, "Defeated Egyptian Judoka Refuses to Shake Israeli Opponent's Hand," *The Telegraph* (August 12, 2016).

146. B. Rumsby, "Rio 2016 Olympics: Anti-Doping Branded 'Worst' in Games History," *The Telegraph* (August 17, 2016).

## CHAPTER 3

1. E. Thomasson, "ADIDAS: We Aren't Selling Reebok," *Reuters* (May 11, 2017).

2. S. Joseph, "How Adidas Is 'Creating the New' to Recapture Its Winning Streak," The Drum.com (March 28, 2015).

3. J. Woolf, "Adidas Tell Us How It Plans to Catch up to Nike," *GQ* (April 27, 2017).

4. R. Weiss and T. Mulier, "New Adidas CEO Plans Fast-Fashion Focus to Catch Up to Nike," Bloomberg.com (March 8, 2017).

5. K. Davidson, "Hard to Find: Workers with Good Soft Skills," *The Wall Street Journal* (August 31, 2016): B1, B6; J. Rodkin and F. Levy, "Recruiting Preferred Skills," *BusinessWeek* (April 13-19, 2015): 43.

6. J.D. Power, "My Advice," *Fortune* (July 1, 2015): 30.

7. H. Mintzberg, quoted in "From the Guest Editors: Change the World: Teach Evidence-Based Practices!" *Academy of Management Learning & Education* 13, no. 3 (2014): 319.

8. E.E. Jervell and S. Germano, "Lagging in U.S., Adidas Aims to Be Cool Again," *The Wall Street Journal* (March 23, 2015): A1, A10.

9. NBA website, www.nba.com (accessed January 15, 2018).

10. E.N. Gamble and R.B. Jelley, "The Case for Competition: Learning About Evidence-Based Management Through Case Competition," *Academy of Management Learning & Education* 13, no. 3 (2014): 433-445.

11. M.T. Wolfe and D.A. Shepherd, "Bouncing Back From a Loss: Entrepreneurial Orientations, Emotions, and Failure Narratives," *Entrepreneurship Theory and Practice* 39, no. 3 (2015): 675-700.

12. P.C. Nutt, "Expanding the Search for Alternatives During Strategic Decision-Making," *Academy of Management Executive* 18, no. 4 (2004): 13-28.

13. Wolfe and Shepherd, "Bouncing Back From a Loss."

14. K. Morrell and M. Learmonth, "Against Evidence-Based Management, for Management Learning," *Academy of Management Learning & Education* 14, no. 4 (2015): 520-533.

15. W.F. Smith, "Dynamic Decision Making: A Model of Senior Leaders Managing Strategic Paradoxes," *Academy of Management Journal* 57, no. 6 (2014): 1592-1623.

16. R. Hennessey, "Decisions, Decisions," *Entrepreneur* (March 2015): 50.

17. E.G.R. Barends and R.B. Briner, "Teaching Evidence-Based Practice: Lessons From the Pioneers," *Academy of Management Learning & Education* 13, no. 3 (2014): 476-483.

18. V. Harnish, "Finding the Route to Growth," *Fortune* (May 19, 2014): 45.

19. A. Erez and A.M. Grant, "Separating Data From Intuition: Bringing Evidence Into the Management Classroom," *Academy of Management Learning & Education* 13, no. 1 (2014): 104-119.

20. L. Iacocca, "Thoughts on Risk," *Forbes* (April 19, 2016): 150.

21. G. Colvin, "The Benefit of Baring It All," *Fortune* (December 10, 2015): 34.

22. T. Monahan, "Revving Up Your Corporate RPMs," *Fortune* (February 1, 2016): 43.

23. Gamble and Jelley, "The Case for Competition."

24. R.L. Hoefer and S.E. Green, "A Rhetorical Model of Institutional Decision Making: The Role of Rhetoric in the Formation and Change of Legitimacy Judgments," *Academy of Management Review* 41, no. 1 (2016): 130-150; J. Shotter and H. Tsoukas, "In Search of Phronesis: Leadership and the Art of Judgment," *Academy of Management Learning & Education* 13, no. 2 (2014): 224-243.

25. R.G. Lord, J.E. Dinh, and E.L. Hoffman, "A Quantum Approach to Time and Organizational Change," *Academy of Management Review* 40, no. 2 (2015): 263-290.

26. L. Weber and K. Mayer, "Transaction Cost Economics and the Cognitive Perspective: Investigating the Sources and Governance of Interpretive Uncertainty," *Academy of Management Review* 39, no. 3 (2014): 344-363.

27. M.T. Wolfe and D.A. Shepherd, "What Do You Have to Say About That?" *Entrepreneurship Theory and Practice* 39, no. 4 (2015): 895-925.

28. Barends and Briner, "Teaching Evidence-Based Practice."

29. M. Parent, "Decision Making in Major Sport Events Over Time: Parameters, Drivers, and Strategies," *Journal of Sport Management* 24 (2010): 291-318.

30. Hennessey, "Decisions, Decisions."

31. Staff, "Building a Culture of Connection," *Costco Connection* (July 2015): 12.

32. A. Stuart, "Damage Control," *INC.* (March 2015): 72-73.

33. G. Colvin, "Humans Are Underrated," *Fortune* (August 1, 2015): 100-113.

34. L. Alexander and D. Van Knippenberg, "Teams in Pursuit of Radical Innovation: A Goal Orientation Perspective," *Academy of Management Review* 39, no. 4 (2014): 423-438.

35. P.M. Picone, G.B. Dagnino, and A. Mina, "The Origin of Failure: A Multidisciplinary Appraisal of the Hubris Hypothesis and Proposed Research Agenda," *Academy of Management Perspectives* 28, no. 4 (2014): 447-468.

36. Alexander and Van Knippenberg, "Teams in Pursuit."

37. Editors, "From the Guest Editors: Change the World: Teach Evidence-Based Practices!" *Academy of Management Learning & Education* 13, no. 3 (2014): 305-319.

38. S. Sonenshein, "How Organizations Foster the Creative Use of Resources," *Academy of Management Journal* 57, no. 3 (2014): 814-848.

39. I. Sager, "Sam Polmisano," *BusinessWeek* (May 1, 2014): 56.

40. M. Cerne, C.G.L. Nerstad, A. Dysvik, and M. Skerlavaj, "What Goes Around Comes Around: Knowledge Hiding, Perceived Motivational Climate, and Creativity," *Academy of Management Journal* 57, no. 1 (2014): 172-192.

41. P. Lencioni, "Innovation Won't Get You Very Far," *INC.* (December 2014/January 2015): 102.

42. D. Rovell, "Adidas Gets Out of Golf Equipment, Selling Businesses for $425 Million," ESPN.com, May 10, 2017.

43. S.H. Harrison and E.D. Rouse, "Let's Dance! Elastic Coordination in Creative Group Work: A Qualitative Study of Modern Dancers," *Academy of Management Journal* 57, no. 5 (2014): 1256-1283.

44. S.H. Harrison and D.T. Wagner, "Spilling Outside the Box: The Effects of Individuals' Creative Behaviors at Work on Time Spent with Their Spouses at Home," *Academy of Management Journal* 59, no. 3 (2016): 841-859.

45. Teradata advertisement, *Forbes* (February 9, 2015): 24.

46. B. Simmons, "Data Wimps," *Forbes* (February 9, 2015): 34.

47. S. Harvey, "Creative Synthesis: Exploring the Process of Extraordinary Group Creativity," *Academy of Management Review* 39, no. 3 (2014): 324-343.

48. P. Lencioni, "When Less Is More," *INC.* (June 2015): 69.

49. E.E. Powell and T. Baker, "It's What You Make of It: Founder Identity and Enacting Strategic Responses to Adversity," *Academy of Management Journal* 57, no. 5 (2014): 1406-1433.

50. C. Tate, "Work Simply," *BusinessWeek* (December 22-28, 2014): 71.

51. Staff, "Building a Culture of Connection," *Costco Connection* (July 2015): 12.

52. S.H. Harrison and E.D. Rouse, "An Inductive Study of Feedback Interactions Over the Course of Creative Projects." *Academy of Management Journal* 59, no. 3 (2016): 841-859.

53. A. Lim, D.C.J. Qing, and A.R. Eyring, "Netting the Evidence: A Review of On-Line Resources," *Academy of Management Learning & Education* 13, no. 3 (2014): 495-503.

54. Rodkin and Levy, "Recruiting Preferred Skills."

55. W. Amos, "Accept the Change," *Costco Connection* (April 2014): 13.

56. Gamble and Jelley, "The Case for Competition."

57. Gamble and Jelley, "The Case for Competition."

58. B. Costa, "Bill and Billy Discuss Big Data in Baseball," *The Wall Street Journal* (September 22, 2105): D6.

59. D. Gage, "What Do Scientists Do All Day at Work?" *The Wall Street Journal* (March 14, 2016): R6.

60. J. Ma, "CEO Wisdom," *BusinessWeek* (October 19-25, 2015): 31.

61. Simmons, "Data Wimps."

62. M.E. Belicove, "Can I Use Big Data Without Going Broke?" *Entrepreneur* (June 2016): 52.

63. Teradata advertisement, *Forbes* (February 9, 2015): 24.

64. R. Charan, "The Algorithmic CEO," *Fortune* (January 22, 2015): 45-46.

65. V. Harnish, "5 Ways to Turn Precision Into Profits," *Fortune* (July 1, 2015): 32.

66. Harnish, "5 Ways."

67. S. Yagan, Book review, *Fortune* (December 1, 2015): 20.

68. R.E. Silverman, J.S. Lublin, and R. Feintzeig, "CEOs Put Less Stock in Predictions," *The Wall Street Journal* (July 13, 2016): B6.

69. S. Yagan, Book review.

70. R. Blumenstein, "The Mistakes Firms Make With Big Data," *The Wall Street Journal* (February 10, 2016): R1.

71. Erez and Grant, "Separating Data From Intuition."

72. G. Spanier, "Adidas Plans $300m Global Media Review," Campaignlive.com (November 30, 2017).

73. J. Bussey, "Leadership Lessons From the Generals," *The Wall Street Journal* (December 12, 2014): R10.

74. Lencioni, "Innovation Won't Get You Very Far."

75. A.P. Petkova, A. Wadhwa, X. Yao, and S. Jain, "Reputation and Decision Making Under Ambiguity: A Study of U.S. Venture Capital Firms' Investments in the Emerging Clean Energy Sector," *Academy of Management Journal* 57, no. 2 (2014): 422-448.

76. A. Chatterji and A. Patro, "Dynamic Capabilities and Managing Human Capital," *Academy of Management Perspectives* 28, no. 4 (2014): 395-408.

77. Y. Zhang, D.A. Waldman, Y.L. Han, and X. Li, "Paradoxical Leader Behaviors in People Management: Antecedents and Consequences," *Academy of Management Journal* 58, no. 2 (2015): 538-566.

78. Hoefer and Green, "A Rhetorical Model."

79. H. Drummond, "Escalation of Commitment: When to Stay the Course," *Academy of Management Perspectives* 28, no. 4 (2014): 430-446.

80. K.Y. Hsieh, W. Tsai, and M.J. Chen, "If They Can Do It, Why Not Us? Competitors as Reference Points for Justifying Escalation of Commitment," *Academy of Management Journal* 56, no. 1 (2015): 38-58.

81. Drummond, "Escalation of Commitment."

82. G. Colvin, "The Art of Doing the Unpopular," *Fortune* (June 15, 2016): 32.

83. Wolfe and Shepherd, "Bouncing Back From a Loss."

84. J. Fortunato, "The Advocacy and Corrective Strategies of the National Football League: Addressing Concussions and Player Safety," *Journal of Conflict Management* 3, no. 1 (2015).

# CHAPTER 4

1. M. Futterman and J. Revill, "Scandal Hits FIFA Reflects President, "*Wall St. Journal* (June 2, 2011).

2. "Sepp Blatter Apologises for Offensive Comments Over Gay Supporters," *The Guardian* (December 17, 2010), https://www.theguardian.com/football/2010/dec/17/sepp-blatter-apologises-gay-supporters.

3. Bagchi, R., "Sepp Blatter and Michel Platini Banned From Football Activity for Eight Years," *The Telegraph* (December 21, 2015).

4. C. Macfarlane and J. Masters, "FIFA Reform is 'Dead,' Says Man Who Helped Bring Down Sepp Blatter," CNN.com (May 10, 2017).

5. R.N. Lussier and C.E. Halabi, "A Three-Country Comparison of the Business Success Versus Failure Prediction Model," *Journal of Small Business Management* 48, no. 3 (2010): 360-377.

6. M.L. Verreynne, D. Meyer, and P. Liesch, "Beyond the Formal-Informal Dichotomy of Small Firm Strategy-Making in Stable and Dynamic Environments," *Journal of Small Business Management* 54, no. 2 (2016): 420-444.

7. North American Society for Sport Management, www.nassm.org (accessed March 7, 2018).

8. A.J. Perez, "XFL Returns: 'Professional Football Re-Imagined,'" usatoday.com (January 25, 2018).

9. Staff, "Controllers," *Entrepreneur* (November 2015): 63.

10. R. Karlgaad, "Vivid Vision for Success," *Forbes* (January 19, 2015): 26.

11. E. Sylvers, "Fiat Set to Spin Off Ferrari in IPO," *The Wall Street Journal* (October 30, 2014): B3.

12. M. Quirk, "6 Things to Know About the 2017 Reebok CrossFit Games," Reebok.com (August 6, 2017).

13. S. Lee, "Reebok Marketing Strategy—How Reebok Relaunched and Became Cool Again," Reebok.com (March 7, 2017).

14. FIFA, "About FIFA," www.fifa.com/about-fifa/who-we-are/explore-fifa.html (accessed March 17, 2018).

15. Found at NASSM.com on March 17, 2018.

16. D. Albert, M. Kreutzer, and C. Lechner, "Resolving the Paradox of Interdependency and Strategic Renewal in Activity Systems," *Academy of Management Review* 40, no. 2 (2015): 210-234.

17. M. Porter, "How Competitive Forces Shape Strategy," *Harvard Business Review* 57, no. 2 (1979): 137-145.

18. Staff, "SWOT Analysis," *Fortune* (June 15, 2015): 12.

19. D.W. Williams and M.S. Wood, "Rule-Based Reasoning for Understanding Opportunity Evaluation," *Academy of Management Perspectives* 29, no. 2 (2015): 218-236.

20. P.R. La Monica, "Skechers Stock Soars as Sneaker Sales Surge," CNN.com (October 20, 2017).

21. E.M. Johnson, "Tiger Woods Signing with TaylorMade Among Equipment Stories of the Year," Golfworld.com (December 26, 2017).

22. R.L. Weinberger, "Surviving Shark Tank," *Costco Connection* (September 2014): 13.

23. Verreynne et al., "Beyond the Formal-Informal Dichotomy."

24. A. Chatterji and A. Patro, "Dynamic Capabilities and Managing Human Capital," *Academy of Management Perspectives* 28, no. 4 (2014): 395-408.

25. K. Dziczek, "Sidebar," *BusinessWeek* (February 23–March 1, 2015): 22.

26. J.M. Ross and D. Sharapov, "When the Leader Follows: Avoiding Dethronement Through Imitation," *Academy of Management Journal* 58, no. 3 (2015): 658-679.

27. S.F. Collins, "Success Steps," *Costco Connection* (January 2016): 29.

28. Collins, "Success Steps."

29. T. Mandoza, "Culture Matters: 7 Ways of Great Leaders," *Forbes* (October 20, 2014): 113.

30. D.T. Welsh and L.D. Ordonez, "Conscience Without Cognition: The Effects of Subconscious Priming on Ethical Behavior," *Academy of Management Journal* 57, no. 5 (2014): 723-742.

31. M. Kelly, *The Four Signs of a Dynamic Catholic* (New York: Beacon, 2012).

32. C. Ricketts, "Hit List/Lou Holtz," *The Wall Street Journal* (December 23-24, 2006): 2.

33. R. Hatman, "Re-Event Yourself," *Costco Connection* (April 2016): 29.

34. Berkshire Hathaway website, www.berkshireha-thaway.com/subs/sublinks.html (accessed March 7, 2018).

35. Russell Athletic website, www.russellathletic.com/history (accessed March 7, 2018).

36. Statista, www.statista.com/statistics/241850/sales-of-nikes-non-nike-brands-2006-2010/ (accessed March 20, 2018).

37. P. Soni, "Nike Sprints Ahead in Footwear Products on Star Power," Marketrealist.com (April 3, 2015).

38. D. Shabotinsky, "Nike Stock Forecast: BCG Matrix & SWOT Indicate Long Term Value," https://iknowfirst.com/rsar-nike-stock-forecast-bcg-matrix-swot-indi-cate-long-term-value (January 25, 2017).

39. M.C. Sonfield and R.N. Lussier, "The Entrepreneurial Strategy Matrix Model for New and Ongoing Ventures," *Business Horizon* 40, no. 3 (May-June, 1997): 73-77.

40. C.E. Pollard and M. Morales, "Exploring the Impact of Aligning Business and IS Strategy Types on Performance in Small Firms," *Journal of Small Business Strategy* 25, no. 1 (2015): 26-32.

41. Williams and Wood, "Rule-Based Reasoning."

42. Staff, "Data Champions," *Entrepreneur* (November 2015): 63.

43. M. Porter, *Competitive Strategy: Techniques for Analyzing Industries and Competitors* (New York: Free Press, 1980).

44. V. Harnish, "Five Questions to Ponder for 2015," *Fortune* (December 22, 2014): 36.

45. W.K. Smith, "Dynamic Decision Making: A Model of Senior Leaders Managing Strategic Paradoxes," *Academy of Management Journal* 57, no. 6 (2014): 1592-1623.

46. D.L. Gamache, G. McNamara, M.J. Mannor, and R.E. Johnson, "Motivated to Acquire? The Impact of CEO Regulatory Focus on Firm Acquisitions," *Academy of Management Journal* 58, no. 4 (2015): 1261-1282.

47. R. Reuteman, "Accentuate the Negative," *Entrepreneur* (February 2015): 44-45.

48. Press release, "Registration Open for 2018 NHL Gaming World Championship, March 9, 2018," NHLcom.

49. G. Wyshynski, "NHL Enters Esports Market with International Tournament," Espn.com (March 9, 2018).

# CHAPTER 5

1. Found at www.hoophall.com/ on April 14, 2018.

2. J. Kinney, "Pro Basketball to Return to Hoop's Birthplace, Springfield to Get ABA Franchise," Masslive.com (July 19, 2106).

3. B.R. Spisak, M.J. O'Brien, N. Nicholson, and M. Van Vugt, "Niche Construction and the Evolution of Leadership," *Academy of Management Review* 40, no. 2 (2015): 291-306.

4. M. Brettel, C. Chomik, and T.S. Flatten, "How Organizational Culture Influences Innovativeness, Proactiveness, and Risk-Taking," *Journal of Small Business Management* 53, no. 4 (2015): 868-885.

5. Spisak et al., "Niche Construction."

6. M.L. Besharov and W.K. Smith, "Multiple Institutional Logics in Organizations: Explaining Their Varied Nature and Implications," *Academy of Management Review* 39, no. 3 (2014): 364-381.

7. Brettel et al., "How Organizational Culture Influences."

8. Staff, "Best Practicers," *Entrepreneur* (November 2015): 59.

9. Brettel et al., "How Organizational Culture Influences."

10. R.C. Liden, S.J. Wayne, C. Liao, and J.D. Meuser, "Servant Leadership and Serving Culture: Influence on Individual and Unit Performance," *Academy of Management Journal* 57, no. 5 (2014): 1434-1452.

11. C. Mims, "Data Is Now the New Middle Manager," *The Wall Street Journal* (April 20, 2015): B1, B2.

12. T. Hahn, L. Preuss, J. Pinkse, and F. Figge, "Cognitive Frames in Corporate Sustainability: Managerial Sensemaking with Paradoxical and Business Case Frames," *Academy of Management Review* 39, no. 4 (2014): 463-487.

13. W.K. Smith, "Dynamic Decision Making: A Model of Senior Leaders Managing Strategic Paradoxes," *Academy of Management Journal* 57, no. 6 (2014): 1592-1623.

14. R.P. Garrett and J.G. Covin, "Internal Corporate Venture Operations Independence and Performance: A Knowledge-Based Perspective," *Entrepreneurship Theory and Practice* 39, no. 4 (2015): 763-790.

15. E. Bernstein, "The Smart Path to a Transparent Workplace," *The Wall Street Journal* (February 23, 2015): R5.

16. S.F. Collins, "Success Steps," *Costco Connection* (January 2016): 29.

17. Y. Zhang, D.A. Waldman, Y.L. Han, and X. Li, "Paradoxical Leader Behaviors in People Management: Antecedents and Consequences," *Academy of Management Journal* 58, no. 2 (2015): 538-566.

18. S.H. Harrison and E.D. Rouse, "Let's Dance! Elastic Coordination in Creative Group Work: A Qualitative Study of Modern Dancers," *Academy of Management Journal* 57, no. 5 (2014): 1256-1283.

19. J. Gaines, "Play with the Big Boxes," *Entrepreneur* (February 2015): 15.

20. G.B. Ryan, "More Happiness, More Revenues: Ryan's Story," *Fortune* (March 15, 2015): 20.

21. Collins, "Success Steps."

22. J.R. Hollenbeck and B.B. Jamieson, "Human Capital, Social Capital, and Social Network Analysis," *Academy of Perspectives* 29, no. 3 (2015): 370-365.

23. Staff, "Best Practicers," *Entrepreneur* (November 2015): 59.

24. Hahn et al., "Cognitive Frames."

25. Staff, "Controllers," *Entrepreneur* (November 2015): 63.

26. Mims, "Data Is Now the New Middle Manager."

27. D. Albert, M. Kreutzer, and C. Lechner, "Resolving the Paradox of Interdependency and Strategic Renewal in Activity Systems," *Academy of Management Review* 40, no. 2 (2015): 210-234.

28. D. Courpasson, F. Dany, and I. Marti, "Organizational Entrepreneurship as Active Resistance: A Struggle Against Outsourcing," *Entrepreneurship Theory and Practice* 40, no. 1 (2016): 131-160.

29. A.M. Kleinbaum and T.E. Stuart, "Network Responsiveness: The Social Structural Microfoundations of Dynamic Capabilities," *Academy of Management Perspectives* 28, no. 4 (2014): 353-367.

30. Staff, "Best Practicers," *Entrepreneur* (November 2015): 59.

31. C.L. Pearce, C.L. Wassenaar, and C.C. Manz, "Is Shared Leadership the Key to Responsible Leadership?" *Academy of Management Perspectives* 28, no. 3 (2014): 275-288.

32. M. Berman, "The No-Boss Company," *The Wall Street Journal* (October 27, 2015): R3.

33. T.A. De Vries, F. Walter, G.S. Van Der Vegt, and P.J.M.D. Essens, "Antecedents of Individuals' Interteam Coordination: Broad Functional Experiences as a Mixed Blessing," *Academy of Management Journal* 57, no. 5 (2014): 1334-1359.

34. Nike website, www.nike.com (accessed March 10, 2018).

35. B.M. Firth, J.R. Hollenbeck, J.E. Miles, D.R. Ilgen, and C.M. Barnes, "Same Page, Different Books: Extending Representational Gaps Theory to Enhance Performance in Multiteam Systems," *Academy of Management Journal* 58, no. 3 (2015): 813-835.

36. Staff, "The M-Form Style," illustration in *BusinessWeek* (November 24-30, 2014): 61.

37. Berkshire Hathaway website, www.berkshirehathaway.com/subs/sublinks.html (accessed March 7, 2018)

38. Russell Athletic website, www.russellathletic.com/history (accessed March 7, 2018).

39. M.R. Barrick, G.R. Thurgood, T.A. Smith, and S.H. Courtright, "Collective Organizational Engagement: Linking Motivational Antecedents, Strategic Implementation, and Firm Performance," *Academy of Management Journal* 58, no. 1 (2014): 111-135.

40. J.P.J. de Jong, S.K. Parker, S. Wennekers, and C.H. Wu, "Entrepreneurial Behavior in Organizations: Does Job Design Matter?" *Entrepreneurship Theory and Practice* 39, no. 4 (2015): 981-995.

41. C. Tate, "Work Simply," *BusinessWeek* (December 22-28, 2014): 71.

42. de Jong et al., "Entrepreneurial Behavior in Organizations."

43. J. Price, "If You Leave Me Now . . . ," *INC.* (January 2015): 20-21.

44. Barrick et al., "Collective Organizational Engagement."

45. De Vries et al., "Antecedents of Individuals' Interteam Coordination."

46. G. Desa, San Francisco State University, reviewer suggestion added May 22, 2015.

47. J. Krasny, "The Latest Thinking About Time," *INC.* (March 2015): 44-45.

48. J. Robinson, "The Refueling Principle," *Entrepreneur* (October 2014): 67-70.

49. M. Whelan, "Productivity Hack," *Fortune* (October 1, 2015): 114.

50. Ad, "More Happiness, More Revenue: Ryan's Story," *Fortune* (March 15, 2015): 20.

51. J. Shotter and H. Tsoukas, "In Search of Phronesis: Leadership and the Art of Judgment," *Academy of Management Learning & Education* 13, no. 2 (2014): 224-243.

52. S. Leibs, "Just Trust," *INC.* (March 2015): 18-19.

53. Whelan, "Productivity Hack."

54. Krasny, "Latest Thinking."

55. J. Wang, "A Delicate Balance," *Entrepreneur* (September 2015): 136.

56. Wang, "Delicate Balance."

57. This section and Skill Builder 5.1 are adapted from Harbridge House training materials (Boston).

58. J. Bercovici, "How Dick Costolo Keeps His Focus," *INC.* (March 2015): 48-57.

59. L. Welch, "A CEO's Job," *INC.* (May 2015): 49-50.

60. J. Buchanan, "Wired for Success," *INC.* (September 2014): 26-52.

61. Buchanan, "Wired for Success."

62. Leibs, "Just Trust."

63. G. Rometty, "Most Powerful Women Advice," *Fortune* (November 17, 2014): 149.

64. J. Fried, "Leading by Letting Go," *INC.* (December 2014–January 2015): 128.

65. Leibs, "Just Trust."

66. R. Abrams, "Gain an Hour a Day," *Costco Connection* (September 2016): 14.

67. C.K. Lam, X. Huang, and S.C.H. Chan, "The Threshold Effect of Participative Leadership and the Role of

Leader Information Sharing," *Academy of Management Journal* 58, no. 3 (2015): 836-855.

68. Staff, "Decoding the DNA of the Entrepreneur," *INC.* (December 2015–January 2016): 53-59.

69. P. Andruss, "What to Delegate," *Entrepreneur* (January 2014): 74-83.

70. Collins, "Success Steps."

71. M. Villano, "Creative Genius," *Entrepreneur* (April 2015): 56-60.

72. R. McCammon, "I'm Going to Need a Bit More Time," *Entrepreneur* (September 2014): 28-30.

73. J. Fenton, "Celtics Struck It Rich with Nets' Picks," Wickedlocal.com (December 6, 2017).

74. D. Perry, "Red Sox Finally Sign the Power Hitting Free Agent They Sorely Needed in J.D. Martinez," CBSSports.com (February 19, 2018).

75. J. Haggerty, "Bruins Young Talent Developing Way Ahead of Schedule," NBCSports.com (January 9, 2018).

76. C. Orr, "For the Patriots, It Felt Like an Ending," SI.com (February, 5, 2018).

## CHAPTER 6

1. M. Katz, N.A. Walker, and L.C. Hindman, "Gendered Leadership Networks in the NCAA: Analyzing Affiliation Networks of Senior Woman Administrators and Athletic Directors," *Journal of Sport Management* 32, no. 2 (2017): 135-149. doi: 10.1123/jsm.2017-0306

2. H. Thorpe and M. Chawansky, "The Gendered Experiences of Women Staff and Volunteers in Sport for Development Organizations: The Case of Transmigrant Workers of Skateistan," *Journal of Sport Management* 31, no. 6 (2017): 546-561.

3. J. Ankeny, "20/20 Visions," *Entrepreneur* (January 2015): 32-36.

4. G.B. Shaw, "Disrupt This," *Entrepreneur* (November 2015): 10.

5. A. Murray, "Lessons From the Fortune 500," *Fortune* (June 15, 2016): 14.

6. D.G. Cosh and J. McNish, "BlackBerry Will Stop Making Its Phones," *The Wall Street Journal* (September 29, 2016): B1, B4.

7. J. Rodkin and F. Levy, "Recruiting Preferred Skills," *BusinessWeek* (April 13-19, 2015): 43.

8. Y. Zhang, D.A. Waldman, Y.L. Han, and X. Li, "Paradoxical Leader Behaviors in People Management: Antecedents and Consequences," *Academy of Management Journal* 58, no. 2 (2015): 538-566.

9. D. Albert, M. Kreutzer, and C. Lechner, "Resolving the Paradox of Interdependency and Strategic Renewal in Activity Systems," *Academy of Management Review* 40, no. 2 (2015): 210-234.

10. Anonymous reviewer of 8th edition suggested this addition.

11. R.D. Costigan and K.E. Brink, "Another Perspective on MAB Program Alignment: An Investigation of Learning Goals," *Academy of Management Learning & Education* 14, no. 2 (2015): 260-276.

12. G. Colvin, "Four Things That Worry Business," *Fortune* (October 27, 2014): 32.

13. A. Murray, "What Do Millennials Want?" *Fortune* (March 15, 2015): 14.

14. G. Klein, "The Myths of Moneyball: The Dangerous Message of a Best-Seller," *Psychology Today* (January 8, 2017).

15. J. Laramore, "Moneyball is Dead. Long Live Moneyball!" Techcrunch.com (April 2, 2016).

16. L. Alexander and D. Van Knippenberg, "Teams in Pursuit of Radical Innovation: A Goal Orientation Perspective," *Academy of Management Review* 39, no. 4 (2014): 423-438.

17. C. Fuzzell, "We're All Connected—And That Will Change Everything," *The Wall Street Journal* (February 28, 2015): R8.

18. G. Colvin, "A CEO's Plan to Defy Disruption," *Fortune* (November 17, 2014): 36.

19. E. Van Oosten and K.E. Kram, "Coaching for Change," *Academy of Management Learning & Education* 13, no. 2 (2014): 295-298.

20. C. Sandler, "Business Lessons From the Art of War," *Costco Connection* (May 2014): 15.

21. G. Colvin, "Ignore These Leadership Lessons at Your Peril," *Fortune* (October 28, 2013): 85.

22. Staff, "Self-Improvement Through Data," *Fortune* (March 15, 2016): 28.

23. E. Bernstein, "The Smart Path to a Transparent Workplace," *The Wall Street Journal* (February 23, 2015): R5.

24. M. Rosenwald, "Bound by Habit," *BusinessWeek* (March 19-25, 2012): 106-107.

25. M. Ulman, margin quote, *Fortune* (December 1, 2015): 28.

26. S. Bing, "How to Kill a Good Idea," *Fortune* (April 1, 2016): 116.

27. Rosenwald, "Bound by Habit."

28. Bing, "How to Kill a Good Idea."

29. G.B. Shaw, "Disrupt This," adapted from a quote from G.B. Shaw, *Entrepreneur* (November 19, 2015): 10.

30. A. Murray, "We Are All Technology Companies Now," *Fortune* (December 1, 2015): 8.

31. Rosenwald, "Bound by Habit."

32. Rosenwald, "Bound by Habit."

33. T. Mendoza, "Culture Matters: 7 Ways of Great Leaders," *Forbes* (October 20, 2014): 113.

34. M. Kelly, *The Four Signs of a Dynamic Catholic* (New York: Beacon, 2012).

35. K. Hultman, *The Path of Least Resistance* (Austin, TX: Learning Concepts, 1979).

36. A. Murray, "The Pinnacles and Pitfalls of Corporate Culture," *Fortune* (March 15, 2016): 14.

37. M.L. Stallard, "Building a Culture of Connections," *Costco Connection* (July 2015): 112.

38. Ad, "84% of Global Executives," *Fortune* (December 15, 2015): S5.

39. Murray, "We Are All Technology Companies Now."

40. G. Colvin, "Lead a Revolution from Within," *Fortune* (August 1, 2016): 22.

41. D.W. Williams and M.S. Wood, "Rule-Based Reasoning for Understanding Opportunity Evaluation," *Academy of Management Perspectives* 29, no. 2 (2015): 218-236.

42. Retrieved from www.amersports.com/about-us/our-business/mission-vision-and-values/ on April 20, 2018.

43. B.R. Spisak, M.J. O'Brien, N. Nicholson, and M. Van Vugt, "Niche Construction and the Evolution of Leadership," *Academy of Management Review* 40, no. 2 (2015): 291-306.

44. D. Antons and F.T. Piller, "Opening the Black Box of 'Not Invented Here': Attitudes, Decision Biases, and Behavioral Consequences," *Academy of Management Perspectives* 29, no. 2 (2015): 193-217; A.C. Cosper, "The Accidental Tourist," *Entrepreneur* (September 2015): 16; T. Monahan, "Revving Up Your Corporate RPMs," *Fortune* (February 1, 2016): 43.

45. Ad, "84% of Global Executives."

46. The Deming Institute website, https://deming.org/explore/fourteen-points (accessed March 15, 2018).

47. W. Beasley, "Listen Up," *Fortune* (December 15, 2015): 12.

48. M. Sytch and A. Tatarynowicz, "Exploring the Locus of Invention: The Dynamics of Network Communities and Firms' Invention Productivity," *Academy of Management Journal* 57, no. 1 (2014): 249-279.

49. M. Blumenstein, "IBM Plans to Thrive as a Digital Company," *The Wall Street Journal* (October 27, 2015): R3.

50. R.B. Briner and N.D. Walshe, "From Passively Received Wisdom to Actively Constructed Knowledge: Teaching Systematic Review Skills as a Foundation of Evidence-Based Management," *Academy of Management Learning & Education* 13, no. 3 (2014): 415-432.

51. J.N. Reyt and B.M. Wiesenfeld, "Seeing the Forest for the Trees: Exploratory Learning, Mobile Technology, and Knowledge Workers' Role Integration Behaviors," *Academy of Management Journal* 58, no. 3 (2015): 739-762.

52. H. Yang, Y. Zheng, and A. Zaheer, "Asymmetric Learning Capabilities and Stock Market Value," *Academy of Management Journal* 58, no. 2 (2015): 356-374.

53. GE ad, "Identifying the Leadership Skills That Matter Most Today," *INC.* (December 2014–January 2015): 78.

54. O.E. Varela and R.G. Watts, "The Development of the Global Manager: An Empirical Study on the Role of Academic International Sojourns," *Academy of Management Learning & Education* 13, no. 2 (2014): 187-207.

55. U.S. Census Bureau website, www.census.gov (accessed March 16, 2018).

56. U.S. Census Bureau website (accessed March 16, 2018).

57. Call for papers, *Academy of Management Review* 40, no. 4 (2015): 669-670.

58. A. Stites, "NFL's Rooney Rule: What Is It and How Does It Work?" *SB Nation* (January 6, 2018).

59. S. Sandberg, "When Women Get Stuck, Corporate America Gets Stuck," *The Wall Street Journal* (September 30, 2015): R3.

60. G. Bensinger, "Airbnb, Under Fire, Promotes Diversity," *The Wall Street Journal* (September 9, 2016): B1.

61. Call for papers, *Academy of Management Review* 40, no. 4 (2015): 669-670.

62. M.L. Besharov, "The Relational Ecology of Identification: How Organizational Identification Emerges When Individuals Hold Divergent Values," *Academy of Management Journal* 57, no. 5 (2014): 1485-1512.

63. F.A. Miller and J.H. Katz, *The Inclusion Breakthrough: Unleashing the Real Power of Diversity* (San Francisco: Berrett-Koehler, 2002).

64. National Public Radio, news, aired April 9, 2015.

65. K. Lanaj and J.R. Hollenbeck, "Leadership Over-Emergence in Self-Managing Teams: The Role of Gender and Countervailing Biases," *Academy of Management Journal* 58, no. 5 (2015): 1476-1494.

66. J. Bercovici, "Inside the Mind of Sheryl Sandberg," *INC.* (October 2015): 78-80.

67. Sandberg, "When Women Get Stuck."

68. U.S. Census data, www.census.gov, accessed April 10, 2015.

69. U.S. Census, NPR news, aired April 7, 2014.

70. J. Adamy and P. Overberg, "Pay Gap Widest for Elite Jobs," *The Wall Street Journal* (May 18, 2016): A1, A10.

71. A. Joshi, J. Son, and H. Roh, "When Can Women Close the Gap? A Meta-Analytic Test of Sex Differences in Performance and Rewards," *Academy of Management Journal* 58, no. 5 (2015): 1516-1545.

72. C. Suddath, "Can Women Ever Win at Work?" *BusinessWeek* (July 28–August 3, 2014): 62.

73. L. Weber and R.L. Ensign, "Promoting Women Is Crucial," *The Wall Street Journal* (September 28, 2016): B1.

74. B. Waber, "Gender Bias by the Numbers," *BusinessWeek* (February 3-9, 2014): 8-9.

75. E.O. Wright and J. Baxter, "The Glass Ceiling Hypothesis: A Reply to Critics," *Gender & Society* 14 (2000): 814-821.

76. Adamy and Overberg, "Pay Gap Widest."

77. Staff, "Gender and GDP," *BusinessWeek* (October 5-11, 2015): 20.

78. EEOC website, www.eeoc.gov (accessed March 18, 2018).

79. Q.N. Huy, K.G. Corley, and M.S. Kraatz, "From Support to Mutiny: Shifting Legitimacy Judgments and Emotional Reactions Impacting the Implementation of Radical Change," *Academy of Management Journal* 57, no. 6 (2014): 1650-1680.

80. A. Lockett, G. Currie, R. Finn, G. Martin, and J. Waring, "The Influence of Social Position on Sensemaking About Organizational Change," *Academy of Management Journal* 57, no. 4 (2014): 1102-1129.

81. S. Giura, SUNY Oneonta, suggestion of 6th edition reviewer, April 2015.

82. C. Blenche, University of Central Florida, reviewer suggestion, added February 3, 2017.

83. A. Von Tobel, "Where Money Meets Morale," *INC.* (April 2014): 48-49.

84. Retrieved from the Ohio State website on Nov. 23, 2018, http://ohiostatebuckeyes.com/staff/gene-smith/.

85. C. Stewart, "6 Things to Know About Ohio State's $170M Athletics Budget," *Daytona Daily News* (June 6, 2017).

86. D. Murphy, "Ohio State Suspends Coach Urban Meyer, AD Gene Smith," ESPN.com (August 23, 2018).

## CHAPTER 7

1. Found at www.teamworkonline.com/other-sports-jobs/ironman/ironman/vice-president-human-resources-1936709 on April 22, 2018.

2. R.L. Dipboye, "Bridging the Gap in Organizations Behavior," *Academy of Management Learning & Education* 13, no. 3 (2014): 487-491.

3. A. Chatterji and A. Patro, "Dynamic Capabilities and Managing Human Capital," *Academy of Management Perspectives* 28, no. 4 (2014): 395-408.

4. L. Jia, J.D. Shaw, A.S. Tsue, and T.Y. Park, "A Social-Structural Perspective on Employee-Organization Relationships and Team Creativity," *Academy of Management Journal* 57, no. 3 (2014): 869-891.

5. B.R. Dineen and D.G. Allen, "Third Party Employment Branding: Human Capital Inflows and Outflows Following Best Places to Work Certifications," *Academy of Management Journal* 59, no. 1 (2016): 90-112.

6. L. Goler and J. de Baubigny, "What Employees Want," *The Wall Street Journal* (March 7, 2017): R1, R2.

7. I. Sager, "Career Services," *BusinessWeek* (May 1, 2014): 56.

8. EEOC website, www.eeoc.gov (accessed March 19, 2018).

9. Staff, "Decoding the DNA of the Entrepreneur," *INC.* (December 2015/January 2016): 53-59.

10. Dineen and Allen, "Third Party Employment Branding."

11. J.C. Molloy and J.B. Barney, "Who Captures the Value Created with Human Capital? A Market-Based View," *Academy of Management Perspectives* 29, no. 3 (2015): 309-325; R. Lussier and J. Hendon, *Human Resource Management*, 2nd ed. (Thousand Oaks, CA: Sage, 2016).

12. J.R. Hollenbeck and B.B. Jamieson, "Human Capital, Social Capital, and Social Network Analysis," *Academy of Management Perspectives* 29, no. 3 (2015): 370-365.

13. C. Orr, "Who Are the NFL's Best General Managers?" SI.com (December 21, 2017).

14. P.K. Thompson, "Help with Hiring," *Costco Connection* (December 2014): 13-14.

15. L. Adler, "4 Big Hiring Mistakes—and How to Avoid Them," *INC.* (March 2015): 10.

16. L. Weber and M. Korn, "Where Did All the Entry-Level Jobs Go?" *The Wall Street Journal* (August 6, 2014): B6.

17. This job description was used with permission from Elms College.

18. L. Adler, "4 Common Leadership Fears and How to Avoid Them," *INC.* (April 2015): 10.

19. C. Blencke, University of Central Florida, review recommendation added May 8, 2017.

20. C. Hann, "Go Get 'Em," *Entrepreneur* (July 2014): 34.

21. S. Frier and A. Satariano, "Big IPO," *BusinessWeek* (December 21-27, 2015): 29-30.

22. Lussier and Hendon, *Human Resource Management*, 2nd ed.

23. Lussier and Hendon, *Human Resource Management*, 2nd ed.

24. DOL, The Occupational Information Network (O*Net) website, www.onetonline.org (accessed March 19, 2018).

25. Staff, "Company Spotlight: First American," *Fortune* (March 15, 2016): 59.

26. "The HR Guide to the Galaxy," *Forbes* (May 25, 2015): 90.

27. Bain & Company survey, reported in *INC.* (October 2014): 112-113.

28. "Bosses Are Creating a New Generation of Leaders," CEO survey reported in *INC.* (September 2014): 76.

29. Staff, "Reader Poll," *Costco Connection* (April 2015): 13.

30. J.C. Marr and D.M. Cable, "Do Interviewers Sell Themselves Short? The Effects of Selling Orientation on Interviewers' Judgments," *Academy of Management Journal* 57, no. 3 (2014): 624-651.

31. A. Handley, "Get Outta Here!" *Entrepreneur* (January 2016): 26.

32. ADP Research Institute study, reported in *Forbes* (November 23, 2015): 102-103.

33. Lussier and Hendon, *Human Resource Management*, 2nd ed.

34. Y. Liu, G.R. Ferris, J. Xu, B.A. Weitz, and P.L. Perrewe, "When Ingratiation Backfires: The Role of Political Skill in the Ingratiation–Internship Performance Relationship," *Academy of Management Learning & Education* 13, no. 4 (2014): 569-586.

35. M. Bidwell and J.R. Keller, "Within or Without? How Firms Combine Internal and External Labor Markets to Fill Jobs," *Academy of Management Journal* 57, no. 4 (2014): 1035-1055.

36. J. Zucker, "LeBron James Reportedly 'Likely' to Join Lakers or Clippers as 2018 Free Agent," Bleacher Report.com (June 14, 2017).

37. Bidwell and Keller, "Within or Without?"

38. A. Von Tobel, "Where Money Meets Morale," *INC.* (April 2014): 48-49.

39. A. Gumbus and R.N. Lussier, "Career Development: Enhancing Your Networking Skill," *Clinical Leadership & Management Review* 17 (2003): 16-20.

40. L.A. Mainiero and K.J. Jones, "Sexual Harassment Versus Workplace Romance: Social Media Spillover and Textual Harassment in the Workplace," *Academy of Management Perspectives* 27, no. 3 (2013): 187-203.

41. T. Monahan, "Revving Up Your Corporate RPMs," *Fortune* (February 1, 2016): 43.

42. ADP Research Institute study, reported in *Forbes*.

43. S.Y. Lee, M. Pitesa, S. Thau, and M.M. Pillutla, "Discrimination in Selection Decisions: Integrating Stereotype Fit and Interdependence Theories," *Academy of Management Journal* 58, no. 3 (2015): 789-812.

44. Von Tobel, "Where Money Meets Morale."

45. G. Anders, "Nice Guys Hire Better," *Forbes* (May 25, 2015): 54.

46. R. Hogan, "Find Out if Your Personality Fits Your Job," *Time* (June 22, 2015): 45.

47. L. Weber, "Drug Use Is on the Rise Among Workers in U.S.," *The Wall Street Journal* (June 3, 2015): B1, B7.

48. L. Weber, "To Get a Job, New Hires Are Put to the Test," *The Wall Street Journal* (April 15, 2015): A1, A10.

49. L. Weber and E. Dwoskin, "As Personality Tests Multiply, Employers Are Split," *The Wall Street Journal* (September 30, 2014): A1, A12.

50. Liu et al., "When Ingratiation Backfires."

51. Von Tobel, "Where Money Meets Morale."

52. ADP Research Institute study, reported in *Forbes*.

53. Von Tobel, "Where Money Meets Morale."

54. Marr and Cable, "Do Interviewers Sell Themselves Short?"

55. P. Lencioni, "Being Smart Is Overrated," *INC.* (October 2014): 128.

56. G. O'Brien, "Honesty Policies," *Entrepreneur* (October 2014): 34-35.

57. Lee et al., "Discrimination in Selection Decisions."

58. O'Brien, "Honesty Policies."

59. O'Brien, "Honesty Policies."

60. Bidwell and Keller, "Within or Without?"

61. G. Colvin, "Ignore These Leadership Lessons at Your Peril," *Fortune* (October 28, 2013): 85.

62. B. Shoot, "HR Made Easier," *Entrepreneur* (June 2015): 80.

63. Y. Dong, M.G. Seo, and K.M. Bartol, "No Pain, No Gain: An Affect-Based Model of Developmental Job Experience and the Buffering Effects of Emotional Intelligence," *Academy of Management Journal* 57, no. 4 (2014): 1056-1077.

64. G. Jones, "Sports Wisdom in the Office," *INC.* (April 2014): 47.

65. Lussier and Hendon, *Human Resource Management*, 2nd ed.

66. Lussier and Hendon, *Human Resource Management*, 2nd ed.

67. Hann, "Go Get 'Em."

68. Von Tobel, "Where Money Meets Morale."

69. Jia et al., "A Social-Structural Perspective."

70. M. Voronov and K. Weber, "The Heart of Institutions: Emotional Competence and Institutional Actorhood," *Academy of Management Review* 41, no. 3 (2016): 456-478.

71. G. O'Brien, "Putting Everyone at Ease," *Entrepreneur* (July 2015): 30.

72. S. Liu, M. Wang, P. Bamberger, J. Shi, and S.B. Bacharach, "The Dark Side of Socialization: A Longitudinal Investigation of Newcomer Alcohol Use," *Academy of Management Journal* 58, no. 2 (2015): 334-355.

73. L.W. Chen and P. Thompson, "Skill Balance and Entrepreneurship Evidence from Online Career Histories," *Entrepreneurship Theory and Practice* 40, no. 2 (2016): 289-304.

74. Information added based on reviewer David Biemer, Texas State University, suggestion May 9, 2017.

75. B.L. Rau, "The Oxford Handbook of Evidence-Based Management," *Academy of Management Learning & Education* 13, no. 3 (2014): 485-487.

76. Chen and Thompson, "Skill Balance and Entrepreneurship Evidence."

77. Rau, "The Oxford Handbook."

78. L. Kolodny, "A New Way to Train Workers, One Small Bite at a Time," *The Wall Street Journal* (March 14, 2016): R6.

79. E. Van Oosten and K.E. Kram, "Coaching for Change," *Academy of Management Learning & Education* 13, no. 2 (2014): 295-298.

80. ADP Research Institute study, reported in *Forbes.*

81. P. Jacquart and J. Antonakis, "When Does Charisma Matter for Top-Level Leaders? Effect of Attributional Ambiguity," *Academy of Management Journal* 58, no. 4 (2015): 1051-1074.

82. C. Hann, "Looking Back," *Entrepreneur* (October 2014): 36.

83. Hann, "Looking Back."

84. Van Oosten and Kram, "Coaching for Change."

85. S. Marikar, "Tools for Your Remote Team," *INC.* (December 2015/January 2016): 88-89.

86. P.B. Whyman and A.I. Petrescu, "Workplace Flexibility Practices in SMEs Relationship with Performance via Redundancies, Absenteeism, and Financial Turnaround," *Journal of Small Business Management* 53, no. 4 (2015): 1097-1126.

87. Whyman and Petrescu, "Workplace Flexibility Practices."

88. E. Bernstein, "The Smart Path to a Transparent Workplace," *The Wall Street Journal* (February 23, 2015): R5.

89. S. Shellenbarger, "It's Not My Fault! A Better Response to Criticism at Work," *The Wall Street Journal* (June 18, 2014): D1, D4.

90. L. Gallagher, "Why Employees Love Marriott," *Fortune* (March 15, 2015): 113-118.

91. Staff, "Nearly Departed," *Forbes* (May 4, 2015): 24.

92. M. Houlihan and B. Harvey, "You Won't Learn This in Business School," *Costco Connection* (April 2014): 13.

93. R. King, "Companies Want to Know: How Do Workers Feel?" *The Wall Street Journal* (November 14, 2015): R3.

94. S. Marikar, "All Hail the King," *INC.* (June 2015): 30.

95. G. Colvin, "Personal Bests," *Fortune* (March 15, 2015): 106-110.

96. Colvin, "Personal Bests."

97. Von Tobel, "Where Money Meets Morale."

98. www.spotrac.com/mlb/boston-red-sox/david-price-7536/ (retrieved April 26, 2018)

99. Von Tobel, "Where Money Meets Morale."

100. E. Schurenberg, "What Do You Owe Your Employees," *INC.* (November 2015): 12.

101. A.W. Mathews, "Cost of a Family Health Plan Tops $17,000," *The Wall Street Journal* (September 23, 2015): B3.

102. C. Flavelle, "Facing America's Other Middle-Class Squeeze," *BusinessWeek* (October 20-26, 2014): 43-44.

103. A. Von Tobel, "Get Financially Fit Before 2015," *INC.* (October 2014): 104.

104. T. Cettina, "Retirement Comes First," *Costco Connection* (January 2016): 27.

105. K. Kristof, "Take Risks When You're Young," *INC.* (March 2017) 56.

106. Cettina, "Retirement Comes First."

107. R. Fagan, "Pro Sports Lockouts and Strikes Fast Facts," Sporting News.com (February 5, 2018).

108. M.L. Call, A.J. Nyberg, R.E. Ployhart, and J. Weekley, "The Dynamic Nature of Collective Turnover and Unit Performance: The Impact of Time, Quality, and Replacements," *Academy of Management Journal* 58, no. 4 (2015): 1208-1232.

109. B.R. Dineen and D.G. Allen, "Third Party Employment Branding: Human Capital Inflows and Outflows Following Best Places to Work Certifications," *Academy of Management Journal* 59, no. 1 (2016): 90-112.

110. M. Medcalf and D. Wilson, "Rick Pitino's Coaching Career: A Timeline," Espn.com (September 27, 2017).

111. S. Axson, "Louisville Head Coach Rick Pitino Officially Fired," SI.com, (October 16, 2017).

112. J. Wertheim, "Throwing in the Chair: The Increasingly Bizarre and Sad Legacy of Bob Knight and Indiana," SI.com (March 10, 2017).

# CHAPTER 8

1. Retrieved from www.usada.org/about/ on May 17, 2018.

2. T. Tygart, "Statement from CEO Travis T. Tygart Regarding Lance Armstrong Interview," www.usada.org (January 17, 2013).

3. D. Andone, "Lance Armstrong to Pay US Government $5 Million to Settle Lawsuit," CNN.com (April 19, 2018).

4. www.theguardian.com/sport/2016/mar/08/meldonium-maria-sharapova-failed-drugs-test (retrieved on May 7, 2018).

5. V. Mather and B. Witz, "Robinson Cano Suspended 80 Games for Positive Drug Test," *The New York Times* (May 15, 2018).

6. W.L. Bedwell, S.M. Fiore, and E. Salas, "Developing the Future Workforce: An Approach for Integrating Interpersonal Skills Into the MBA Classroom," *Academy of Management Learning & Education* 13, no. 2 (2014): 171-186; L. Weber and M. Korn, "Where Did All the Entry-Level Jobs Go?" *The Wall Street Journal* (August 6, 2014): B6.

7.  D.X.H. Wo, M.L. Ambrose, and M. Schminke, "What Drives Trickle-Down Effects? A Test of Multiple Mediation Processes," *Academy of Management Journal* 58, no. 6 (2015): 1848-1868.

8.  S.D. Charlier, "Incorporating Evidence-Based Management Into Management Curricula: A Conversation with Gary Latham," *Academy of Management Learning & Education* 13, no. 3 (2014): 467-475.

9.  D.L. Ferris, H. Lian, D.J. Brown, and R. Morrison, "Ostracism, Self-Esteem, and Job Performance: When Do We Self-Verify and When Do We Self-Enhance?" *Academy of Management Journal* 58, no. 1 (2015): 279-297.

10. A.S. DeNisi, "Some Further Thoughts on the Entrepreneurial Personality," *Entrepreneurship Theory and Practice* 39, no. 5 (2015): 997-1003.

11. G. O'Brien, "It's All Your Fault!" *Entrepreneur* (February 2015): 30.

12. D. Sterling, "Advice to My 20-Year-Old Self," *Fortune* (October 1, 2015): 116.

13. M. Kelly, https://dynamiccatholic.com (accessed April 1, 2018).

14. M.S. Cardon and C.P. Kirk, "Entrepreneurial Passion as Mediator of the Self-Efficacy to Persistence Relationship," *Entrepreneurship Theory and Practice* 39, no. 5 (2015): 1027-1050.

15. J. Gaines, "Playing with the Big Boxes," *Entrepreneur* (February 2015): 15.

16. E. Bernstein, "Beat Back the Self-Doubt," *The Wall Street Journal* (June 14, 2016): D1, D2.

17. M. Kelly, *Rediscovering Catholicism* (New York: Beacon, 2010).

18. P.M. Picone, G.B. Dagnino, and A. Mina, "The Origin of Failure: A Multidisciplinary Appraisal of the Hubris Hypothesis and Proposed Research Agenda," *Academy of Management Perspectives* 28, no. 4 (2014): 447-468.

19. R. Lewis, "My Advice," *Fortune* (December 22, 2014): 34.

20. S. Shellenbarger, "When the Only Thing Holding You Back Is Self-Doubt," *The Wall Street Journal* (April 15, 2015): D3.

21. C. Rose, "Charlie Rose Talks to Tory Burch," *BusinessWeek* (October 20-26, 2014): 24.

22. DeNisi, "Some Further Thoughts."

23. F.P. Morgeson, T.R. Mitchell, and D. Liu, "Event System Theory: An Event-Oriented Approach to the Organizational Sciences," *Academy of Management Review* 40, no. 4 (2015): 515-537.

24. S.F. Collins, "Success Steps," *Costco Connection* (January 2016): 29.

25. Kelly, *Rediscovering Catholicism.*

26. W. Amos, "Agent of Change," *Costco Connection* (August 2015): 15.

27. M. Rosenwald, "Bound by Habit," *BusinessWeek* (March 19-25, 2012): 106-107.

28. Bernstein, "Beat Back the Self-Doubt."

29. C. Kenny, "The Economic Power of Positive Thinking," *BusinessWeek* (January 12-18, 2015): 8-9.

30. B. Cohen, "The Power of Ohio State's Positive Thinking," *The Wall Street Journal* (January 9, 2015): D6.

31. M. Angelica, *Suffering and Burnout* (EWTN Publishing, 2016).

32. Bernstein, "Beat Back the Self-Doubt."

33. L. Holtz, "Setting a Higher Standard," *Success Yearbook* (Tampa, FL: Peter Lowe International, 1998): 74.

34. Staff, "4 Habits of Truly Resilient People," *INC.* (March 2016): 10.

35. News, National Public Radio (NPR) (aired November 23, 2015).

36. E. Bernstein, "Self-Talk, or a Heart-to-Heart with Your Closest Friend," *The Wall Street Journal* (May 6, 2014): D1, D2.

37. Ziglar, www.ziglar.com (accessed May 17, 2017).

38. V. Williams, "Top Videos," *INC.* (December 2016/January 2017): 10.

39. Bernstein, "Self-Talk."

40. Bernstein, "Beat Back the Self-Doubt."

41. Staff, "What's on Entrepreneur.com?" *Entrepreneur* (December 2014): 12.

42. Rosenwald, "Bound by Habit."

43. E. Bernstein, "We Actually Get Nicer with Age," *The Wall Street Journal* (April 22, 2014): D1, D2.

44. E. Grijalva and P. D. Harms, "Narcissism: An Integrative Synthesis and Dominance Complementarity Model," *Academy of Management Perspectives* 28, no. 2 (2014): 108-127.

45. T. Hahn, L. Preuss, J. Pinkse, and F. Figge, "Cognitive Frames in Corporate Sustainability: Managerial Sensemaking with Paradoxical and Business Case Frames," *Academy of Management Review* 39, no. 4 (2014): 463-487.

46. DeNisi, "Some Further Thoughts."

47. Bernstein, "We Actually Get Nicer with Age."

48. DeNisi, "Some Further Thoughts."

49. T. Georgens, "Trust Your People to Innovate, Take Risk," *Forbes* (October 29, 2014): 113.

50. V. Bamiatzi, S. Jones, S. Mitchelmore, and K. Nikoogpulos, "The Role of Competencies in Shaping the Leadership Style of Female Entrepreneurs," *Journal of Small Business Management* 53, no. 3 (2015): 627-644.

51. J. Robinson, "Where There's Willpower, There's a Way," *Entrepreneur* (July 2015): 50-54; K. Tindell, "Top Videos," *INC.* (March 2016): 10.

52. L. Buchanan, "Wired for Success," *INC.* (September 2014): 26-52.

53. J. Ankeny, "The Six Entrepreneurial Profiles," *Entrepreneur* (February 2015): 37.

54. Ankeny, "Six Entrepreneurial Profiles."

55. T.A. Judge and C.P. Zapata, "The Person-Situation Debate Revisited: Effect of Situation Strength and Trait Activation on the Validity of the Big Five Personality Traits in Predicting Job Performance," *Academy of Management Journal* 58, no. 4 (2015): 1149-1179.

56. B. Antoncic, T.B. Kregar, G. Singh, and A.F. DeNoble, "The Big Five Personality-Entrepreneurship Relationship: Evidence from Slovenia," *Journal of Small Business Management* 53, no. 3 (2015): 819-841.

57. Judge and Zapata, "Person-Situation Debate Revisited."

58. L. Weber and E. Dwoskin, "As Personality Tests Multiply, Employers Are Split," *The Wall Street Journal* (September 30, 2014): A1, A12; L. Weber, "To Get a Job, New Hires Are Put to the Test," *The Wall Street Journal* (April 15, 2015): A1, A10.

59. K. Lanaj and J.R. Hollenbeck, "Leadership Over-Emergence in Self-Managing Teams: The Role of Gender and Countervailing Biases," *Academy of Management Journal* 58, no. 5 (2015): 1476-1494.

60. D. Roberts, "The Rock," *Fortune* (November 17, 2014): 146.

61. Staff, "Margin Note," *BusinessWeek* (July 20-26, 2015): 21.

62. Wo et al., "What Drives Trickle-Down Effects?"

63. R. Fehr, K.C. Yam, and C. Dang, "Moralized Leadership: The Construction and Consequences of Ethical Leader Perceptions," *Academy of Management Review* 40, no. 2 (2015): 182-209.

64. O. Ybarra, E. Kross, and J.S. Burks, "The Big Idea That Is Yet to Be: Toward a More Motivated, Contextual, and Dynamic Model of Emotional Intelligence," *Academy of Management Perspectives* 28, no. 2 (2014): 93-107.

65. A. Meister, K.A. Jehn, and S.M.B. Thatcher, "Feeling Misidentified: The Consequences of Internal Identity Asymmetries for Individuals at Work," *Academy of Management Review* 38, no. 4 (2014): 488-512.

66. A.C. Peng, J.M. Schaubroeck, and Y. Li, "Social Exchange Implications of Own and Coworkers' Experience of Supervisory Abuse," *Academy of Management Journal* 57, no. 5 (2014): 1385-1405.

67. G. Colvin, "What Really Has the 99% Up in Arms," *Fortune* (November 7, 2011): 87.

68. P. Harvey, K. Madison, M. Martinko, T.R. Crook, and T.A. Crook, "Attribution Theory in the Organizational Sciences: The Road Traveled and the Path Ahead," *Academy of Management Perspectives* 28, no. 2 (2014): 128-146; Peng et al., "Social Exchange Implications."

69. P. Jacquart and J. Antonakis, "When Does Charisma Matter for Top-Level Leaders? Effect of Attributional Ambiguity," *Academy of Management Journal* 58, no. 4 (2015): 1051-1074.

70. V. Desai, "Learning Through the Distribution of Failures Within an Organization," *Academy of Management Journal* 58, no. 4 (2015): 1032-1050.

71. D. Ariely, "Ask Ariely," *The Wall Street Journal* (September 27-28, 2014): D4.

72. Picone et al., "The Origin of Failure."

73. Wo et al., "What Drives Trickle-Down Effects?"

74. M.E. Chan and D.J. McAllister, "Abusive Supervision Through the Lens of Employee State Paranoia," *Academy of Management Review* 39, no. 1 (2014): 44-66.

75. Wo et al., "What Drives Trickle-Down Effects?"

76. A. Kirkman, "It's All About Attitude," *Fortune* (November 17, 2014): 34.

77. T. Gimbel, "CEO 101," *Fortune* (November 17, 2014): 147.

78. D. Antons and F.T. Piller, "Opening the Black Box of 'Not Invented Here': Attitudes, Decision Biases, and Behavioral Consequences," *Academy of Management Perspectives* 29, no. 2 (2015): 193-217.

79. Antons and Piller, "Opening the Black Box."

80. Harvey et al., "Attribution Theory."

81. S.J. Creary, B.B. Caza, and L.M. Roberts, "Out of the Box? How Managing a Subordinate's Multiple Identities Affects the Quality of a Manager-Subordinate Relationship," *Academy of Management Review* 40, no. 4 (2015): 538-562.

82. Harvey et al., "Attribution Theory."

83. Chan and McAllister, "Abusive Supervision."

84. Peng et al., "Social Exchange Implications."

85. J. Wooden, www.coachwooden.com (accessed April 2, 2018).

86. S. Diestel, J. Wegge, and K.H. Schmidt, "The Impact of Social Context on the Relationship Between Individual Job Satisfaction and Absenteeism: The Roles of Different Foci of Job Satisfaction and Work-Unit Absenteeism," *Academy of Management Journal* 57, no. 2 (2014): 353-382.

87. Diestel et al., "The Impact of Social Context."

88. B.P. Owens and D.R. Hekman, "How Does Leader Humility Influence Team Performance? Exploring the Mechanism of Contagion and Collective Promotion Focus," *Academy of Management Journal* 59, no. 3 (2016): 1088-1111; A. Lashinsky, "Larry Page Interview," *Fortune* (February 6, 2012): 98-99.

89. R. McCammon, "I'm Sure You're Wondering Why I've Called You All Here," *Entrepreneur* (March 2015): 28-29.

90. J. Robinson, "Your Brain on Power," *Entrepreneur* (March 2014): 61.

91. Picone et al., "The Origin of Failure."

92. D. Eng, "How to Get Over Yourself," *Fortune* (March 1, 2015): 36; L. Tomkins and E. Ulus, "Is Narcissism Undermining Critical Reflection in Our Business Schools?" *Academy of Management Learning & Education* 14, no. 4 (2015): 595-606.

93. Q.N. Huy, K.G. Corley, and M.S. Kraatz, "From Support to Mutiny: Shifting Legitimacy Judgments and Emotional Reactions Impacting the Implementation of Radical Change," *Academy of Management Journal* 57, no. 6 (2014): 1650-1680.

94. J.D. Westphal and G. Shani, "Psyched-Up to Suck-Up: Self-Regulated Cognition, Interpersonal Influence, and Recommendations for Board Appointments in the Corporate Elite," *Academy of Management Journal* 59, no. 2 (2016): 479-509.

95. I. Sutherland, J.R. Gosling, and J. Jelinek, "Aesthetics of Power: Why Teaching About Power Is Easier Than Learning for Power, and What Business Schools Could Do About It," *Academy of Management Learning & Education* 14, no. 4 (2015): 607-624.

96. C.L. Pearce, C.L. Wassenaar, and C.C. Manz, "Is Shared Leadership the Key to Responsible Leadership?" *Academy of Management Perspectives* 28, no. 3 (2014): 275-288.

97. N.M. Lorinkova, M.J. Pearsall, and H.P. Sims, "Examining the Differential Longitudinal Performance of Directive Versus Empowering Leadership in Teams," *Academy of Management Journal* 56, no. 2 (2013): 573-596; F. Aime, S. Humphrey, D.S. Derue, and J.B. Paul, "The Riddle of Heterarchy: Power Transitions in Cross-Functional Teams," *Academy of Management Journal* 57, no. 2 (2014): 327-352.

98. F. Sobral and G. Islam, "He Who Laughs Best, Leaves Last: The Influence of Humor on the Attitudes and Behavior of Interns," *Academy of Management Learning & Education* 14, no. 4 (2015): 500-518.

99. D. Ma, M. Rhee, and D. Yang, "Power Source Mismatch and the Effectiveness of Interorganizational Relations: The Case of Venture Capital Syndication," *Academy of Management Journal* 56, no. 3 (2014): 711-734.

100. A.A. Cannella, C.D. Jones, and M.C. Withers, "Family- Versus Lone-Founder-Controlled Public Corporations: Social Identity Theory and Boards of Directors," *Academy of Management Journal* 58, no. 2 (2015): 436-459.

101. Aime et al., "The Riddle of Heterarchy."

102. H. Lian, D.J. Brown, D.L. Ferris, L.H. Liang, L.M. Keeping, and R. Morrison, "Abusive Supervision and Retaliation: A Self-Control Framework," *Academy of Management Journal* 57, no. 1 (2014): 116-139.

103. D. Wescott, "Field Guide to Office Bullies," *Business-Week* (November 26–December 2, 2012): 94-95; B.M. Galvin, D. Lange, and B.E. Ashforth, "Narcissistic Organizational Identification: Seeing Oneself as Central to the Organization's Identity," *Academy of Management Review* 40, no. 2 (2015): 163-181.

104. A. Bitektine and P. Haack, "The Macro and the Micro of Legitimacy: Toward a Multilevel Theory of the Legitimacy Process," *Academy of Management Review* 40, no. 1 (2015): 49-75.

105. D.J. Harmon, S.E. Green, G.T. Goodnight, "A Model of Rhetorical Legitimation: The Structure of Communication and Cognition Underlying Institutional Maintenance and Change," *Academy of Management Review* 40, no. 1 (2015): 76-95.

106. S.S. Wiltermuth, "Power, Moral Clarity, and Punishment in the Workplace," *Academy of Management Journal* 56, no. 4 (2013): 1002-1023.

107. J. Naisbitt, "Thoughts: On Power," *Forbes* (November 23, 2015): 160.

108. A. Joshi and A.P. Knight, "Who Defers to Whom and Why? Dual Pathways Linking Demographic Differences and Dyadic Deference to Team Effectiveness," *Academy of Management Journal* 58, no. 1 (2015): 59-84.

109. P. Lencioni, "Being Smart Is Overrated," *INC.* (October 2014): 128.

110. Lencioni, "Being Smart Is Overrated."

111. Y. Liu, G.R. Ferris, J. Xu, B.A. Weitz, and P.L. Perrewe, "When Ingratiation Backfires: The Role of Political Skill in the Ingratiation–Internship Performance Relationship," *Academy of Management Learning & Education* 13, no. 4 (2014): 569-586.

112. Liu et al., "When Ingratiation Backfires."

113. M. Berman, "The No-Boss Company," *The Wall Street Journal* (October 27, 2015): R3.

114. C.H. Chang, C.C. Rosen, and P.E. Levy, "The Relationship Between Perceptions of Organizational Politics and Employee Attitudes, Strain and Behavior: A Meta-Analytic Examination," *Academy of Management Journal* 52, no. 4 (2009): 779-801.

115. D.R. Soriano, "Political Skills in Organizations: Do Personality and Reputation Play a Role?" *Academy of Management Perspectives* 22, no. 1 (2008): 66-68.

116. R. McCammon, "Do Me a Solid," *Entrepreneur* (March 2014): 32-33.

117. Peng et al., "Social Exchange Implications."

118. Creary et al., "Out of the Box?"

119. McCammon, "Do Me a Solid."

120. Ziglar website, www.ziglar.com (accessed May 18, 2017).

121. Liu et al., "When Ingratiation Backfires."

122. R. McCammon, "I'm Going to Need a Bit More Time . . . ," *Entrepreneur* (September 2014): 28-30.

123. R. McCammon, "How to Own the Room," *Business-Week* online (accessed May 18, 2017).

124. E. Bernstein, "Don't Apologize So Fast," *The Wall Street Journal* (July 15, 2014): D1, D4.

125. Staff, "The Reconciliation Game," *The Wall Street Journal* (November 17, 2015): D1.

126. S. Fisher, "How to Turn Foes Into Friends," *Costco Connection* (April 2016): 13.

127. S. Shellenbarger, "Leader? No, Be a Follower," *The Wall Street Journal* (September 30, 2015): D1, D3.

128. M. Sytch and A. Tatarynowicz, "Friends and Foes: The Dynamics of Dual Social Structures," *Academy of Management Journal* 57, no. 2 (2014): 585-613.

129. E. Bernstein, "I'm Sorry, I'm Allergic to You," *The Wall Street Journal* (July 1, 2014): D1, D2.

130. S. Shellenbarger, "To Fight or Not to Fight? When to Pick Workplace Battles," *The Wall Street Journal* (December 17, 2014): D1, D2; E. Bernstein, "The Year in Relationship Troubles, and How Talk Can Help," *The Wall Street Journal* (December 30, 2014): D1, D2.

131. Bernstein, "Don't Apologize So Fast."

132. Shellenbarger, "To Fight or Not to Fight?"

133. E. Bernstein, "You Can Do It! Be a Motivator," *The Wall Street Journal* (June 16, 2016): D1, D3.

134. R. McCammon, "I'm Sure You're Wondering Why I've Called You All Here," *Entrepreneur* (March 2015): 28-29.

135. Wo et al., "What Drives Trickle-Down Effects?"

136. Wo et al., "What Drives Trickle-Down Effects?"

137. R. McCammon, "Can We Talk," *Entrepreneur* (May 2015): 25-26.

138. Wo et al., "What Drives Trickle-Down Effects?"

139. P. Lencioni, "Innovation Won't Get You Very Far," *INC.* (December 2014/January 2015): 102.

140. K. Clark, "Why the Seahawks Like Confrontation," *The Wall Street Journal* (January 8, 2015): D6.

141. T. Perrotta, "The Secret Power of Twins: Amnesia," *The Wall Street Journal* (May 27, 2014): D6.

142. Shellenbarger, "To Fight or Not to Fight?"

143. D. Horowitz and A. Horowitz, "When Customer Service Goes Wrong," *Costco Connection* (October 2014): 15.

144. K. Leavitt and D.M. Sluss, "Lying for Who We Are: An Identity-Based Model of Workplace Dishonesty," *Academy of Management Review* 40, no. 4 (2015): 587-610.

145. N. Brodsky, "Shut Up and Listen," *INC.* (March 2015): 58.

146. D.T. Kong, K.T. Dirks, and D.L. Ferrin, "Interpersonal Trust Within Negotiations: Meta-Analytic Evidence, Critical Contingencies, and Directions for Further Research," *Academy of Management Journal* 57, no. 5 (2014): 1235-1255.

147. G. Colvin, "Where Disrupters Meet Aristocrats," *Fortune* (December 1, 2015): 28.

148. Kong et al., "Interpersonal Trust Within Negotiations."

149. Charlier, "Incorporating Evidence-Based Management."

150. R. Lussier, "The Negotiation Process," *Clinical Leadership & Management Review* 14, no. 2 (2000): 55-59.

151. Brodsky, "Shut Up and Listen."

152. A. Coombs, "The Biggest Mistakes Executives Make When Negotiating a Retirement Package," *The Wall Street Journal* (June 13, 2016): R1, R2.

153. Coombs, "The Biggest Mistakes Executives Make."

154. Coombs, "The Biggest Mistakes Executives Make."

155. C. Hann, "Always Be Closing," *Entrepreneur* (August 2015): 30.

156. Brodsky, "Shut Up and Listen."

157. Coombs, "The Biggest Mistakes Executives Make."

158. Horowitz and Horowitz, "When Customer Service Goes Wrong."

159. Brodsky, "Shut Up and Listen."

160. Coombs, "The Biggest Mistakes Executives Make."

161. Kong et al., "Interpersonal Trust Within Negotiations."

162. C. Hann, "Fair Pay," *Entrepreneur* (May 2016): 23.

163. McCammon, "Can We Talk."

164. T. Robbins, "Robbins' Rules," *Fortune* (November 17, 2014): 131.

165. Bernstein, "The Year in Relationship Troubles."

166. McCammon, "Can We Talk."

167. Bernstein, "I'm Sorry, I'm Allergic to You."

168. Shellenbarger, "To Fight or Not to Fight?"

169. L.R. Weingart, K.J. Behfar, C. Bendersky, G. Todorova, and K.A. Jehn, "The Directness and Oppositional Intensity of Conflict Expression," *Academy of Management Review* 40, no. 2 (2015): 235-262.

170. Charlier, "Incorporating Evidence-Based Management."

171. Fisher, "How to Turn Foes Into Friends."

172. R.D. Costigan and K.E. Brink, "Another Perspective on MBA Program Alignment: An Investigation of Learning Goals," *Academy of Management Learning & Education* 14, no. 2 (2015): 260-276; Bedwell et al., "Developing the Future Workforce."

173. The term *eustress* was added at the suggestion of reviewer Carl Blencke, University of Central Florida, on May 23, 2017.

174. E. Agnvall, "Stress: Don't Let It Make You Sick," *AARP Bulletin* (November 2014): 26-27.

175. Y. Zhang, J.A. Lepine, B.R. Buckman, and F. Wei, "It's Not Fair . . . Or Is It? The Role of Justice and Leadership in Explaining Work Stressor–Job Performance Relationships," *Academy of Management Journal* 57, no. 3 (2014): 675-697.

176. Zhang et al., "It's Not Fair . . . Or Is It?"

177. J. Fried, "In Praise of Deadlines," *INC.* (December 2015/January 2016): 128.

178. L.M. Maruping, V. Vewnkatesh, S.M.B. Thatcher, and P.C. Patel, "Folding Under Pressure of Rising to the Occasion? Perceived Time Pressure and the Moderating Role of Team Temporal Leadership," *Academy of Management Journal* 58, no. 5 (2015): 1313-1333.

179. A.J. Lombardi, "Tech Neck," *Strength & Conditioning* online (accessed May 23, 2017).

180. J. Schramm, "Manage Stress, Improve the Bottom Line," *HR Magazine* (February 2013): 80.

181. H. Mitchell, "Does Being Stressed Out Make You Forget?" *The Wall Street Journal* (March 17, 2015): D1.

182. D. Ariely, "Better Off Bed," *INC.* (March 2015): 52.

183. S. Reddy, "Sleep Experts Close in On the Optimal Night's Sleep," *The Wall Street Journal* (July 22, 2015): D1, D2.

184. G.D. Redford, "Why Sleep Is Precious," *AARP the Magazine* (December 2014/January 2015): 22.

185. E. Bernstein, "Changing the Clock Wasn't Good for Your Relationship," *The Wall Street Journal* (March 10, 2015): D1, D2.

186. Staff, "Drinking Diet Soda," *AARP the Magazine* (December 2014/January 2015): 19.

187. M. Gulati, "The Higher Your Stress, the Higher Your LDL," *The Wall Street Journal* (February 9, 2016): D1, D2; S. Shellenbarger, "Are You Hard-Wired to Boil Over From Stress?" *The Wall Street Journal* (February 13, 2013): D3.

188. Gulati, "The Higher Your Stress."

189. Lombardi, "Tech Neck."

190. G. Brown, "Springfield College Grad Savors Role in Minor League Team's Front Office," *The Republican* (April 21, 2018): B1.

191. A. Kirshner, "College Football's Cupcake Games Are About More Than Just Easy Wins," *SB Nation* (June 22, 2016).

192. D. Rovell, "'Guarantee' Games to Fetch $12.9M," ESPN.com (August 29, 2014).

193. S. Rottenberg, "The Baseball Player's Labor Market," *Journal of Political Economy* 64, no. 3 (1956): 242-258.

194. M.A. Leeds, P. von Allmen, and V.A. Matheson, *The Economics of Sports,* 5th ed. (Abingdon, UK: Taylor & Francis, 2013).

195. K. Dosh, "How College Football Playoff's Payouts Compare with BCS's: A Conference-By-Conference Breakdown," *Forbes, Sports Money* (January 1, 2018).

196. J. Thomas, "UMass Football in Line for More Than $6 Million From Nonconference Games," MassLive.com (*The Republican*) (April 23, 2012).

197. Kirshner, "Cupcake Games."

198. D. Malone, "UMass Athletic Director John McCutcheon Leaving for AD Job at UC Santa Barbara," MassLive.com (January 29, 2015).

199. M. Wiedmer, "Did Public Rebuff for Tennessee Job Eventually Cost UTC AD His Job?" *Times Free Press* (June 14, 2017).

## CHAPTER 9

1. Boys and Girls Club of Brattleboro, Vermont, http://bgcbrattleboro.com/about/mission/ (accessed November 29 2018).

2. R. Riley, T. Peterson, A. Kanter, G. Moreno, and W. Goode, *After-School Programs: Keeping Children Safe and Smart* (Washington, DC: U.S. Department of Education, 2000).

3. NBA Communications: Official Release, "NBA All-Star 2018 Community Efforts to Impact Youth, Families and Charitable Organizations Across Los Angeles" (February 14, 2018).

4. L.M. Maruping, V. Vewnkatesh, S.M.B. Thatcher, and P.C. Patel, "Folding Under Pressure of Rising to the Occasion? Perceived Time Pressure and the Moderating Role of Team Temporal Leadership," *Academy of Management Journal* 58, no. 5 (2015): 1313-1333; A. Joshi and A.P. Knight, "Who Defers to Whom and Why? Dual Pathways Linking Demographic Differences and Dyadic Deference to Team Effectiveness," *Academy of Management Journal* 58, no. 1 (2015): 59-84.

5. R.D. Costigan and K.E. Brink, "Another Perspective on MBA Program Alignment: An Investigation of Learning Goals," *Academy of Management Learning & Education* 14, no. 2 (2015): 260-276.

6. K. Davidson, "Hard to Find: Workers With Good Soft Skills," *The Wall Street Journal* (August 31, 2016): B1, B6; J. Rodkin and F. Levy, "Recruiting Preferred Skills," *BusinessWeek* (April 19, 2015): 43.

7. Costigan and Brink, "Another Perspective."

8. Costigan and Brink, "Another Perspective."

9. Staff, "Margin Note," *INC.* (June 2016): 106.

10. N.M. Lorinkova, M.J. Pearsall, and H.P. Sims, "Examining the Differential Longitudinal Performance of Directive Versus Empowering Leadership in Teams," *Academy of Management Journal* 56, no. 2 (2013): 573-596.

11. J. Hu and R.C. Liden, "Making a Difference in the Teamwork: Linking Team Prosocial Motivation to Team Processes and Effectiveness," *Academy of Management Journal* 58, no. 4 (2015): 1102-1127.

12. Lorinkova et al., "Examining the Differential Longitudinal Performance."

13. B. Murphy Jr., "Super Bowl LI: 9 Things to Learn from Tom Brady," Inc.com (February 3, 2017).

14. "Sports Money: 2017 NFL Valuations," www.forbes.com/teams/dallas-cowboys/ (retrieved May 13, 2018).

15. S.H. Harrison and E.D. Rouse, "Let's Dance! Elastic Coordination in Creative Group Work: A Qualitative Study of Modern Dancers," *Academy of Management Journal* 57, no. 5 (2014): 1256-1283.

16. L. Alexander and D. Van Knippenberg, "Teams in Pursuit of Radical Innovation: A Goal Orientation Perspective," *Academy of Management Review* 39, no. 4 (2014): 423-438.

17. C.L. Pearce, C.L. Wassenaar, and C.C. Manz, "Is Shared Leadership the Key to Responsible Leadership?" *Academy of Management Perspectives* 28, no. 3 (2014): 275-288; Lorinkova et al., "Examining the Differential Longitudinal Performance."

18. C.C. Manz, "Taking the Self-Leadership High Road: Smooth Surface or Potholes Ahead?" *Academy of Management Perspectives* 29, no. 1 (2015): 132-151; Pearce et al., "Shared Leadership."

19. L. Jia, J.D. Shaw, A.S. Tsue, and T.Y. Park, "A Social-Structural Perspective on Employee-Organization Relationships and Team Creativity," *Academy of Management Journal* 57, no. 3 (2014): 869-891.

20. M. Sytch and A. Tatarynowicz, "Exploring the Locus of Invention: The Dynamics of Network Communities and Firms' Invention Productivity," *Academy of Management Journal* 57, no. 1 (2014): 249-279.

21. C. Blencke, University of Central Florida, review suggestion, added April 10, 2017.

22. J. Bussey, "Leadership Lessons from the Generals," *The Wall Street Journal* (December 12, 2014): R10.

23. F. Aime, S. Humphrey, D.S. Derue, and J.B. Paul, "The Riddle of Heterarchy: Power Transitions in Cross-Functional Teams," *Academy of Management Journal* 57, no. 2 (2014): 327-352.

24. M.L. Turner, "Remote Control," *Entrepreneur* (January 2016): 75-79.

25. Blencke, review suggestion.

26. C. Clifford, "My Advice," *Fortune* (August 11, 2014): 32.

27. P. Lencioni, "When Less Is More," *INC.* (June 2015): 69.

28. Manz, "Taking the Self-Leadership High Road."

29. Blencke, review suggestion.

30. Staff, "Leader Board: Business Library," *Forbes* (November 23, 2015): 32.

31. Staff, "Leader Board."

32. Editors, "Call for Papers," *Academy of Management Review* 40, no. 4 (2014): 664-665; A.M. Grant, J.M. Berg, and D.M. Cable, "Job Titles as Identity Badges: How Self-Reflective Titles Can Reduce Emotional Exhaustion," *Academy of Management Journal* 57, no. 4 (2014): 1201-1225.

33. S. Yagan, "Book Review," *Fortune* (December 1, 2015): 20; R. Karlgaard, "Diversity's Central Paradox," *Forbes* (May 4, 2015): 34.

34. Joshi and Knight, "Who Defers to Whom."

35. Joshi and Knight, "Who Defers to Whom."

36. C. Ricketts, "Hit List: Lou Holtz," *The Wall Street Journal* (December 23, 2006): P2; L. Holtz, "Setting a Higher Standard," *Success Yearbook* (Tampa, FL: Peter Lowe International, 1998): 74.

37. M. Sytch and A. Tatarynowicz, "Friends and Foes: The Dynamics of Dual Social Structures," *Academy of Management Journal* 57, no. 2 (2014): 585-613.

38. Sytch and Tatarynowicz, "Exploring the Locus of Invention."

39. Maruping et al., "Folding Under Pressure"; N. Li, B.L. Kirkman, and C.O.H. Porter, "Toward a Model of Work Team Altruism," *Academy of Management Review* 39, no. 4 (2014): 541-565.

40. T.A. De Vries, F. Walter, G.S. Van Der Vegt, and P.J.M.D. Essens, "Antecedents of Individuals' Interteam Coordination: Broad Functional Experiences as a Mixed Blessing," *Academy of Management Journal* 57, no. 5 (2014): 1334-1359.

41. A. Lockett, G. Currie, R. Finn, G. Martin, and J. Waring, "The Influence of Social Position on Sensemaking About Organizational Change," *Academy of Management Journal* 57, no. 4 (2014): 1102-1129.

42. J.N. Reyt and B.M. Wiesenfeld, "Seeing the Forest for the Trees: Exploratory Learning, Mobile Technology, and Knowledge Workers' Role Integration Behaviors," *Academy of Management Journal* 58, no. 3 (2015): 739-762.

43. Hu and Liden, "Making a Difference."

44. Li et al., "Work Team Altruism."

45. B.M. Galvin, D. Lange, and B.E. Ashforth, "Narcissistic Organizational Identification: Seeing Oneself as Central to the Organization's Identity," *Academy of Management Review* 40, no. 2 (2015): 163-181.

46. H. Delehanty, "A Conversation With S. Lyubomirsky," *AARP Bulletin* (June 2016): 30.

47. Sytch and Tatarynowicz, "Friends and Foes."

48. B.R. Spisak, M.J. O'Brien, N. Nicholson, and M. Van Vugt, "Niche Construction and the Evolution of Leadership," *Academy of Management Review* 40, no. 2 (2015): 291-306.

49. D. Chandler, "Morals, Markets, and Values-Based Business," *Academy of Management Review* 39, no. 3 (2014): 396-397.

50. G. Di Stefano, A.A. King, and G. Verona, "Sanctioning in the Wild: Rational Calculus and Retributive Instincts in Gourmet Cuisine," *Academy of Management Journal* 58, no. 3 (2015): 906-931.

51. R.C. Liden, S.J. Wayne, C. Liao, and J.D. Meuser, "Servant Leadership and Serving Culture: Influence

on Individual and Unit Performance," *Academy of Management Journal* 57, no. 5 (2014): 1434-1452.

52. Y.R.F. Guillaume, D. Van Knippenberg, and F.C. Brodbeck, "Nothing Succeeds Like Moderation: A Social Self-Regulation Perspective on Cultural Dissimilarity and Performance," *Academy of Management Journal* 57, no. 5 (2014): 1284-1308.

53. R. Durand and P.A. Kremp, "Classical Deviation: Organizational and Individual Status as Antecedents of Conformity," *Academy of Management Journal* 59, no. 1 (2016): 65-89.

54. A. Meister, K.A. Jehn, and S.M.B. Thatcher, "Feeling Misidentified: The Consequences of Internal Identity Asymmetries for Individuals at Work," *Academy of Management Review* 38, no. 4 (2014): 488-512.

55. Staff, "Self-Improvement Through Data," *Fortune* (March 15, 2016): 28.

56. Liden et al., "Servant Leadership."

57. Turner, "Remote Control."

58. E. Frauenheim, "Lessons from the Warriors," Fortune.com (accessed April 12, 2017).

59. Frauenheim, "Lessons from the Warriors."

60. S.J. Creary, B.B. Caza, and L.M. Roberts, "Out of the Box? How Managing a Subordinate's Multiple Identities Affects the Quality of a Manager-Subordinate Relationship," *Academy of Management Review* 40, no. 4 (2015): 538-562.

61. A.G. Pollock and A.G. Acharya, "Shoot for the Stars? Predicting the Recruitment of Prestigious Directors at Newly Public Firms," *Academy of Management Journal* 56, no. 5 (2013): 1396-1419.

62. Aime et al., "Riddle of Heterarchy."

63. Durand and Kremp, "Classical Deviation."

64. J.C. Marr and S. Thau, "Falling from Great (and Not-So-Great) Heights: How Initial Status Position Influences Performance After Status Loss," *Academy of Management Journal* 57, no. 1 (2014): 233-248.

65. Marr and Thau, "Falling from Great."

66. D. Ma, M. Rhee, and D. Yang, "Power Source Mismatch and the Effectiveness of Interorganizational Relations: The Case of Venture Capital Syndication," *Academy of Management Journal* 56, no. 3 (2014): 711-734.

67. Creary et al., "Out of the Box?"

68. Guillaume et al., "Nothing Succeeds Like Moderation."

69. Joshi and Knight, "Who Defers to Whom."

70. L.R. Weingart, K.J. Behfar, C. Bendersky, G. Todorova, and K.A. Jehn, "The Directness and Oppositional Intensity of Conflict Expression," *Academy of Management Review* 40, no. 2 (2015): 235-262.

71. R.L. Hoefer and S.E. Green, "A Rhetorical Model of Institutional Decision Making: The Role of Rhetoric in the Formation and Change of Legitimacy Judgments," *Academy of Management Review* 41, no. 1 (2016): 130-150.

72. Sytch and Tatarynowicz, "Friends and Foes."

73. Lorinkova et al., "Examining the Differential Longitudinal Performance"; Li et al., "Work Team Altruism."

74. C. Blencke, University of Central Florida, review suggestion to add the name, added April 12, 2017.

75. Lorinkova et al., "Examining the Differential Longitudinal Performance."

76. Costigan and Brink, "Another Perspective."

77. E. Whitford, "Management Playbook," *INC.* (April 2014): 46-47.

78. T.C. Bednall, K. Sanders, and P. Runhaar, "Stimulating Informal Learning Activities Through Perceptions of Performance Appraisal Quality and Human Resource Management System Strength: A Two-Wave Study," *Academy of Management Learning & Education* 13, no. 1 (2014): 45-61.

79. AACSB website, www.aacsb.edu (accessed April 12, 2018).

80. W.L. Bedwell, S.M. Fiore, and E. Salas, "Developing the Future Workforce: An Approach for Integrating Interpersonal Skills Into the MBA Classroom," *Academy of Management Learning & Education* 13, no. 2 (2014): 171-186.

81. R.E. Silverman, "Going Bossless Backfires at Zappos," *The Wall Street Journal* (May 21, 2015): A1, A10.

82. C. Blencke, University of Central Florida, review suggestion, added April 17, 2017.

83. Silverman, "Going Bossless."

84. A. Dizol. "Meeting Overload," *Fortune* (May 1, 2015): 68-70.

85. J.D. Power, "My Advice," *Fortune* (July 1, 2015): 30.

86. Dizol, "Meeting Overload."

87. J. Libert, "Secrets of Effective Meetings," *Fortune* (May 1, 2015): 67.

88. Dizol, "Meeting Overload."

89. A. Gogo, "Productivity Hack," *Fortune* (October 1, 2015): 114.

90. Dizol, "Meeting Overload."

91. S. Shellenbarger, "Stop Wasting Everyone's Time," *The Wall Street Journal* (December 3, 2014): D1, D3.

92. C. Tate, "Work Simply," *BusinessWeek* (December 22-28, 2015): 71.

93. Shellenbarger, "Stop Wasting Everyone's Time."

94. Dizol, "Meeting Overload."

95. R. McCammon, "Zap! Session," *Entrepreneur* (February 2014): 32-33.

96. Shellenbarger, "Stop Wasting Everyone's Time."

97. B. Lanks, "You Can't Beat the Clock," *BusinessWeek* online (accessed May 28, 2015).

98. M. Whelan, "Productivity Hack," *Fortune* (October 1, 2015): 114.

99. Dizol, "Meeting Overload."

100. S. Shellenbarger, "Don't Be Late or You'll Be a Schedule-Wrecker," *The Wall Street Journal* (July 8, 2015): D1, D3.

101. McCammon, "Zap! Session."

102. J.P. Pullen, "A Better Brainstorm," *Entrepreneur* (April 2015): 63.

103. Karlgaard, "Diversity's Central Paradox."

104. A. Webb, "Don't Forget to Meet," *INC.* (December 2015–January 2016): 90.

105. Dizol, "Meeting Overload."

106. Dizol, "Meeting Overload."

107. Libert, "Secrets of Effective Meetings."

108. V. Harnish, "5 Ways to Get More From Your PR," *Fortune* (March 1, 2015): 38.

109. Shellenbarger, "Don't Be Late."

110. Shellenbarger, "Don't Be Late."

111. Lanks, "You Can't Beat the Clock."

112. Dizol, "Meeting Overload."

113. Shellenbarger, "Stop Wasting Everyone's Time."

114. N.J. Fast, E.R. Burris, and C.A. Bartel, "Managing to Stay in the Dark: Managerial Self-Efficacy, Ego Defensiveness, and the Aversion to Employee Voice," *Academy of Management Journal* 57, no. 4 (2014): 1013-1034.

115. Joshi and Knight, "Who Defers to Whom."

116. Silverman, "Going Bossless."

117. D. Eng, "How to Get Over Yourself," *Fortune* (March 1, 2015): 36.

118. Sytch and Tatarynowicz, "Friends and Foes."

119. Silverman, "Going Bossless."

120. S. Shellenbarger, "Meet the Meeting Killers," *The Wall Street Journal* (May 16, 2012): D1, D3.

121. Joshi and Knight, "Who Defers to Whom."

122. C. Hann, "Dedicated to You," *Entrepreneur* (September 2013): 24.

123. Shellenbarger, "Meet the Meeting Killers."

124. Lanks, "You Can't Beat the Clock."

125. Eng, "How to Get Over Yourself."

126. R. McCammon, "Put Down the Phone!" *Entrepreneur* (August 2014): 44-45.

127. McCammon, "Put Down the Phone!"

128. Manz, "Taking the Self-Leadership High Road."

129. Li et al., "Work Team Altruism."

130. J. Edwards, "Stat to the Future: Explaining WAR and Why it's Still an Imperfect Stat," *Sporting News* (January 9, 2018).

131. A. de Vogue and Maegan Vasquez, "Supreme Court Lets States Legalize Sports Gambling," CNN.com (May 14, 2018).

132. M. Arsenault and A. Rosen, "If It's Legalized in Massachusetts, Sports Betting Could Take Many Forms," *Boston Globe* (May 16, 2018).

# CHAPTER 10

1. R. Leuty, "2017 Executive of the Year Joe Lacob Is at the Top of His Game with the Golden State Warriors (Video)," *San Francisco Business Times* (December 27, 2017).

2. S. Norton, "Golden State Warriors General Manager Bob Myers on Building a Winning Team," *The Wall Street Journal* (March 6, 2018).

3. R.D. Costigan and K.E. Brink, "Another Perspective on MBA Program Alignment: An Investigation of Learning Goals," *Academy of Management Learning & Education* 14, no. 2 (2015): 260-276.

4. L. Tomkins and E. Ulus, "Is Narcissism Undermining Critical Reflection in Our Business Schools?" *Academy of Management Learning & Education* 14, no. 4 (2015): 595-606.

5. K.E. Brink and R.D. Costigan, "Oral Communication Skills: Are the Priorities of the Workplace and AACSB-Accredited Business Programs Aligned?" *Academy of Management Learning & Education* 14, no. 2 (2015): 205-221.

6. K. Davidson, "Hard to Find: Workers with Good 'Soft Skills,'" *The Wall Street Journal* (August 31, 2016): B1, B6.

7. D.M. Ames and A.S. Wazlawek, "How to Tell If You're a Jerk in the Office," *The Wall Street Journal* (February 23, 2015): R2.

8. GE ad, "Identifying the Leadership Skills That Matter Most Today," *INC.* (December 2014–January 2015): 78.

9. J. Robinson, "Up, Down and Sideways," *Entrepreneur* (December 2015): 59.

10. GE ad, "Identifying the Leadership Skills."

11. F.P. Morgeson, T.R. Mitchell, and D. Liu, "Event System Theory: An Event-Oriented Approach to the Organizational Sciences," *Academy of Management Review* 40, no. 4 (2015): 515-537.

12. GE ad, "Identifying the Leadership Skills."

13. N.J. Fast, E.R. Burris, and C.A. Bartel, "Managing to Stay in the Dark: Managerial Self-Efficacy, Ego Defensiveness, and the Aversion to Employee Voice," *Academy of Management Journal* 57, no. 4 (2014): 1013-1034.

14. B. Snyder, "Tech's Next Disruption: The Org Chart," *Fortune* (June 15, 2015): 90.

15. Snyder, "Tech's Next Disruption."

16. G. Colvin, "The Benefit of Baring It All," *Fortune* (December 2015), 34.

17. J. Rodkin and F. Levy, "Recruiting Preferred Skills," *BusinessWeek* (April 13-19, 2015): 43.

18. E. Bernstein, "The Hidden Benefits of Chitchat," *The Wall Street Journal* (August 13, 2013): D1, D2.

19. B.B. Baekgaard, "My Advice," *Fortune* (September 15, 2015): 40.

20. S. Pinker, "When Being Too Smart Ruins Writing," *The Wall Street Journal* (September 27-28, 2014): C3.

21. B.M. Cole, "Lessons From a Martial Arts Dojo: A Prolonged Process Model of High-Context Communication," *Academy of Management Journal* 58, no. 2 (2015): 567-591.

22. E. Bernstein, "Honey, You Never Said . . .," *The Wall Street Journal* (March 24, 2015): D1, D4.

23. W.L. Bedwell, S.M. Fiore, and E. Salas, "Developing the Future Workforce: An Approach for Integrating Interpersonal Skills Into the MBA Classroom," *Academy of Management Learning & Education* 13, no. 2 (2014): 171-186.

24. N. Brodsky, "Shut Up and Listen," *INC.* (March 2015): 58.

25. J. Robinson, "Pay Attention!" *Entrepreneur* (September 2014): 60-65.

26. Robinson, "Pay Attention!"

27. Editors, "Putting Communication Front and Center in Institutional Theory and Analysis," *Academy of Management Review* 40, no. 1 (2015): 10-27.

28. Bedwell et al., "Developing the Future Workforce."

29. Bedwell et al., "Developing the Future Workforce."

30. R. McCammon, "Zap! Session," *Entrepreneur* (February 2014): 32-33.

31. S. Shellenbarger, "You Really Look Smart," *The Wall Street Journal* (January 4, 2015): D1, D2.

32. Shellenbarger, "You Really Look Smart."

33. S. Reddy, "Walk This Way: Acting Happy Can Make It So," *The Wall Street Journal* (November 18, 2014): D3.

34. C. Hann, "Keep a Level Head," *Entrepreneur* (January 2016): 23.

35. A. McConnon, "To Be a Leader, Watch Your Body Language," *The Wall Street Journal* (October 3, 2016): R8.

36. Shellenbarger, "You Really Look Smart."

37. Reddy, "Walk This Way."

38. R.K. Ross, "Recognizing Employee Disengagement . . . and Taking Steps to Re-engage," *Costco Connection* (December 2014): 13-14.

39. S. Dembling, "Should I Stay or Should I Go?" *Entrepreneur* (August 2014): 28.

40. Dembling, "Should I Stay or Should I Go?"

41. Ad, "Mutual of America," *INC.* (June 2017): 95.

42. S. Sandberg, quote in *Fortune* (October 1, 2015): 114.

43. A. Gogo, "Productivity Hack," *Fortune* (October 1, 2015): 114.

44. J. Queenan, "Speak No Evil," *The Wall Street Journal* (June 14-15, 2014): C1, C2.

45. D. Eng, "How to Get Over Yourself," *Fortune* (March 1, 2015): 36.

46. S. Shellenbarger, "Raise a Glass, Give a Speech, Without a Stumble," *The Wall Street Journal* (December 23, 2015): D3.

47. McConnon, "To Be a Leader."

48. Brink and Costigan, "Oral Communication Skills."

49. I. Khrennikov, "Now the Boss Can Monitor Your Phone," *BusinessWeek* (June 27–July 3, 2016): 31-32.

50. A.C. Cosper, "Creating Relevance," *Entrepreneur* (May 2015): 10.

51. Survey, "CEO Survey," *INC.* (September 2014): 78.

52. Gogo, "Productivity Hack."

53. A. Handley, "Words of Wisdom," *Entrepreneur* (October 2014): 38.

54. S. Shellenbarger, "Stop Wasting Everyone's Time," *The Wall Street Journal* (December 3, 2014): D1, D3.

55. A. Handley, "Before You Hit Send," *Entrepreneur* (January 2015): 28-29.

56. A. Handley, "Detox Your Inbox," *Entrepreneur* (November 2014): 34.

57. Handley, "Words of Wisdom."

58. N. Best, "Entercom Executive Explains Mike Francesa's Return to WFAN," *Newsday* (April 30, 2018).

59. Editors, "Putting Communication Front and Center in Institutional Theory and Analysis," *Academy of Management Review* 40, no. 1 (2015): 10-27.

60. Bedwell et al., "Developing the Future Workforce."

61. R. McCammon, "I'm Sure You're Wondering Why I've Called You All Here," *Entrepreneur* (March 2015): 28-29.

62. Ames and Wazlawek, "How to Tell."

63. Ames and Wazlawek, "How to Tell."

64. S.H. Harrison and E.D. Rouse, "An Inductive Study of Feedback Interactions Over the Course of Creative Projects," *Academy of Management Journal* 59, no. 3 (2016): 841-859.

65. T. Robbines, "Questions Are the Answer," *Fortune* (November 17, 2014): 140.

66. E. Bernstein, "You Can Do It! Be a Motivator," *The Wall Street Journal* (June 16, 2016): D1, D3.

67. E. Bernstein, "How Well Are You Listening?" *The Wall Street Journal* (January 13, 2015): D1, D4.

68. F. Feiberbaum, "Forget-Me-Nots," *Costco Connection* (June 2016): 37.

69. Feiberbaum, "Forget-Me-Nots."

70. Feiberbaum, "Forget-Me-Nots."

71. Feiberbaum, "Forget-Me-Nots."

72. J. Steinberg, Advice quote, *Fortune* (October 1, 2015): 116.

73. R.B. Pollock, "CEO 101," *Fortune* (November 17, 2014): 130.

74. Brodsky, "Shut Up and Listen."

75. Brodsky, "Shut Up and Listen."

76. Bernstein, "You Can Do It!"

77. B. Murphy, "4 Habits of Exceptional Bosses," *INC.* (June 2016): 12.

78. Bernstein, "You Can Do It!"

79. Bernstein, "You Can Do It!"

80. Bernstein, "How Well Are You Listening?"

81. R. McCammon, "Can We Talk," *Entrepreneur* (May 2015): 25-26.

82. G. Colvin, "What Really Has the 99% Up in Arms," *Fortune* (November 7, 2011): 87.

83. S. Flowler, "Improve Your Motivation," *Costco Connection* (January 2015): 15.

84. S. Shellenbarger, "To Fight or Not to Fight? When to Pick Workplace Battles," *The Wall Street Journal* (December 17, 2014): D1, D2.

85. S. Shellenbarger, "Find Out What Your Boss Really Thinks About You," *The Wall Street Journal* (June 29, 2016): D1, D2.

86. McCammon, "Can We Talk."

87. E. Bernstein, "Venting Isn't Good for Us," *The Wall Street Journal* (August 11, 2015): D1, D4.

88. R. McCammon, "Don't Pop Your Top," *Entrepreneur* (May 2016): 15-16.

89. J. Whalen, "Angry Outbursts Really Do Hurt Your Health, Doctors Find," *The Wall Street Journal* (March 24, 2015): D1, D4.

90. E. Bernstein, "Thou Shalt Not Send in Anger," *The Wall Street Journal* (October 21, 2014): D1.

91. C. Sandler, "Business Lessons from the Art of War," *Costco Connection* (May 2014): 15.

92. Bernstein, "You Can Do It!"

93. Bernstein, "Venting Isn't Good for Us."

94. I. Berkovich, "Between Person and Person: Dialogical Pedagogy in Authentic Leadership Development," *Academy of Management Learning & Education* 13, no. 2 (2014): 245-264.

95. Murphy, "4 Habits."

96. R. McCammon, "So, Here's the Bad News . . ." *Entrepreneur* (July 2015): 24-25.

97. K. Clark, "Why the Seahawks Like Confrontation," *The Wall Street Journal* (January 8, 2015): D6.

98. R. Feintzeig, "When Nice Is a Four-Letter Word," *The Wall Street Journal* (December 31, 2015): D1, D3.

99. S. Shellenbarger, "It's Not My Fault! A Better Response to Criticism at Work," *The Wall Street Journal* (June 18, 2014): D1, D4.

100. M. Kelly, *Rediscovering Catholicism* (New York: Beacon, 2010).

101. Feintzeig, "When Nice Is a Four-Letter Word."

102. Feintzeig, "When Nice Is a Four-Letter Word."

103. L. Adler, "4 Common Leadership Fears and How to Avoid Them," *INC.* (April 2015): 10.

104. Shellenbarger, "Find Out."

105. Fast et al., "Managing to Stay in the Dark."

106. Shellenbarger, "Find Out."

107. Shellenbarger, "It's Not My Fault!"

108. D.S. Mason and T. Slack, "Evaluating Monitoring Mechanisms as a Solution to Opportunism by Professional Hockey Agents," *Journal of Sport Management* 15, no. 2 (April 2001): 107-134.

109. Associated Press, "Revisions to Sports Agent Act that Protects NCAA Athletes get Approved," www.espn.com/college-football/story/_/id/13263390/law-commission-approves-changes-strengthen-uniform-athlete-agents-act (July 15, 2015).

110. MLBPA Regulations Governing Player Agents (As Amended Effective December 8, 2017), http://reg.mlbpaagent.org/Documents/AgentForms/Agent%20Regulations.pdf (accessed on November 29, 2018).

111. M. Sherman, "Everything You Need to Know About the College Basketball Scandal," ESPN.com (February 23, 2018).

112. C.W. Henninger, "Report: NBA Investigated LeBron James to See if He Had Stake in Klutch Sports Agency," CBSSports.com (August 1, 2017).

# CHAPTER 11

1. H. Hutrya, "115 Vince Lombardi Quotes To Use In The Game Of Life," https://www.keepinspiring.me/vince-lombardi-quotes/ (accessed November 30, 2018).

2. A. Burke, "'Brave in the Attempt,'" *Chicago Tribune* (July 19, 2008).

3. G. Liebman, "5 Great Quotes by Legendary Coach Daryl Royal," www.espn.com/espn/page2/index/_/id/5639164.

4. Ironoctopus Fitness, "31 Epic Mental Toughness Quotes," http://ironoctopusfitness.com/blog/31-epic-mental-toughness-quotes/ (accessed November 30, 2018).

5. General Electric ad, "Identifying the Leadership Skills That Matter Most Today," *INC.* (December 2014–January 2015): 78.

6. P. Wahba, "She Thanks You for Not Smoking," *Fortune* (September 15, 2015): 125-130.

7. R. Fehr, K.C. Yam, and C. Dang, "Moralized Leadership: The Construction and Consequences of Ethical

Leader Perceptions," *Academy of Management Review* 40, no. 2 (2015): 182-209.

8. S. Shellenbarger, "Leader? No, Be a Follower," *The Wall Street Journal* (September 30, 2015): D1, D3.

9. J. Rodkin and F. Levy, "Recruiting Preferred Skills," *BusinessWeek* (April 13-19, 2015): 43.

10. N. Li, B.L. Kirkman, and C.O.H. Porter, "Toward a Model of Work Team Altruism," *Academy of Management Review* 39, no. 4 (2014): 541-565.

11. M. E. Chan and D.J. McAllister, "Abusive Supervision Through the Lens of Employee State Paranoia," *Academy of Management Review* 39, no. 1 (2014): 44-66.

12. R.K. Ross, "Recognizing Employee Disengagement . . . and Taking Steps to Re-Engage," *Costco Connection* (December 2014): 13-14.

13. C. Hann, "Dedicated to You," *Entrepreneur* (September 2013): 24.

14. F.K. Matta, B.A. Scott, J. Koopman, and D.E. Conlon, "Does Seeing Eye to Eye Affect Work Engagement and Organizational Citizenship Behavior? A Role Theory Perspective on LMX Agreements," *Academy of Management Journal* 58, no. 6 (2015): 1686-1708.

15. A.C. Peng, J.M. Schaubroeck, and L. Li, "Social Exchange Implications of Own and Coworkers' Experiences of Supervisor Abuse," *Academy of Management Journal* 57, no. 5 (2014): 1385-1405.

16. C.K. Lam, X. Huang, and S.C.H. Chan, "The Threshold Effect of Participative Leadership and the Role of Leader Information Sharing," *Academy of Management Journal* 58, no. 3 (2015): 836-855.

17. O. Ybarra, E. Kross, and J.S. Burks, "The Big Idea That Is Yet to Be: Toward a More Motivated, Contextual, and Dynamic Model of Emotional Intelligence," *Academy of Management Perspectives* 28, no. 2 (2014): 93-107.

18. www.nba.com/coachfile/pat_riley/ (accessed April 23, 2018)

19. T. Mitchell, "Victory Dance," *INC.* (April 2014): 47.

20. W. Buffett and M. Barra, "Most Powerful Women Advice!" *Fortune* (November 17, 2014): 149.

21. Y. Zhang, D.A. Waldman, U.L. Han, and X.B. Li, "Paradoxical Leader Behaviors in People Management: Antecedents and Consequences," *Academy of Management Journal* 58, no. 2 (2015): 538-566.

22. E. Bernstein, "You Can Do It! Be a Motivator," *The Wall Street Journal* (June 16, 2016): D1, D3.

23. A. Maslow, "A Theory of Human Motivation," *Psychological Review* 50 (1943): 370-396; A. Maslow, *Motivation and Personality* (New York: Harper & Row, 1954).

24. K. Schnitzer, "Cardinals Trade Bussing Outfielder to Be Closer to Sick Mom," *New York Post* (December 14, 2017).

25. R.L. Dipboye, "Bridging the Gap in Organizational Behavior," *Academy of Management Learning & Education* 13, no. 3 (2014): 487-491.

26. C. Alderfer, "An Empirical Test of a New Theory of Human Needs," *Organizational Behavior and Human Performance* (April 1969): 142-175; C. Alderfer, *Existence, Relatedness, and Growth* (New York: Free Press, 1972).

27. F. Herzberg, "One More Time: How Do You Motivate Employees?" *Harvard Business Review* (January/February 1968): 53-62.

28. S. Diestel, J. Wegge, and K.H. Schmidt, "The Impact of Social Context on the Relationship Between Individual Job Satisfaction and Absenteeism: The Roles of Different Foci of Job Satisfaction and Work-Unit Absenteeism," *Academy of Management Journal* 57, no. 2 (2014): 353-382.

29. A. Liveris, "CEO 101," *Fortune* (November 17, 2014): 129; P. Keegan, "The New Rules of Engagement," *INC.* (December 2014–January 2015): 86-132.

30. P. Diamandis, "The Future of . . . Technology," *Entrepreneur* (January 2015): 36.

31. D. McClelland, *The Achieving Society* (New York: Van Nostrand Reinhold, 1961); D. McClelland and D.H. Burnham, "Power Is the Great Motivator," *Harvard Business Review* (March/April 1978): 103.

32. Rodkin and Levy, "Recruiting Preferred Skills."

33. M. Mursthorn, "More Brokers Say No to Being Boss," *The Wall Street Journal* (online) (accessed June 18, 2015).

34. J.S. Adams, "Toward an Understanding of Inequity," *Journal of Abnormal and Social Psychology* 67 (1963): 422-436.

35. B.A. Scott, A.S. Garza, D.E. Conlong, and Y.J. Kim, "Why Do Managers Act Fairly in the First Place? A Daily Investigation of Hot and Cold Motives and Discretion," *Academy of Management Journal* 57, no. 6 (2014): 1571-1591.

36. G. O'Brien, "It's All Your Fault!" *Entrepreneur* (February 2015): 30.

37. D.T. Kong, K.T. Dirks, and D.L. Ferrin, "Interpersonal Trust Within Negotiations: Meta-Analytic Evidence, Critical Contingencies, and Directions for Further Research," *Academy of Management Journal* 57, no. 5 (2014): 1235-1255.

38. Peng et al., "Social Exchange Implications."

39. K. Leavitt, S.J. Reynolds, C.M. Barnes, P. Schilpzan, and S.T. Hannah, "Different Hats, Different Obligations: Plural Occupational Identities and Situated Moral Judgments," *Academy of Management Journal* 55, no. 6 (2012): 1316-1333.

40. G.O. Trevor, G. Reilly, and B. Gerhart, "Reconsidering Pay Dispersion's Effect on the Performance of

Interdependent Work: Reconciling Sorting and Pay Inequality," *Academy of Management Journal* 55, no. 3 (2012): 585-610.

41. E. Locke, "Guest Editor's Introduction: Goal-Setting Theory and Its Applications to the World of Business," *Academy of Management Executive* 18, no. 4 (2004): 124-125.

42. Ybarra et al., "The Big Idea."

43. C.L. Pearce, C.L. Wassenaar, C.C. Manz, "Is Shared Leadership the Key to Responsible Leadership?" *Academy of Management Perspectives* 28, no. 3 (2014): 275-288.

44. D. Baden and M. Higgs, "Challenging the Perceived Wisdom of Management Theories and Practice," *Academy of Management Learning & Education* 14, no. 4 (2015): 539-555.

45. Locke, "Guest Editor's Introduction."

46. C. Duhigg, "Smarter Faster Better," *Fortune* (March 15, 2016): 28.

47. S.D. Charlier, "Incorporating Evidence-Based Management Into Management Curricula: A Conversation with Gary Latham," *Academy of Management Learning & Education* 13, no. 3 (2014): 467-475.

48. C. Ricketts, "Hit List: Lou Holtz," *The Wall Street Journal* (December 23, 2006): P2; L. Holtz, "Setting a Higher Standard," *Success Yearbook* (Tampa, FL: Peter Lowe International, 1998): 74.

49. S.F. Collins, "Success Steps," *Costco Connection* (January 2016): 29.

50. J. Fried, "In Praise of Deadlines," *INC.* (December 2015–January 2016): 128; V. Harnish, "5 Crucial Performance Metrics," *Fortune* (August 1, 2016): 322.

51. V. Vroom, *Work and Motivation* (New York: John Wiley & Sons, 1964).

52. N.J. Fast, E.R. Burris, and C.A. Bartel, "Managing to Stay in the Dark: Managerial Self-Efficacy, Ego Defensiveness, and the Aversion to Employee Voice," *Academy of Management Journal* 57, no. 4 (2014): 1013-1034.

53. B.F. Skinner, *Beyond Freedom and Dignity* (New York: Alfred A. Knopf, 1971).

54. H. Geffen, "36. Laffer," *BusinessWeek* (December 8-14, 2014): 70-71.

55. S.D. Levitt and S.J. Dubner, "SuperFreakonomics," *Academy of Management Perspectives* 25, no. 2 (2011): 86-87.

56. N. Pasricha, "The Happiness Equation," *Fortune* (March 15, 2016): 28.

57. Li et al., "Work Team Altruism."

58. E. Bernstein, "If You Want to Persuade People, Try Altercasting," *The Wall Street Journal* (September 5, 2016): D1, D2.

59. Based on the author's consulting experience.

60. K. Blanchard and S. Johnson, *The One-Minute Manager* (New York: Morrow, 1982).

61. Pearce et al., "Shared Leadership."

62. R. McCammon, "Words of Encouragement," *Entrepreneur* (October 2015): 26.

63. Li et al., "Work Team Altruism."

64. M.R. Barrick, G.R. Thurgood, T.A. Smith, and S.H. Courtright, "Collective Organizational Engagement: Linking Motivational Antecedents, Strategic Implementation, and Firm Performance," *Academy of Management Journal* 58, no. 1 (2015): 111-135.

65. Fast et al., "Managing to Stay in the Dark."

66. M. Cerne, C.G.L. Nerstad, A. Dysvik, and M. Skerlavaj, "What Goes Around Comes Around: Knowledge Hiding, Perceived Motivational Climate, and Creativity," *Academy of Management Journal* 57, no. 1 (2014): 172-192.

67. R.C. Liden, S.J. Wayne, C. Liao, and J.D. Meuser, "Servant Leadership and Serving Culture: Influence on Individual and Unit Performance," *Academy of Management Journal* 57, no. 5 (2014): 1434-1452.

68. Zhang et al., "Paradoxical Leaders."

69. Collins, "Success Steps."

70. L. Daska, "4 Pieces of Advice Most People Ignore (but Great Entrepreneurs Don't)," *INC.* (July–August 2015): 8.

71. M. Rosenwald, "Bound by Habit," *BusinessWeek* (March 19-25, 2012): 106-107.

72. Rosenwald, "Bound by Habit."

73. M. Leonard, "Sheldon Rosenthal Memorial Junior Tennis Tournament Wraps Another Successful Run," Masslive.com (July 16, 2013).

# CHAPTER 12

1. G. Wyshynski, "Longtime Predators Executive Paul Fenton Named GM of Wild," Espn.com (May 22, 2018).

2. S. Clinebell, "Snapshots of Great Leaders," *Academy of Management Learning & Education* 13, no. 1 (2014): 139-149.

3. https://scholar.google.com/ (accessed April 27, 2018)

4. Based on the suggestion of reviewer David Biemer, Texas State University.

5. B.R. Spisak, M.J. O'Brien, N. Nicholson, and M. Van Vugt, "Niche Construction and the Evolution of Leadership," *Academy of Management Review* 40, no. 2 (2015): 291-306.

6. J. Rodkin and F. Levy, "Recruiting Preferred Skills," *BusinessWeek* (April 13-19, 2015): 43.

7. R. Hennessey, "Decisions, Decisions," *Entrepreneur* (March 2015): 50.

8. B. O'Keefe, "The Chosen One," *Fortune* (June 15, 2015): 134-139.

9. Spisak et al., "Niche Construction."

10. www.vincelombardi.com/quotes.html (accessed November 30, 2018)

11. R.L. Dipboye, "Bridging the Gap in Organizational Behavior," *Academy of Management Learning & Education* 13, no. 3 (2014): 487-491.

12. N.M. Lorinkova, M.J. Pearsall, and H.P. Sims, "Examining the Differential Longitudinal Performance of Directive Versus Empowering Leadership in Teams," *Academy of Management Journal* 56, no. 2 (2013): 573-596.

13. D. Wakabayshi, "Tim Cook's Vision for His Apple Emerges," *The Wall Street Journal* (July 8, 2014): B1, B5.

14. A. Lashinsky, "Being Tim Cook," *Fortune* (April 1, 2015): 60-63.

15. GE ad, "Identifying the Leadership Skills That Matter Most Today," *INC.* (December 2014–January 2015): 78.

16. D. Collinson and D. Tourish, "Teaching Leadership Critically: New Directions for Leadership Pedagogy," *Academy of Management Learning & Education* 14, no. 4 (2015): 576-594.

17. C.K. Lam, X. Huang, and S.C.H. Chan, "The Threshold Effect of Participative Leadership and the Role of Leader Information Sharing," *Academy of Management Journal* 58, no. 3 (2015): 836-855.

18. J. Clegg, "And the Oregon Ducks Prefer to Avoid It," *The Wall Street Journal* (January 8, 2015): D6.

19. Clegg, "Oregon Ducks Prefer to Avoid It."

20. R.E. Boyatzis, "Possible Contributions to Leadership and Management Development From Neuroscience," *Academy of Management Learning & Education* 13, no. 2 (2014): 300-301.

21. T.A. Judge and C.P. Zapata, "The Person-Situation Debate Revisited: Effect of Situation Strength and Trait Activation on the Validity of the Big Five Personality Traits in Predicting Job Performance," *Academy of Management Journal* 58, no. 4 (2015): 1149-1179.

22. A.C. Cosper, "O Captain! My Captain!" *Entrepreneur* (March 2015): 14.

23. K. Lanaj and J.R. Hollenbeck, "Leadership Over-Emergence in Self-Managing Teams: The Role of Gender and Countervailing Biases," *Academy of Management Journal* 58, no. 5 (2015): 1476-1494; E. Grijalva and P. D. Harms, "Narcissism: An Integrative Synthesis and Dominance Complementarity Model," *Academy of Management Perspectives* 28, no. 2 (2014): 108-127.

24. E. Ghiselli, *Explorations in Management Talent* (Santa Monica, CA: Goodyear, 1971).

25. A. Bornstein and J. Bornstein, "What Makes a Great Leader?" *Entrepreneur* (March 2016): 36-44.

26. G. Colvin, "From High-Minded to High Value," *Fortune* (December 22, 2014): 38.

27. R. Fehr, K.C. Yam, and C. Dang, "Moralized Leadership: The Construction and Consequences of Ethical Leader Perceptions," *Academy of Management Review* 40, no. 2 (2015): 182-209.

28. D.A. Waldman and R.M. Balven, "Responsible Leadership: Theoretical Issues and Research Directions," *Academy of Management Perspectives* 28, no. 3 (2014): 224-234.

29. A. Murray, "The Moral Imperative for Leaders," *Fortune* (December 1, 2016): 6.

30. Edgewalkers International website, https://edgewalkers.org (accessed May 2, 2018).

31. J. Saraceno, "Conversation with Phil Jackson," *AARP Bulletin* (January–February 2014): 10.

32. Zig Ziglar website, www.ziglar.com (accessed April 27, 2018).

33. K. Lewin, R. Lippert, and R.K. White, "Patterns of Aggressive Behavior in Experimentally Created Social Climates," *Journal of Social Psychology* 10 (1939): 271-301.

34. R. Likert, *New Patterns of Management* (New York: McGraw-Hill, 1961).

35. R.M. Stogdill and A.E. Coons, eds., *Leader Behavior: Its Description and Measurement* (Columbus: Ohio State University Bureau of Business Research, 1957); Likert, *New Patterns of Management*.

36. R. Blake and J. Mouton, *The Leadership Grid III: Key to Leadership Excellence* (Houston: Gulf Publishing, 1985); R. Blake and A.A. McCanse, *Leadership Dilemmas—Grid Solutions* (Houston: Gulf Publishing, 1991).

37. P. Harvey, K. Madison, M. Martinko, T.R. Crook, and T.A. Crook, "Attribution Theory in the Organizational Sciences: The Road Traveled and the Path Ahead," *Academy of Management Perspectives* 28, no. 2 (2014): 128-146.

38. C.L. Pearce, C.L. Wassenaar, and C.C. Manz, "Is Shared Leadership the Key to Responsible Leadership?" *Academy of Management Perspectives* 28, no. 3 (2014): 275-288; M.L. Besharov, "The Relational Ecology of Identification: How Organizational Identification Emerges When Individuals Hold Divergent Values," *Academy of Management Journal* 57, no. 5 (2014): 1485-1512.

39. A.C. Peng, J.M. Schaubroeck, and Y. Li, "Social Exchange Implications of Own and Coworkers' Experience of Supervisory Abuse," *Academy of Management Journal* 57, no. 5 (2014): 1385-1405.

40. F.K. Matta, B.A. Scott, J. Koopman, and D.E. Conlon, "Does Seeing 'Eye to Eye' Affect Work Engagement and Organizational Citizenship Behavior? A Role Theory Perspective on LMX Agreements," *Academy of Management Journal* 58, no. 6 (2014): 1686-1708.

41. S.J. Creary, B.B. Caza, L.M. Roberts, "Out of the Box? How Managing a Subordinate's Multiple Identities Affects the Quality of a Manager–Subordinate Relationship," *Academy of Management Review* 40, no. 4 (2015): 538-562.

42. Ad, "Lynne Doughtie," *Fortune* (June 15, 2015).

43. D.L. Shapiro, P. Hom, W. Shen, and R. Agarwal, "How Do Leader Departures Affect Subordinates' Organizational Attachment? A 360-Degree Relational Perspective," *Academy of Management Review* 41, no. 3 (2015): 479-502.

44. S. Berfield, "The Clutter in Kip Tindell," *BusinessWeek* (February 23–March 1, 2015): 41-45.

45. K. Helin, "Warriors Respond to Trump, Say Trip to D.C. will 'Celebrate Equality, Diversity and Inclusion,'" NBCSports.com (September 23, 2017).

46. A. Wolfe, "Jack and Suzy Welch," *The Wall Street Journal* (February 21-22, 2015): C11.

47. D.L. Gamache, G. McNamara, M.J. Mannor, and R.E. Johnson, "Motivated to Acquire? The Impact of CEO Regulatory Focus on Firm Acquisitions," *Academy of Management Journal* 58, no. 4 (2015): 1261-1282.

48. Collinson and Tourish, "Teaching Leadership Critically."

49. Grijalva and Harms, "Narcissism."

50. Grijalva and Harms, "Narcissism."

51. W. Isaacson, "Steve Jobs: The Biography . . . His Rivalry With Bill Gates," *Fortune* (November 7, 2011): 97-112.

52. Cosper, "O Captain! My Captain!"

53. A.M. Carton, C. Murphy, and J.R. Clark, "A (Blurry) Vision of the Future: How Leader Rhetoric About Ultimate Goals Influences Performance," *Academy of Management Journal* 57, no. 6 (2014): 1544-1570.

54. R. Ackoff, *Creating the Corporate Future* (New York: Wiley, 1981).

55. Carton et al., "A (Blurry) Vision."

56. M.A. LePine, Y. Zhang, E.R. Crawford, and B.L. Rich, "Turning Their Pain to Gain: Charismatic Leader Influence on Follower Stress Appraisal and Job Performance," *Academy of Management Journal* 59, no. 3 (2016): 1036-1059.

57. J. Antonakis, M. Fenley, and S. Liechti, "Can Charisma Be Taught? Test of Two Interventions," *Academy of Management Learning & Education* 10, no. 3 (2011): 374-396.

58. Spisak et al., "Niche Construction."

59. Y. Zhang, J.A. Lepine, B.R. Buckman, and F. Wei, "It's Not Fair . . . Or Is It? The Role of Justice and Leadership in Explaining Work Stressor–Job Performance Relationships," *Academy of Management Journal* 57, no. 3 (2014): 675-697.

60. Collinson and Tourish, "Teaching Leadership Critically."

61. Creary et al., "Out of the Box."

62. C. Dieterich and B. Eisen, "Amazon Stock Breaches $1,000," *The Wall Street Journal* (June 3-4, 2017): B1.

63. D. Haught, "The Theo Factor: Epstein Turns His Vision Into Reality with Cubs," Chicago Tribune.com (October 24, 2017).

64. Matta et al., "Seeing 'Eye to Eye.'"

65. Creary et al., "Out of the Box."

66. M. Kelly, *Rediscovering Catholicism* (New York: Beacon, 2010).

67. B.M. Galvin, D. Lange, and B.E. Ashforth, "Narcissistic Organizational Identification: Seeing Oneself as Central to the Organization's Identity," *Academy of Management Review* 40, no. 2 (2015): 163-181.

68. Cosper, "O Captain! My Captain!"

69. J. Clemmer, "Leadership Strategies," *Costco Connection* (April 2015): 13.

70. R.C. Liden, S.J. Wayne, C. Liao, and J.D. Meuser, "Servant Leadership and Serving Culture: Influence on Individual and Unit Performance," *Academy of Management Journal* 57, no. 5 (2014): 1434-1452.

71. Kelly, *Rediscovering Catholicism*.

72. A. McConnon, "To Be a Leader, Watch Your Body Language," *The Wall Street Journal* (October 3, 2016): R8.

73. Galvin et al., "Narcissistic Organizational Identification."

74. R. McCammon, "Faking It Right," *Entrepreneur* (December 2015): 15-16.

75. Saraceno, "Conversation with Phil Jackson."

76. I. Berkovich, "Between Person and Person: Dialogical Pedagogy in Authentic Leadership Development," *Academy of Management Learning & Education* 13, no. 2 (2014): 245-264.

77. A.S. Amezcua, M.G. Grimes, S.W. Bradley, and J. Wiklund, "Organizational Sponsorship and Founding Environments: A Contingency View on the Survival of Business-Incubated Firms, 1994-2007," *Academy of Management Journal* 56, no. 6 (2013): 1628-1654.

78. T.L. Stanko and C.M. Beckman, "Watching You Watching Me: Boundary Control and Capturing Attention in the Context of Ubiquitous Technology Use," *Academy of Management Journal* 58, no. 3 (2015): 712-738; O. Ybarra, E. Kross, and J. S. Burks, "The Big Idea That Is Yet to Be: Toward a More Motivated, Contextual, and Dynamic Model of Emotional Intelligence," *Academy of Management Perspectives* 28, no. 2 (2014): 93-107.

79. F. Fiedler, *A Theory of Leadership Effectiveness* (New York: McGraw-Hill, 1967).

80. R. Tannenbaum and W. Schmidt, "How to Choose a Leadership Pattern," *Harvard Business Review* (May/June 1973): 166.

81. R. House, "A Path–Goal Theory of Leadership Effectiveness," *Administrative Science Quarterly* 16, no. 2 (1971): 321-329.

82. V.H. Vroom, "Leadership and the Decision-Making Process," *Organizational Dynamics* 28, no. 4 (2000): 82-94.

83. Vroom, "Leadership and the Decision-Making Process."

84. Robert N. Lussier developed the Contingency Management Model and Self-Assessment Exercise 12.2, and they are used with his permission.

85. S. Kerr and J. Jermier, "Substitutes for Leadership: The Meaning and Measurement," *Organizational Behavior and Human Performance* 22 (1978): 375-403.

86. K. Belson, "Carolina Panthers Will Be Sold for $2.2 Billion to David Tepper," New York Times.com (May 15, 2018). Retrieved from www.forbes.com/profile/david-tepper/ on May 24, 2018.

# CHAPTER 13

1. Information in the case taken from personal interviews with Pete and Korby Clark and The Ranch website https://www.theranchgolfclub.com (accessed November 30, 2018).

2. M.R. Barrick, G.R. Thurgood, T.A. Smith, and S.H. Courtright, "Collective Organizational Engagement: Linking Motivational Antecedents, Strategic Implementation, and Firm Performance," *Academy of Management Journal* 58, no. 1 (2015): 111-135.

3. V. Harnish, "5 Ways to Stay Ahead of Rising Costs," *Fortune* (April 28, 2014): 32; A. Murray, "Should Leaders Be Modest?" *Fortune* (September 15, 2015): 28; R. Krause and G. Brunton, "Who Does the Monitoring?" *Academy of Management Review* 39, no. 1 (2014): 111-112.

4. International Organization for Standardization (ISO), www.iso.org (accessed May 2, 2018).

5. American Society for Quality (ASQ), https://asq.org (accessed May 2, 2018).

6. Editors, "Rethinking Governance in Management Research," *Academy of Management Journal* 57, no. 6 (2014): 1535-1543; C. Blencke, University of Central Florida, reviewer suggestion, added June 14, 2017.

7. V.F. Misangyi and A.G. Acharya, "Substitutes or Complements? A Configurational Examination of Corporate Governance Mechanisms," *Academy of Management Journal* 57, no. 6 (2014): 1681-1705.

8. R.P. Garrett and J.G. Covin, "Internal Corporate Venture Operations Independence and Performance: A Knowledge-Based Perspective," *Entrepreneurship Theory and Practice* 39, no. 4 (2015): 763-790; L. Weber, "Nowhere to Hide for 'Dead Wood' Workers," *The Wall Street Journal* (August 22, 2016): A1, A10.

9. B. Haislip, "There Is Never Enough Time," *The Wall Street Journal* (October 26, 2015): R4.

10. Haislip, "Never Enough Time."

11. R. Reuteman, "Accentuate the Negative," *Entrepreneur* (February 2015): 44-45.

12. Dialogue, "Is Decoupling Becoming Decoupled from Institutional Theory? A Commentary on Wijen," *Academy of Management Review* 40, no. 2 (2015): 307-313.

13. E. Van Oosten and K.E. Kram, "Coaching for Change," *Academy of Management Learning & Education* 13, no. 2 (2014): 295-298.

14. A. Canato, "Coerced Practice Implementation in Cases of Low Cultural Fit: Cultural Change and Practice Adaptation During the Implementation of Six Sigma at 3M," *Academy of Management Journal* 56, no. 6 (2013): 1724-1753.

15. D.A. Waldman and R.M. Balven, "Responsible Leadership: Theoretical Issues and Research Directions," *Academy of Management Perspectives* 28, no. 3 (2014): 224-234.

16. C. Hann, "Dedicated to You," *Entrepreneur* (September 2013): 24.

17. V. Harnish, "5 Crucial Performance Metrics," *Fortune* (August 1, 2016): 32.

18. L. Jia, J.D. Shaw, A.S. Tsue, and T.Y. Park, "A Social-Structural Perspective on Employee-Organization Relationships and Team Creativity," *Academy of Management Journal* 57, no. 3 (2014): 869-891.

19. J. Tozzi, "What Does Good Medical Look Like?" *BusinessWeek* (May 5-11, 2015): 28-29.

20. B. Dummett, "Cost Cuts Narrow BlackBerry's Loss," *The Wall Street Journal* (September 27-28, 2014): B3.

21. D. Chandler, "Morals, Markets, and Values-Based Business," *Academy of Management Review* 39, no. 3 (2014): 396-397.

22. Dialogue, "Is Decoupling Becoming Decoupled."

23. Dialogue, "Is Decoupling Becoming Decoupled."

24. T.S. Liao, J. Rice, and J.C. Lu, "The Vicissitudes of Competitive Advantage: Empirical Evidence from Australian Manufacturing SMEs," *Journal of Small Business Management* 53, no. 2 (2015): 469-481.

25. R.L. Hoefer and S.E. Green, "A Rhetorical Model of Institutional Decision Making: The Role of Rhetoric in the Formation and Change of Legitimacy Judgments," *Academy of Management Review* 41, no. 1 (2016): 130-150.

26. M.T. Wolfe and D.A. Shepherd, "Bouncing Back From a Loss: Entrepreneurial Orientations, Emotions, and Failure Narratives," *Entrepreneurship Theory and Practice* 39, no. 3 (2015): 675-700.

27. Garrett and Covin, "Internal Corporate Venture Operations."

28. H. Lian, D.J. Brown, D.L. Ferris, L.H. Liang, L.M. Keeping, and R. Morrison, "Abusive Supervision and Retaliation: A Self-Control Framework," *Academy of Management Journal* 57, no. 1 (2014): 116-139.

29. W.E.D. Creed, B.A. Hudson, G.A. Okhuysen, and K.S. Crowe, "Swimming in a Sea of Shame: Incorporating Emotion Into Explanations of Institutional Reproduction and Change," *Academy of Management Review* 39, no. 3 (2014): 275-301.

30. R.C. Liden, S.J. Wayne, C. Liao, and J.D. Meuser, "Servant Leadership and Serving Culture: Influence on Individual and Unit Performance," *Academy of Management Journal* 57, no. 5 (2014): 1434-1452.

31. C.C. Manz, "Taking the Self-Leadership High Road: Smooth Surface or Potholes Ahead?" *Academy of Management Perspectives* 29, no. 1 (2015): 132-151.

32. Y. Zhang, D.A. Waldman, Y.L. Han, and X. Li, "Paradoxical Leader Behaviors in People Management: Antecedents and Consequences," *Academy of Management Journal* 58, no. 2 (2015): 538-566.

33. Harnish, "5 Ways to Stay Ahead of Rising Costs."

34. I. Filatotchev and C. Nakajima, "Corporate Governance, Responsible Managerial Behavior, and Corporate Social Responsibility: Organizational Efficiency Versus Organizational Legitimacy," *Academy of Management Perspectives* 28, no. 3 (2014): 289-306.

35. "Rethinking Governance in Management Research."

36. W. Su and E.W.K. Tsang, "Product Diversification and Financial Performance: The Moderating Role of Secondary Stakeholders," *Academy of Management Journal* 58, no. 4 (2015): 1128-1148.

37. D.L. Yohn, "Olympics Advertisers Are Wasting Their Sponsorship Dollars," Forbes.com (August 3, 2016).

38. A. Sauer, "Rio 2016: Nike Nails Landing As First-Time Official Olympics Sponsor" *Brand Channel* (August 6, 2016).

39. J. Baumbach, "Yankees' Ticket Revenue Falls Again," *Newsday* (May 28, 2016).

40. Associated Press, News release, Charter.net (posted on homepage news August 10, 2011).

41. T. Cettina, "Dump That Debt!" *Costco Connection* (January 2016): 26.

42. N. Brodsky, "Don't Fear the Numbers," *INC.* (December 2015–January 2016): 80.

43. J. Worth, "Mr. Finance Fix-It," *Entrepreneur* (August 2015): 62-63.

44. D. Seetharaman, "Facebook Investors Press Suit on Shares," *The Wall Street Journal* (December 10, 2016): B1, B2.

45. K. Stock, "Briefs," *BusinessWeek* (November 2-8, 2015): 26; J. Reinsdorf, "Newcomer Michael Jordan," *Forbes* (March 23, 2015): 151; S. Gummer, "Michael Jordan," *Fortune* (June 13, 2011): 38.

46. A. Von Tobel, "Get Financially Fit Before 2015," *INC.* (October 2014): 104.

47. Zhang et al., "Paradoxical Leader Behaviors."

48. Liden et al., "Servant Leadership and Serving Culture"; Barrick et al., "Collective Organizational Engagement."

49. Van Oosten and Kram, "Coaching for Change"; C. Hann, "Goofing Off Online," *Entrepreneur* (November 2014): 36.

50. Jia et al., "A Social-Structural Perspective."

51. M. Weber, "Culture Matters: 7 Ways of Great Leaders," *Forbes* (October 20, 2014): 113.

52. L. Weber, "Nowhere to Hide."

53. A. Von Tobel, "Where Money Meets Morale," *INC.* (April 2014): 48-49.

54. A.L. Kenworthy, "Introduction; Coaching and Positive Emotions," *Academy of Management Learning & Education* 13, no. 2 (2014): 295-298.

55. Van Oosten and Kram, "Coaching for Change."

56. Von Tobel, "Where Money Meets Morale."

57. B.L. Rau, "The Oxford Handbook of Evidence-Based Management," *Academy of Management Learning & Education* 13, no. 3 (2014): 485-487.

58. Rau, "Evidence-Based Management."

59. D. Biemer, Texas State University, reviewer suggestion (added June 15, 2017).

60. S. Johnston, "The Benefits of Walking Meetings," *Costco Connection* (October 2014): 13.

61. R. McCammon, "The Worst of Times," *Entrepreneur* (February 2016): 15-16.

62. C. Blencke, University of Central Florida, reviewer data, added June 16, 2017.

63. C. Hann, "Caught in the Cookie Jar," *Entrepreneur* (December 2014): 41.

64. J.A. Clair, "Procedural Injustice in the System of Peer Review and Scientific Misconduct," *Academy of Management Learning & Education* 14, no. 2 (2015): 159-172.

65. Hann, "Caught in the Cookie Jar"; Canato, "Coerced Practice Implementation."

66. Hann, "Caught in the Cookie Jar."

67. L.A. Mainiero and K.J. Jones, "Sexual Harassment Versus Workplace Romance: Social Media Spillover and Textual Harassment in the Workplace," *Academy of Management Perspectives* 27, no. 3 (2013): 187-203.

68. S. Reddy, "Why Are You Always Late? It Could Be a Planning Fallacy," *The Wall Street Journal* (February 3, 2015): D1, D2.

69. R. Hennessey, "Decisions, Decisions," *Entrepreneur* (March 2015): 50.

70. Hann, "Caught in the Cookie Jar."

71. E. Fry, "We Were Promised a 20-Hour Workweek," *Fortune* (April 1, 2016): 18.

72. R. Foroohar, "Hard Math in the New Economy," *Time* (March 16, 2015): 32.

73. S. Forbes, "Free Trade Means More Jobs," *Forbes* (June 15, 2015): 11.

74. M. Philips and P. Coy, "Look Who's Driving R&D Now," *BusinessWeek* (June 8-14, 2015): 18-20.

75. R. Miller, "How Productive Is the U.S.?" *BusinessWeek* (March 2-8, 2015): 16-17.

76. A. Murray, "Lessons From the Fortune 500," *Fortune* (June 15, 2016): 14.

77. J. Robinson, "The Refueling Principle," *Entrepreneur* (October 2014): 67-70.

78. J. Chew, "Be Better!" *Fortune* (January 2016): 18.

79. S. Bing, "Productivity Now!" *Fortune* (January 1, 2016): 100.

80. J. Sparshott, "Weakening Productivity Augurs Ill for Wages," *The Wall Street Journal* (June 5, 2015): A2; Fry, "20-Hour Workweek."

81. Chew, "Be Better!"

82. TaylorMade website, www.taylormadegolf.com (accessed May 8, 2018).

83. Gatorade website, www.gatorade.com (accessed May 8, 2018).

84. A. Gaskell, "Nike Strikes Gold with Lean Manufacturing," *PEX Process Excellence Network* (May 6, 2002).

85. Lean Institute of Ukraine, "Lean Institute of Ukraine" (February 28, 2018).

86. G. Christ, "Research and Strategy: Sustainability: Just Do It," *Industry Week* (February 6, 2004).

# CHAPTER 14

1. https://www.maccabi.org/sport/maccabiah (accessed December 4, 2018)

2. P. Pedersen and L. Thibault (editors), *Contemporary Sport Management*, 6th ed. (Champaign, IL: Human Kinetics, 2019).

3. Springfield College website, www.springfieldcollege.edu (accessed May 14, 2018).

4. Pedersen and Thibault, *Contemporary Sport Management*.

5. www.linkedin.com/in/joseph-esile-1765917b/

6. SMG Worldwide website, www.smgworld.com (accessed May 14, 2018).

7. SMG Worldwide website (accessed May 14, 2018).

8. A. Handley, "Having a Plan," *Entrepreneur* (December 2014): 41.

9. R.N. Lussier and C.E. Halabi, "A Three-Country Comparison of the Business Success Versus Failure Prediction Model," *Journal of Small Business Management* 48, no. 3 (2010): 360-377.

10. M.L. Verreynne, D. Meyer, and P. Liesch, "Beyond the Formal-Informal Dichotomy of Small Firm Strategy-Making in Stable and Dynamic Environments," *Journal of Small Business Management* 54, no. 2 (2016): 420-444.

11. O. Schilke, "Second-Order Dynamic Capabilities: How Do They Matter?" *Academy of Management Perspectives* 28, no. 4 (2014): 366-380.

12. Dialogue, "Is Decoupling Becoming Decoupled from Institutional Theory? A Commentary on Wijen," *Academy of Management Review* 40, no. 2 (2015): 307-313.

13. D.J. Jones, C.R. Willness, and S. Madey, "Why Are Job Seekers Attracted by Corporate Social Performance? Experimental and Field Tests of Three Signal-Based Mechanisms," *Academy of Management Journal* 57, no. 2 (2014): 383-404.

14. F. Wijen, "Means Versus Ends in Opaque Institutional Fields: Trading Off Compliance and Achievement in Sustainability Standard Adoption," *Academy of Management Review* 39, no. 3 (2014): 302-323.

15. A. Chatterji and A. Patro, "Dynamic Capabilities and Managing Human Capital," *Academy of Management Perspectives* 28, no. 4 (2014): 395-408.

16. G. Di Stefano, M. Peteraf, and G. Verona, "The Organizational Drivetrain: A Road to Integration of Dynamic Capabilities Research," *Academy of Management Perspectives* 28, no. 4 (2014): 307-327.

17. Di Stefano et al., "Organizational Drivetrain."

18. Editors, "Putting Communication Front and Center in Institutional Theory and Analysis," *Academy of Management Review* 40, no. 1 (2015): 10-27.

19. C. Hann, "Caught in the Cookie Jar," *Entrepreneur* (December 2014): 41.

20. B.A. Scott, A.S. Garza, D.E. Conlon, and Y.J. Kim, "Why Do Managers Act Fairly in the First Place? A Daily Investigation of Hot and Cold Motives and Discretion," *Academy of Management Journal* 57, no. 6 (2014): 1571-1591.

21. M.J. Waller, Z. Lei, and R. Pratten, "Focusing on Teams in Crisis Management Education: An Integration and Simulation-Based Approach," *Academy of Management Learning & Education* 13, no. 2 (2014): 208-221.

22. F. Feiberbaum, "Forget-Me-Nots," *Costco Connection* (June 2016): 37.

23. S. Bing, "Productivity Now!" *Fortune* (January 1, 2016): 100; M. Adams, "There Is Never Enough Time," *The Wall Street Journal* (October 26, 2015): R4.

24. S. Shellenbarger, "Put a Dollar Value on Your Time, With Help From New Tools," *The Wall Street Journal* (July 22, 2015): D1, D2; R.G. Lord, J.E. Dinh, and E.L. Hoffman, "A Quantum Approach to Time and Organizational Change," *Academy of Management Review* 40, no. 2 (2015): 263-290; R. Abrams, "Gain an Hour a Day," *Costco Connection* (September 2016): 14.

25. V. Harnish, "Five Ways to Get Organized," *Fortune* (September 1, 2014): 42.

26. J. Bercovici, "How Dick Costolo Keeps His Focus," *INC.* (March 2015): 48-57.

27. Bercovici, "How Dick Costolo Keeps His Focus."

28. NPR, news (aired January 12, 2015).

29. J. Robinson, "Pay Attention!" *Entrepreneur* (September 2014): 60-65.

30. A. Handley, "Detox Your Inbox," *Entrepreneur* (November 2014): 34.

31. Bercovici, "How Dick Costolo Keeps His Focus."

32. V. Shmidman, "Advise," *Fortune* (October 1, 2015): 111.

33. M. Whelan, "Productivity Hack," *Fortune* (October 1, 2015): 114.

34. J. Krasny, "The Latest Thinking About Time," *INC.* (March 2015): 44-45.

35. Robinson, "Pay Attention!"

36. V. Harnish, "5 Crucial Performance Metrics," *Fortune* (August 1, 2016): 32.

37. J. Wang, "A Delicate Balance," *Entrepreneur* (September 2015): 136.

38. Krasny, "Latest Thinking About Time."

39. Bercovici, "How Dick Costolo Keeps His Focus."

40. S.S. Wang, "Never Procrastinate Again," *The Wall Street Journal* (September 1, 2015): D1, D2.

41. Staff, "When Good Habits Go Bad," *AARP Magazine* (January 2015): 19.

42. M. Kelly, *Rediscovering Catholicism* (New York: Beacon, 2010).

43. Robinson, "Pay Attention!"

44. D. Meyer, "One Thing at a Time," *Entrepreneur* (September 2014): 64.

45. Robinson, "Pay Attention!"

46. Feiberbaum, "Forget-Me-Nots."

47. A.J. Lombardi, "Tech Neck," *Strength & Conditioning* online (accessed January 27, 2017).

48. Staff, "Self-Improvement Through Data," *Fortune* (March 15, 2016): 28.

49. Abrams, "Gain an Hour a Day."

50. Bercovici, "How Dick Costolo Keeps His Focus."

51. G. Mark, "One Thing at a Time," *Entrepreneur* (September 2014): 64.

52. Robinson, "Pay Attention!"

53. "Five Trends for 2017 in Sport Event and Operations," GlobalSportsJobs, www.globalsportsjobs.com/article/five-trends-in-sports-events-and-operations-for-2017-/ (January 25, 2017; retrieved on May 25, 2018).

54. K. Belson, "Before Game Decided, Superdome Goes Dark," New York Times.com (February 3, 2013).

55. I. Edwards, "Euro 2012: 183 Arrested after Polish and Russian Clash as March Descends into Violence on Russia Day," www.telegraph.co.uk (June 13, 2012).

56. R. Polidoro, "Bryan Stow's Friends Describe Brutal Attack Outside Dodger Stadium," http://rockcenter.msnbc.com (December 19, 2011).

57. "Queens Man in San Francisco for One Day Catches Famous Ball," http://espn.com (August 9, 2007).

## AFTERWORD

1. "Five Trends for 2017 in Sport Event and Operations," GlobalSportsJobs, www.globalsportsjobs.com/article/five-trends-in-sports-events-and-operations-for-2017-/ (January 25, 2017; retrieved on May 25, 2018).

2. E. James, "Former Louisville Operations Director Acted Unethically, Head Coach Failed to Monitor," NCAA.org (June 15, 2017).

3. T. Connor, "Gymnastics Doctor Larry Nassar Gets 40 to 175 Years for Sex Abuse," NBCNews,com (January 24, 2018).

4. R. Blum, "Mariners All-Star Cano Suspended 80 Games for Drug Violation," USA Today.com (May 15, 2018).

5. R. Pérez-Peña and T. Panja, "28 Russian Athletes Win Appeals of Doping Bans" (February 1, 2008).

6. R. Ulrich, H.G. Pope, L. Cléret, A. Petróczi, T. Nepusz, J. Schaffer, G. Kanayama, R.D. Comstock, and P. Simon, "Doping in Two Elite Athletics Competitions Assessed by Randomized-Response Surveys," *Sports Medicine* 48, no. 1 (January 2018): 211-219. https://doi.org/10.1007/s40279-017-0765-4

7. N. Davidson, "NHL Becomes Latest Sporting League to Join eSports," www.cbc.ca/sports/hockey/nhl/nhl-esports-inaugural-world-championship-1.4569261 (March 9, 2018).

# INDEX

*Note:* The italicized *f* and *t* following page numbers refer to figures and tables, respectively.

# ABOUT THE AUTHORS

**Robert N. Lussier, PhD**, is a professor of management at the birthplace of basketball, Springfield College, where more than one-third of the students compete in 27 intercollegiate athletic teams. He has taught undergraduate and graduate sport management students for more than 30 years. He has also supervised sport internships and serves as an advisor for sport management research projects. To view his 73-page CV, visit www.publishdonotperish.com.

Lussier was an intercollegiate cross country and track athlete and has coached at the college, high school, and youth levels. He is a prolific writer with more than 444 publications, including articles in top refereed journals. Over one million people globally have used his textbooks, earning him an unsurpassed national and international reputation as an author and keynote speaker.

**David C. Kimball, PhD**, is a professor of management and the director of the sport management program at Elms College. He teaches sport management and sport marketing courses. As coordinator of the sport management internship program, he has placed many students in internships that offer real-world experience.

Kimball has helped develop and promote sporting events for organizations such as Junior Achievement and the JCC Maccabi Games, and he coaches and supervises Maccabi athletes each summer. He has an expansive network of friends and acquaintances in the sport management field; many of the case studies in this book arose from these relationships.